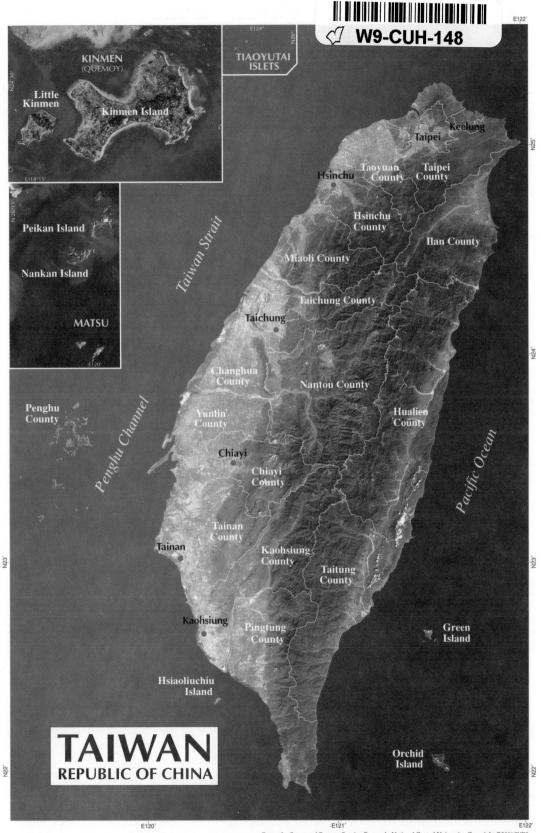

W9-CUH-148

KINMEN
(QUEMOY)

Little
Kinmen

Kinmen Island

Peikan Island

Nankan Island

MATSU

TIAOYUTAI
ISLETS

Taiwan Strait

Penghu Channel

Penghu
County

Keelung

Taipei

Taoyuan
County

Taipei
County

Hsinchu

Hsinchu
County

Ilan County

Miaoli County

Taichung County

Taichung

Changhua
County

Nantou County

Hualien
County

Yunlin'
County

Chiayi

Chiayi
County

Tainan
County

Tainan

Kaohsiung
County

Taitung
County

Pacific Ocean

Kaohsiung

Pingtung
County

Green
Island

Hsiaoliuchiu
Island

Orchid
Island

TAIWAN
REPUBLIC OF CHINA

UNIVERSITY OF THE PACIFIC

The Republic of China Yearbook— Taiwan 2002

With the extremely rapid political, economic, and social changes affecting the modern world, it is difficult to prevent information overload, particularly with regard to the Republic of China on Taiwan, which has now entered a new transitional period of democratization after the historic change of governing party in 2000.

The Republic of China Yearbook—Taiwan has consistently provided the most current and authoritative information on the Republic of China on Taiwan with its annual updates of major events, political and social trends, statistics, and historical information. This yearbook contains new facts, figures, and developments in an even more timely and objective format to clearly describe the Republic of China of 2001.

The yearbook provides a comprehensive and cohesive overview of most fields of interest concerning the Republic of China. The 25 chapters provide details on history, government, national defense, foreign relations, education, economics, environmental protection, science and technology, labor, religion, relations with the Chinese mainland, and other important aspects of the Republic of China.

The yearbook is far more than a repository of individual facts, which can be used to answer specific questions. Each chapter presents in-depth essays, color photos, graphs, charts, and statistical tables to provide balanced and comprehensive information and assist the reader in understanding the Republic of China in the context of the 21st century's era of globalization.

Nine appendices cover the historical chronology; the history of the ROC; the Constitution of the Republic of China; directories of ROC government offices, ROC representatives abroad, and foreign representatives in the ROC; weights and measures; national holidays and festivals; and a comparison of romanization systems.

The "Who's Who in the ROC" section formerly included in *The Republic of China Yearbook* is now a separate publication.

To assist bilingual readers, the yearbook provides extensive Chinese annotation throughout the text and index. *The Republic of China Yearbook—Taiwan 2002* is the essential reference work on one of Asia's most dynamic societies.

The Republic of China Yearbook

Taiwan 2002

The Republic of China *Yearbook*

Taiwan 2002

Published by the Government Information Office
2 Tientsin Street, Taipei 100, Taiwan, ROC

Printed by China Color Printing Co., Inc.
229 Pao Chiao Road, Hsintien, Taipei County 231, Taiwan, ROC

1st edition, C36 June 2002
Catalog Card No.:GIO-EN-BO-91-023-I-1

ISBN 957-01-1071-6
ISSN 1013-0942
G P N 1009101325

Beginning in 2001, the print editions of *The Republic of China Yearbook* and *Who's Who in the Republic of China*, which were formerly published together as a single volume, were split into two separate books. *The Republic of China Yearbook—Taiwan 2002* alone is available in both hardcover and paperback formats:

  Hardcover: NT$950 US$35
  Paperback: NT$550 US$20

Who's Who in the Republic of China—Taiwan 2002, which is only available in paperback, can be ordered by adding an additional NT$250 (US$10) to the above prices.

The CD-ROM version continues to contain both publications and is available for NT$600 (US$20).

For information on ordering
The Republic of China Yearbook—Taiwan 2002, please contact
SINORAMA MAGAZINE
5th Floor, 54 Chung Hsiao East Road, Section 1, Taipei 100, Taiwan, ROC
Phone: (+886-2) 2397-0633 Fax: (+886-2) 2397-0655
or
KWANG HWA PUBLISHING (USA), Inc.
6300 Wilshire Boulevard, Suite 1510A Los Angeles, California 90048, USA
Phone: (323) 782-8770 Fax: (323) 782-8761

Cover: Scenic Sun Moon Lake is again ready to welcome tourists after reconstruction following the September 21, 1999 earthquake. (Photo by Chen Chih-ming 陳志明, courtesy of the Sun Moon Lake National Scenic Area Administration, Tourism Bureau, Ministry of Transportation and Communications)
Cover design: HU Ru-yu 胡如瑜

Contents

Foreword from the Publisher

Over the past year, the Republic of China experienced major domestic and international political and economic challenges. The world economic downturn, which began in the second half of 2000, continued to adversely affect Taiwan's export industry, particularly the high-tech sector. Nonetheless, significant accomplishments were made in cross-strait and foreign relations, as well as democratization.

The complex relationship with the Chinese mainland was considerably enhanced at the very beginning of the year 2001, when the "Three Small Links" (direct trade, postal, and transportation) between the ROC's offshore islands Kinmen and Matsu and the Chinese mainland coastal cities of Xiamen and Fuzhou in Fujian were formally established on January 1. The expansion of direct social and economic ties will encourage both sides of the Taiwan Strait to seek peaceful and mutually beneficial solutions to their political differences.

Early in the year, the controversy surrounding the cabinet's decision to terminate the construction of the Fourth Nuclear Power Plant was settled by the Council of Grand Justices. On February 14, the premier announced the resumption of construction, thus reassuring industrialists, who had expressed concern over the future adequacy of Taiwan's electric power supply.

Two thousand one was a year of numerous accomplishments in foreign affairs. Heads of state, premiers, and other eminent leaders from the ROC's diplomatic partners and other friendly nations visited Taipei for high-level discussions.

President Chen began a 16-day state visit on May 21 to Latin America, with transit stops in Houston and New York. This trip was extremely important in solidifying relations with Latin American nations and upgrading substantive relations with the United States. Premier Chang Chun-hsiung also represented the ROC abroad by visiting four of the ROC's Caribbean allies in September.

Vice President Lu's state visit to The Gambia for the inauguration of President Yahya Jammeh in December was instrumental in strengthening relations with the ROC's African partner. In addition, Vice President Lu sponsored the 2001 Global Peace Assembly attended by five Nobel Peace Prize recipients and representatives from major international NGOs in August.

For their outstanding efforts, President Chen and Vice President Lu were both honored with prestigious international awards in 2001. On November 6, President Chen received the "2001 Prize for Freedom" from the London-based Liberal International, with First Lady Wu Shu-jen accepting the prize in France on his behalf. Then, on December 9, Vice President Lu received the World Peace Prize for her dedication to human rights, democracy, and peace.

In August, President Chen convened the Economic Development Advisory Conference (EDAC), composed of leaders from all sectors of society, to identify methods of promoting sustainable economic development at a time of worldwide recession. The month-long conference yielded 322 items of consensus for reform, including 36 recommendations for developing closer economic ties with the mainland.

After years of negotiations with other World Trade Organization (WTO) members, the ROC finally gained approval for accession on November 11 at the WTO 4th Ministerial Meeting in Doha, Qatar. WTO membership will bring many new challenges to Taiwan's economy, but the expected benefits will outweigh the difficulties in the long term.

Democratic development was uniquely elevated with the December 1, 2001, Legislative Yuan election. For the first time, the DPP became the largest political party in the legislature with 87 of the 225 seats, giving President Chen additional political authority to form a DPP-led cabinet.

These and other major events and trends are all covered in *The Republic of China Yearbook—Taiwan 2002*. With objective facts and accurate figures, the 2002 edition of the yearbook presents a comprehensive and cohesive overview of the most important aspects of the Republic of China on Taiwan, which readers around the world will certainly find useful and informative.

Throughout the text, an exchange rate of NT$31.23 to US$1 has been used to give meaning to financial statistics for non-Taiwan readers.

We invite readers to visit the GIO website at *www.gio.gov.tw* for the most recent information on the ROC.

National Symbols

National Designation

The Founding Father of the ROC, Dr. Sun Yat-sen, first proposed naming what was to ultimately become our country the "Republic of China" 中華民國 at the first official meeting of the Tung-meng Hui 同盟會 (Revolutionary Alliance) in Tokyo in 1905. Dr. Sun said: "It was not until the day in autumn of 1905 when outstanding individuals of the entire country gathered to found the Tung-meng Hui in Tokyo that I came to believe the great revolutionary task could indeed be achieved. Only at this point did I dare to propose the national designation of 'Republic of China' and announce it to the members of our party, so that each could return to his respective province and proclaim the message of the revolution and disseminate the ideas behind the founding of the Republic of China."

Dr. Sun's suggestion was officially adopted when the Provisional Assembly 臨時國民大會 was established in 1912.

ROC Year Designations

In official and most ordinary usages, years in the Republic of China are calculated from the year of the republic's founding, 1912. Thus, 1912 was referred to as "the first year of the Republic of China," and 2000 is "the 89th year of the Republic of China," and so on. This is a continuation of the millennia-old system in China of beginning new year designations with the ascension of a new emperor.

National Anthem

The words of the ROC national anthem were first delivered as an exhortation at the opening ceremony of the Whampoa Military Academy 黃埔軍校 on June 16, 1924, by Dr. Sun Yat-sen. This exhortation was designated as the Kuomintang's (KMT) party song in 1928, after which the KMT then publicly solicited contributions for a tune to fit the words. The melody submitted by Cheng Mao-yun 程懋筠 was the undisputed winner out of 139 contenders.

In the late 1920s and early 1930s, the Ministry of Education held two separate competitions for lyrics for a national anthem, using the KMT party song in the meantime as a temporary national anthem. None of the entries reviewed by the Ministry of Education were deemed appropriate, so Dr. Sun's composition was finally adopted as the official national anthem of the Republic of China in 1937.

The anthem first declares the Three Principles of the People to be the foundation of the nation and guides to a world commonwealth of peace and harmony; and then calls upon the people to be brave, earnest and constant in striving to fulfill the nation's goals.

The piece was honored as the world's best national anthem at the 1936 Berlin Olympics.

National Flag

The "white sun in a blue sky" portion of the Republic of China's national flag was originally designed by Lu Hao-tung 陸皓東, a martyr of the Chinese revolution. Lu presented his design upon the founding of the Hsing-chung Hui 興中會 (Society for Regenerating China) in Hong Kong on February 21, 1895. It was redesigned to include a crimson background during the years just prior to the revolution. This design is still used today as the national emblem.

Before the Wuchang Uprising 武昌起義 in 1911, the revolutionary armies in different provinces had different flags: the one used in the Wuhan area had 18 yellow stars, representing the 18 administrative divisions of China at the time; the Shanghai army adopted a five-color flag of red, yellow, blue, white, and black, representing the five main ethnic groups of China; and Guangdong, Guangxi, Yunnan, and Guizhou provinces used the "white sun in a blue sky."

When the Provisional Government 臨時政府 was first established, the five-color flag was adopted as the national flag, the 18-star flag was used by the army, and the "white sun in a blue sky" by the navy. The five-color national flag was replaced by the current ROC national flag on May 5, 1921; however, it was only used in the south. It was officially adopted by the new national government on December 17, 1928, following the successful completion of the Northern Expedition and the unification of China. Thereafter, it was used nationwide.

The 12 points of the white sun in the emblem represent the 12 two-hour periods of the day, symbolizing unceasing progress. At one level, the three colors of blue, white, and crimson stand for the Three Principles of the People: nationalism 民族, democracy 民權, and social well-being 民生. At another level, the colors embody qualities that evoke other concepts enumerated in the Three Principles: the blue signifies brightness, purity, freedom, and thus a government that is of the people 民有; the white—honesty, selflessness, equality, and thus a government that is by the people 民治; and the crimson—sacrifice, bloodshed, brotherly love, thus a government that is for the people 民享.

National Flower

The plum blossom, *prunus mei*, was officially designated by the Executive Yuan of the Central Government to be the national flower on July 21, 1964. The plum blossom, which produces shades of pink and white and gives off a delicate fragrance, has great symbolic value for the Chinese people because of its resilience in harsh winter weather. The triple grouping of stamens (one long and two short) represents Dr. Sun Yat-sen's Three Principles of the People, while the five petals symbolize the five branches of the ROC government.

NATIONAL ANTHEM OF THE REPUBLIC OF CHINA

Dr. Sun Yat-sen
Translated by Tu Ting-hsiu
Maestoso

Music by Cheng Mao-yun
Accompaniment by Huang Tzu

三　民　主　義，吾　黨　所　宗，以　建　民
San - min - chu - i, wu - tang so tsung, i - chien min
San - min - chu - i, our aim shall be; To found a free

國，以　進　大　同，咨　爾　多　士，為　民　前　鋒；
kuo, i - chin ta - t'ung. Tzu erh to - shih wei min chien - feng, su-
land, world peace be our stand. Lead on, com - rades, van - guards ye are; Hold

夜　匪　懈，主　義　是　從，矢　勤　矢　勇，必　信　必
yeh fei - hsieh, chu - i shih ts'ung. Shih ch'in, shih yung; pi hsin, pi
fast your aim, by sun and star. Be ear - nest and brave, your coun - try to

忠，一　心　一　德，貫　徹　始　終！
chung; i - hsin, i - te, kuan - ch'e shih - chung.
save; One heart, one soul, one mind, one goal!

3

Sun Yat-sen 孫中山

Founding Father, Republic of China

Dr. Sun Yat-sen, also known as Sun Chung-shan and Sun Wen, was born in 1866 in a coastal village of Hsiangshan County 香山縣, Guangdong Province. After receiving his early education in both Chinese and Western schools, he moved to Hawaii in 1879, where he attended Iolani and Oahu Colleges. In 1883, he returned to China to continue his studies, concentrating on the Chinese classics and history. He later moved to Hong Kong to attend Queen's College and in 1892 graduated from Hong Kong Medical College.

Seeing the weakness of the imperial Manchu court and the encroachment on China by foreign powers, Sun gave up his medical career to pursue political reform. In 1894, together with a group of overseas Chinese youths, Sun established his first revolutionary organization, the Hsing-chung Hui 興中會 (Society for Regenerating China), in Honolulu, Hawaii. His political ideals are summarized in a set of doctrines called the Three Principles of the People—nationalism, democracy, and the people's well-being—which were designed to build an independent, democratic, and prosperous China.

Over the next 16 years, Sun and his followers launched ten futile attempts to topple the corrupt imperial Manchu court. Finally, on October 10, 1911, forces loyal to Sun took over Wuchang, the capital of Hubei Province. Thereafter, other provinces and important cities joined the revolutionary camp and declared independence from the Manchu government. On December 29, 1911, Sun was elected provisional president of the new republic by delegates from 16 of the 17 provinces gathered in Nanjing. He was inaugurated on January 1, 1912, the founding day of the ROC.

To preserve national unity, Sun relinquished the presidency on April 1, 1912, to military strongman Yuan Shih-kai 袁世凱, who declared himself emperor in 1915. Sun and other leaders moved the revolutionary effort to Japan until Yuan Shih-kai's death in 1916. In 1917, the Provisional Assembly elected Sun to lead the Chinese Military Government 軍政府 based in Guangzhou, and in 1921 Sun assumed office as president of the newly formed government in Guangzhou. He devoted the rest of his life to uniting China's feuding factions.

Dr. Sun denied the inevitability of communism in China. He believed that class struggle, an intrinsic element of communism, was not a requirement of human progress. He reiterated this point in a joint declaration issued with Soviet envoy Adolf Joffe in 1923, which stated that the communist system was not suitable for China. He also believed that cooperation rather than class struggle was the motive force for social development.

Sun died of illness on March 12, 1925, at the age of 59 in Beijing. In 1940, he was posthumously declared the Founding Father of the Republic of China for his life-long contributions to the revolution.

Chen Shui-bian 陳水扁

Tenth-term President, Republic of China

Chen Shui-bian was born on February 18, 1951, in Kuantien, Tainan County, to a poor farming family. In 1969, he passed the Joint College and University Entrance Examination with the highest score possible. Mr. Chen received his LL.B. from National Taiwan University in 1974, graduating with the Outstanding Performance Award.

He was a highly successful attorney at the Formosan International Marine and Commercial Law Office, serving as a senior partner from 1976 until 1989. In 1980, Mr. Chen took his first political case, defending the staff and supporters of *Formosa* magazine, who had been charged with sedition and riot following the 1979 "Kaohsiung Incident" 美麗島事件.

Mr. Chen first ran for public office in 1981, winning a seat in the Taipei City Council as an independent and becoming its youngest member ever. After serving for five years, he joined the Democratic Progressive Party 民主進步黨 (DPP), which became the first major opposition party following the lifting of martial law in 1987.

Mr. Chen quickly advanced in the DPP and served as a member of the DPP Central Standing Committee from 1987 to 1989. He was elected to the Legislative Yuan in 1989 and served until 1994; was executive director of the DPP caucus of legislators from 1990 to 1993; and served on the DPP Central Executive Committee from 1991 to 1996. In the Legislative Yuan, Mr. Chen served as co-convener of both the National Defense Committee and the Rules Committee.

In 1994, Mr. Chen was recognized by *Time* magazine in its "Global 100" list of forthcoming young leaders for the new millennium. Mr. Chen left the legislature that year to run in the Taipei mayoral election. With 44 percent of the vote in a three-way race, Chen won a great victory for both himself and the DPP. During Mr. Chen's four-year tenure as Taipei mayor, his administration maintained a consistent approval rating of over 70 percent. Mr. Chen cracked down on the sex industry, eradicated corruption, fought crime, and tackled traffic problems, earning Taipei a place in *Asiaweek*'s top five best cities in Asia.

On March 18, 2000, Chen Shui-bian was elected the tenth-term president of the Republic of China. Major themes of Mr. Chen's administration are to develop Taiwan into a high-tech "Green Silicon Island," promote lasting peace in the Taiwan Strait, uphold the Taiwan spirit, and share the island's achievements with the rest of the world.

To reinforce relations with the ROC's diplomatic partners throughout the world, President Chen made highly successful state visits to the Dominican Republic, Nicaragua, Costa Rica, The Gambia, Burkina Faso, and Chad from August 14 through August 25, 2000. In his October 10, 2000 National Day Message, President Chen announced: "The people of Taiwan now stand up. Taiwan is now part of the worldwide trend of democracy and freedom."

On June 5, 2001, President Chen returned from his second trip to the Americas. During these 16 days, he visited heads-of-state in Honduras, Paraguay, Panama, Guatemala, and El Salvador, and made transit stops in the United States, where he held historic meetings with several US congressmen and senators.

In August 2001, President Chen convened the Economic Development Advisory Conference (EDAC), consisting of representatives from all sectors of society. The EDAC reached a total of 322 points of consensus on revitalizing Taiwan's economy, promoting cross-strait and international relations, and preparing for WTO accession. President Chen was awarded the 2001 Prize for Freedom by Liberal International. Although he was unable to travel to France due to Beijing's interference, First Lady Wu Shu-jen accepted the prize on his behalf in Strasbourg on November 14, 2001.

In his "Meeting Challenges, Moving Forward" New Year's address on January 1, 2002, President Chen emphasized that national unity in times of uncertainty is essential to the continuation of peace, stability, and prosperity for the people of Taiwan.

Lu Hsiu-lien 呂秀蓮
Tenth-term Vice President, Republic of China

Lu Hsiu-lien was born on June 7, 1944, in Taoyuan, Taiwan. She studied law at National Taiwan University, graduating first in her class in 1967. She earned a master's degree in comparative law from the University of Illinois at Urbana-Champaign in 1971, and an LL.M. from Harvard in 1978.

In the 1970s, Lu introduced feminist ideas to Taiwan through a series of important newspaper articles and books, and later became the country's leading women's rights activist. She established a publishing house, a coffee shop/resource center, and hotlines for women before she left Taiwan in 1977 to study at Harvard.

In 1978, foreseeing that the United States would soon sever diplomatic relations with the ROC, she gave up her studies at Harvard and returned to Taiwan. She ran for a seat in the National Assembly that autumn, but when the US announced recognition of the PRC on December 16, the government canceled the election scheduled for December 23.

Lu then became increasingly active in *tangwai* 黨外, the local opposition movement. In 1979, she delivered a 20-minute speech criticizing the government at an International Human Rights Day rally that turned into a riot, known as the "Kaohsiung Incident." She was tried under martial law and found guilty of sedition, and harshly sentenced to 12 years in prison. In 1985, she was released.

Lu resumed her campaign for women's rights, democracy, and international recognition for Taiwan. In 1993, she founded the Taiwan International Alliance to press for Taiwan's membership in the UN. As a member of the opposition Democratic Progressive Party, Lu was elected to the Legislative Yuan, where she served on the Foreign Relations Committee beginning in 1993. In 1994, Lu chaired the Global Summit of Women, and in 1995, she hosted the Feminist Summit for Global Peace held in Taipei.

In 1996, President Lee Teng-hui appointed her National Policy Advisor, breaking away from the usual practice of appointing only members of the ruling party. Lu was elected Taoyuan County magistrate in a March 1997 by-election on a platform of reform and ending government corruption. Nine months later, she was re-elected in the regular election by a large margin.

On March 18, 2000, Lu was elected the tenth-term vice president of the ROC. After her inauguration on May 20, she actively participated in government affairs, effectively promoting the new government as a symbol of "social equality and harmony" between men and women and of "political rule by both sexes." In foreign affairs, she redefined cross-strait relations as "distant relatives, close neighbors."

In September 2000, she made her first overseas state visit to the ROC's Central American diplomatic partners, including El Salvador, Honduras, Belize, and Guatemala. During the trip she emphasized the ROC's "Soft Power" of "democracy, human rights, peace, love, and high technology."

Focusing on peace and prosperity in the Asia-Pacific region, Vice President Lu called for a Union of Asian States that was modeled after the European Union and would promote resource-sharing, cooperation, and peaceful co-existence.

In August 2001, Vice President Lu organized the "Global Peace Assembly: Voice from Taiwan" with local non-governmental organizations, inviting five winners of the Nobel Peace Prize to Taiwan to promote peace in the Taiwan Strait and the rest of the world.

On December 9, 2001, Vice President Lu became the first woman to be awarded the World Peace Prize from the World Peace Corps Academy for her significant contributions to world peace. Later that month, she led a special delegation to The Gambia for the inauguration of President Yahya Jammeh in Banjul.

In January 2002, she left Taiwan for New York to bring the condolences of the people of Taiwan to the victims of the September 11 terrorist attack. She then traveled to Nicaragua to attend the inauguration of President Enrique Bolanos Geyer in Managua. Subsequently, she made a state visit to Paraguay, the ROC's only diplomatic partner in South America.

Yu Shyi-kun 游錫堃

Premier, Republic of China

Yu Shyi-kun was born on April 25, 1948, in Taiho Village, Tungshan, Ilan County, Taiwan. Raised in a poor tenant farming family near the Tungshan River that always flooded, he worked very hard during his childhood. In 1961, his father died of tuberculosis. As the eldest son in the family, he was forced to quit junior high school to work full-time as a farmer on six acres of land, but he was not content to give up his opportunity to get an education.

At the age of 19, Mr. Yu passed the entrance exam to study at the supplementary night school of the Lotung Commercial High School. It was not until he was 37 that Mr. Yu graduated from the department of politics at Tunghai University. Every stage of Mr. Yu's education was completed by will power.

Before he reached the age of 20, Mr. Yu joined the Youth Party and followed senior political leader Kuo Yu-hsin as a "political apprentice." Later, Mr. Yu served as Lin I-hsiung's campaign manager for the provincial assembly election.

In 1978, Mr. Yu married Yang Pao-yu. The couple has two sons.

When Mr. Yu served in the provincial assembly, he impressed everyone with his outstanding performance. On September 28, 1986, Mr. Yu announced a conference to form a political party, and the Democratic Progressive Party (DPP) was born as the first opposition party under martial law. Mr. Yu was re-elected four times to the DPP Central Standing Committee. In 1990, after being elected magistrate of Ilan County, Mr. Yu resigned his DPP position and began to concentrate his efforts on Ilan County.

During the eight years he served as magistrate, Mr. Yu recruited talented individuals. He tried to develop a unique style of administration in such areas as tourism, environmental protection, culture, and information. After completing his term as county magistrate in 1997, Taipei Mayor Chen Shui-bian invited Mr. Yu to join the Taipei City Government as chairman of the Taipei Rapid Transit Corporation (TRTC). Following Mr. Chen Shui-bian's loss of the Taipei mayoral election at the end of 1998, Mr. Yu resigned his position in the Taipei City Government and accepted an appointment by DPP Chairman Lin I-hsiung as the party's secretary-general.

During his tenure as secretary-general, Mr. Yu helped Chairman Lin manage and promote DPP party affairs. In addition, his previous eight years of experience as Ilan County magistrate established Mr. Yu as an expert on cultural administration. He taught several classes on the subject at the graduate school of traditional arts at the National Institute of the Arts, now the Taipei National University of the Arts.

During the 2000 election for tenth-term president and vice president, Mr. Yu served concurrently as DPP secretary-general and director and chief spokesman for the DPP presidential campaign. With the DPP victory on March 18, 2000, Mr. Yu was appointed vice premier of the new government that same year.

In July 2000, the "Pachang Creek Tragedy" occurred, resulting in unprecedented public outrage. Vice Premier Yu, who was serving concurrently as chairman of the Council of Disaster Prevention, immediately tendered his resignation to take political responsibility for the incident and help ease public anger. After a six-month hiatus from politics, Mr. Yu was once again pressed into service by President Chen Shui-bian, who appointed him secretary-general to the Office of the President.

In February 2002, President Chen Shui-bian appointed Mr. Yu premier. In his first administrative report to the Legislative Yuan, he announced four new primary policy objectives for the cabinet. These four goals are "to establish a new style of politics based on maintaining a simple, straightforward, results-oriented attitude; creating a new economy centered around technology; setting up a new society founded on the spirit of cooperation; and building a new Taiwan rooted in human values."

1

Geography

The Taroko Gorge, a spectacular marble-walled cleft towering near the east coast city of Hualien, is one of Taiwan's most attractive natural wonders.

What's New

1. Typhoons in 2000
2. Updated climatic statistics

S ince the government's withdrawal to Taiwan in 1949, the term Republic of China has been taken to apply to the territory under the government's effective control: the islands of Taiwan, Penghu, Kinmen, Matsu, and a number of smaller islands. For the sake of simplicity, these are sometimes referred to collectively as "Taiwan."

Taiwan

Off the eastern coast of Asia lie the mountainous island arcs of the Western Pacific. The island chain closest to the continent marks the edge of the Asiatic Continental Shelf. Taiwan, one of the islands of this chain, is the largest body of land between Japan and the Philippines.

The island of Taiwan is 394 km long and 144 km at its widest point, shaped like a tobacco leaf. It is located between 21°53'50" and 25°18'20" N latitude and between 120°01'00" and 121°59'15" E longitude.

With a total area of nearly 36,000 sq. km, Taiwan is separated from the Chinese mainland by the Taiwan Strait, which is about 220 km at its widest point and 130 km at its narrowest. The island is almost equidistant from Shanghai and Hong Kong.

The surface geology of the island varies in age from very recent alluvial deposits to early sedimentary and crystalline rocks. The structure is formed by a tilted fault block running roughly northeast to southwest along the entire length. The steep slope of this tilted block faces east and the rock mass slopes more gently to the west. This block is composed primarily of old rocks, some of which have been subjected to heat and pressure. Only one-third of the land area is arable. The mountains are

Eroded sandstone shaped like frozen yogurt is one of the many topographical rock formations typically found in the Northeast Coast National Scenic Area.
(Photo by Liao Tai-chi)

mostly forested, with some minerals, chiefly coal, at the northern end.

On the east coast, the mountains rise steeply from the Pacific. To the west, the level sediments lie just below the surface of the sea. As a result, river deposits have filled the shallow waters and extended the land 15 to 30 km westward from the foothills, giving Taiwan a larger proportion of useful level land than either

Position of Taiwan				
Locality	Longitude		Latitude	
	Aspect	Apex	Aspect	Apex
Total Taiwan Area	Eastern Point	124°34'09"	Southern Point	21°45'18"
	Western Point	119°18'03"	Northern Point	25°56'21"
Taiwan Proper	Eastern Point	121°59'15"	Southern Point	21°53'50"
	Western Point	120°01'00"	Northern Point	25°18'20"
Penghu Islands	Eastern Point	119°42'54"	Southern Point	23°09'40"
	Western Point	119°18'03"	Northern Point	23°45'41"

Japan or the Philippines. Natural resources and agricultural potential make this coastal plain of great importance.

The shoreline of Taiwan is relatively smooth and unbroken with a total length of 1,566 km (including the Penghu Islands). Off the southern end of the island lie small area of coral reefs, which have built up along the island's shores.

The most important feature of Taiwan's topography is the central range of high mountains running from the northeast corner to the southern tip of the island. Steep mountains over 1,000 meters high constitute about 31 percent of the island's land area; hills and terraces between 100 and 1,000 meters above sea level make up 38 percent; and alluvial plains below 100 meters in elevation, where most communities, farming activities, and industries are concentrated, account for the remaining 31 percent. Based on differences in elevation, relative relief character of rock formations, and structural patterns, the island can be divided physiographically into five major divisions: the mountain ranges, volcanic mountains, foothills, tablelands, and coastal plains and basins.

Mountain Ranges

Taiwan's five longitudinal mountain ranges occupy almost half of the island. As a group, they extend 330 km from north to south and average about 80 km from east to west. They include more than two hundred peaks with elevations of over 3,000 meters.

Central Range

The Central Range 中央山脈 extends from Suao 蘇澳 in the north to Oluanpi 鵝鑾鼻 in the south, forming a ridge of high mountains and serving as the island's major watershed for rivers and streams. The range is predominantly composed of hard rock formations resistant to weathering and erosion, although heavy rainfall has deeply scarred the sides with gorges and sharp valleys. The relative relief of the terrain is usually extensive, and the forest-clad mountains with their extreme ruggedness are almost impenetrable. The east side of the Central Range is the steepest mountain slope in Taiwan, with fault scarps ranging in height from 120 to 1,200 meters.

Mount Snow Range

The Mount Snow Range 雪山山脈 lies northwest of the Central Range, beginning at Santiao Chiao 三貂角 in the northeast and gaining elevation as it extends toward the southwest. Mount Snow 雪山, the main peak, is 3,884 meters high.

Mount Jade Range

The Mount Jade Range 玉山山脈 runs along the southwestern flank of the Central Range. It includes the island's tallest peak, the 3,952-meter Mount Jade 玉山.

Mount Ali Range

The Mount Ali Range 阿里山山脈 lies west of the Mount Jade Range, with major elevations between 1,000 and 2,000 meters. The main peak, Mount Ta 塔山, towers 2,484 meters.

Area of Taiwan			
Locality	*Number of Islands*	*Area (sq. km)*	*Coastline (km)*
Taiwan Area	86	35,961.17	1,566.34
Taiwan Proper & 21 offshore islands	22	35,834.30	1,239.58
Penghu Islands	64	126.86	326.76

Source: Department of Land Administration, Ministry of the Interior

East Coastal Range

The East Coastal Range 東部海岸山脈 extends from the mouth of the Hualien River 花蓮溪 in the north to Taitung County 臺東縣 in the south, and chiefly consists of sandstone and shale. Although Mount Hsinkang 新港山, the highest peak, reaches an elevation of 1,682 meters, most of the range is composed of large hills. Small streams have developed on the flanks, but only one large river cuts across the range. Badlands are located at the western foot of the range, where the ground water level is the lowest and rock formations the least resistant to weathering. Raised coral reefs along the east coast and the frequent occurrences of earthquakes in the rift valley indicate that the fault block is still rising.

Volcanic Mountains

Although igneous rocks are not commonly found in Taiwan, smaller outcroppings of extrusive bodies are scattered over the island, representing at least five periods of igneous activity.

The Tatun mountain area 大屯山 is a prominent group of volcanic peaks, lying at the promontory between Keelung Port 基隆港 and the Tamsui River 淡水河 overlooking the Taipei metropolitan area. The entire area is covered by lava that poured out of the volcanic craters which now stand as conical notches of over 1,000 meters. The area is unique for its hot springs and fumaroles.

Foothills

The foothills are found in a narrow zone surrounding the Central Range. This zone, with an elevation of from 100 to 500 meters, is connected with the Central Range and linked with the tablelands in continuous slopes. Low hills with gentle slopes and longitudinal valleys woven with transverse gullies are characteristic topographic features of this zone, as are broad escarpments and short hogbacks formed on fault scarps or along rock formations.

Along the Central Range, the Keelung-Miaoli foothills and those extending from Chiayi 嘉義 to Pingtung 屏東 are the broadest. The Keelung-Miaoli foothills start from the coast at Keelung 基隆 and end at south of Miaoli 苗栗. The Chiayi foothills rise below Mount Ali, with their northern border on the Choshui River 濁水溪 and the southern border between Kaohsiung 高雄 and Pingtung. There is a shallow-faulted region between these foothills and the Fengyuan foothills, extending from Fengyuan 豐原, just north of Taichung 臺中, to Nantou 南投, some distance to the south. This is the widest section of western foothills in Taiwan. It is intersected by three rivers: the Tachia 大甲溪, Tatu 大肚溪, and Choshui. Included in this region is the Sun Moon Lake Basin 日月潭盆地, which lies about 765 meters above sea level and forms a graben basin. At the southern flank of the Central Range are the Hengchun foothills that occupy most of the Hengchun Peninsula 恆春半島. The topography is down-graded on the eastern and western sides.

Terrace Tablelands

From the foothills, the terrain is gradually reduced to tableland from 100 to 500 meters in height. These thick deposits of well-rounded sandstone gravel are accumulations of eroded material washed down from higher areas. The gravel beds may have been deposited near the sea and then raised into flat-topped tablelands by recent tilting. The broadest tableland is the one between Taoyuan 桃園 and Hsinchu 新竹 in northern Taiwan. Next in size are the Houli Terrace 后里臺地 in Taichung, the Tatu Terrace 大度臺地 and the Pakua Terrace 八卦臺地 in Changhua 彰化, and the Hengchun Terrace 恆春臺地 in southern Taiwan.

Coastal Plains, Basins, and Valleys

To the west, the physical character of Taiwan changes through the foothills zone to the alluvial plain. Topographically, the coastal plains and basins are monotonously flat, except near the foothills. All of the larger rivers running through the plains have their sources in the high mountains. Flowing out of the western foothills, these rivers diverge into a number of channels and meander to the ocean, forming large alluvial deltas. Many of these have been linked by irrigation and drainage canals.

The coastal plains are generally covered with gravel, sand, and clay, with an average slope of between 0.5 meters and one km. Slopes are gentle enough to eliminate the need for major terracing and are rarely subject to serious soil erosion. The western edge of the plain, where it meets the Taiwan Strait, is marked by wide tidal flats and the coast is swampy. Shore currents have built up a series of spits and offshore bars, with many lagoons formed by shoreward shifting of the sandbars.

The Chianan Plain 嘉南平原 is the broadest in southwestern Taiwan, extending from Changhua to Kaohsiung. It is about 180 km long and 43 km wide at its broadest point, making up more than 12 percent of the total land area of Taiwan. Next largest are the Pingtung Plain 屏東平原 and the Ilan Plain 宜蘭平原. Finally, there are two major basins, the Taipei Basin 臺北盆地 and the Taichung Basin 臺中盆地.

The East Longitudinal Valley 臺東縱谷 is an extremely narrow fault valley in proportion to its length. It has a general elevation of about

High Peaks in Taiwan (meters)	
Mount Jade (Mt. Morrison) 玉山:	
Main Peak 主峰	3,952
Eastern Peak 東峰	3,940
Northern Peak 北峰	3,920
Southern Peak 南峰	3,900
Mount Snow 雪山	3,884
Mount Hsiukuluan 秀姑巒山	3,860
Mount Wulameng 烏拉孟山	3,805
Mount Nanhu 南湖大山	3,740
Central Range Point 中央尖山	3,703
Mount Kuan 關山	3,666
Mount Chilai 奇萊山:	
Northern Peak 北峰	3,605
Main Peak 主峰	3,559
Mount Hsiangyang 向陽山	3,600
Mount Tachien 大劍山	3,593
Cloud Peak 雲峰	3,562
Mount Pintien 品田山	3,529
Mount Tahsueh 大雪山	3,529
Mount Tapachien 大霸尖山	3,505
Mount Tungchun 東郡大山	3,500
Mount Wuming 無明山	3,449
Mount Nengkao 能高山:	
Southern Peak 南峰	3,349
Main Peak 主峰	3,261
Mount Choshe 卓社大山	3,343
Mount Hsinkang 新康山	3,335
Mount Tao 桃山	3,324
Mount Paiku 白姑大山	3,341
Mount Taroko 太魯閣大山	3,282
Mount Tan 丹大山	3,240
Mount Hohuan 合歡山	3,146

Source: Ministry of the Interior

120 meters above sea level and dips slightly toward the east. Coalescing alluvial fans have developed at the foot of both sides, and the river beds are filled with gravel. Due to repeated movements along the fault line and frequent shocks, subordinate watersheds have developed in the valley.

Rivers

The Central Mountain Range is the major watershed for Taiwan's rivers and streams; thus,

Major Rivers in Taiwan

River	Drainage (sq. km)	Length (km)	Passes Through
Lanyang River 蘭陽溪	979	73	Ilan County
Tamsui River 淡水河	2,726	159	Taipei City, and Taipei and Taoyuan counties
Touchien River 頭前溪	566	63	Hsinchu City and County
Houlung River 後龍溪	537	58	Miaoli County
Taan River 大安溪	759	96	Miaoli and Taichung counties
Tachia River 大甲溪	1,236	124	Taichung County
Wu River 烏溪	2,026	119	Taichung, Changhua, and Nantou counties
Choshui River 濁水溪	3,155	186	Nantou, Changhua, and Yunlin counties
Peikang River 北港溪	645	82	Yunlin and Chiayi counties
Putzu River 朴子溪	400	76	Chiayi City and County
Pachang River 八掌溪	475	81	Chiayi and Tainan counties
Chishui River 急水溪	410	30	Tainan County
Tsengwen River 曾文溪	1,177	139	Tainan City, and Chiayi and Tainan counties
Yenshui River 鹽水溪	222	87	Tainan City and County
Erhjen River 二仁溪	350	65	Tainan City, Tainan and Kaohsiung counties
Kaoping River 高屏溪	3,257	171	Kaohsiung and Pingtung counties
Tungkang River 東港溪	472	44	Pingtung County
Linpien River 林邊溪	344	42	Pingtung County
Peinan River 卑南溪	1,603	84	Taitung County
Hsiukuluan River 秀姑巒溪	1,790	81	Hualien County
Hualien River 花蓮溪	1,507	57	Hualien County

Source: Ministry of the Interior

most rivers in Taiwan flow in either an easterly or westerly direction. They are short and steep, especially on the eastern side of the island, and become torrential during heavy rainstorms, carrying heavy loads of mud and silt. The riverbeds tend to be wide and shallow, making them difficult to manage and develop as water resources.

Taiwan has 151 rivers and streams. The Choshui River is the longest (186 km), while the Kaoping River 高屏溪 has the largest drainage basin (3,257 sq. km).

Natural Vegetation and Soils

Because of Taiwan's location, plant species are diverse and abundant. The high altitude of the island's mountains provides climatic and vegetation zones ranging from subtropical to alpine. Except for the western coastal plain and the Penghu Islands, Taiwan was once entirely covered by forests. The forested area today is estimated at 1.9 million hectares.

Acacia trees are ubiquitous on lower hills. Bamboo groves and forests are found naturally in central and northern Taiwan, whereas in the south, most stands of bamboo are cultivated on farms. Outside of forests, bamboo is normally confined to relatively moist areas; thus, it can be cultivated almost anywhere in the Taiwan area.

The flora of Taiwan resembles that of the Chinese mainland. A wide range of Asian subtropical species are found in the lowlands, and low altitude flora is closely related to that of the southern Chinese provinces. Mountain flora is related to that of western China, and high alpine flora to that of the Himalayan region.

Soils vary in fertility. Many have lost their natural fertility after centuries of irrigation and heavy rainfall. In the north, the soils of arable land are primarily acid alluvials and latosols of diluvial, some of which are residuals. In the southwest, where agricultural production is concentrated, most of the arable soils are alluvials of neutral to weak alkalinity and planosol-like alluvials. Upland soils of mountainous areas are mostly lithosols, which are usually thin and infertile.

Climate

Situated off the east coast of Asia and in the path of warm ocean currents, Taiwan has an oceanic and subtropical monsoon climate, conspicuously influenced by its topography. Summers are long and accompanied by high humidity, while winters are short and usually mild. In the coldest months, snow is visible on the peaks of high mountains. Frost is rare in the lowlands, where most of the population lives and works. The mean monthly temperature in the lowlands is about 16°C in the winter, and ranges between 24°C and 30°C the rest of the year. The relative humidity averages about 80 percent.

Taiwan is in the trade wind belt of the planetary wind system and is greatly affected by the seasonal exchange of air masses between the continent and the ocean. Besides location and topography, the winter (northeast) and summer (southwest) monsoons are the main factors controlling the climate of Taiwan.

The different directions of the winter and summer monsoons cause seasonal distribution of rainfall in northern Taiwan to be different from that in the south. The northeast monsoon 東北季風 in the winter lasts about six months from October to late March and brings steady rain to the windward (northeast) side of the island. The central and southern parts of the island, however, are on the leeward side of the northeast monsoon; thus, they have sunny winters, with less than 30 percent of their annual precipitation falling at this time.

The annual "plum rain" season in May and June brings a lot of precipitation. In the summer, the southwest monsoon 西南季風 prevails for about five months, beginning in early May and ending in late September. During this period, southern Taiwan usually has wet weather, while northern Taiwan is relatively dry. The moisture, carried by the southwest monsoon and local terrestrial winds, falls largely in convectional form. Thundershowers and typhoons bring Taiwan heavy rainfall during the summer months.

Taiwan lies in the path of severe tropical cyclones known in East Asia as typhoons. With their violent winds and extremely heavy rainfall,

Climatic Statistics for Selected Locations in Taiwan						
City	Period	Average Temperature (°C)			Average Annual Rainfall (mm)	Average Rainy Days Per Year
		Annual	January	July		
Taipei	(1897-2000)	22.1	15.3	28.5	2,160.8	182
Keelung	(1903-2000)	22.1	15.6	28.5	3,373.4	209
Taichung	(1897-2000)	22.6	15.9	28.1	1,712.2	122
Hualien	(1911-2000)	22.8	17.4	27.8	2,095.5	183
Kaohsiung	(1932-2000)	24.5	18.7	28.5	1,760.8	97
Hengchun	(1897-2000)	24.8	20.5	27.9	2,174.3	140

Source: Central Weather Bureau

Typhoons in 2000					
Month	Name of Typhoon	Strength	Warning Issued	Warning Terminated	Damages
July	Kaitak	Medium	Sea:6th, 11:43 Land: 8th, 5:45	Sea: 10th, 3:00 Land: 9th, 23:05	Torrential rains Agricultural loss
August	Bilis	Strong	Sea: 21st, 8:25 Land: 21st, 14:45	Sea: 23rd, 20:05 Land:23rd, 20:05	11 deaths 434 houses collapsed Power failure Landslides Agricultural loss: NT$ 4.74 billion
August	Prapiroon	Light	Sea: 27th, 20:45 Land: 28th, 14:45	Sea: 30th, 14:20 Land: 30th, 8:40	Light
September	Bopha	Light	Sea: 8th, 15:15 Land: 8th, 20:40	Sea: 10th, 15:00 Land: 10th, 8:40	Light
October	Yagi	Medium	Sea: 23rd, 20:20 Land: 24th, 14:50	Sea: 26th, 8:50 Land: 26th, 3:25	None
November	Xangsane	Medium	Sea: Oct. 30th, 20:15 Land: Oct. 31st, 2:45	Sea: 1st, 20:05 Land: 1st, 17:45	64 deaths Floods Power failure Agrucultural loss: NT$ 3.6 billion
November	Bebinca	Light	Sea: 6th,10:15	Sea: 7th, 8:55	None

Source: Central Weather Bureau

these storms often cause severe damage, especially to crops. However, they are the greatest source of water in the Taiwan area. During a typhoon, windward mountain slopes may receive as much as 300 mm of rainfall in 24 hours. An average of three to four typhoons hit Taiwan every year, usually in July, August, or September. However, in 2000 seven typhoons, Kaitak, Bilis, Prapiroon, Bopha, Yagi, Xangsane, and Bebinca hit the Taiwan area (see chart). Kaitak, Bilis, and Xangsane brought torrential rains. Xangsane alone caused 64 deaths. And the agricultural losses of Bilis and Xangsane were estimated at US$152 million and US$115 million respectively.

According to a statistical analysis by the Water Resources Bureau (WRB) of the Ministry of Economic Affairs 經濟部水資源局 based on data collected from 1949 to 1990 at 440 rainfall gauging stations, the mean annual rainfall in the Taiwan area is 2,515 mm, with the hills receiving more than 5,600 mm, and lowland areas at least 1,200 mm. Rainfall is most abundant in the north with mean annual rainfall at 2,934 mm, followed by the eastern region at 2,715 mm, the southern region at 2,501 mm, and the central region at 2,081 mm. The southern area of Taiwan receives 90 percent of its rainfall between May and October. In the north, the seasonal distribution of precipitation is more even, with 60 percent falling between May and October. Throughout the entire Taiwan area, the driest months occur between November and February.

Earthquakes

Taiwan has a high degree of seismic activity due to its location at the junction of the Manila Trench and the Ryukyu Trench along the west side of the Philippine Sea plate. The collision of the two tectonic plates—the Philippine Sea plate and the Eurasia plate—which created the uplift of land that became Taiwan's four major mountain ranges, continue to push against each other. In addition, the Philippine plate has been forced beneath the South China Sea plate to the south. The majority of earthquakes occur off the coast of eastern Taiwan and are deep beneath the seabed causing little damage. Plate tectonics have created numerous fault lines that crisscross the island.

The largest earthquakes in the past 100 years include a 7.1 magnitude temblor that killed more than 3,250 people in 1935, and a 6.8 magnitude quake on November 14, 1986, which killed 15 and injured 44. A powerful and devastating earthquake struck at 1:47 A.M. on September 21, 1999, toppling high-rise buildings, damaging roads and bridges, and severing powerlines across the island. The quake registered a magnitude of 7.3 on the Richter scale with the epicenter at Chichi township in Nantou County. More than 1,300 aftershocks were reported by the morning of September 22, with the strongest registering a magnitude of 6.8 in central Taiwan.

According to statistics from the National Fire Administration of the Ministry of the Interior 內政部消防署, as of December 30, 1999, the massive "921 Earthquake" caused the deaths of 2,415 people, injured 11,305, and left 29 still unaccounted for. The greatest number of casualties was in Taichung County with 1,175 dead and 6,190 injured.

On October 22, 1999, another major earthquake occurred 2.5 km northwest of Chiayi City at 10:19 A.M., registering 6.4 on the Richter scale. Although there were no deaths, 122 were injured, ten buildings were severely damaged or collapsed. There were 37 cases of gas leaks, and 4 cases of fire.

The release of tectonic energy in the aftershock area of the "921 Earthquake" continued in 2000. Three strong aftershocks with magnitudes of 5.3, 6.7, and 6.1 were reported in the area on May 17, June 11, and July 29, respectively. In addition, a strong earthquake with a magnitude of 6.2 occurred to the north of Hualien in eastern Taiwan on September 10.

Penghu Islands

Lying between 119°18'03" and 119°42'54" E, 23°09'40" and 23°45'41" N, the Penghu Islands (the Pescadores) 澎湖群島 consist of 64 islets situated in the Taiwan Strait, midway between the Chinese mainland and Taiwan. They form a natural demarcation between the East China Sea and the South China Sea. In the past they were a key stop for ships sailing throughout the Far East and crossing the Pacific. Penghu is the only county that is an archipelago.

Only 20 of the islands of Penghu are inhabited. Two of the three main islands, Yuweng 漁翁島 and Paisha 白沙島 are connected by two causeways, and the Cross-sea Bridge 跨海大橋, with its 76 spans, is the longest inter-island bridge in the Far East.

The total area of the islands is 126.86 sq. km. Penghu, the largest island of the archipelago, accounts for half of the total area and is home to 70 percent of the population.

The islands were formed by a mass of basalt rising from the sea through volcanic action. Due to long-term underwater erosion, the islands have a relatively flat terrain. Their highest elevation, located on Mao Yu 貓嶼 (Greater Cat Islet), is only 79 meters above sea level. There is some arable land on the three main islands, with altitudes varying from three to five meters above sea level. The islands have no rivers and are marked by winding coastlines forming numerous natural

harbors. The shallow, warm water around the Penghu Islands favors the growth of coral. Numerous reefs shelter the coral from sea waves.

Climate

The Penghu Archipelago's climate is characterized by hot summers, cold winters, and strong winds. From October to March, the northeasterly wind (known as the northeast monsoon) blows at a high velocity of nine meters per second. This often brings sea water to the islands in the form of "salt rain." From June to October, the southwesterly wind is mild. Typhoons frequently hit the islands during the summer.

Annual rainfall in Penghu County is about 1,000 mm, only half the rainfall of the plains of Taiwan. Moreover, the strong monsoon winds result in a high rate of evaporation. Over 1,800 mm of water, or 1.8 times the annual rainfall, evaporate every year. Therefore, maintaining water supplies is a high priority. At present, there are five reservoirs in the Penghu area: Chengkung 成功, Hsingjen 興仁, Tungwei 東衛, Paisha Chihkan 白沙赤崁 (an underground reservoir with a capacity of 1,761,774 cubic meters) and Hsian 西安. Virtually every household has its own well.

Kinmen (Quemoy)

The 12 islands of the Kinmen金門 group are located off the southeastern coast of Fujian Province, covering an area of 150.45 sq. km. They lie at approximately 118°24' E longitude and 24°27' N latitude, a key position in the Taiwan Strait that blocks the mouth of the Xiamen (Amoy) Bay and protects Taiwan and the Penghu Islands.

The Kinmen Islands are 82 nautical miles west of the Penghu Islands and 150 nautical miles from Kaohsiung in southern Taiwan. The shortest distance from the main island of Kinmen to communist-held territory is only 2,310 meters.

Although the satellite islets are low and flat, Kinmen itself is hilly. Mount Taiwu 太武山 is the highest point of the island, rising to 253 meters in the eastern part of the island. Mount Shuhao 菽蒿山 stretches into the sea where precipitous cliffs have formed as a result of sea wave erosion. Most rivers in Kinmen are short and narrow with unsteady flows, so it is necessary to construct reservoirs for water supply and irrigation.

Due to the hilly terrain, there are several harbors around Kinmen. Liaolo Bay 料羅灣 on

The Lanyang Plain, the largest plain in northeastern Taiwan, is home to many people.
(Courtesy of Liao Tai-chi)

the south of the island is the most famous. Tzukan Harbor 子感港 of Liaolo Bay is deep enough to accommodate ships of several thousand tons.

Rain showers in the Kinmen area usually occur from April to August, and typhoons often strike the islands in July and August. East winds last for about eight months a year. The average temperature varies from 13˚C to 28˚C. The average relative humidity is 85 percent.

Matsu

Situated outside the mouth of the mainland Chinese Min River 閩江, the Matsu Islands form the northern anchor of the offshore defense line. The main island of the complex is Nankan 南竿, more commonly known as Matsu 馬祖 from the name of the major port of the island. It is 114 nautical miles northwest of Keelung, the port city on the northern tip of Taiwan and is the same distance north from the Kinmen Islands. There are two harbors in Nankan: Fuao 福澳 and Matsu. Other major islands of the group are Peikan 北竿, Kaoteng 高登, Liang Island 亮島, Tachiou 大坵, Hsiaochiou 小坵, Tungyin 東引, Hsiyin 西引, Tungchu 東莒, and Hsichu 西莒. Nankan is the largest, with an area of 10.4 sq. km. Kaoteng is located only 5.5 nautical miles (9,250 meters) from the Chinese mainland.

The islands are composed of an uplift of igneous rock. Granite is the Matsu area's major natural resource. The climate is characterized by monsoon rains from August to December and typhoons during the summer.

Although the hilly terrain is not well suited for agriculture, ten reservoirs, 15 sea dikes, and two ponds have been constructed and 320 irrigation wells drilled to facilitate farming. Vegetable production has reached the point of self-sufficiency.

South China Sea

The ROC maintains a historical claim to the islands of the South China Sea. All are part of the territory of the Republic of China. Four groups of coral reef archipelagoes are scattered over this immense area. They are the Tungsha (the Pratas) Islands 東沙群島, Nansha (the Spratly) Islands 南沙群島, Hsisha (the Paracel) Islands 西沙群島, and Chungsha (the Macclesfield Bank) Islands 中沙群島. Currently the ROC's effective jurisdiction includes the Tungsha and Taiping 太平 Islands.

Since 1993, the government's policy towards the region has been set by the Executive Yuan's *Policy Guidelines for the South China Sea* 南海政策綱領, which expresses Taiwan's desire to resolve all disputes peacefully, to step up the exploration and management of resources in the South China Sea, to promote cooperation with the other claimant states, and to protect the ecology of the region. In keeping with its peaceful intentions, the government has pursued a policy of shifting authority from the military to civilian authorities over the Tungsha and Taiping Islands. In 1999, responsibility for defending both islands was transferred from the Ministry of National Defense to the newly created Coast Guard Administration of the Executive Yuan 行政院海岸巡防署, and the administration of the Tungsha and Taiping Islands was officially transferred to the Kaohsiung City Government.

Tungsha (Pratas) Islands

Tungsha Islands comprise Tungsha Island 東沙島 and two coral reefs, the North Vereker Bank 北衛灘 and the South Vereker Bank 南衛灘. The archipelago is located in a strategically important position along the major sea route connecting the Pacific and Indian oceans, between 116˚40' and 116˚55' E longitude, and 20˚35' and 20˚47' N latitude. The group is 140 nautical miles south of Shantou 汕頭 in Guangdong Province, 430 nautical miles northwest of Manila, 170 miles southeast of Hong Kong, and 240 nautical miles southwest of Kaohsiung. Tungsha Island is a coral atoll with a land area of 2.4 sq. km. Shaped like a horseshoe, it extends 0.9 km from east to west, and 2.7 km from north to south. Among these islands, only Tungsha is always above water. North and South Vereker Banks are completely submerged at high tide. On Tungsha Island, the

ROC government set up a national monument and a corridor on June 30, 1989, and May 18, 1992, respectively, to assert its sovereignty over the archipelago.

Tungsha Islands enjoy a subtropical climate, which is influenced by northeast winds during the winter. They experience their warmest weather in July, with an average temperature of 29.8°C. Temperatures are lowest in January, when the average is 22°C.

The areas around Tungsha provide excellent fishing grounds, and ROC fishermen visit the region during March and April. In addition to being a source of salt, fish, and minerals, the islands are an outpost for the ROC navy in the South China Sea. A hospital, power station, satellite tracking station, and runway have been built on Tungsha Island. A fishermen's service center also provides emergency shelter for fishermen operating in the South China Sea. There are three jetties and an onshore service center, which gives directions to fishing boats.

Nansha (Spratly) Islands

Nansha Islands consist of 180 islands, reefs, cays, and banks, in an area that stretches 810 km from north to south and 900 km from east to west. Taiping Island, the major island of the group, is located in the center of the island group. Six hundred and eighty miles to its north lies Hong Kong; 700 miles to its northeast is Kaohsiung; and Singapore is located 880 miles southwest of the island. James Shoal at the south of the island complex is the southernmost Chinese territory.

Taiping Island is located at 114°22' E longitude and 10°23' N latitude. The island has a land area of only 489,600 sq. meters, and stretches 1,360 meters from east to west and 350 meters from north to south. Its average altitude is 3.8 meters above sea level. A cross-island highway runs about one km and a trip round the island can be completed in 30 minutes. The area has abundant fishing, mineral, and petroleum resources.

Nansha Islands have a strategic importance, and ROC coast guards are currently stationed on Taiping Island. Facilities on the island include a radar station, meteorological center, power plant, library, and activities center.

Pacific Coast Islands

The two major islands located off the Pacific coast of Taiwan are Green Island 綠島 and Orchid Island 蘭嶼. (For further information on these islands, see Chapter 22, Tourism.)

To the northeast of Taiwan are the Tiaoyutai Islets 釣魚臺列嶼, a tiny archipelago of Tiaoyutai 釣魚臺, Huangwei Islet 黃尾嶼, Chihwei Islet 赤尾嶼, Nan Hsiao-tao 南小島, Pei Hsiao-tao 北小島, and three neighboring reefs. The group has a total area of 6.3 square kilometers, and lies just 75 nautical miles northeast of Pengjia Islet (彭佳嶼), Keelung. These islets were officially included as Chinese territory as early as the Ming dynasty.

Further Reading (in Chinese):

Nei-cheng Tung-chi Ti-yao 內政統計提要 (Statistical Abstract of the Interior of the Republic of China). Taipei: Ministry of the Interior, annual. (The Ministry of the Interior also publishes numerous maps, atlases, and local gazetteers of the Republic of China and Taiwan Province.)

Wang Lu 王魯. Chung-kuo Ti-li Tung-lun 中國地理通論 (General Introduction to the Geography of China). Taipei: New Learning Publishing Center, 1988.

Related Websites
1. Ministry of the Interior: http://www.moi.gov.tw
2. Central Weather Bureau, MOTC: http://www.cwb.gov.tw

2

People

A group of youth perform a folk dance at the Double Ten National Day celebrations.

2 PEOPLE

What's New
1. Figures updated
2. Taiwan's population distribution by locality
3. Recognition of the Shao tribe of aborigines

Taiwan's total population was 22.35 million as of July 2001. This chapter presents a comprehensive view of Taiwan's population distribution and composition, as well as a summary of the emergence of the majority Han group, which forms the cultural core of both the Chinese mainland and Taiwan.

Taiwan's Population Distribution

The population density of the ROC on Taiwan is 616 persons per square kilometer, making it the second highest in the world after Bangladesh. Taipei City, which covers 272 sq. km, is Taiwan's most crowded urban area with 9,737 persons per square kilometer. Kaohsiung City (154 sq. km) is next, with 9,704 persons per square kilometer; and Taichung City (163 sq. km), the third most populated area, has 5,910 persons per square kilometer.

Heavily populated urban areas have grown outside the official limits of major cities, forming large metropolitan areas, which are now home to 68.65 percent of Taiwan's total population. Among the island's metropolitan areas, the Chungli-Taoyuan Greater Metropolitan Area grew the fastest in 2000, with a population increase of 2.54 percent. The Taichung-Changhua Greater Metropolitan Area was second with a 1.89 percent growth rate. The metropolitan area with the highest population remains the Taipei-Keelung Greater Metropolitan Area, with 6.52 million residents and 42.61 percent of Taiwan's urban population. The Kaohsiung Greater Metropolitan Area is second with 2.73 million residents, and the Taichung-Changhua Greater Metropolitan Area is the third most populous, with 2.09 million people.

The earliest census taken in Taiwan recorded the island's population at 3.12 million in 1905. After 40 years, the figure nearly doubled to 6.02 million. The population further increased to 7.39 million in 1949 due to the influx of migrants from the Chinese mainland. The next year, the natural rate of population increase peaked at 3.84 percent. A baby boom in the postwar years put excessive population pressure on Taiwan's economy, and the ROC government began encouraging family planning. By 2000, the population growth rate had dropped to 0.83 percent.

The birth rate rose from 1.29 percent in 1999 to 1.38 percent in 2000, while the death rate slightly dropped from 0.573 percent in 1999 to 0.568 percent in 2000. Clearly, the population structure has undergone great changes over the last few decades. As those born during the baby boom have grown to maturity, the economically

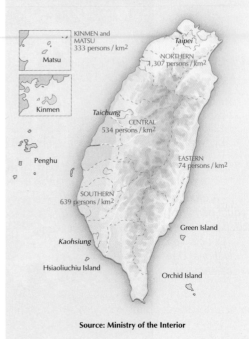

Population Density of the Taiwan Area December 2000

KINMEN and MATSU
333 persons / km²

Matsu

Kinmen

Penghu

Taipei

NORTHERN
1,307 persons / km²

Taichung

CENTRAL
534 persons / km²

EASTERN
74 persons / km²

SOUTHERN
639 persons / km²

Green Island

Kaohsiung

Hsiaoliuchiu Island

Orchid Island

Source: Ministry of the Interior

Population Statistics for the Taiwan and Fujian Areas by Locality

Locality	Population (persons)				Population Density
	Total		Male	Female	(persons per km²)
	Persons	(%) of population			
December 2000	22,276,672	100.00	11,392,050	10,884,622	615.58
Taiwan Area	22,216,107	99.73	11,360,358	10,855,749	617.01
Taiwan Province	18,079,073	81.16	9,298,274	8,780,799	508.11
Taipei County	3,567,896	16.02	1,801,773	1,766,123	1,738.26
Ilan County	465,186	2.09	240,691	224,495	217.01
Taoyuan County	1,732,617	7.78	890,755	841,862	1,419.07
Hsinchu County	439,713	1.97	230,167	209,546	308.01
Miaoli County	559,703	2.51	293,952	265,751	307.48
Taichung County	1,494,308	6.71	766,922	727,386	728.41
Changhua County	1,310,531	5.88	679,393	631,138	1,219.78
Nantou County	541,537	2.43	282,873	258,664	131.88
Yunlin County	743,368	3.34	392,911	350,457	575.88
Chiayi County	562,305	2.52	296,936	265,369	295.69
Tainan County	1,107,687	4.97	572,550	535,137	549.45
Kaohsiung County	1,234,707	5.54	641,615	593,092	442.13
Pingtung County	907,590	4.07	473,928	433,662	326.99
Taichung County	245,312	1.10	131,806	113,506	69.79
Hualien County	353,630	1.59	187,174	166,456	76.40
Penghu County	89,496	0.40	46,877	42,619	705.45
Keelung City	388,425	1.74	199,061	189,364	2,925.79
Hsinchu City	368,439	1.65	187,972	180,467	3,539.40
Taichung City	965,790	4.34	477,183	488,607	5,909.66
Chiayi City	266,183	1.19	133,793	132,390	4,434.49
Tainan City	734,650	3.30	369,942	364,708	4,182.57
Taipei City	2,646,474	11.88	1,309,308	1,337,166	9,736.85
Kaohsiung City	1,490,560	6.69	752,776	737,784	9,703.98
Fujian Province	60,565	0.27	31,692	28,873	333.04
Kinmen County	53,832	0.24	27,901	25,931	351.71
Lienchiang County	6,733	0.03	3,791	2,942	233.78

Source: Ministry of the Interior

productive 15-to-64 age group increased to 70.26 percent of the total population in 2000. Meanwhile, the proportion of dependents dropped from 64 percent in 1975 to 42 percent in 2000.

Longer education, delayed marriages, and comparatively fewer potential mothers between the ages of 20 and 34 have reduced the birth rate. Since 1984, the population replacement rate has remained below 1 percent, dropping to 0.8 percent in 2000.

Population Policy

The average age in the Taiwan area is rising. According to 1999 figures from the Ministry of the Interior, the average life expectancy in the Taiwan area was 75.04 years, with men living an average of 72.46 years, and women, 78.12 years. In 2000, 8.62 percent of the population was over 65 years of age, up from 8.44 percent in 1999. This puts Taiwan midway between "older" countries like Great Britain (16 percent), France (15 percent), Japan (13 percent), and the United States (13 percent) and "younger neighbors" like the Chinese mainland and South Korea (6 percent each), and Thailand and the Philippines (4 percent each).

The Taiwan index of aging, calculated by dividing the number of people over 65 years of age by the number under the age of 15, is 40.9 percent. A national population policy and policy guidelines on Taiwan's aging population were revised by the Ministry of the Interior and approved by the Executive Yuan in November 1992. Contrary to past family planning programs aimed at curtailing population growth, the ministry now proposes a moderate increase. "Two are just right" 兩個恰恰好 is the new family planning slogan. The ROC government's population policy and national family planning program received top marks among developing countries from the US Population Crisis Committee in 1987, 1992, and 1997.

Gender Imbalance

Among the 307,200 births registered in the Taiwan area in 2000, there were 109.45 boys for every 100 baby girls.

The ratio in Taiwan reflects the traditional preference among Asian parents for boys, which has led to an imbalance, as certain private hospitals and small clinics in Taiwan ignore the ban on using chorionic villus sampling to determine fetus gender and perform abortions for parents who do not want a girl.

Many young Taiwan newlyweds plan to have only one child for economic and lifestyle reasons. In 1965, 72 percent of parents wanted two children, but the percentage had decreased to 24 percent by 1991. Tradition favors male descendants, thus, parents who only want one child usually prefer a boy. In 1965, only 6 percent of potential mothers preferred their first child to be a baby boy; but by 1991, some 52 percent preferred boys.

According to 2000 figures, among families having more than one child, the male-to-female ratio was 107:100 for the first born, 108:100 for the second child, 119:100 for the third; and 135:100 for the fourth.

Some medical professionals have suggested that the situation is a result of the 1985 promulgation of the *Genetic Health Law* 優生保健法, which allows abortion 24 weeks into pregnancy if the fetus is found to have a congenital defect. The law may have been used by some doctors as a pretext for performing otherwise illegal abortions. However, according to a survey by the Family Planning Institute, the abortion rate in Taiwan increased only slightly after the *Genetic Health Law* was enacted.

Taiwan's Ethnic Composition

The Han 漢, the largest ethnic group in Taiwan, comprise roughly 98 percent of the ROC's population. The remaining 2 percent consists of indigenous peoples from Taiwan's ten different aboriginal tribes, as well as almost 60 other non-Han minorities from the Chinese mainland.

The Han on Taiwan are usually classified into two different groups: early Han Chinese immigrants, who are often referred to as "Taiwanese," and immigrants who moved to Taiwan with the ROC government in 1949, generally referred to as "mainlanders." The Taiwanese group comprises 85 percent of the Han population and is often subdivided even further into the Hakka, who are mostly from Guangdong Province; and the Southern Fujianese. The Fujianese outnumber the Hakka by approximately three to one. The mainlanders comprise slightly less than 15 percent of the Han population. Intermarriage between all four groups—indigenous peoples, Hakkas, Southern Fujianese, and mainlanders—is quite common, so the distinguishing characteristics of each group grow fainter with the passage of time.

On October 25, 1998, Taiwan's Retrocession Day, former President Lee Teng-hui first proposed the concept of the "new Taiwanese" to promote ethnic unity. Its highest ideal is to see future generations no longer discriminating between those whose ancestors came to Taiwan earlier and those who came more recently. This concept of the "new Taiwanese" still retains the principle that people in the Taiwan area are

Field trips provide valuable and fun learning experiences for kindergarten students.
(Courtesy of Yi Hsing Kindergarten)

ethnically and culturally Chinese, but emphasizes the attachment of the people to Taiwan.

The term "Chinese" includes all these peoples and is mainly a cultural designation. Throughout China's long history, numerous ethnic groups from diverse areas were united by a set of complex and generally consistent national characteristics; however, the origins of some of these groups remain unidentified. What is today called the majority Han people has been, from the outset, an aggregate ethnic group named after the Han dynasty. The ancient predecessors of the Han people were the Hua-Hsia 華夏 people. Similarly, *Cina* was an Indian transliteration of the name of the influential state of Chin 秦, during the Warring States Period 戰國時代. *Cina* was later transformed into the word "China," which still serves as the western name of the nation.

Taiwan's Indigenous Peoples

An excellent place to get a comprehensive introduction to Taiwan's ten major tribes is the Aboriginal Culture Park 原住民文化園區, located in Machia Rural Township 瑪家鄉 in Pingtung County 屏東縣. Designated areas of the village display and explain the common traditional dwellings, utensils, clothing, activities, and customs of the nine major peoples. Performances of tribal music and dance are held daily.

In historical records, Taiwan's indigenous peoples were called the Eastern Ti 東鯷 or Eastern Fan 東番, terms which translate as "savages." During the Ching dynasty, the indigenous peoples were assimilated into Han culture to varying degrees (for details see Chapter 4, History).

Archaeologists have found evidence of prehistoric human habitation in Taiwan that dates back 12,000 to 15,000 years, indicating that Taiwan's tribes came from at least two different places: southern China and Austronesia. In general, early settlers from southern China settled in northern and central Taiwan, while Australoid settlements were mainly in southern Taiwan and along the eastern coast.

There are currently ten major indigenous peoples in Taiwan Province: the Atayal 泰雅族, Saisiyat 賽夏族, Bunun 布農族, Tsou 鄒族, Shao 邵族, Paiwan 排灣族, Rukai 魯凱族, Puyuma 卑南族, Ami 阿美族, and Yami 雅美族. Plains-dwelling tribes, or the Pingpu 平埔 people (including the

Ketagalan, Luilang, Favorlang, Kavalan, Taokas, Pazeh, Papora, Babuza, Hoanya, Siraya, and Sao), have ceased to exist as distinct groups due to assimilation with Han Chinese over the last three centuries. The mountain peoples have maintained their cultural identities by resisting intermarriage. In May 2001, the number of indigenous people in the Taiwan area was approximately 413,519. The Ami account for over one third of the indigenous population, followed by the Atayal and Paiwan. The Yami is the smallest group. Many indigenous people live in mountainous reservations, which cannot be sold to non-aborigines.

Each indigenous group has its own tribal language. These languages are called "Formosan" to distinguish them from "Taiwanese," which is the Southern Fujianese dialect of Chinese spoken widely in Taiwan. These languages belong to the Proto-Austronesian linguistic family, an agglutinative language type, to which both Malaysian and Hawaiian belong. The Austronesian language that is spoken in Taiwan can be subdivided into three branches: Atayalic, Tsouic, and Paiwanic. There is, however, a greater diversity among the Formosan languages than among those Philippine languages and dialects that are related to the Formosan languages. For this reason, some scholars believe that Taiwan may have been the original homeland of the vast Austronesian linguistic group.

Cultural characteristics formerly common to all or most of the groups include animism; lack of shrines or sanctuaries within tribal settlements (except for the *kuba* of the Paiwan people); lack of written language; horizontal back-strap loom weaving and in-woven designs; bark cloth making tapa; ironsmithing to make knives, spearpoints, and other implements; slash-and-burn cultivation; cultivation of millet and tuber crops, such as sweet potatoes and taro; production of fermented-grain wine (except among the Yami); treatment of disease by female shamans; the hunting of deer, wild boar, and other animals with bow and arrow, harpoon-like spears, snares, and traps; and head-hunting (except among the

Yami). Below are some of the distinctive historical traits of the ten main tribes in Taiwan.

Atayal

The Atayal are distributed over a large area in the northern part of Taiwan's central mountain regions: northern Nantou and Hualien 花蓮, Ilan 宜蘭, and Taipei Counties. They can also be found in Taoyuan, Hsinchu 新竹, Miaoli 苗栗, and Taichung Counties. Their language is divided into the Atayal and Sedeg branches and is apparently not closely related to any other aboriginal language. In the past, their staple foods were corn, rice, sweet potatoes, and taro. The typical Atayal house was semi-subterranean and made of stacked branches and cordwood of varying lengths placed between upright roof supports, with gable roofs made of thatch, bark shingles, or slate. Clothing design was typified by rectilinear woven and beaded motifs. Facial tattooing among both men and women for personal adornment and to ward off evil was a special feature of this people. Their traditions of tattooing, head-hunting, and burial of the dead under dwelling structures ended almost a century ago.

The Atayal kinship system is ambilineal, with a tendency for nuclear families preferring patrilocal residence. All three Atayal branches, the Segoleg, Tseole, and Sedeg, have patriarchal social systems. Several leaders from community ritual groups, or *gaga*, usually controlled the political authority and economy. Atayal society was relatively closed and did not readily accept outsiders. The Atayal believe in spirits and unnamed supernatural powers, which they call *utux,* as well as spirits of the dead.

Saisiyat

In terms of population, the Saisiyat are the second smallest of the island's aboriginal peoples. Their language is divided into northern and southern dialect groups. The northern Saisiyat live in the mountainous region of Hsinchu County. Most of the Saisiyat of the southern branch live in Miaoli's highlands. The Saisiyat were long threatened by their aggressive Atayal neighbors, and their culture has been strongly influenced by the Atayal. The early Saisiyat practiced crop rotation, slash-and-burn mountain cultivation, hunting, and river fishing. Later, they turned to settled agriculture and forestry.

The Saisiyat were among the first to be acculturated by the Han Chinese and adopted Chinese surnames that were transliterations of such Saisiyat totemic surnames as bee, spider, and crab. The basic structural unit of Saisiyat society is the totemic clan linked by geographical and family ties. Three or four households of the same clan name or totem constitute a settlement and clan worship group. Several neighboring settlements might unite to form a village with shared farmland, fishing zones, and mutual assistance units.

The Saisiyat habit of tattooing disappeared long ago. However, the Saisiyat in Miaoli County continue to observe a unique rite, the Ceremony of the Dwarfs, or *Pastáai,* once every two years in November. According to legend, a group of three-foot tall, dark-skinned dwarfs once taught the Saisiyat to farm, sing, and dance, but also harassed and threatened the Saisiyat women. The Saisiyat retaliated by inviting the dwarfs to a ceremony and then pushing them into a ravine as they crossed a narrow footbridge. The original purpose of the ceremony was to appease the souls of these dwarfs.

Bunun

The Bunun live in mountainous regions of central Taiwan, including Hualien, Taitung 臺東, and parts of Nantou, and Kaohsiung Counties. Six cognate groups are included under the designation Bunun: the Taketodo, Takebaka, Takevatan, Takbanuath, Isibukun, and Takopulan. Alternating cultivation of corn and beans by slash-and-burn agriculture was typical of the Bunun. Corn was their staple food, and beans were an economic crop. Making liquor from corn was also typical of the Bunun. Hunting was a key occupation, and it figures importantly in the Bunun oral literary tradition. Traditional houses were made by digging into the slope of a hillside and constructing an earth and stone

terrace in front to provide a level or split-level foundation for the house and a large courtyard.

The Bunun are patrilineal, with extended family households grouped in small villages. Usually, these extended families have more than 20 members living in the same house. Patriarchal rule is absolute regarding familial division of labor, but every member has fair access to the settlement's resources, such as arable land and hunting grounds. Their production-consumption mode of living and the group-sharing norm made accumulation of wealth impossible; thus, social stratification did not emerge in Bunun society. Close family ties give Bunun communities greater cohesion than in some other aboriginal groups. They have been relatively accepting of outsiders and have incorporated cultural traits, such as clothing styles and facial tattooing from other peoples, including the Atayal, Tsou, Rukai, and Paiwan. The Bunun practiced the extraction of certain teeth as a sign of social identity and adulthood.

Bunun pottery features impressed geometric designs. The Bunun have a strong musical tradition, which was developed partly through the use of song to communicate over long distances. Early Bunun religious beliefs mentioned in oral literature include periodic offerings to the moon. The Bunun also believe in the existence of *hanido,* or guardian spirit, which determines the innate ability of a person. Bunun male and female shamans, were responsible for treating illnesses through sorcery.

Tsou and Shao

The Tsou depend mainly on mountain agriculture for their livelihood, but supplement it

Population of Indigenous Peoples in Taiwan, 2001	
Plains Dwellers	193,889
Mountain Dwellers	219,630
Total	413,519
Source: Ministry of the Interior	

by hunting, fishing, and raising animals. Traditional Tsou houses had rounded corners and dome-shaped roofs of thatch, which extended nearly to the ground-level packed-mud floor. The men's meeting hut, or *kuba,* serves as a religious and political center. The activities carried out in the *kuba* enhance clan social solidarity. The coming-of-age ceremony takes place in these meeting huts, which also once housed the cage for enemy heads and the box of fire-striking implements. The *hosa* was the basic political unit composed of several small tribes or clans, which established the hierarchy of power and distributed wealth.

The Tsou are patrilineal, with high positions, such as chiefs, war leaders, and elders. The former prominence of hunting among the Tsou is demonstrated by the extensive use of leather in their clothing. Their pottery, like that of the Bunun, is also adorned with impressed geometric designs.

The Tsou speak one of three languages: Tsou, Kanakanabu, or Saaroa. Spirits are called *hicu,* *ucu,* and *i'icu* in the three language groups, but unlike the Atayal and Bunun, the Tsou also have many particularized names for gods and spirits. Of all aboriginal tongues, the Tsou language has the least in common with the other Formosan languages, suggesting that it was separated from the common ancestral language in the very distant past. Tsou people are found in Chiayi 嘉義 (Mt. Ali 阿里山), Nantou (Sun Moon Lake 日月潭), and Kaohsiung Counties.

On August 8, 2001, the Executive Yuan formally approved the Shao, as the tenth aboriginal tribe in Taiwan. The Shao are the smallest of the island's aboriginal peoples with a population between 355-450, living in the Sun Moon Lake area (Yuchi Rural Township 魚池鄉 and Shuili Rural Township 水里鄉) of Nantou County.

Because of geography, the Shao were categorized as members of the Tsou in the past. Actually, they are quite different from the Tsou in language, lifestyle, and customs.

Paiwan and Rukai

The Paiwan, closely related in material culture to the Rukai, are divided into the Raval and Butaul

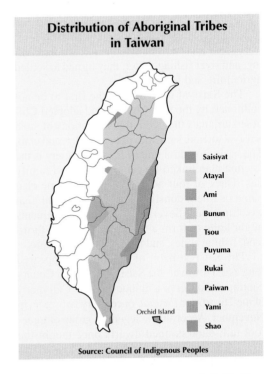

Distribution of Aboriginal Tribes in Taiwan

- Saisiyat
- Atayal
- Ami
- Bunun
- Tsou
- Puyuma
- Rukai
- Paiwan
- Yami
- Shao

Orchid Island

Source: Council of Indigenous Peoples

peoples. The Butaul can be further subdivided into the Paumaumaq, Chaoboobol, Parilarilao, and Pagarogaro groups. The main occupation of the Paiwan and Rukai is agriculture.

The traditional houses of the Paiwan and Rukai are similar to those of the Bunun. A site was leveled by digging into a slope, and then an earth and stone terrace was extended outward to provide a slightly lower than ground level floor and a slightly higher courtyard. Houses of the southern and eastern Paiwan, however, were frequently constructed at ground level. The Paiwan and Rukai are noted for their outstanding wood and stone sculpture. Ancestral figures were often carved in shallow relief into house posts, slate, or plank panels.

Paiwan kinship was originally matrilineal but is now ambilineal. The custom is, however, not consistent among all branches. Most marriages are matrilocal. The hereditary chieftainship plays an important role in their oral literature. In the past, the Paiwan observed class distinctions between nobility and commoners, and interclass marriage was forbidden.

Puyuma

Traditionally, the Puyuma depended on growing millet, taro, sweet potatoes, and beans on hillside plots cleared by burning. They supplemented farming with fishing and hunting. The Puyuma live in a flatland area of Taitung County, and they have been greatly influenced by Paiwan and Rukai culture. The Puyuma have a multilineal kinship system with ritual groups. The extended family inheritance goes to the eldest daughter, but the kinship system is ambilineal. The positions of chieftains and shamans are patrilineal. Like the closely-related Paiwan, Puyuma society is stratified into "chiefly" (noble) families and commoners. Marriage between the two classes is, however, not prohibited. The more prominent ritual groups in each village cluster around the various "chiefly" families.

The clergy come from the leading clans' ancestral worship groups, which are called *karumangan*. Since 1964, there have been only three groups, which are responsible for performing ceremonies during harvests twice a year. The largest basic unit of a Puyuma settlement is called a *samawan*. Each *samawan* has a *karumahan*, or center of ancestor worship, and a *parakoang*, or men's meeting house. *Karumahan* of the same name belong to the same ancestor. Men's meeting houses accept members at age 15.

Samawan are divided into *saja munan*. The latter are composed of groups of families, which share the same ancestor and bear the collective name of their leading clan. A chief's power is symbolized by his role in ancestor worship and the transfer of tribal knowledge, not from monopolization of land, as in the Paiwan and Rukai.

Ami

The Ami, the largest indigenous group in terms of population, are mainly plains dwellers, living in the valleys of the Hualien-Taitung area. The Ami can be divided into five groups based

Minority Studies in Taiwan

Scholarly research on China's minority peoples and cultures is conducted by the Institute of Ethnology at the Academia Sinica 中央研究院民族學研究所.

Courses on the languages, histories, and cultures of the Mongolian, Tibetan, Manchu, Uighur, and Taiwan indigenous peoples are offered in both the Department and the Graduate School of Ethnology at National Chengchi University 政治大學民族學系暨研究所. The Tibetan language is offered at National Taiwan Normal University 臺灣師範大學. Some courses on China's minorities are offered through the Department of Anthropology at National Taiwan University 臺灣大學人類學系, the Institute of Sociology and Anthropology at National Tsinghua University 清華大學社會人類學研究所, the College of Indigenous Study at National Dong Hwa University 東華大學原住民民族學院, and the Graduate School of Indigenous Culture at National Tainan Teachers College 臺南師範學院鄉土文化研究所.

Missionaries and others serving in the United Bible Societies in Taiwan have compiled numerous materials on indigenous languages and continue their work of translating the Bible into these languages.

on geography, customs, and language: the northern Ami are also known as the Nanshih 南勢 group; the central Ami belong to the coastal and Hsiukuluan 秀姑巒 groups; and the southern Ami can be classified into the Peinan 卑南 and Hengchun 恆春 groups. The Ami began to use oxen to cultivate paddy fields relatively early. They continue to fish, but now hunt only for recreation.

Ami houses are traditionally built flat on the ground, with the main beams and posts made of hard wood, and subsidiary beams usually of bamboo or betel palm. Walls were made of double layers of plaited dwarf bamboo, with grass thatch in between to keep out the cold wind. Due to a comparatively advanced level of agriculture capable of supporting a considerable number of people, traditional Ami villages were relatively large, with populations of between 200 and 1,000.

The Ami are the only indigenous group living on the island of Taiwan to preserve the art of pottery making. Pottery in the form of food vessels, water ewers, rice pots, and earthenware steamers is made by women. Sacrificial vessels in varying sizes are also made, and these are buried with their owner at death.

Ami society is matrilineal, and the oldest woman in the extended family is generally the household head. Men, however, exercise authority when village councils of leading men from each village ward are held in the men's meeting houses. A rigid system of authority based on age is enforced. The Ami have elaborate cosmogonic myths, which may be recited only by trained male "lineage priests" and are subject to strict recitation-related taboos.

Yami

The Yami live almost exclusively on Orchid Island (Lanyu 蘭嶼), 44 nautical miles off the eastern coast of Taitung County. Culturally, the Yami are closely related to the inhabitants of the Batan Islands of the Philippines, and the Yami language and Ivatan dialect of the Batanes are mutually intelligible. The Yami language also seems to be quite closely related to the Paiwanic languages on Taiwan.

Fishing is central to the Yami economy, and many of the fish caught are preserved by drying. The basic cooperative and distributive units of the Yami are fishing groups formed by kinsmen in villages from the same region. Ceremonies related to fishing have become part of the Yami culture. The Yami grow taro extensively, as well as sweet potatoes, yams, and millet. Men are responsible for laying out fields, building boats, fishing, constructing homes, and making baskets, pottery, and metalwork. Women tend the fields, gather taro, cook, and weave cloth.

Yami dwellings are somewhat similar to those of the Paiwan, Rukai, and Bunun: a rectangular pit is first dug, then low stone walls line the top of the house pit as protection against frequent and fierce typhoons. Elevated "rest houses" called

tagakal are used for sleeping or working when it is too hot to work in the house. The Yami live in nuclear families and tend towards patrilocality. Inheritance is patrilineal.

The Yami are constantly haunted by a fear and hatred of ghosts. They think ghosts exercising evil influence are the cause of all mischief. The Yami do not have regular shamans, but they do believe magical amulets to be effective against mischief.

The Yami are known for their unique and beautifully decorated dugout canoes, which can carry eight to ten people. The Yami are Taiwan's only indigenous group known to practice silversmithing, and the only people that have never practiced headhunting or made alcohol. There is no chieftainship. One of the more notable of the many colorful Yami celebrations is an elaborate ceremony held upon the launching of a newly-completed boat.

The Life of Taiwan's Indigenous Peoples Today

Changes are taking place in tribal culture and lifestyles, as the descendants of Taiwan's earliest inhabitants adjust to rapid modernization. Young people are leaving traditional occupations, such as farming, hunting, and fishing, and are taking up factory and construction work in the cities.

The use of Formosan languages varies according to area. On Orchid Island, for example, Yami is still widely spoken; however, throughout Taiwan, native speakers are dwindling in number, and young people are usually not as fluent in their ancestral language as they are in Mandarin or Taiwanese. Bilingual education is being promoted and the publication of stories and legends is being undertaken as oral literary traditions attenuate (see Chapter 3, Language). A six-year research program covering a comprehensive history of Taiwan's indigenous peoples, was started in 1993 by the Historical Research Commission of Taiwan Province 臺灣省文獻會.

Some native traditions, such as periodic tribal festivals that celebrate a rich harvest with singing and dancing, are still maintained and, although most tribes have switched to Western attire, loincloths are still common attire on Orchid Island. By adopting Han Chinese dietary habits, most indigenous people now eat a much more varied diet than did their forefathers. Animistic and shamanistic beliefs have largely given way to Christianity, due to intensive missionary efforts.

Education is increasingly providing a way for the young to improve their lives. During the Japanese occupation, only 19 tribe members graduated from Taiwan's middle school. In 1999, the number of aboriginal students totaled 85,203, with 6,780 in university or college, and 11,765 in high school. Since 1991, the government has given 25 special scholarships for aboriginal students to study overseas.

Members of Taiwan's indigenous peoples are increasingly active in local and national politics. More than 6,000 work in various government agencies, 252 serve in central or local representative organizations, and the number is growing. As of June 2001, two served as ambassadors-at-large and national policy advisors to the president, nine held seats in the Legislative Yuan, two were councilors in special municipalities, and 55 were city and county council members. Thirty serve as magistrates of rural townships with predominantly indigenous constituents. Taitung County, where indigenous peoples comprise a large proportion of the electorate.

The overall educational and income levels of Taiwan's indigenous people, however, still lag behind those of Han Chinese, and many face acute social problems such as alcoholism, unemployment, and prostitution. Therefore, in 1992 the Ministry of the Interior began implementing a six-year Living Guidance Plan for Aborigines Residing in Cities 都市原住民生活輔導計畫. The plan calls for spending approximately US$8 million to promote indigenous culture and to provide urban-based indigenous people with subsidized medical care, legal advice, adolescent educational guidance, employment counseling, and business loans. Additionally, a construction plan to improve the roads linking tribal villages with nearby metropolitan communities was begun in 1992, further reducing the gap in living standards.

The cabinet-level Council of Indigenous Peoples of the Executive Yuan 行政院原住民族委員會 is the agency responsible for indigenous affairs at the central government level. Corresponding organizations at the local government level are the Taipei City Government's Council of Aboriginal Affairs 臺北市政府原住民事務委員會, and the Kaohsiung City Government's Commission of Indigenous Affairs 高雄市政府原住民事務委員會. In addition to government agencies, over 40 private organizations are devoted to tribal welfare, including World Vision of Taiwan 臺灣世界展望會.

Search for an Appropriate Name

Heated controversy flared in Taiwan during the 1992 constitutional amendment process in the Second National Assembly, regarding the official name to be used for the island's indigenous peoples. For years, the various indigenous peoples had been collectively called *shan-pao* 山胞 "mountain compatriots," and the term is incorporated into the Constitution of the Republic of China. Many indigenous people proposed that this be changed, claiming that the term conveyed a degree of discrimination. They asserted that the term *yuan-chu-min* 原住民 (aborigines or indigenous peoples) is more suitable.

Parliamentarians representing indigenous people said that they wanted appropriate wording in the Constitution as a step toward giving these citizens the "dignity and justice" they seldom experienced in society. Indigenous people were looking forward to gaining greater social status via a constitutional amendment, which they felt would enhance their legal protection and lead to increased assistance from the government to improve the overall standard of living among the indigenous population.

During the fourth extraordinary session of the Second National Assembly at its 32nd plenary meeting in July 1994, National Assembly members adopted the term *yuan-chu-min* to replace the expression *shan-pao,* when they passed a series of Additional Articles of the ROC Constitution 中華民國憲法增修條文. According to

The Rukai, like the Paiwan people, believed their founding chieftain was a snake in human form. The legend serves as a popular motif in decorating their garments.

the articles, "The state shall accord the aborigines in the free area legal protection of their status and the right to political participation. It shall also provide assistance and encouragement for their education, cultural preservation, social welfare, and business undertakings. The same protection and assistance shall be given to the people of the Kinmen and Matsu areas."

Mongolian and Tibetan Affairs

The ROC government agency which serves Mongolians and Tibetans worldwide, is the Mongolian and Tibetan Affairs Commission 蒙藏委員會 of the Executive Yuan. The commission has organizations in many foreign countries, including the United States, Canada, Germany, Switzerland, India, and Nepal, to serve local Mongolian and Tibetan communities. The commission's goals are to build and maintain a worldwide

liaison network for Mongolians and Tibetans, offering programs to improve their living conditions and raise the level of education. The commission has established a scholarship program for outstanding overseas Tibetan students to complete their education.

The commission publishes a colorful monthly pictorial, *Mongolian Tibetan Friendship* 蒙藏之友, with articles in Chinese, English, Mongolian, and Tibetan, featuring current political affairs, as well as Mongolian and Tibetan culture, history, and art. The commission also provides regular Mongolian and Tibetan language broadcasts.

Related Websites
1. Ministry of the Interior:*http://www.moi.gov.tw*
2. Council of Indigenous Peoples:*http://www.apc.gov.tw*
3. Mongolian & Tibetan Affairs Commission:*http://www.mtac.gov.tw*

3
Language

The "King of Calligraphy," Wang Hsi-chih (307-365), was known for his unrestrained style of running script.
(Courtesy of the National Palace Museum)

The National Language

Mandarin, the national language of the Republic of China and of the Chinese mainland, is based on the Beijing dialect. Formerly referred to as Official Speech 官話, the Beijing dialect has had approximately 1,000 years of history as the common language of politics and commerce in China, particularly in the North.

The Choice of Mandarin

The need to establish an official national language was felt as early as the 17th century when the Ching dynasty established a number of "correct pronunciation institutes" to teach standard Beijing pronunciation, particularly in the Cantonese and Fujianese-speaking southern provinces. The success of these schools, however, was extremely limited.

The concept of a national language coalesced around 1910. In 1913, the Ministry of Education (MOE) 教育部 convened a Commission on the Unification of Pronunciation 讀音統一會 to establish a standard national tongue. Delegates with linguistic backgrounds from all of China's provinces voted to decide on official pronunciations for each individual Chinese character. Wu Ching-heng 吳敬恆 (also known as Wu Chih-hui 吳稚暉), a philosopher and one of the founders of the ROC, was chosen to direct the task of creating a truly national language that would transcend locality and dialect. The Beijing dialect was the general foundation of the new national language, but features of various local dialects were also incorporated. This hybrid is now known to English speakers as Mandarin.

Phonetic Symbols

There was a great deal of disagreement as to the best way to notate the sounds of Mandarin. The three main options were modified Chinese characters, a new set of phonetic symbols, and romanization. The system that was eventually adopted and developed was the predecessor of today's Mandarin Phonetic Symbols (MPS) 注音符號. This collection of 39 symbols (later 40)

plus four tone marks and a voicing symbol was designed by Chang Ping-lin 章炳麟 (also known as Chang Tai-yen 章太炎).

Once the phonetic alphabet was approved and promulgated by the MOE in November 1918, primary school textbooks were required to use it alongside Chinese characters. In April 1919, the MOE formally established the Preparatory Committee for the Unification of the National Language 國語統一籌備委員會. Mandarin became the required language of instruction in elementary and middle schools. Gramophone records recorded by Wang Pu 王璞 in Shanghai and Y.R. Chao 趙元任 in the US in 1920 and 1921 were used as a standard reference for correct pronunciation. The tonal system used was basically that of the Beijing dialect, but originally a fifth tone marker for words pronounced in the "entering" tone of Middle Chinese (i.e., syllables ending in a -*p*, -*t*, or -*k* stop) was added, based on the Nanjing dialect. Since the Beijing dialect had not preserved this distinction for over 500 years, this feature was eliminated in 1924. In 1932, a new system was devised for indicating the tone of a word, and three initials which were not used in standard Beijing dialect were dropped, bringing the total number of MPS to today's 37.

Romanization

In 1928, the MOE promulgated a system of romanization for Mandarin, *Gwoyeu Romatzyh* 國語羅馬字, dubbed the National Phonetic Symbols II 國音字母第二式. This intricate system incorporated the tone of each character into its romanized spelling. In spite of the system's official status, however, it has never been widely studied or used for two reasons: its complexity and the dominance of the Wade-Giles romanization system, which predates it. In 1984, the MOE announced the adoption of a modified form of *Gwoyeu Romatzyh*, in which tone spellings were replaced by tone marks. This, however, did not succeed in improving public acceptance of the system.

Since the Mandarin Phonetic Symbols (MPS) were promulgated by the MOE in November 1918, all ROC primary school students have been required to learn the phonetic alphabet in the first grade.
(Courtesy of the K.S.T. Education Corp.)

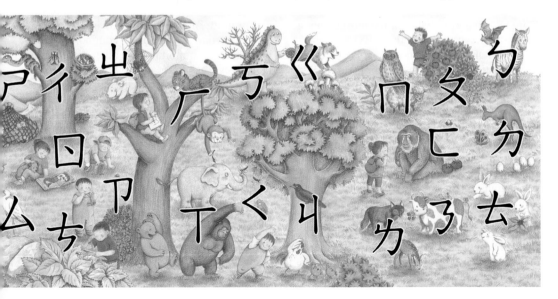

Wade-Giles is currently the de facto standard in Taiwan, despite official use of the Postal Standard by the Directorate General of Posts under the Ministry of Transportation and Communications 交通部郵政總局 and occasional utilization in the public and private sectors of spellings based on other romanization standards. The simultaneous use of different romanization systems to represent the same Chinese pronunciation often confuses non-Chinese speakers attempting to identify street or place names in Taiwan.

In December 1996, the Educational Reform Council 教育改革委員會, led by Dr. Lee Yuan-tseh 李遠哲, recommended that the government adopt a new romanization system—Tongyong Pinyin 通用拼音, chiefly devised by Dr. B.C. Yu 余伯泉 of Academia Sinica 中央研究院. According to Dr. Yu, Tongyong Pinyin can be used to romanize not only Mandarin Chinese but also local languages in Taiwan, including Southern Fujianese and Hakka, and it is "compatible" with the Hanyu Pinyin 漢語拼音 system promoted by the Chinese mainland. At a time when Hanyu Pinyin has become internationally accepted, Tongyong Pinyin represents a conscious effort to promote a romanization system suited to Taiwan's culture and society (see Appendix VIII to find a comparison table of the most common romanization systems and the MPS).

The MOE also saw a need to solve problems in the existing phonetic system. In January 1998, the MOE promulgated the Taiwan Language Phonetic System 臺灣語言音標系統, which was proposed by an MOE task force aimed at compiling guidelines for teaching dialects and aboriginal languages in March 1995. This system includes phonetic systems for Southern Fujianese and Hakka as well as phonetic symbols for aboriginal languages. Except for part of the phonetic symbols for aboriginal languages, the MOE's system has been registered with the International Organization for Standardization (ISO). By doing so, the MOE hopes to facilitate the use of information worldwide. However, the Taiwan Language Phonetic System and the MOE's actions have aroused criticism from academic groups. Some academicians have been developing their own system and are declining the use of this system.

Academia Sinica's Second Conference on Chinese Romanization System, held on May 27, 2000, demonstrated the diversity of views and the complexity of these issues. Topics such as establishing a norm for local pronunciation, developing a compatible romanization system for all local languages, remodeling programs for overseas Chinese, and taking into account non-linguistic elements were all discussed at the conference. Nevertheless, despite recommendation of the MOE's Mandarin Promotion Council in late 2000, a final decision is still pending until the minister of education convenes a new round of meetings to decide between the Tongyong and Hanyu Pinyin systems.

Languages in Taiwan Today

The Native Languages

For many years, native languages like Southern Fujianese (often called Taiwanese 臺灣話, spoken natively by perhaps 70 percent of the people of Taiwan) and Hakka, as well as the aborigine languages, were not given much official attention in Taiwan. In the process of making sure everyone mastered the common national language, the importance of other dialects and languages was played down. For example, Taiwanese dialect pop songs tended in the past to be stereotyped and relegated to a subordinate position in the market. In recent years, however, Southern Fujianese has entered the mainstream of popular culture. Singers are often expected to produce at least a few songs or an album in Southern Fujianese. Use of Southern Fujianese in advertising and business—from TV commercials to restaurant names—is considered fashionable. Bookstores now offer entire sections of literature written in a style reflecting spoken Southern Fujianese. Hakka, on the other hand, is being spoken less by younger generations who favor Mandarin and Southern Fujianese.

Distribution of Regional Dialects in Taiwan

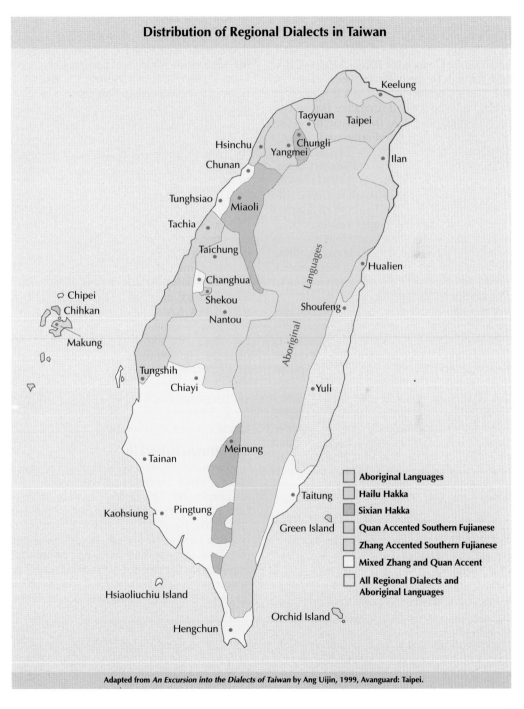

Keelung

Taoyuan
Taipei

Hsinchu
Chungli
Yangmei
Ilan

Chunan

Tunghsiao
Miaoli

Tachia

Taichung

Changhua
Hualien

Chipei
Shekou
Chihkan
Shoufeng
Nantou

Makung

Tungshih
Chiayi
Yuli

Languages

Aboriginal

Meinung

Tainan

Taitung

Kaohsiung
Pingtung

Green Island

Hsiaoliuchiu Island

Orchid Island

Hengchun

☐ **Aboriginal Languages**
☐ **Hailu Hakka**
☐ **Sixian Hakka**
☐ **Quan Accented Southern Fujianese**
☐ **Zhang Accented Southern Fujianese**
☐ **Mixed Zhang and Quan Accent**
☐ **All Regional Dialects and Aboriginal Languages**

Adapted from *An Excursion into the Dialects of Taiwan* by Ang Uijin, 1999, Avanguard: Taipei.

There are nearly four million Hakka people in Taiwan, but many of the young generation can no longer speak their mother tongue well. Therefore, the Council for Hakka Affairs (CHA) 客家委員會 was formally established on June 14, 2001. The top priority of the CHA is to preserve the Hakka language and revitalize Hakka culture. Following the CHA, the Research and Development Association on Formosan Language and Culture 福爾摩莎語言文化研究發展協會 became operational on June 17, 2001, in Hsinchu County, which has a high concentration of ethnic Hakka. Headed by Professor Ku Kuo-shun 古國順, who is also the director of the Institute of Applied Linguistics at National Taipei Teachers' College, the association works on projects such as compiling Hakka language textbooks, training Hakka language teachers, operating Hakka broadcasting study centers, and hosting various Hakka arts and cultural events.

Many aboriginal people are bilingual and have been assimilated into mainstream society. Although more people today are willing to identify with their aboriginal ancestry than in the past, the new generation who grew up in cities can no longer converse in their ancestral tongues. To rectify this, in June 2001, the Taipei City Government's Council of Aboriginal Affairs (CAA) 原住民事務委員會 cosponsored two aboriginal radio programs—one on the Taipei Broadcasting Station and the other on the Broadcasting Corp. of China—to introduce aboriginal languages, cultures, activities, as well as the latest policies and welfare packages to the aborigines in Taipei. Around the same time, the first program to combine the concept of local language education and childcare was also launched by the Taipei City Government, which has 632 Taiwanese-, 86 Hakka-, one Ami- 阿美, and two Ataya- 泰雅 speaking nannies. The aim was to expose children to native languages during their preschool years, as this is believed to be the critical stage for language learning.

Although the majority of the aborigines in Taipei's primary schools are either Ami, Ataya, Paiwan 排灣, or Bunun 布農 (500, 164, 92, and 67 students respectively), most are scattered throughout different schools. Therefore, in July 2001, the CAA adapted New Zealand's Köhanga Reo programme for the Mäoris and implemented the Scheme of Aboriginal Language Networks 原住民語言巢方案 in its 12 districts to provide total immersion education. This scheme facilitates aboriginal tutors and parents to build up the best approaches and curriculum for their own particular groups. As only one Yami 雅美 student studied in Taipei City, the CAA invited one Yami tutor and two from each of the other tribes to work with the children.

The Taipei Bureau of Education's statistics only include children who are formally registered as aborigine. Many children with maternal aborigine heritage were thus excluded, in accordance with the *Aborigine Identification Law* 原住民身分法 implemented in January 2001. Such children would need to change their surname to their mothers' in order to obtain formal recognition. The CAA's scheme, however, not only welcomes aboriginal children who were formerly excluded by the above law, but also embraces all non-aborigine family members of registered aborigine children. Nonetheless, only aboriginal students who obtain a Certification of Aboriginal Language Proficiency will be able to apply for a 25 percent increase in school entrance examination scores beginning in 2005.

Language Education

To encourage research on Southern Fujianese, Hakka, other Chinese dialects, and non-Han languages, the MOE offers various levels of financial support in the form of awards for scholarly publications in these areas. Taiwan society is a rich mixture of diverse cultures, and more people on the island are becoming aware of the importance of preserving various languages and dialects. This awareness has become the propelling force behind government efforts to promote "nativist" education 鄉土教育 in elementary and secondary schools. The goal of nativist education is to teach students about the natural history, geography, environment, dialects, arts, and culture of Taiwan, and thus cultivate an affection for Taiwan and respect for the island's

Main Chinese Language Centers in Taiwan		
Language Center	*Mailing Address*	*E-mail & Website*
• Center for Chinese Language and Culture Studies, National Taiwan Normal University	162 Hoping East Rd., Sec. 1, Taipei 10610	Mtc@mtc.ntnu.edu.tw http://www.ntnu.edu.tw/ mtc/index.htm
• Mandarin Studies Program, Language Center, National Chengchi University	64 Chihnan Rd., Sec. 2, Wenshan, Taipei 116	Mandarin@nccu.edu.tw http://140.19.190.90-mandarin.htm
• Language Center, Fu Jen Catholic University	510 Chungcheng Rd., Hsinchuang, Taipei 242	Flcg1013@mails.fju.edu.tw http://www.lc.fju.edu.tw
• Mandarin Learning Center, Chinese Culture University	B1, 231 Chienkuo South Rd., Sec. 2, Taipei 106	Mandarin@cec.pccu.edu.tw http://www.cec.pccu.edu.tw
• International Chinese Language Program, National Taiwan University	P.O. Box 13-204, Taipei 106	Tdiclc@ms.cc.ntu.edu.tw http://ccsun57.cc.ntu.edu.tw/ ~tdiclc
• Chinese Language Center, Tunghai University	Campus Box 898, Tunghai Uni., Taichung 407	Clc@mail.thu.edu.tw http://www.mail.thu.edu.tw/~clc

different cultures and ethnic groups. Under initial plans adopted by the MOE in 1997 for promoting nativist education, bilingual education is a primary focus.

Bilingual education has been introduced in the Taiwan area as a way of reversing the previous neglect of Chinese dialects other than Mandarin. The central government has been lagging behind several steps in its proponents for bilingual education; thus, the magistrates of three counties, making good on campaign promises, chose to "jump the gun" and institute programs in the areas under their jurisdiction prior to any decision by the central authorities.

Ilan County was the first to initiate Southern Fujianese courses in elementary and junior high schools. The program was heralded by a county order in June 1990. Pingtung County followed suit in September 1991, and elective courses in Southern Fujianese, Hakka, and the Paiwan and Rukai 魯凱 aboriginal languages are now taught in county schools. Additional activities, such as speech and singing contests, have also been held to further motivate students.

Extracurricular Atayal language lessons made their debut in 1990 at Taipei County's Wulai elementary and junior high schools, where the majority of students are Atayal aborigines. In the absence of ready-made teaching materials, teachers depended almost solely on a blackboard and their own ingenuity. Some were not very fluent in their ancestral language, and had to learn it themselves as they went along. Materials were compiled as courses were developed. In 1992, the Taipei County Government commissioned its Bureau of Education and the Taipei County Cultural Center to compile teaching materials for the two most prevalent Chinese dialects in Taiwan, Southern Fujianese and Hakka, and two aboriginal languages, Ami and Atayal.

However, the promotion of bilingual education by local governments has faced many obstacles. One of the obstacles comes from parents who do not support bilingual instruction programs. Some parents worry that instruction time spent gaining competence in a chosen Chinese dialect or aboriginal language might negatively affect a student's ability to compose in standard written Chinese, and possibly result in lower scores on college entrance exams. Other parents feel that the usefulness of their native language is limited. "Wouldn't it be better to teach English or Japanese instead?" they reason. For aborigines who are less well off, economic and social advancement is a much more urgent concern; bilingual education may be a luxury they feel they cannot afford.

To remedy the situation, the MOE revised guidelines and amended curriculum standards for elementary and junior high schools. Started in September 2001, primary school students are required to take at least one course on a local language, such as Southern Fujianese, Hakka, or an aboriginal language. For junior high school students, however, such language courses remain an elective. Furthermore, the revised guidelines clearly stipulate that schools may teach in dialects. The government supports such courses with various levels of funding for compiling teaching materials, publishing teacher handbooks, holding teacher workshops, producing audio and video cassettes, and collecting teaching materials.

Another obstacle is the absence of generally agreed-upon standard written forms for each of the Chinese dialects and aboriginal languages. Different phonetic systems have been proposed and tried. The choices for representing aboriginal languages in the written content of textbooks range from a number of romanization schemes to a phonetic symbol-based system similar to that for Mandarin. For Southern Fujianese and Hakka, the use of Chinese characters with no phonetic alphabet is a third option. However, simply using standard Chinese characters is problematic, since they may only indirectly indicate pronunciation, and some dialects lack widely known, written characters for some of their words.

Mandarin Phonetic Symbols (MPS) have sometimes been adapted to represent Chinese dialects and aboriginal languages. But because MPS is a part-alphabet, part-syllabary system created primarily for the language's relatively simple phonological and tonal structure, they are not particularly well-adapted for use with other local languages. This is especially true with multisyllabic Austronesian languages like Taiwan's aboriginal tongues.

Romanization systems are perhaps the most flexible and precise and are well suited to serve as the primary writing system for aboriginal languages. In addition, they can serve as an auxiliary system for teaching Chinese dialects. For example, the romanization system developed by missionaries for Southern Fujianese has a long history and is currently in widespread use, so it would seem a natural candidate as a standard phonetic alphabet. As things stand, each method tends to start from scratch and contribute yet another idiosyncratic system to the existing jumble. Thus, progress is often held back simply due to indecision about which system to adopt in education. Nonetheless, a new system must be decided to accommodate both localization and globalization.

In August 1994, the MOE established a task force, composed of experts from the Institute of History and Philology of Academia Sinica, to research dialects and aboriginal languages and establish guidelines for teaching them. A guidebook of auxiliary teaching materials for dialects in secondary schools which proposed a Taiwan language phonetic system was published by the task force in March 1995. The project also involves developing materials for aboriginal languages, including Atayal, Ami, Yami, Paiwan, Rukai, Puyuma 卑南, Tsou 鄒, Bunun, Saisiyat 賽夏, Kavalan 噶瑪蘭, and Sedeka 賽德克. Moreover, the Legislative Yuan passed the *Aboriginal Education Act* 原住民教育法 in 1998, which stipulates that the government should provide aborigines with opportunities to learn their native languages, history and culture at preschools and elementary schools in their hometowns.

In order to promote the internationalization of the ROC, on the other hand, the MOE has extended the teaching of foreign languages to the primary-school level. The MOE has focused

In view of the need for globalization, all fifth and sixth grade students in Taiwan have been required to study English as part of their formal education since September 2001.

on English as its first target in foreign language education and has scheduled the teaching of English to fifth and sixth grade students from September 2001. In view of the need for globalization, the MOE also promotes the Second Foreign Language Education Five-year Program for Senior High Schools 高級中學第二外語教育五年計畫 (July 1999-December 2004), in addition to the compulsory English courses scheduled for primary school students. Although other languages are not excluded from the program, the focus is on Japanese, French, German and Spanish. Under the multitrack admission policy (see Chapter 17, Education), students attending these classes will have the advantage of gaining admission to related language departments in universities.

A Cross-Strait Comparison

Although Mandarin is standardized, each region speaks its own local version of it, usually reflecting influence from the native dialects of the area. These regional variations of Mandarin are perhaps not even as great as the differences between British and American English, but are definable. The typical Taiwan Mandarin exhibits four major differences from the Mandarin spoken in Beijing:

- The retroflex series of initials *tʂ-, tʂ'-, ʂ-* has generally merged with the dental sibilants *ts-, ts'-, s-*.
- The retroflex -ɹ suffix common in Beijing is rarely used in Taiwan.
- The neutral tone is used much less often than in Beijing.
- The third tone, which in Beijing falls sharply and then rises back up, tends in Taiwan to conclude in the speaker's lowest voice pitch, without rising.

These characteristics are likely attributable, at least in part, to influence from the Southern Fujianese dialect widely spoken throughout the Taiwan area. Apart from these four major differences, there are also some relatively minor vocabulary and grammatical differences between the Mandarin spoken in Taiwan and on the Chinese mainland.

In October 2000, the Chen Mao-pang Cultural and Educational Foundation 陳茂榜文教基金會 invited Tianjin and Suzhou college students and educational committee representatives to Taiwan to discuss commonly used colloquialisms with Taiwanese counterparts. During the seminar, which was hosted by Associate Professor Wei Hsiu-ming 魏岫明 of National Taiwan University's Chinese literature department, the participants summarized the different methods of creating slangs into the following five categories:

- Metaphor: the most common type of slang, such as using *kung lung* (恐龍 "dinosaur") to describe unattractive girls and *kuei mao* (龜毛 "turtle hair" in Taiwanese) to characterize a picky person;
- Homonym: often used between Mandarin and English words or Mandarin and Taiwanese words, such as *cha bao* (茶包 "tea bag") for "trouble" and *yao bai* (搖擺 "swinging") for "arrogance" or "domineering" (based on its Taiwanese pronunciation);
- Abbreviation: the most convenient way to produce slang terms, such as *liao bu liao?* for *liao bu liao chieh?* (瞭不瞭解 "Understood?") or "LKK" for *lao ko ko*, the Taiwanese pronunciation for "oldie";
- Affix: usually used for emphasis, such as *bi le* (斃了 "dead") becoming *ku bi le* (酷斃了 "deadly cool") and or *dai le* (呆了 "dumbstruck") becoming *shuai dai le* (帥呆了 "stunningly hunky"); and
- Internet usage: more and more specialized usages are being created in Chinese-language Internet chat rooms by young web surfers, such as "c.u.l." for "see you later" and "dd" for *di di* (弟弟 "younger brother").

These are just some of the terms commonly used by young people in both Taiwan and on the Chinese mainland, according to university students who attended the seminar. However, not all slang terms created are used by youths on both sides of the Taiwan Strait. Communication among Chinese-language Internet users, which is the fourth largest language group in cyberspace, is occasionally obstructed by dialect differences, such as terms only known to Southern Fujianese, Cantonese, or other dialect speakers. The former two groups were developed mainly in Taiwan and Hong Kong, while the latter, which consists of overseas Chinese and Chinese mainland web surfers, are at a disadvantage in developing dialect slang due to their relatively smaller numbers online.

From a sociolinguistic point of view, slang is a valid dialect. Slang that is prevalent today could some day be absorbed into the written system and formalized. For example, dictionaries published by Taiwan's Mandarin Daily News Publishing Company have already incorporated several "new" phrases that have been widely used for a considerable period of time. However, the process is arbitrary and cannot be regulated by any particular language policy.

Chinese Language Resources Online

According to Euro-Marketing Associates, there are nearly 900 million people who can read Chinese, the largest group in the world, and approximately 6.4 million of them use the Internet. Over the past three years, the Overseas Chinese Affairs Commission has been developing the Global Chinese Language and Culture Center Online 全球華文網路教育中心 (http://edu.ocac.gov.tw) to serve overseas Chinese. As Taiwan is one of the world's largest producer of Chinese publications, with approximately 30,000 new books, more than 150 magazines, and a score of newspapers published annually, it has many advantages in terms of both language materials and information technology. The online center provides various Mandarin, Taiwanese, and Hakka courses for English, Spanish, Portuguese, and French speakers. The Chung Hwa Correspondence School 中華函授學校, established in 1940, also provides online training courses for teachers working in schools for overseas Chinese students.

Professor Chen Hsin-hsi 陳信希 of the Department of Computer Science and Information Engineering at National Taiwan University has developed several Taiwan Native Language Translation and Text-to-Speech Synthesizers (see website at http://nlg3.csie.ntu.edu.tw) under the sponsorship of the National Science Council. These synthesizers, which are aimed at promoting dialogues between different language groups, provide options for Zhangzhou and Quanzhou accented Taiwanese. Programs for providing literary and colloquial Taiwanese and Hakka pronunciations are also under construction. By

October 2001, however, audio programs were only available in Taiwanese.

Further Reading

(in Chinese unless otherwise noted):

Ang Uijin 洪惟仁. *Tai-wan fang-yen chih lu* 臺灣方言之旅 (An Excursion into the Dialects of Taiwan). Taipei: Avanguard Publishing Co. 前衛出版社, 1992.

Chang Tsung-chih 張宗智. "Ka-ma-lan yu te wei-lai" 噶瑪蘭語的未來 (The Future of the Kavalan Language). Taipei: Master's thesis, National Taiwan University, 1994.

Chao Yuan Ren 趙元任. *A Grammar of Spoken Chinese*. Berkeley (in English). University of California Press, 1970.

Cheng, Robert L. 鄭良偉. *Yen-pien-chung te Tai-wan she-hui yu-wen: to-yu she-hui chi shuang-yu chiao-yu* 演變中的臺灣社會語文：多語社會及雙語教育 (Taiwan's Society and Language in Transition: A Multilingual Society and Bilingual Education). Taipei: Independence Evening News Publishing Co. 自立晚報出版社, 1990.

Forrest, R.A.D. *The Chinese Language* (in English). London: Faber and Faber, 1973.

Huang Tung-chiu 黃東秋, ed. *Tai-wan yuan-chu-min yu-yen min-su yen-chiu* 臺灣原住民語言民俗研究 (A Study of Tai-wan Aborigine Languages and Customs). Taipei: Crane Publishing Co., Ltd. 文鶴出版社, 1993.

Kuo-wen tien-ti 國文天地 (The World of Chinese Language and Literature). Taipei, monthly.

Kuo-yin hsueh 國音學 (A Study of Mandarin Phonology). National Taiwan Normal University, Committee for the Compilation of Mandarin Phonology Teaching Materials, ed. Taipei: Cheng Chung Book Co., Ltd. 正中書局, 1982; 1993.

Li Jen-kuei 李壬癸, Lin Ying-chin 林英津. *Tai-wan nan-tao min-tsu mu-yu yan-chiu lun-wen chi* 臺灣南島民族母語研究論文集 (Research Essays on the Mother Tongues of the Austronesian People of Taiwan). Taipei: The Educational Research Center of the Ministry of Education, 1995.

Lin Ying-chin 林英津. "*Pa-ze-hai yu: pu-li ai-lan tiao-cha pao-kao*" 巴則海語:埔里愛蘭調查報告 (The Pazeh Language: A Survey at the Ailan Tableland in Puli Township). *The Taiwan Folkways* 臺灣風物 39, no. 1 (1989).

Lo Chao-chin 羅肇錦. *Ke-yu yu-fa* 客語語法 (A Grammar of the Hakka Dialect). Taipei: Student Book Store 學生書局, 1985.

—*Kuo-yu hsueh* 國語學 (A Study of the National Chinese Language). Taipei: Wunan Book Inc. 五南圖書, 1990.

Norman, Jerry. *Chinese* (in English). Cambridge: Cambridge University Press, 1988.

Tai-yu wen-chai 臺語文摘 (Taiwanese Digest). Taipei, monthly.

Tung Kun 董琨. *Han-tzu fa-chan shih-hua* 漢字發展史話 (The Evolution History of the Chinese Characters). Taipei: Taiwan Commercial Publication Co. Ltd. 臺灣商務印書館, 1993.

Yang Hsiu-fang 楊秀芳. *Tai-wan Min-nan-yu yu-fa kao* 臺灣閩南語語法稿 (A Grammar of the Southern Fujianese Dialect in Taiwan). Taipei: Tah-an Publishing Co. 大安出版社, 1991.

4
History

This engraving shows the surrender negotiations of Frederic Coyett, the last Dutch governor of Taiwan, with Koxinga in 1662. (Photo by SMC Publishing Inc.)

What's New
Taiwan chronology

The beauty of Taiwan was recognized by the Portuguese in the mid-16th century, when they called it *Ilha Formosa*, or "beautiful island." In less than four hundred years, the island has developed into one of the most modernized countries in the world, with a current population of 22.35 million. The self-sufficient agrarian economy of Taiwan was transformed in the second half of the 20th century into a vigorous and advanced economy, with an income of more than US$11,000 per capita. Despite being ruled under colonial regimes in the 17th and 20th centuries and martial law for forty years after World War II, Taiwan peacefully evolved into a democratic country, and has been acclaimed as a "silent revolution." All these miracles took place in a short period, which was unique in Chinese history.

This chapter briefly summarizes the history of Taiwan. An additional chapter on the history of the ROC before 1949 is included in the Appendix II.

History of Taiwan

The history of Taiwan is a story of both frustration and miracles. Taiwan, isolated and poorly developed, had been a neglected island before the 17th century. But during the age of exploration and maritime conquest by Europeans, Taiwan attracted world attention owing to its strategic location and natural resources. First came the Dutch (1624) and the Spanish (1628), who colonized parts of northern and southern Taiwan. Cheng Cheng-kung, who was loyal to the fallen Ming dynasty, defeated the Dutch in 1662 and set up a government on Taiwan to defy the Manchus, who had established the Ching dynasty. The Manchus conquered Taiwan in 1683, and ruled it until 1895 when Taiwan was ceded to Japan after the First Sino-Japanese War. Eventually, Taiwan returned to Chinese rule under the Nationalist government at the end of World War II.

Earliest Inhabitants

Taiwan's first inhabitants left no written records of their origins. Anthropological evidence suggests that Taiwan's indigenous peoples are from proto-Malayan ancestry. Their vocabulary and grammar belong to the Malayan-Polynesian family of modern day Indonesia, and they once shared many Indonesian customs such as tattooing, using identical names for father and son, gerontocracy, head-hunting, spirit worship, and indoor burials. Over 500 prehistoric sites in Taiwan, including many dwelling areas, tombs, and shell mounds, have provided more and seemingly contradictory clues to the origins of Taiwan's aborigines. The majority of prehistoric artifacts discovered so far, such as flat axes, red unpolished pottery, decorated bronze implements, and glass beads, suggest an Indonesian connection. However, other items, such as painted red pottery, red polished pottery, chipped stone knives, black pottery, stone halberds, pottery tripods, and bone arrowheads, suggest that Taiwan's earliest settlers might have come from the Chinese mainland. Many other questions remain unanswered. Were these prehistoric remains left by the ancestors of today's indigenous peoples? The question is a complex one, but many anthropologists have suggested that the remains discovered so far have no proven connection to the present indigenous cultures in Taiwan.

What is known for certain is that large tribes of indigenous peoples, plus many Han people from the Chinese mainland, were already living in Taiwan when the Portuguese first visited the island in 1582 after a shipwreck.

European Colonization

When Portuguese navigators first came upon Taiwan in mid-16th century, struck by the tremendous beauty of its green mountains rising steeply of the blue-green waters of the Pacific, they exclaimed *Ilha Formosa*, meaning "beautiful island." The island has thus been known as

Formosa in the West for centuries after. Portuguese interest in the island was limited, for survivors of the shipwreck left Formosa for Macao and never returned after staying for only six weeks on the southwest coast.

The next groups of Europeans to come to Taiwan were the Dutch and the Spanish. In 1622, the Dutch East India Company established a military base on the Pescadores Islands (Penghu 澎湖), but were forced out by the Chinese and moved to the much larger island of Taiwan in 1624, where they established a colonial capital and ruled for the next 38 years. Two years later, the Spanish also occupied Northern Taiwan to counter-balance the Dutch expansion, building Keelung and Tamsui as their bases for trade and Christian missions, but were ousted by the Dutch in 1642.

The Dutch carried out an economic policy of mercantilism. Taiwan became a trading and transshipment center for goods between a number of areas, such as Japan, China, Batavia (Jakarta), Persia, and Holland. To increase the trade surplus, the Dutch induced the Chinese to migrate to Taiwan to grow sugarcane and rice in 1630s and thus initiated an agricultural revolution. The amount of land under cultivation was largely increased, and sugar and rice had since become principal products until recent years.

Taiwan mainly played a role of a Dutch entrepot for trading among China, Japan, Southeast Asia, and Europe. Taiwan's exports to China included rattan, deer hides, deer horns, and medical herbs. The island's imports from China included raw silk and silk textiles, porcelain, and medicine, but most products were re-exported either to Japan, Batavia, or Europe. Imports to Taiwan from Batavia included spices, amber, tin, lead, cotton, and opium, most of which were traded to China or Japan. Before the Dutch arrived, the Chinese on Taiwan had enjoyed free trade with the Japanese without taxation, trading mainly silk and deer hides in exchange for silver. Continuing the same trade, the Dutch added with a new item, sugar. The Dutch efforts proved to be successful, Taiwan turned to be one of the most profitable branches of the Dutch East India Company in the Far East, accounting for 26 percent of the company's world profits in 1649.

In addition to economic development, Dutch missionaries were also active in converting Taiwan's population to Christianity. Protestant missionaries established schools where religion and the Dutch language were taught. It was recorded in 1659 that the Dutch had converted to Christianity more than 6,078 out of 10,109 inhabitants in their parishes.

Settlement by Han people in Taiwan dates back to the 16th century, but large-scale immigration did not begin until 1630s when the Dutch started developing Taiwan's agriculture. While the Dutch were colonizing Taiwan, China was going through a period of civil wars, followed by the invasion of the Manchus, who eventually established the Ching Dynasty in 1644, and the resistance wars in the south until 1661. At the same time, pirates repeatedly ravaged coastal towns. The endless wars, famines and robberies severely threatened the peaceful life of average Chinese. Consequently, thousands of people, especially from the coastal provinces of Fujian 福建 and Guangdong, migrated across the Taiwan Strait to Taiwan. It has been estimated that about 40,000 Chinese were living in Taiwan in 1662.

Mass migration to Taiwan changed the character of the island. Recognizing the urgent need for industrious farmers, the Dutch employed the new immigrants, providing them with oxen, seeds, and implements. Because all land in these areas belonged to the Dutch East India Company, the Dutch were able to profit enormously from collecting heavy rents from the Chinese tenants. Although settlers petitioned to be allowed to buy and own the land they were tilling, so that they could pay taxes instead of rent, the Dutch rulers refused. Unemployment, mistreatment by the colonial rulers and collection of a new poll tax increased tensions. In September 1652, frustrated Chinese farmers revolted against the Dutch. The rebellions were violently suppressed by the Dutch, who slaughtered about 3,000 peasants.

Cheng Cheng-kung and Defeat of the Dutch

As Manchu troops poured into northern China, many Ming loyalists escaped southwards, where they resisted the foreign invasion for over 20 years. One of the most celebrated resistance fighters was Cheng Cheng-kung 鄭成功, also known as Koxinga 國姓爺. Son of an international trader and pirate Cheng Chi-lung 鄭芝龍 and his Japanese wife, Cheng forced the Dutch out in 1662 and made Taiwan his base for counter-attacking the Manchus on the mainland until 1683.

Cheng Cheng-kung and his son built the first Confucian temple in Taiwan, set up schools for the young, and enacted Chinese laws and customs. During their rule, a steady stream of Chinese continued to arrive in Taiwan and settlements sprang up in increasing numbers along the western coast. Agriculture developed primarily in the southern part of the island. Industry consisted of refining sugar, tile manufacturing, and salt production. Trade, which had begun under the Dutch, continued with neighboring areas, such as China, Japan, and Southeast Asian countries.

Ching Rule Over the Island

Cheng's son and grandson ruled Taiwan for 22 years before surrendering control of the island to the Manchus in 1683, following military defeat. Taiwan was ruled by the Manchus for 212 years until 1895.

Under Ching rule, agriculture expanded northward and southward, and increasing numbers of Chinese left the mainland to settle on the island, despite laws restricting emigration. Rice and sugar, first developed under the Dutch rule, were cultivated all over the island and exported to China, Japan, and even Australia for some time.

Four ports in Taiwan were forcibly opened to foreign trade following the Treaty of Tianjin in 1858. Tea and camphor, which had large markets in the world, became major cash crops for earning foreign exchange. Being the producing areas of new crops, as well as coal, northern Taiwan surpassed southern Taiwan as new economic center, resulting in Taipei's superseding Tainan as the new political capital. However, the conflicts between the immigrant and the aborigines intensified due to the Chinese encroachment on the mountainous areas for producing tea and camphor.

The new resources of Taiwan attracted international attention. Apart from trading with Taiwan, some countries even attempted to occupy Taiwan. Japan occupied southern Taiwan for a short time in 1874 and the French attacked northern Taiwan in 1884-85.

Foreign interest in the island made the Ching court realize Taiwan's importance as a gateway to the seven provinces along China's southeastern coast. Consequently, through the 1870s and 1880s, a number of progressive and ambitious Ching officials sent to Taiwan succeeded in strengthening defenses, exploiting coal, and constructing telegraph lines between central and southern Taiwan, as well as with Fujian Province across the Taiwan Strait. In 1885, the Ching dynasty made Taiwan its 22nd province. During the more than two centuries of Ching rule, Taiwan was fully integrated into the Chinese empire, with numerous Taiwanese attending traditional academies and passing civil service examinations.

Japanese Colonization

Achievements by the Ching administration were disrupted when Taiwan was ceded to Japan in 1895, under the terms of the Treaty of Shimonoseki. When Japanese troops formally entered Taipei on June 6 of that year, armed resistance broke out. By the time resistance was broken in October, over 7,000 Chinese soldiers had been killed and civilian casualties numbered in the thousands.

During its 50-year rule of Taiwan, Japan developed programs designed to supply the Japanese empire with agricultural products, create demand for Japanese industrial products, and provide living space for emigrants from an increasingly overpopulated home country. The colonial government eventually introduced an

On the 13th of the fifth lunar month, crowds gather to celebrate the birthday of the City God in one of the oldest areas of Taipei City.
(Photo by Wang Neng-yu; courtesy of Taipei Archives Commission)

industrialization program aimed at building Taiwan as a base for executing a "South Forward Policy" of colonial expansion into Southeast Asia.

The period of Japanese colonization can be roughly divided into three periods. The first, from 1895 to 1918, involved establishing administrative mechanisms and militarily suppressing armed resistance by local Chinese and indigenous peoples. One of the largest revolts, the Tapani Incident 噍吧哖事件 of 1915, resulted in the deaths of several thousand Taiwanese. During this period, the Japanese introduced strict police controls, carried out a thorough land survey, standardized measurements and currencies, monopolized the manufacture and sale of important products (such as salt, sugar, and pineapple), began collecting census data, and made an ethnological study of the island's indigenous peoples.

During the second period from 1918 to 1937, Japan consolidated its hold over Taiwan. Compulsory Japanese education and cultural assimilation were emphasized, while economic development was promoted to transform the island into a secure stepping stone from which Japan could launch its southward aggression.

The third period, which started in 1937 and lasted until 1945, entailed the naturalization of Taiwan residents as Japanese. The Chinese on Taiwan were forced to deny their heritage by adopting Japanese names, wearing Japanese-style clothing, eating Japanese food, and observing Japanese religious rites. Chinese dialects and customs were discouraged and Chinese language schools closed. Heavy industry and foreign trade was strongly emphasized during this period, coinciding with the Second World War.

Japanese development of its Taiwan colony was extensive in areas such as railroads, agricultural research and development, public health, banking, education and literacy, cooperatives, and business.

Transportation Infrastructure: Recognizing the importance of transportation to Taiwan's economy, the colonial rulers constructed 2,857 miles of railroad lines, modernized harbors, and built 2,500 miles of highways.

Irrigation and Agriculture: Irrigation was considered the key to further developing Taiwan's agriculture, which was plagued by uneven rainfall. Concrete dams, reservoirs, and large aqueducts formed an extensive irrigation project that brought thousands of acres of poor farmland into production. Arable land for rice production increased by more than 74 percent and sugar cane, by 30 percent. The enormous increase in sugar cane production is considered to be one of the most spectacular achievements of Japanese colonization. Over a period of 30 years (1905-1935) the area planted in sugar cane increased 500 percent and output skyrocketed. By 1939, Taiwan was the world's seventh largest sugar producer.

Industry: The Japanese policy of an agricultural Taiwan and industrial Japan did not call for significant development of Taiwan's industry. Factories during the period were small—95 percent had fewer than 30 workers. Finally, during World War II, military necessity led the Japanese to develop in Taiwan strategic industries including aluminum, chemicals, oil refining, metals, and shipbuilding. Around 90 percent of Taiwan's foreign trade was with Japan, mostly agricultural.

Hydroelectric Power: Heavy rainfall and swift mountain streams on the island made hydroelectric power attractive to colonial administrators. In the 1930s, a large-scale project utilizing Sun Moon Lake 日月潭 and the Choshui River 濁水溪, greatly increased electric power, thus boosting aluminum, chemical, and steel alloy production.

Despite the Japanese success in transforming Taiwan into a society that, economically, was rather modern in comparison with its neighbors, alien rule came at a heavy cost. Economic development was primarily for the benefit of Japan and not Taiwan. The Taiwanese were denied self-government and democracy and kept out of high positions at all levels of society. People were taught to see themselves as Japanese instead of Chinese, and in fact, during the Second World War, tens of thousands joined the Japanese military. Liberation from colonial rule would only come with the total defeat of Japan in 1945 and Taiwan's return to China.

The ROC on Taiwan

The history of Taiwan after 1949 is one of rapid and sweeping change over a short period.

Following 50 years of Japanese colonization, an influx of around one and half million soldiers and civilians from the Chinese mainland turned the island into a frontline of the cold war. Over the last five decades, intensive economic development made the island one of the world's largest economies, and rapid industrialization, urbanization, and modernization over a few decades has dramatically transformed the lives of the island's residents. The scale of this transformation has seldom been witnessed anywhere in world history.

Tragic Early Days

Following Japan's defeat and surrender in 1945 at the end of World War II, Taiwan was retroceded to the Republic of China on October 25 of the same year. After having been occupied by the Portuguese, Dutch, Spanish, Manchus, and Japanese, Taiwan was under Chinese rule again.

The first years after the Japanese surrender were not smooth and resulted in one of Taiwan's greatest tragedies, the February 28 Incident 二二八事件. The first troops sent to take over Taiwan were poorly trained and undisciplined, while the major fighting component of Nationalist troops remained on the Chinese mainland battling the communist rebellion. Most importantly, high inflation, shortages of daily necessities, unequal treatment by the Nationalist troops, unjust appropriation of personal property, and unchecked profiteering angered Taiwanese natives.

The tension finally exploded on February 28, 1947, following an incident in Taipei where an elderly woman was beaten while resisting arrest for selling untaxed cigarettes in Taipei, and a bystander was shot in the commotion. Crowds rioted across the island, seizing police stations, arms, and radio stations and killing a number of mainlanders. In the succeeding months, after the arrival of troop reinforcements from the mainland, the governor, Chen Yi 陳儀, proceeded to arrest and kill thousands of people who demanded government reform. Chen Yi was thus discharged from his governor post. Later he was

Taiwan Chronology (1544-2001)

1544 The Portuguese sailing to Japan spot Taiwan and refer to it as *Ilha Formosa* (beautiful island).

1662 Cheng Cheng-kung, also known as Koxinga, defeats Dutch forces, marking the end of Dutch rule.

1684 Manchus replace the Cheng family as the new rulers of Taiwan. Taiwan becomes a dependency of the Fujian provincial administration.

1885 Taiwan is made a province of China and Liu Ming-chuan becomes the first governor of Taiwan.

1895 Treaty of Shimonoseki concludes Sino-Japanese War; Taiwan is ceded to Japan.

1945 World War II ends with Japan's surrender to the Allies. Taiwan is retroceded to China after 50 years of Japanese occupation.

1947 Due to bad administration, ethnic tension, and other factors, an islandwide uprising breaks out, known as the February 28 Incident.

1949 The central government of the Republic of China relocates to Taiwan after the mainland falls to the Communists.

1950 In March, Chiang Kai-shek resumes the presidency of the Republic of China.

In June, with the outbreak of the Korean War, US President Truman orders the Seventh Fleet to protect Taiwan against attack by the Chinese Communists.

1953 The Legislative Yuan adopts the *Land-to-the-Tiller Act.*

1967 The Executive Yuan extends period of compulsory education from six to nine years.

1971 The Republic of China withdraws from the United Nations.

1973 The Ten Major Construction Projects begin.

1978 Chiang Ching-kuo is elected president.

1979 The US grants diplomatic recognition to the People's Republic of China and breaks ties with the Republic of China.

A demonstration organized by opposition politicians and the *Formosa Magazine* to commemorate Human Rights Day, turns into the bloody riot known as the "Kaohsiung Incident."

1986 The Democratic Progressive Party (DPP) announces its formation.

1987 The Emergency Decree is lifted.

The government announces that residents of Taiwan are officially allowed to visit relatives on the mainland.

1988 President Chiang Ching-kuo dies on January 13, and Vice President Lee Teng-hui is sworn in as president of the Republic of China.

1990 Lee Teng-hui is elected the eighth-term president of the ROC by the National Assembly.

1991 The Executive Yuan approves a Six-Year National Development Plan aimed at improving the nation's economic infrastructure.

The Period of National Mobilization for Suppression of the Communist Rebellion is ended in May.

1992 The election for the Second Legislative Yuan is held, the first popular election to the legislature since 1947.

1996 The first direct presidential election is held, and incumbent president and KMT candidate Lee Teng-hui is elected.

1998 The Legislative Yuan passes the statute to streamline the Taiwan Provincial Government.

1999 On September 21, Taiwan is hit by its deadliest earthquake in more than 60 years. The 7.3 magnitude quake claims more than 2,000 lives and injures over 8,000.

2000 Democratic Progressive Party candidate Chen Shui-bian is elected president of the Republic of China, ending the KMT's more than 50-year hold on the presidency in Taiwan.

2001 The World Trade Organization Ministerial Conference formally approves Taiwan's accession to the WTO on November 11.

tried and executed in 1950 for conspiring with the communists to overthrow the ROC government while serving as governor of Zhejiang Province 浙江省. The incident was a source of tension between Taiwanese and those who came from the mainland after 1945.

Rapid Development after 1950

With the outbreak of the Korean War in late June 1950, US President Harry S. Truman ordered the US Seventh Fleet to protect Taiwan against attack by the Chinese communists, and the US began to provide Taiwan with considerable economic and military assistance. The international community sided with Taiwan and the internal situation began to stabilize. Taiwan became the focus of world attention again in August 1958, when the communists, who wished to take over Taiwan, began shelling the island of Kinmen (Quemoy) in the Battle of the Taiwan Strait. The attack eventually subsided, and on October 23, 1958 八二三戰役, the US and ROC governments issued a joint communiqué reaffirming solidarity between the two countries. This invaluable military support continued through the 1960s and 70s, and prevented Taiwan from becoming communist.

Miraculous Economic Transformation

When the ROC government moved to Taipei in 1949, the economy of Taiwan was still trying to recover from the heavy Allied bombing that had occurred during the war. Only a few industries remained, including sugar refining and some textile manufacturing. In the initial years, two factors stabilized the situation and laid the foundations for a future economic takeoff: aid from the US and the land reform program. From 1951 to 1965, large amounts of economic and military aid came from the US as part of its cold war efforts to preserve this valuable ally in Asia. Much of the aid was used in infrastructure and the agricultural sector. Advisors stationed in Taiwan and Taiwanese sent abroad for education were all directed at rebuilding the economy. The highly successful land reform program, which

was completed in 1953, reduced land rents, distributed public land, and purchased and resold land from large landlords. Farmers were supplied with fertilizer, seeds, pesticides, expert advice, and credit. By 1959, 90 percent of exports were agriculture or food related. Increased production and higher income resulted in low inflation and capital accumulation, as importing food was unnecessary.

After land reform policies and economic assistance had laid a solid foundation for the economy, two policies of the 1950s and 60s led to the remarkable takeoff of the 1970s. The first was an "import substitution policy" aimed at making Taiwan self-sufficient by producing inexpensive consumer goods, processing imported raw materials, and restricting other imports. When far-sighted government planners realized the economic bottleneck poised by the narrow base of Taiwan's domestic economy, a second policy of "export promotion" was adopted in the late 1950s and continued throughout the 1960s. Using Japan as a model and employing US advice, the resource-poor, labor-abundant island began to expand light industries. Export processing zones, free of bureaucratic red-tape and with special tax incentives, were set up to attract overseas investment. Soon, Taiwan secured an international reputation as an exporter to the world.

Between 1962 and 1985, Taiwan's economy witnessed the most rapid growth in its history: an average annual rate of nearly 10 percent, over twice the average economic growth rate of industrialized countries during this period. Equitable distribution of income was a major objective in the government's economic planning. In 1953, the average income of the top one-fifth of families was estimated at 20 times that of the lowest one-fifth. In the 1980s this 1:20 ratio was further reduced to a range of between 1:5 and 1:4, indicating a highly equitable distribution of income.

The economic structure of the nation shifted from reliance on agricultural exports in the 1950s to light manufacturing in the 1960s and 70s;

One year after the signing of the Sino-American Mutual Defense Treaty (1954), US Secretary of State John Foster Dulles visited Taiwan and Minister of Foreign Affairs George K. C. Yeh delivered a speech after the exchanges of document ratifiation.

and on to high technology and chemical product exports in the 1980s and 90s. By 1995, technology-intensive products constituted 46.7 percent of exports.

A new and significant economic trend beginning in the 1980s was the rise of investments by the ROC business community on the Chinese mainland. After the *Emergency Decree* 戒嚴令 was lifted in 1987, non-government civilian contacts between Taiwan and the Chinese mainland were allowed, and, by 2000, Taiwan's business sector had invested over US$17.1 billion on the mainland, according to official ROC statistics. (Beijing's statistics indicated a much higher figure of US$26.4 billion.) The sharp increase of Taiwan exports to the Chinese mainland beginning in 1990 decreased Taiwan's dependence on the US market, but raised new concerns of growing economic reliance on the ROC's long-time foe. Although politically divided, investment and trade by the business community have begun a process of bringing the two sides closer together.

Education

Much of the credit for Taiwan's steady economic growth must go to the spread of universal education throughout the island. After 1949, the government expanded education and raised literacy rates. From 1950 to 2000 the number of university students, including those at private colleges and universities, increased by more than 100 times to 647,920. Although there were only five M.A. candidates in 1950, and Taiwan had its first Ph.D. student in 1956, by 2000 there were 70,039 students in 2,734 master's degree programs, with 13,822 students studying in 873 Ph.D. programs. Thousands of others were enrolled in graduate programs abroad in the US, Japan, Canada, Australia, Britain and European countries. The number of high school students also increased from around 34,000 in the 1950s to more than 350,000 in 2000. Most noticeable has been the change in the rate of illiteracy. In 1951, 34.6 percent of the population six years and older were illiterate. This figure had dropped to 15.3 percent by 1969. At present, less than 6 percent of the population is illiterate, mostly the elderly.

Politics and Foreign Relations

Despite restrictions under martial law, the ROC government has long promoted local

53

self-government. Beginning in 1950, all the chief executive and representative bodies under the provincial level were directly elected by the people, and in 1951, 16 county and five city governments and councils were established. In June 1959, the first Taiwan Provincial Assembly was established, extending political participation from the county to the provincial level.

Following the death of Chiang Kai-shek in 1975, Yen Chia-kan 嚴家淦 briefly served as president until Chiang's son, Chiang Ching-kuo 蔣經國, was elected in 1978. It was under his rule that full democratization began, starting with the lifting of martial law in 1987 shortly before his death in 1988. In fact, the first major opposition party, the Democratic Progressive Party 民主進步黨 (DPP), was formally established on September 28, 1986, marking the beginning of multiparty democracy in the ROC. Chiang Ching-kuo's successor, President Lee Teng-hui 李登輝, continued to reform the rigid political system that had been developed after decades of civil war and martial law. Under his administration, press freedoms were guaranteed, opposition political parties developed, visits to the mainland continued, and revisions of the constitution encouraged.

Representatives of the National Assembly, the Legislative Yuan and the Control Yuan, who had been frozen in office since 1947, were also asked to step down during Lee's administration. Elections for total seats in the National Assembly and the Legislature were first held in 1991 and 1992. The Control Yuan was transformed into a semi-judicial institution following the 1992 constitutional amendment. On March 23, 1996, the democratization process peaked with the election of the ROC president, the first direct election of the head-of-state in the history of China. Provoking considerable debate and controversy, the provincial government was largely dissolved in 1998 in a government-downsizing move.

On March 18, 2000, the second direct presidential election was held, with five pairs of candidates contending for the positions of president and vice president of the Republic of China. In a tight, three-way campaign, former Taipei City Mayor Chen Shui-bian of the DPP narrowly defeated his rivals with 39.3 percent of the vote. He was closely followed by former Taiwan Provincial Governor James Soong (independent) with 36.8 percent, and Vice President Lien Chan of the KMT with 23.1 percent.

The election not only brought a record 82 percent turnout, but also ended the KMT's five-decade hold on the presidency. President Lee Teng-hui was forced to resign his chairmanship of the KMT, as a result of street protests by KMT grassroots members over his role in the defeat. In April, supporters of James Soong combined with some of the KMT and New Party members to form the People First Party.

These domestic political changes were closely intertwined with Taiwan's experience in the international arena. The ROC was a founding member of the UN in 1945. However, after the withdrawal of the government to Taiwan and the establishment of the PRC, diplomatic competition emerged between the two rivals. In 1971, supported by most of the newly independent states, the PRC succeeded in gaining admission to the UN General Assembly, and the ROC walked out. Since then, most of the remaining UN members have switched their ties from Taipei to Beijing. A low point was reached at the end of the 1970s, when the United States was the last major power to sever diplomatic ties, including the 1954 Mutual Defense Treaty. The US has continued economic ties and sold defensive military equipment to Taiwan in accordance with the *Taiwan Relations Act* 臺灣關係法 of 1979.

With the beginning of democratization, the people's dissatisfaction with this state of affairs led to a new effort to increase Taiwan's participation in the international arena. Collectively known as pragmatic diplomacy, this policy included a revived effort to expand and consolidate formal diplomatic ties, a new campaign to re-enter international organizations, and increased emphasis on substantive ties with the US, Japan, and Europe. During the 1990s, these efforts resulted in some progress, although the ultimate goal of UN membership still faced many obstacles.

Until 1987, the ROC remained under "martial law." During that forty-year period, opposition political parties were banned, publishing and the media were restricted, and relations with the mainland were forbidden. However, religious and business activities were essentially free, and citizens regularly traveled around the island and the world. This policy was adopted because of the continued military threat from the Chinese mainland. As Taiwan prospered economically and the mainland undertook radical reforms and began to open up to the outside world, reasons for martial law were no longer seen as valid. On November 2, 1987, the ROC officially permitted its citizens to visit relatives on the Chinese mainland. Since then, cross-strait ties have grown, and, by the late 1990s, Taiwan residents made millions of trips, involving visits to relatives, tourism, and scholarly, cultural, and sports exchanges. The number of trips made by mainland Chinese to Taiwan for cultural and educational activities has totaled more than 34,000.

In February 1991, the semi-private Straits Exchange Foundation 海峽交流基金會 (SEF) was set up to deal with matters arising from contact between people from both sides of the Strait. Its mainland counterpart, the Association for Relations Across the Taiwan Straits 海峽兩岸關係協會 (ARATS), was established ten months later. These organizations have met intermittently to discuss matters of a technical or business nature across the Strait, such as the repatriation of hijackers and illegal entrants and solutions for fishing disputes.

Two recent developments that will strongly affect Taiwan's future is its entry into the World Trade Organization (WTO) and its increasing economic involvement with the Chinese mainland. After more than 12 years of negotiations and waiting, Taiwan signed its WTO accession accord in November 2001, with official entry on January 1, 2002. Membership in the WTO will enable Taiwan's industrial and business sector to fully participate in the world economy on a more equal footing. However, opening the domestic economy to the world will also expose the island to increased competition which could have a negative impact on some industries, most notably agriculture.

A second major development has been the substantial increase of Taiwan investment and business activity on the Chinese mainland. Many businesses have sought cheap labor and potential markets on the mainland, and are acting in preparation for full integration into the WTO. What impact this new development will have on Taiwan's economy in the long-term, as well as on political relations with Beijing, is still uncertain.

To meet this new reality and prepare for entry in to the WTO, the Cabinet announced in October 2001 that the "patience over haste" policy restricting investment on the Chinese mainland would be replaced with a managed liberalization policy of "active opening, efficient management." Most limits on individual investment projects on the mainland will be scrapped, and offshore banking units of Taiwanese banks will be permitted to engage in direct business exchanges with mainland financial institutions.

Limited transportation links have been allowed between the outlying islands of the ROC (Kinmen and Matsu) and the Chinese mainland, and establishing direct transportation links between Taiwan and the mainland remain under discussion.

Present and Future

Although the greatest change in post-1949 Taiwan has been the island's economic revolution and spectacular rise in income and living standards, the social transformation brought about following the lifting of martial law in 1987 cannot be overlooked. The legalization of labor strikes, demonstrations, and the formation of new political parties all gave greater power to the people. The lifting of restrictions on newspapers and publishing has produced an explosion in media growth and broadened the perspectives of an increasingly sophisticated audience.

As the nation enters the 21st century, the forces of global capitalism, democracy, and the information age are carrying Taiwan further into a new era, one in which its future and the rest of the world's is undivided.

5

Government

As part of the Double Ten National Day celebrations, a group of high school students participates in a drawing contest of the Office of the President.

Freedom and democracy are more than just slogans in the Republic of China (ROC). They are the tangible results of constitutional government and rule of law. This chapter outlines the Republic of China's Constitution and governmental system. First, the essential concepts of the Constitution are explained, followed by a description of various units of the central government. This chapter concludes with a description of the municipal and local governments. Readers may locate information on a specific government agency most quickly by first referring to the index at the back of this book.

The Constitution

"The Republic of China, founded on the Three Principles of the People, shall be a democratic republic of the people, to be governed by the people and for the people." (Article 1, *Constitution of the Republic of China*)

The ROC Constitution is based on the principles of nationalism, democracy, and social well-being formulated by Dr. Sun Yat-sen, the founding father of the Republic of China. His political doctrine is known as the Three Principles of the People 三民主義.

The Principle of Nationalism 民族主義 postulates the equal treatment and sovereign status for the Republic of China internationally as well as equality for all ethnic groups within the nation. The Principle of Democracy 民權主義, assuring each citizen the right to exercise political and civil liberties, is the foundation for the organization and structure of the ROC government. The Principle of Social Well-being 民生主義 indicates that the powers granted to the government must ultimately serve the welfare of the people by building a prosperous economy and a just society. The three principles have extensively shaped current policies and legislation in many areas, such as education, land reforms, social welfare, and relations with mainland China. More recently, they have contributed heavily to political and economic liberalization.

The Constitution delineates the rights, duties, and freedoms of the people, the overall direction for political, economic, and social policies, and the organization and structure of the government. (The full text of the Constitution and its 11 *Additional Articles* can be found in Appendix III.)

Constitutional Rights and Freedoms

The ROC Constitution guarantees various rights and freedoms to all citizens. Modeled after American constitutional concepts, the rights include equality, work, livelihood, and property, as well as the four political powers of election, recall, initiative, and referendum. The people have the duty to pay taxes and perform military service as prescribed by law. Obtaining an education is considered both a right and a duty of the people.

The people are also entitled to the freedoms of speech, residence, travel, assembly, confidential communication, religion, and association. Personal freedom is also guaranteed. Rights and freedoms not specified in the Constitution are also protected, if they do not violate social order and public interest.

The law may not restrict freedoms stipulated in the Constitution, unless the freedoms are abused, the freedoms of others are infringed, or public order is threatened. Even in these situations, the Constitution permits restrictions on constitutional rights and freedoms only under specific circumstances. This is designed to prevent legislative bodies from enacting laws that exceed the limits established by the Constitution. Restrictions on constitutional freedoms are valid only if contained in legislation necessary to prevent restrictions against the freedom of others, to respond to emergencies, to maintain social order, or to enhance social interest. In any

ROC Constitutional Amendments

On May 1, 1991, the ROC president promulgated ten *Additional Articles of the Constitution of the Republic of China* 中華民國憲法增修條文, which had just been passed by the first National Assembly. The articles were designed to reflect the fact that Taiwan and the Chinese mainland are administered by two separate political entities. The *Additional Articles* also provided the legal basis for the election of the second National Assembly and the second Legislative Yuan, which would be representative of the people on Taiwan and overseas Chinese.

After the second National Assembly took office on January 1, 1992, its delegates adopted *Additional Articles* 11 through 18. These articles were promulgated on May 28, 1992, laying the groundwork for the popular election of the president and vice president of the Republic of China, the transformation of the Control Yuan from a parliamentary body to a quasi-judicial organ, and the implementation of provincial and local self-governance.

On July 28, 1994, the second National Assembly revised the 18 *Additional Articles*, reducing the number to ten. Under the revised *Additional Articles of the Constitution,* the president was to be directly elected from the ninth-term and the term was reduced from six to four years. The National Assembly no longer had the right to recall the president and the vice president. Instead, when recall of the president was proposed by one-fourth and passed by two-thirds of the delegates, additional confirmation from more than half of the voters out of at least half of the total voting population was still required for recall. The president was entitled to nominate the president and committee members of the Control Yuan, Examination Yuan and Judicial Yuan, as well as the grand justices, with the consent of the National Assembly. Although the committee members of the Control Yuan were no longer elected, their right to impeach the president remained. When passed by two thirds of the entire National Assembly, the impeached person would be dismissed.

From May to July, 1997, the *Additional Articles* were further amended.
- The Provincial Government was streamlined and the popular elections of the governor and members of the provincial council were suspended.
- A resolution on the impeachment of the president or vice president is no longer initiated by the Control Yuan, but rather by the Legislative Yuan.
- The Legislative Yuan has the power to pass a no-confidence vote against the president of the Executive Yuan (premier), and the president of the Republic has the power to dissolve the Legislative Yuan.
- The president of the Executive Yuan is to be directly appointed by the president of the Republic, without consent of the Legislative Yuan.
- Educational, scientific, and cultural budgets, especially the compulsory education budget, will be given priority, but are no longer restricted by Article 164 of the Constitution requiring at least 15 percent of the total national budget.

In September 1999, the ROC third National Assembly passed another round of constitutional amendments, which extend the term of delegates from May 2000 to June 2002. Due to the controversial nature of the tenure extension, constitutional interpretation was requested and the Council of Grand Justices ruled the amendments invalid, and the previous amendment promulgated on July 21, 1997, was revived from March 24, 2000.

Another series of constitutional amendments were promulgated on April 25, 2000, to terminate the third National Assembly on May 19, 2000, and establish a unicameral legislative system. Under this newest revision:
- Three hundred delegates shall be elected by proportional representation to the National Assembly, within three months of the expiration of a six-month period following the public announcement of a proposal by the Legislative Yuan to amend the Constitution or alter the national territory, or within three months of a petition initiated by the Legislative Yuan for the impeachment of the president or the vice president.
- Recall of the president or the vice president shall be initiated upon the proposal of one-fourth of all members of the Legislative Yuan, and passed by two-thirds of all the members. The measure must be passed by more than one-half of the valid ballots in a vote in which more than one-half of the electorate in the free area of the Republic of China participates.
- When the Legislative Yuan convenes each year, it may hear a report on the state of the nation by the president.
- Grand justices shall not hold office for life unless they are judges.

case, arrest, trial, and punishment must be implemented strictly in accordance with proper legal procedures. If human rights are violated by the government, the victims are entitled to compensation by the state.

Government, Economic, and Social Policies

The ROC Constitution contains provisions for legislation and procedures addressing important government, economic, and social issues. Chapter XIII of the Constitution (Fundamental National Policies 基本國策) contains articles on national defense, foreign policy, national economy, social security, education and culture, and frontier regions. The policies outline the government's responsibility to provide necessary support for the welfare and well-being of the people and enable them to engage in various business and professional activities. Article 10 of the *Additional Articles of the Constitution* prescribes specific policy orientations on several modern issues including scientific development, industrial modernization, environmental protection, national health insurance, and the elimination of sexual discrimination.

Governmental Structure

The ROC government is divided into central, provincial/municipal, and county/city levels, each of which has specifically defined powers. The central government consists of the Office of the President 總統府, the National Assembly 國民大會, and five branches (called "yuan" 院), namely the Executive Yuan 行政院, the Legislative Yuan 立法院, the Judicial Yuan 司法院, the Examination Yuan 考試院, and the Control Yuan 監察院.

At the provincial level, the provincial governments exercise administrative authority. Since the ROC government administers only Taiwan Province and two counties in Fujian Province, only two provincial governments are currently operational—the Taiwan Provincial Government 臺灣省政府 and the Fujian Provincial Government 福建省政府. The Fujian Provincial Government oversees the regional affairs of Kinmen County 金門縣 and Lienchiang County 連江縣. Likewise, the Taiwan Provincial Government exercises full jurisdiction over Taiwan's 16 counties and all the cities except for Taipei and Kaohsiung, which are special municipalities directly under the jurisdiction of the central government.

At the local level and under the Taiwan Provincial Government, there are five cities—Keelung 基隆, Hsinchu 新竹, Taichung 臺中, Chiayi 嘉義, and Tainan 臺南—and 16 counties. Under each county there are county municipalities 縣轄市.

The Presidency

The president of the Republic of China is the head of state and is granted specific constitutional powers to conduct national affairs. Scores of agencies and advisors, including senior advisors, national policy advisors, military advisors, and organizations and institutions such as the Academia Sinica 中央研究院, Academia Historica 國史館, National Security Council 國家安全會議, and National Unification Council 國家統一委員會 provide information on state affairs to the president.

The May 20, 2000, inauguration of President Chen Shui-bian (for more information, see Biographies) as the tenth-term president of the ROC, demonstrated that Taiwan's democratic system had further matured. The Nationalist Party (KMT) lost its 50-year hold on the presidency in Taiwan and was peacefully replaced by the Democratic Progressive Party (DPP), despite the threat of possible military action by the Chinese mainland.

Functions

As head of state, the president represents the country in foreign relations and at state functions. All acts of state are conducted in the president's name: commanding the land, sea, and air forces; promulgating laws and decrees; declaring martial law with the approval of the Legislature; concluding treaties; declaring war and making peace; convening the National Assembly; granting amnesty and commutations; appointing and removing civil service officials and military officers; and conferring honors and

Organization of the Central Government

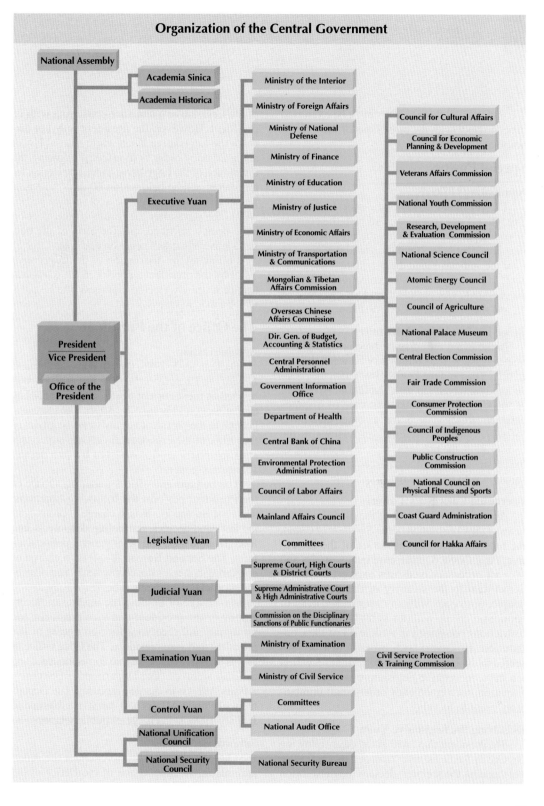

National Assembly

President
Vice President

Office of the President

Academia Sinica
Academia Historica

Executive Yuan

- Ministry of the Interior
- Ministry of Foreign Affairs
- Ministry of National Defense
- Ministry of Finance
- Ministry of Education
- Ministry of Justice
- Ministry of Economic Affairs
- Ministry of Transportation & Communications
- Mongolian & Tibetan Affairs Commission
- Overseas Chinese Affairs Commission
- Dir. Gen. of Budget, Accounting & Statistics
- Central Personnel Administration
- Government Information Office
- Department of Health
- Central Bank of China
- Environmental Protection Administration
- Council of Labor Affairs
- Mainland Affairs Council

- Council for Cultural Affairs
- Council for Economic Planning & Development
- Veterans Affairs Commission
- National Youth Commission
- Research, Development & Evaluation Commission
- National Science Council
- Atomic Energy Council
- Council of Agriculture
- National Palace Museum
- Central Election Commission
- Fair Trade Commission
- Consumer Protection Commission
- Council of Indigenous Peoples
- Public Construction Commission
- National Council on Physical Fitness and Sports
- Coast Guard Administration
- Council for Hakka Affairs

Legislative Yuan — Committees

Judicial Yuan
- Supreme Court, High Courts & District Courts
- Supreme Administrative Court & High Administrative Courts
- Commission on the Disciplinary Sanctions of Public Functionaries

Examination Yuan
- Ministry of Examination
- Ministry of Civil Service
- Civil Service Protection & Training Commission

Control Yuan
- Committees
- National Audit Office

National Unification Council

National Security Council — National Security Bureau

decorations. All these powers must be exercised in accordance with the provisions of the Constitution and the law.

Special Powers

Nominating Officials

The president appoints the president of the Executive Yuan (premier), and with the consent of the Legislature, appoints the president 院長, vice president 副院長, and the grand justices 大法官 of the Judicial Yuan; the president, vice president, and members of the Examination Yuan; and the president, vice president, auditor-general 審計長, and members of the Control Yuan.

Resolving Inter-branch Disputes

In the event of a dispute among the various branches, such as a controversy between the Executive Yuan and the Legislative Yuan, the president may intervene to seek a solution. Article 44 of the Constitution states: "In case of disputes between two or more branches other than those for which there are relevant provisions in the Constitution, the president may call a meeting of the presidents of the branches concerned for consultation with a view to reaching a solution."

Exercising Emergency Powers

According to Article 2 of the *Additional Articles of the Constitution of the Republic of China*, the president may, by resolution of the Executive Yuan Council, issue emergency orders and take all necessary measures to avert an imminent threat to the security of the state or the people, or to cope with any serious financial or economic crisis, without being subject to the restrictions prescribed in Article 43 of the Constitution. However, such orders must be presented to the Legislature for confirmation within ten days. Should the Legislature withhold confirmation, such emergency orders shall immediately cease to be valid.

Dissolving the Legislative Yuan

The president may, within ten days following passage by the Legislative Yuan of a no-confidence vote against the premier, declare the dissolution of the Legislative Yuan after consulting with its president. However, the president may not dissolve the Legislative Yuan while martial law or an emergency order is in effect. Following the dissolution of the Legislative Yuan, an election for legislators will be held within 60 days. The new Legislative Yuan will convene of its own accord within ten days after the results of the election have been confirmed, and the term of the new Legislative Yuan will begin on that date.

Following the dissolution of the Legislative Yuan by the president and prior to the inauguration of its newly elected members, the Legislative Yuan is in recess.

The Office of the President

Administration

On January 5, 1996, the 50-year-old *Organic Law of the Presidential Office* 總統府組織法 was revised to meet current needs, and the new law took effect on February 24, 1996. The secretary-general to the president administers the affairs of the Office of the President, directs and supervises staff members, and is assisted by two deputy secretaries-general.

The bureaus and offices under the Office of the President perform the following functions: The First Bureau 第一局 is in charge of promulgating laws and decrees, translating documents into foreign languages, and other general political affairs. The Second Bureau 第二局 is in charge of conferring honors, safekeeping seals, and distributing official documents. The Third Bureau 第三局 is in charge of holding the inauguration ceremony of the president and vice president and arranging and receiving foreign guests of the president and vice president. The Code Office 機要室 is in charge of telegraphic correspondence and national archives. The Department of Security Affairs 侍衛室 is in charge of security. The Department of Public Affairs 公共事務室, established in January 1996, is in charge of public relations.

Subordinate Offices

There are four institutions under the direct administrative supervision of the Office of the

President: Academia Sinica, Academia Historica, the National Unification Council, and the National Security Council.

Academia Sinica, the leading research institution in the ROC, was established in Nanjing on June 9, 1928, to conduct scientific research and to direct, coordinate, and promote scientific research throughout the ROC. Although it is a unit of the government, Academia Sinica enjoys virtually independent status. The most important body within Academia Sinica is the Assembly of Members 院士會議. The members, commonly known as academicians 院士, are elected for life from among distinguished Chinese scholars. On July 6, 2000, 22 new members—12 from outside the ROC and ten based in Taiwan—were elected. The 22 new members brought the total number of academicians to 213. Their duties include formulating national research policy and pursuing specific research at the request of the government. As of mid-2001, the Academia Sinica had 25 institutes, six of which are in the preparatory stage, including the two newly established Institute of Bioagriculture and Institute of Linguistics. The Academia Sinica is staffed by 1,150 full-time research fellows.

Academia Historica was founded in 1914 and was reestablished in Taiwan 43 years later. It is responsible for preserving documents and conducting research in modern Chinese history, particularly the republican period. The academy has a collection of 7.5 million publications and national records, mainly from the Office of the President, the Executive Yuan, provincial and local governments, plus some personal and other archives. Most of the records are open to the staff of Academia Historica and researchers.

Founded in 1990, the National Unification Council recommends national unification policies to the president, helps the government to devise a national unification framework, and builds a consensus in society and among political parties concerning the issue of national unification.

The National Security Council, established in 1967 and chaired by the president, is an advisory body to the president. The main functions of the National Security Council and its subsidiary organ, the National Security Bureau 國家安全局, are to set national security policies and to assist in planning security strategy.

The National Assembly

After six constitutional amendments between April 1991 and 2000, the National Assembly is now a non-standing body and its delegates will be nominated by political parties on the basis of proportional representation. Most of its functions have been transferred to the Legislative Yuan (see Appendix III for details).

Delegates

A 300-member non-standing body will be selected by proportional representation, according to laws to be passed by the Legislative Yuan. The National Assembly's functions will be limited to voting on Constitution amendments, presidential impeachment, or alteration of the national boundaries, as proposed by the Legislative Yuan. Its former powers, including hearing the president's state of the nation address and approving the president's nominations of the grand justices and the heads of the Examination and Control Yuan, have been transferred to the Legislative Yuan.

Five Government Branches

The ROC Constitution provides for a central government with five "yuan" (branches)—the Executive Yuan, the Legislative Yuan, the Judicial Yuan, the Examination Yuan, and the Control Yuan.

Executive Yuan

The Executive Yuan has a president, usually referred to as the premier of the ROC; a vice premier; a number of ministers and chairpersons of commissions; and five to seven ministers-without-portfolio. The premier is appointed by the president of the Republic. If the premier resigns or if his office becomes vacant, office functions are temporarily exercised by the vice premier. The vice premier, ministers, and

chairpersons are appointed by the president of the Republic on the recommendation of the premier. In addition to supervising the operations of the various subordinate agencies of the Executive Yuan, the premier is also responsible for the following: performing the duties of the president of the Republic in the event of vacancies in both the presidency and the vice presidency (limited to three months); presenting administrative policies and reports to the Legislature and responding, either orally or in writing, to the interpellations of legislators; countersigning laws and decrees promulgated by the president of the Republic; and requesting, with the approval of the president, the Legislative Yuan to reconsider its resolutions.

Executive Yuan Council

The Executive Yuan Council is a policymaking organization, which consists of the premier, who presides over its meetings, the vice premier, ministers-without-portfolio, the heads of the ROC's eight ministries, and the heads of the Mongolian and Tibetan Affairs Commission and the Overseas Chinese Affairs Commission. According to Article 58 of the Constitution, the council

evaluates statutory and budgetary bills and bills concerning martial law, amnesty, declarations of war, conclusion of peace or treaties, and other important affairs, which are to be submitted to the Legislature, as well as matters of common concern to the various ministries and commissions. The council may invite heads of other Executive Yuan organizations to attend council meetings and answer any questions that may arise pertaining to affairs under their jurisdiction. The secretary-general and the deputy secretary-general also attend the meetings; however, they have no vote.

Ministries and Other Organizations

There are eight ministries under the Executive Yuan: Interior 內政, Foreign Affairs 外交, National Defense 國防, Finance 財政, Education 教育, Justice 法務, Economic Affairs 經濟, and Transportation and Communications 交通.

In addition to the Mongolian and Tibetan Affairs Commission and the Overseas Chinese Affairs Commission, a number of commissions and subordinate organizations have been formed with the resolution of the Executive Yuan council and the Legislature to meet new demands and handle

Under the supervision of Peng Ming-min, senior advisor to the president, the outgoing Premier Chang Chun-hsiung hands the seal of his office to incoming Premier Yu Shyi-kun.
(Photo by the Central News Agency)

new affairs. Examples include the Environmental Protection Administration 環境保護署, which was set up in 1987; the Mainland Affairs Council 大陸委員會, which was established in 1990 to handle the relations between Taiwan and the Chinese mainland; the Fair Trade Commission 公平交易委員會, which was established in 1992 to promote a fair trade system; and the Consumer Protection Commission 消費者保護委員會, which was set up in July 1994 to study and review basic policies on consumer protection.

Since 1995, additional commissions have been set up to provide a wider scope of services: the Public Construction Commission 公共工程委員會 was set up in July 1995, the Council of Indigenous Peoples 原住民族委員會 in December 1996, the National Council on Physical Fitness and Sports 體育委員會 in July 1997, the Coast Guard Administration 海岸巡防署 in January 2000, and the Council for Hakka Affairs 客家委員會 in June 2000.

In accordance with the *File Law* 檔案法 promulgated by the ROC president on December 15, 1999, the National Archives of the ROC 檔案管理局 was placed under the authority of the Executive Yuan's Research, Development, and Evaluation Commission 行政院研究發展考核委員會 on November 23, 2001. The new organization formulates laws and policies on file management and assists all government agencies in managing their files.

Relationship with the Legislative Yuan

The Executive Yuan presents the Legislative Yuan with an annual policy statement and an administrative report. When the Legislative Yuan is in session, its members have the right to interpellate the premier, ministers, and chairpersons of commissions of the Executive Yuan.

If the Legislative Yuan disagrees with an important policy of the Executive Yuan, it may, by resolution, request the Executive Yuan to alter it. The Executive Yuan may, with the approval of the president of the Republic, request the Legislature's reconsideration. If after reconsideration one-half of the attending members of the Legislature uphold the original resolution, the premier must either abide by the resolution or resign from office. Similar procedures apply, if the Executive Yuan considers a resolution on a statutory, budgetary, or treaty bill passed by the Legislative Yuan difficult to execute. The Executive Yuan shall, three months prior to the end of each fiscal year, present to the Legislative Yuan the budgetary bill for the following fiscal year.

With the signatures of more than one-third of the total number of legislators, the Legislative Yuan may propose a no-confidence vote against the premier. Seventy-two hours after the no-confidence motion is made, an open-ballot vote must be taken within 48 hours. Should more than one-half of the total number of Legislative Yuan members approve the motion, the premier must resign from office within ten days and at the same time may request that the president dissolve the Legislative Yuan. Should the no-confidence motion fail, the Legislative Yuan may not initiate another no-confidence motion against the same premier for one year.

Relationship with the Judicial Yuan

According to the constitutional amendment completed in July 1997, the proposed budget submitted by the Judicial Yuan may not be eliminated or reduced by the Executive Yuan. The Executive Yuan may instead indicate its opinions on the budget and include it in the central government's proposed budgetary bill for submission to the Legislative Yuan for deliberation.

Relationship with the Examination Yuan

Public officials to be appointed by the Executive Yuan must be qualified by examinations held by the Examination Yuan.

Relationship with the Control Yuan

The Control Yuan has the authority to request the Executive Yuan and its ministries and subordinate organizations to submit original orders issued for examination. It may set up a number of committees to investigate the activities of the Executive Yuan and its ministries and

subordinate organizations to determine whether they violated the law or are derelict in their duties. It may propose and forward corrective measures to the Executive Yuan and the agencies concerned. The Executive Yuan shall, within four months after the end of each fiscal year, present final accounts of revenues and expenditures to the Control Yuan for audit.

Legal Affairs

The Ministry of Justice 法務部 handles legal affairs for the Executive Yuan, including prosecution procedures, investigation of crimes, and management of prisons and rehabilitation programs. It consists of the departments of Prosecutorial Affairs 檢察司, Corrections 矯正司, Rehabilitation and Social Protection 保護司, and Legal Affairs 法律事務司. The Investigation Bureau 調查局 is also under its jurisdiction.

Legislative Yuan

The Legislative Yuan (Legislature) is the highest legislative body of the state, consisting of popularly elected representatives who serve for three years and are eligible for reelection. Elections for the fifth Legislative Yuan were held in December 2001.

Functions and Powers

In accordance with the Constitution, the Legislature has the following functions and powers:

- General legislative power: The Legislature exercises legislative power on behalf of the people. The term "law" as used in the Constitution includes any legislative bill passed by the Legislature and promulgated by the president of the Republic.
- Confirmation of emergency orders: Emergency orders and measures proclaimed by the president in the case of an imminent threat to national security or a serious financial or economic crisis, during the recess of the Legislature, are presented to the Legislature for confirmation within ten days of issuance. Should the president issue an emergency order after dissolving the Legislative Yuan, the Legislative Yuan convenes of its own accord within

three days and has seven days to decide whether to ratify the order.

- Hearing reports on administration and revision of government policy: The Executive Yuan presents a statement of its administrative policies and a report on its administration to the Legislative Yuan. If the Legislative Yuan does not concur with any important Executive Yuan policy, it may request the Executive Yuan to alter such a policy.
- Examination of budgetary bills and audit reports: The Legislative Yuan has the power to decide by resolution upon budgetary bills, which the Executive Yuan is required to present to the Legislative Yuan three months before the beginning of each fiscal year. The auditor-general, within three months after presentation by the Executive Yuan of the final accounts of revenues and expenditures, completes the audit in accordance with the law, and submits an audit report to the Legislative Yuan.
- Right of consent: The presidents of the Control, Examination, and Judicial Yuan are nominated and appointed by the president of the Republic with the consent of the Legislative Yuan.
- Amendment of the Constitution: Upon the proposal of one-fourth of the members of the Legislative Yuan and by resolution of three-fourths of the members present at a meeting having a quorum of three-fourths of the members of the Yuan, a bill to amend the Constitution may be submitted to the National Assembly for deliberation.
- Settlement of disputes concerning self-governance: The Legislature settles any disputes over items and matters of self-governance of special municipalities, counties/cities, or other administrative units.

Article 4 of the *Additional Articles of the Constitution of the Republic of China* has given the Legislature power to institute impeachment proceedings against the president or vice president of the Republic. Impeachment of the president or vice president will be initiated upon the agreement of more than two-thirds of all members of the Legislative Yuan, after proposal by more than one-half of the legislators. The resolution will be submitted to the National Assembly.

Election and Tenure of Office

According to Article 4 of the *Additional Articles of the Constitution of the Republic of China*, beginning with the fourth Legislative Yuan, the Legislative Yuan will have 225 members, elected as follows: First, 168 members shall be elected from the special municipalities, counties, and cities in the ROC. At least one member shall be elected in each county and city. Second, four members each shall be elected from among the plains and mountain aborigines in the ROC. Third, eight members shall be elected from among Chinese citizens who reside abroad. Fourth, 41 members shall be elected from the nationwide constituency.

Members in the third and fourth categories above shall be selected by proportional representation of political parties. Where the number of seats for each special municipality, county, and city as set forth in the first item, and for each political party as set forth in the third and fourth items, is not less than five and not more than ten, one seat shall be reserved for a female candidate. Where the number exceeds ten, one seat out of each additional ten shall be reserved for a female candidate.

Procedures pertaining to the election of members shall be conducted openly by universal, equal, and direct vote by single and secret ballot. The election shall be completed three months prior to the expiration of the current term. If more than 2 percent of the total voters in a district feel that their elected representative has not properly performed, they may file a petition for recall, after the member has been in office for one year. (Article 133 of the Constitution and Article 69 and 70 of the *Public Officials Election and Recall Law* 公職人員選舉罷免法)

Immunity and Restrictions

According to Article 73 of the Constitution, "No member of the Legislative Yuan shall be held responsible outside the Yuan for opinions expressed or votes cast in the Yuan." This is to protect members from outside threats or disturbances, so that they can express their views and cast ballots freely.

According to Article 4 of the *Additional Articles of the Constitution of the Republic of China*, no member of the Legislative Yuan may, except in case of *flagrante delicto*, be arrested or detained without the permission of the Legislative Yuan when that body is in session. The provisions of Article 74 of the Constitution shall cease to apply.

Article 75 of the Constitution states: "No member of the Legislative Yuan shall concurrently hold a government post." This provision completely separates legislative and executive powers to avoid a monopolization of power by members of the Legislature.

Organization and Functions

The Legislature operates through sessions of the Yuan, committees, and the secretariat. The Yuan holds two sessions each year and convenes of its own accord. The first session lasts from February to the end of May, and the second from September to the end of December. Whenever necessary, a session may be extended. An extraordinary session may be held at the request of no less than one-fourth of its members. Regular meetings of the Legislature require a quorum of one-third of the total membership. Unless otherwise stipulated, resolutions at meetings of the Legislature are adopted by a simple majority vote. In case of a tie, the chairman casts the deciding vote.

In exercising the power of consent in accordance with Article 104 of the Constitution, the Legislative Yuan may vote on the matter, after hearing the report of the committee of the whole Yuan. The chairman is elected by and from the members present at a meeting of the committee of the whole Yuan, when the president and vice president of the Yuan are both absent.

The Legislative Yuan has the following 12 standing committees: Home and Border Affairs 內政及邊政委員會, Foreign and Overseas Chinese Affairs 外交及僑政委員會, Technology and Information 科技及資訊委員會, National Defense

國防委員會, Economics and Energy 經濟及能源委員會, Finance 財政委員會, Budget and Final Accounts 預算及決算委員會, Education and Cultural Affairs 教育及文化委員會, Transportation and Communications 交通委員會, Judiciary 司法委員會, Organic Laws 法制委員會, and Health, Environment and Social Welfare 衛生環境及社會福利委員會. Each of the committees is composed of not more than 21 members, and no member may serve on more than one committee. The Legislature has the following five special committees: Discipline 紀律委員會, Rules 程序委員會, Accounts 經費稽核委員會, Publications 公報指導委員會, and Constitutional Amendment 修憲委員會.

Judicial Yuan

The Judicial Yuan (Judiciary) is the highest judicial organization of the state, with the Council of Grand Justices 大法官會議 as its main body. According to Article 3 of the *Organic Law of the Judicial Yuan* 司法院組織法, there shall be 17 grand justices, even though there are only 15 at present. However, Article 5 of the *Additional Articles of the Constitution* reduced the number to 15, including the president and the vice president of the Judicial Yuan to be selected from among the members. The grand justices are nominated and appointed by the president of the Republic, with the consent of the Legislative Yuan. This will take effect from the year 2003, and the provisions of Article 79 of the Constitution will no longer apply. The subordinate units of the Judicial Yuan are the Supreme Court 最高法院, the high courts 高等法院, the district courts 地方法院, the Supreme Administrative Court 最高行政法院, the high administrative courts 高等行政法院, and the Commission on the Disciplinary Sanctions of Public Functionaries 公務人員懲戒委員會. The Judiciary exercises administrative supervision of the ROC court system, while enforcing compliance by ROC court personnel with constitutionally mandated judicial independence.

The Council of Grand Justices

The sixth Council of Grand Justices 大法官會議 took office on October 1, 1994, following confirmation by the National Assembly for a nine-year term. However, according to Article 5 of the *Additional Articles of the Constitution*, each grand justice serves a term of eight years, regardless of the order of appointment to office and cannot serve an additional term. The president and vice president of the Judicial Yuan are not guaranteed an eight-year term.

Among the grand justices to be nominated by the president in the year 2003, eight members, including the president and the vice president of the Judicial Yuan, will serve for four years. The remaining grand justices will serve eight years. The provisions of the preceding paragraph regarding term of office will not apply.

The Council of Grand Justices interprets the Constitution and unifies the interpretation of laws and ordinances. The Council meets three times a week and holds additional meetings as necessary. Oral proceedings may be held whenever the need arises. After an interpretation of the Constitution or unified interpretation of a law is made, the Judiciary publishes the text of the interpretation, the reasons supporting it, and any dissenting opinions.

Interpretation of the Constitution

From 1948 to July 20, 2001, the Council of Grand Justices rendered 529 interpretations of the Constitution at the request of government agencies, individuals, juridical persons, and political parties. Constitutional interpretations are made when there are doubts or disputes concerning:
• the application of the Constitution;
• the constitutionality of laws, regulations, or decrees; and
• the constitutionality of local self-government laws, regulations, and matters.

Unified Interpretation of Laws and Ordinances

A petition for a unified interpretation of a law or ordinance may be filed with the Council of Grand Justices if:
• a government agency, when applying a law or ordinance, has an interpretation, which is different from one already expressed by itself or another government organ, unless it is legally

bound to obey the expressed opinion or has the authority to revise it;
- an individual, juridical person, or political party whose rights have been infringed and believes that the final decision of the court of last resort was based on an interpretation of the applicable law or regulation that is different from precedents by other courts. (Such requests will not be accepted if the petitioner has not yet exhausted all judicial remedies or the opinion adopted in an earlier decision has been altered by a later one.)

The Constitutional Court

In December 1993, the Judiciary formally established a Constitutional Court 憲法法庭, in accordance with Article 13 of the previous version of the *Additional Articles of the Constitution* and the revised *Organic Law of the Judicial Yuan*, to adjudicate cases concerning the dissolution of political parties that have violated the Constitution. The Constitutional Court is composed of the grand justices and presided over by its most senior member.

The Ministry of the Interior may, as the agency overseeing political parties, petition the Constitutional Court for the dissolution of a political party whose objectives and activities are found to endanger the existence of the ROC or its free and democratic constitutional order.

Commission on the Disciplinary Sanctions of Public Functionaries

The Control Yuan may impeach a public official for malfeasance, dereliction of duty, other neglect of duty, or if the head of any of the various branches, ministries or commissions or the highest local administrative head requests a disciplinary measure against a public official for these reasons. The Commission on the Disciplinary Sanctions of Public Functionaries, under the Judicial Yuan, exercises jurisdiction over such cases.

The Commission consists of nine to 15 senior members, one of whom serves as the Chief Commissioner. Cases are decided without outside interference. The Commission orders the impeached public official to submit a written

reply within a prescribed period of time and, when it deems necessary, may summon the person to appear before the Commission to defend himself. The conference is not open to the public and its proceedings are strictly confidential.

There are six disciplinary measures which the Commission may order: dismissal, suspension from office, demotion, reduction of salary, demerit, and reprimand. Only dismissal and reprimand are applicable to political appointees.

The ROC Court System

The judiciary of the Republic of China has three levels: district courts and their branches that hear civil and criminal cases in the first instance; high courts and their branches at the intermediate level that hear appeals against judgments of district courts or their branches; and the Supreme Court at the highest appellate level, which reviews judgments by lower courts for compliance with pertinent laws or regulations. Issues of fact are decided in the first and second levels, while only issues of law are considered by the Supreme Court. However, there are exceptions to this system. Criminal cases relating to rebellion, treason, and offenses against friendly relations with foreign states are handled by high courts, as the court of first instance; and appeals may be filed with the Supreme Court.

District Courts

There are 20 district courts in the Taiwan area. Each has a president, appointed from among the judges, who is in charge of the administrative work of the court. Each court is divided into civil 民事庭, criminal 刑事庭, and summary divisions 民刑事簡易庭. Currently there are 45 summary divisions in the Taiwan area to adjudicate cases in a prompt and expeditious manner. Summary proceedings are conducted by a single judge. In addition, there is the Juvenile Court of Kaohsiung 高雄少年法院 established in accordance with the *Law Governing the Disposition of Juvenile Cases* 少年事件處理法. Appeals may be filed with the civil or criminal division of the district court for review by a three-judge panel.

Specialized divisions may also be set up by district courts to deal with juvenile, family, traffic, financial, and labor cases, as well as motions to set aside rulings on the violations of the *Statute of the Maintenance of Social Order* 社會秩序維護法. Cases to be tried by a district court are heard before a single judge, although more important cases may be heard by three judges.

High Courts

At present there is one high court in Taipei serving all of Taiwan and the Pescadores, with four branch courts in Taichung, Tainan, Kaohsiung, and Hualien. In the part of Fujian Province under the control of the ROC, there is the Kinmen Branch Court of the Fujian High Court 福建高等法院金門分院, which exercises jurisdiction over appellate cases in Kinmen County and Lienchiang County. A senior judge of the High Court is appointed to serve concurrently as president of the court in charge of the administrative work of the court and its subordinate units.

The High Court is divided into civil and criminal, as well as specialized divisions dealing with juvenile, traffic, and labor cases. Each division has a presiding judge and associates. Cases to be tried by the High Court are heard before a three-judge panel. However, one of the judges may conduct the preliminary proceedings alone.

The High Court and its branches exercise jurisdiction over the following cases:
• civil, criminal, and election cases on appeal from judgments of district courts or their branches;
• motions to set aside rulings of district courts or their branches;
• criminal cases relating to rebellion, treason, and offenses against friendly relations with foreign states, as the court of first instance; and
• other lawsuits prescribed by law.

The Supreme Court

Although it is under the administrative supervision of the Judicial Yuan, the entire ROC court system has judicial independence in criminal and civil matters of law. The Supreme Court is the court of final appeal in the ROC judicial system.

The Supreme Court has a president, who is responsible for the administrative work of the Court and is concurrently a judge. The Supreme Court is divided into eight civil divisions and 12 criminal divisions. An appeal may be made to the Supreme Court only on grounds that the lower court's decision violates a law or ordinance. Since the Supreme Court does not decide questions of fact, documentary proceedings are the rule, while oral arguments are the exception. Cases before the Supreme Court are tried by five judges.

The Supreme Court exercises jurisdiction over the following kinds of cases:
• appeals against judgments in civil and criminal cases by high courts or their branches as court of second instance;
• appeals against judgments of high courts or their branches in criminal cases as court of first instance;
• motions to set aside rulings of high courts or their branches in civil and criminal cases;
• appeals against or motions to set aside rulings of district courts or their branches as the court of second instance in civil summary proceedings; and
• cases of extraordinary appeal.

The Supreme and High Administrative Courts

On July 1, 2000, the amended *Organic Law of the Administrative Court* 行政法院組織法 became effective. The new law adopts the "two-level and two-instance system" for administrative litigation. As a result, one Supreme Administrative Court and three high administrative Courts have been established in Taipei, Taichung and Kaohsiung to adjudicate administrative cases.

The administrative courts have a different authority from that of the other courts in the system. Any person who claims that his rights or legal interests are violated by an unlawful administrative action rendered by a government agency may institute administrative proceedings before the high administrative court. This right is available on objection to the decision on an administrative appeal submitted in accordance with the

Law of Administrative Appeal 訴願法, or if no decision is rendered over three months after the submission of an administrative appeal, or over two months of extension after the prescribed period for decision has expired. An administrative action, which exceeds the legal authority of the government agency or which results from an abuse of power, is unlawful.

Cases before a high administrative court are tried by three judges. Appeals may be filed with the Supreme Administrative Courts for review by a five-judge panel. The high administrative courts decide questions of both fact and law, while the Supreme Administrative Court decides only questions of law.

Judicial Reform

Significant reforms are being carried out to reorganize the ROC judicial system and ensure fair trials. The National Conference on Judicial Reform held in July 1999, proposed that experts be brought into Taiwan's courts to assist in the trying of cases which involve family affairs, juvenile crimes, labor and medical disputes, and intellectual property rights. Also, assessors may be called into court on major criminal and administrative cases to assist presiding judges who may not necessarily be equipped with a technical expertise in specialized areas.

A framework for transforming the role of the judicial branch was reached. The Judiciary's short-term reform plan will establish civil, criminal, constitutional, and administrative courts. The long-term reform plan will seat 13 to 15 grand justices, who will be responsible for civil, criminal, and administrative litigation, as well as cases on disciplining public functionaries, dissolving political parties, and interpreting the Constitution. Changes in the Judiciary are expected to increase public confidence in the independence of the judicial system.

Examination Yuan

The Examination Yuan is responsible for the civil service system in the Republic of China. Specifically, the Examination Yuan oversees examination; qualification screening; security

of tenure; pecuniary aid in case of death; retirement of civil servants; and all legal matters relating to the employment, discharge, performance evaluation, scale of salaries, promotion, transfer, commendation, and award of civil servants.

The examination system is applicable to all Chinese civil servants, high- or low-ranking, appointed or elected and is applicable to Chinese and foreign professionals and technicians. The examination function, exercised solely by the Examination Yuan at the central government level, is separated from the executive power and is free from partisan influence.

Organization and Functions

The Examination Yuan currently has a president and 17 members, all of whom were appointed on September 1, 1996, for six-year terms by the president of the ROC with the approval of the National Assembly. However, the appointment of the tenth-term Examination Yuan council shall be approved by the Legislative Yuan, in accordance with Article 6 of the *Additional Articles of the Constitution*. The Examination Yuan consists of a council, a secretariat, the Ministry of Examination 考選部, the Ministry of Civil Service 銓敘部, the Civil Service Protection and Training Commission 公務員保障暨培訓委員會, and the Supervisory Board for the Civil Servant Pension Fund 公務人員退休撫卹基金監理委員會. The Examination Yuan also supervises the operations of the Central Personnel Administration 人事行政局, established under the Executive Yuan in 1967.

The council of the Examination Yuan 考試委員會 makes policy and decides all significant matters within the jurisdiction of the Examination Yuan. Various examination boards are formed each year under the chairmanship of the president, the vice president, or a member of the Examination Yuan. Members of examination boards formulate questions for and grade the examinations. They also determine the number of successful candidates in each examination. In addition, committees may be set up to facilitate the administration of examinations and personnel projects. The Ministry of Examination oversees all civil service, professional, and technological

examinations. The Ministry of Civil Service is in charge of the government personnel system throughout the nation.

Examinations

The two main types of government examinations in the ROC are Civil Service Examinations 公務人員考試 and Examinations for Professionals and Technologists 專門職業及技術人員考試. Civil Service Examinations are divided into the following types:

• Senior-grade Civil Service Examinations 高等考試: Divided into Level I, for holders of Ph.D.; Level II, for holders of M.A. and M.S. degrees; and Level III, for holders of B.A. and B.S. degrees and for people who have passed the Senior Qualifying Examinations or those who passed the Junior-grade Civil Service Examinations at least three years prior to taking the exam;

• Junior-grade Civil Service Examinations 普通考試: Primarily for graduates of senior high schools or senior vocational schools and secondarily for those who passed the Junior Qualifying Examinations or those who passed Special Examination D at least three years prior to taking the exam;

• Special Examination A 特種考試（一等）: Corresponding to the Senior-grade Civil Service Examination Level I;

• Special Examination B 特種考試（二等）: Corresponding to the Senior-grade Civil Service Examination Level II;

• Special Examination C 特種考試（三等）: Corresponding to the Senior-grade Civil Service Examination Level III;

• Special Examination D 特種考試（四等）: Corresponding to the Junior-grade Civil Service Examination;

• Special Examination E 特種考試（五等）: Primarily for ROC citizens 18 years of age or older;

• Promotion Examinations 升等考試; and

• Qualifying Examinations 檢定考試.

Examinations for Professionals and Technologists are divided into the following types:

• Junior Examinations 普通考試;

• Senior Examinations 高等考試; and

• Special Examinations 特種考試: including tests for merchant seamen, harbor pilots, ship surveyors, crew of fishing boats, ship radio operators, doctors of Chinese medicine, and nutritionists.

The Ministry of Examination also screens qualifications for candidates running for elected posts, military personnel transferring to the civil service, and Chinese nationals and non-nationals for their technical skills.

Examinations for senior and junior civil servants are conducted every year, every other year, or whenever necessary. Categories of personnel needed, subjects to be tested, and dates are announced by the Ministry of Examination two months before the examination.

Civil Servants

There were 602,407 civil servants in the ROC at the end of 2000. ROC civil servants are well-educated, with 77.23 percent holding college degrees or higher. The majority—58.47 percent—were male, however, an increasing number of women have joined the civil service in recent years.

Unlike the political appointees whom they serve, civil servants are classified into senior 簡任 (grades 10-14), intermediate 薦任 (grades 6-9), or junior 委任 (grades 1-5) levels. The 14 levels of administration reflect an employee's abilities, experience, and seniority. Salary increases with grade, and civil servants at grade 14 can earn up to five times that of those at grade one. Each year civil servants are reviewed by their superiors. Those who receive good reviews receive an annual increase in grade. However, it is necessary to either pass a difficult civil service exam or be specially recommended by a superior to enter grades six and ten.

Control Yuan

The Control Yuan is the highest control organization of the state, exercising the powers of impeachment, censure, and audit. The Control Yuan was formerly a parliamentary body, with its members elected by provincial and municipal councils. However, constitutional amendments in May 1992 transformed it into a quasi-judicial organization. The new Control Yuan began operations on February 1, 1993. From July 1997 onwards, it no longer had the power to institute the impeachment against the president and vice president of the Republic, and the Legislative Yuan was empowered by constitutional amendment to take over the duty. The 29 current members took office on February 1, 1999. The president, vice president, and members were nominated and appointed by the president of the ROC with the consent of the National Assembly, as required by the earlier version of the *Additional Articles of the Constitution.* However, according to the present version of the *Additional Articles of the Constitution*, nominations of the fourth-term members require the consent of the Legislative Yuan. The term of office for all members is six years.

Organization

The Control Yuan council, which is composed of the president, vice president, and 27 other members, makes policy on significant matters. Meetings are held monthly with the president acting as chairman. The Control Yuan has seven committees, which handle cases on domestic and ethnic minority affairs 內政及少數民族委員會, foreign and overseas Chinese affairs 外交及僑政委員會, national defense and intelligence affairs 國防及情報委員會, finance and economic affairs 財政及經濟委員會, education and cultural affairs 教育及文化委員會, transportation, communications and purchase affairs 交通及採購委員會, and judicial affairs and prison administration 司法及獄政委員會. Each Control Yuan member may join three of the seven committees and participate in other committees as a nonvoting member. Each committee elects a convener from among its members to handle routine affairs.

Members

Control Yuan members are responsible for correcting government officials at all levels and generally monitoring the government. Members of the Control Yuan must be beyond party control, exercise their powers independently, and discharge their responsibilities in accordance with the law. Article 103 of the Constitution also stipulates that "no member of the Control Yuan shall concurrently hold any other public office or engage in any other profession."

Functions

The Constitution defines the Control Yuan as the highest control organization of the Republic. It is empowered to institute impeachment proceedings against public officials of the central or local government, except for the president and the vice president of the Republic, if that individual is guilty of dereliction of duty or violation of law. A decision concerning a motion for impeachment requires the concurrence of nine Control Yuan members other than those who initiated the motion. If the case is affirmed in the Control Yuan it goes to the appropriate authority for action—the Commission on the Disciplinary Sanctions of Public Functionaries in the case of a civil servant, or the Ministry of National Defense for military personnel.

A Control Yuan member may, with the support of three other members, file a written censure against a public official, whose offense requires immediate suspension of duty or punishment. Pending legal proceedings, the superior of a censured official must follow the *Law on Discipline of Public Functionaries* 公務員懲戒法 within one month of receiving the written censure.

The Control Yuan may investigate the operations of the Executive Yuan and its subordinate organizations and propose corrective measures to be examined by relevant committees and referred to the relevant ministry or commission, which must take appropriate action and report to the Control Yuan in writing.

Under the *Control Law* 監察法, citizens are authorized to initiate proceedings against public officials by filing a written complaint with the Control Yuan. The complaint and any supporting evidence is considered by the member on duty, who will decide appropriate action.

The members of the Control Yuan or their designees may conduct field investigations of public or private organizations based on complaints or press reports regarding dereliction

of duty or violation of law. They may also initiate investigations.

The Control Yuan exercises its power of audit through its National Audit Office 審計部, which establishes audit departments in provinces and special municipalities and sets up county and city audit offices. Audit departments or offices may be established within special government agencies, state-run enterprises, or public institutions.

According to the Constitution, the auditor-general is nominated by the president of the Republic of China and appointed with the consent of the Legislature. The auditor-general is responsible for auditing central government expenditures.

The National Audit Office monitors public affairs, properties, institutions, as well as enterprises in which the state owns at least 50 percent. Auditing duties and functions include supervision of all government organization budgets, approval of receipts and disbursements, investigation of irregularities and abuse of power in property and financial administration, evaluation of the efficiency of financial administration, decisions on financial responsibilities, and other auditing functions prescribed by law. The audit agencies also monitor government bids, contract awards, and proceedings concerning the redemption of bonds and conduct random inspections of ongoing construction projects.

The Control Yuan established the Department of Assets Disclosure for Public Functionaries 公職人員財產申報處 in August 1993. In accordance with Article 4 of the *Public Functionary Assets Disclosure Law* 公職人員財產申報法, the Control Yuan receives assets disclosure reports from the president and vice president of the Republic, the presidents and vice presidents of the five Yuan, political appointees, paid advisors to the president of the Republic, elected officials at the level of township magistrates or above, and elected representatives of counties and cities under provincial jurisdiction and higher administrative units.

Provincial Government

A provincial government is the highest local administrative organization prescribed by the *Constitution of the Republic of China*. Although the ROC Constitution designates 35 provinces (see map on the inside of the back cover), Taiwan (see map on the inside of the front cover) is the only one complete province under the effective control of the ROC. The Fujian Provincial Government, headquartered in Kinmen County, has delegated most of its powers to county governments.

The Role of the Provincial Government

At the end of 1996, the National Development Conference was convened to draft a plan for development in the new century. In this conference, the following measures to streamline the provincial government were proposed:

- The functions, operations, and organization of the provincial government should be reorganized and streamlined; a committee to plan and implement these projects should be established; and elections for provincial offices should be suspended starting from the second term.
- Elections for rural township, urban township, and county municipality offices should be suspended, and the heads of these townships and municipalities should be appointed in accordance with the law.
- The offices of deputy magistrate (for counties) and deputy mayor (for provincial municipalities) should be created, and greater power delegated to the county and provincial municipality governments.
- The legislation governing local taxes and the revision of the *Law Governing the Allocation of Government Revenues and Expenditures* should be completed quickly in order to provide an effective financial base for local governments.

The foregoing projects were instituted by constitutional amendment in July 1997, providing the legal foundation to streamline the Taiwan Provincial Government (TPG).

The first phase of the plan involved the appointment of Chao Shou-po 趙守博 as the new provincial governor to succeed popularly elected Taiwan Governor James Soong 宋楚瑜, whose

Budget Allocation

All governments from the central down to the county/city levels are required to submit their budget bills for review by the legislative body at their respective levels three months before the beginning of each fiscal year. Cities under county jurisdiction and urban and rural townships are required to submit their proposed budgets to their respective representative offices two months in advance.

Funding for these budgets comes mainly from national and local taxes, which are proportionally allocated to each government level, in accordance with the *Law Governing the Allocation of Government Revenues and Expenditures* 財政收支劃分法. Each year, the Executive Yuan reviews the financial conditions of each government level and may revise the law to adjust the percentage of tax revenues to be appropriated to the different levels of government. The tax revenues shall, however, account for an appropriate proportion of the fiscal expenditures at each government level, which is also required to maintain a certain proportion of local financial resources. The figures for these two proportions, which are proposed by the Executive Yuan, require the approval of the Legislature.

On July 19, 2000, the Executive Yuan announced the new tax revenue ratio allocated to each level of local government. According to the new ratio, 39 percent of the tax revenue was distributed to county/city government in fiscal year 2001, a 4 percent increase over the previous year. The rural and urban townships obtained 12 percent of the tax revenue since the Taiwan Provincial Government no longer has any major responsibilities to local governments. However, the percentage for the special municipalities of Taipei and Kaohsiung was reduced from 47 percent to 43 percent. The central government was holding 6 percent of the revenue as an emergency reserve, while reducing the allocations for Taipei and Kaohsiung. The same tax revenue ratio will also apply in fiscal year 2002.

The local county/city governments not only requested a fair distribution formula based on population, area, financial needs, and efforts made in boosting revenues, but also demanded an allocation of the entire business tax revenue. The Executive Yuan also encouraged local governments to develop their own sources of income, such as lotteries and taxes on alcohol and cigarettes. Under the *Self-governance Law for Provinces and Counties* 省縣自治法, and the *Municipal Self-governance Law* 直轄市自治法, local governments from the provincial level down may increase their revenues by levying taxes or charging fees for specific purposes in the areas under their jurisdiction. The fees may be charged in accordance with pertinent regulations or with the approval of the legislative body or representative conference at that level of government.

As the supervisory organization of provincial and municipal self-governance, the Executive Yuan may provide subsidies or financial aid to the said governments with the approval of the Legislative Yuan. Such subsidies or financial aid may be cut if the government concerned does not levy taxes or fees which are permitted under the law. This is also true for governments of counties, provincial municipalities, county municipalities, and urban and rural townships. Such subsidies and aid are provided with the approval of the respective county/city council or representative conference. The provincial government may demand funding for such purposes from counties/cities that are in better financial conditions.

term in office expired in December 1998. Gubernatorial elections were indefinitely suspended, making Mr. Soong the first and only popularly elected Taiwan Provincial Governor in the ROC history. The incumbent Taiwan Governor is Fan Kuang-chun 范光群.

The plan entered a second phase on July 1, 1999, with a structural adjustment. The TPG has been downsized and divided into six sections, five offices, two committees, and 13 affiliated organizations. The 149 administrative units, 36 health-care organizations, and 170 provincial high schools originally listed under the provincial administration have been recategorized as units of the central government. Also, 58 organizations were either eliminated or merged. Altogether, 16 former TPG departments were transformed into the regional offices of the ministries and agencies under the Executive Yuan and three under the Examination Yuan. By the end of

2000, all restructuring have been completed. After January 1, 2001, the organization, functions and administrative affairs of local-level governments have returned to normal, in accordance with regulations in the *Law on Local Government Systems* 地方制度法, which was passed by the Legislature on January 25, 1999.

Article 9 of the *Additional Articles of the Constitution* stipulates:

The system of self-government in the provinces and counties shall include the following provisions: (1) A province shall have a provincial government of nine members, one of whom shall be the provincial governor. All members shall be nominated by the president of the Executive Yuan and appointed by the president of the Republic. (2) A province shall have a provincial advisory council made up of a number of members, who shall be nominated by the president of the Executive Yuan and appointed by the president of the Republic. (3) A county shall have a county council; members of which shall be elected by the people of the said county. (4) The legislative powers vested in a county shall be exercised by the county council of the said county. (5) A county shall have a county government headed by a county magistrate who shall be elected by the people of the said county. (6) The relationship between the central government and the provincial and county governments. (7) A province shall execute the orders of the Executive Yuan and supervise matters governed by the counties.

The modifications of the functions, operations, and organization of the TPG may be specified by law.

The Provisional Statute on the Adjustment of the Function, Business, and Organization of the Taiwan Provincial Government

The Provisional Statute on the Adjustment of the Function, Business, and Organization of the Taiwan Provincial Government 臺灣省 政府功能業務及組織調整暫行條例 was passed in October 1998, and suspended all provisions for provincial autonomy in the existing *Self-governance Law for Provinces and Counties* effective December 21, 1998. After streamlining the provincial government, the central government assumed all of its assets and liabilities. The statute provides a two-year deadline for the completion of the streamlining process. The downsized provincial administration is now a branch of the central government. The statute also states that regulations governing the streamlined provincial administration should be issued by the Executive Yuan and acknowledged by the Legislature. Two additional bills were passed in 1999 on the downsizing project: a new *Law on Local Government Systems* and a revised version of the *Law Governing the Allocation of Government Revenues and Expenditures*.

The Fujian Provincial Government

The ROC government administers only two counties in Fujian Province: Kinmen County, which includes Kinmen, and Lienchiang County, which includes Matsu. In July 1956, the ROC military assumed full administrative responsibility for these two counties. Military administration lasted until August 7, 1992, when President Lee Teng-hui promulgated the *Statute for the Security and Guidance of Kinmen, Matsu, and the Pratas and Spratlys Areas* 金門、馬祖、東沙、南沙地區安全及輔導條例. The return of local autonomy to Kinmen County and Lienchiang County is part of the ROC's recent constitutional reforms. The residents of these counties now have the same rights and freedoms as all people in Taiwan.

Like its Taiwan counterpart, the Fujian Provincial Government has a council. Fujian Governor Yen Chung-cheng 顏忠誠 presides over the council when it convenes.

The Kinmen County Government is responsible for the administration of six rural and urban townships, which are subdivided into 37 villages and boroughs. Although elections for township magistrates and village mayors as well as for

Taipei City Mayor Ma Ying-jeou (third from the right) attends the lottery issuance celebration party given by Taipei Bank.
(Photo by the Central News Agency)

representatives of the local and central governments have been held regularly since 1971, local self-government was fully implemented after the area was formally demilitarized in 1992. The first popular election for county magistrate took place in November 1993, followed by an election for county council in January 1994.

Lienchiang County contains four urban and rural townships, subdivided into 22 villages and boroughs. Like Kinmen County, Lienchiang County held its first popular election for county magistrate in November 1993, followed by an election for county council in January 1994. This elected council took office on February 1, 1994, replacing the Provisional Lienchiang County council set up on November 7, 1992.

The incumbent magistrates of Kinmen and Lienchiang counties are Lee Chu-feng 李炷烽 and Chen Hsueh-sheng 陳雪生 respectively.

Special Municipality Government

The passage of the *Municipal Self-governance Law* in 1994 provides a clear demarcation of the powers to be exercised by the central and local governments. One distinct move towards local autonomy has been the popular election of Taipei and Kaohsiung city mayors, who, prior to 1994, were nominated by the premier and appointed by the president of the Republic. The mayors serve a four-year term and may be reelected to a second term in office. They may appoint two deputies, one in charge of political affairs and the other in charge of administrative affairs. The political deputy mayor must resign if the mayor who appointed him is no longer in office.

Taipei City Government

The Taipei City Government 臺北市政府 is headed by Mayor Ma Ying-jeou 馬英九, a member of the KMT. It has a secretariat, 16 bureaus, eight departments, five commissions, the Bank of Taipei, the Civil Worker Training Center, the Taipei Rapid Transit Company, and an administrative office for each district (see Appendix IV, ROC Government Directory). In March 1990, the 16 districts of Taipei City were reorganized into 12 districts. These districts include a total of 435 boroughs.

Kaohsiung City Government

Frank Hsieh 謝長廷 won the election for mayor of Kaohsiung City in December 1998. He was also elected chairman of the Democratic Progressive Party in June 2000 unopposed. The Kaohsiung City Government 高雄市政府 consists of seven departments, a secretariat, 12 bureaus, five commissions, the Human Resource Development Institute, the Bank of Kaohsiung, and an administrative office for each of its 11 districts (see Appendix IV, ROC Government Directory).

City Councils

According to Article 15 of the *Municipal Self-governance Law*, the main functions of the Taipei and Kaohsiung city councils are:

- to adopt municipal statutes and regulations;
- to approve the municipal budget;
- to approve special taxes, temporary taxes and sur-taxes in the special municipality;
- to approve the disposal of municipal properties;
- to approve the organic laws of the municipal government and municipally owned businesses;
- to approve proposals made by the city government;
- to screen the auditor's reports on municipal accounts;
- to approve proposals made by the council members;
- to hear petitions from citizens; and
- to carry out other functions as prescribed by law or endowed by laws promulgated by the central government.

The term of office for a city councilor is four years. Councils meet for 70 days at most (including holidays) every six months. A session may be extended by ten days at the request of the mayor, council speaker, or one-third of the council members. At each session, various committees are formed to scrutinize proposals. A councilor may join only one committee.

City Government and Council Relationship

The municipal council sends its resolutions to the city government for implementation. In case of delay or otherwise unsatisfactory performance on the part of the city government, the municipal council may ask for an explanation or request that the Executive Yuan invite pertinent agencies for consultation to reach a resolution.

If a municipal council resolution is considered impractical, the municipal government may request reconsideration. If two-thirds of the council members present uphold the previous resolution, the municipal government is obliged to abide by their decision.

When the municipal council is in session, the mayor must periodically submit an oral or written report on the city government's administrative policies, on the administration of previous municipal council resolutions, and on other major activities of the municipal government. Directors of departments in the municipal government must also submit reports on matters under their jurisdiction. The members of the council may interpellate the mayor and his subordinates. The mayor or officials may be asked by the municipal council to submit special reports on important matters.

Every year the municipal government submits an administrative budget for the next fiscal year to the municipal council. Details of expected revenues and projected expenditures must be listed, but the council cannot propose spending increases.

County and Provincial Municipality Governments

Taiwan Province has 16 counties 縣: Taipei, Taoyuan, Hsinchu, Miaoli, Taichung, Changhua, Yunlin, Chiayi, Tainan, Kaohsiung, Pingtung, Taitung, Hualien, Nantou, Ilan, and Penghu; and five provincial municipalities 省轄市: Keelung, Hsinchu, Taichung, Chiayi, and Tainan. Each county/city has a county/city government and a county/city council to check and balance the county/city government. County governments are headed by magistrates, and city governments are headed by mayors who are directly elected for up to two four-year terms. County and city councilors are elected for four-year terms. The number of county or city councilors is determined by the population of each county, and several county and city council seats are reserved for women and aborigines.

City Ranking

There are three levels of cities in the Taiwan area: special municipalities 直轄市, which, like provinces, fall under the direct jurisdiction of the central government; provincial municipalities 省轄市, which are under direct provincial jurisdiction; and county municipalities 縣轄市, which are under direct county jurisdiction.

The Taiwan area currently has two special municipalities: Taipei City, which was elevated to this status in 1967; and Kaohsiung City, which gained similar status in 1979, when its population exceeded one million. The *Municipal Self-governance Law* passed in July 1994 raised this population requirement to 1.5 million.

Under Article 3 of the *Self-governance Law for Provinces and Counties*, an area with a population of over 600,000, which is politically, economically, and culturally important, shall be considered a provincial municipality. There are five such cities directly under Taiwan Province: Keelung City, Hsinchu City, Taichung City, Chiayi City, and Tainan City. These cities are equivalent to counties in status.

There are 29 county municipalities in the Taiwan area. According to the *Self-governance Law for Provinces and Counties*, an area with a population of over 150,000 may become a county municipality, if it is industrially and commercially developed and has sufficient financial resources, convenient transportation links, and complete public facilities.

Special and provincial municipalities are subdivided into districts 區. Each district has an office headed by a chief administrator, who is appointed by the mayor. Districts and county municipalities are subdivided into boroughs 里. Each borough has a borough office headed by a chief, who is elected by popular vote for a four-year term. The chief is assisted by an executive officer. Boroughs are subdivided into neighborhoods 鄰, which are the basic unit of urban governance. Each neighborhood is represented by a warden, who is nominated by the borough chief and contracted to a four-year term by the district office.

The International Lantern Festival is held for the first time in Kaohsiung City in 2001.

Cities and Townships under County Governments

Counties are subdivided into county municipalities, rural townships 鄉, or urban townships 鎮, depending on population density. Each city, rural township and urban township has a magistrate, who is popularly elected for up to two four-year terms. Taiwan currently has 29 county municipalities, 220 rural townships, and 60 urban townships under county jurisdiction.

Villages and Boroughs

Rural townships are subdivided into villages 村, and urban townships are subdivided into boroughs 里. The residents of each village or borough elect their own chiefs for four-year terms of office. The chiefs work with executive officers to handle the administrative affairs of their village or borough. Villages and boroughs are subdivided into neighborhoods 鄰. Heads of neighborhoods are routinely recommended by chiefs for appointment to the rural township or urban township office.

Reinvention of Government

The ROC has placed the reinvention of government at the top of its administrative agenda. The goal is the transformation of the entire government into a streamlined, flexible, innovative, and resilient organization that functions like a well-managed private company. To achieve this goal, government agencies will be streamlined and the organization and functions of the central government will be modified to suit present needs. The government also plans to promote a more flexible hierarchy and personnel structure within government organizations and modify the government budgetary system.

By computerizing operations and using information technology and networked systems, the ROC is establishing "electronic" government to provide an information service network, increase administrative efficiency, and enhance public services. Finally, government ethics are being heavily emphasized.

Harmony and cooperation between the central and local governments are vital to the smooth implementation of any government policy. As part of the streamlining efforts, the administrative and financial responsibilities of the Taiwan Provincial Government have been delegated to other local and central government offices.

Further Reading
(in Chinese unless otherwise noted):

Chien-cha-yuan kai-kuang 監察院概況 (An Introduction to the Control Yuan). Taipei: Control Yuan.

Chung-hua min-kuo cheng-fu tsu-chih yu kung-tso chien-chieh 中華民國政府組織與工作簡介 (An Introduction to ROC Government Organizations and Their Tasks). Taipei: Research, Development and Evaluation Commission, Executive Yuan.

Chung-hua min-kuo fa-lu hui-pien 中華民國法律彙編 (Compendium of Laws in the Republic of China). 10 vols. Taipei: Legislative Yuan.

Chung-hua min-kuo hsien-hsing fa-kui hui-pien 中華民國現行法規彙編 (Compendium of Current Laws and Regulations in the Republic of China). 1981– . Taipei: Compendium Compilation Steering Committee 中華民國現行法規彙編編印指導委員會印行. A looseleaf edition with supplementary editions issued quarterly.

Chung-hua min-kuo hsing-cheng kai-kuang 中華民國行政概況 (*Annual Review of Government Administration of the Republic of China*; in Chinese and English editions). Taipei: Research, Development and Evaluation Commission, Executive Yuan, annual.

Chung-hua min-kuo kao-hsuan hsing-cheng kai-kuang 中華民國考選行政概況 (An Introduction to the Examination Administration in the Republic of China). Taipei: Ministry of Examination.

Chung-hua min-kuo kuo-min ta-hui 中華民國國民大會 (*The National Assembly of the Republic of China*; Chinese-English bilingual). Taipei: Secretariat of the National Assembly.

Chung-hua min-kuo nien-chien 中華民國年鑑 (Yearbook of the Republic of China). Taipei: ROC Yearbook Publishers, annual.

Chung-hua min-kuo szu-fa-yuan 中華民國司法院 (The Judicial Yuan of the Republic of China). Taipei: Judicial Yuan.

Control Yuan, Republic of China (in English). Taipei: Secretariat, Control Yuan.

2000 Directory of Taiwan, Republic of China (in English).

Taipei: China News.

The Examination Yuan of the Republic of China (in English). Taipei: Examination Yuan.

Kao-hsiung shih hsing-cheng kai-kuang 高雄市行政概況 (An Introduction to Kaohsiung Municipal Administration). Kaohsiung: Kaohsiung Municipal Government.

Legislative Yuan, Republic of China (in English). Taipei: Legislative Yuan.

Li-fa-yuan kung-pao 立法院公報 (Legislative Yuan Gazette). Taipei: Legislative Yuan, semiweekly.

Statistics on Chinese Examination and Personnel Administrations (Chinese-English bilingual). Taipei: Examination Yuan, annual.

Tai-pei shih yi-hui chien-chieh 臺北市議會簡介 (*A Guide to the Taipei City Council*; Chinese-English bilingual). Taipei City Council.

Related Websites

1. Office of the President: *http://www.president.gov.tw*
2. National Unification Council: *http://www.president.gov.tw*
3. National Assembly: *http://www.nasm.gov.tw*
4. Academia Sinica: *http://www.sinica.gov.tw*
5. Academia Historica: *http://www.drnh.gov.tw*
6. Executive Yuan: *http://www.ey.gov.tw*
7. Legislative Yuan: *http://www.ly.gov.tw*
8. Judicial Yuan: *http://www.judicial.gov.tw*
9. Examination Yuan: *http://www.exam.gov.tw*
10. Ministry of Examination: *http://www.moex.gov.tw*
11. Ministry of Civil Service: *http://www.mocs.gov.tw*
12. Civil Service Protection and Training Commission: *http://www.csptc.gov.tw*
13. Control Yuan: *http://www.cy.gov.tw*
14. National Audit Office: *http://www.audit.gov.tw*
15. Ministry of the Interior: *http://www.moi.gov.tw*
16. Ministry of Foreign Affairs: *http://www.mofa.gov.tw*
17. Ministry of National Defense: *http://www.mnd.gov.tw*
18. Ministry of Finance: *http://www.mof.gov.tw*
19. Ministry of Education: *http://www.edu.tw*
20. Ministry of Justice: *http://www.moj.gov.tw*
21. Ministry of Economic Affairs: *http://www.moea.gov.tw*
22. Ministry of Transportation and Communications: *http://www.motc.gov.tw*
23. Mongolian and Tibetan Affairs Commission: *http://www.mtac.gov.tw*
24. Overseas Chinese Affairs Commission: *http://www.ocac.gov.tw*
25. Directorate General of Budget, Accounting and Statistics: *http://www.dgbas.gov.tw*
26. Central Personnel Administration: *http://www.cpa.gov.tw*
27. Government Information Office: *http://www.gio.gov.tw*
28. Department of Health: *http://www.doh.gov.tw*
29. Central Bank of China: *http://www.cbc.gov.tw*
30. Environmental Protection Administration: *http://www.epa.gov.tw*
31. Council of Labor Affairs: *http://www.cla.gov.tw*
32. Mainland Affairs Council: *http://www.mac.gov.tw*
33. Council for Cultural Affairs: *http://www.cca.gov.tw*
34. Council for Economic Planning and Development: *http://www.cepd.gov.tw*
35. Veterans Affairs Commission: *http://www.vac.gov.tw*
36. National Youth Commission: *http://www.nyc.gov.tw*
37. Research, Development and Evaluation Commission: *http://www.rdec.gov.tw*
38. National Science Council: *http://www.nsc.gov.tw*
39. Atomic Energy Council: *http://www.aec.gov.tw*
40. Council of Agriculture: *http://www.coa.gov.tw*
41. National Palace Museum: *http://www.npm.gov.tw*
42. Central Election Commission: *http://www.cec.gov.tw*
43. Fair Trade Commission: *http://www.ftc.gov.tw*
44. Consumer Protection Commission: *http://www.cpc.gov.tw*
45. Council of Indigenous Peoples: *http://www.apc.gov.tw*
46. Public Construction Commission: *http://www.pcc.gov.tw*
47. National Council on Physical Fitness and Sports: *http://www.ncpfs.gov.tw*
48. Coast Guard Administration: *http://www.cga.gov.tw*

6

Democratic Electoral System

President Chen took to the campaign trail in 2001 to urge voters to give his Democratic Progressive Party more support within the Legislative Yuan.

What's New

1. Figures updated
2. 2001 Elections for Legislative Yuan and County Magistrates and City Mayors
3. Statistical charts

Over the past 15 years, the Republic of China has moved rapidly toward full democracy. Elections for important posts in the government are held regularly, political parties have matured, and people actively participate in elections. ROC citizens now have a greater control over affairs of state than ever before. Taiwan's lively politics prove that the ROC's democratization has progressed considerably.

In fact, more posts are filled by election in Taiwan than in many other democratic countries in the world, and there is usually election every year. Average turnout rates in ROC elections are around 70 percent of eligible voters, lower than in some European countries, but much higher than in the United States.

Voting eligibility is defined broadly: the minimum voting age is 20, and there are no gender, property, or educational requirements. Voter registration is automatic. The government notifies

Central Election Commission

Founded in 1980, the Central Election Commission 中央選舉委員會 (CEC) under the Executive Yuan 行政院 is responsible for holding and supervising national and local elections, screening candidate qualifications, recalling elected officials, and drafting or amending laws concerning elections. The CEC is led by a chairman and consists of 11 to 19 commissioners who, after nomination by the premier and then approval by the president, serve a term of three years. To guarantee the impartiality of the CEC, the *Public Officials Election and Recall Law* 公職人員選舉罷免法 rules that commissioners from any single political party shall not constitute more than two-fifths of the whole commission.

citizens of an impending election and distributes a bulletin or gazette that identifies and describes all candidates and their platforms in their districts.

Normally, voting is scheduled for Saturdays. A large number of election workers, typically teachers and other dedicated local citizens, administer paper ballots at convenient polling stations. The workers count the votes accurately and quickly, reporting the results just a few hours after the polls close. By any standard, election administration in Taiwan is honest and highly efficient.

Electoral Systems

Taiwan's electoral process varies with the type of office. For such executive posts as president and vice president (forming a single ticket), special municipality mayors 直轄市市長, county magistrates 縣長, provincial municipality mayors 省轄市市長, rural and urban township magistrates 鄉鎮長, county municipality mayors 縣轄市市長, each voter casts one vote in a single-member district, and the candidate who receives a plurality of the vote is elected.

Elections for the Legislative Yuan 立法院, special municipal councils 直轄市議會, county or city councils 縣市議會, and township councils 鄉鎮市民代表會, use the single nontransferable vote (SNTV) method. Normally, several representatives are elected from a single electoral district, which is based essentially on existing administrative boundaries. Each voter casts only one vote, and several leading candidates are elected.

Since 1991, a certain number of seats have been reserved for a national constituency and the overseas Chinese communities in the National Assembly and Legislative Yuan elections. These seats are allocated by proportional representation (PR). Prior to the election, each party submits two lists of candidates, one for the national constituency and the other for overseas Chinese communities. However, Taiwan voters do not vote directly for candidates on the party lists. Instead, they vote in their respective SNTV districts, and the votes obtained by all candidates are totaled according to party affiliation. The seats for the national constituency and overseas Chinese communities are then distributed proportionally among the parties that get at least 5 percent of total valid votes nationwide. Thirty percent of the seats in the National Assembly election of 1996 and 22 percent of those in the Legislative Yuan election of 2001 were filled this way.

According to the latest amendment to the Constitution passed by the National Assembly on April 24, 2000, the future National Assembly will consist of 300 members and will be elected by PR. If the Legislative Yuan passes a proposal to amend the Constitution, to alter the national territory, or to impeach the president or vice president, the new National Assembly will then convene to ratify the Legislative Yuan's proposal.

In general, both the SNTV and PR systems benefit the smaller parties, for as long as they win a certain number of votes, they are able to secure at least a few seats.

As of December 2001, a total of 97 political parties had registered with the Ministry of the Interior, but most are insignificant in electoral politics. The five significant parties are the Democratic Progressive Party 民主進步黨 (DPP), the Kuomintang 中國國民黨 (KMT), the New Party 新黨 (NP), the People First Party 親民黨 (PFP), and the newly formed Taiwan Solidarity Union 台灣團結聯盟 (TSU). All won seats in the Legislative Yuan election of 2001. In 1996, the Green Party 綠色本土清新黨 won a seat in the election for National Assembly. In the Legislative Yuan election of 1998, the Taiwan Independence Party 建國黨 (TAIP), which was formed two years before the election by former DPP members and supporters who were dissatisfied with recent DPP policy changes, captured a seat. The New Nation Association 新國家連線, Democratic Alliance 民主聯盟, and Non-Party Alliance 全國民主非政黨聯盟 also won one, four, and three seats, respectively, in that election. In 2001, the Taiwan No. One Party 台灣吾黨 won one seat in the Legislative Yuan.

Since 1991, the National Assembly has amended the ROC Constitution six times, changing, to a certain degree, the electoral mechanism in Taiwan. First, the terms of office for the ROC president and for National Assemblymen were shortened from six years to four (the term for Legislative Yuan members remains three years), and proportional representation was introduced to the Legislative Yuan and National Assembly elections. As a result of the latest constitutional amendment, the National Assembly has become an ad hoc body. Second, the offices of president and vice president are now elected by direct popular vote of all eligible citizens in the free area of the ROC, rather than indirectly by the National Assembly as in the past. To be elected, a presidential and vice presidential ticket needs only a plurality, not a majority, of the vote. Third, the method of selecting members of the Control Yuan 監察院 has changed. Previously, Control Yuan members were elected by provincial assemblies and special municipal councils. They are now nominated and appointed by the president with the consent of the Legislative Yuan. This reform has transformed the Control Yuan from a parliamentary body to a semi-judicial institution. Fourth, the constitutional amendment passed in mid-1997 streamlined the provincial government. As a consequence, the provincial governor and the Taiwan Provincial Assemblymen are no longer directly elected.

The SNTV system currently in use for the legislative elections has been criticized for minimizing the role of parties and policies in the elections and for increasing corruption and factional politics. This topic was put on the agenda for recent discussions on constitutional reform. However, no changes were made so far, because the political parties could not agree on an alternative system.

Political Parties

Democratic Progressive Party

The Democratic Progressive Party 民主進步黨, formed on September 28, 1986, now has

approximately 450,000 members. The party's organizational structure closely resembles that of the Kuomintang. The DPP's National Congress elects 31 members to the Central Executive Committee 中央執行委員會 and 11 members to the Central Review Committee 中央評議委員會. The Central Executive Committee, in turn, elects the 11 members of the Central Standing Committee 中央常務執行委員會. The members of these committees all serve two-year terms.

Previously, the National Congress elected the party chairman. The second plenary meeting of the DPP's seventh National Congress, held in September 1997, adopted a provision that the chairman be directly elected by party members. Current chairman Frank Hsieh 謝長廷 was elected in July 2000, following the DPP's victory in the March 2000 presidential election. The chairman appoints a secretary-general, one or two deputy secretaries-general, and a number of department directors. Wu Nai-jen 吳乃仁 is the current secretary-general of the DPP.

The nominating process for DPP candidates has been more open compared to that of the KMT, but it has been changed quite frequently. At the DPP's Sixth National Congress, held in April and May of 1994, a two-tier primary system was initiated in which ordinary members of the DPP voted for candidates in one primary election and party cadres voted in a second primary. The results of the two elections were combined, with equal weight given to each.

At the second plenary meeting of the Sixth National Congress held in March 1995, the nomination process for the presidential and gubernatorial candidates was modified to add open primaries for DPP members and non-members alike. It was also decided that candidate slots on the party's list of national constituency representatives for the Legislative Yuan and National Assembly would be allocated equally among three groups: (1) scholars and experts, (2) representatives of disadvantaged groups, and (3) politicians.

At the Seventh National Congress held in June 1996, additional changes were made to the nominating process. It was decided that the primary reserved for the party leadership would be abolished. A two-stage process, involving a closed primary for party members and an open primary for all eligible voters, with each given equal weight, would be used to nominate candidates for president, provincial governor, special municipality mayors, county magistrates, provincial municipality mayors, Legislative Yuan members, National Assembly members, and special municipal councilmen. However, this procedure was repealed at the provisional meeting of the Seventh National Congress held in December 1996. The second stage, an open primary for all eligible voters, was replaced by opinion polls. It was further decided at the meeting that the party chairman would be elected directly by all members of the party starting in 1998.

At the second meeting of the Eighth National Congress held in May 1999, a special rule was adopted for the 2000 presidential election: A qualified candidate must be recommended by more than 40 party leaders, and if there is only one such candidate, the National Congress must be convened to ratify the nomination by a three-fifths majority. At the provisional meeting of the National Congress in July, former Taipei City Mayor Chen Shui-bian 陳水扁 was officially nominated to represent the DPP in the 2000 presidential election.

Perhaps what most distinguishes the DPP from the KMT, the People First Party, and the New Party is its inclination toward Taiwan independence, or the permanent political separation of Taiwan from China. However, recently, the DPP leadership has tried to downplay the party's independence theme in an attempt to broaden voter support. At the Eighth National Congress in 1999, the DPP ratified a resolution, stipulating that:

• Taiwan is a sovereign state, whose official name is the Republic of China.
• Any change of Taiwan's status quo should first require a plebiscite.

(Top) KMT Chairman Lien Chan earnestly supported Wang Chien-shien in the 2001 campaign for Taipei County magistrate.
(Photo by the Central News Agency)

(Bottom) James Soong, who proved to be a strong vote-getter in the 2000 presidential election, spearheaded the campaign activities of the People First Party.

- Taiwan is not part of the People's Republic of China, and the so-called "one country, two systems" or "one China" declaration unilaterally declared by the PRC falls short of the interests of the people of Taiwan.
- Taiwan and China should seek to establish perpetual peace by building up a communication mechanism based on mutual understanding and consensus through dialogue across the Taiwan Strait.

Downplaying the independence theme has led to dissatisfaction among the more radical advocates of Taiwan independence. Several of these disaffected DPP members left the party and established the Taiwan Independence Party (TAIP).

At the second meeting of the DPP's Ninth National Congress held in October 2001, party members passed a motion that any resolutions adopted in response to major government policies should be considered equivalent to the party platform. In addition, the national congress also approved a resolution acknowledging the importance of trade liberalization with the mainland and stressing the party's determination to improve the national economy.

The Kuomintang

The Kuomintang 中國國民黨, also known as the KMT or Nationalist Party, celebrated its one hundredth anniversary on November 24, 1994. The KMT has a membership of approximately 1.08 million and had won almost every major election until recently. It lost to the Democratic Progressive Party in the 1997 election for county magistrates and city mayors, the 2000 presidential election, and the 2001 Legislative Yuan election. As a result of its defeat in the 2000 presidential election, the KMT initiated a major reorganization, including re-registration of its members.

At the grassroots level, members are organized into cells. Moving upwardly, there are district, county, and city congresses and committees. The highest level is the National Congress 全國代表大會 and the Central Committee 中央委員會.

The National Congress is the highest authority of the party. Its delegates are selected to serve four-year terms. The congress amends the party charter, determines the party platform and other important policies, elects the party chairman and the Central Committee members, and approves candidates nominated by the chairman to serve as vice chairmen and members of the Central Advisory Council 中央評議委員會. When the National Congress is in recess, the supreme

party organization is the Central Committee, which holds a plenary session every year.

The Central Standing Committee 中央常務委員會, which represents the Central Committee when that body is not in session, is the most influential organization in the KMT. It meets every week to discuss and approve important policies and nominate candidates for important positions.

General party affairs are managed by the secretariat under current secretary-general Lin Fong-cheng 林豐正. The secretariat manages various party departments and commissions. At lower levels, party organizations have their own secretariats and administrative staffs. All of these organizations, from the national to the local level, are funded primarily by profits from party-owned and -operated business enterprises, ranging from newspapers and TV stations to electrical appliance companies and computer firms.

The first meeting of the KMT's 14th National Congress held in August 1993 approved significant changes in the conduct of party affairs, deciding that the National Congress would elect the party chairman through secret ballot. ROC President Lee Teng-hui 李登輝 won 83 percent of the votes and was reelected chairman of the party. In addition, four vice-chairmen, nominated by the chairman and approved by the National Congress, were added to the Central Committee. The KMT also decided that the chairman would appoint only 10 to 15 of the 31 members of the Central Standing Committee, with the remaining members elected by the Central Committee. Finally, it decided to hold the National Congress every two years, instead of four years. The second meeting of the 14th National Congress was held in August 1995 to nominate the party's presidential candidate for the March 1996 election (see section on the First Direct Presidential Election in this chapter).

In August 1997, the 15th National Congress was convened. President Lee Teng-hui was reelected chairman of the party with 93 percent of the votes. The congress also approved four vice-chairmen, one of whom was Vice President Lien

Chan 連戰, and elected 230 Central Committee members. In the first plenary session of the 15th Central Committee held immediately after the congress, 17 members were elected to the enlarged Central Standing Committee, and 16 were appointed by the chairman. In August 1998, a new Central Standing Committee was elected in the second plenary session of the 15th Central Committee.

In August 1999, the second meeting of the 15th National Congress ratified the nomination of Lien Chan and Vincent Siew 蕭萬長 as the KMT's presidential and vice-presidential candidates for the 2000 presidential election. At the third plenary session of the 15th Central Committee held later, the Central Standing Committee was reorganized.

After the KMT lost the presidential election in March 2000, President Lee resigned as party chairman. Lien Chan succeeded him as the acting chairman. At the provisional meeting of the 15th National Congress held three months later, Lien was elected party chairman. Five new vice-chairpersons, including one woman, were nominated by Lien and approved by the congress. At the fourth plenary session of the 15th Central Committee following the provisional meeting of the National Congress, 31 members were elected to the new Central Standing Committee, none of whom were appointed from above.

The provisional meeting also revised the party charter, eliminating the provincial party organization. Another important change is the direct election of future party chairmen by all party members. On March 24, 2001, Lien Chan became the first directly elected party chairman by winning 97 percent of the vote.

The 16th National Congress was convened in July 2001. The five incumbent vice-chairpersons were re-nominated by Lien and approved by the Congress. A new 210-member Central Committee was also elected, which, in turn, elected the 31 members of the Central Standing Committee. In order to boost the party image, the Congress revised the party charter by barring those who committed criminal and sexual offenses from seeking nomination for public offices.

New Party

In August 1993, shortly before the Kuomintang's 14th National Congress, a group of dissatisfied KMT members, including six Legislative Yuan members and one former lawmaker, broke away from the KMT to establish the New Party 新黨 (NP). The seven quit because of ideological differences and the "undemocratic practices of the KMT." Such prominent individuals as the former Finance Minister Wang Chien-shien 王建煊 and former head of the Environmental Protection Administration Jaw Shau-kong 趙少康 were among the founders of the NP, which adopted an anticorruption and social justice platform. The goal of the NP was to attract voters who were dissatisfied with the performance of the ruling KMT and opposed to the DPP's advocacy of Taiwan independence. The NP now claims a registered membership of nearly 68,000.

The New Party differs from the KMT and the DPP in organizational structure, stressing the leadership of those holding public office. At the head of the party is the National Campaign and Development Committee 全國競選暨發展委員會. The convener of the committee serves as the leader of the party, currently held by Hsieh Chi-ta 謝啟大.

In the 2001 election for Legislative Yuan members and county magistrates and city mayors, the NP fared poorly, immediately calling into question the future of the party (see section on the 2001 Elections for Legislative Yuan and County Magistrates and City Mayors in this chapter).

People First Party

In the 2000 presidential election, former KMT provincial governor James Soong 宋楚瑜, running as an independent, lost by less than three percentage points to DPP's Chen Shui-bian. In fact, Soong's vote far exceeded that received by KMT candidate Lien Chan. Immediately after the election, Soong's supporters called on him to form a new party. Eventually, the People First Party 親民黨 was established, attracting many KMT and NP lawmakers. It is now the third largest party after the DPP and the KMT in the Legislative Yuan.

According to the party charter, the highest policy-making body is the National Council 全國委員會, which consists of current or former office-holders in the executive or legislative branches of the government (at either national or local levels), current or former party officials, and representatives from different sectors of society. This council elects a central executive committee with 21 members and seven alternate members for two-year terms. Every two years, all party members directly elect the party chairman.

James Soong was elected the first PFP chairman. He appointed former KMT Deputy Secretary-General David J.C. Chung 鍾榮吉 as secretary-general of the new party.

Taiwan Solidarity Union

The Taiwan Solidarity Union 台灣團結聯盟 is a new addition to Taiwan's party system. It registered with the Ministry of the Interior on July 31, 2001, and held its inaugural meeting twelve days later. With the endorsement of former President Lee Teng-hui, it attracts supporters from the KMT, the DPP, and other political groupings. Its aim is to "stabilize the political situation, promote the economy, consolidate democracy, and strengthen Taiwan."

In terms of internal structure, it has a Party Congress serving as the highest authority of the party. The Congress elects seven members and three alternate members of the Central Executive Committee every two years. In addition, the party chairman and the secretary-general are ex officio members of the Central Executive Committee. The party chairman is directly elected by party members for two-year terms.

The current party chairman is Huang Chu-wen 黃主文. He appointed Su Chin-chiang 蘇進強 as the secretary-general.

Elections

The ROC has a long history of elections. Even during the period of martial law, elections for county magistrates, municipality mayors,

provincial assemblymen, county and city councilmen, etc. were held quite regularly. With the exception of 1978, when the United States announced that it would sever diplomatic ties with the ROC, supplementary elections for members of the Legislative Yuan and the National Assembly were held regularly since 1969.

In 1986, under the leadership of President Chiang Ching-kuo 蔣經國, political reform was accelerated. After Chiang passed away, his successor, President Lee Teng-hui, continued liberalization and democratization programs. As a result of these reforms all senior members of the First National Assembly, Control Yuan, and Legislative Yuan, who had been elected to office in the late 1940s either on the Chinese mainland or Taiwan, were retired. Beginning with the National Assembly election of 1991 and the Legislative Yuan election of 1992, the general public in Taiwan has elected all members of the national legislative bodies.

The following sections will outline elections in the ROC, beginning with an account of the ROC's first direct presidential and the Third National Assembly elections held in March 1996; a summary of the elections for county magistrates and city mayors held in 1997; a discussion of the elections for county councilors, city councilors, and township magistrates held in early 1998; a report on the "three-in-one" elections for legislators, mayors, and city council members held in December 1998; an account of the 2000 presidential election; and finally, a discussion of the elections for Legislative Yuan members, county magistrates, and city mayors in 2001.

First Direct Presidential Election

Democratic reforms in the ROC have made significant progress during the last decade. Ever since the first steps were taken to liberalize and expand the political process, each election has carried Taiwan politics closer to the goal of full democracy. On March 23, 1996, the ROC held its first direct presidential election.

Recent amendments to the ROC Constitution provide the legal foundation for the direct popular election of the president and vice president. These amendments also specify that the winning candidate need only a plurality of the vote. In addition to the changes to the Constitution, a number of supporting laws have been passed to ensure that presidential elections are carried out efficiently and fairly.

In July 1995, the Legislative Yuan passed the *Presidential and Vice Presidential Election and Recall Law* 總統副總統選舉罷免法, which states that presidential and vice presidential candidates may be nominated by any political party gaining at least 5 percent of the vote in the most recent provincial-level or higher election, or by collecting the signatures of no less than 1.5 percent of eligible voters in the most recent parliamentary election. The law also requires that the Central Election Commission provide no less than 30 minutes of national television time for each candidate. Furthermore, when two or more candidates agree to participate, the committee will provide funding for nationally televised presidential debates.

Four teams of candidates campaigned to become the first directly elected president and vice president. The KMT nominated President Lee Teng-hui, who picked Premier Lien Chan as his running mate. The DPP, after a fierce primary process, nominated veteran political dissident and professor, Peng Ming-min 彭明敏, as its presidential candidate. Peng then chose prominent legislator Frank Hsieh as his running mate.

Other candidates entered the race via petition. Lin Yang-kang 林洋港 and his running mate Hau Pei-tsun 郝柏村 were both former vice chairmen of the KMT, but decided to run as independents under the endorsement of the New Party. The fourth team was Chen Li-an 陳履安 and Wang Ching-feng 王清峰, a woman member of the Control Yuan. Chen was also a member of the KMT and the president of the Control Yuan, but gave up both of these positions when he announced his candidacy.

The KMT ran a very successful campaign. Almost from the very beginning, the Lee-Lien ticket was well ahead of the other three. Lee Teng-hui, as the ROC's first Taiwan native president, not only received the backing of traditional KMT supporters, but was also supported by some in the DPP camp. Missile tests off the coast of Taiwan and military exercises conducted by the Chinese mainland prior to the election further increased support for Lee by motivating people to "rally around the flag."

On March 23, slightly over 76 percent of eligible voters turned out to cast their ballots and reelected Lee Teng-hui, giving him an impressive 54 percent of the vote. The DPP's Peng Ming-min trailed with 21.1 percent. Lin and Chen obtained 14.9 percent and 10 percent of the vote, respectively.

Third National Assembly

Voters were not only deciding who would become the ROC's first directly elected president on March 23, 1996, but they were also electing members to the Third National Assembly. Although this contest was largely overshadowed by the presidential election, many parties fielded candidates, and several constituencies saw hotly contested races.

The KMT captured 49.7 percent of the vote and remained the largest party in the new Assembly. Of the 334 seats contested, KMT candidates won 183, or 54.8 percent. While the KMT retained its majority, the result still represented a significant decline from the 75.4 percent of the seats it had held in the previous Assembly. The DPP added considerably to the 66 Assembly seats it had won in 1991. DPP candidates obtained 29.9 percent of the vote and 99 seats, or 29.6 percent of the total. The 1996 election was the first National Assembly election for the New Party. Its candidates captured 46 seats, or 13.8 percent of the total, with 13.7 percent of the vote, similar to the NP's performance in the Legislative Yuan election of December 1995. Of the remaining seats, one went to the newly-formed Green Party, while five others went to independents.

County Magistrates and City Mayors

The outcome of the November 29, 1997, elections for county magistrates and city mayors took many by surprise, including senior officials of both the ruling KMT and the largest opposition party, the DPP. With 23 seats contested, the KMT lost almost half of its previous 15 seats, retaining only eight. Meanwhile, the DPP doubled its number of seats from six to 12. Although the DPP won only a marginal victory over the KMT by 43 percent to 42 percent of the vote, the results were still quite impressive, because the DPP had only existed as a political party for 11 years, whereas the KMT commemorated its 100th anniversary in 1994. As a result of these elections, the DPP was able to exercise administrative power over 70 percent of the country's population.

The outcome of this election meant more than a decline of the KMT's executive power. When implementing administrative policies, the central government began to encounter resistance from subordinate local governments held by the DPP. In addition, independent candidates were elected to head Chiayi City, as well as Miaoli and Nantou Counties. One was a former member of the KMT, while another was formerly of the DPP.

The New Party and the Taiwan Independence Party failed to win a single seat in the 1997 mayoral and county magistrate elections. The NP obtained only 1.4 percent of the total vote, a sharp decline from the 13 percent it won in the election for the Third Legislative Yuan election in 1995.

County and City Councilors and Township Magistrates

Immediately following the election for county magistrates and city mayors, elections were held for county and provincial municipality councils, rural and urban township magistrates, and county municipality mayors on January 24, 1998. A total of 890 legislative seats and 319 executive offices were contested. Although the KMT lost to the DPP in the election for county magistrates

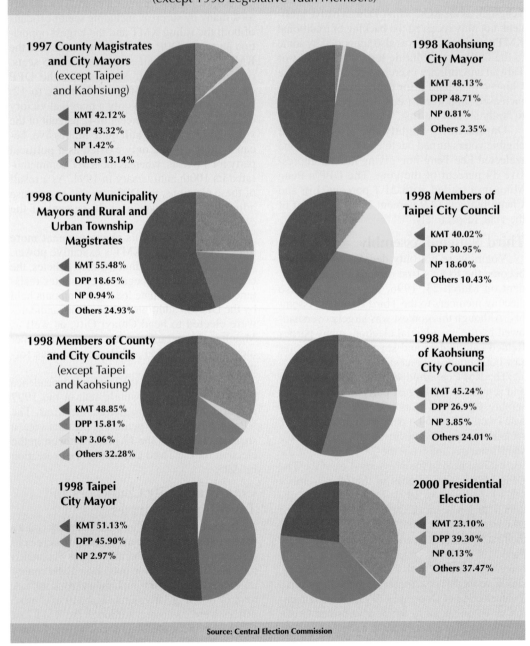

Percentage of Votes Obtained in Major Elections Between 1997 and 2000
(except 1998 Legislative Yuan Members)

**1997 County Magistrates
and City Mayors**
(except Taipei
and Kaohsiung)

◀ KMT 42.12%
◀ DPP 43.32%
NP 1.42%
◀ Others 13.14%

**1998 Kaohsiung
City Mayor**

◀ KMT 48.13%
◀ DPP 48.71%
NP 0.81%
◀ Others 2.35%

**1998 County Municipality
Mayors and Rural and
Urban Township
Magistrates**

◀ KMT 55.48%
◀ DPP 18.65%
NP 0.94%
◀ Others 24.93%

**1998 Members of
Taipei City Council**

◀ KMT 40.02%
◀ DPP 30.95%
NP 18.60%
◀ Others 10.43%

**1998 Members of County
and City Councils**
(except Taipei
and Kaohsiung)

◀ KMT 48.85%
◀ DPP 15.81%
NP 3.06%
◀ Others 32.28%

**1998 Members
of Kaohsiung
City Council**

◀ KMT 45.24%
◀ DPP 26.9%
NP 3.85%
◀ Others 24.01%

**1998 Taipei
City Mayor**

◀ KMT 51.13%
◀ DPP 45.90%
NP 2.97%

**2000 Presidential
Election**

◀ KMT 23.10%
◀ DPP 39.30%
NP 0.13%
◀ Others 37.47%

Source: Central Election Commission

and city mayors two months earlier, it regained seats in the new elections.

Kuomintang candidates captured 58.9 percent of the county and city council seats, slightly down from their performance four years ago. Its candidates also won 73.3 percent of the township magistrates and county municipality mayors, an increase from earlier gains. In fact, these figures underestimate the KMT's strength in the elections, because many successful candidates were KMT members who had failed to receive their party's nomination.

The Democratic Progressive Party won 12.7 percent of the council seats and 8.8 percent of the magistrate positions. While these results represented an increase from the party's previous showings, the DPP had yet to win a majority of the seats in a single county or city council.

The New Party won ten council seats (1.1 percent), but no magistrate positions. The Taiwan Independence Party captured only one council seat. The remaining 27.2 percent of council seats and 9 percent of magisterial and mayoral seats went to independent candidates, who outperformed DPP nominees and were the KMT's main competitors.

The 1998 "Three-in-One" Elections

On December 5, 1998, the ROC completed the "three-in-one" elections for legislators, mayors, and city council members. In the Fourth Legislative Yuan election, the KMT retained a majority of the seats, improving its performance over the same election three years earlier. The KMT captured 46.43 percent of the vote nationwide, with 123 (54.67 percent) out of a total of 225 seats, benefiting from the New Party's internal bickering. The NP obtained only 7.06 percent of the vote, much less than the 13 percent it had gained in 1995, and won 11 (4.89 percent) of the total seats. The DPP did not fare well, either. With 29.56 percent of the vote, it captured 70 seats (31.11 percent). The DPP's setback had much to do with an internal split and the formation of the TAIP and the New Nation Association. These two groups obtained one seat each.

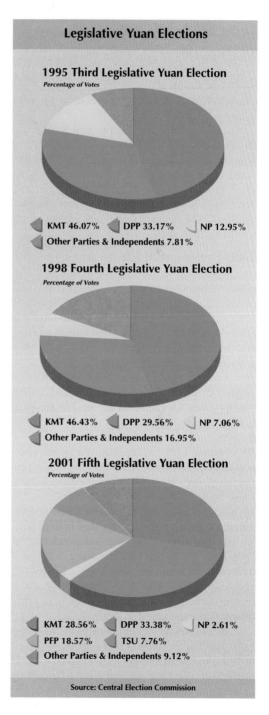

Legislative Yuan Elections

1995 Third Legislative Yuan Election
Percentage of Votes

KMT 46.07%   DPP 33.17%   NP 12.95%
Other Parties & Independents 7.81%

1998 Fourth Legislative Yuan Election
Percentage of Votes

KMT 46.43%   DPP 29.56%   NP 7.06%
Other Parties & Independents 16.95%

2001 Fifth Legislative Yuan Election
Percentage of Votes

KMT 28.56%   DPP 33.38%   NP 2.61%
PFP 18.57%   TSU 7.76%
Other Parties & Independents 9.12%

Source: Central Election Commission

In addition, KMT candidate Ma Ying-jeou 馬英九 was elected Taipei City mayor, defeating incumbent DPP Mayor Chen Shui-bian. However, in the Kaohsiung mayoral election, DPP candidate Frank Hsieh defeated the KMT incumbent Mayor Wu Den-yih 吳敦義 by a narrow margin of 4,565 votes.

In the elections for Taipei and Kaohsiung city councils, the KMT also gained strength by winning 23 (44.3 percent) and 25 (56.8 percent) seats, respectively. The DPP obtained 19 seats (36.5 percent) in Taipei, and nine seats (20.5 percent) in Kaohsiung. The New Party obtained nine seats (17.3 percent) in Taipei and a single seat in Kaohsiung.

2000 Presidential Election

On March 18, 2000, 82.7 percent of all eligible voters went to the polls to elect the new president of the Republic of China. The heated competition among the top three candidates was quite dramatic. The PRC did not launch missiles this time, but did severely warn Taiwan voters of the danger of making "wrong" decisions. However, harsh words had little effect on the election results. DPP candidate Chen Shui-bian and his running mate Lu Hsiu-lien 呂秀蓮 won the election, ending the Kuomintang's 50-year hold on the presidency in Taiwan. Chen and Lu received 39.3 percent of the vote, followed by the independent James Soong, formerly the KMT provincial governor, and his running mate Chang Chao-hsiung 張昭雄 with 36.84 percent.

Kuomintang candidate Lien Chan and his running mate Vincent Siew finished in third place with 23.1 percent of the vote. Independents Hsu Hsin-liang 許信良 and Chu Hui-liang 朱惠良 won 0.63 percent, while the New Party's Li Ao 李敖, and his running mate Fung Hu-hsiang 馮滬祥 received a only 0.13 percent, after Li Ao urged his supporters to vote for James Soong.

Chen's victory was a major political comeback. Elected as Taipei's first opposition mayor in 1994, he lost the Taipei mayoral race to KMT challenger Ma Ying-jeou in 1998. Chen Shui-bian, at the age of 49, is the youngest president

of the Republic of China under the 1947 Constitution, while Vice President Lu Hsiu-lien is the highest-ranking woman in the ROC's political history.

The 2001 Elections for Legislative Yuan and County Magistrates and City Mayors

On December 1, 2001, more than 66 percent of eligible voters in Taiwan went to the polls to vote for the 225 members of the Legislative Yuan and 23 county magistrates and city mayors. It was the first major election after the DPP's victory in the 2000 presidential election, and given the fact that there had been a stalemate between the DPP government and the KMT-controlled Legislative Yuan since then, the new Legislative Yuan election was of particular significance for Taiwan's political development. During the campaigning, the election was often depicted as the contest between the Pan-Blue (KMT's color) and Pan-Green (DPP's color) camps. The former refers to the KMT, the PFP, and the NP, and the latter to the DPP and the TSU.

It was widely expected that the KMT would lose its majority status in the Legislative Yuan, but as it turned out, it performed even worse than expected. It won only 68 seats or 30.22 percent of total seats available with 28.56 percent of the total popular vote. The DPP became the largest party in the new legislature by capturing 87 (or 38.67 percent) out of 225 seats with 33.38 percent of the vote. Two other newly formed parties, PFP and TSU, performed quite well. The PFP obtained 46 seats with 18.57 percent of the vote, and the TSU garnered 13 seats with 7.76 percent of the vote. The NP was unable to reach the 5 percent threshold for the PR allocation. It received merely 2.61 percent of the vote and won one seat. One seat went to the Taiwan No. One Party and the remaining nine to independents.

In the election for county magistrates and city mayors, the KMT fared slightly better by capturing nine seats, the same as the DPP. In

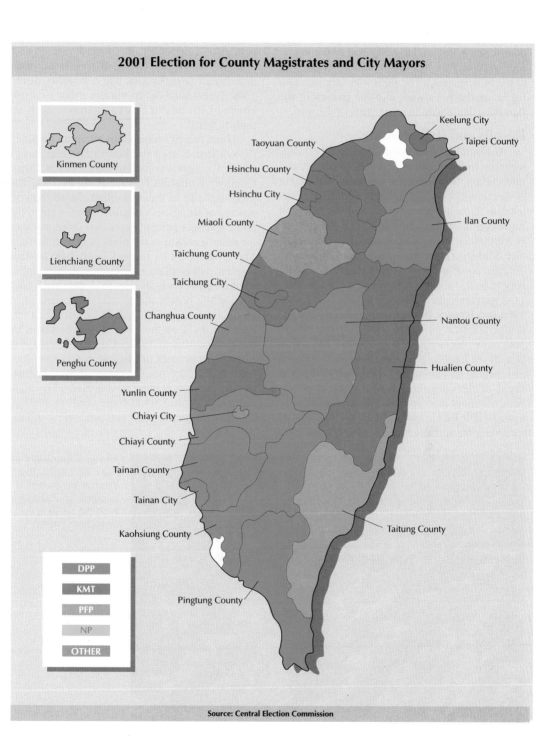

2001 Election for County Magistrates and City Mayors

Kinmen County

Lienchiang County

Penghu County

Taoyuan County

Keelung City

Taipei County

Hsinchu County

Hsinchu City

Miaoli County

Ilan County

Taichung County

Taichung City

Changhua County

Nantou County

Hualien County

Yunlin County

Chiayi City

Chiayi County

Tainan County

Tainan City

Kaohsiung County

Taitung County

Pingtung County

DPP
KMT
PFP
NP
OTHER

Source: Central Election Commission

95

addition, the PFP and the NP won two and one seats respectively with the remaining two going to the independents. The DPP was very successful in southern Taiwan, and the parties in the Pan-Blue camp won in other parts of Taiwan.

Recalls and Referendums

According to the Constitution, ROC citizens have the rights of election, recall, initiative, and referendum. In practice, however, only the right of election has been effectively exercised. Legislation to regulate the exercise of the rights of initiative and referendum has yet to be passed. Nevertheless, there has been an occasional referendum in certain areas; however, without a detailed legal framework, the results are advisory at best.

Two recall attempts were held in November 1994 and January 1995 in Taipei County and the southern district of Taipei City, respectively. In both cases, the targets of recall were KMT members of the Legislative Yuan, who were accused of reneging on campaign promises by voting in favor of the construction of a nuclear power plant. Turnout rates in both incidents were very low. In Taipei County, only 21.4 percent of those eligible actually voted, and in the southern district of Taipei City, the turnout rate was 8.6 percent. Since the *Public Officials Election and Recall Law* requires that a majority of eligible voters turn out to vote in order to recall elected officials or representatives, both attempts failed.

Three recent referendum attempts involved the construction of the Fourth Nuclear Power Plant. The first was held in May 1994 in Taipei County's Kungliao Township 臺北縣貢寮鄉, the proposed site of the new plant. More than 58 percent of Kungliao's eligible voters went to the polls, and 96.1 percent expressed disapproval of the plan to construct the plant in their township. The government of Taipei County held another nuclear power plant referendum in November of the same year. While 87.1 percent voted against the power plant, only 18.5 percent of eligible voters participated. The most recent referendum held on the issue was undertaken by the government of Taipei City in March 1996. Fifty-eight percent of eligible voters cast their ballots, and 51.5 percent opposed the construction of the new nuclear power plant. The plant remains a controversial issue, and referendum has often been mentioned as the means for solving the problem.

The 225 members of the Fifth Legislative Yuan were sworn in to office on February 1, 2002. (Photo by the Central News Agency)

Another referendum was held in March 1995 by the government of Hsichih Township in Taipei County 臺北縣汐止鎮 to decide on public works proposals. The turnout rate was only 17 percent, but 95 percent of the ballots cast were in favor of the local government's proposals.

In the "three-in-one" elections of 1998, three counties and cities also held referendums. These included a referendum on Taiwan independence; one on the construction of a new airport in Tainan City; the use of a parcel of public land in the Neihu district of Taipei City 臺北市內湖區; and the construction of the new Fourth Nuclear Power Plant in Taipei County. The voting rates ranged from 25 percent in Tainan to around 60 percent in the Neihu district.

Related Websites
1. Central Election Commission: *http://www.cec.gov.tw*
2. Democratic Progressive Party: *http://www.dpp.org.tw*
3. Kuomintang: *http://www.kmt.org.tw*
4. People First Party: *http://www.pfp.org.tw*
5. New Party: *http://www.np.org.tw*
6. Taiwan Solidarity Union: *http://www.tsu.org.tw*

7

Cross-Strait Relations

In August 2001, scholars and performers from Taiwan and the Chinese mainland met in Ilan County for a conference on the development of Taiwanese opera and Hsiang opera (popular in Southern Fujian).

Potential conflict in the Taiwan Strait remains a serious threat to the stability of the Asia-Pacific region and world peace. Beginning in 1927, the Chinese civil war brought death and destruction to untold millions of people. After the government of the Republic of China relocated to Taipei in 1949, major battles erupted during the 1950s, and lesser incidents continued throughout the 1960s. Even today, when trade, business, and people-to-people contacts between the two sides of the Taiwan Strait are rapidly expanding, the authorities on the Chinese mainland refuse to renounce the use of force against Taiwan.

Consequently, seven decades of strife between the Republic of China and the Chinese Communists make the peaceful unification of China one of the world's greatest challenges. Nonetheless, guided by the principles of reason, peace, parity, and reciprocity, the government of the Republic of China has consistently and creatively sought new approaches to solving the complications and difficulties related to a divided China.

The Status of a Divided China

The Republic of China was founded in 1912, and it maintained sovereignty over the territories that have been administered by a succession of Chinese dynasties and emperors through the ages. The international community has referred to these territories as "China."

Ten years after the founding of the Republic of China, the Chinese Communist Party (CCP) was established with the support of international communist activists. In 1949, the Chinese Communists gained control of the Chinese mainland through military force, and on October 1, 1949, they proclaimed the establishment of the People's Republic of China. In December 1949, the ROC

government moved to Taiwan. Since that time, two distinct societies, with different ideologies and contrasting political, economic, and social systems, have existed simultaneously on opposite sides of the Taiwan Strait.

For many years after gaining control of the Chinese mainland, the Chinese communists sought to "liberate" Taiwan by force. Beginning in the early 1950s, they launched a series of military attacks against areas controlled by the ROC government in an effort to achieve reunification by force: the artillery bombardment of Kinmen (Quemoy) 金門 in 1958 was the largest of these attacks, with up to 60,000 artillery shells fired at Kinmen per day for a week. Beijing changed its policy toward Taiwan after establishing diplomatic relations with the United States in 1979, and began pursuing a course of peaceful confrontation. Although references to "liberation" in propaganda concerning Taiwan were dropped in favor of the term "peaceful reunification," Beijing has refused to renounce the use of military force to solve the "Taiwan problem."

Since 1979, Beijing launched an intensive united front campaign through a series of proposals, beginning with the National People's Congress's "Letter to Taiwan Compatriots," which claimed the two sides should establish "three links" (trade, postal, and transportation) and "four exchanges" (economic, cultural, technological, and sports). In 1981, Ye Jianying 葉劍英 announced nine points of principles for peaceful reunification, in which he suggested a third-time cooperation between the KMT and the Chinese Communist Party and introduced the preliminary idea of the "one country, two systems" 一國兩制 formula. Deng Xiaoping 鄧小平 further elaborated the idea with another six points of principles in 1983. After the Chinese mainland reached an agreement with the United Kingdom in 1984 over the handover of Hong Kong, Beijing's tactic of "peaceful reunification under 'one country, two systems'" was formed. In the meantime, Beijing still refused to renounce the use of force and continued to suppress Taiwan by isolating the ROC in the international community.

A Statistical Comparison

	Republic of China (Also known internationally as ROC, Taiwan, Republic of China on Taiwan, or Free China)	People's Republic of China (Also known internationally as PRC, China, Communist China, Red China, mainland China, or the Chinese mainland)
Land area	13,969 sq mi[1]	3,706,566 sq mi[2]
Population	22.28 million[1]	1.26 billion[6]
Type of government	Democracy[3]	Communist Party-led state[3]
Per capita GNP	US$14,188[1]	US$842[2]
Foreign trade	US$288.33 billion[1]	US$474.3 billion[2]
Foreign exchange reserves	US$110.6 billion[1] (March 2001)	US$175.9 billion[2] (March 2001)
Foreign debt	US$34.8 million[1]	US$145.7 billion[2]
Investment climate	5th/50[5]	22nd/50[5]
Human rights condition	Free (1.5)[4]	Not free (6.5)[4]
Literacy	98.12%[1]	84.86% (1999)[2]
Mobile phone penetration rate	80.24%[1]	6.8%[7]
Internet accounts	6.26 million[1]	22.5 million[2]

[1] ROC statistics
[2] PRC statistics
[3] The World Almanac and Book of Facts 2001
[4] Freedom House, Freedom in the World: The Annual Survey of Political Rights & Civil Liberties, 2000-2001 (on a scale of 1.0 to 7.0, with 1.0 being the freest)
[5] Business Environment Risk Intelligence (BERI), Switzerland
[6] China Economic Information Center (Hong Kong)
[7] Strategis Group

All figures are as of 2000, unless otherwise noted.

In response to Beijing's united front offensive, the ROC government implemented the "three no's" policy (no contacts, no negotiations, and no compromise) in 1979 while at the same time calling for "reunification under the Three Principles of the People."

Throughout the 1980s, economic liberalization, social diversification, and political democratization increased in Taiwan, and, with the lifting of martial law in July 1987, the government adopted a more open policy toward the Chinese mainland. In November 1987, the ROC government allowed people residing in the Taiwan area to visit relatives on the Chinese mainland. This decision moved cross-strait relations away from complete estrangement and began private-level exchanges.

In 1990, prominent individuals from inside and outside Taiwan's ruling party were invited to sit on the National Unification Council 國家統一委員會 (NUC) and drafted the Guidelines for National Unification 國家統一綱領 in February 1991, specifying that national unification is to be pursued through peaceful and democratic means. On May 1 of that year, President Lee Teng-hui announced the termination of the "period of national mobilization for suppression of the Communist rebellion," 動員勘亂時期 acknowledging on a constitutional level the fact that the two sides of the Strait were under separate rule, and thus bringing cross-strait relations into a new stage.

Since tourism, trade, investment, and cultural and academic exchanges between the two sides of the Taiwan Strait required a more systematic

approach to deal with a range of issues, the ROC government also established a legal and organizational foundation to administer relations between Taiwan and the Chinese mainland.

Guidelines for National Unification

The *Guidelines for National Unification* state that China's unification should be achieved in three phases: a short-term phase of exchanges and reciprocity, a mid-term phase of mutual trust and cooperation, and a long-term phase of consultations and unification. The phased approach was chosen with the full realization that the unification of China will be a long and arduous process. China's unification will not be achieved quickly, because the two sides have vast social, political, economic, and lifestyle differences. However, there is no fixed time for each stage. Progress may increase or decrease, depending on the mainland authorities' response to the ideas outlined in the guidelines.

In the short-term phase, neither side should deny the other's existence as a political entity, and both sides should expand unofficial contacts. In addition, the guidelines call for Beijing to renounce the use of force against Taiwan and respect Taiwan's position in the international community.

The first task in the medium-term phase is to set up channels for official communication between the two sides on the basis of parity. The goals of the second phase also include the establishment of direct postal, commercial, and transportation links across the Taiwan Strait, as well as exchange of visits by high-ranking officials from both sides. Only after the goals of this phase have been achieved can the process of national unification be actively considered.

In the long-term phase, a bilateral consultative body should be established to jointly discuss the overall political and economic structure of a unified China, in accordance with the wishes of the people on both sides of the Taiwan Strait. A peaceful, democratic, and prosperous China will have a significant stabilizing effect on the Asia-Pacific region and world peace.

Currently, relations between the two sides are in the short-term phase, although exchanges in many areas have already reached the second phase.

Statute Governing Relations

The ROC is a constitutional democracy, and all major governmental policies are formulated in accordance with due process of law. The policy toward the Chinese mainland is no exception. At present, the most significant piece of legislation on cross-strait affairs is the *Statute Governing the Relations Between the People of the Taiwan Area and the Mainland Area* 臺灣地區與大陸地區人民關係條例, promulgated in September 1992. The statute covers administrative, civil, and criminal affairs and recognizes the rights of the people living under the control of the authorities on the mainland.

Organizational Structures

In addition to a clear set of principles and laws guiding the development of relations, appropriate channels of communication are also an obvious necessity. In 1990 and 1991, the ROC government set up a three-tier network of government and private-sector institutions to handle relations with the Chinese mainland. The National Unification Council was established in September 1990. Then, in January 1991, the Executive Yuan's Mainland Affairs Council 行政院大陸委員會 (MAC) was formed. In February 1991, MAC approved the formation of a private non-profit organization, the Straits Exchange Foundation 海峽交流基金會 (SEF).

National Unification Council

The National Unification Council functions as an advisory board and provides the president with research findings and ideas. The NUC is generally headed by the president, with opposition party members as deputies, and respected civic leaders as members. The tenure for NUC members is one year, renewable at the president's

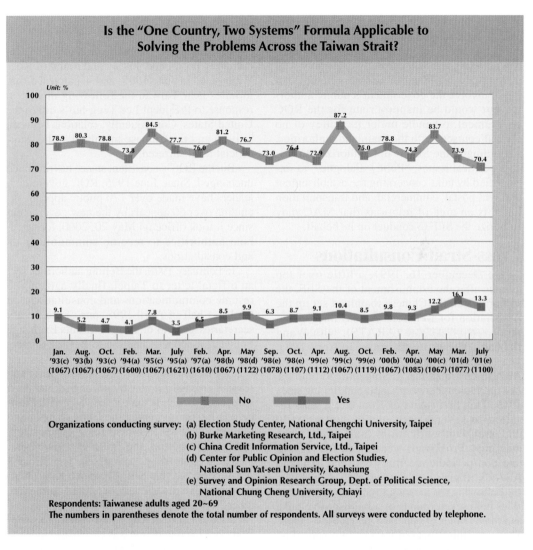

Is the "One Country, Two Systems" Formula Applicable to Solving the Problems Across the Taiwan Strait?

Unit: %

	Jan. '93(c) (1067)	Aug. '93(b) (1067)	Oct. '93(c) (1067)	Feb. '94(a) (1600)	Mar. '95(c) (1067)	July '95(a) (1621)	Feb. '97(a) (1610)	Apr. '98(b) (1067)	May '98(d) (1122)	Sep. '98(e) (1078)	Oct. '98(e) (1107)	Apr. '99(e) (1112)	Aug. '99(c) (1067)	Oct. '99(e) (1119)	Feb. '00(b) (1067)	Apr. '00(a) (1085)	May '00(c) (1067)	Mar. '01(d) (1077)	July '01(e) (1100)
No	78.9	80.3	78.8	73.8	84.5	77.7	76.0	81.2	76.7	73.0	76.4	72.9	87.2	75.0	78.8	74.3	83.7	73.9	70.4
Yes	9.1	5.2	4.7	4.1	7.8	3.5	6.5	8.5	9.9	6.3	8.7	9.1	10.4	8.5	9.8	9.3	12.2	16.1	13.3

■ No   ■ Yes

Organizations conducting survey: (a) Election Study Center, National Chengchi University, Taipei
(b) Burke Marketing Research, Ltd., Taipei
(c) China Credit Information Service, Ltd., Taipei
(d) Center for Public Opinion and Election Studies, National Sun Yat-sen University, Kaohsiung
(e) Survey and Opinion Research Group, Dept. of Political Science, National Chung Cheng University, Chiayi

Respondents: Taiwanese adults aged 20~69
The numbers in parentheses denote the total number of respondents. All surveys were conducted by telephone.

discretion. As a multiparty board, the NUC attempts to reach a consensus on the reunification of China.

Mainland Affairs Council

The Mainland Affairs Council, a formal administrative agency of the Executive Yuan, is responsible for the overall planning, coordination, evaluation, and implementation of the ROC government's policy toward the Chinese mainland. As a decision-making body, it also oversees rules and regulations proposed by various ministries concerning cross-strait relations. MAC is headed by a chairman and three vice chairmen and is organized into seven departments and three divisions.

Straits Exchange Foundation

The Straits Exchange Foundation, headed by a chairman and drawing its funds from both the

private sector and the government, is the only private organization authorized by the government to handle relations with the mainland. Nevertheless, the SEF currently deals only with matters of a technical or business nature that might involve the government's public authority, but would be inappropriate for the ROC government to handle under its policy of no official contacts with the mainland authorities. Accordingly, the SEF is not authorized to discuss political issues. "Policy dialogue," as exemplified by talks concerning the establishment of direct postal, commercial, and transportation links, is an area of relations that MAC may authorize the SEF to conduct on its behalf.

Cross-Strait Consultations

On December 16, 1991, a little over ten months after the establishment of the SEF, the authorities on the Chinese mainland set up the Association for Relations Across the Taiwan Strait 海峽兩岸關係協會 (ARATS), with Wang Daohan 汪道涵 as its chairman. In April 1993, SEF chairman Koo Chen-fu 辜振甫 and the ARATS chairman met in Singapore to hold the first discussions between Taipei and Beijing since 1949. This first round of Koo-Wang talks resulted in several agreements dealing with document authentication, mail, and future meetings. Provisions were made for regular and non-periodic meetings between SEF and ARATS officials.

Following the meeting in Singapore, the two sides held seven rounds of administrative talks and three rounds of secretary-general-level talks. These meetings focused largely on practical issues and led to a number of agreements in areas such as the repatriation of hijackers, illegal entrants, and fishing disputes. Dates for future talks were also set. At a preparatory meeting held in May 1995, it was decided that a second round of Koo-Wang talks would be held in Beijing on July 20, 1995. Both sides agreed that the talks would cover such issues as the implementation of accords signed during the first round of Koo-Wang talks, Taiwan investment rights on the

Chinese mainland, and a wide range of unofficial exchanges.

Unfortunately, the mainland authorities indefinitely postponed this second round of Koo-Wang talks in June 1995, and began test-firing missiles near Taiwan the following month, in response to President Lee Teng-hui's trip to the United States. Consequently, relations between Taiwan and the Chinese mainland at the semi-official level suffered.

But the ROC's consistent stance has remained unchanged. Since June 1995, ROC government leaders have made over 170 public appeals, including over 60 appeals by the new government since it took office on May 20, 2000, for mainland authorities to resume communications and consultations.

In February 1998, the Beijing authorities sent an official letter to Taipei, finally agreeing to resume communications and consultations. In the latter half of April 1998, one of the deputy secretaries-general of Taipei's Straits Exchange Foundation led a delegation to Beijing to meet their mainland counterparts from the Association for Relations Across the Taiwan Strait and resume cross-strait consultations that had been suspended for nearly three years. When US President Bill Clinton visited the Chinese mainland to meet with PRC President Jiang Zemin 江澤民 at the end of June, the issue of Taiwan and mainland relations was discussed. The SEF and ARATS agreed that SEF Chairman Koo Chen-fu would visit the Chinese mainland during October 14-19, 1998.

It was Chairman Koo's first visit to the mainland since the foundation was established in 1991. Also, Koo became the highest-ranking negotiator from Taiwan to visit the mainland since the Chinese civil war divided the two sides of the Taiwan Strait in 1949.

Koo's 12-member delegation visited Shanghai and Beijing during the trip. In Shanghai, Koo met with his mainland counterpart, ARATS chairman Wang Daohan. During their meetings, Koo and Wang agreed on four points to encourage closer cross-strait ties. Wang agreed

Top executives from TransAsia Airways (left) and Air Macau (right) shake hands after signing a new contract to jointly operate cargo transportation flights for the increasingly busy Taiwan-Macau route. (Photo by the Central News Agency)

to visit Taiwan at an appropriate time, and the two intermediary bodies would resume contacts and negotiations. It was also agreed that the SEF and ARATS should reinforce Taiwan-mainland exchanges at various levels. Fourth, the two organizations should provide more assistance on matters concerning protection of the property and personal safety of visitors from both sides.

Despite this Koo-Wang consensus, no significant breakthroughs were achieved on difficult issues during the meetings on the mainland. The two sides had different definitions of the "one China" principle. Also, the mainland authorities still refuse to acknowledge that the two sides of the Strait have separate governments. Moreover, Beijing refused to renounce the use of military force against Taiwan as a possible means of unification.

2000-2001 Cross-Strait Relations

Chen Shui-bian of the DPP won the March 18, 2000, presidential election. In his May 20 inaugural speech, he stated that as the directly elected tenth-term president of the Republic of China, he must abide by the Constitution; maintain the sovereignty, dignity, and security of the country; and ensure the well-being of all citizens. Therefore, so long as the mainland authorities do not use military force against Taiwan, he pledged that, during his term in office, he would not declare independence, change the national title, push for the inclusion of the so-called "state-to-state" description in the Constitution, nor promote a referendum on the question of independence or unification. Furthermore, he said there is no question of abolishing the *Guidelines for National Unification* or the National Unification Council. These remarks are often referred to as the "five no's policy."

Efforts of Goodwill Reconciliation

During Chen's first year in office, cross-strait situation remained stable, and the new administration made consistent efforts to end

deadlock on cross-strait talks. Following Chen's election, a supra-party task force 跨黨派小組 was set up under the Office of the President as a consultative body to integrate public opinion into the formulation of policies on cross-strait relations. After several rounds of discussion, it presented three acknowledgements and four recommendations 三個認知、四個建議 in November 2000 as national consensus, noting that the current state of cross-strait affairs is a result of the development of history and neither side represents or belongs to the other, and that any change to the current cross-strait situation should be approved by the people of Taiwan through democratic measures. Also, it acknowledged that people are the pillar of a nation and the purpose of a nation is to safeguard their security and well-being. As the two sides of the Strait use a similar language and are closely situated, their people should share long-term and mutual benefits.

Furthermore, after months of preparation, the "Three Mini-Links" 小三通 (see section on the "Three Mini-Links") were established in January 2001 between the Chinese mainland and the offshore islands of Kinmen and Matsu, as a prelude to direct transportation links between the two sides.

Chen made another appeal in his 2001 New Year's Eve address by suggesting that the two sides use economics, trade, and culture as a starting point for gradually building faith and confidence in each other, which in turn can be made into the basis for a new framework of lasting peace and political integration 統合. Meanwhile, KMT chairman Lien Chan proposed his version of a future "one China," which is under the framework of "confederation," 邦聯 but was opposed by Beijing.

In May 2001, on a state visit to Central and South America, Chen proposed the new "five no's policy," stressing that Taiwan would not provoke the Chinese mainland; misjudge the cross-strait situation; give up its sincerity and goodwill to improve cross-strait relations; nor

would it be a pawn of any country and consider cross-strait relations as a zero-sum game.

Later in the year, during Beijing's bid to host the 2008 Olympic Games, the ROC government expressed its support and congratulations in goodwill.

Despite continuous efforts of the Chen administration, Beijing, however, made no positive responses and continued to suspend talks by insisting on its "one China" principle, while blockading Taiwan in the international community with "large country diplomacy." Qian Qichen revised his Taiwan-is-part-of-China statement into both the mainland and Taiwan are part of China in 2000, and this has been interpreted by some as showing more flexibility in cross-strait policy. However, Beijing's later rhetoric has not been consistent, showing a lack of a fundamental change in its attitude.

Other factors that might have contributed to the cross-strait impasse in 2001 included the Chinese mainland's imminent leadership changes in 2002, the adjustment of Asia-Pacific and cross-strait policies by the new US administration, and Taiwan's lack of national consensus on certain issues of cross-strait relations.

New Prospects

In 2001, there have been controversies on the island about the "patience over haste" 戒急用忍 policy, adopted by former President Lee Teng-hui in 1996, and disputes over whether a consensus had been reached on the principle of "one China with respective verbal interpretations" during the 1992 cross-strait consultations. After five years of implementation, the "patience over haste" policy finally drew to a close when President Chen reiterated the new policy of "active opening and effective management" 積極開放、有效管理 in response to proposals made by the Economic Development Advisory Conference (EDAC) in August 2001 (for details, see Chapter 10), marking a more open attitude on cross-strait relations on Taiwan's side. According to the proposals of the EDAC's division on cross-strait relations, "Taiwan first, global perspectives, mutual benefit, and risk management"

Unification or Independence?

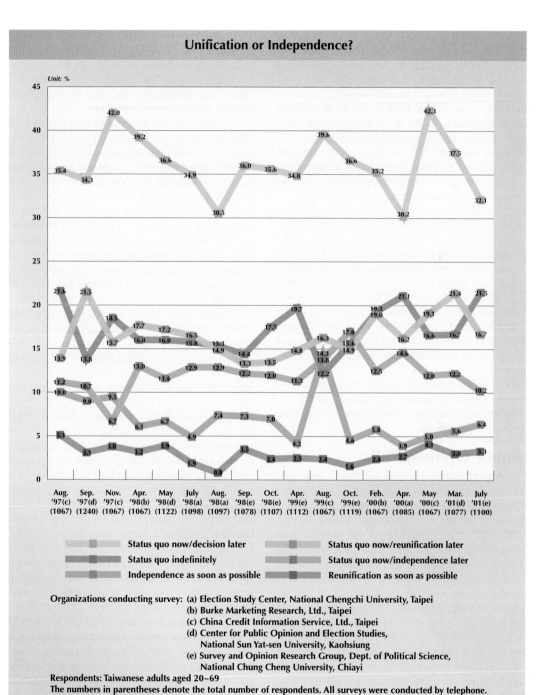

Unit: %

	Aug. '97(c) (1067)	Sep. '97(d) (1240)	Nov. '97(c) (1067)	Apr. '98(b) (1067)	May '98(d) (1122)	July '98(a) (1098)	Aug. '98(a) (1097)	Sep. '98(e) (1078)	Oct. '98(e) (1107)	Apr. '99(e) (1112)	Aug. '99(c) (1067)	Oct. '99(e) (1119)	Feb. '00(b) (1067)	Apr. '00(a) (1085)	May '00(c) (1067)	Mar. '01(d) (1077)	July '01(e) (1100)

Legend:
- Status quo now/decision later
- Status quo now/reunification later
- Status quo indefinitely
- Status quo now/independence later
- Independence as soon as possible
- Reunification as soon as possible

Organizations conducting survey: (a) Election Study Center, National Chengchi University, Taipei
(b) Burke Marketing Research, Ltd., Taipei
(c) China Credit Information Service, Ltd., Taipei
(d) Center for Public Opinion and Election Studies,
National Sun Yat-sen University, Kaohsiung
(e) Survey and Opinion Research Group, Dept. of Political Science,
National Chung Cheng University, Chiayi

Respondents: Taiwanese adults aged 20~69
The numbers in parentheses denote the total number of respondents. All surveys were conducted by telephone.

will be the principles for cross-strait economic and trade development. Additionally, restrictions of Taiwan investment on the Chinese mainland will be relaxed, flexible mechanisms for cross-strait capital flow will be established, operations relating to the "Three Links" will be liberalized in accordance with the WTO accession process; and tourism will be opened to visitors from the Chinese mainland. The panel also suggested the government to quickly establish a consensus between the governing and opposition parties to resolve differences over the 1992 consensus.

The World Trade Organization's (WTO) 4th Ministerial Conference held in Doha, Qatar admitted the Chinese mainland and the ROC to membership on November 10 and 11, 2001, respectively, with the Protocols of Accession signed 24 hours later. After the protocol was ratified by the Legislative Yuan and deposited with the WTO secretariat for 30 days to allow completion of membership, the ROC became the WTO's 144th member in January 2002, and the Chinese mainland became the 143rd member. Now that the two sides have joined the WTO, cross-strait trade and economic activities can be conducted under a rule-based framework, and interactions across the Taiwan Strait have entered a new phase.

Public Opinion Polls

A poll commissioned by MAC and conducted by the China Credit Information Service 中華徵信所 from May 21-23, 2000, found 89.6 percent of the respondents agreed to the president's "five no's policy," and only 5.2 percent disagreed. Overall, 83.2 percent of the people thought that President Chen had extended in his inauguration speech goodwill to the Chinese mainland and that the mainland should respond in kind. Moreover, 87.6 percent agreed with the view that cross-strait dialogue can be possible only if both sides are equal. Meanwhile, 76.6 percent also agreed with the view that, in order to have dialogue on the issue of unification, the Chinese mainland must implement democratization.

In addition, the cabinet-level MAC has been polling residents on the same subjects for a decade. Subjects being regularly polled include key issues such as "unification or independence," "direct transportation links," and Beijing's "one country, two systems" formula.

Recent poll results showed that cross-strait relations are a major concern of ROC citizens. In a MAC-commissioned poll conducted by the Center for Public Opinion and Election Studies of National Sun Yat-sen University 國立中山大學民意調查中心 from March 25-28, 2001, Taiwan people for the first time regarded progress in cross-strait relations as more important than development of foreign relations. In the poll, 36.5 percent of respondents viewed cross-strait progress as more important, while 33 percent chose foreign relations development as priority.

Respondents' views toward Beijing's "one country, two systems" formula for unification also underwent certain changes in 2001. Although the majority of the people (70.4 percent in the July poll) still rejected the proposal, respondents who regarded the formula as applicable had risen to over 10 percent since May 2000, peaking at 16.1 percent in March 2001, but was down to 13.3 percent in July. Some observers ascribed this to the strong economic growth along the mainland's southeastern coast and politico-economic troubles in Taiwan.

On the question of unification or independence, the latest MAC-commissioned poll, conducted by the Survey and Opinion Research Group of National Chung-cheng University 國立中正大學民意調查研究中心 between July 6-9, 2001, showed that 80.5 percent of the respondents approved maintaining the status quo (including status quo now, decision later; status quo now, unification later; status quo now, independence later; status quo forever), with approximately one-third of the people supporting "status quo now, decision later." Those supporting independence or reunification as soon as possible accounted for only 6.4 and 3.3 percent respectively, a result consistent with past polls.

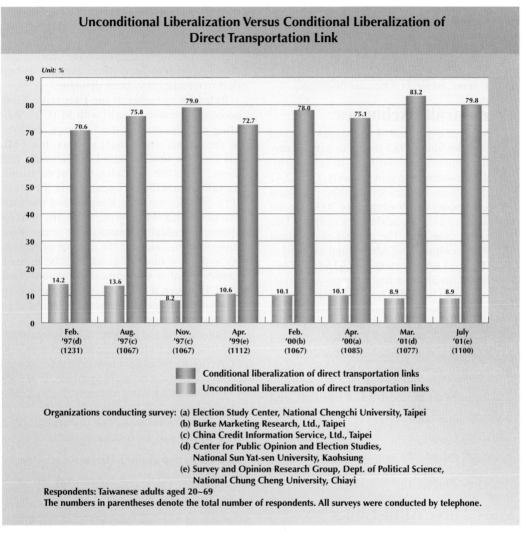

Unconditional Liberalization Versus Conditional Liberalization of Direct Transportation Link

Unit: %

	Feb. '97(d) (1231)	Aug. '97(c) (1067)	Nov. '97(c) (1067)	Apr. '99(e) (1112)	Feb. '00(b) (1067)	Apr. '00(a) (1085)	Mar. '01(d) (1077)	July '01(e) (1100)
Conditional	70.6	75.8	79.0	72.7	78.0	75.1	83.2	79.8
Unconditional	14.2	13.6	8.2	10.6	10.1	10.1	8.9	8.9

◼ Conditional liberalization of direct transportation links
◼ Unconditional liberalization of direct transportation links

Organizations conducting survey: (a) Election Study Center, National Chengchi University, Taipei
(b) Burke Marketing Research, Ltd., Taipei
(c) China Credit Information Service, Ltd., Taipei
(d) Center for Public Opinion and Election Studies, National Sun Yat-sen University, Kaohsiung
(e) Survey and Opinion Research Group, Dept. of Political Science, National Chung Cheng University, Chiayi

Respondents: Taiwanese adults aged 20~69
The numbers in parentheses denote the total number of respondents. All surveys were conducted by telephone.

On the issue of direct transportation between the two sides, the same poll showed that 79.8 percent of the respondents supported "conditional liberalization," which means direct transportation links between the two sides should be established with the ROC's national security, dignity, and the principle of parity taken into account. Only 8.9 percent of the respondents prefer liberalization without any condition, a result close to earlier findings. When asked to comment on the government's restrictions on Taiwan investment in mainland China, 56.8 percent of the respondents hoped to see them tightened and 23.8 percent relaxed.

Currently the two sides still hold different definitions for "one China." When asked about their attitude toward Beijing's preposition that "Taiwan must first admit it is part of China

before any cross-strait talks can resume," 52.8 percent of the respondents in the July 2001 poll disagreed, whereas 32.4 percent agreed. In addition, 46.8 percent of the respondents agreed the two sides may hold negotiations over the "one China" issue, while 31.7 percent disagreed.

Cross-strait Exchanges

The rapid expansion of exchanges between the two sides since 1987 seems to have generated momentum for continued development. Travel has continued to grow steadily. Over 2.41 million Taiwan visitors went to the mainland between January and November of 2000. On the other hand, 123,978 mainlanders came to Taiwan in the same year. The number of mainland visitors for cultural and educational exchanges grew from 11,662 in 1999 to 12,154 in 2000, registering an all time high. Cross-strait religious activities have also been popular in recent years. Numerous pilgrimage trips were made each year to the mainland. In addition, reporters from the Chinese mainland have been allowed to be based in Taipei since November 2000.

According to statistics of the Mainland Affairs Council, Taiwan investment on the Chinese mainland in 2000 registered US$2.61 billion, and Taiwan-mainland trade of the year amounted to US$31.25 billion. Taiwan has become the fourth largest source of foreign investment of the Chinese mainland, and the mainland was the largest source of Taiwan's trade surplus in 2000 (for details, see Chapter 10).

The "Three Mini-Links"

The transportation, postal, and trade links between the Chinese mainland and the offshore islands of Kinmen, Matsu, and Penghu are referred to as the "three mini-links."

On June 13, 2000, the 23rd meeting of the Legislative Yuan passed the following resolution: "First, the government shall complete the assessment of the three mini links (TML) within three months. Upon completion, the government shall immediately prioritize decriminalization and implementation of areas within our jurisdiction.

Second, within this framework, the government shall first begin, on a trial basis, shipping links that are related to religious purposes. Third, as the government undertakes assessments and plans, it shall at the same time, exercise its best effort to resume cross-strait dialogue."

Relevant agencies of the Executive Yuan conducted the assessment, with MAC coordinating and integrating the findings. Following the impact assessment studies, the TML will be first implemented on Kinmen and Matsu. After the normalization of relations, an evaluation will be conducted on the feasibility of links between Penghu and the Chinese mainland. Moreover, the TML will be expanded gradually. Initially, the scale of the transportation links and the number of passengers and the volume of goods will be limited. Transshipment or side-trip calls will not be permitted. However, if necessary, permission may be considered on a special case-by-case basis, e.g., religious pilgrimages.

The planning and implementation of the three mini-links will follow these major principles: (1) giving national security first priority; (2) keeping with the legislative spirit of the *Statute of Offshore Island Development* 離島建設條例; (3) integrating and complementing the "three links" within WTO rules; and (4) establishing a stable and normal cross-strait relationship.

Implementation of the TML for Kinmen and Matsu

In the short term, there will be limited opening of Kinmen and Matsu to trade, visitors, ships, and postal service with the Fujian area of the mainland.

Stage one: Priority will be given to decriminalization and implementation of areas within our jurisdiction. The priority order of items to be opened will be established according to the prevailing conditions.

Stage two: Additional areas will be subject to bilateral consultation between the two sides.

In the medium and long term, the Kinmen and Matsu areas may be used as a way station for visitors and the exchange of personnel and goods between the two sides. Sea traffic may be

Exchanges Between Taiwan and the Chinese Mainland in 2000

Category	Quantity	Annual change
Total cross-strait trade[1]	US$31.25 billion	20.93%
Mainland trade dependence on Taiwan[1]	6.60%	—
Taiwan trade dependence on the mainland[1]	10.84%	—
Taiwan investment in the mainland[2]	US$2.61 billion	108.11%
Cross-strait remittances[3]	US$1,978.91 million	46.41%
Remittances to the mainland[3]	US$1,208.62 million	43.44%
Remittances to Taiwan[3]	US$770.29 million	51.32%
Cross-strait postal exchanges[4]	14.75 million	9.10%
Letters to the mainland[4]	5.41 million	7.55%
Letters to Taiwan[4]	9.34 million	10.01%
Cross-strait telephone exchanges[5]	583.80 million min.	16.72%
Calls to the mainland	342.98 million min.	19.91%
Calls to Taiwan	240.82 million min.	12.45%
Cross-strait travel[6]	—	—
Taiwan visits to the mainland (Jan.-Nov.)	2.41 million	40.47%
Mainland visits to Taiwan	117,125	9.77%

[1] MAC estimates based on ROC and Hong Kong customs data
[2] Investment Commission, Ministry of Economic Affairs, ROC 經濟部投資審議委員會
[3] Foreign Exchange Department, Central Bank of China, ROC 中央銀行外匯局
[4] Directorate General of Posts, Ministry of Transportation and Communications, ROC 交通部郵政總局
[5] Chunghwa Telecommunications Co. Ltd., ROC 中華電信公司
[6] China Travel Service 中國旅行社 in Hong Kong and the Bureau of Immigration, Ministry of the Interior, ROC 內政部警政署入出境管理局

further adjusted, whereas air traffic will be authorized only under appropriate conditions. And economic cooperation may be developed with the Fujian area on the mainland.

Shipping Link

Initially, air traffic will not be opened. Sea transportation will be limited to one port per region, with "fixed points, fixed periods, and fixed courses" 定點,定期,定航. The sea routes selected will be from Liaoluo port 料羅港 on Kinmen to Xiamen, and Fuao port 福澳港 on Matsu to Fuzhou. In principle, only passenger and cargo ships, not fishing boats, will be used. However, fishing boats refurbished for passenger-cargo service will be authorized in accordance with the *Law of Ships* 航舶法 and the *Law of Marine Transportation* 航業法.

Merchandise Trade

In the trade of goods, priority will be given to the basic needs of residents on Kinmen and Matsu. The next priority will be the transshipment of semi-processed goods. The main effort will be decriminalization of imports. A positive list system will be adopted. Goods that were publicly announced and permitted for indirect imports will be implemented as the first step.

In the next step, the list of items will be expanded according to the needs and development of the offshore island. Other than contraband, no other restrictions will be imposed on exports.

Quarantine measures will be strengthened on Matsu and Kinmen, and agricultural products imported to Kinmen and Matsu will be restricted from entering Taiwan proper.

Entry and Exit of Personnel

Residents of Kinmen and Matsu entering the Chinese mainland will be limited to such daily activities as enhancing offshore island development and humanitarian efforts. A flexible policy will be adopted on length of stay and the number of trips. However, to protect national security, a quota system will be adopted for residents of the mainland area entering Kinmen or Matsu. Each day, a maximum of 700 mainland residents will be allowed to enter Kinmen and 100 to Matsu for commercial activities.

Decriminalization

Activities, such as smuggling, illegal entry and exit of personnel, and illegal sailing directly to the mainland will be legalized or punishment for such activities will be reduced.

Activities that are based on daily requirements and have no effect on national security (e.g., smuggling basic necessities), will be decriminalized or the relevant restrictions adjusted. In contrast, activities which affect national security or are not related to local necessities (e.g., smuggling mainland products to Taiwan), will not be legalized.

The TML began on January 1, 2001. Operations of trade, visitor, and financial exchanges between Kinmen/Matsu and the mainland have begun successively and progressed at a good and steady pace. By the end of October 2001, 139 voyages and 10,515 visits had been made between the two sides. Many elderly natives of Kinmen who live in Xiamen were able to visit their birthplace. Illegal trading has significantly decreased. Although still in a trial stage and facing obstruction from the Chinese mainland, overall, the TML has had a positive effect on cross-strait relations and people-to-people exchanges.

The government has carried out a mid-term review on the TML. On September 5, 2001, the Executive Yuan approved to expand the operations of the TML and broaden its scope to include Penghu, another offshore island located even closer to Taiwan proper. The new measures allow mid- and low-ranking public functionaries (excluding police officers and personnel involved in national security affairs or highly confidential research) of Kinmen and Matsu to visit mainland China. Travelers who accompany patients to seek medical treatment in mainland China will no longer be restricted to family members living in the same household. Also, residents from the Chinese mainland who have been granted permission to visit Kinmen or Matsu can make the trip within a maximum of 30 days upon receiving the permission. In addition, ships will soon be able to sail from Penghu to the mainland with government approval on a case-by-case basis, but not vice versa.

Hong Kong and Macau

Chinese reunification cannot be discussed without mentioning Hong Kong and Macau. The ROC government realizes that the people of Hong Kong and Macau have special positions in the East Asian economy and have contributed to positive change on the Chinese mainland. The ROC fully supports the rights and achievements of these two areas.

History of Hong Kong

After losing the Opium War, the Ching government was compelled to sign the Treaty of Nanking in 1842, ceding Hong Kong Island to Britain. Another military defeat ended with the 1860 Convention of Beijing, under which the Ching rulers leased southern Kowloon and Stonecutters Island to the British. Finally, the New Territories and 235 outlying islands were leased to Great Britain for 99 years under the Convention for the Extension of Hong Kong, signed on June 9, 1898. (In this chapter, the term Hong Kong refers to Hong Kong Island, southern Kowloon, the New Territories, and the offshore islands, that is, the whole area administered by the British beginning in 1898.)

In 1982, Britain opened negotiations with the authorities on the Chinese mainland to discuss the return of Hong Kong. On September 24, 1984, London and Beijing signed the Sino-British Joint Declaration in which they agreed that Hong Kong was to be returned to the mainland authorities on July 1, 1997, after 150 years of British rule. Beijing made plans to establish the Hong Kong Special Administrative Region and promised to keep Hong Kong's system intact for 50 years after 1997. In April 1990, the mainland authorities promulgated the *Basic Law of the Hong Kong Special Administrative Region* 香港特別行政區基本法. In March 1996, a provisional legislature was selected to take the place of Hong Kong's popularly elected Legislative Council, and in December of the same year, Tung Chee-hwa 董建華, a shipping tycoon, was appointed as Hong Kong chief executive by Beijing, effective July 1997. The handover of Hong Kong and the return of Macau in 1999 marked the end of Europe's colonial presence in Asia.

History of Macau

Like Hong Kong, Macau has also experienced a history separate from that of the rest of China for over a century. Macau consists of a small peninsula projecting from the province of Guangdong, as well as the islands of Taipa and Coloane, with a total area of only 23.8 square kilometers. At the end of 1999, Macau's resident population totaled 438,000, composed of 68.7 percent Chinese, 27.2 percent Portuguese, and 4.1 percent others. The Portuguese leased Macau from China during the 16th, 17th, and 18th centuries and used the port as an entrepôt for trade with China and Japan. Under a treaty signed in 1887, the Ching rulers ceded Macau to the Portuguese. In August 1979, Portugal established diplomatic relations with the authorities on the Chinese mainland and redefined Macau as a part of China temporarily administered by Portugal. In 1987, Lisbon and Beijing issued the Sino-Portuguese Joint Declaration stating that Macau would be returned to China on December 20, 1999.

With the signing of this Joint Declaration, the period of transition began. The *Basic Law of the Macau Special Administrative Region* 澳門特別行政區基本法 was approved by the National People's Assembly and promulgated by the President of the People's Republic of China on March 31, 1993. It functions as a mini-constitution, containing the fundamental statutes concerning the territory's autonomy; the exclusive powers of the Chinese central authorities; the statute and rights of the permanent residents of the Macau Special Administrative Region; the political structure; and the economic, cultural, and social affairs of the region.

The second phase of the period of transition, from the beginning of 1993 to the end of 1995, was marked by the completion of various large infrastructure projects, including the new Macau-Taipa Bridge, the Outer Harbor Ferry Terminal, and the airport. The emphasis has since been placed on education, including technical training and advanced education, cultural development, and social welfare to improve the quality of life. The founding of the University of Macau, which replaced the private University of East Asia, was the first step in expanding higher education. The creation of the Polytechnic, the Tourism Training Institute, and the establishment of courses run by the University of the United Nations have since followed.

Edmund Ho Hau-wah 何厚鏵 was elected by the Selection Committee and then appointed by Beijing as the chief executive of the Macau Special Administrative Region on May 20, 1999. The transfer to Chinese jurisdiction was smooth, and Macau will hopefully continue to enjoy a high degree of autonomy, prosperity, and stability.

Policy Toward Hong Kong and Macau

The ROC maintains very close ties with both Hong Kong and Macau. Taiwan residents made 1.85 million trips to Hong Kong in 2000, while residents of Hong Kong made 263,943 trips to Taiwan. Economic ties are also strong, with the volume of trade between Taiwan and Hong Kong reaching US$33.94 billion in 2000. Taiwan-Macau trade grew to US$363 million. In the same year, there were 53 cases of Taiwan-to-Hong Kong investment, totaling US$47.51 million; and 92 Hong Kong-to-Taiwan investment projects, totaling US$270.65 million. In addition to Hong Kong's importance for direct investment, the territory also serves as a transshipment point for cross-strait trade. Hong Kong customs officials estimated that in 2000, US$11.57 billion in Taiwan-mainland trade passed through Hong Kong. Capital goods and funds for investment on the Chinese mainland are also typically transferred through the territory.

In light of such close and comprehensive links, it should come as no surprise that policy concerning Hong Kong and Macau is a high priority of the ROC government. The ROC responded to the negotiations between Britain and the mainland authorities by forming a special Hong Kong Affairs Task Force in August 1983. After London and Beijing signed the Joint Declaration, the Task Force was upgraded to a Coordination Panel, under the direct supervision of the ROC vice premier. Following the signing of the Sino-Portuguese Joint Declaration in April 1987, the name of the Hong Kong Affairs Task Force was changed to the Hong Kong and Macau Affairs Task Force 行政院港澳小組. At the end of January 1991 when the ROC government set up MAC, the Task Force was incorporated into the new organization as its Department of Hong Kong and Macau Affairs 港澳處 to coordinate ROC government policies toward the two areas.

The ROC government has maintained a consistent and continuous policy in its dealings with Hong Kong and Macau. To promote the various relations with Hong Kong after 1997 and with Macau after 1999, the ROC government has defined the two places as "special districts" to distinguish them from the mainland. The original direct traffic between the people of Taiwan and Hong Kong and Macau has been maintained in the hope that healthy interaction can be furthered.

The new administration, aware of the peculiarity and importance of the two places, has handled Taiwan's relationship with them in an open and forward-looking way, in keeping with the spirit of "goodwill reconciliation, active cooperation, and lasting peace" that President Chen Shui-bian declared in his inaugural address. The ROC has been actively strengthening the functions of government agencies in Hong Kong and Macau and expanding contact with various circles in Hong Kong and Macau to increase mutual understanding.

Overall, relations between Taiwan and these two places have had positive developments. A major breakthrough is that starting from August 8, 2001, Hong Kong and Macau residents visiting Taiwan (excluding first-time visitors) can obtain 14-day landing visas, greatly enhancing the exchanges between Taiwan and Hong Kong/Macau. Hong Kong officials have also agreed to allow Chung Hwa Travel Service 中華旅行社 to establish an office in Hong Kong International Airport to facilitate transit procedures of visitors transferring from mainland China to Taiwan. Furthermore, ROC citizens can now apply for Hong Kong visa via the Internet, a measure that will shorten the current 14 work-day period and facilitate bilateral ties as Taiwan has long been one of Hong Kong and Macau's three main sources of visitors.

Looking to the Future

A stable and democratic China is in the world's best interest. The ROC government has repeatedly emphasized that its participation in the international community does not challenge the existing interests of the People's Republic of China. The ROC must further develop its international relations to ensure its continued existence and development.

The two sides should avoid the use of force and instead apply the principles of reason, peace, reciprocity, and mutual benefit to systematically improve cross-strait relations. Only in this way can Taipei and Beijing bring the greatest possible benefit to the people on both sides of the Taiwan Strait and contribute to the long-term peace and stability of the Asia-Pacific region.

Related Websites
1. Mainland Affairs Council: *http://www.mac.gov.tw*
2. Straits Exchange Foundation: *http://www.sef.org.tw*

8

National Defense

The ROC's military preparations are purely defensive and help to maintain peace and stability in the Taiwan Strait.

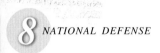

What's New
1. Reorganization of GSH
2. Courses offered at military academies
3. Important R&D achievements

The objective of the nation's armed forces is to defend the territory of the Republic of China on Taiwan (including the islands of Taiwan, Penghu, Kinmen, and Matsu). This requires maintaining a sufficient self-defense capability to safeguard the nation and protect its people. The direct and most serious threat to the ROC's national security comes from the Chinese mainland, as Beijing refuses to renounce the use of military force against Taiwan. Thus, while the ROC's national defense strategy calls for a balanced development of the three armed forces, naval and air supremacy receive first priority. In addition to current defensive preparations, the long-term policy requires developing an elite fighting force and self-sufficiency in defense technology through restructuring the armed forces, streamlining command levels, renovating logistical systems, merging or reassigning military schools and high-ranking staff units, and reducing the total number of personnel.

Current Defense Policy

The ROC must maintain a strong military to deter the Chinese mainland from using force against Taiwan, which would upset the peace in the Asia-Pacific region. Furthermore, effective armed forces allow Taipei to conduct dialogue and negotiations with Beijing from a position of strength. The ROC's military preparations are purely defensive to maintain peace and stability in the Taiwan Strait.

Budgetary Reductions

The defense budget for the ROC military has generally been reduced each year over the past decade, and an increasing percentage has become open to public scrutiny. The defense budget for 2002 was US$8.39 billion (NT$626 billion), or 16.5 percent of the total national budget.

Maximizing Effectiveness

The changes to the ROC's Armed Forces over the past few years reflect a shift from balancing offensive and defensive capabilities to simply assuring defense. The total number of personnel in the Armed Forces, which was at 450,000 in 1997, was reduced to 380,000 in 2001 when the Armed Forces Refining Program was completed.

Other results of the Armed Forces Refining Program include:
- Since July 1, 1998, the MND, General Staff Headquarters, and commands of the three services have been reorganizing staff units at all levels, changing their designations according to each unit's functions. So far, 78 first grade staff units and 324 second grade staff units have been reduced by 27.44 percent each.
- The ROC Army has adjusted the structuring of its forces, cutting several divisions and independent brigades while forming division-level commands and more than 30 joint-branch brigades. Other organizational restructuring has also been carried out.
- The ROC Navy has acquired new combat ships, including Lafayette-class, Chengkung-class, Knox-class, and Chinchiang-class ships. In addition, an Aviation Command has been set up, and the ROC's anti-submarine group has been reassigned to it. Two division level units of the Chinese Marine Corps have been reorganized into two marine brigades and a base garrison brigade.
- The ROC Air Force has gradually upgraded its combat wings with the acquisition of new combat aircraft, including F-16, IDF, and Mirage 2000-5 fighters. In addition, the Air Force's Eastern Command has been transformed into the Education, Training, and Doctrine Development Command.
- On July 1, 1999, the Combined Services Headquarters completed its mission of reorganizing the ROC Armed Forces' common logistics units.
- The ROC Military Police Command has reorganized its structure.

Facing the threat of high-tech warfare from the Chinese mainland, the ROC's Armed Forces have streamlined their organization and introduced more cost-effective measures by de-centralizing organizations, shortening the chain of command, accelerating reaction times, and promoting increased efficiency. Management and processing have shortened process flow times, fostered the creativity of grassroots units and individuals, and eliminated outdated approaches, resulting in a new military organization.

Command Structure

Article 36 of the *ROC Constitution* stipulates that the president of the republic "shall have supreme command of the land, sea and air forces of the whole country," and Article 3 of the *Organic Law of the Executive Yuan* 行政院組織法 states that "the Executive Yuan shall establish (among others) a Ministry of National Defense (MND)." According to the *Organization Law of the MND* 國防部組織法, this ministry shall be in charge of the defense affairs of the whole country.

Within the Ministry of National Defense is the General Staff Headquarters (GSH), under which are the various services, including the Army, Navy, Air Force, Combined Services Forces, Armed Forces Reserve Command 軍管區司令部, and Military Police Command 憲兵司令部. The GSH is headed by the chief of the general staff, who is in charge of military affairs. In the military command system, he acts as the chief of staff to the president for operational matters, while in the administrative system, he serves as chief of staff to the minister of national defense.

Ministry of National Defense

The Ministry of National Defense 國防部, under the command of the Executive Yuan, is responsible for formulating military strategy, setting military personnel policies, formulating draft and mobilization plans, delineating supply distribution policies, arranging the research and development of military technology, compiling the national defense budget, setting military regulations, conducting court martial proceedings,

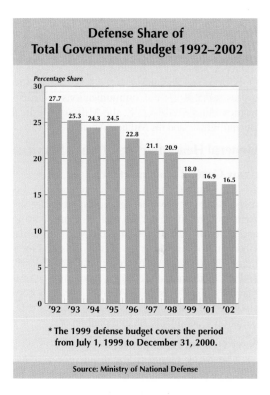

Defense Share of Total Government Budget 1992–2002

Percentage Share

* The 1999 defense budget covers the period from July 1, 1999 to December 31, 2000.

Source: Ministry of National Defense

and administering military law. The ministry consists of Minister's Office 部長辦公室; Departments of Manpower 人力司, Material 物力司, and Law 法制司; Bureau of the Comptroller 主計局; the Judge Advocates Bureau 軍法局; Procurement Bureau 採購局; Military History and Translation Bureau 史政編譯局; Chungshan Institute of Science and Technology中山科學研究所; the Appeals and Deliberation Committee訴願審議委員會; and Office of National Mobilization全民防衛動員準備綜合作業室.

General Staff Headquarters, MND

In accordance with the *Organizational Statute of the General Staff Headquarters* (GSH), MND 國防部參謀本部組職條例, the GSH is responsible for the planning and supervision of joint war activities, political warfare, personnel, military intelligence, operations, education and training, logistics, organization and equipment calibration, communications, and medical services.

It includes the offices of Joint War Training and Standard Development 聯合作戰訓練暨準則發展室, the Deputy Chiefs of the General Staff for Personnel 人事參謀次長室, Intelligence 情報參謀次長室, Operations and Planning 作戰及計劃參謀次長室, Logistics 後勤參謀次長室, Communications and Electronics 通信電子資訊次長室; the Military Medical Bureau 軍醫局; and the Military Affairs 總務局.

General Headquarters of Each Service

Army General Headquarters

The Army General Headquarters 陸軍總部 is responsible for developing and maintaining the Army's combat power, as well as commanding and supervising all subordinate troops and units. Under its command are the Army Logistics Command 後勤司令部, Army Commands 軍團司令部, and the Airborne and Special Operations Command 航空特戰司令部. The Army's hierarchy consists of the army 軍團, division 師, brigade 旅, battalion 營, company 連, and platoon 排.

Navy General Headquarters

The Navy General Headquarters 海軍總部 is in charge of developing and maintaining the Navy's combat readiness, as well as commanding and supervising all of its subordinate fleets and ground units. Under its command are the Naval Fleet Command 艦隊司令部, the Marine Corps Headquarters 陸戰隊司令部, the Navy Logistics Command 後勤司令部, the Educational Training and Standard Development Command 教育訓練暨準則發展司令部, and the Bureau of Maritime Survey 海洋測量局. The subordinate Navy units are under the direct supervision of the Naval Fleet Command 艦隊司令部 and are organized into fleet 艦隊, group 戰隊, and ship 艦 levels. The Marine Corps units, like those of the Army, extend from the Marine Corps Headquarters 陸戰隊司令部 and, in descending order, consist of brigade 旅, battalion 營, company 連, and platoon 排.

Air Force General Headquarters

The Air Force General Headquarters 空軍總部 is responsible for the Air Force's combat strength and commands and supervises all subordinate troops and units. Its units include the Air Force Operations Command 作戰司令部, the Air Force Logistics Command 後勤司令部, the Air Defense Artillery Command 防砲警衛司令部, the Educational Training and Standard Development Command 教育訓練暨準則發展司令部, and various tactical wings 聯隊. In descending order under the wing are the group 大隊, squadron 中隊, and flight 分隊.

By February 1, 2003, the Army General Headquarters, the Navy General Headquarters, and the Air Force General Headquarters will have been re-designated as the Army Headquarters, the Navy Headquarters, and the Air Force Headquarters.

Combined Services Force General Headquarters

The Combined Services Force General Headquarters 聯勤總部 is responsible for acquiring ordnance, military maps, and communication equipment for the ROC Armed Forces. It also provides support and services commonly needed by all of the branches of the Armed Forces, such as surveying, engineering, rear echelon administration, purchase and procurement, and armament appraisal and testing.

Armed Forces Reserve Command

The Armed Forces Reserve Command manages reserve troops and other mobilization affairs.

Military Police Command

The Military Police 憲兵 guard military and certain governmental installations, enforce military law, maintain military discipline, support combat troops, and serve as supplementary police when necessary to maintain public security. The Military Police have four sub-command centers and one training center. The Military Police Command 憲兵司令部 has a Department of Political Warfare 政治作戰部 and offices of Personnel 人事軍務處, Intelligence 情報處, Police Affairs 警務處, Logistics 後勤處, Planning 計畫處, and Comptroller 主計處.

The ROC defense strategy calls for maintaining a minimum force in peacetime and mobilizing a large number of troops in the event of war.
(Courtesy of Military News Agency)

Manpower Structure

A member of the ROC military may be an officer 軍官, a noncommissioned officer (NCO) 士官, or an enlisted man 士兵. He may be serving on either a volunteer 志願役 or conscript 義務役 basis, and may be on active duty 常備 or reserve 預備 status.

Officers

Officers in the ROC military generally come from one of the three backgrounds. They might be graduates of military academies who become career officers 正期軍官, graduates of different specialized military schools who serve shorter terms of duty 專科軍官, or college graduates who have passed a written test to become reserve officers 預官.

Approximately 20 percent of the officers commissioned each year are graduates of different military academies, another 35 percent are graduates of specialized military schools, and the remaining 45 percent are reserve officers.

The ratio of officers to NCOs is about 1:1.77, and officers to enlisted men is 1:1.97. Thus, the ratio of officers to soldiers is 1:3.74.

Noncommissioned Officers (NCO)

NCOs are the backbone of the Armed Forces' smaller units, and are required to train troops and develop their combat performance. In recent years, however, most senior NCOs have retired, leaving the current proportion of career NCOs too low and the percentage of NCO reservists in service too high. Reservists are on active duty for a very limited period of time, making it difficult for them to keep up with changes in the operation and maintenance of sophisticated weapons and equipment. To overcome this problem, it is necessary to reorganize the NCO structure and recruit additional career NCOs.

Conscripts

The *Military Service Law* 兵役法 of the ROC stipulates that all males in the Republic of China shall fulfill military service. Article 3 of the law states: "Male persons shall be liable for military service on January 1 of the year immediately following the year during which they reach the age of 18, and shall no longer be drafted for service beginning on December 31 of the year during which they reach the age of 40." Citizens who have been sentenced to imprisonment for

five years or have served a total time in prison of 3 years are ineligible for service.

Under the *Military Service Law*, military conscription is administered jointly by the Ministry of National Defense and the Ministry of the Interior (MOI) 內政部. The MND is responsible for securing an adequate number of conscripts and training them, while the MOI determines the sources of the conscripts and ensures their rights and benefits. Generally, conscripts undergo 22 months of training.

The *Implementation Regulations for Substitutive Conscription* was promulgated on February 2, 2000, and went into effect on July 1, 2000. The categories for these services include domestic security (police and fire fighters), social services (social, environmental protection, medical, and educational), and other categories designated by the Executive Yuan.

Male senior high school, vocational high school, and college students whose studies would be interrupted by military conscription can defer their induction until after graduation. Young men in poor health are exempt from military conscription. Those in average health may serve in the militia 國民兵.

Manpower and Equipment

Ground Forces

The ROC Army totals 200,000 personnel. The Army is organized into combat, combat support, and service support troops and is organized into the following units:
- Army Corps
- Defense Command
- Aviation and Special Warfare Command
- Division Commands
- Airborne Cavalry Brigades
- Armored Brigades
- Armored Infantry Brigades
- Motorized Rifle Brigades
- Infantry Brigades
- Special Warfare Brigades
- Missile Command

The primary weapon systems of the ROC Army include AH-1W attack helicopters, OH-58D scout helicopters, M-48H and M-60A-3 tanks, portable Stinger surface-to-air missiles, Chaparral self-propelled air-defense missiles, M-109A-5 self-propelled howitzers, Sky Bow air defense missiles, and Patriot air defense systems.

Military Police

The ROC Military Police consists of around 10,000 officers and men and is organized into the following units:
- Military Police Headquarters
- Military Police Command
- Investigation Units
- Military Police Battalions
- Military Police Squadrons

Navy

The ROC Navy maintains control and surveillance of the waters surrounding Taiwan. The Navy also participates in joint operations with the Army and Air Force. The Navy GHQ oversees operational and land-based forces. The main operational units in the ROC Navy include the following:
- Fleet Command
- Marine Corps Command
- Destroyer Fleet
- Frigate Fleet
- Amphibious Fleet
- Service Fleet
- Submarine Squadron
- Fast-Attack Missile Boat Force
- Land-based Missile Force
- Naval Aviation Command
- Surveillance and Communications System Command
- Marine Corps Force

The primary weapon systems of the ROC Navy include missile destroyers, missile frigates, missile corvettes, fast-attack missile boats, mine warfare ships, submarines, fixed-wing anti-submarine warfare (ASW) aircraft, ASW helicopters, amphibious ships, and landing vehicles. Newly established forces in the ROC Navy include:

An F-16 of the 401 Wing launches a Harpoon anti-ship missile, which successfully hits the target.
(Courtesy of the Air Force General Headquarters)

• Marine Brigade

The ROC's Marine Corps Force focuses on maintaining amphibious capabilities while making changes to its mission and organization. These changes include phasing out two basic divisions from the Chinese Marine Corps and establishing two marine brigades and a base garrisson brigade in their place.

• Naval Aviation Command

Since ASW involves 3-dimensional operations requiring quick mobilization and a unified command, the S-2T ASW aircraft were transferred from the Air Force to the Navy, and the ASW Command was merged into the Naval Aviation Command.

Air Force

Taiwan's geographical location makes air defense crucial for overall defense of the nation. At present, the ROC Air Force has some 50,000 officers and men. Personnel are divided into operational and logistical support systems under the command of the Air Force GHQ.

The main operational units in the ROC Air Force include the following:

• Air Combat Command
• Air Defense Artillery, Guard Command, and Guard Troops
• Tactical Fighter Wings
• Transport/Electronic Warfare Wing
• Air Tactical Control Wing
• Communications and ATC Wing
• Weather Forecasting Wing

The primary weapon systems of the ROC Air Force include IDF, F-16, and Mirage 2000-5 fighters; Sidewinder, Maverick, Sparrow, Mica, and Magic missiles; and Sky Sword I and II missiles.

Military Mobilization

The ROC defense strategy calls for maintaining a minimum force in peacetime and mobilizing a large number of troops in the event of war. In peacetime, the primary mobilization missions are to test both the preparedness of reservists for instant action and the capabilities of industries supplying military equipment to expand production.

121

At present, registered reservists in the ROC number about 3 million, or more than 15 percent of the general population. After being discharged from active duty, all reservists must report to their local military reserve units, which are sub-units of the Armed Forces Reserve Command. Reservists are organized into different units according to their military occupational specialty 軍職專長 (MOS).

Since a prolonged mobilization recall might adversely affect both the livelihood of a reservist and the overall economic development of the country, annual reservist training is usually conducted through recalls. An MOS refresher training course is conducted, and each reservist is notified of his unit's combat mission and relative location.

The purpose of muster calls is two-fold: to maintain readiness by practicing immediate report on call-up and to keep data on reservists current. Methods for streamlining call-up procedures and maximizing public convenience are periodically reviewed.

Military Education

Military education includes preparatory education, fundamental education, in-service education, and advanced education. After completing fundamental education, a career officer must receive short-term specialized training at a number of military-branch schools, such as the infantry, armor, and artillery branch schools of the Army.

Candidates for colonel (captain) or major general 少將 (rear admiral) must complete advanced military education at National Defense University 國防大學.

National Defense University, formerly the Armed Forces University, was integrated with the Chung-cheng Institute of Science and Technology, the National Defense Medical College, and the National Defense Management School on May 8, 2000.

The professional track is for specialized military personnel—including medical personnel, engineers, and technicians—at various specialized military schools, such as Fu Hsing Kang College and the National Defense Medical College.

Military Academies

The Chinese Military Academy 陸軍軍官學校 (CMA) offers electrical engineering, civil engineering, information, physics, chemistry, and management courses. All students must complete 128 credits worth of studies in four years.

Immediately following graduation, the young lieutenants receive further training in a branch specialty, such as infantry, armor, artillery (missiles), engineering, transportation, communications (electronics), chemistry, or military police.

The Chinese Naval Academy 海軍軍官學校 (CNA) offers cadets courses such as marine science, applied science, marine engineering, electrical engineering, and information management. All students must complete 128 credits worth of studies in four years. They also must serve an apprenticeship aboard a ship.

Just prior to graduation, all CNA cadets will sail abroad in the "Fleet of Friendship" 敦睦艦隊 for two months of shipboard training. In recent years, the "Fleet of Friendship" has sailed to the Middle East and South Africa. During the long voyage, future naval officers are given a chance to practice combat skills, tactics, and navigation.

The Chinese Air Force Academy 空軍軍官學校 (CAFA) trains pilots for jet fighters and other combat and transport aircraft. Cadets learn aeronautics, navigation, avionics, aviation management, and related skills in a program that lasts four years. They participate in supervised flight operations during their second year. At the beginning of their junior year, cadets are divided into five sections to receive either specialized training in flight skills, aviation equipment, electronic communication, air defense, or air control.

Fu Hsing Kang College 政治作戰學校 (FHKC), located in the Peitou 北投 district of Taipei, was established in 1951 to train political warfare officers for the Armed Forces. There are three levels of education at FHKC: basic, advanced, and graduate. The college has five departments and three graduate schools offering master's and doctoral degree programs.

The National Defense Medical College 國防醫學院 (NDMC) trains military medical specialists, providing a basic college education plus medical training in such fields as dentistry, pharmacology, nursing, and public health. It also has 11 master's and doctoral programs. The Tri-Service General Hospital 三軍總醫院 is the main teaching hospital of the NDMC.

The Chung-cheng Institute of Science and Technology 中正理工學院 conducts research and development of weapon systems, maintains arms and equipment, and educates technical military officers. It has one doctoral program, six master's degree programs, and 11 undergraduate departments.

The National Defense Management School 國防管理學院 is responsible for educating the planning, decision-making, and management personnel of the Armed Forces. It has a Graduate School of Information Management 資訊管理所, a Graduate School of Law 法律研究所, and departments of accounting, statistics, business management, information management, and law.

The Chung-cheng Armed Forces Preparatory School 中正國防幹部預備學校, founded in 1976, provides senior high school education to students who wish to continue in one of the three service academies or FHKC following graduation. It combines a regular senior high school education with basic military training through innovative teaching methods.

The ROC Armed Forces also operate a number of branch schools, such as the Infantry 陸軍步兵學校, Armor 陸軍裝甲兵學校, and Artillery 陸軍炮兵學校 branch schools of the Army, and specialized schools, such as the Air Technical School 空軍技術學校 and the Navy Technical School 海軍技術學校.

Defense R&D

Research and development of national defense technology is crucial to national defense modernization. The ROC's industrial sector has made considerable progress over the past decade, especially in the areas of aviation, ship-building, electronics, information, machinery, chemical industry, and systems integration. The MND has provided long-term assistance to public and private enterprises for operations and development. In addition, the MND has used the Industrial Cooperation Program Credit to demand that contract companies invest in production, purchase facilities, transfer advanced technology, and perform R&D within Taiwan. Through this, both key advanced technology and foreign funds have been introduced from other countries to enhance industrial upgrading and establish long-term global economic cooperation. In addition, it has also helped develop a more sophisticated production base, which has helped the defense industry to become self-sufficient.

The MND issued the Defense Science and Technology Development Plan 國防科技發展方案 to strengthen cooperation between the academic and industrial sectors. It also set up the Executive Committee for the Development of Defense Science and Technology 國防科技發展推行委員會 (ECDDST) in collaboration with several other cabinet-level institutions, such as the National Science Council 國家科學委員會 and the Ministry of Economic Affairs 經濟部. With its two subdivisions, the Academic Cooperation Group 學術合作小組 and the Industrial Cooperation Group 工業合作小組, the ECDDST uses academic resources for defense technology research and employs the industrial sector to develop and manufacture weapons and equipment.

Chungshan Institute of Science and Technology

As the ROC's leading institution for the research, design, and development of defense technology, the Chungshan Institute of Science and Technology 中山科學研究院 (CSIST) employs approximately 4,000 scientists and more than 5,000 technicians.

Headquartered at Lungtan 龍潭 in Taoyuan County 桃園縣, the CSIST has facilities covering nearly 4,000 acres in various locations around Taiwan. It is divided into six major research divisions: aeronautics and missiles, rockets, electronics, information and communications, materials, and chemistry. The CSIST also has three centers for systems development, systems maintenance, and systems production. Each research division or research center has a director in charge of the R&D, and all planning units have project chairmen responsible for R&D program management and system integration. The CSIST jointly conducts R&D on weapon systems with some manufacturing units of the Combined Services Force, academic institutions, and public and civilian industries.

A number of weapon systems have already been domestically designed, tested, and produced by the CSIST and deployed by the three armed services. These include the Kung-feng 6A multiple rocket launcher system, the Tien-kung I and Tien-kung II surface-to-air missile systems, the Hsiung-feng I and Hsiung-feng II surface-to-surface naval missile systems, the Tien-chien I and Tien-chien II air-to-air missiles, the Tsu Chiang AT-3 advanced jet trainer attack aircraft, and the Ching-kuo indigenous defense fighter aircraft (IDF).

Important R&D achievements made between July 2000 and June 2001 include advances in electronic warfare systems and conventional information warfare. Successful test firings have been done on both the Thunder-2000 multiple-launch rocket system and the vehicle-carried Sky Sword-1 air defense missile. Both the PRC-37A man-carried and vehicle-carried frequency-hopping communications equipment have entered the strategic appliance test stage, as have the VHF/UHF frequency-hopping communications network, the IR reconnaissance system, and frequency-hopping communications countermeasures. A protection system on the national defense information network has been established. Research is also being done on key radar technology to integrate existing radar facilities with long-range 3D air defense warning radar. The Unmanned Aerial Vehicle (UAV) system, whose uses include day-or-night surveillance and reconnaissance, real-time data transmission, automatic flying control, and geostationary navigation, is also being researched.

Related Website
Ministry of National Defense: *http://www.mnd.gov.tw*

9
Foreign Relations

President Chen
Shui-bian wel-
comes Nicara-
guan President
Arnoldo Aleman
Lacayo at the
Hsinchu County
Government.
(Courtesy of the Office
of the President)

The Republic of China (ROC) is a sovereign state with a population of 23 million and a defined territory consisting of the islands of Taiwan, Penghu, Kinmen, Matsu, and several islets. Since the establishment of the People's Republic of China (PRC) in 1949, the two sides of the Taiwan Strait have been governed separately, with neither subject to the other's rule.

The Republic of China maintains its own national defense and conducts its own independent foreign policy, including full diplomatic relations with nearly 30 countries and substantive ties with more than 140 others. Its democratically elected government represents the 23 million people living in Taiwan, and no other government in the world can legitimately claim to represent them or speak on their behalf.

The continuing consolidation of Taiwan's democracy further reinforces the fact that recognition of the international and legal status of Taiwan is entirely in accord with the principles, obligations and values professed in the United Nations Charter. This fundamental truth is buttressed by Taiwanese public opinion, which overwhelmingly supports Taiwan's participation in international organizations. In response to this democratic aspiration, the government will resolutely encourage the participation of individuals and NGOs of the ROC in international forums and UN-sponsored activities.

The international community has steadily increased its recognition of the achievements of Taiwan in democracy, directly benefiting the ROC's diplomacy. For example, President Chen Shui-bian 陳水扁 was awarded the 2001 Prize for Freedom by Liberal International. In addition, President Chen's stopovers in the United States on his second trip to Latin America represented a significant improvement in the treatment accorded to the ROC's highest elected official.

The tragic terrorist attacks of September 11, 2001, and the ensuing conflict in Afghanistan have had a massive impact on the international system; however, the values of democracy and international cooperation have only been strengthened. These events have also highlighted the rapid acceleration of interdependence, where what takes place in one country affects the whole world. As a result, foreign relations in the post-cold war period have been increasingly characterized by the development of multilateral institutions dedicated to economic development, peace and security, democracy and human rights.

Clearly, exclusion of any single nation from these mechanisms severely compromises their integrity and effectiveness. Taiwan, one of the world's largest economies and trading nations, could help deal much more effectively with issues ranging from the provision of international aid to the conservation of endangered species, if it were a signatory to relevant international conventions and were allowed to attend multilateral forums within the United Nations and other frameworks.

People's Diplomacy

Since taking office, the Chen administration has placed particular emphasis on "people's diplomacy." This concept includes, first, the engagement of the whole of the Taiwanese people with the peoples of other countries in transnational or intersocietal networks, not merely interstate ones. Second, it implies the democratization of foreign policy making, including the principles of accountability and transparency, bringing the public more fully into the process.

The Ministry of Foreign Affairs (MOFA) has launched a series of measures to put these principles into practice. Beginning in September 2000, the MOFA's Foreign Affairs Institute has held seminars for the public and civil society leaders to build their capacity in international affairs through training in topics such as cross-strait relations, international law and politics, negotiation, and the international role of non-governmental organizations. In the second year of the alternative military service program (see Chapter 8), 37 young men were sent to work in technical missions overseas; at the conclusion of their training in October 2001, President Chen called for a "volunteer Taiwan" where more and more Taiwanese young people participate in overseas development work.

In October 2000, the NGO Affairs Committee was established as a new standing body within MOFA to assist Taiwan's NGOs in their engagement of international NGO activities. By the end of November 2001, it had already approved 387 grant applications from Taiwan's NGOs to hold international events, meetings, and conferences in Taiwan or to travel to participate in such activities overseas; in addition, when necessary, it facilitated visa processing for these activities. It also assumed responsibility for coordinating NGO participation in humanitarian assistance projects, such as the relief efforts following earthquakes in El Salvador and India.

In the area of capacity-building, the Committee sponsored a number of training camps and internships for NGO workers and overseas volunteers. In 2001, the Committee successfully encouraged Taiwanese participation in activities in celebration of the UN International Year of Volunteers. In fact, Taiwanese non-governmental organizations have become members of over 1,000 international NGOs in a wide variety of fields. These undertakings are not only further mobilizing the prodigious resources of Taiwan's civil society in facing global challenges, but also helping further consolidate Taiwan's democracy.

Human rights have also become a new focal point for ROC diplomacy. As the universal values of human rights have also become core national values, it is only natural that they be expressed in the nation's foreign policy. President Chen has committed the government to move towards full integration of Taiwan in the international human rights system spearheaded by the United Nations. As a crucial first step, in April 2001 the two most important international human rights treaties were sent to the Legislative Yuan for ratification.

ROC Membership in International Non-governmental Organizations	
Nature of Organization	*Number*
Science and Technology	100
Medicine and Hygiene	227
Agriculture, Forestry, Fisheries and Animal Husbandry	44
Religion	61
Charity and Social Welfare	47
Education	28
Journalism	3
Culture and Arts	34
Law and Police Administration	15
Labor	81
Transportation and Tourism	21
Leisure and Recreation	26
Women, Family, and Youth	8
Business, Finance, and Economics	68
Engineering	16
Industrial Technology	31
Electronics and Mechanical Science	11
Mining and Energy	18
R&D and Management	73
Wildlife Conservation and Environmental Protection	25
Sports	100
Total	1037

Multilateral Relations

Increasing global interdependence renders the traditional concept of national sovereignty ever more abstract. Since Taiwan, like all other countries, is intimately affected by "globalization," it has a legitimate right to actively participate in multilateral mechanisms to address relevant issues.

Taiwan has continued to make progress in obtaining membership in international organizations. It is now a member of 17 intergovernmental organizations, including the World Trade Organization (WTO), Asia Pacific Economic Cooperation (APEC), the Asian Development Bank (ADB), and the Governmental Advisory Committee of the Internet Cooperation for Assigned Names and Numbers (ICANN).

The United Nations

Because the ROC is not a member of the UN, and because the PRC capitalizes on its position in the UN to attempt to choke Taiwan's diplomatic space, the 23 million people of Taiwan have neither representation nor participation in the international decision-making process in many fields. Moreover, they are even hindered from efforts to participate in international humanitarian assistance and NGO activities.

The government began actively promoting Taiwan's UN membership bid in 1993. The campaign is carried out through proposals made by many of the ROC's diplomatic allies at the UN General Assembly, urging it to "examine the exceptional international situation pertaining to the Republic of China on Taiwan, to ensure that the fundamental right of its 23 million people to participate in the work and activities of the UN is fully respected."

In 2001, the request was formally submitted by ten member states, four of which (The Gambia, Grenada, Nicaragua, and Tuvalu) also held a joint press conference in August with the ROC's New York representative to explain their stance. However, once again it met resistance at the UN General Assembly's General Committee and failed to be included in the UN agenda for discussion. Due to the September 11 terrorist attacks, the General Debate was postponed until November, and each country's time to speak was also reduced. Nevertheless, 26 allied countries made statements in support of Taiwan's participation in the UN, and the Czech Republic noted the need to maintain universality. In addition, during the UN Special Session on HIV/AIDS in June, eight countries noted the role and contributions of the ROC in the fight against the disease. Nicaragua's foreign minister Francisco Xavier Aguirre Sacasa also took the floor at the special General Assembly debate on terrorism on October 1 to plead for Taiwan's UN membership, arguing that "like all the citizens of the world, its 22 million inhabitants suffer the effects of terrorism and should, in the United Nations, add their own voice."

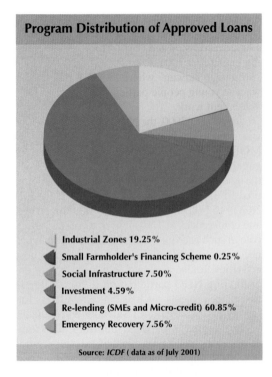

Program Distribution of Approved Loans

- Industrial Zones 19.25%
- Small Farmholder's Financing Scheme 0.25%
- Social Infrastructure 7.50%
- Investment 4.59%
- Re-lending (SMEs and Micro-credit) 60.85%
- Emergency Recovery 7.56%

Source: *ICDF* (data as of July 2001)

The World Trade Organization

Taiwan has long sought to expand its role in international economic organizations, and in 1990 applied for membership of the General Agreement on Tariffs and Trade (GATT) under the name of "Separate Customs Territory of Taiwan, Penghu, Kinmen and Matsu," which application was transferred to the WTO when it was created in 1995. After conducting bilateral negotiations with 30 member countries, this vital goal was finally achieved at the WTO summit in Qatar. On November 11, 2001, the trade ministers unanimously approved Taiwan's membership bid, and the formal accession protocols were signed the following day. With swift ratification by the Legislative Yuan on November 16, formal membership took effect on January 1, 2002.

Following the successful entry, trade ministers of several ROC allies, the United States, the EU, and other important members issued congratulatory remarks, and then Minister of

Economic Affairs Lin Hsin-yi 林信義 stated, "As a new member with a very free and open trade regime, we will honor our commitments by following the rules and principles of WTO." The ROC government looks forward to active participation in the Qatar Round of trade talks, where it hopes to make a valuable contribution in accordance with its status as a developed trading country.

The World Health Organization

In 1997, based on humanitarian concerns and on the fact that diseases know no borders, Taiwan also began a bid for observer status at the WHO. Its allies have repeatedly submitted proposals to the annual meetings of the World Health Assembly (WHA) urging the international community to respect the health rights of Taiwan's 23 million people by inviting Taiwan to join the WHO. Such a move would on the one hand enable Taiwan to benefit from participating in WHO activities, and on the other allow the WHO to benefit from Taiwan's resources and experience in promoting public sanitation and combating infectious diseases.

In addition, Taiwan also actively participated in bilateral and multilateral international medical cooperation programs. For example, the ROC government donated 5 million condoms in January 2001 to help implement an anti-AIDS program in Liberia promoted by the WHO's Liberia office. In November, the ROC signed an agreement with CARE France to donate a total of US$1.02 million over a three-year period to support an AIDS prevention program in Chad.

Asia Pacific Economic Cooperation

At the regional level, the ROC joined APEC in the name of "Chinese Taipei" in 1991. Taiwan has played an active role in the 21-member economic forum, taking charge of several working groups in recent years. Currently, Taiwan is the international coordinator of the Education Network (EDNET) of the Human Resources Working Group. In 2001, Taiwan actively participated in a wide range of APEC meetings. CEPD Chairman Chen Po-chih 陳博志 attended the "High Level Meeting on Human Capacity Building" in Beijing in May; Minister of Economic Affairs Lin Hsin-yi attended the trade ministers meeting in Shanghai in June; Minister of Finance Yen Ching-chang 顏慶章 attended the finance ministers meeting in Suzhou in September, and, in the same month, Council of Labor Affairs Chairwoman Chen Chu 陳菊 attended the 4th Human Resources Ministerial Meeting in Kumamoto, Japan.

At the APEC ministerial meeting in Shanghai in October 2001, Taiwan was represented by CEPD Chairman Chen Po-chih and Minister of Economic Affairs Lin Hsin-yi. APEC Ministers reiterated strong support for Taiwan's accession to the WTO and welcomed the participation of Taiwan in the APEC Business Travel Card Scheme. Furthermore, Taiwan's contributions in hosting the symposium "Guidelines of Best Practices for Entrepreneurship and Start-up Companies" as well as the phase I work on the project "Transforming the Digital Divide into a Digital Opportunity" were endorsed by the ministers. Unfortunately, due to inhospitable treatment by the host government, which failed to follow established APEC precedents, Taiwan was not able to send a representative to the Economic Leaders' Meeting.

Bilateralism

The ROC maintains full diplomatic relations with 28 countries. On the basis of pragmatic diplomacy and mutual interest, Taiwan continues to endeavor to establish diplomatic ties or substantially enhance relations with the rest of the world's countries, maintaining 95 representative offices in the capitals and major cities of 62 countries. Although these offices carry various names, such as "Taipei Representative Office," "Taipei Economic and Cultural Office," or "Trade Mission of the Republic of China," they perform most of the functions of embassies and consulates general.

Reciprocally, 45 countries that do not have formal diplomatic relations with Taiwan have established 53 representative offices or visa

issuing centers in Taiwan. (for a complete list of ROC embassies and representative offices abroad and foreign embassies and offices in the ROC, see appendices V and VI.)

Asia and the Pacific

The ROC is an East Asian country, strategically located in the West Pacific. Therefore, the security and prosperity of Taiwan are intimately related to the peace and stability in the Asia-Pacific, and in turn they serve the interests of all the nations in the region.

The MOFA's Department of East Asia and the Pacific is responsible for the area from Japan and Korea in the north to Australia and New Zealand in the south, and from India in the west to the islands of the Central and South Pacific in the east, except for the People's Republic of China. At present, the ROC maintains diplomatic relations with and embassies to the Republic of Marshall Islands, the Republic of Nauru, the Republic of Palau, the Solomon Islands, and Tuvalu. In addition, Taiwan has signed communiqués of mutual recognition with Fiji, Papua New Guinea, and the Republic of Vanuatu and conducts substantive relations with the rest of the countries of the region through 14 representative offices and eight branch offices.

Taiwan works to promote regional integration in a number of venues. The most important is APEC, of which Taiwan is a full member (see the "Multilateral Relations" section). Taiwan is also a productive member of the Asian Development Bank, contributing both financial support and its own experience to the balanced development of the region. In the security field, Taiwan is active in numerous "track two" regional dialogue processes. Although Taiwan is not yet a full member of the most prominent of these efforts, the Council for Security Cooperation in the Asia-Pacific (CSCAP), Taiwanese experts participate constructively in their individual capacities.

Northeast Asia

Northeast Asia, including Japan and the Korean Peninsula, is a strategic fulcrum, and Taiwan holds a key location at the southern end of this region. It has had close ties with Japan and Korea throughout history, including trade, culture, technical cooperation and professional exchanges. It is of vital importance to enhance Taiwan's security dialogue and regional cooperation with Northeast Asian countries to strengthen the security and prosperity of all of Asia.

Japan is Taiwan's second largest trading partner, and it maintains unofficial substantive relations with Taiwan under the terms of the 1972 Japan-China Joint Communiqué. Taiwan has welcomed Japan's unwillingness to bend that framework in the PRC's favor, for example refusing to enunciate its opposition to Taiwan's entry into international organizations. In the security realm, Japan passed legislation in 1999 to put the revised US-Japan Defense Guidelines into effect. The PRC repeatedly asked Japan to exclude Taiwan from a chapter on cooperation in cases of "situations in areas surrounding Japan"; however, Japan insisted on the need for flexibility in this regard. Furthermore, many members of Japan's Diet have expressed support for Taiwan.

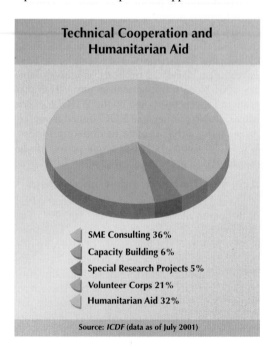

Technical Cooperation and Humanitarian Aid

- SME Consulting 36%
- Capacity Building 6%
- Special Research Projects 5%
- Volunteer Corps 21%
- Humanitarian Aid 32%

Source: *ICDF* (data as of July 2001)

The parliamentary friendship association has expanded to 212 members, and an appeal by a cross-party group of 64 MPs helped former President Lee Teng-hui 李登輝 obtain a visa for his first visit to Japan in March 2001.

There has been an increase in contacts and exchanges between Taiwan and South Korea. In November 2000, the Korea-Taiwan Economic Cooperative Council, a grouping of business leaders, met for the first time since formal ties were broken off and discussed the restoration of full air links, as well as cooperation on economic exchanges with North Korea. Former Korean President Kim Young Sam visited Taipei in July 2001 and held meetings with President Chen and other officials.

Southeast Asia

Historic, cultural, and geographic factors; the presence of strong overseas Chinese communities; and complementary economic conditions all contribute to close ties between Taiwan and Southeast Asia. The ROC has seven representative offices in Brunei, Indonesia, Malaysia, the Philippines, Singapore, Thailand, and Vietnam.

In the 1990s, Taiwan promoted a "go south" policy of investment in Southeast Asia. To enhance economic ties and substantive mutual interests with the region, Taiwan has signed agreements on the protection of mutual investment, avoidance of double taxation, customs cooperation, agricultural cooperation, technical cooperation, tourism cooperation, and aviation rights with most of the nations of Southeast Asia. In addition, since the region is the major source of foreign workers in Taiwan (see Chapter 20, Labor), Taiwan has signed labor agreements with relevant countries. In January 2001, the Philippines became the second country after Vietnam to sign a direct labor employment agreement with Taiwan, allowing Taiwanese employers to hire Filipino workers without intermediary brokers, and in July the sixth meeting of the ROC-Thailand joint labor committee was held in Taipei.

The Association of Southeast Asian Nations (ASEAN) has expanded its membership to ten countries and took concrete steps to create an ASEAN Free Trade Area. Therefore, Taiwan is seeking closer contacts with the grouping, building on its strong bilateral relations with most of the members of ASEAN, as well as its collective contacts in APEC and other venues. The eventual goal is to become an ASEAN dialogue partner and a member of the ASEAN Regional Forum political dialogue.

South Asia

Taiwan's diplomatic efforts in this region focus on India, which hosts the ROC's only representative office in South Asia. Since the mutual establishment of representative offices in 1995, bilateral trade has more than trebled, and now exceeds US$1.2 billion per year. Taiwanese investment in and tourists to this area have also been increasing. Taiwan and India have signed a memorandum of understanding on civil aviation and initialed an Agreement on Promotion and Protection of Mutual Investments. Taiwan will continue to strengthen its trade relations with India and promote the signing of the Agreement on the Avoidance of Double Taxation, the Agreement on Customs Deposits for Temporary Admission of Goods. A relief effort following the Gujarat earthquake in January 2001 was the first major Taiwanese humanitarian activity in the region, and the ROC will try to increase such assistance as needed in the future.

Oceania

Oceania consists of the continent of Australia and the island states of the South Pacific. Except for Australia and New Zealand, physical constraints such as great distances and fragile climates have hindered economic development. Therefore, the ROC has signed technical cooperation agreements with Fiji, Nauru, and the Solomon Islands. In addition, given the importance of fisheries to these countries' economies and the extent of Taiwanese fishing activity in the region, Taiwan has signed a number of fisheries agreements with these countries.

Substantive relations with Australia and New Zealand are historically strong. They have been

further reinforced in recent years by economic and people-to-people contacts, of which the most prominent are the annual ROC-Australia and ROC-New Zealand Bilateral Economic Consultations, which were both held in May 2001. In addition, the 16th joint meeting of ROC-Australia Business Council and the Australia-Taiwan Business Council in Taipei and the 10th joint meeting of ROC-New Zealand Business Council and the New Zealand-Taiwan Business Council were both held in Taipei in September. Also in 2001, a "Memorandum on Agriculture and Agribusiness" was signed with Australia.

The 16 countries in the region comprise the membership of the Pacific Islands Forum (PIF). Following its annual summit of heads of government, dialogue partners from outside the region are invited to participate in the "post-Forum dialogue." In 1992, the PIF passed a resolution to allow "Taiwan/the Republic of China" to participate in the "post-Forum dialogue." Since then, Taiwan has sent a delegation each year, including the one after the 2001 Forum held in Nauru in August. Through the Forum, Taiwan provides regional programs of economic and technological assistance and educational training, further strengthening its relations with South Pacific nations.

West Asia

West Asia extends from Pakistan in the east to Turkey in the west, and from Russia in the north to the Arabian Peninsula in the south. It includes the 12 nations of the Commonwealth of Independent States (CIS), 17 nations in the Middle East, and Palestine.

Based on economic exchanges and technical cooperation as well as religious, academic and cultural exchanges, the bilateral relations between Taiwan and West Asia have developed steadily. Taiwan has representative offices or economic and cultural offices in 10 West Asian countries, including Bahrain, Belarus, Israel, Jordan, Kuwait, Oman, Russia, Saudi Arabia, Turkey, and the United Arab Emirates. Israel, Jordan, Oman, Russia, Saudi Arabia, and Turkey also have trade offices in Taiwan.

Taiwan also closely interacts with a number of significant regional organizations in West Asia. The Taipei Economic and Trade Mission in Minsk remains in close contact with the Executive Secretariat of the CIS located in that city. Ivan Korotchenya, its First Deputy Executive Secretary, visited Taiwan in 1999. The primary intergovernmental organization of the Muslim world is the Organization of the Islamic Conference (OIC). Taiwan plans to establish a cooperative relationship with the OIC's Islamic Development Bank following the pattern of its cooperation with the European Bank for Reconstruction and Development. In addition, the Muslim World League (MWL), the non-governmental leader of Muslim organizations worldwide, has developed regular exchanges with Taiwan. Following the visit of its Secretary General to Taiwan in June 2000, the MWL participated in the Islamic exhibition at the Museum of World Religions in Taipei, which opened in November 2001, including a display of donated Islamic religious artifacts.

During the 17th Economic Cooperation Meeting between the ROC and Saudi Arabia, held in Taipei in October 2000, the two countries signed a memorandum of understanding on the promotion and protection of investment, and the ROC and Saudi Chambers of Commerce also signed an agreement. Chao Kang 趙鋼, Director-General of the National Fire Administration, visited Moscow in late December 2000 to participate in the tenth anniversary of the Russian Ministry for Civil Defense, Emergencies and Elimination of Consequences of Natural Disasters. He also signed a memorandum of understanding with Russia's Assistance Foundation, a key inter-regional charitable public foundation, regarding rescue work and the consequences of natural disasters. Likewise, in October 2001 the Science and Technology Information Center of the National Science Council signed a cooperation agreement with its Russian counterpart for cooperation on seminars, exchanges, and joint research programs.

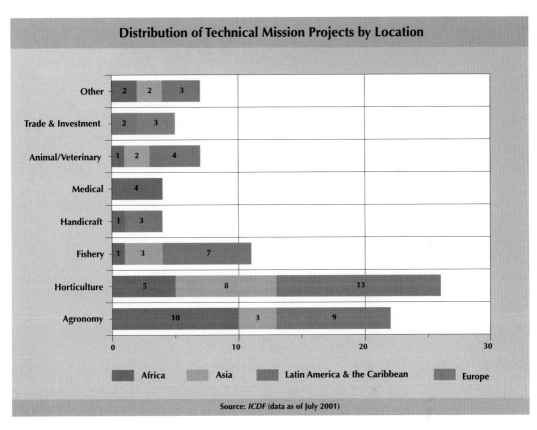

Distribution of Technical Mission Projects by Location

	Africa	Asia	Latin America & the Caribbean	Europe
Other	2	2	3	
Trade & Investment	2	3		
Animal/Veterinary	1	2	4	
Medical	4			
Handicraft	1	3		
Fishery	1	3	7	
Horticulture	5	8	13	
Agronomy	10	3	9	

Source: *ICDF* (data as of July 2001)

Africa

Africa's political scene has recently seen many changes. Over half of the continent's countries have carried out multiparty presidential and parliamentary elections and embraced democratization and the rule of law. Yet 38 out of the 53 nations of Africa are still heavily indebted and mired in poverty, and the spread of AIDS is severely impacting economic development and creating serious social problems in many African countries. In May 2001, the African Union (AU) was founded to speed up regional integration, promote regional economic growth, raise African standards of living, and consolidate democratic achievements. The AU, which replaces the Organization of African Unity, will establish a council, a pan-African parliament, a central bank, and a court of justice patterned on the institutions of the European Union.

Eight African countries maintain official diplomatic relations with Taiwan: Burkina Faso, Chad, The Gambia, Liberia, Malawi, São Tomé and Principe, Senegal, and Swaziland. Taiwan has embassies in all of these countries, and they also maintain embassies in Taiwan. Furthermore, Taiwan has set up representative offices or liaison offices in Cote d'Ivoire, Mauritius, Nigeria, and South Africa, of which Nigeria and South Africa have also established trade and liaison offices in Taipei.

The ROC's African allies have long supported Taiwan's participation in international organizations. In October 2001, Senegal hosted an international seminar on Africa's stance

regarding Taiwan's participation in the United Nations. The event, organized by the Dakar regional center of the Center for Diplomatic and Strategic Studies (CEDS), gathered participants not only from countries that have diplomatic relations with Taiwan but also from the rest of the region. Senegalese President Abdoulaye Wade hosted the opening ceremony, and Deputy Minister of Foreign Affairs Wu Tzu-dan 吳子丹 led the delegation of Taiwanese participants.

Taiwan's successful political and economic development is serving as a role model for friendly countries in Africa. In 2001, Taiwan budgeted NT$526.9 million to strengthen its technical and medical cooperation with African countries. Currently there are 14 technical cooperation missions comprising 109 experts and other technical personnel working in Africa, including 8 agricultural technical missions, 4 medical missions, 1 handicraft mission, and 1 vocational training advisory mission. These missions help revitalize agricultural production and improve medical services in allied countries, and they also help realize Taiwan's ideal of active humanitarian diplomacy.

Taiwan NGOs have also become more involved in humanitarian aid to Africa. The Taiwan Root Medical Peace Corps 臺灣路竹會醫療服務團 carried out a mission to Liberia in January 2001, including distributing condoms to help with AIDS prevention. The Buddha's Light International Association 國際佛光會 donated wheel chairs and medicines to Mauritius, Nigeria, and Swaziland in 2001.

High-level visits to Africa consolidate relations, increase understanding of the scope and results of cooperation projects, and promote Taiwan's democratic achievements. President Chen Shui-bian made a landmark visit to the Gambia, Burkina Faso and Chad, the first trip by an ROC president to West Africa, in August 2000. In August 2001, Control Yuan President Frederick Chien 錢復 represented President Chen to attend the inauguration of the President of Chad, Idriss Deby. In the same month, Deputy Foreign Minister Wu Tzu-dan, also as President

Chen's special envoy, attended the inauguration of Fradique de Menezes as President of São Tomé and Principe.

Europe

Taiwan has always maintained close relations with the nations of Western Europe, including commercial, cultural, technological, educational, and tourism exchanges. Taiwan warmly welcomed the fall of the Berlin Wall and the restoration of democracy in the countries of the former Warsaw Pact, and in recent years it has energetically extended its hand of friendship eastward to encompass Central Europe, the Balkan Peninsula, and the Baltic States (other states of the former Soviet Union are discussed under "West Asia"). Taiwan's experiences in political and social reconstruction have proven very valuable for these countries.

Relations with Europe are conducted both bilaterally and with European institutions, especially the European Union (EU). The ROC has an embassy to the Holy See and representative offices in the capitals of each of the 15 EU members and in the Czech Republic, Hungary, Latvia, Norway, Poland and Switzerland, as well as additional economic and cultural offices in Edinburgh, Geneva, Hamburg, and Munich. The Taipei Representative Office in Belgium is also in charge of EU affairs. In addition to the embassy of the Holy See, Austria, Belgium, the Czech Republic, Denmark, Finland, France, Germany, Great Britain, Hungary, Ireland, Italy, the Netherlands, Norway, Poland, Spain, Sweden, and Switzerland have established representative offices in Taipei. In July 2001, the European Commission published a report indicating its consideration of the establishment of a representative office in Taipei, which is expected by the end of 2002.

Interparliamentary exchanges have become an increasingly important feature of Taiwan-Europe relations. At present, 20 European nations and the European Parliament (EP) have established parliamentary groupings to promote ties with Taiwan. The EP in particular, with its

European Parliaments with "Friends of Taiwan" Groupings	
France	1984
Germany	1989
European Parliament	1991
Belgium	1993
Italy	1994
Czech Republic	1994
Spain	1995
Denmark	1995
Finland	1995
Hungary	1995
Switzerland	1995
Norway	1996
Great Britain	1997
Lithuania	1997
Estonia	1997
Sweden	1997
Latvia	1998
Poland	1998
Greece	1999
Macedonia	1999
Austria	2001

strong interest in human rights and democracy, has on several occasions adopted resolutions in favor of Taiwan. These resolutions have supported Taiwan's right to participate in international organizations and called on the EU member states and the European Commission to strengthen their relations with Taiwan, including the early establishment of a Commission representative office in Taipei.

Taiwan has signed over 100 agreements, protocols and memorandums with 22 European countries and the EU. In 2001, such agreements included the Agreement on Educational and Cultural Matters with the UK; double taxation exemption and tax evasion prevention agreements with the Netherlands and Sweden; and two conventions on cultural and scientific exchanges as well as guidelines for the conduct of international aviation accident investigations with France. The ROC government also welcomes European multilateral financial institutions to issue bonds in Taiwan to expand their sources of funds. To date, the European Bank for Reconstruction and Development, the Nordic Investment Bank, the European Investment Bank, and the Council of Europe Social Development Fund have done so.

In November 2001, First Lady Wu Shu-jen 吳淑珍 traveled to France and the Czech Republic. In Strasbourg, she addressed the European Parliament and received the Prize for Freedom on behalf of President Chen Shui-bian; in Prague, she met with Czech President Vaclav Havel and his wife.

In order to help Taiwan's businessmen understand the investment environment, economic and trade conditions, and potential for tourism in Eastern and Southern Europe, MOFA and the Ministry of Economic Affairs held the "Eurogate 2001—New European Products and Trade Fair" at the Taipei World Trade Center in September. Companies from Eastern Europe and the Baltic States exhibited their products at the show.

North America

The United States

The United States plays a special role in Taiwan's foreign policy, both as Taiwan's largest trading partner and in its historical role of maintaining peace and stability in the Asia-Pacific. In addition, person-to-person ties are strong, primarily due to the large community of Taiwanese-Americans, and the two countries share a wide range of political and cultural values.

The democratic development of Taiwan has earned the affirmation of the American people. The US government has repeatedly stressed Taiwan's democratic achievements and urged the PRC to resume cross-strait dialogue. Democratic links between Taiwan and the US are consolidated through extensive mutual exchanges among legislators, local governments, and political parties. Twenty-one US states have established representative offices in Taipei to promote commercial and cultural ties, and 140 US counties and cities have established sister city relationships with local governments in Taiwan. Moreover, Taiwanese contacts and exchanges

with civil society in the US, including the religious community, labor unions and NGOs, are increasing.

Immediately following the tragic terrorist attacks of September 11 which took the lives of thousands of Americans and hundreds of citizens of other countries, including 8 ROC citizens, President Chen and the government immediately made statements of profound condolences to the victims and to the American people, as well as clear condemnations of terrorism in all its forms, and ROC flags were flown at half-mast for two days. Taiwan offered its full support for the global mobilization against terrorism, and has indicated its willingness to play a role in related humanitarian assistance efforts. In November, Control Yuan President Frederick Chien, as President Chen's special envoy, visited New York and Washington to convey a message of humanitarian concern to the American people and to make a US$1 million contribution for the bereaved families of policemen and firefighters killed at the World Trade Center.

The bilateral trade volume between Taiwan and the US in 2000 was US$59.9 billion, making Taiwan the seventh largest importer of US products and its eighth largest trading partner overall. The US was the second largest recipient of Taiwan's investment in 2000, as the Ministry of Economic Affairs approved 801 investment cases towards the US worth US$860 million, a jump of 86 percent from the previous year. This brought Taiwan's officially approved accumulative investment in the US to US$5.43 billion.

Substantive relations are currently conducted under the framework of the 1979 *Taiwan Relations Act*, the 1982 "six assurances," and the 1994 Taiwan Policy Review. In 2001, high-level visits between the two countries continued apace, and the restrictions on such visits were further relaxed in 2001. On President Chen Shui-bian's transit stopovers in New York and Houston in May and June, he met many significant people, including almost thirty members of Congress, New York Mayor Rudolph Giuliani, and Houston Mayor Lee Brown. Expanding on the existing

principles of "safety, comfort and convenience," the US government for the first time also treated President Chen with "respect and goodwill."

The *Taiwan Relations Act* obligates the US to "make available to Taiwan such defense articles and defense services in such quantity as may be necessary to enable Taiwan to maintain a sufficient self-defense capability." To this end, in April 2001 President Bush agreed to sell Taiwan four Kidd-class guided-missile destroyers, eight diesel-powered submarines, and a dozen P-3C Orion anti-submarine aircraft. President Bush also exhibited his resolve to abide by the *Taiwan Relations Act*, stating that the US will "help Taiwan defend herself."

The Taiwan Policy Review also mandates the US to "support Taiwan's membership in international organizations accepting non-states as members and look for ways to have Taiwan's voice heard in organizations of states where Taiwan's membership is not possible." In line with this objective, the US has supported Taiwan's membership in international organizations more actively. Secretary of Health and Human Services Tommy Thompson announced US support for Taiwan's membership in the World Health Organization (WHO) while in Geneva for the World Health Assembly (WHA) in mid-May. This followed steadily increasing calls for such support from the US Congress, culminating in the passage into law of Resolution H.R.428 mandating the State Department to take effective action to achieve observer status for Taiwan in the WHO. At the WTO summit in Qatar in November, the US delegation was instrumental in ensuring that Taiwan's entry to that body proceeded smoothly.

Canada

The relationship between Taiwan and Canada has developed steadily based on long-standing economic, cultural and social ties, as well as shared values of democracy, peace, and human rights. Taiwan maintains a representative office in Ottawa and branch offices in Toronto and Vancouver. In addition to the Federal Government,

British Columbia, Alberta, and Quebec have set up trade representative offices in Taiwan. Parliamentary exchanges center on the Canada-Taiwan Parliamentary Friendship Group, and nine Federal MPs visited Taiwan in 2001.

Academic and cultural exchanges are also flourishing, with over 6,000 Taiwanese students studying in Canada. Important events in 2001 included the fifth international conference on Taiwan-Canada Relations in Taipei in March and a seminar on Taiwan's economy in Vancouver in April. A series of activities were held commemorating the one-hundredth anniversary of the death of Canadian missionary George Leslie Mackay, in recognition of his great contributions to Taiwan.

Latin America and the Caribbean

The region of Latin America and the Caribbean has long been a stronghold of Taiwan's diplomacy: among the region's 33 countries, the ROC maintains full diplomatic relations with 14. It has embassies in each of their capitals, along with ROC consulates general in Oriental City of Paraguay, Colon of Panama, and San Pedro Sula of Honduras, and 10 of these allies have embassies in Taipei. Taiwan also maintains substantive relations with many other countries in the region and has established representative offices in ten of these. In return, six of the ten have established trade offices in the ROC.

The "Third Wave" of democracy, of which Taiwan is an integral part, has also been felt quite strongly in Latin America and the Caribbean: since the late 1980s, military dictatorships have nearly disappeared from the region. Thus, mutual strengthening and consolidation of democratization has become a focus of Taiwan's relations with the region. In addition, Taiwan is increasing its participation in regional international organizations in Latin America and the Caribbean. In 2000, the ROC became an official observer of the System for the Integration of Central America (SICA), the first from outside the Western Hemisphere. Moreover, to enhance Taiwan's contribution to the development of the region, the International Cooperation and Development Fund 財團法人國際合作發展基金會 (ICDF) has established formal working relations with the Inter-American Development Bank and the Central American Bank for Reconstruction and Development.

A number of major events in the year 2001 indicated a continuing strengthening of ties between Taiwan and the region. The most prominent was the trip by President Chen Shui-bian, who led a large delegation to El Salvador to attend the third ROC-Central America Summit in May. At this event, he discussed major issues with heads of state or deputy heads of state of Costa Rica, El Salvador, Guatemala, Honduras, Nicaragua, Panama, Belize, and the Dominican Republic, and he followed the summit with official visits to Guatemala, Honduras, Panama, and Paraguay. In September, former Premier Chang Chun-hsiung 張俊雄 led another delegation to the Commonwealth of Dominica and Saint Vincent and the Grenadines.

The growth of parliamentary cooperation and exchanges has greatly accelerated in recent years. The ROC has become an observer with the Central American Parliament (PARLACEN) and the Forum of the Presidents of the Legislative Powers of Central America (FOPREL), and the latter organization traveled to Taipei for the first time in November 2000 to hold its 11th conference. Seven countries in the region have established parliamentary friendship associations with the ROC, including Guatemala (1991), the Dominican Republic (1991), Panama (1997), Brazil (1999), Argentina (1997), Peru (1999) and Chile (2000). Military exchanges in 2001 were highlighted by the three-ship Midshipmen Cruising and Training Squadron, which over three months sailed to and made port visits in Guatemala, St. Vincent, St. Kitts and Nevis, the Dominican Republic, Belize, and Honduras, in the longest journey ever made by the Navy.

In addition to long-term development projects, Taiwan also continued to provide timely aid and humanitarian relief assistance to our allies in the region. The largest such effort in 2001 followed

the pair of devastating earthquakes which hit El Salvador in January and February. The ROC immediately made donations for emergency aid and dispatched a 30-member rescue team to the disaster areas. Moreover, several Taiwanese NGOs also dispatched rescuers and paramedical workers or provided assistance in money and goods.

Development Cooperation and Humanitarian Aid

Taiwan's economic development was greatly assisted in the early stages by development aid from other countries, which to a great extent enabled the "Taiwan miracle." In addition, Taiwan's political democratization was also greatly enhanced by overseas support. Therefore, Taiwan has a responsibility to return this generosity to the international community by assisting other countries in their development.

In the year 2001, the ROC government's annual budget for foreign assistance equaled 0.15 percent of Taiwan's GDP, still well short of the target of 0.7 percent of GDP set by the UN for advanced economies and the average of 0.39 percent of GDP reached by OECD members in 2000. Despite domestic needs for major

infrastructure projects and new social welfare programs, the government hopes to raise this ratio in order to strengthen our feedback to the international community.

Through its international cooperation programs, Taiwan actively shares its successful development experience with friendly developing nations. In 1996, as these programs expanded, the ICDF, an independent foundation, was established to consolidate their planning and implementation. (For further information, please see the ICDF website at http://www.icdf.org.tw)

The programming of the ICDF includes investment and lending, technical cooperation, human resources development, as well as humanitarian assistance, and it aims to reduce poverty by stimulating economic activity, especially in the private sector. The ICDF has established long-term technical missions in partner countries; at the end of 2001, 40 such missions were operating in 34 countries, staffed by 284 technical specialists in agriculture, fisheries, horticulture, animal husbandry, handicrafts, medicine, transport, industry, mining, electricity production, printing, vocational training, trade and investment, etc.

In keeping with the new focus on "people's diplomacy," the role of volunteers in the ICDF's

international cooperation has been steadily expanding. As of December 2001, the ICDF had recruited and dispatched 74 volunteers to 16 different nations. In addition, the first group of young men reporting to be sent overseas in fulfillment of their obligations under the alternative military service scheme (see Chapter 8, National Defense) finished their training in November 2001, and were sent on two-year assignments to assist the ICDF's technical missions abroad. Among the 37 participants were 4 veterinarians, 3 doctors, 2 aquaculturists, 1 civil engineer, and many other master's degree holders. The number of participants is projected to double in 2002.

Taiwan has created a graduate program at National Pingtung University's Institute of Tropical Agriculture with full scholarships for agricultural technicians from allied nations. Thirty students have participated to date, and the existing master's degree program has been extended to include Ph.D. studies, with the first doctoral student attending in fall 2001. Similarly, an international MBA (IMBA) program has been established at National Chengchi University to train entrepreneurs from allied countries, and plans are under way to create a similar scholarship program in technology.

Taiwan continues to strengthen its international cooperation and foreign assistance efforts based on several basic principles. First, in order to further institutionalize such efforts, the new *International Cooperation and Development Law* 國際合作發展法 was passed by the Executive Yuan in May 2001 and submitted for legislative review; it will enable proper legislative supervision of foreign assistance budgets and evaluation processes, rendering foreign aid policy more accountable to public opinion. Second, a comprehensive approach that combines civil society, private sector and government resources will be developed. Third, a proper balance will be found between foreign assistance and economic and trade investment. Fourth, the scope of Taiwan's foreign assistance programs will be enlarged to actively share the entire "Taiwan Experience." This includes helping recipient countries to strengthen government agencies, upgrade human resources, develop SMEs, expand the middle class, and promote human rights and democracy.

Finally, collaboration with international organizations will be further emphasized. The ICDF has established working relations with the Inter-American Development Bank, the Central American Bank for Reconstruction and Development, the Asian Development Bank, the European Bank

Eight ROC allies reaffirm their support for Taiwan's UN bid and its access to the future "American Free Trade Area" during President Chen Shui-bian's "Friendship and Cooperation Trip for Mutual Prosperity" to Central America.
(Courtesy of the Office of the President)

for Reconstruction and Development, the West African Development Bank, and the World Trade Organization. This substantive interaction raises the effectiveness of Taiwan's aid programs and provides many mutual benefits both for these organizations and for Taiwan.

Humanitarian Assistance

In addition to long-term development programs, Taiwan is also very active in promoting humanitarian assistance. The heavy loss of life and property caused by the 921 earthquake in Taiwan in 1999 received worldwide attention and concern, for which the Taiwanese people are eternally grateful. This experience strengthened Taiwan's determination to care actively for the poor and the distressed.

Following the pair of earthquakes in January and February 2001 in El Salvador, the ROC government dispatched a 30-member rescue team and gave monetary and material assistance. Also in January, another massive earthquake struck the western Indian state of Gujarat. A public relief campaign called "Sending Love and Care to India" was launched in

Taiwan which raised US$700,000 and 100 tons of relief supplies. In November, an official delegation led by Control Yuan President Frederick Chien delivered a US$1 million donation to assist the bereaved families of policemen and firefighters killed in the September 11 terrorist attacks in New York City. In December, a long-term aid effort for displaced persons in Afghanistan was launched. In one program, the government donated over NT$87 million worth of supplies to the US-based Mercy Corps' "Campaign for the Afghan Children." In addition, an initial shipment of relief supplies donated by the government and various charitable organizations, worth NT$20 million in total, was sent to the Iran Red Crescent Society for distribution in camps along the Iranian border.

Some relief and reconstruction programs, such as the large program carried out in Central America in the aftermath of Hurricane Mitch, are executed by the ICDF. In addition, twenty-four Taiwanese private international charity organizations, such as the Tzu Chi Foundation 慈濟功德會, World Vision Taiwan 臺灣世界展望會, the Taiwan Root Medical Peace Corps, and the

While the development of technology has shortened the distance between nations, World Vision Taiwan is building bridges to connect the world with love, extending a helping hand to the suffering no matter where they are.
(Photo by the Central News Agency)

Chinese Fund for Children and Families 中華兒童暨家庭扶助基金會 have directly provided relief to Africa, Latin America, and Oceania, winning international recognition with their quick mobilization and flexibility. A number of private organizations are also working to arrange individual sponsorships for poor children, an increasingly popular form of international assistance among Taiwanese citizens.

Overseas Chinese

Aside from diplomatic endeavors and attempts to participate in international organizations, the ROC government has in recent years stepped up contacts with overseas Chinese around the world and strengthened efforts to serve their interests. By tradition, any person of Chinese descent living outside the borders of the Republic of China is considered a *hua chiao* 華僑, or overseas Chinese. Earlier overseas Chinese referred mainly to emigrants pursuing their fortunes or higher studies abroad during the 19th and early 20th centuries. In the past few decades, emigrants from Taiwan have increased, initially for academic reasons and more recently for business as the ROC has continued to experience rapid economic growth and growing prosperity. These relatively new overseas Chinese 新僑, comprising mainly of intellectuals and businessmen, face different challenges in their new environment compared with those encountered by the old overseas Chinese 舊僑.

Therefore, while equal attention will still be given to both old and new emigrants, the ROC government has adjusted its overseas Chinese policy to meet new demands arising from this demographic change in the overseas Chinese population. Previously, the emphasis was on preserving ethnic ties with the overseas Chinese by maintaining contact, providing education to new generations born overseas, offering economic assistance to overseas Chinese businessmen, and encouraging investment in the ROC. Recent trends have led to a policy shift toward planned and guided emigration by Taiwan residents, as

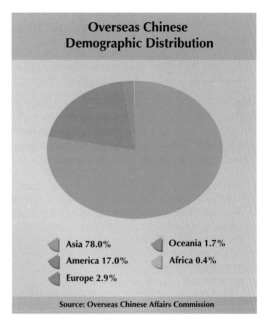

Overseas Chinese Demographic Distribution

Asia 78.0%   Oceania 1.7%
America 17.0%   Africa 0.4%
Europe 2.9%

Source: Overseas Chinese Affairs Commission

well as the integration of the business interests of the established overseas Chinese with those of recent emigrants who are completely unfamiliar with their new adopted cultures. Meanwhile, the earlier focus on keeping overseas Chinese informed of domestic developments has been replaced by an effort to increase domestic understanding of Chinese residing overseas.

Emigration Trends and ROC Policy

According to OCAC statistics, some 8.7 million Chinese were living overseas in 1948. The latest figures indicated that over 35 million Chinese resided outside the Chinese mainland at the end of 2000 (not including Hong Kong and Macau). About 78 percent make their homes in Asia, mainly in Indonesia, Thailand, Hong Kong, Malaysia, and Singapore. About 17 percent of overseas Chinese who live in North or South America are concentrated in the United States. Europe is home to 2.9 percent, while Oceania and Africa are home to about 1.7 percent and 0.4 percent, respectively. Most overseas Chinese come from Guangdong and Fujian.

Overseas Chinese Affairs Commission

In 1926, the ROC government established the Overseas Chinese Affairs Commission (OCAC) 僑務委員會 to ensure the welfare and interests of overseas Chinese, and it was placed under the Executive Yuan in 1932. The OCAC is organized into eight divisions: an overseas Chinese student center, an overseas Chinese passport and visa office, four departments, and two subsidiaries—the Overseas Chinese News Agency 華僑通訊社 and the Chung Hwa Correspondence School 中華函授學校.

The student center is known as the Office for Overseas Chinese Students Guidance 僑生輔導室 and is in charge of overseas Chinese studying in the ROC. The center also provides guidance, counseling, and post-graduation services. Areas handled by the passport and visa office, known as the Overseas Passport and Visa Service Office 華僑證照服務室, include the approval and transfer of entry and exit applications, applications to travel or settle in Taiwan, matters relating to military service, applications for re-entry visas, and the issuance of overseas Chinese ID cards and name chop certificates.

As for the OCAC's four departments, the first department is in charge of keeping track of the number of overseas Chinese, as well as providing services to overseas Chinese communities and to overseas Chinese on homecoming visits. The second department is responsible for fulfilling the formal educational, social service, and mass communication needs of overseas Chinese, as well as for promoting cultural and educational programs. Assisting overseas Chinese to invest in the ROC and providing economic and banking assistance to overseas Chinese enterprises are included in the third department's duties. The fourth department takes care of general affairs.

The Overseas Chinese News Agency provides news and media services pertaining to overseas Chinese affairs. The Chung Hwa Correspondence School provides educational services for overseas Chinese.

By profession, the majority are engaged in engineering or business.

Since the peaceful transfer of power in May 2000, the ROC's overseas Chinese policy has remained unchanged. The OCAC will continue to strengthen its contacts with, and services for, all overseas Chinese. It is hoped that overseas Chinese and the ROC government will form a common entity and that overseas Chinese everywhere, irrespective of party identity or ethnic origin, can unite in harmony and support one another.

Reception Services

Every year, large numbers of overseas Chinese come from everywhere to Taiwan to celebrate the ROC's National Day on October 10. In 2001, 1,759 overseas Chinese arrived for the purpose. To facilitate their visits, the OCAC runs a special reception center during this period.

To encourage greater participation by overseas Chinese in these and other activities, the OCAC has been improving entry and exit services. The OCAC has reduced the amount of paperwork required for entry and exit applications and has made a special effort to provide the most friendly and efficient reception services possible. The same applies to overseas Chinese applying for overseas Chinese ID cards and name chop certificates. In 2000, the number of entries and exits by overseas Chinese totaled 9,392, and 17,878 overseas Chinese ID cards and name chop certificates were issued.

Culture and Education

Maintaining cultural solidarity among overseas Chinese is one of the OCAC's primary missions. The OCAC has 19 overseas Chinese cultural and educational centers in major US cities, Toronto, Manila, Sydney, Melbourne, Paris, and Bangkok. The Overseas Chinese Culture and Education Foundation 海華文教基金會, set up with a US$15 million fund provided by the OCAC, subsidizes outstanding overseas Chinese youths in the areas of education, arts, and culture. The OCAC also subsidizes the establishment and management of Chinese TV and radio stations overseas. By the end of 2000, it had sponsored 107 Chinese-language TV stations worldwide. The Overseas Chinese News Agency 華僑通訊社, an OCAC subsidiary, provides the latest information on current events in the Taiwan area to overseas Chinese publications. The agency also puts out press releases to local news agencies to keep Taiwan residents well-informed of overseas Chinese affairs.

Traditionally, overseas Chinese education has been aimed at teaching cultural traditions—particularly Chinese customs, the Chinese family system, and Chinese literature—to new generations of foreign-born Chinese. When overseas Chinese have settled down in new areas, they may also set up schools to pass on their cultural heritage. Currently, there are 2,945 overseas Chinese-language schools. The OCAC provides free teaching materials, subsidizes school facilities, and assists in training school teachers. In order to meet the growing need for Chinese education resulting from the increasing number of Chinese emigrants, the OCAC established an overseas Chinese volunteers' education group in September 1997 in Taiwan, which assigns domestic volunteers (mostly retired teachers) to overseas Chinese-language schools to assist in training teachers. In addition, the OCAC has commissioned domestic academic institutions to sponsor training programs for teachers of overseas Chinese-language schools.

An alternative form of Chinese education for overseas Chinese is the Chung Hwa Correspondence School 中華函授學校, which was formally established in 1940. Mandarin lessons, vocational training, and general educational courses are provided free of charge. In 2000, more than 14,382 students from around the world registered for courses. Educational programs are broadcast via two international shortwave broadcast stations—the CBS Radio Taipei International and the Voice of Asia. The OCAC has also made available on its web page information regarding overseas Chinese-language schools, various Mandarin teaching materials and Chinese culture.

Economic Integration

For many decades, overseas Chinese have been contributing financially to the development of the ROC. As the world moves towards economic alignment, and more and more Taiwan businessmen invest overseas, the OCAC has become aware of the need to integrate the business strength of Taiwan entrepreneurs. Toward this end, the OCAC has guided the establishment of Taiwan chambers of commerce. In order to help coordinate the activities of regional Taiwan chambers of commerce, a continental council was set up in North America in 1987, and in 1994, a World Taiwanese Chambers of Commerce 世界臺灣商會聯合總會 was established. Any businessman from the Taiwan area who has invested overseas may participate in these chambers of commerce. Because most Taiwan investments are in export-oriented areas, and as the earlier Chinese emigrants are largely engaged in local trade, the integration of these two groups could foster economic strength among overseas Chinese, which in turn could help the ROC achieve further economic growth.

The scope of the Overseas Chinese Credit Guarantee Fund 華僑貸款信用保證基金 has been expanded in the last few years to enhance the economic status of overseas Chinese. Originally set up to encourage overseas Chinese investment in the Taiwan area and to offer credit guarantees to overseas Chinese businesses which lacked collateral and bank credit lines, the fund has extended its services to include Taiwan investors overseas.

From its inception to the end of 2000, the fund had concluded 2,812 credit guarantee cases worth a total of US$447 million. The fund also helped overseas Chinese to obtain US$668 million from various financial institutions to develop their businesses during the same period. In 2000 alone, the number of cases handled by the fund rose 6.7 percent from 1999 to 397 cases.

Overseas Chinese are important investors in Taiwan. According to the Investment Commission under the Ministry of Economic Affairs 經濟部投資審議委員會, 82 new overseas Chinese investment projects worth a total of US$83.7 million were approved in 2000. These projects were concentrated primarily in Taiwan's service, financial, and insurance sectors, as well as electronics and electrical appliances, textiles, and the paper industry. To encourage even greater participation from overseas Chinese investors and professionals in Taiwan, the government has improved the overall investment environment in Taiwan by amending the *Regulations Governing the Investment in Taiwan by Overseas Chinese* 華僑回國投資條例.

Political Participation

Article 10 of the *Additional Articles of the ROC Constitution* 中華民國憲法增修條文 promulgated on April 25, 2000, states that "the state shall accord to nationals of the Republic of China residing overseas protection of their rights of political participation." Article 4 of the *Additional Articles* provides that beginning with the 1998 election of the fourth Legislative Yuan 立法院, 8 overseas Chinese (who must, however, retain ROC citizenship) of the 225 members shall be elected to the Legislature. As the result of the 2001 legislative election, three members from the Democratic Progressive Party, two from the Kuomintang, two from the People First Party, and one from the Taiwan Solidarity Union were elected from among the Chinese citizens residing abroad. Overseas Chinese who hold ROC passports and who are not citizens of a foreign country have the right to take ROC civil service exams and serve in government posts. The right to vote is regulated by the ROC's *Public Officials Election and Recall Law* 公職人員選舉罷免法 and the *Nationality Law* 國籍法. A special clause was also included in the *Presidential and Vice Presidential Election and Recall Law* 總統副總統選舉罷免法 to allow overseas Chinese to return to vote in the direct popular election of the ROC president. Overseas Chinese who no longer hold an ROC passport can participate indirectly in ROC politics by becoming advisory members of the OCAC.

Conclusion: An End to the Obstruction of Taiwanese Participation

The people and government of the ROC are ready and willing to participate in all types of international activities. In bilateral cooperation, humanitarian relief, scientific exchanges, promotion of human rights, protection of the environment, maintenance of global and regional peace, and even the fight against terrorism, the sincerity and enthusiasm of the Taiwanese is apparent. However, for political and ideological reasons, the PRC has sought to court allegiance of overseas Chinese and obstruct Taiwan's relations with the world community, in order to compel the people of Taiwan to accept the rule of a communist dictatorship and to deny them the right to pursue their own foreign policy. Beijing even severs or downgrades relations with any country establishing or strengthening relations with Taiwan, which is a serious affront to the freedom and rights of many sovereign countries and peoples.

It is the sincere wish of the people of Taiwan that the PRC leadership will soon realize that this attitude only brings harm to the peoples on both sides of the Taiwan Strait, as well as to overseas Chinese groups and the international community as a whole. The Chinese mainland should adopt a more constructive stance, so that both sides can contribute fully to the great tasks of promoting peace, stability, development, and prosperity around the world.

Related Websites
1. Ministry of Foreign Affairs: *http://www.mofa.gov.tw*
2. Overseas Chinese Affairs Commission: *http://www.ocac.gov.tw*

10
The Economy

The 15-story Core Pacific City, currently Taiwan's largest shopping mall, sports a fancy, modern look and can accommodate nearly 1,000 retail outlets.

I
n 2000, the ROC economy grew by 5.86 percent, while consumer prices rose by only 1.26 percent, outperforming many other economies of Asia. This was due to the strong growth of world economy and world trade in the first three quarters. The ROC's gross national product (GNP) in 2000 was US$313.9 billion, and per capita GNP increased to US$14,188.

However, since the fourth quarter of 2000, Taiwan's economic growth has slowed sharply. Influenced by the world economic downturn and sluggish domestic demand, the economic growth rate in the first two quarters of 2001 dropped to 0.91 percent and -2.35 percent, respectively. For the January-July period of 2001, export orders were down 8.62 percent from a year earlier, and the unemployment rate climbed to 4.92 percent by the end of July.

To revive the economy, the ROC government launched the "8100 Taiwan Starts Moving" infrastructure project in March 2001 to increase domestic demand and create jobs. Furthermore,

the Economic Development Advisory Conference (EDAC) convened by President Chen Shui-bian in August 2001 made 322 recommendations pertaining to finance, industry, investment, employment, and cross-strait relations. Financial reforms, deregulation of investments, relaxation of the "patience over haste" cross-strait policy, and other policy changes were proposed and are being implemented.

This chapter profiles the ROC's economy in the following sections: macroeconomic indicators, trade, investment, economic ties with the Chinese mainland, the Economic Development Advisory Conference, services, industry, and energy.

Macroeconomic Indicators

Taiwan's GDP increased by 7.5 percent to US$309.4 billion in 2000, of which 32.38 percent was contributed by the industrial sector and only 2.09 by agriculture. The service sector, which has been particularly robust and generating more than 50 percent of Taiwan's GDP since 1988, accounted for 65.53 percent of the GDP in 2000. The wholesale price index for the year increased slightly by 1.8 percent, while the consumer price index was up by 1.26 percent.

Trade

In 2000, Taiwan's foreign trade increased 24.1 percent to US$288.3 billion, making the ROC the world's 14th largest trading nation. Total exports for the year grew by 22 percent

Major Economic Indicators				
Item	*Unit*	*1998*	*1999*	*2000*
Economic growth rate (real GDP increase)	%	4.57	5.42	5.86
Gross national product (GNP)	US$ billion	268.6	290.5	313.9
Per capita GNP	US$	12,333	13,235	14,188
Changes in consumer prices (CPI)	%	1.7	0.18	1.26
Exchange rate (average)	NT$ per US$	33.44	32.27	31.23
Unemployment rate	%	2.7	2.9	3.0
Foreign exchange reserves (end of the year)	US$ billion	90.3	106.2	106.7

Source: Council for Economic Planning and Development

to US$148.3 billion, allowing Taiwan to register a trade surplus of US$8.3 billion. Imports also increased significantly by 26.5 percent to US$140 billion.

However, the gradual cooling of the global economic climate since the second half of 2000 has slowed Taiwan's external trade. Exports were down 18.5 percent year-on-year in the first nine months of 2001, to US$89.6 billion, while imports fell 23.7 percent to US$80.3 billion. This, however, led to a trade surplus of US$9.3 billion, an increase of 102.6 percent.

Foreign trade—exports in particular— has played a vital role in the ROC economy. Brisk foreign trade in the 1970s and 1980s enabled the ROC to amass huge foreign exchange reserves. This annual trade surplus peaked at US$18.7 billion in 1987. Taiwan's trade surpluses soon evoked protests from major trading partners, the United States in particular, which demanded that the ROC remove trade barriers, allow more foreign products to enter the domestic market at reduced import tariffs, and allow the NT$ to float against the US$. In 1992, Taiwan's trade surplus

was reduced to only US$9.5 billion, down nearly 30 percent from the preceding year. This downward trend continued through the 1990s until 1996, when the ROC trade surplus began to increase again. These trade surpluses have allowed Taiwan to accumulate additional foreign exchange reserves, which at the end of 2000 stood at US$106.7 billion, the fourth highest in the world.

Exports

Exports increased by 22 percent to US$148.3 billion in 2000. The United States, Hong Kong, and Japan continued to remain the top buyers of Taiwan's exports, accounting for 55.8 percent. Other major recipients of Taiwan exports for the year included Europe and Southeast Asia.

In 2000, exports to the US rose 12.7 percent to US$34.81 billion. With the continued health of the US economy, including robust domestic demand and capital investment, US import demand remained strong. The global expansion of trade in information technology (IT) products has also been an important factor in the growth in ROC

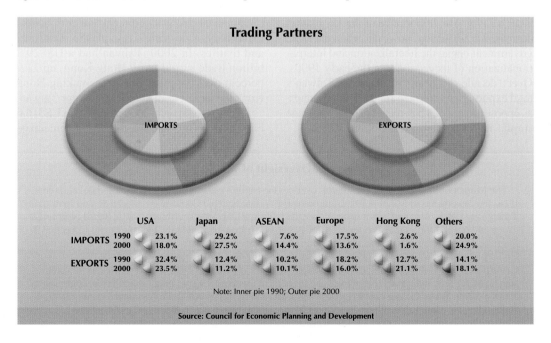

Trading Partners

		USA	Japan	ASEAN	Europe	Hong Kong	Others
IMPORTS	1990	23.1%	29.2%	7.6%	17.5%	2.6%	20.0%
	2000	18.0%	27.5%	14.4%	13.6%	1.6%	24.9%
EXPORTS	1990	32.4%	12.4%	10.2%	18.2%	12.7%	14.1%
	2000	23.5%	11.2%	10.1%	16.0%	21.1%	18.1%

Note: Inner pie 1990; Outer pie 2000

Source: Council for Economic Planning and Development

China External Trade Development Council

The principal organization in Taiwan designed to facilitate closer cooperation between government and industry, as well as between Taiwan and its trading partners, is the China External Trade Development Council (also known as CETRA) 中華民國對外貿易發展協會, which is co-sponsored by the government and both private industrial and business organizations. The council maintains 37 branch offices, design centers, and trade centers in 27 countries.

CETRA gathers trade information, conducts market research, promotes made-in-Taiwan products, organizes exhibitions, promotes product and packaging designs, offers convention venues, and trains business people. Assisted by CETRA, 16 US states and the American Institute in Taiwan maintain trade offices at the Taipei World Trade Center 臺北世界貿易中心 (see Appendix V). An additional 11 nations—Bolivia, Canada, Chile, Finland, France, Ireland, Nigeria, the Oman, the Philippines, Spain, and Thailand—have also set up trade offices at the Taipei World Trade Center. Most recently, Costa Rica, El Salvador, Guatemala, Honduras, and Nicaragua have established a joint Central America Trade Office there to further promote trade relations with the ROC.

exports to the US. Mechanical appliances and accessories, electronics and electrical appliances, personal computers and peripherals, metal products, transportation equipment, furniture, and garments comprised the bulk of Taiwan's exports to the United States.

For decades, the US market has been the most important export destination for the ROC, and this has resulted in huge trade surpluses in the ROC's favor. The importance of the US market decreased dramatically, however, when the ROC government began the liberalization and internationalization of its economy in the early 1990s. Over a decade ago, nearly 40 percent of Taiwan's total exports were destined for the United States, as opposed to only 23.5 percent in 2000. The trade surplus in 2000 was US$9.7 billion.

The ROC's exports to Hong Kong increased 20.5 percent to US$31.34 billion in 2000, accounting for 21.1 percent of Taiwan's exports. Since 1990, Hong Kong has been the second largest export destination for Taiwan products. The main reason is Taiwan's trade with the Chinese mainland, which must be carried out indirectly via a third party, usually Hong Kong. Major items exported to or through Hong Kong include electrical and electronic equipment and peripherals, machinery, accessories, raw plastic materials, and textiles. In 2000, Taiwan had a US$29.2 billion trade surplus with Hong Kong, up 21.9 percent over the preceding year, making Hong Kong the largest trade surplus region for Taiwan.

Exports to Japan in 2000 increased to US$16.6 billion, or by 39.5 percent, the largest percentage

Government Oversight of the Economy

The Ministry of Economic Affairs 經濟部 oversees the nation's economic administration and development. It has the departments of Mines 礦業司, Commerce 商業司, International Cooperation 國際合作處, and Industrial Technology 技術處. Also under its jurisdiction are the Industrial Development Bureau 工業局, Board of Foreign Trade 國際貿易局, Intellectual Property Office 智慧財產局, Bureau of Standards, Metrology and Inspection 標準檢驗局, Energy Commission 能源委員會, Bureau of Water Resources 水資源局, Small and Medium Enterprise Administration 中小企業處, Export Processing Zone Administration 加工出口區管理處, Central Geological Survey 中央地質調查所, Commission of National Corporations 國營事業委員會, Investment Commission 投資審議委員會, Industrial Development and Investment Center 投資業務處, International Trade Commission 貿易調查委員會, Water Conservancy Agency 水利處, Bureau of Mines 礦務局, Professional Training Institute 專業人員研究中心, and Taipei Water-Resources Management Commission 臺北水源特定區管理委員會.

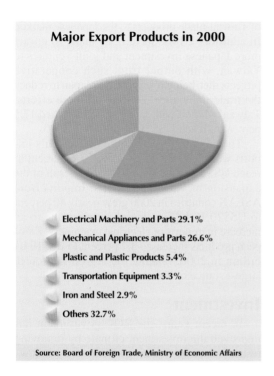

Major Export Products in 2000

- Electrical Machinery and Parts 29.1%
- Mechanical Appliances and Parts 26.6%
- Plastic and Plastic Products 5.4%
- Transportation Equipment 3.3%
- Iron and Steel 2.9%
- Others 32.7%

Source: Board of Foreign Trade, Ministry of Economic Affairs

gain among the ROC's major export markets. Consumption of IT products accelerated in Japan in 2000, and many large corporations launched or stepped-up technological cooperation with Taiwan electronics firms. The effect was an expansion of Japanese demand for personal computer components and liquid crystal displays, leading to a significant growth of Taiwan's exports of mechanical appliances, electrical machinery, and optical instruments.

Europe has been a target of the ROC's market diversification policy, and in 2000, Taiwan's exports to Europe grew by 16.7 percent to US$23.71 billion. Exports and employment in Europe increased after the Euro's devaluation in 1999-2000, leading to a rise in demand for imports. Germany, the Netherlands, the United Kingdom, and France were the top European buyers of Taiwan products, accounting for more than 67 percent of Taiwan's exports to the continent.

To cope with the trade barriers created by the European Union's (EU) single market, a dozen of Taiwan's largest firms gained access to the EU by establishing factories or merging with companies that already existed in the United Kingdom, the Netherlands, and Germany. Investment in Europe has mostly centered on electrical appliances, electronics, and information technology products.

Exports to ASEAN countries grew by 28.8 percent to US$18.08 billion in 2000. Southeast Asia became a strong trade alternative in recent years under the government's "southward policy." Many Taiwan enterprises established factories in this region to take advantage of the lower labor, raw material, and land prices. Most of the key components of the products produced in these countries, as well as the machinery used for production, were imported directly from Taiwan. This has contributed to the importance of Southeast Asian nations as a destination for Taiwan exports. In 1997, Taiwan's exports to ASEAN accounted for 13.3 percent of its total exports, up from only 5.5 percent in 1987. Since then, however, ASEAN's share of Taiwan's total exports gradually declined to 10.1 percent in 2000.

Imports

The ROC economy has been able to sustain high-levels of growth since 1960s, as a result of various government export policies. For decades, imports, which actually constitute one-third of the island's foreign trade, were discouraged by the government through such barriers as high import tariffs and foreign exchange controls. The accumulated wealth from exports brought about a more prosperous Taiwan, and as a result, the spending power of both the government and the private sector has increased immensely. This is easily seen by examining the value of imports, which has quintupled during this period.

In 2000, Taiwan's imports totaled US$140.01 billion, up 26.5 percent from the previous year. The demand for raw industrial and agricultural materials, the preponderance of Taiwan's imports, increased by 26.5 percent to US$89.78 billion. Capital goods imports increased 34.3 percent to US$39.26 billion, while consumer products imports grew 4.8 percent to US$10.98

billion. The large increase in imports can be traced to a steep climb in international commodity prices, especially petroleum; greater demand for imports due to the expansion of exports; and aggressive capacity expansion in the semiconductor and optoelectronics industries.

Over a quarter (US$38.56 billion) of Taiwan's 2000 imports were from Japan. Major import items included machinery, auto parts, electrical appliances, electronics, chemicals, and metal products. Many of Taiwan's industries rely heavily on the supply of key parts and the transfer of technology from Japan, especially the information technology and automobile industries. Every year, much of Taiwan's trade surplus with other nations is offset by its trade deficit with Japan. Continuous growth of Japanese imports by over 10 percent annually has led to a serious trade deficit with Japan, prompting the ROC government to take a series of measures to help restore a more favorable trade balance. For example, the ROC government has encouraged more exports

Major Import Products in 2000

- Electrical Machinery and Parts 27.3%
- Mechanical Appliances and Parts 19.9%
- Fossil Fuels 9.3%
- Optical Instruments 6.3%
- Organic Chemical Products 4.0%
- Others 33.2%

Source: Board of Foreign Trade, Ministry of Economic Affairs

of Taiwan-made products to the Japanese market. In addition, efforts have been made to attract more Japanese investment and joint-ventures to Taiwan, with output from such cooperative projects then being re-exported to Japan to reduce the trade imbalance. Despite all these efforts, Taiwan's deficit with Japan again increased 17.5 percent to reach US$21.96 billion in 2000.

The second largest source of Taiwan's imports was the United States, up 27.6 percent to reach US$25.13 billion in 2000 as a result of the expansion in Taiwan's exports. Imports from ASEAN countries in 2000 grew nearly 40 percent to US$20.19 billion, mainly attributable to an increase in imports of electrical machinery. European products increased 8.1 percent to US$19.01 billion in 2000, making the region the fourth largest source of Taiwan's imports.

Investment

In recent years, the ROC government has improved the investment climate by removing restrictions, implementing a "one-stop window" 單一窗口 policy, and encouraging participation by the private sector in public construction projects. Numerous Build-Operate-Transfer (BOT) infrastructure projects, including the high-speed rail line through Taiwan's western corridor and eight private power plants, have been approved and significantly helped the ROC to capitalize on private resources and accelerate national development. In 2000, private fixed capital formation increased by 15.74 percent to US$50.14 billion (NT$1,566 billion), mainly attributed to large expansion projects in the semiconductor, optoelectronics, and electronics industries. In addition to the high-speed rail line and private power plants, other private investment projects in 2000 and 2001 include fixed networks telecommunications, industrial parks, and large shopping malls.

According to the *World Investment Report 2000* published by the United Nations, by the end of 1999, the ROC had accumulated a total foreign investment of approximately US$23 billion, about 0.48 percent of all global foreign investment, ranking 32nd in the world. The same report listed accumulated outward investment from the ROC at approximately US$42.5 billion, accounting for 0.89 percent of the global total and ranking 16th in the world.

Inward Investment

In 2000, there were 1,410 approved inward foreign investments, totaling US$7.6 billion. Compared to the previous year, the total number of approved inward foreign investments increased by 79.79 percent, a record high. Most of Taiwan's inward foreign investments in 2000 came from British Territories in Central America (mainly the British Virgin Islands and the Cayman Islands), the United States, Singapore, Japan, and the United Kingdom. The total amount from these areas equaled about 83.36 percent of inward foreign investment in 2000.

The ROC has already opened its finance, insurance, transportation, telecommunications, and real estate sectors to foreign investment. At present, except for a small number of ratio restrictions on foreign investment, such as in telecommunications services, foreign investors enjoy equal treatment in most cases. Manufacturing is completely open to foreign investment, except for a small number of items that affect national security, health, and environmental protection. The degree of liberalization has reached 99 percent in the manufacturing sector and 95 percent in services.

The top five sectors for foreign investment were banking and insurance (invested mostly in holding companies), telecommunications (mostly in fixed networks and mobile communication services), electronic and electrical appliances, services, and wholesale and retail marketing. These five categories together accounted for 85.92 percent of all investment by overseas Chinese and foreign nationals.

Outward Investment

Overseas investments (not including the Chinese mainland) by Taiwan businesses in 2000 totaled 1,391 cases (US$5.08 billion), representing a growth of 55.31 percent over 1999. Most of this investment went to the British Virgin Islands

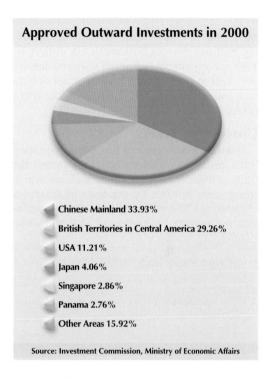

Approved Outward Investments in 2000

Chinese Mainland 33.93%

British Territories in Central America 29.26%

USA 11.21%

Japan 4.06%

Singapore 2.86%

Panama 2.76%

Other Areas 15.92%

Source: Investment Commission, Ministry of Economic Affairs

and Cayman Islands, the United States, other areas in the Americas, Japan, and Singapore. Together, these five areas accounted for 83.92 percent of all outward investment from the ROC in 2000. The top five sectors for outward investment were banking and finance, services, electronic and electrical appliances, wholesale and retail marketing, and transportation.

Economic Ties with the Chinese Mainland

The ROC government lifted its ban on cross-strait exchanges by the private sector in 1987 in order to allow family reunions. In 1992, investment in the mainland by Taiwan businesses was legalized, quickly pushing the Chinese mainland to the top of the list of Taiwan's foreign investment. By 2000, Taiwan had become the fourth largest source of foreign investment of mainland China.

Over the past decade, economic relations between the two sides have developed from sporadic

trading activities by Taiwan's small and medium enterprises into large-scale investments involving millions or even billions of US dollars by Taiwan conglomerates. These Taiwan businesses are eager to invest in the mainland not only to seek cost advantages, but also to gain access to a potentially large market.

Cross-strait Trade

Despite the absence of direct transportation links, economic ties between Taiwan and the Chinese mainland have never been closer than in recent years. In 1987, Taiwan had a trade surplus of just over US$1 billion with the Chinese mainland, but by 2000 it had reached US$18.81 billion.

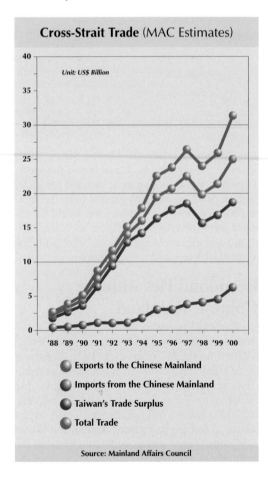

Cross-Strait Trade (MAC Estimates)

Unit: US$ Billion

- 🔵 Exports to the Chinese Mainland
- 🔴 Imports from the Chinese Mainland
- ⚫ Taiwan's Trade Surplus
- 🔘 Total Trade

Source: Mainland Affairs Council

According to the ROC's Mainland Affairs Council 行政院大陸委員會, the value of two-way trade between Taiwan and the Chinese mainland amounted to US$31.25 billion in 2000. Over 80 percent of this indirect trade was exports from Taiwan, totaling US$25.03 billion, up 17.2 percent from 1999. Major export items to the mainland included electronic equipment and parts, mechanical appliances and parts, plastics and plastic products, iron and steel, and artificial fibers. Imports from the Chinese mainland increased 37.5 percent to US$6.22 billion in 2000. The bulk of the imports was industrial raw materials or agricultural products for which domestic supply is inadequate. In addition, according to the Board of Foreign Trade 經濟部國際貿易局, exports to the Chinese mainland (via Hong Kong) represented 17.6 percent of the ROC's total exports in 2000, making the Chinese mainland Taiwan's second largest export market, next to the US. Goods from mainland China represented 4.4 percent of the total imports, and the Chinese mainland was the source of Taiwan's largest trade surplus.

Investment on the Chinese Mainland

The Chinese mainland has opened up its economic system gradually in recent years to prepare for entry into the World Trade Organization (WTO) and comply with international norms. The mainland's relatively low production costs has attracted large amounts of foreign direct investment. Taiwan enterprises have gradually made the Chinese mainland a major base in global logistics. A large number of Taiwan's labor-intensive industries have set up factories on the Chinese mainland to take advantage of the cheap labor and low overhead costs. Many of these manufacturers receive orders in Taiwan, produce their goods on the Chinese mainland, and ship the goods from the mainland directly to their overseas buyers. As the market on the Chinese mainland becomes more open and lucrative, more of Taiwan's large enterprises, including firms in the information technology, plastics, and food and beverage sectors, are beginning to undertake large-scale projects on the Chinese mainland.

The Investment Commission of the Ministry of Economic Affairs 經濟部投資審議委員會 indicates that approved investment by Taiwan companies in the Chinese mainland amounted to a total of 22,974 cases with a value of US$17.1 billion from 1991 to the end of 2000. This accounted for 38.82 percent of the US$44.1 billion in overall approved outward investment recorded during that period, making the Chinese mainland the foremost destination of outward investment from Taiwan and ranking Taiwan the fourth-largest source of foreign investment in the Chinese mainland. In 2000, there were 840 cases of approved indirect investment in the Chinese mainland, totaling US$2.61 billion, an increase of 108.11 percent over the previous year in terms of value and 72.13 percent in the number of cases. Most of the capital went into electronic and electrical apparatus manufacturing (56.18 percent of the total) and plastic products manufacturing (7.09 percent). Taiwan businessmen are also beginning to invest in areas other than export manufacturing, setting up mainland offices to handle real estate, insurance, banking, and tourism. The majority (nearly 90.94 percent) of Taiwan investors concentrate on the southeastern coast of the mainland, as transportation facilities in this area are far more developed than in the interior. However, Taiwan investment has recently begun to spread beyond the coastal provinces of Jiangsu, Guangdong, and Fujian.

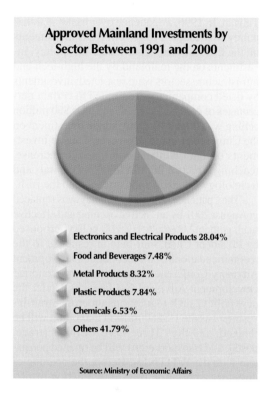

Approved Mainland Investments by Sector Between 1991 and 2000

- Electronics and Electrical Products 28.04%
- Food and Beverages 7.48%
- Metal Products 8.32%
- Plastic Products 7.84%
- Chemicals 6.53%
- Others 41.79%

Source: Ministry of Economic Affairs

Active Opening, Effective Management

Increasing economic dependence on the Chinese mainland and the hollowing-out of the Taiwan economy have become major concerns for

---

Taiwan as a Green Silicon Island

Taiwan's economic achievements were primarily based on labor-intensive industries and low-tech export products. In 1987, for example, approximately 48 percent of Taiwan's total exports were low-tech products, with only 18 percent considered high-tech. This proportion has been gradually reversed in the past decade, and by 2000, approximately 54 percent of Taiwan's exports were high-tech products and only 14 percent were considered low-tech. Taiwan is now the world's fourth largest IT hardware producer.

President Chen Shui-bian proposed developing Taiwan into a "green silicon island" during his inauguration speech to ensure a balance between environmental conservation and economic development. On May 7, 2001, the Executive Yuan passed the "green silicon island" plan, which is based on three major concepts: a knowledge-based economy, a sustainable environment, and a just society.

Developing Taiwan into a "green silicon island" has become the main national development policy and is being implemented over a ten-year period through the "National Development Plan for the New Century" and other relevant projects by all ministries.

Taiwan. In 1996, a "patience over haste" 戒急用忍 policy was adopted to govern ROC investments on the Chinese mainland. Under this policy, investments on the mainland by the high-tech and infrastructure sectors were restricted; investments by listed companies were limited to certain percentages of company capital; and a US$50 million ceiling was imposed on any single investment on the Chinese mainland. However, Taiwan investments on the mainland continued to increase, reaching a record high in 2000, as capital- and technology-intensive industries joined the rush.

The "patience over haste" policy was replaced in August 2001 by an "active opening and effective management" 積極開放,有效管理 policy, proposed by President Chen Shui-bian in response to the recommendations of the Economic Development Advisory Conference (see section on Economic Development Advisory Conference). Under the new policy, such regulations on cross-strait investment as the US$50 million maximum will be relaxed, and the "Three Direct Links" (trade, postal, and transportation) will be opened consistent with the WTO rules. Before the opening of direct transportation links, the function of offshore transshipment centers 境外航運中心 will be enlarged to facilitate cross-strait trade.

Direct cross-strait sea-air transshipment service began with the first air shipment of cargo from Xiamen to Europe via Kaohsiung's offshore transshipment center on August 15, 2001. Furthermore, on October 31, 2001, the Executive Yuan approved the additional expansion of the scope and functions of the offshore transshipment center. Raw materials and semi-finished goods from the Chinese mainland can be processed at Taiwan's export processing zones, science-based industrial parks, bonded factories, and bonded warehouses for export to third destinations. Also, the government will allow both secondary processing (with added value of over 35 percent) and simple processing (less than 35 percent added value) in the manufacturing zone. Goods that have undergone secondary processing can carry the "Made in Taiwan" label. While the offshore transshipment center will still be

initially limited to Kaohsiung Harbor, mainland cargo arriving through Kaohsiung can be transshipped to a third destination via Taiwan's other international harbors and two international airports. Cargo can also be airlifted from third countries to Taiwan's two international airports and then transshipped to the mainland through Kaohsiung. The new policy is expected to help reduce transportation time and costs and improve cross-strait division of labor, thereby upgrading competitiveness of local manufacturers and encouraging businesses to stay in Taiwan.

A big step in relaxing the "patience over haste" policy came on November 7, 2001, when the Executive Yuan announced its plan to implement the EDAC consensus on "active opening, effective management."

According to the implementation plan, a new mechanism will be adopted to review Taiwan businesses' investment on the Chinese mainland. The US$50 million cap on any single investment on the Chinese mainland will be abolished, meaning that there will no longer be upper limits for the amount of any single investment. In addition, the new regulations allow a simple review process for investments of less than US$20 million. Investments higher than US$20 million will be reviewed by the Investment Commission through clear standards and streamlined process on a case-by-case basis. Also, the upper limit on aggregate investments by individuals or small and medium enterprises will be raised from NT$60 million (US$1.92 million) to NT$80 million (US$2.56 million).

Moreover, restrictions on spending capital for mainland investment by publicly listed and OTC-traded companies have been relaxed. To provide flexible mechanisms for cross-strait capital flow, offshore banking units (OBUs) of Taiwan banks will be allowed to engage in direct business exchanges with mainland financial institutions. Cross-strait capital remittances through the OBUs will be viewed as company capital deployment, which does not involve taxation.

In relaxing restrictions on investment items, a positive listing will be adopted. The list will be decided and regularly reviewed by a panel of representatives from the industries, the government, and the academia. The panel will decide whether items such as upstream petrochemical products, silicon wafers, and notebook computers will be allowed in mainland-bound investment.

The Chinese mainland and the ROC became members of the World Trade Organization at the end of 2001 and the beginning of 2002, respectively, bringing the two sides under a rule-based multilateral framework, which is expected to accelerate the economic integration.

Economic Development Advisory Conference

The Economic Development Advisory Conference 經濟發展諮詢委員會議 (EDAC), which was organized to reach a consensus among ruling and opposition parties, concluded on August 26, 2001, with 322 proposals, 36 majority opinions, and 12 other opinions. The proposal to relax the "patience over haste" policy on investment in mainland China drew the most attention. The proposals and opinions were sent to the executive and legislative branches for implementation. According to preliminary estimates, they will result in the revision of 43 laws, constituting the biggest regulatory relaxation ever and will strengthen international economic competitiveness. The major proposals of the conference include the following:

- Changing of the "patience over haste" policy to "active opening and effective management" to facilitate the upgrading of the competitiveness of domestic industries and corporate global logistics capabilities.
- Establishing "Taiwan first, global perspectives, mutual benefit, and risk management" as the basic principles of cross-strait economic and trade development.
- Coordinating the process of WTO entry by opening direct cross-strait trade, transportation, and telecommunications and expanding the range of commodities imported from the mainland.
- Planning for cross-strait shipping and, prior to the signing of a cross-strait shipping agreement,

expanding the functions and scope of Taiwan's offshore shipping center by allowing goods to clear customs and enter the territory of the Republic of China, so as to reduce the inconvenience of indirect cross-strait shipping.

- Expanding the term of service in Taiwan for technical personnel from mainland China to five years or more and enhancing Taiwan's attraction for such personnel by providing them with long-term residence rights or tax exemptions.
- Further opening direct correspondent relations between Taiwan's offshore banking units and mainland Chinese financial institutions and planning for direct remittances.
- Opening business investment in the mainland or establishing branches or subsidiaries there by domestic financial services in an orderly fashion and in accordance with international practice.
- Relaxing restrictions on investment in the mainland by companies listed on the stock or over-the-counter market and allowing of stock dividends for the employees of overseas subsidiaries.
- Allowing stock market or over-the-counter listing for venture capital companies that meet certain conditions.
- Establishing a mechanism for licensing intellectual property rights and technology and providing incentives for the development of the R&D services industry.
- Revising laws and regulations governing corporate operations to facilitate mergers.
- Relaxing restrictions on working hours of female employees to make them consistent with those that apply to men to alleviate problems of human resources utilization and relaxing restrictions on night-time work by female employees to increase job opportunities for women.
- Re-engineering government organizations to improve administrative efficiency and reduce government expenditures.
- Simplification of approval procedures for foreign investment in the domestic stock

SMEs

For decades, small and medium enterprises (SMEs) have been the backbone of the ROC's economic development. Unlike many advanced nations, where conglomerates dominate the economy, Taiwan's manufacturing and foreign trade are built up and fortified by countless SMEs.

SMEs began emerging after World War II, when Japanese conglomerates withdrew from Taiwan, and the local market was dominated by state-run enterprises and large private companies. The island's SMEs focused on foreign markets to survive. At first, agricultural products and agricultural processed goods made up the bulk of exported items. These were eventually replaced by light industrial products, especially after the government set up several export-processing zones to spur the export economy. An export-oriented policy in the 1960s also created a favorable environment for SMEs to penetrate international markets. SME entrepreneurs are characterized by high adaptability to market trends, hard work, thrift, and a tendency to pass their businesses on to their children. According to the Ministry of Economic Affairs, over 98 percent of Taiwan's 1,091,245 registered enterprises are SMEs. These SMEs employ nearly 80 percent of the total work force and account for half of the island's aggregate export value.

The 2000 revision to the *Small and Medium Enterprises Development Statute* 中小企業發展條例 defines small and medium enterprises by sector, paid-in capital/annual turnover, and the number of employees. Industries, including manufacturing, construction, and mining and quarrying, that have a paid-in capital not exceeding NT$80 million (an equivalent of US$2.56 million) or hire less than 200 regular workers, are categorized as SMEs. Companies in the commercial, service, and transportation sectors with an annual turnover not exceeding NT$100 million (an equivalent of US$3.2 million) or that hire less than 50 employees are also considered SMEs.

Most SMEs (60.39 percent) are in the commercial sector, followed by manufacturing (13.21 percent). Many manufacturers work closely with trading companies to export products, and a large number of the SMEs still rely heavily on OEM and ODM orders. On average, SMEs spend less than 3 percent of their annual operating income on research and development (R&D).

For decades, Taiwan has been an Asian production center for many multinational conglomerates, proof that Taiwan can produce high-quality goods. Today, made-in-Taiwan products, ranging from packaging to toys and from garments to personal computers, are found in shops around the world. The SMEs also constitute a large portion of Taiwan's investment overseas, as the ROC has become a major investor worldwide.

To create an environment for SMEs to increase productivity, the government has made five revisions to the *Small and Medium Enterprise Guidance Regulations* 中小企業輔導準則, first issued in 1967. It has also set up SME service centers in 23 cities and counties around the island and a development fund that provides assistance in case of recession and indemnification for damages caused by natural disasters. Other measures include automation and computerization programs and marketing and managerial seminars.

In recent years, Taiwan's SMEs have encountered many challenges. A shortage of laborers, increases in wages, and prohibitive land prices have plaqued both large-scale firms and SMEs. Fluctuating exchange rates and keen competition from other nations also had direct impact on SME operations. As the focus of Taiwan's industrial structure shifts to high-tech industries, the role of SMEs in Taiwan's economy has gradually changed from direct exporters of final products to component suppliers to large enterprises. Many SMEs face the problem of relocation and industrial upgrading. Additionally, the business environment of the knowledge-based economy after Taiwan's accession to the WTO is likely to become more volatile and challenging to SMEs.

To assist SMEs in upgrading and transformation, over 50 centers have been established around the island by February 2001, currently focusing on IT, biotechnology, marine transport, and other high-tech businesses. A number of enterprise owners, managers, and specialists in management, who have a wide network of local contacts, have been chosen as enterprise service volunteers. Over 3,300 SME "honorary directors" have been appointed and are actively involved in consulting, strengthening existing local service networks, and implementing localized guidance services.

market and relaxation of related administrative systems.

- Privatization under market conditions of government-owned companies, whether profitable or not, for which the Executive Yuan determines that government operation is no longer necessary.

At the closing ceremony of the conference, President Chen Shui-bian emphasized that the government would take concrete actions to invest in emerging industries, and that the goal for R&D spending growth would be at least 12 percent per year. The president also expressed support for the establishment of a government committee to work out a re-engineering program for submission to the Legislative Yuan.

President Chen had proposed the convening of the Economic Development Advisory Conference on May 18 to mark the first anniversary of his inauguration. A total of 120 representatives from business, government, the legislature, academia, and political parties participated. They were divided into five panels: manufacturing, investment, finance, cross-strait relations, and employment.

The Executive Yuan responded quickly to the EDAC proposals by approving revisions to the *Statute Governing the Relations Between the People of the Taiwan Area and the Mainland Area* 臺灣地區與大陸地區人民關係條例 in September 2001. According to the revisions, Taiwan's real estate market will be opened to mainland investors. Individuals and companies from the mainland will be able to purchase property in Taiwan under certain conditions. Taiwan businesspeople will be exempted from double taxation on profits from mainland investment. Companies that have invested in the mainland without approval from the ROC government will be given six months to register once the amendments take effect.

Services

In the Republic of China, the service sector is divided into seven main categories: (1) finance, insurance, and real estate; (2) commerce, including wholesale, retail, food and beverage, and

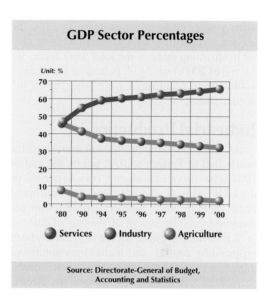

GDP Sector Percentages

Unit: %

Services   Industry   Agriculture

Source: Directorate-General of Budget, Accounting and Statistics

international trade; (3) social and individual services; (4) transportation, storage, and telecommunications; (5) commercial services, including legal, accounting, civil engineering, information, advertising, designing, leasing, etc.; (6) governmental services, and (7) others. During the 1960s and 1970s, the rapid growth of manufacturing almost caught up with Taiwan's service sector in terms of GDP percentage. Roughly two decades ago, however, Taiwan's service sector was revitalized. By 2000, the service sector accounted for 65.53 percent of Taiwan's GDP, a percentage very similar to that of many advanced nations. The total GDP value for the service sector that year reached US$202.78 billion, up 6.08 percent over the preceding year.

Finance, insurance, and real estate comprised the bulk of the service sector, accounting for over 30.6 percent.

Commerce rebounded to account for 29.45 percent of the service sector, with wholesale, retail, international trade, and the food and beverage industry all performing better than the year before, with growth rates in 2000 of 6.14, 4.14, 12.37, and 8.27 percent, respectively.

Taiwan's thriving service sector, particularly in the financial and stock market areas, has attracted

many young people in recent years. In 1988, the service sector surpassed the manufacturing sector in attracting more of the total work force. By the end of 2000, over 54.98 percent of the island's 9.49 million employees were working in the service sector.

Industrial Production

In 1986, industrial production accounted for nearly half of Taiwan's GDP, but by the end of 1987, it had dropped to slightly over 40 percent of the GDP. This downward trend has continued ever since. In 2000, industrial production accounted for 32.38 percent of Taiwan's GDP.

Labor-intensive industries have gradually been replaced by capital- and technology-intensive industries, such as the production of chemicals, petrochemicals, information technology, electrical equipment, and electronics, all of which experienced moderate to strong growth rates in 2000 despite a general recession. Electronics and information technology have become the mainstay of industrial production, accounting for nearly 27 percent of total output by value. Manufacturing output constituted over 80 percent of the total industrial production and engaged over 27 percent of the workforce.

Information Technology Industry

In 2000, Taiwan's hardware information technology (IT) industry domestic and overseas production was US$47 billion, up 17.9 percent from the previous year's US$39.9 billion, making it the ROC's most important foreign exchange earner. Taiwan has been the world's third-largest computer hardware supplier from 1995 to 1999 and ranked fourth in 2000, trailing only the United States, Japan, and the Chinese mainland. Taiwan's 1,000 plus computer hardware manufacturers provide jobs for approximately 130,000 employees. In 2000, laptop computers, monitors, desktop PCs, and motherboards accounted for about 80 percent of the production value of the IT industry. Taiwan manufacturers have a large share of the world market because of their competitive prices and high quality. According to the Institute

for Information Industry 財團法人資訊工業策進會, Taiwan has already supplanted Singapore to become Japan's second largest supplier of information products, second only to the United States.

Despite the generally lackluster performance of the domestic economy in recent years, Taiwan's IT hardware industry still managed to register significant growth. This can be attributed to many factors, including the rapid growth of the Internet, the increased popularity of multimedia computers, and the expansion of production by local PC manufacturers. Taiwan's IT industry has grown from a minor role to a major contributor to the island's export-based economy. This is partly a result of governmental inducements and partly because of the extreme flexibility of domestic small and medium enterprises (SMEs), which are able to quickly adapt to the latest market trends and adjust their production accordingly. Nevertheless, the industry still faces problems that are common to all manufacturing industries.

The structure of Taiwan's IT industry is best described as a pyramid. A handful of companies at the top of the pyramid commit themselves to product innovation through costly and time-consuming R&D (see Chapter 18, Science and Technology), while small and medium enterprises at the base of the pyramid account for the vast majority (85 percent) of the actual output. The latter comprise a weak and unstable downstream foundation. As in other manufacturing sectors,

SMEs generally produce goods on an OEM (original equipment manufacturer) and ODM (original design manufacturer) basis, and therefore spend a negligible percentage of their revenue on R&D. This has led to the inability of these companies to make in-depth assessments for investment, production, and marketing of new and innovative products. Moreover, heavy reliance on the importation of key parts and advanced technology from the United States and Japan has tied Taiwan's IT sector to the economic strength of these two countries, thereby offsetting a substantial portion of Taiwan's trade surplus each year.

Automobile Industry

Taiwan is currently home to ten automobile manufacturers, the majority of which have contractual joint ventures with foreign makers, mostly from Japan. These companies both produce and import automobiles. The production value of the automotive industry reached US$10 billion in 2000, equivalent to 4.04 percent of Taiwan's aggregate manufacturing production value for the year. Approximately 372,613 automobiles were produced in Taiwan in 2000.

Due to limited parking space and the operation of several mass rapid transit system lines in urban districts, total automobile demand in Taiwan dropped from 542,000 units sold in 1995 to 420,446 in 2000. Although sedans for private use continued to dominate demand, accounting for 74.2 percent, the number of domestically made cars sold in 2000 decreased 1.5 percent to 249,657, and the number of imported cars increased 8.7 percent from the previous year. Domestically made commercial vans accounted for 95 percent of the market. Recently, competition between locally made and imported vehicles has gradually declined. In 2000, the domestic automobile industry, threatened by imports from Japan and the US, still managed to capture around 84.4 percent of the market, proving that the quality of domestic vehicles has been accepted by local consumers.

In 2000, over 86 percent of the 249,657 domestically made sedans were supplied by four

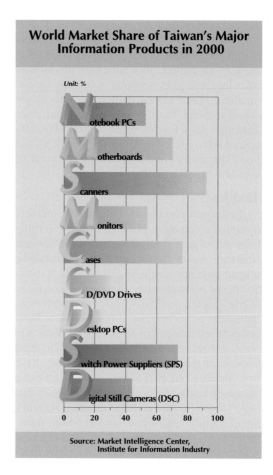

World Market Share of Taiwan's Major Information Products in 2000

Unit: %

- Notebook PCs
- Motherboards
- Scanners
- Monitors
- Cases
- CD/DVD Drives
- Desktop PCs
- Switch Power Suppliers (SPS)
- Digital Still Cameras (DSC)

0   20   40   60   80   100

Source: Market Intelligence Center,
Institute for Information Industry

companies: Ford Lio Ho Motor Co., Ltd. 福特六和汽車股份有限公司 (17 percent), Yulon Motor Co., Ltd. 裕隆汽車製造股份有限公司 (20 percent), Kuozui Motors, Ltd. 國瑞汽車股份有限公司 (23 percent), and China Motor Corporation 中華汽車工業股份有限公司 (26 percent). In the commercial vehicle market, China Motor Corporation maintained its long-held top position, producing over 58.7 percent of the 101,417 commercial vehicles sold.

Although the ROC imposes a quota on autos imported directly from Japan, Japanese vehicles have, like many other commercial products, successfully penetrated the Taiwan market and built up a solid customer base. In 2000, nearly one-third of the imported vans were Japanese brands

that had been made in American factories. Toyota alone took 14 percent of the Taiwan market share of imported sedans. Of the top ten best sellers in the Taiwan market, all were either products of Sino-Japanese joint ventures or directly carried Japanese brand names. Domestic automobile manufacturers have long worried that once Taiwan's door for imported cars is officially opened with reduced tariffs, foreign vehicles will flood the market and threaten the survival of domestic manufacturers.

Textiles

In the past five decades, the textile industry occupied an eminent place in exports, earning large amounts of foreign exchange for Taiwan. However, since the second half of the 1980s, several problems, including the sharp appreciation of the NT dollar, labor shortages, increasing overhead costs, prohibitive land prices, and environmental protection, have forced textile businesses to relocate part or all of their production to Southeast Asia and the Chinese mainland in order to maintain their competitiveness. Textiles have been dubbed one of Taiwan's labor-intensive "sunset industries." Those textile companies that have stayed in Taiwan have initiated reforms. Small, family-run businesses have been transformed into medium-sized or large enterprises, with cost-effective measures and innovative management introduced to raise quality and productivity. Since Taiwan does not produce cotton, wool, silk, linen, or other natural raw materials, the domestic textile industry has developed man-made fabrics, which have proven to be an excellent alternative to natural products.

Today, Taiwan's man-made fibers have earned a prominent place in the world's textile industry. In 2000, Taiwan produced over four million tons of man-made fiber, ranking third in the world. Polyester accounted for 80 percent of the total output and placed Taiwan as the world's second largest producer of this fiber. That same year, Taiwan exported and imported over US$18 billion worth of textiles, including fiber, yarn, fabric, garments, and accessories. Hong Kong was the primary destination for Taiwan's textile exports, followed by the US and ASEAN countries. Taiwan's textile industry has been one of ROC's prime contributors in maintaining the island's favorable trade balance with other nations.

Petrochemicals

Taiwan's petrochemical industry primarily consists of 45 upper- and middle-stream manufacturers located in Kaohsiung's special chemical zone. In 2000, the industry had a production value of US$14.2 billion (excluding textile and plastics-related industries), of which 81 percent was sold on the domestic market. However, Taiwan's petrochemical production capacity (as measured by ethylene output) could only satisfy about 51 percent of actual domestic demand in 1999; therefore, the Formosa Plastics Group 臺灣塑膠工業股份有限公司 (FPG), the major plastics conglomerate in Taiwan, applied for government approval to build a sixth naphtha cracking plant 第六輕油裂解廠. The company launched the project several years ago in Yunlin County's Mailiao 麥寮. The massive project was built in an industrial zone that includes 57 plants, including an oil refinery, naphtha cracking plant, cogeneration plant, coal-fired power plant, heavy machinery plant, boiler plant, wafer fabrication plant, and petrochemical-related plants on 2,500 hectares of reclaimed land, a great portion of which lies below sea level.

The FPG began its initial operations in the industrial zone at the end of 1998 and is expected to produce 1,350 thousand tons of ethylene annually. Taiwan's ethylene self-sufficiency rose to 79 percent since the US$40 billion (naphtha cracking plant) project was completed in 2000.

WTO Accession and Impact

The ROC applied to join the General Agreement on Tariffs and Trade (GATT), the predecessor of the World Trade Organization, in January 1990 under the name of Separate Customs Territory of Taiwan, Penghu, Kinmen and Matsu, and was granted observer status in September 1992. The application was transferred to the

WTO after its establishment in 1995. On January 31, 1995, the ROC was formally admitted as an observer to the WTO, and the WTO's working party successfully concluded negotiations on the ROC's terms of membership on September 18, 2001. After a long, 12-year accession process, the WTO's 4th Ministerial Conference held in Doha, Qatar admitted the ROC to membership on November 11, 2001, with the protocols of accession signed 24 hours later. The ROC became the 144th member of the WTO in January 2002.

Upon Taiwan's accession, import restrictions, tariffs, and local subsidies for agricultural and industrial products will be comprehensively reduced. Markets at home and abroad will be liberalized and made more transparent. The monopoly on wine and cigarettes will be eliminated. Twenty-eight signatories of the Government Procurement Agreement (GPA) will be allowed to bid for government contracts once Taiwan joins the agreement. Reduced prices on imported raw materials are expected to help local companies lower production costs and, along with low-priced imports, increase consumer spending.

The WTO entry is expected to impact certain sectors in Taiwan, especially the agricultural sector. Imports of agricultural products are expected to increase, resulting in lower market prices and reduced agricultural production. Approximately 100,000 farmers and fruit growers will need to seek new jobs and production will decrease by 12 percent upon WTO entry.

Export-oriented industries, such as electrical and electronics, information technology, plastics, and textile, will benefit from reduced tariffs and open markets under the WTO framework. As a WTO member, Taiwan's export textile products will be free from quota restrictions beginning in 2005. Taiwan's IT and telecommunications products, many of which account for over 50 percent of world marketshare, will benefit from zero tariff in the world's major markets as Taiwan has joined the Information Technology Agreement (ITA).

Industries relying on the domestic market, on the other hand, will face greater competition due

Now that Taiwan has joined the WTO, local retailers will be facing keener competition from international chain stores. Pictured is the interior of a Starbucks coffeehouse in Taipei City.

to a substantial reduction of average nominal duty rates. Industries likely to be affected by the accession include automobiles, paper, heavy electrical machinery, home electrical appliances and a few other less competitive traditional industries.

The impact of the WTO accession on the service sector may include freer personnel exchanges, capital flow, and land use, as well as keener business competition. However, as liberalization of services is already well under way, impact on this sector should be relatively limited.

To reduce negative impact on agriculture and industry, the ROC government has adopted a phased

tariff reduction plan and sought special safeguard provisions (SSG) on 14 sensitive items of agricultural products against a sudden surge in imports or a fall in import price below a specified reference price for the products. It is also assisting businesses to increase competitiveness by improving R&D capabilities, reducing operational costs by promoting e-commerce, and pursuing internationalization through overseas investments.

Overall, it is expected that WTO membership will bring new business opportunities, facilitate industrial upgrading, boost Taiwan's international profile, and help Taiwan resolve unfair trade charges via an institutionalized mechanism.

Energy

Taiwan has insufficient energy natural resources. Its coal reserves amount to only 98 million tons, most of which are distributed throughout the northern part of the island. Oil and natural gas reserves, found mostly in the northern Taiwan counties of Hsinchu and Miaoli, and near the southern city of Kaohsiung, total 0.4 million tons and 2,400 billion cubic feet, respectively. Total hydropower reserves have been estimated at 5,047 megawatts, of which 1,973 megawatts have been developed, primarily along several major rivers. Given such limited energy resources, Taiwan must import fossil fuels to meet the bulk of its energy needs.

Supply

The total energy supply in Taiwan increased from 34.29 million kiloliters of oil equivalent in 1980 to 106.23 million kiloliters in 2000, with an average annual growth of 5.8 percent. Over the past two decades, local energy supplies have accounted for a progressively smaller portion of annual usage, declining from 14 percent in 1980 to 3 percent in 2000. Of the total energy supply, oil accounted for 51 percent and nuclear power accounted for 9 percent.

Expenditures for imported energy totaled US$11.93 billion in 2000, of which imported oil accounted for 77 percent, or US$9.19 billion. Imported energy accounted for 8.5 percent of the total value of imports in 2000 and 3.8 percent of GDP, with per capita energy imports at US$544.

Consumption

Taiwan's annual energy consumption increased from 29.58 million kiloliters of oil equivalent in 1980 to 90.91 million kiloliters in 2000, marking an average growth rate of 5.8 percent per year. By comparison, GDP grew by an average of 7.2 percent during the same period, with an energy demand elasticity of about 0.81. Per capita energy consumption increased from 1,677 liters of oil equivalent in 1980 to 4,109 liters in 2000, an annual growth rate of 4.6 percent.

Over the past 20 years, the industrial sector has been the greatest energy consumer; however, its share of total energy consumption dropped from 65 percent in 1980 to 55 percent in 2000. Energy consumption for transportation increased from 12 percent in 1980 to 16 percent in 2000; and for agriculture, it declined from 3 percent to 2 percent; for residential use, it increased from 10 percent to 12 percent; for commercial use, it increased from 2 percent to 6 percent; for other sectors, it remained around 6 percent. Non-energy use was close to 3 percent in 2000.

Since the second worldwide energy crisis, coal has accounted for a growing percentage of Taiwan's overall energy consumption, rising from 8 percent in 1980 to 11 percent in 2000. By contrast, petroleum products accounted for only 37 percent of overall energy consumption in 2000, down from 52 percent in 1980.

Oil and Natural Gas

Taiwan is heavily dependent on imported oil. In 2000, approximately 59 percent of Taiwan's imported crude oil came from the Middle East, and 41 percent came from Indonesia, the Congo, and Australia. Consumption of petroleum products totaled 41.12 million kiloliters of oil equivalent in 2000, of which 33 percent was for industrial use, 35 percent for transportation, 17 percent for power generation, 2 percent for agriculture, 4 percent for residential use, and 9 percent for other purposes.

To liberalize the oil market, the government authorized the establishment of petroleum refining enterprises and granted them permission to engage in petroleum production, import, export, and marketing in June 1996. The Chinese Petroleum Corporation 中國石油股份有限公司 (CPC) is responsible for exploring, producing, importing, refining, and marketing petroleum and natural gas in Taiwan. The CPC operates three oil refineries with a total refining capacity of 770,000 barrels per day. In addition, the private Formosa Petrochemical Corporation 台塑石化股份有限公司 will operate an oil refinery, with a total capacity of 450,000 barrels per day. The first stage, with a capacity of 150,000 barrels per day, was completed in 2000.

In 1987, the government began allowing privately operated gas stations to sell gasoline and diesel oil. At the end of May in 2001, there were 2,060 gas stations, 1,477 (72 percent) of which were privately owned. In 2000, domestic petroleum production amounted to 51.4 million kiloliters of oil equivalent and 747 million cubic meters of gas respectively.

The domestic market for the importation of fuel oil, jet fuel, and LPG was opened in January 1999. All petroleum products will be imported, within three months after passing of the Petroleum Administration Law. Even if the Petroleum Administration Law does not pass the Legislative Yuan, the oil market is scheduled to be fully liberalized by the end of 2001.

To diversify energy supplies, CPC began importing LNG from Southeast Asia in 1990. In 2000, the total amount of natural gas supply was 6.55 billion cubic meters, of which only 0.75 billion cubic meters (11 percent) were locally produced, and 5.8 billion cubic meters (equivalent to 4.4 million tons) were imported LNG, accounting for 89 percent of the total. Of the latter, 58 percent came from Indonesia, and the other 42 percent was from Malaysia. Natural gas consumption in 2000 totaled 6.4 billion cubic meters, of which 26 percent was for industrial use, 58 percent for power generation, 13 percent for residential use, and 3 percent for commercial use.

Coal

Coal production has continued to decline, dropping from five million tons in 1969 to 80 thousand tons in 2000. The local coal industry was once the prime source of energy for Taiwan, supplying over 60 percent of the energy used by industry in the 1950s and employing some 65,000 coal miners in over 400 mines around the island. Due to the high costs of coal production under increasingly difficult mining conditions, as well as competition from imported coal, the number of coal mines and miners in Taiwan has decreased dramatically. On January 9, 2001, the government rescinded rules that protected local coal production, and the last coal mine in Taiwan closed in January 2001.

The coal supply in Taiwan totaled 45.51 million tons in 2000. Of this, 0.2 percent was domestically produced, while the remaining 99.8 percent was imported from Australia, Indonesia, South Africa, the Chinese mainland, and the United States. In 2000, some 56 percent of the total coal consumption went to power generation, 5 percent to the cement industry, 13 percent to steelworks, and 26 percent to other industries and users.

Electricity

In 2000, gross power generation by the Taiwan Power Company 臺灣電力公司 (Taipower) totaled 145 billion KWH, a 0.6 percent increase from 1999. Of this total, 6 percent was generated by hydropower, 39 percent by coal, 17 percent by oil, 11 percent by LNG, and the remaining 27 percent by nuclear fission. Power cogeneration by auto producers created another 30.2 billion KWH in 2000. Electricity consumption in 2000 rose to 172 billion KWH, up 10 percent over the preceding year. At present, almost everyone in Taiwan has electricity service.

Taipower is the agency responsible for developing, generating, supplying, and marketing electric power for almost the entire Taiwan area. By the end of 2000, the Taiwan area had 17 EHV substations (345/161 KV), with a total capacity of 29,500 MVA; 45 primary substations (161/69

KV), with a total capacity of 22,830 MVA; and 60 primary distribution substations (69/22-11 KV), with a total capacity of 10,600 MVA. A total of 39 hydropower, 30 thermal, and three nuclear plants supply power to these stations. Taipower's installed plant capacity totaled 27,385 megawatts, of which 16 percent was from hydropower, 30 percent coal-fired, 16 percent gas-fired, 19 percent oil-fired, and 19 percent nuclear. By the end of 2000, the installed capacity of auto producer cogeneration was 5,138 megawatts, equivalent to 15 percent of Taipower's installed capacity.

With the continuous growth of the domestic economy, the peak load in 2000 reached 25,854 MW, up 6.8 percent over 1999. The average load was 17,289 MW, a 7.4 percent increase compared with the previous year. In the face of ever increasing demands for power, the government has already taken several steps to alleviate future potential shortages. The government has allowed private investors to participate in the power generation industry in 2 stages beginning in January 1995 and August 1995. To promote gas-fired power plants, the government issued "Program for the Private Sector to Apply for Constructing Power Plants in Current Stages" in January 1999. At present, there are ten Independent Power Producers (IPPs) with approved capacity of 9,180 MW, of which 2,250 MW is in operation, 3,020 MW under construction, and 3,910 MW in the planning stage. In 1999, units five, six, seven, and eight of the Taichung Thermal Power Plant 臺中火力發電廠, unit six of the Tunghsiao Power Plant 通霄發電廠, and unit five of the Hsinta Power Plant 興達發電廠 were all put into operation, generating an additional 377 megawatts electricity per year.

In June 1999, Mailiao Power Corporation, located in the Yunlin County naphtha cracker complex established by the Formosa Plastics Group, began its initial commercial operations, with an annual power generating capacity of 1,200 megawatts. This new independent power plant is expected to alleviate the island's power shortages during the summer. In addition, companies operating at the Hsinchu Science-based Industrial Park (HSBIP) suffered a loss of over US$3 million due to the power outage that resulted from the devastating September 21 earthquake in 1999. Consequently, the government instructed the Science-based Industrial Park Administration to construct a second cogenerator in HSBIP to supply additional electricity to the park.

Nuclear Power

The six nuclear power units in Taiwan provided 14.8 percent of the island's total installed capacity (5,144 megawatts of 34,773 megawatts), but produced 27 percent of Taiwan's total electrical power in 2000. The six nuclear units are housed in three nuclear power stations, all of which are owned and operated by Taipower. With increasing demands for electricity, especially for industrial use, the government began plans to construct the Fourth Nuclear Power Plant in 1980. Environmental and anti-nuclear protests generated opposition in the Legislative Yuan, especially among legislators representing constituencies near the construction site. The Legislative Yuan passed budgets for the plant and construction began in 1998. However, the new administration announced the termination of the project in October 2000, resulting in serious disputes between the executive and legislative branches. With a constitutional interpretation delivered by the Grand Justices and weeks of negotiation, the project was resumed in February 2001, with a goal of establishing Taiwan as a "nuclear-free homeland" in the future.

Renewable Energy Sources

Taiwan is expected to have great potential for developing solar energy resources. A number of solar thermal and photovoltaic testing systems are already in service in Taiwan, with the total area of solar collectors reaching 961,300 square meters at the end of 2000. In addition, after launching of the five-year subsidy program for the promotion of wind energy in 2000, the first 2.64 MW wind-farm was successfully installed and operated in Mailiao in November 2000. Technologies for biogas purification and the assembly of biogas power generators have been investigated over the last decade, and a number of pig farms already

As Taiwan continues to develop its renewable energy resources, solar collectors—such as these found at the Jade Mountain Meteorological Station—are becoming more and more prevalent.

have biogas power generators in operation, with capacities of 625 kilowatts. In 2000, these generators produced approximately 23 megawatts.

Energy Prices

The price structure for electrical power is set to reflect the cost of supplying energy at different seasons (seasonal rates) and different times of the day (TOU rates). Seasonal rates and TOU rates are designed to encourage peak clipping, valley filling, and/or load shifting. Currently, the electrical service is divided into three categories: lighting, combined lighting and power, and power (metered and flat-rated). Seasonal rates are applied to all customer classes except flat-rated customers. TOU rates are mandatory for those with a contracted capacity of 100 KW and are voluntary for those with a contracted capacity below 100 KW. At present, TOU rates are applied to all customer classes except lighting customers.

Low-tension metered lighting service is applicable to residential as well as small commercial and noncommercial customers. Charges for metered lighting service are calculated solely upon KWH consumed. Low-tension combined lighting and power service is applicable to medium commercial and noncommercial customers. Low-tension metered power service is applicable to small and medium industrial/agricultural customers. High or extra-high tension service is applicable to customers with a contracted capacity of around 100 KW. Charges for power service and combined lighting and power service are separated into demand charge and energy charge (a two-part rate). Demand charge is billed on contracted KW, and energy charge is calculated according to KWH consumed.

In order to directly reduce the summer peak load, Taipower also offers a menu of interruptible rates (seven options) on a voluntary basis to customers taking high or extra-high tension service. Interruptible rates are designed to reflect capacity cost savings for customers' interruptible loads. The rates require that customers reduce their peak demand to a predetermined level in accordance with the contract in return for demand credits. The latest rate schedules for electrical service came into effect on June 1, 1999.

Domestic oil price has been allowed to reflect the cost of imported oil as world price fluctuates. The government abolished the "Domestic Petroleum Price Formula" in September 2000. Now, all prices of petroleum products are determined by the market mechanism.

Further Reading

2000 Tai-wan neng-yuan tung-chi nien-pao 臺灣能源統計年報 (Annual Report on Energy Statistics in the Taiwan Area; in Chinese). Taipei: Energy Commission, Ministry of Economic Affairs, 2001.

Chih-tsao-yeh hsien-kuang yueh-pao 製造業現況月報 (Monthly Bulletin of the Manufacturing Industry; in Chinese). Taipei: Industrial Development Bureau.

Chung-hwa min-kuo tai-wan ti-chu neng-yuan chien-chieh 中華民國臺灣地區能源簡介 (Introduction to Energy in the Taiwan Area, ROC; in Chinese). Taipei: Energy Commission, Ministry of Economic Affairs, 2001.

Cross-strait Economic Statistics Monthly 兩岸經濟統計月報 (Chinese-English bilingual). Taipei: Mainland Affairs Council, Executive Yuan.

Economic Development, Taiwan, Republic of China 2001 (in English). Taipei: Council for Economic Planning and Development, Executive Yuan.

Kung-yeh fa-chan nien-chien 工業發展年鑑 (Yearbook of Industrial Development in Taiwan, ROC; Chinese-English bilingual). Taipei: Industrial Development Bureau, Ministry of Economic Affairs, annual.

Kung-yeh sheng-chan tung-chi yueh-pao 工業生產統計月報 (Monthly Bulletin of Statistics in Industrial Production; in Chinese). Taipei: Statistics Department, Ministry of Economic Affairs.

Monthly Bulletin of Manpower Statistics, Taiwan Area, ROC 人力資源統計月報 (Chinese-English bilingual). Taipei: Directorate-General of Budget, Accounting, and Statistics.

Monthly Bulletin of Statistics of the Republic of China 主計月報 (Chinese-English bilingual). Taipei: Directorate-General of Budget, Accounting, and Statistics.

Monthly Statistics of Finance 財政統計月報 (Chinese-English bilingual). Taipei: Ministry of Finance.

News Bulletin 財政部新聞稿 (Chinese-English bilingual). Taipei: Ministry of Finance, monthly.

Newsletter, Taiwan New Economy 臺灣新經濟簡訊 (Chinese-English bilingual). Taipei: Center for Economic Deregulation and Innovation, Council for Economic Planning and Development, monthly.

Quarterly National Economic Trends, Taiwan Area, the Republic of China 經濟動向統計月報 (Chinese-English bilingual). Taipei: Directorate-General of Budget, Accounting, and Statistics.

Statistical Abstract of National Income in Taiwan Area, ROC 中華民國臺灣地區國民所得統計摘要 (Chinese-English bilingual). Taipei: Directorate-General of Budget, Accounting, and Statistics.

Statistics on Overseas & Foreign Investment, Outward Investment, Outward Technical Cooperation, Indirect Mainland Investment, and Guide of Mainland Industry Technology, the Republic of China 中華民國華僑及外國人投資,對外投資,對外技術合作,對大陸間接投資,大陸產業技術引進統計月報 (Chinese-English bilingual). Taipei: Investment Commission, Ministry of Economic Affairs, 2001.

The Development of International Trade in the Republic of China 中華民國國際貿易發展概況 (Chinese-English bilingual). Taipei: Board of Foreign Trade, Ministry of Economic Affairs, annual.

White Paper on Small and Medium Enterprises in Taiwan 中小企業白皮書 (Chinese-English bilingual). Taipei: Small and Medium Enterprise Administration, Ministry of Economic Affairs, Executive Yuan, annual.

World Investment Report 2000. New York: United Nations.

Related Websites

1. Board of Foreign Trade: *http://www.trade.gov.tw*
2. Council for Economic Planning and Development: *http://www.cepd.gov.tw*
3. Directorate-General of Budget, Accounting, and Statistics: *http://www.dgbas.gov.tw*
4. Industrial Development Bureau: *http://www.moeaidb.gov.tw*
5. Energy Commission: *http://www.moeaec.gov.tw*
6. Mainland Affairs Council: *http://www.mac.gov.tw*
7. Ministry of Economic Affairs: *http://www.moea.gov.tw*
8. Small and Medium Enterprise Administration: *http://www.moeasmea.gov.tw*
9. Taiwan Transportation Vehicle Manufacturers Association: *http://www.ttvma.org*

11

Finance and Banking

As a member of the WTO, Taiwan will continue liberalization of its financial system.

What's New

1. Financial situation on the downturn
2. Record-high issuance of bonds
3. Depreciation of the NT dollar
4. Weak stock market

The Republic of China's financial situation in 2000 was not encouraging. The real domestic economy, which had experienced a boom since the Asian financial crisis in 1997, experienced a sharp downturn. Moreover, the financial side of the domestic economy continued to deteriorate as a result of the increasing number of non-performing loans.

In the first quarter, domestic economic growth peaked at 7.94 percent as the global economy strongly expanded. The Taiwan Stock Exchange (TSE) composite index, which took a strong comeback to 8,448 points at the end of 1999, continued to escalate to 10,202 points on February 17, 2000. Meanwhile, the New Taiwan dollar appreciated against the greenback, as the exchange rate rose from US$1:NT$31.395 at the end of 1999 to US$1:NT$30.302 on April 10.

However, the financial situation took a dive in the second half of 2000 despite good performance by the real side of the domestic economy. GDP grew 6.73 percent, and exports and imports jumped 29.9 percent and 34.5 percent respectively in the third quarter. But bearish sentiments in global stock markets began to affect domestic stock markets.

The situation became even worse when Premier Tang Fei resigned in October 2000 because of turmoil caused by the problem of the Fourth Nuclear Power Plant. In addition, weak global demand for IT products wreaked havoc on the domestic economy and the GDP growth declined sharply to 3.82 percent.

The TSE index slid to the bottom at the end of 2000 and closed at 4,739 points. The New Taiwan (NT) dollar also had a large depreciation against the US dollar. All of these developments indicated that both the real side and financial side of the domestic economy was losing ground even though annual GDP growth for 2000 reached 5.86 percent.

The government continued to relax regulations on capital markets and reform financial institutions. For instance, a second board market, Taiwan Innovative Growing Entrepreneurs (TIGER), was created in April 2000 for over-the-counter (OTC) trading. On October 13, 2000, the Legislative Yuan passed the revised *Banking Law* 銀行法部分條文修正案, increasing the limit of individual shareholding in the same bank to 25 percent. The Legislative Yuan also passed the *Financial Institutions Merger Law* 金融機構合併法 on November 24, 2000, serving as the enabling law for establishing asset management corporations (AMCs) to accelerate the disposition of non-performing loans.

Despite the worsening economic situation in the first half of 2001, deregulation and reform in the financial sector continued. The *Financial Holding Company Act* 金融控股公司法 and other related laws were passed during an extended session of the Legislative Yuan. All these developments indicated that the government was determined to solve the non-performing loan problems and adapt the financial sector to world standards.

In this chapter, we use an average exchange rate of US$1:NT$32.27 for the year 1999 and US$1:NT$31.23 for 2000. As for fiscal year 1999 (from July 1, 1998 to June 30, 1999), an average rate of US$1:NT$33.12 is used. And for fiscal year 2000 (from July 1, 1999 to June 30, 2000), an average rate of US$1:NT$31.44 is used. To avoid confusions resulting from currency fluctuations, this chapter will use the NT dollar as the unit of calculation where appropriate, unless otherwise noted.

Public Finance

Government Expenditures

In FY2000, government expenditures reached US$97.6 billion, up 57.7 percent from the FY1999 level of US$61.9 billion. The increase was mainly due to the extension of FY2000 from

Government Revenues and Expenditures

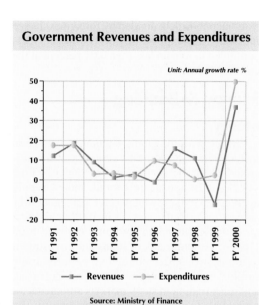

Unit: Annual growth rate %

Revenues   Expenditures

Source: Ministry of Finance

12 months to 18 months in order to synchronize the fiscal and calendar years beginning in 2001. The appreciation of the NT dollar also contributed to the increase. In terms of the NT dollar, government expenditures only increased 49.7 percent from NT$2,050 billion in FY1999 to NT$3,069 billion in FY2000. A breakdown of the FY2000 government expenditures showed that education, science, and culture was the largest area for spending, accounting for 20.8 percent of the total.

Other major spending items included general administration at 16.1 percent, social welfare at 15.3 percent, economic development at 13 percent, national defense at 11.5 percent, pension and survivors' benefits at 9.5 percent, obligations at 9.2 percent, community development and environmental protection at 2.9 percent, and miscellaneous expenditures at 1.8 percent. Overall current expenditures at all levels of government were 84.1 percent, while capital expenditures were 15.9 percent. Except for community development and environmental protection expenditures on all areas were on the rise. Besides miscellaneous expenditures, obligations

led the increased expenditures with a 100.1 percent growth in FY2000, followed by general administration with a 76.7 percent growth. The government has shifted policy priorities from economic development and national defense to social welfare; pension and survivors' benefits; and education, science and culture. Funding for social welfare; pension and survivors' benefits; and education, science and culture gained 67.3 percent, 60.9 percent, and 48.4 percent respectively. Meanwhile, spending on national defense and economic development increased to a lesser extent 23.4 percent and 13.8 percent respectively.

Overall current expenditures at all levels of government rose by 66.1 percent to reach NT$2,581 billion, while capital expenditures declined 1.8 percent to NT$486.7 billion. In consequence, the share of current expenditures to total expenditures increased from 75.8 percent in FY1999 to 84.1 percent in FY2000, while the share of capital expenditures declined from 24.2 percent to 15.9 percent.

Government Revenues

Government revenues also increased in FY2000, but growth was less than expenditures. With increases in revenues from taxes, monopoly sales, public enterprises and public utilities, public properties, fees, and fines and indemnities, the total revenue for all levels of government increased by 37.1 percent in FY2000 to NT$2,748 billion. However, revenues from donations and contributions, sales of properties and recalled capital, and miscellaneous items declined.

Overall the share of current revenues was up from 93.1 percent in FY1999 to 96.2 percent in FY2000, while the share of capital expenditures declined from 6.9 percent in FY1999 to 3.8 percent in FY 2000. This indicated that the government relied less on capital accounts and more on current accounts in FY2000. Tax revenues, which accounted for 70 percent of government revenues, increased 47.9 percent in FY2000 to reach NT$1,922 billion. Surplus revenue from public enterprises and public utilities, the second largest source of government revenues, increased

25.7 percent to NT$408.2 billion. Revenues from monopolies, fees, and fines and indemnities were also up 56 percent, 53.5 percent, and 25.3 percent respectively to reach NT$86.3 billion, NT$103.1 billion and NT$48.5 billion. Profits of public properties increased only 3.7 percent to reach NT$26.4 billion. On the down side were revenues from donations & contributions, declining 6.9 percent to NT$1.4 billion; sales of properties and recalled capital, declining 24.2 percent to NT$104 billion; and miscellaneous items, declining 12.2 percent to NT$47.7 billion.

Debt Obligations

Because expenditures outpaced revenues at all levels of the government, the outstanding government bonds accumulated from NT$1,245 billion at the end of 1999 to NT$1,480 billion at the end of 2000, up 18.9 percent. Meanwhile, the outstanding debt to GNP ratio for the central government increased from 14.6 percent in FY1999 to 25.3 percent in FY2000. Nevertheless, external public debt reduced 36.2 percent from US$47 million at the end of 1999 to US$30 million at the end of 2000. The external public debt servicing ratio, which is equal to the

Money Supply

Unit: Annual growth rate %

—■— M$_{1A}$ —●— M$_{1B}$ —▲— M$_2$

Source: Central Bank of China

external public debt divided by foreign exchange income from exports of goods and services, continued to remain less than 0.01 percent at the end of 2000.

Money & Banking

Money

Along with the global economic expansion in 2000, the ROC domestic economy also accelerated. Nevertheless the Central Bank of China 中央銀行 (CBC) set a target for the money supply aggregate M$_2$ to grow between 6 percent and 11 percent in 2000, the same as in 1999. In the first quarter, the domestic economy enjoyed high growth. Growth rates of loans and investment by domestic banks rebounded, exports, trade surplus and foreign capital inflow all increased, and brisk trading in stock markets attracted a lot of money from investors. Consequently the growth rate of the M$_2$ in terms of daily average increased from 7.08 percent of December 1999 to 8.27 percent in the first quarter of 2000. To keep the economy from overheating, the CBC on March 24 raised both the rediscount rate and the prime rate for accommodation with collateral by 0.125 percentage points to 4.625 percent and 5 percent respectively. On June 27, the CBC once again raised both the rediscount rate and the prime rate for accommodation with collateral by 0.125 percentage points to 4.75 percent and 5.125 percent. In April, US stocks faced a serious adjustment and bearish sentiment spread to domestic stock markets, and foreign portfolio investment began to pull out of Taiwan. The trade surplus also shrank in the second quarter, as a result, the growth rate of the M$_2$ declined. Furthermore, traditional industries, which rely heavily on domestic banks for financing, did not grow as strongly as the IT industry. The attitude of domestic banks toward granting new loans to traditional industries was therefore affected. Compared to the relatively high base of 1999, the growth rate of the M$_2$ declined to the year-low of 5.96 percent in July. Since August foreign portfolio investment again increased. But domestic economy began to cool down in the second half of 2000. Demand for money was weakened. Thus from August to December the growth rates of the M_2 fluctuated between 6 percent and 7 percent. Overall the annual average of M_2 growth rates was 7.04 percent in 2000, slightly lower than the 8.33 percent registered in 1999.

Similarly, the growth rates of the narrowly defined money supply aggregate M_{1b} also rose with the fast expansion of the domestic economy, continued inflow of foreign capital, increase in stock values, and growing demand deposits. The growth rates of the M_{1b} climbed from 14.08 percent in December 1999 to the peak of 19.88 percent in March 2000. The growth rates of the M_{1b} remained in double digits from January to June, but with growth rates declining. In the second half of 2000, a cool domestic economy, less trading in the stock market, and investor's transferring money from demand deposits to time deposits caused the growth rates of the M_{1b} to decline sharply. The growth rates of the M_{1b} fell from 7.32 percent in July to merely 0.37 percent in December. Still, the annual average of M_{1b} growth rates was 10.8 percent in 2000, which was slightly higher than 1999's 9.86 percent.

Financial Institutions

Financial institutions include monetary and other financial institutions. The former consists of the Central Bank of China, domestic banks, medium business banks, local branches of foreign banks, credit cooperatives, and the credit departments of farmers' and fishermens' associations. The latter are made up of the postal savings system, investment and trust companies, and life insurance institutions. By the end of December 2000, the number of financial institutions in Taiwan had decreased by four from the

Financial Institutions			
	1995	*1999*	*2001*
Domestic Banks	34	47	54
Branches	1,361	2,288	2,992
Medium Business Banks	8	5	5
Branches	446	288	289
Taiwan Branches of Foreign Banks	38	41	38
Branches	58	70	69
Credit Cooperatives	73	50	39
Branches	556	416	373
Credit Departments of Farmers' Associations	285	287	260
Branches	886	971	887
Credit Departments of Fishermen's Associations	27	27	25
Branches	44	49	44
Postal Savings System	1	1	1
Branches	1,269	1,296	1,316
Investment and Trust Companies	5	3	3
Branches	49	36	33
Life Insurance Companies	29	31	18
Branches	76	108	117
Source: Central Bank of China			

end of the previous year to reach a total of 491. Two local branches of foreign banks were closed, and nine new domestic banks were formed from either the combining credit cooperatives or from merging of credit cooperatives with existing banks. In addition, two investment and trust companies were transformed into domestic banks, one industrial bank was established, and one insurance institution was terminated. Including branches, the total number of financial institutions increased from 6,026 at the end of 1999 to 6,127 at the end of 2000.

At the end of 2000, loans and investment of monetary institutions grew 3.11 percent from the previous year, and monthly growth rates fluctuated between 2.76 percent and 4.15 percent. The annual average of growth rates for loans and investment of financial institutions was 3.63 percent in 2000, less than 1999's 5.33 percent.

Several factors contributed to the slowdown in lending growth. First, domestic banks continued to aggressively write off past-due and non-performing loans and were more conservative toward new loans. Second, cash-rich insurance institutions sought business in lending and therefore replaced some lending by monetary institutions. Third, traditional industries and the construction industry continued to shrink and thus their borrowing needs decreased. Fourth, the trend of direct financing continued to increase while indirect financing became less popular. Fifth, the shadow of a financial crisis in some domestic conglomerates loomed over monetary institutions and made them more reluctant to grant new loans.

Among loans to different sectors, the share of private enterprises declined from 84.83 percent at the end of 1999 to 83.08 percent at the end of 2000. Meanwhile, loans to government agencies, influenced by increasing borrowing from the government treasury, increased from 12.54 percent to 14.3 percent, while loans to public enterprises declined minutely from 2.63 percent to 2.62 percent. Investment of monetary institutions declined 8.37 percent from the end of 1999 to the end of 2000, with monthly growth

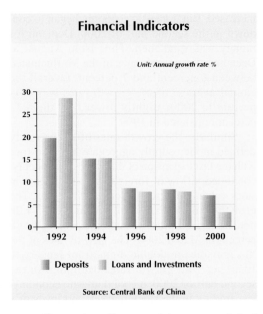

Financial Indicators

Unit: Annual growth rate %

Deposits ▮ Loans and Investments

Source: Central Bank of China

rates all negative. Commercial papers weighed 41.96 percent of bank investment, declining from 49.94 percent at the end of 1999. Investment in government bonds and treasury bills, however, increased from 28.4 percent to 29.3 percent. Overall, the ratio of direct financing of business decreased from 30.11 percent in 1999 to 23.29 percent in 2000, while indirect financing increased from 69.89 percent to 76.71 percent.

The non-performing loan ratio for domestic financial institutions rose steadily from 5.67 percent in December 1999 to 6.26 percent in September 2000 and then dropped slightly to 6.2 percent in December 2000. The reason for the increase was due to the effects of continued difficulties facing traditional industries, a rising unemployment rate, and continued recession in the real estate market. In the fourth quarter, increased government borrowing and appropriation of large private investment projects caused loans to increase and the ratio of non-performing loans was able to decline a little.

Money Market

Transactions in money markets varied in 2000. While transactions in the inter-bank call-loan market expanded mildly, transactions in short-term bills declined. In the first quarter, continued inflow of foreign capital filled money markets with excess funds. But beginning in the second quarter, a change in the global and domestic economic situation induced capital outflow. Stock values reduced sharply and the NT dollar faced a pressure to depreciate as more investors switched deposits from the NT dollar to foreign currencies, especially to the US greenback. Consequently, the domestic money markets tightened. Overall, transactions in the inter-bank call-loan market amounted to NT$9.54 trillion in 2000, increasing NT$1,691 billion or 1.8 percent from 1999. Among different maturities, overnight call-loans accounted for 69.57 percent, followed by one-week maturity loans with 21.67 percent. In 2000, short-term bills valued at NT$10.32 trillion were issued, down NT$3,519 billion or 3.3 percent from 1999. Commercial papers constituted 87.49 percent of total issues, followed by 11.15 percent of negotiable certificates of deposit, while bankers' acceptance had the smallest share of 0.57 percent.

The decline in the issues of short-term bills was attributed to weak money demand from private firms. In addition, banks and bill-financing companies reduced the business of guaranteeing short-term bills to control credit risks. A third factor came from the CBC's inclination to purchase fewer short-term bills and grant more loans so as to reduce the non-performing loan ratio.

At the end of 2000, the outstanding balance on short-term bills amounted to NT$1.81 trillion, down NT$2,283 billion or 11.23 percent from the end of 1999. Nevertheless, transactions of short-term bills in the secondary market gained NT$4.26 trillion or 7.14 percent in 2000 to reach NT$63.92 trillion. Commercial papers accounted for 89.09 percent of those transactions.

The trend in the short-term interest rates was influenced by both global and domestic factors. Global factors included rising crude oil prices, setbacks in international stock markets, and concerns about the slowdown in the US economy. Domestic factors included the 2000 presidential election, the controversy over the Fourth Nuclear Power Plant, plunge in the stock index, an increasing non-performing loan ratio, and other factors. Generally speaking, the money supply in money markets changed from loose to tight in 2000.

At the beginning of 2000, the entire banking system had much excess money and short-term interest rates were kept at low levels. However, uncertainty before the presidential election led to a temporary depreciation of the NT dollar. In addition, increasing crude oil prices and the US Fed's raise of interest rates three times in the first half of the year caused the interest rate spread to enlarge. Expectation for inflation also increased. To prevent the NT dollar from depreciation and to keep inflation in control, the CBC raised both the rediscount rate and the prime rate for accommodation with collateral by 0.125 percentage points to 4.625 percent and 5 percent respectively on March 24. As a result, the average interest rate for the overnight call-loan market rose from 4.61 percent in January to 4.64 percent in March. On June 27, the CBC once again raised the rediscount rate and the prime rate for accommodation with collateral by another 0.125 percentage points to reach 4.75 percent and 5.125 percent respectively. The average interest rate for the overnight call-loan market also increased to a peak of 4.8 percent in June. The domestic financial situation continued to worsen in the second half of the year and pushed up short-term interest rates. But under the moderation of the CBC, short-term interest rates were relatively stable. As global economy began to show weakness in the fourth quarter, the short-term interest rate began to decrease. The CBC reduced the rediscount rate and the prime rate for accommodation with collateral back to 4.625 percent and 5 percent on December 29. The average interest rate for the overnight call-loan market declined to 4.72 percent in December and 4.73 for the year, the lowest since 1988. The weighted average rates for 1-to-30-day and 31-to-90-day commercial papers in the secondary market also declined to 5.34 percent and 5.18 percent respectively in 2000.

Bond Market

With the government's fiscal deficit widening in 2000, the government bond issues broke historic records. The central government issued NT$346.5 billion in bonds during 2000, an increase of 22.52 percent over 1999. Taipei City also issued bonds twice, totaling NT$16 billion. As a result, the new issuance of bonds by all levels of governments increased 28.17 percent to reach NT$362.5 billion.

The outstanding balance for bonds issued by all levels of governments also rose 18.88 percent to NT$1.48 trillion. In addition, low interest rates and falling share prices encouraged firms to favor issuing corporate bonds, which increased 31.8 percent to NT$181.2 billion, while bank debentures increased 28.29 percent. The outstanding balance for corporate bonds increased by 19.85 percent to reach NT$707.3 billion, and bank debentures declined by 6.27 percent to NT$91.67 billion.

Low interest rates and more issues of bonds boosted the secondary bond market in 2000. In addition, slumping stock markets induced many investors to switch into bond trading. Therefore, transitions in the secondary bond markets increased 30.36 percent to reach a historic high of NT$68.35 trillion in 2000. Bond repurchase transactions increased 15.44 percent to NT$52.15 trillion, while outright transactions grew 123.3 percent to NT$16.2 trillion. Trading in government bonds constituted 99.3 percent of total bond transactions.

Interest Rates

The CBC's monetary policy in the first half of 2000 was relatively neutral and loosened up in the second half of the year, primarily to acclimatize the economic situation. On March 24, the CBC raised the rediscount rate from 4.5 percent to 4.625 percent. Simultaneously, the prime rate for accommodation with collateral was raised from 4.875 percent to 5 percent. On June 27, the CBC raised again the rediscount rate and the prime rate for accommodation with collateral to 4.75 percent and 5.125 percent respectively. On

December 29, the CBC lowered both rates back to 4.625 percent and 5 percent respectively. The prime lending rate for five major commercial banks was up slightly from 7.667 percent at the end of 1999 to 7.71 percent in December 2000.

Foreign Exchange Market

In the first quarter of 2000, the NT dollar appreciated against the US dollar, as a result of the strong expansion of the domestic economy an exports, as well as the huge amount of capital inflow. The exchange rate of the NT dollar against the US dollar reached NT$30.302:US$1 on April 14. However, the effects of US interest hikes and a weak Japanese yen caused the US dollar to remain strong against other currencies. Consequently, the NT dollar began to depreciate.

Political gridlock over the construction of the nuclear power plant and the slowdown of domestic economic growth caused further depreciation of the NT dollar in the fourth quarter. Investors rushed money into foreign currency deposits, and the NT dollar sank to a low of NT$33.18:US$1 on December 22. Nevertheless, the average exchange rate of the NT dollar was NT$31.225:US$1 in 2000, up 3.33 percent from the previous year. The NT dollar depreciated 2.08 percent against the Japanese yen and appreciated 19.33 percent against the euro in 2000.

Foreign exchange transactions expanded in 2000, with net transactions at authorized foreign exchange banks and local branches of foreign financial institutions totaling US$1,205 billion, up 15.5 percent from 1999. Trading between banks and customers made up 44.5 percent of foreign exchange transactions, while trading among banks made up 55.5 percent. Spot transactions were the most popular accounting for 65.8 percent of total foreign exchange transactions in 2000, followed by foreign exchange rate swaps with 14.6 percent, options with 9.3 percent, forwards with 8.3 percent, margin trading with 1.7 percent, and cash-and-carry swaps with 0.3 percent. Compared to 1999, except for margin trading which declined 40.1 percent, all others experienced growth. Options had the highest growth rate of

63.6%, followed by cash-and-carry swaps at 30.4 percent, forwards at 23.2 percent, spot at 13.3 percent, and swaps at 12.3 percent.

As the trade surplus expanded and foreign portfolio investment grew, the foreign reserves of the CBC accumulated quickly in the first half of 2000. But in the second half, a worsening domestic situation caused foreign reserves to decline to US$106.7 billion at the end of the year, compared to US$106.2 billion at the end of 1999.

Stock Market

The Taiwan Stock Exchange started strong but finished weak in 2000. In the first quarter, an expected economic boom and huge inflow of foreign portfolio investment pushed the TSE composite index to as high as 10,202 points on February 17. Afterwards, the uncertainty before the presidential election and rising cross-strait tension caused the TSE index to temporarily decline. But once the election results came out, the TSE index bounced back to 10,186 points on April 5. Between April and May, the US Nasdaq stocks faced a downward adjustment as Internet stocks collapsed. The TSE was affected and the index slid to 8,438 points on May 25, and downward to 4,614 points on December 27.

Several factors caused the stock downturn in the second half of the year. First, foreign institutional investors sell stocks heavily in September. Second, international crude oil prices reached another peak in September and October, adding to investor's worries about a slowdown in the global economy. Third, news of a financial crisis among some domestic conglomerates and the ever-increasing non-performing loan ratio by financial institutions decreased investor's confidence. Fourth, the Executive Yuan announced in October the termination of the Fourth Nuclear Power Plant construction, increasing instability in domestic politics. Fifth, several foreign news media reported in November that a financial crisis could take place in Taiwan. Last but not the least, signs of a weaker US economy appeared and hi-tech stocks faced another downward

In recent years, the ROC has strengthened financial re-regulation and supervision in response to changes in the financial environment.

adjustment pressure. For 2000, the TSE index plunged 43.9 percent.

The number of listed companies increased to 531 in 2000, compared to 462 in 1999. The number of shares increased 18.86 percent to 363 billion in 2000. Total trading value also increased 4.22 percent to reach NT$30.53 trillion in 2000. The average daily trading amounted to NT$112.6 billion, compared to NT$110.1 billion in 1999. With the fall in stock prices and trading volume, the turnover rate also dropped from 238 percent in 1999 to 195 percent in 2000. In addition, the market value of all companies listed on the TSE index declined 30.5 percent to NT$8.2 trillion in

2000. Among all indexes, electronics suffered the largest decline of 49.7 percent in 2000, followed by a 49.4 percent decline in construction, and a 48.3 percent decline in textiles. Other indexes also declined.

Financial Restructuring

The ROC economy grew at a phenomenal pace through the 1970s and 1980s. The rapid accumulation of assets which accompanied this growth led to a tremendous increase in financial activity and brought about profound structural changes in the local financial markets. Increasing labor costs and the appreciation of the NT dollar in the 1980s sped up the globalization of Taiwanese capital by encouraging investment and other financial involvement in overseas financial markets. This trend, in turn, exerted competitive pressure on the domestic financial system and forced the ROC to liberalize itself more to attract foreign investors and financial institutions.

The ROC's financial system has been undergoing restructuring since 1987. Among many changes that have been made is the relaxation of restrictions on cross-border capital flows. Interest rates have also been gradually liberalized, beginning with discount rates on CDs and bank debentures in 1980 and extending to include deposit interest rates. In 1989, the revised *Banking Law* 銀行法 was passed, lifting all restrictions on interest rates and bringing an end to Taiwan's long history of interest rate controls. In addition, the island has developed its short-term money market and long-term capital market to help meet the requirements of supply and demand, thereby allowing market mechanisms to play a more active role in the financial system.

When the ROC set up its money market in 1975, it was limited to inter-bank call loans and other short-term monetary instruments. Since then, it has evolved into the second largest money market in Asia with an annual turnover exceeding US$1.6 trillion. The size of the bond market also expanded drastically after 1989 due to the heavy issuance of government bonds for economic development. As for the stock market, the revised *Securities Transaction Law* 證券交易法 of 1989 allowed new entries into the brokerage business and loosened restrictions on inward remittances of foreign capital for portfolio investment, thereby making Taiwan's financial markets more competitive internationally.

In recent years, the ROC has strengthened financial re-regulation and supervision in response to changes in the financial environment. The rapid expansion of financial markets, including the deregulation of financial activities, financial innovations, and new entries in the financial sector, and the possible disorder associated with financial realignment have all made re-regulation necessary. In line with the Bank of International Settlements, the ROC has set its capital adequacy ratio at 8 percent of risk assets. The government also established the Central Deposit Insurance Corporation 中央存款保險公司 in 1987 to provide a better safety net for depository institutions. The *Banking Law* of 1989, while allowing new entrants into the banking industry, also tightened regulations dealing with problem banks. Regulating some areas while deregulating others has been the most important task of financial restructuring in Taiwan.

After a number of bank runs on local credit cooperatives in the past few years, the CBC and the MOF decided to form a temporary joint committee to monitor all banking institutions. The MOF also made a proposal to revise the *Statute of Deposit Insurance* 存款保險法 requiring all financial institutions to participate in a system of compulsory deposit insurance.

To promote an active market of corporate bonds and to introduce more positive competition among banking institutions, the first credit rating company began its operation in May 1997. With the passage of the *Futures Trading Law* 期貨交易法, the local futures exchange was opened in October 1997 and the Taiwan International Mercantile Exchange (TAIMEX) was inaugurated in July 1998. Trading on indexes of electronic and financial stocks was open in 1998 to make firms and individuals more flexible in hedging their risks against the volatility of commodity prices, exchange rates, interest rates and stock prices. Some new financial instruments, including warrant contracts on approved stocks, exchange rate options and foreign exchange futures, were also listed on the Taiwan Stock Exchange or allowed to be traded over-the-counter in 1997. To mobilize the domestic stock markets for international competitiveness, the MOF also gradually loosened up the regulation on foreign capital. The limit on the ownership ratio of domestically listed firms by a single foreign investor was raised from 15 percent to 50 percent, and for foreign investors from 30 percent to 50 percent in February 1999. The MOF also raised the quota of portfolio investment by a single foreign investor from US$600 million to US$1.2 billion in November 1999 and to US$1.5 billion in October 2000. At the same time, foreign investors are allowed to participate in the TAIMEX trading. The Securities and Futures Commission under the MOF announced in October 1999 the Regulatory Principle for Consolidation of Security Firms 證券商合併原則 to further encourage domestic security firms to consolidate and develop globally or toward the direction of investment banking. To help firms with potential to overcome the hurdle of listing regulation, a second board market, Taiwan Innovative Growing Entrepreneurs (TIGER) for over-the-counter trading, was created in April 2000.

Several laws regarding financial reform were passed in 2000. On June 30, the *Enterprise Act* 信託業法 was passed so that the increasing demand for management of trust properties could be met by diversifying the trust enterprise's business scope, encouraging the development of an asset management corporations mechanism. This act is viewed as one of the key statutes in the development of securitization structures.

On October 13, 2000, the Legislative Yuan passed the revised *Banking Law*. Key amendments include: (1) authorizing additional administrative powers to the Ministry of Finance for dealing with financial institutions encountering difficulties; (2) relaxing limits on the holding of bank shares, increasing the individual bank ownership ceiling from 15 percent to 25 percent to allow greater equity participation; (3) expanding bank's business scope, such as allowing banks to issue debit cards and subordinated financial debentures; and (4) increasing punitive liability. The purpose of these amendments is to bring Taiwan's banking system in line with international standards, improve the asset quality of banks, and facilitate mergers of financial institutions.

On November 24, the Legislative Yuan passed the *Financial Institutions Merger Law*. The law offers tax and non-tax incentives to financial institutions that take the initiative to merge on their own. For instance, merged financial institutions are exempt from land value increment taxes, stamp taxes, and other taxes. Losses resulting from the sale of bad debts because of a merger can be amortized over a 15-year period. The law also facilitates domestic and foreign bank mergers by permitting foreign financial institutions to acquire 100 percent of a domestic financial institution. More importantly, the law provides a legal basis for establishing asset management corporations. The AMCs will help dispose of non-performing assets in the banking sector. The impaired assets foreclosed by an AMC may be auctioned through an independent third party, bypassing the usual lengthy court procedures.

After accession to the World Trade Organization (WTO) in 2001, Taiwan has continued its liberalization process in the financial system. Other issues, such as allowing domestic financial institutions to set up branches in mainland China, will be dealt with under the principle of globalization. In the future, Taiwan's financial institutions will do their best to compete in the global financial platform and to meet the challenges of a rapid changing finance world.

Related Websites
1. Ministry of Finance: *http://www.mof.gov.tw*
2. Central Bank of China: *http://www.cbc.gov.tw*
3. Security and Futures Commission: *http://www.sfc.gov.tw*

Los Angeles

London

Hong Kong

Singapore

Tokyo

Guam

Phnom Penh

Palau

El Salvador

Any banking service you need, when you are in

Guam Palau
Tokyo Hong Kong
Singapore Phnom Penh
Los Angeles New York
El Salvador London

Please contact.........

Head Office
30, Chung King South Road, Sec. 1
Taipei 100, Taiwan, R.O.C.
Tel: 886-2-2348-1111
Fax: 886-2-2361-0036
http://www.firstbank.com.tw
e-mail: fcb@mail.firstbank.com.tw

第一商業銀行
FIRST COMMERCIAL BANK

THE ART OF CHINESE GOURMET
GOES ON AND ON.

滿漢大餐
蔥燒牛肉麵

 統一企業公司
UNI-PRESIDENT ENTERPRISES CORP.

Creative the Healthy & Joyful Feature

12 Agriculture

Consistent with the ROC's accession to the World Trade Organization in January 2002, the government has revised relevant laws and regulations to soften the impact of imported foreign agricultural products on local farmers.

Agricultural development in Taiwan has been facing an increased pressure in recent years due to the rapid changes in political, economic, and social conditions both at home and abroad. The global promotion of trade liberalization has enabled a growing number of imported agricultural products to enter Taiwan, making local products less and less competitive in the market. Taiwan's admittance into the World Trade Organization (WTO) in January 2002 exacerbated this situation, as the ROC government further reduced tariffs on agricultural products, canceled separate customs protective measures, and eased the domestic support for agricultural development in Taiwan in accordance with WTO requirements. In 2000, Taiwan's farmers made up only 7.4 percent of the workforce, down from 8.3 percent in 1999, and produced less than 3 percent of the island's GDP. Soaring labor costs in Taiwan and greater demand by consumers for high-end agricultural products have forced Taiwan to adjust the structure of its agricultural industry and map out a new overall plan on the future use of land, water, and man power resources, as well as the development of farm villages.

Taking into account the aforementioned circumstances, the ROC government continues to formulate agricultural policies that can adjust the role and function of agriculture in Taiwan, facilitate systematic and structural reforms for its agricultural industry, and attach greater importance to environmental protection. Sustainable agricultural development in Taiwan can only be ensured when agriculture becomes a highly competitive and modernized green industry.

The New Plan on Agriculture for the 21st Century 邁進二十一世紀農業新方案 implemented in January 2001 was designed not only to realize the goal of a sustainable development of the green industry, but also to create a dignified and dynamic life for farmers and establish an ideal living environment for all. In accordance with this plan, the government has attached greater importance to the quality rather than the quantity of agricultural production. The number of farmers in the farming, livestock, and fishery industries will be reduced from 776,000 in 1999 to 633,000 by 2004. The labor productivity in the agricultural sector will also be raised by 4.17 percent each year from 2001 through 2004. The production value of farming, livestock, and fishery industries will be adjusted from 43.6, 33.2, and 23.2 percent to 42, 35, and 23 percent, respectively, by 2004, and the annual income from agricultural products for every farming household will be increased from US$5,411 to US$5,860 by 2004.

Farmers

In 2000, there were nearly 851,495 hectares of land farmed by 782,566 farming households, meaning that each household on average farmed only 1.08 hectares (2.65 acres). For the past decade, Taiwan farmers have derived nearly 80 percent of their annual income from non-farming activities. The rise of part-time farming households, which have accounted for over 80 percent of all farming households since 1980, concerns economic planners, who argue that only full-time farmers are likely to invest in the capital and training necessary to develop large and profitable businesses.

Efficient farming is also being inhibited by the rapidly aging agrarian workforce. The number of farmers over the age of 65 has increased annually, and in 2000 they accounted for around 10 percent of the total farming population. Many youths are leaving family farms for the better-paying jobs in the cities. Farming incomes have grown, but they have not kept pace with other sectors.

The Council of Agriculture 農業委員會 (COA) has tried to persuade graduates of agricultural institutes and young members of farming families to stay on the farm. Local agricultural authorities encourage potential young farmers to improve farm management and raise farm income, after determining that they are capable of farming on their own. Rural projects are also being developed to make rural life more acceptable to today's youth.

The long-term solution for maintaining agriculture competitiveness is for the remaining farmers to increase their efficiency as older farmers retire. The COA and the Council of Labor Affairs 行政院勞工委員會 (CLA) have been conducting training programs and job counseling over the past several years in accordance with the *Agricultural Development Act* 農業發展條例. Recognizing the difficulty of training older farmers and the need to provide alternative forms of assistance, the government promulgated a temporary statute on May 31, 1995, to grant elderly farmers a monthly stipend of US$96. Eligible farmers included those who:

• have reached the age of 65;
• have been covered by the farmers' health insurance program for more than six months;
• are not receiving any old-age pensions from social insurance (such as labor insurance), living allowances, or other types of government assistance;
• are solely employed in the agricultural sector;
• have lands and houses (private farmlands and farmhouses excluded) whose value does not exceed US$185,185; and
• have an individual income that does not exceed the annual minimum wage.

To further enhance the welfare of farmers, the Legislative Yuan passed several revisions to the temporary statute in October 1998, removing items 3 through 6 above, and expanding the act to cover fishermen. These amendments allowed 150,000 more people in the farming and fishing industries to receive the stipend. From July 1999 through the end of 2000, a total of US$1.22 billion had been distributed through the stipend to approximately 680,000 farmers.

Land

In mountainous Taiwan, farming is largely restricted to the island's arable western slope lands and alluvial plains. Farm plots tend to be small: 76 percent of all farming households have less than one hectare of arable land. The small average size of farms is a significant obstacle to Taiwan's agricultural modernization, since mechanization and advanced management depend on size to be cost-efficient.

To address this situation, the government has been working in cooperation with farmers' organizations and other agencies to convert unprofitable farmland to other uses, consolidate plots into larger areas of land that are easier to farm, and gradually reduce excess farmland. On July 11, 1996, the Legislative Yuan passed amendments to the *Agricultural Development Act*, lifting restrictions on the transfer, inheritance, and division of farmland.

Farmland Rezoning

On August 4, 1995, the Executive Yuan instituted the Farmland Release Program 農地釋出方案 to ease restrictions on rezoning farmland. Some 160,000 hectares of farmland have been scheduled for release, including 78,000 hectares of coastal subsidence areas, 50,000 hectares of polluted areas, and 27,000 hectares of low productivity farmland. Fish farms in subsidence areas are given priority for release, with the goal of reducing the present 50,000 hectares by 40 percent over the next ten years.

The minimum area for plots released for the construction of labor housing or industrial and commercial use is five hectares, and for residential use is ten hectares. To ensure safe and efficient land use, all development on rezoned farmland must follow the government's environmental and development policies.

To prevent windfall profits, those who transfer farmland for industrial or commercial use are required to pay a usage fee of up to 12 percent on the current assessed price of the transferred land. Half of this money goes to government agricultural agencies while the other half goes to local governments. To encourage businesses to move to eastern Taiwan and to accelerate offshore island development, farmland released in Ilan 宜蘭, Hualien 花蓮, Taitung 臺東, the Penghu Islands 澎湖群島, Kinmen 金門, and Matsu 馬祖 is exempt from usage fees. As of December 2000, 13,604 hectares had been released under the Farmland Release Program, and an additional 2,012 hectares were in the process of being released.

Farmland Consolidation

The farmland consolidation program 農地重劃 is designed to combine odd-shaped plots of scattered farmland into larger contiguous plots, that are easier to farm. The reshaped plots of land are then redistributed, giving each farmer a plot of land about the same size as the one he formerly owned, but much better proportioned. Farm roads and irrigation ditches that serve these areas are also being improved, rebuilt, and repaired. This program is helping to overcome a few of the shortcomings of small-scale farming by reducing production and marketing costs and increasing operational efficiency.

Farmland

According to Article 3, Item 10 of the *Agricultural Development Act,* farmland includes any property necessary to the farming, forestry, animal husbandry, or aquaculture industries—such as farm houses, animal stalls or coops, storage facilities, drying areas, collection areas, farm roads, irrigation ditches, and catchment areas. It also includes land used for warehouses, refrigeration facilities, equipment centers, silkworm houses, and collection centers that have been provided by farmers' associations or agricultural cooperatives and stations.

Farmland Utilization Project

The COA, in cooperation with the now defunct Taiwan Provincial Department of Agriculture and Forestry, enacted a long-term General Farmland Utilization Project 農地利用綜合規劃 in 1992. This project guides county and city governments and grassroots organizations in setting up agricultural districts to meet the needs of farmers based on environmental, economic, and technical requirements. In fiscal 2000, the COA spent US$5.3 million on the project, affecting over 94,650 hectares of farmland.

Water

Farming is dependent on large quantities of clean water, and although Taiwan has an annual average precipitation of 2,515 millimeters, its water resources are unevenly distributed. Regional and seasonal water shortages necessitate careful planning and conservation. The Water Resources Bureau 水資源局 (WRB) of the Ministry of Economic Affairs reported Taiwan's water usage in 1999 to be 16.87 billion cubic meters (bcm); and of that amount, agriculture accounted for 12.05 bcm or 71.44 percent of the total. In comparison, the total water used in 1999 by the residential and industrial sectors was only 18.35 percent and 10.21 percent, respectively.

Crops

Both the types and quantities of crops produced in Taiwan have changed over the past two decades. The ROC's pending acceptance into the WTO has pressured farmers to diversify crop production into horticulture, agritourism, exotic fruits and vegetables, chemical-free organic produce, and other high-value products. The Taiwanese people have changed their dietary habits and are now eating more wheat-based foods and dairy products and consuming less rice. The island's rising standard of living has also boosted demand for such products as exotic flowers and processed foods.

Rice ranked as Taiwan's most valuable crop in 2000, followed by betel nuts, corn, pineapple, mangoes, sugar cane, pears, tea, bamboo shoots,

Rice harvesters have greatly increased labor and production efficiency.

and peanuts. In terms of harvested area, rice ranked first, followed by betel nuts, sugar cane, peanuts, bamboo shoots, tea, mangoes, corn, watermelons, and sorghum.

Rice

According to the COA, there were 339,949 hectares of rice-fields in Taiwan in 2000, producing 1.54 million tons of brown rice during the island's two crop seasons. This surplus exceeded the island's annual demand and was largely attributed to changes in people's dietary habits, which caused per capita rice consumption to fall by 60 percent between 1974 and 2000, from 134 kilograms to 55 kilograms. As Taiwan entered the WTO in January 2002, foreign competition further exacerbated the problem of oversupply and intensify the downward pressure on rice prices.

To help Taiwan rice growers adapt, the government is working to balance rice supply with falling demand through the Rice Production and Rice-field Diversion Program implemented in July 1984 稻米生產及稻田轉作計畫 and the initiation of several programs for purchasing rice. In May 1997, the *Food Management Law* 糧食管理法 was promulgated to further stabilize the price by upgrading the quality and regulating the supply and demand of rice.

Rice-field Diversion Program

The Rice Production and Rice-field Diversion Program was carried out to reduce rice production in Taiwan. Through subsidies and incentives, this program encouraged farmers to leave rice paddies fallow, rotate crops, or fully convert their land to more profitable uses. The program was concluded at the end of June 1997

Taiwan Agricultural Research Institute

The Taiwan Agricultural Research Institute 農業試驗所 (TARI) was established in Taipei in 1895. The headquarters of this institute, which currently occupies 140 hectares of buildings and experimental farms, was moved from Taipei to Wufeng, Taichung, in 1977. The goal of the institute is to help farmers in Taiwan increase crop yields by developing elite cultivars with better resistance to pests and stress. TARI carries out its mission through R&D on crop improvement, production systems, and international cooperation. The institute employs 266 well-educated and -trained researchers and administrative staff.

TARI is also home to the National Plant Genetic Resources Center 國家作物種原中心, which is equipped with sophisticated long-term vaults capable of preserving up to 240,000 crop accessions for as long as 50 years. Currently, over 870 crop species and 70,000 accessions have been collected, preserved, and inputted into a computerized database to provide valuable information for domestic and international germ plasm exchanges. By the end of 2000, the center had sent out 36,199 seed samples to cooperators in foreign countries.

Recently, TARI released 50 and 26 new agronomic and horticultural crop varieties, respectively, such as the high-yielding, good quality Tainung No. 71 rice, and the Tainung No. 17, 18, and 19 pineapple that can be grown all year round. TARI regularly provides farmers with training programs on pest management and fertilizer application, as well as other advanced technologies to assist them in overcoming problems related to crop production. TARI also conducts basic, applied, conventional, and advanced biotechnological research for various fields. The improved varieties and technologies developed by the institute have contributed greatly to the remarkable increase of agricultural production in Taiwan, as well as to the rapid progress made in rural economic development.

and replaced by the Program for Rezoning Paddy Fields and Dry Farmland 水旱田利用調整計畫 a month later to further balance the supply and demand of rice. By 2000, these two programs combined had: diverted nearly 182,000 hectares of paddies, of which about 130,000 hectares were laid fallow and the remainder was planted with other crops; reduced the total area of rice cultivation from 429,000 hectares in 1991 to about 340,000 hectares in 2000; and decreased rice yields by 1.66 million metric tons to 1.54 million metric tons.

Rice Purchasing Program

Since April 1974, the government has been buying rice from farmers through the Food Stabilization Fund 糧食平準基金. Altogether, the government purchased 16 million metric tons of rice for US$8.5 billion between 1974 and 2000, increasing growers' income by US$1.4 billion. In 2000 alone, some 507,500 metric tons of rice were purchased in this manner for US$292 million, directly increasing growers' total income by nearly US$51 million. Since the government buys rice

and then sells it at a loss, by fiscal 2000 the Food Stabilization Fund had accumulated a deficit of US$3.3 billion.

Rice Quality Improvement

The High Quality Rice Production and Marketing Program 良質米產銷計畫 was enacted in fiscal 1986 and included in the Six-Year National Development Plan 國建六年計畫 of fiscal 1992. In fiscal 2000, 29 farmers' associations participated in this program to improve rice quality, and 74 grain traders contracted with farmers to produce high-quality rice.

Vegetables

Most vegetables produced in Taiwan are for domestic consumption. In 2000, 175,138 hectares of land were devoted to vegetable cultivation, down from a high of 239,707 hectares in 1986, but still considerably higher than the 1945 figure of 35,438 hectares. The main vegetable producing areas were concentrated in Yunlin, Tainan, Changhua, and Chiayi Counties. In 2000, bamboo shoots, watermelons, potatoes, cabbages, vegetable soybeans, garlic, cantaloupes, scallions, Chinese cabbages, and radishes were the leading vegetables in terms of area planted.

Vegetable production in 2000 was 3,222,088 metric tons. Through technological improvements such as new cultivars, growth regulators, and mechanization, crop yields per hectare of land increased from 8,970 kilograms in 1945 to 18,720 kilograms in 2000. Taiwan's most important vegetable crops in 2000 by value were watermelons, bamboo shoots, cantaloupes, garlic, cabbages, scallions, radishes, water bamboo shoots, Chinese cabbages, and Chinese mustard. Currently, more than 100 kinds of vegetables are produced in Taiwan. In northern Taiwan, radishes, Chinese cabbages, leaf-mustard, and garlic thrive in the cooler climate. In southern Taiwan, tomatoes, cauliflower, bamboo shoots, and beans are cultivated.

Fruits

Over 30 types of fruit are cultivated in Taiwan. Such deciduous varieties as apples, pears, and peaches thrive at high elevations, while citrus fruits, bananas, pineapples, lychees, longans, mangoes, papayas, persimmons, loquats, and guavas are grown in the lower plains and undulating slope lands. The main crops are citrus fruits, mangoes, lychees, bananas, pineapples, wax apples, and Asian pears. In 2000, almost 2.45 million metric tons of fruit were grown in Taiwan on a total planted area of 224,431 hectares.

Local growers have suffered tremendously from foreign fruit imports, which have flooded the domestic market in response to the reduction or elimination of tariffs on imported fruit. To face this growing competition, Taiwan fruit growers have applied advanced horticulture technology to modernize their operations. Through the effective control of diseases, adjustments of fruit maturation, cultivation of improved fruit strains, and implementation of multiple annual harvests, fruit farming has become a profitable and growing industry. Orchards are also diversifying into the agritourism business (see section on Agritourism below).

Sugar Cane

Taiwan's sugar industry has lost most of its former vitality due to a stagnation in global sugar prices and the importation of sugar into the domestic market. Both of these signs spell "transition" for the state-run Taiwan Sugar Corporation 臺灣糖業公司 (TSC), which has expanded its product line and diversified into biotechnology, land development, and overseas investments in order to remain competitive.

Taiwan was formerly one of the world's leading sugar exporters. In the 1950s and 1960s, the island had over 100,000 hectares of sugar cane fields and produced over one million metric tons of sugar annually. By 2000, however, farm labor shortages and a steady decline in world prices had reduced Taiwan's sugar cane fields to 12,000 hectares, half of which were owned by the TSC. Decreases in domestic sugar production led to a subsequent increase in sugar imports, and Taiwan now imports almost 190,000 metric tons of sugar annually.

In an effort to bring down sugar prices even further, the Executive Yuan passed the Sugar Industry Management Policy and Sugar Price Adjustment Program 糖業經營策略與糖價調整方案 in June 1996 to progressively reduce domestic production and increase imports.

Tea

Tea is symbolic of China and was once a mainstay of Taiwan's economy. At one time, Taiwan exported 80 percent of its tea production. In 1973, tea exports topped 21,000 metric tons. This situation has since reversed, however, and the island has been a major tea importer since 1991. Nearly 13,000 metric tons of tea were imported in 2000. The transformation of Taiwan from seller to buyer has been driven by local demand.

According to the Council of Agriculture, ever since the government opened Taiwan's market to Southeast Asian tea in 1990, annual tea imports have nearly tripled. In 2000, tea imports increased to12,891 metric tons while local production dropped to 20,349 metric tons (see chart). Taiwan has transferred tea processing techniques to

Taiwan Area Tea Industry
(unit: metric tons)

Year	Local Production	Imports	Exports
1990	22,299	2,604	6,194
1991	21,380	6,045	5,696
1992	20,164	6,752	5,577
1993	20,515	10,237	5,606
1994	24,485	10,685	4,948
1995	20,892	8,354	4,150
1996	19,955	7,365	3,475
1997	23,505	7,692	2,918
1998	22,641	9,034	3,188
1999	21,119	11,302	3,539
2000	20,349	12,891	3,774

Source: Council of Agriculture

Vietnam, Indonesia, and Thailand in order to take advantage of these nations' lower labor costs, and the tea produced in these countries is usually exported back to the Taiwan market.

Flowers

With a wide variety of fresh, beautiful flowers to choose from, Taiwan's horticulture industry has been flourishing in recent years. Between 1986 and 2000, output value increased from about US$74 million to US$305 million, while export value increased from US$3.7 million to US$46.5 million. Farmland used for raising flowers expanded from 3,500 hectares to 10,973 hectares. Major markets for export include Japan, Hong Kong, and the US. Flower farms usually devote half of the planting area to producing cut flowers, while the other half is used for nursury production.

Recreational Agriculture

Agritourism

From 1982 to 2000, some 2,045 hectares of land producing 20 different crops were officially converted into tourist farms 觀光農園, where visitors could pick their own fruits and vegetables. In 1990, the government began to encourage traditional farm owners to transform their farms into recreational farms 休閒農場. Recreational farms were similar to tourist farms, but also offered visitors picnicking, bird watching, and other low-impact activities, in addition to the opportunity to harvest their own agricultural products. In the early 1990s, however, it became clear that the agritourism industry was developing to an extent and in a direction that violated some environmental protection laws and land utilization regulations.

Major Livestock Production in Taiwan

Year	Hogs (millions of metric tons)	Chickens (millions)	Chicken Eggs (billions)	Milk (metric tons)
1990	1.22	226	4.03	203,830
1991	1.36	233	3.89	225,656
1992	1.36	257	4.75	246,281
1993	1.37	288	4.91	278,476
1994	1.45	301	5.20	289,574
1995	1.49	319	5.71	317,806
1996	1.53	345	6.13	315,927
1997	1.24	390	7.10	330,469
1998	1.08	389	7.15	338,369
1999	0.99	385	7.27	338,005
2000	1.16	390	7.27	258,049

Source: Council of Agriculture

In an effort to bring tourist and recreational farms under the rule of law, the government passed a revised set of *Recreational Agriculture Guidance and Management Measures* 休閒農業輔導管理辦法 in July 2000. The purpose of these regulations was to protect the environment; use land wisely and appropriately; and promote agricultural, educational, and recreational activities to increase the income of farmers and strengthen farm communities. As of June 2001, the COA had assisted 19 tourist and recreational farms in obtaining legal documents from the government for setting up such farms.

Fishing Industry

Over the past half-century, the island's fishing industry has developed from small-scale coastal fishing to deep-sea commercial fishing. In 1945, only a hundred or so trawlers produced an annual catch of about 40,000 metric tons. By 2000, the island's fishing fleet totaled 26,623 ships (of which 25,109 were powered craft), with an annual catch of some 1.10 million metric tons. The total fishery production, including aquacultural products, was 1.36 million metric tons in 2000.

In 2000, Taiwan produced US$2.8 billion worth of fish. Of this, 52 percent came from deep-sea fishing, 29 percent from aquaculture, 14 percent from offshore fishing, and 3 percent from coastal fishing. More than 36 percent of Taiwan's total production was exported, led by skipjack, squid, and tilapia.

The expanding role of deep-sea fishing in Taiwan's fishing industry largely resulted from declining fish stocks close to home caused by overfishing and pollution from industrial and household waste. In 1990, the government began to work on restoring its declining fish stocks. By 2000, a total of US$21 million had been allocated to set up 23 fishery conservation zones, 78 artificial reefs, and 70 reef protection zones along the coasts of Taiwan and the Penghu Islands 澎湖群島. Sea bream, abalone, grouper, mullet, threadfin, and brown croaker were then released into these areas to restore depleted fish stocks.

The development of offshore aquaculture is part of Taiwan's efforts to enter the world's fishery market. This offshore aquaculture farm managed by the Pan Asia Ocean Company in Liuchiu Rural Township, Pingtung County, is raising Cobia fish (Rachycentron cancadum).

The COA is also working to reduce the size of Taiwan's fishing fleet through a boat buy-back program. Approximately 2,342 old boats have been bought back since the initiation of the program, and displaced fishermen have been retrained to work in other occupations. Furthermore, the ROC government has been active in international fishery management organizations and promoted international fishery cooperation. By 2000, the ROC had signed official or private fishery agreements with 29 countries.

Aquaculture

Taiwan's aquaculture has been growing steadily over the years. In 2000, total aquacultural production was 256,399 tons, accounting for 19 percent of Taiwan's total seafood production. Taiwan's geography and climate are ideal for aquaculture, offering fish farmers tropical, sub-tropical, and temperate climate to raise a wide variety of fish. Even the North American rainbow trout can be cultivated in some of Taiwan's mountains.

One of Taiwan's most important aquacultural products is eel. Annual production of eels has been around 30,500 metric tons, worth more than US$7.04 million. Other important aquacultural products in Taiwan include milkfish, tilapia, grouper, tiger prawn, giant fresh water prawn, oyster, hard clam, and small abalone.

Livestock Industry

Starting from backyard farms in poor villages during the 1950s, the livestock industry in Taiwan had grown to a US$3.3 billion business, accounting for 39.44 percent of Taiwan's total agricultural production value in 2000. Hog production ranked first in value, followed by chickens, chicken eggs, and milk.

The *Animal Protection Law* was promulgated in October 1998. In addition, the *Animal Husbandry Law* 畜牧法 went into effect in June 1998 to better balance animal production and consumption, thereby ensuring a steadier income for farmers.

In accordance with the *Animal Husbandry Law*, the COA now has the responsibility for meat inspection. It promulgated the *Standards for Establishing Slaughterhouses* 屠宰場設置標準 in November 1999, the *Regulations on Slaughter Operations* 屠宰作業規範 in March 2000, and the *Meat Inspection Rules* 屠宰衛生檢查規範 in April 2000.

Agricultural Prospects

Perhaps the single biggest challenge confronting Taiwan farmers today is the increased competition they are facing after the ROC was admitted into the WTO. To meet WTO requirements, the ROC government has systematically reduced the trade barriers to its traditionally well-protected agricultural market. The average tariff on Taiwan's agricultural imports used to be 20 percent. After gaining admittance to the WTO, the ROC has reduced this average to 15.2 percent by the first year and will cut it down to 12.9 percent by the sixth year. After accession, all area restrictions were completely eliminated, tariffs were cut substantially, and products used to be subject to import control were subject to tariff-based conversion measures instead.

Consistent with the ROC's accession to the WTO, the government has taken legal steps to soften the impact of imports on local farmers, with the COA revising the *Agricultural Producer Import Damage Compensation Guidelines* 農產品受進口損害救助辦法 on March 29, 2000. In order to prevent harmful organisms from entering Taiwan through imported animals and plants, the Bureau of Animal and Plant Health Inspection and Quarantine 動植物防疫檢疫局 (BAPHIQ) was established under the COA in August 1998. Four branches of the bureau were set up near the airports and harbors in Keelung, Hsinchu, Taichung, and Kaohsiung, with three or four inspection stations established under each branch.

Related Websites:
1. Council of Agriculture: *http://www.coa.gov.tw*
2. Council of Labor Affairs: *http://www.cla.gov.tw*
3. Water Resources Bureau: *http://www.wrb.gov.tw*
4. Taiwan Agricultural Research Institute: *http://www.tari.gov.tw*

13

Environmental Protection

Coral reefs are one of the most important global ecosystems and a precious ecological heritage. (Photo by Jeng Ming-shiou)

What's New

1. Figures updated
2. Emergency Response Plan for Severe Marine Oil Pollution formulated
3. Two new wildlife refuges

Following four decades of rapid industrial development, a growing public and government awareness of the severe extent and ultimate cost of pollution is propelling the environmental protection movement in the Republic of China. A number of factors have shifted the focus of policymaking: First, the predominant concern in the 1960s and 1970s of stimulating economic growth has given way over the last decade or so to a more balanced consideration of the needs for additional growth versus the short- and long-term environmental costs. Second, as Taiwan approaches developed-nation status, people are starting to demand a quality of life commensurate with their level of economic achievement. Finally, the World Trade Organization (WTO) set up a Trade and Environment Committee to mediate disputes and solve problems between trade and environmental protection, which shows that environmental problems have already won global attention. As a member of the international community, Taiwan must keep in step with the pulse of the global environmental movement by actively participating in global environmental events and respecting international environmental conventions and regulations.

In all respects, the key to continued improvement is strict enforcement of already existing laws, coupled with a sustained campaign to inculcate a positive environmental protection and wildlife conservation ethic among the public. This chapter recounts the vicissitudes of environmental protection and wildlife conservation in Taiwan and describes the mandates, as well as legal and financial resources, at the disposal of the various government agencies that work to preserve the environment, conserve Taiwan's natural resources, and protect the island's wildlife.

Air Quality

Air pollution is one of the most serious problems in Taiwan, due to heavy traffic and a high concentration of industrial plants. The Environmental Protection Administration 環境保護署 (EPA) reported in 2000 that there were 2.76 registered factories and 445 motor vehicles for every square kilometer in the Taiwan area. Overall, there were some 16.32 million vehicles (5.36 million cars and 10.96 million motorcycles) registered in the Taiwan area, nearly three for every four people. According to the EPA, vehicular exhaust comprises more than 95 percent of the air pollution in Taipei, Taiwan's largest city.

According to EPA measurements of air quality in 2000, ozone and suspended particles were the primary air pollutants in the Taiwan area. On average, the percentage of days in 2000 in which the pollution standard index (PSI) recorded over 100 for the entire Taiwan area was 5.18. In the Kaohsiung and Pingtung areas, the PSI exceeded 100 during 18 percent of the days in 1996. Thus, in August 1997, the EPA established an office in the area and began the Air

---

Environmental Protection Administration

The only government agency at the national level that is solely devoted to protecting the environment is the Environmental Protection Administration (EPA) under the Executive Yuan 行政院環境保護署. The EPA sets the standards used to measure the amount of pollution in Taiwan's environment and drafts laws to elicit environmentally friendly behavior. As of 1998, the EPA had 582 full-time employees, 262 environmental investigators charged with collecting evidence in pollution cases, and 85 lab technicians responsible for analyzing test samples of pollutants brought back to the EPA's National Institute of Environmental Analysis 環境檢驗所. The EPA had a budget of US$540 million in fiscal 1999.

Pollution Improvement Project. The purpose of this office was to conduct total quality control and assist the local governments' environmental protection bureaus in reducing pollution from stationary and mobile sources and eliminating illegal ones. By the end of 2000, the percentage of days in these two areas with PSI values greater than 100 had been lowered to 11.7.

To more effectively monitor air pollution, the EPA set up the Taiwan Area Air Quality Monitoring Network 臺灣地區空氣品質監測網, which began operations in September 1993. The network includes 72 stationary automatic air quality monitoring stations, two mobile monitoring stations, and one air quality assurance laboratory. In January 1996, the EPA divided Taiwan into eight air quality prediction areas and began issuing next-day air quality forecasts islandwide.

On July 1, 1995, the EPA began collecting a broad surcharge on fuel in the form of an air pollution control (APC) fee. Under this scheme, a per-liter fee of US$0.006 was imposed on both premium diesel fuel and leaded gasoline. Since January 1, 2000, leaded gasoline has been phased out, and a per-liter fee of US$0.003 and US$0.01 has been imposed on Grade 2 and Grade 3 unleaded gasoline, respectively. The fee has not been levied on Grade 1, the best unleaded gasoline.

APC fees were also levied on exhausted NOx 氮氧化物 (US$0.094-0.375 per kg) and exhausted SOx 硫氧化物 (US$0.016-0.313 per kg) in air pollution control zones. In fiscal year 2000, the APC fee system generated almost US$96 million.

The funds collected from APC fees are earmarked for carrying out air pollution control programs, such as implementing air quality improvement plans at the local level, establishing environmental conservancy parks, subsidizing the purchase of electric motorcycles, and converting automobile engines to allow them to run on liquefied petroleum gas (LPG). The first LPG station for such converted automobiles was opened in Taipei City on March 15, 1996, and today there are nine LPG stations in Taiwan.

Noise Pollution

The *Noise Control Act* 噪音管制法 was promulgated in 1983 and later amended in 1992. Regrettably, noise pollution controls have not kept pace with the evolution of living quality in Taiwan over the past decade. In response, the EPA added a number of regulatory articles to address recent societal changes.

The proposed amendments shift responsibility for the subsidy, distribution, and administration of the aircraft noise control fee to competent

Percentage of Measurement Days by Pollutant Standard Index (PSI)

Level in the Taiwan Area

All Monitoring Stations

Period	Good 0-50	Moderate 51-100	Unhealthy 101-199	Very Unhealthy 200-299	Hazardous 300&Above	PSI>100
1994	34.41	58.76	6.82	0.01	0	6.83
1995	37.08	57.19	5.72	0.01	0	5.73
1996	40.39	53.49	6.08	0.04	0	6.12
1997	40.67	54.11	5.20	0.03	0	5.23
1998	47.98	47.41	4.60	0.02	0	4.61
1999	46.68	48.63	4.68	0	0	4.69
2000	45.32	49.51	5.18	0	0	5.18

Source: Bureau of Environmental Monitoring and Data Processing, EPA.

aviation authorities while relegating environmental agencies to the delineation of aircraft noise prevention zones. In terms of work site controls, the EPA has expanded the scope of control from "work sites, construction and equipment" to encompass all site types. Additionally, noise control standards have been defined according to type of work site, nature of the noise, control areas, and control periods.

The draft amendments have also taken into consideration noises that disturb the peace. In addition to setting controls on the activities that generate such noises, the amendments also target sources of low-frequency or temporary noises, such as air coolers and air conditioning systems. Even though such noises may be low in volume, they still impart discomfort, and therefore the amendments have brought such noises under their scope of control.

Also worth noting are changes that have been made to noise pollution inspection procedures. Because noises are ephemeral also, and because noise levels are often reduced when pollution inspectors arrive, 70 percent of noise complaints cannot be appropriately verified. This has posed a great deal of difficulty in the inspection and prosecution of violators. The new amendments address this by allowing inspection personnel to order facilities suspected of generating noise pollution to turn on the equipment in question while inspectors are present. Should the Legislative Yuan pass these amendments, this new approach would become the basis for future inspections and penalization.

The ROC Executive Yuan has approved the third amendment draft of the *Noise Control Act*. The revisions to this act would not only strengthen controls on all types of sites, but also limit the noise generation in residential areas. The draft amendment has already been submitted to the Legislative Yuan for review.

Water Resources

Most of Taiwan's rivers and coastal waters have long been seriously polluted. Urban communities are major culprits, primarily because of the island's long-term inaction to develop a comprehensive sewage system. Most industrial, agricultural, and residential wastewater drains directly into rivers, seriously polluting the water

---

Legislative Developments

The Environmental Protection Administration (EPA) under the Executive Yuan has taken the system of laws and regulations regarding environmental protection and separated them into five different categories: basic laws, administrative organizations, prevention, control, and relief. With the exception of the *Basic Environmental Protection Law*, which is still being reviewed by the Legislative Yuan, the remaining four categories are nearly complete in the structuring of their laws and regulations. Drafts are currently being formulated for the *Ocean Pollution Control Act* and the *Amendment to the Noise Control Act*. At the same time, revisions are being made to the *Noise Control Act* and several other related environmental protection laws that require modification due to changes in the official function and organization of the Taiwan Provincial Government. A total of 140 pieces of legislation have been completed, including 13 laws and amendments and 127 regulations and administrative orders. The thirteen environmental protection laws and amendments passed thus far consist of: (1) the *Environmental Impact Evaluation Law*, (2) the *Air Pollution Control Act*, (3) the *Noise Control Act*, (4) the *Water Pollution Control Act*, (5) the *Amendment to the Waste Disposal Act*, (6) the *Amendment to the Toxic Chemical Control Act*, (7) the *Amendment to the Drinking Water Management Act*, (8) the *Environmental Agents Control Act*, (9) the *Amendment to the Public Nuisance Dispute Settlement Law*, (10) the *Amendment to the Regulations Governing the Structure of the EPA under the Executive Yuan*, (11) the *Regulations Governing the EPA's Institute for Training Environmental Protection Personnel under the Executive Yuan*, (12) the *Regulations Governing the EPA's National Institute of Environmental Analysis under the Executive Yuan*, and (13) *the Soil and Groundwater Pollution Remediation Act*.

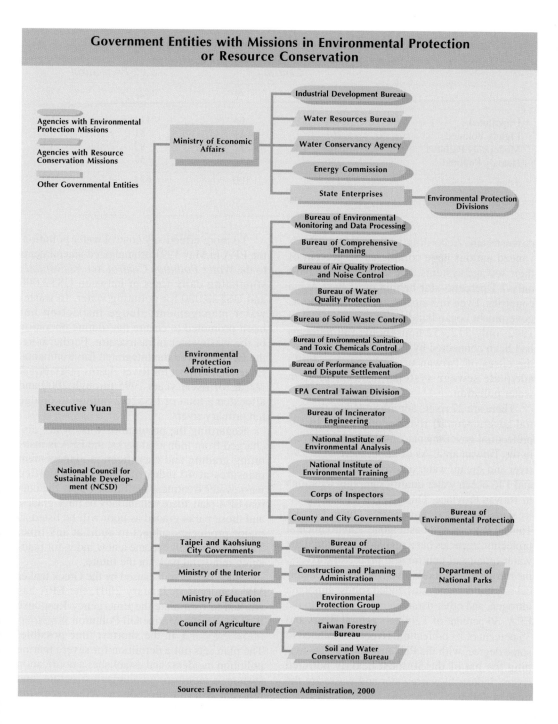

Government Entities with Missions in Environmental Protection or Resource Conservation

Agencies with Environmental Protection Missions

Agencies with Resource Conservation Missions

Other Governmental Entities

Ministry of Economic Affairs
- Industrial Development Bureau
- Water Resources Bureau
- Water Conservancy Agency
- Energy Commission
- State Enterprises — Environmental Protection Divisions

Environmental Protection Administration
- Bureau of Environmental Monitoring and Data Processing
- Bureau of Comprehensive Planning
- Bureau of Air Quality Protection and Noise Control
- Bureau of Water Quality Protection
- Bureau of Solid Waste Control
- Bureau of Environmental Sanitation and Toxic Chemicals Control
- Bureau of Performance Evaluation and Dispute Settlement
- EPA Central Taiwan Division
- Bureau of Incinerator Engineering
- National Institute of Environmental Analysis
- National Institute of Environmental Training
- Corps of Inspectors
- County and City Governments — Bureau of Environmental Protection

Executive Yuan

National Council for Sustainable Development (NCSD)

Taipei and Kaohsiung City Governments — Bureau of Environmental Protection

Ministry of the Interior — Construction and Planning Administration — Department of National Parks

Ministry of Education — Environmental Protection Group

Council of Agriculture
- Taiwan Forestry Bureau
- Soil and Water Conservation Bureau

Source: Environmental Protection Administration, 2000

195

Condition of Taiwan's Central and Prefectural Rivers

	Central		Prefectural	
	km	*%*	*km*	*%*
Unpolluted	1,434	64	414	65
Lightly Polluted	263	11	81	13
Moderately Polluted	265	12	82	13
Heavily Polluted	296	13	57	9
Total	2,258	100	634	100

Source: Environmental Protection Administration, 2000

downstream. According to the EPA, most advanced nations have completed 95 percent of their sewage systems, while Taiwan has built only 7.1 percent—far behind most East Asian countries. Even in Taipei City, where the ROC government began building a sewage system in 1972, only 317,752 households (36 percent) had been connected by the end of 2000. Thus, the cities of Taiwan urgently need to build adequate sewage systems in order to stem water pollution.

There are 27 rivers administrated by the central government, 91 rivers administrated by the prefectural governments, and 11 drainage rivers in the Taiwan area. As of 2000, there were 290 river and stream water quality sampling stations and 146 ocean water quality sampling locations in Taiwan Province. Thirty-two river water quality sampling stations have been set up in Taipei's Tamsui River 淡水河 basin alone. Environmental protection agencies have regularly monitored the water quality of central and prefectural rivers, measuring levels of dissolved oxygen, biochemical oxygen demand, suspended solids, ammonia nitrogen, and other parameters. According to the EPA, 36 percent of Taiwan's central rivers and 35 percent of its prefectural rivers are polluted to some degree, with the Peikang River 北港溪 topping the list of the 50 most heavily polluted rivers. Industrial wastewater and waste are the main pollutants.

To more effectively control water pollution, the EPA in May 1991 promulgated amendments to the *Water Pollution Control Act* 水污染防治法, stipulating daily fines of between US$2,000 and US$20,000 for polluting water. In wastewater management, sludge inspection has been promoted to ensure the routine operation of the wastewater infrastructure. Furthermore, the EPA renewed the Integrated Environmental Protection Project for River Basins 流域整體性環保計畫 for fiscal years 1995 through 2000 and allocated a total of US$26.2 million to dredge ten primary rivers.

Regarding the problem of wastewater discharged from industrial parks, the EPA is instituting grading and classification management measures at 40 industrial parks with unified wastewater treatment facilities. Under the current EPA plan, there will initially be three grades, and those parks graded as poor will be listed as major producers subject to audit at any time. This measure will become a new index for managing industrial parks in the future.

Since the oil spill caused by the Greek tanker MV Amorgos in January 2001, the EPA has worked to formulate the Emergency Response Plan for Severe Marine Oil Pollution 重大海洋油污染緊急應變計畫 in the shortest time possible. The plan sets out a definition for severe marine pollution incidents and establishes a notification system, a monitoring-command structure, and relevant working procedures. After receiving

Environmental Nuisance Complaints

In 2000, environmental protection agencies in the Taiwan area registered 102,200 environmental nuisance complaints, mostly concerning waste disposal. The public has not only become increasingly intolerant of companies that do not offer environmentally friendly products or services, but has also become more willing to do something about pollution control now that the government has set up channels for handling complaints and resolving disputes.

The *Public Nuisance Dispute Settlement Law* 公害糾紛處理法, which was promulgated in February 1992 and whose enforcement rules were announced in February 1993, was amended in January 2000. This legislation provides a legal basis for the Public Nuisance Arbitration Panel 公害糾紛裁決委員會 under the EPA and all of the subordinate public nuisance mediation committees 公害糾紛調處委員會 in every city and county in the Taiwan area. These committees are open for public participation and usually consist of academic and environmental specialists to insure objectivity. Decisions reached by the mediation committees and/or the EPA's arbitration panel are reviewed by the courts, and thus carry the weight of legal judgments.

Yearly Tabulation of Selected Environmental Nuisance Complaint Categories

	Waste Disposal	Noise	Air Pollution	Noxious Odors	Total* Complaints
1991	31,322	15,726	12,966	3,814	67,438
1992	29,805	20,328	16,916	5,603	77,547
1993	32,319	19,165	18,676	8,186	84,273
1994	34,855	20,265	12,957	10,049	86,517
1995	52,462	21,149	12,277	11,950	117,788
1996	51,557	19,432	10,962	12,655	114,431
1997	43,015	20,546	12,454	13,072	95,711
1998	31,702	19,343	14,575	14,309	85,768
1999	32,135	22,036	14,411	19,657	93,555
2000	32,875	26,158	11,091	24,087	102,200

*Includes categories not listed
Source: Environmental Protection Administration

Executive Yuan approval in April 2001, this plan became the basis for mobilizing government agencies when responding to severe marine pollution incidents.

There are 40 reservoirs in the Taiwan area, and the water quality at 20 primary reservoirs is regularly monitored. In 1999, seven of the 20 primary reservoirs were heavily polluted and eutrophic. The Fengshan Reservoir 鳳山水庫 and the Cheng Ching Lake Reservoir 澄清湖水庫 have been considered heavily polluted for two consecutive years. The Techi Reservoir 德基水庫 has the best water quality.

The development of industrial zones, golf courses, and real estate presents yet another challenge. Mountain deforestation has severely damaged watersheds. Soil in upstream areas is washed away, turning into silt and filling the reservoirs downstream, thereby reducing both the quantity and quality of water available for use. There seems to be no easy remedy for such upstream pollution beyond spending more money on downstream water cleanup or finding new water sources.

With this in mind, the Ministry of Economic Affairs 經濟部 (MOEA) plans to add nine new reservoirs to the island's current 40. However, environmentalists worry about environmental degradation resulting from reservoir construction, and reservoir proposals almost always provoke public protest. To win over the public, the MOEA in April 1996 drafted the *Water Resource Development and Conservation Incentive Regulations* 水資源開發保育回饋條例, which established an incentive fund for residents near new reservoirs. Furthermore, the MOEA implemented a five-year, US$1.55 billion integrated reservoir conservation program to clean up 38 reservoirs in the Taiwan area between 1997 and 2001. The EPA has also provided funds for local governments to carry out reservoir pollution control programs.

Land Subsidence

Lured by profits, many farmers in the coastal areas of Yunlin 雲林, Changhua 彰化, Pingtung 屏東, Chiayi 嘉義, and Ilan 宜蘭 have expanded into aquaculture. As a result, aquaculturalists have dug 170,000 illegal wells and pumped out excessive amounts of precious groundwater because it is cheap and stable in temperature. In addition to being used in aquaculture, groundwater is also being pumped for industrial, residential, and standard agricultural uses. Recent data shows that while 5.94 billion cubic meters of groundwater is being pumped annually, only four billion cubic meters is being replaced. This deficit has caused land in many areas to subside,

especially along Taiwan's southwestern coast and on the Ilan Plain 宜蘭平原. Overall, almost 865 square kilometers of Taiwan's plains, or a full 8 percent, have subsided. The most serious subsidence has occurred around Chiatung 佳冬 in Pingtung County, where sites have sunk by as much as 3.06 meters. The average rate of subsidence in the coastal areas is between 5 and 15 centimeters per year.

In November 1995, the Executive Yuan's Council of Agriculture 行政院農業委員會 passed a land subsidence control program drawn up jointly with the MOEA. This program allotted for US$56 million to be spent from July 1995 to June 2000 to control land subsidence in seven counties and cities.

Solid Waste Disposal

There has been a great increase in the amount of solid waste as a result of rapid industrial and economic development. According to the EPA, the amount of household garbage produced per person per day in Taiwan has nearly doubled over the past 15 years, going from 0.67 kilograms in 1985 to 1.05 kilograms in 2000. A daily average of 22,964 metric tons, or 8.38 million metric tons annually, of household garbage

The building of incinerators is expected to help resolve Taiwan's solid waste disposal problems.

2000 Recycling Amount (Tons)	
General Packaging	227,306
Lubricant Oil	11,996
Lead Acid Batteries	31,688
Tires	100,283
Waste Cars & Motorcycles	503,702
Source: Environmental Protection Administration	

was collected in 2000. Overall, 20,773 metric tons of garbage are properly treated in landfills or by incineration every day; the rest is disposed of in landfills that do not meet EPA standards. In addition, industries produce on average 18 million metric tons of waste each year, of which only 62 percent is properly treated.

Another problem is that many landfills are either full or nearing their capacity, and constructing replacement is difficult since available land resources are extremely scarce in Taiwan. In 1998, 66 of the island's 316 garbage treatment sites had reached full capacity, leaving more than half of Taiwan's rural and urban townships with no place to dispose of their garbage. The third stage of the Taiwan Area Solid Waste Disposal Project 臺灣地區垃圾處理第三期計畫, initiated in July 1997, called for the additional construction of eight regional landfills, 135 local sites, and 19 large-scale incinerators. At the close of the second stage of this project at the end of 1996, nine regional landfills, 161 local sites, and two large-scale incinerators had already been completed.

Recycling

A study performed by the EPA shows that about 40 percent of Taiwan's garbage is recyclable, including paper, glass, plastics, and metals. The recycling of these materials can not only lessen environmental burdens, lower the costs of waste disposal, and reduce Taiwan's dependence on resources, it can also create job opportunities and increase GDP. Thus, the ROC has recently devoted much effort to formulating regulations and programs for waste reduction and resource recycling. In Taipei, for example,

the city government began a "fee per package" policy on July 1, 2000, requiring residents to use special trash bags designated by the city government. This, in turn, caused residents to seek ways to reduce the amount of trash they produce while boosting recycling efforts. Recycling trucks now visit Taipei neighborhoods three times each week. After Article 10.1 of the *Waste Disposal Act* 廢棄物清理法 was amended on March 28, 1997, a new system for recycling resources was put into force. Through the market mechanism, the manufacturing and recycling systems are now integrated to the effect that communities, local garbage collection teams, scrap dealers, and the recycling fund all work together to carry out recycling activities.

The Four-in-One Resource Recycling Program 資源回收四合一計畫, which has been in operation since January 1997, combines the efforts of industry, auditing groups, scrap dealers, the government, and the public. In accordance with stipulations made by the Review Committee of Recycling Fee Rates, all responsible parties must pay fees to a recycling fund. Independent auditing groups selected by the EPA then examine the recycling rate and determine its value by taking into account materials, volume, weight, recycling value, and the recycling rate in the previous year. Based on the stipulated fee rate and their revenues, the responsible parties pay fees to a designated bank to form a recycling fund, which was originally managed by eight councils responsible for different aspects of the recycling program: waste containers, waste vehicles, waste tires, waste lubricant oil, waste lead acid batteries, waste agricultural pesticide containers, waste electronic appliances, and waste computers. After receiving pressure from many legislators and several non-governmental organizations, council members selected from relevant government agencies, academia, and non-governmental organizations were appointed by the EPA's administrator to have the management and use of recycling funds made more transparent and supervised by the Legislative Yuan. The EPA integrated the eight councils managing the recycling fund and, in FY1999, divided the collected recycling fund into a trust fund and a non-commercial fund.

Industrial Waste Management

Industrial wastes are produced principally from factories, agriculture, medicine and other business organizations. According to statistical data from the Industrial Waste Control Center, the total amount of industrial waste generated in Taiwan in 2000 was approximately 19.47 million tons, consisting of 1.61 million tons of hazardous and 17.86 million tons of non-hazardous waste. Under the guidance of the Industrial Waste Control Clean Strategy approved by the Executive Yuan on January 17, 2001, the EPA now coordinates and cooperates with other responsible agencies, such as the Industrial Development Bureau, to raise the percentage of industrial waste receiving proper treatment. This percentage is expected to approach 100 by the end of 2003.

Nearly 20,000 chemical substances are regularly used in the Taiwan area, of which 6,000 are highly toxic. Pursuant to the *Toxic Chemicals Control Act* 毒化物管理法, the EPA has released a list of 252 toxic chemicals for which the production, import, export, sale, or use must first be approved. Under another EPA program aimed at gathering information on pollution sources, all enterprises that use toxic substances or discharge waste gas, wastewater, or industrial waste are required to file plans covering the proper disposal of all toxins. Companies are then assigned deadlines for setting up disposal systems. A company that has filed a report and received a deadline is free from prosecution until the deadline passes. A company that does not file a plan or is found to be polluting the environment after the deadline has passed is subject to the heaviest fine under the law, which ranges from US$11,111 to US$37,037. Under the *Waste Disposal Act* amended in October 2001, manufacturers must assume responsibility for managing waste, and violators face fines of between US$1,921 and US$9,606. Those who dump hazardous waste resulting in the loss of life may be sentenced to life imprisonment.

The establishment of an ideal waste control and treatment system requires the concerted effort of government agencies and private groups. For example, the area of providing guidance to industry on waste cleanup and treatment requires a combined effort by the businesses, the Ministry of National Defense, the Ministry of Economic Affairs' Industrial Development Bureau, the Ministry of the Interior's Construction and Planning Administration, the Department of Health, and the Council of Agriculture. With the participation and oversight of citizens and private groups to prevent illegal dumping, the goal of appropriate treatment and handling of all industrial waste can be achieved. However, accomplishing this will require concerted efforts by everyone.

The EPA is currently using its Industrial Waste Enforcement Center facilities not only to improve the enforcement structure, but also to provide guidance to private investors in establishing waste cleanup and treatment organizations, industrial waste storage centers, and final waste disposal sites. The EPA is also encouraging sustainable management of environmental protection businesses to effectively manage waste treatment. These actions will improve the image of ROC enterprises, raise the competitiveness of Taiwanese products, and help Taiwan achieve its goal of balancing environmental protection with economic development.

Wildlife Conservation

Over the past decade, the ROC government and private environmental groups in Taiwan have been acting to stop international traffic in illegal wildlife products. Beginning with the promulgation of the *Wildlife Conservation Law* 野生動物保育法 in 1989 and continuing through 1995 with the formation of an interministerial task force designed to investigate and supervise wildlife conservation and crack down on the smuggling of wildlife products, Taiwan has repeatedly demonstrated its commitment to domestic conservation and support for global wildlife protection efforts.

However, some well-intentioned environmental groups felt that Taiwan's conservation efforts came "too little, too late." The United States therefore invoked the Pelly Amendment to impose trade sanctions on Taiwan in April 1994, and went on to announce a ban on imports of wildlife and wildlife products from Taiwan, effective August 19, 1994.

To avert international trade sanctions, the ROC legislature pushed through amendments to the *Wildlife Conservation Law* and toughened penalties against violators. The government also made greater and more visible efforts to abide by international agreements to halt the trafficking of endangered species and illegal wildlife products. On June 30, 1995, the United States lifted its trade sanctions on Taiwan. A little over a year later, on September 11, 1996, Taiwan's achievements were further confirmed when the US announced that Taiwan was being removed entirely from the Pelly Amendment's "watch list." The United States cited the ROC government's comprehensive efforts and cooperation with international endeavors as being behind the decision.

Legal Framework

Trafficking in certain wildlife products in Taiwan is proscribed by the *Cultural Heritage Preservation Law* 文化資產保存法, enacted in 1981, and the *Wildlife Conservation Law*. The former law mandates the creation of a system of nature reserves and designates 11 species of rare and valuable plants and 23 species of rare and valuable animals for protection; the latter law classifies over 1,955 species of rare flora and fauna into three levels of protection. Species listed either as "endangered" 瀕臨絕種 (meaning that their population size is at or below a critical level) or as "rare and valuable" 珍貴稀有 (referring to endemic species or those with a very low population) may not be disturbed, abused, hunted, captured, traded, exchanged, owned, killed, or processed. Species considered to "require conservation measures" 應予保育 may be utilized once the population has reached a

sustainable level, as determined by the Council of Agriculture (COA).

A newly revised *Wildlife Conservation Law* went into effect on October 29, 1994. The revised law is among the most severe in Asia: The trade or display for commercial purposes of protected, endangered, or rare and valuable wildlife products, as well as the unauthorized import or export of live protected wildlife or products made from protected wildlife, is punishable by a prison term of between six months and five years and/or a fine of between US$9,000 and US$45,000. Habitual offenders face prison terms of between one and seven years and/or fines of between US$15,000 and US$75,000. A person who falsely labels merchandise as containing protected wildlife or protected wildlife products shall be subject to a fine of between US$4,500 and US$22,500.

Further progress was achieved with the promulgation of the *Wildlife Conservation Law Implementation Regulations* 野生動物保育法施行細則 on April 29, 1995. These regulations stipulate that

Council of Agriculture

The Executive Yuan's Council of Agriculture 行政院農業委員會 (COA) is the highest government agency after the EPA, responsible for enforcing Taiwan's conservation laws. The COA drafts the nation's conservation policies and oversees their implementation. The COA spent approximately US$8.8 million of its budget on wildlife conservation in fiscal year 1999, and has allocated US$12.8 million for fiscal 2000. A Wildlife Conservation Investigation and Supervisory Task Force 野生動物保育查緝督導小組, which was set up in September 1993, coordinates conservation activities at various national and local government agencies, boosts conservation awareness, trains conservation personnel, and institutes crackdowns on illicit traffic in wildlife products. This task force consists of vice ministerial officials from selected government ministries, is convened by the chairman of the COA, and meets regularly to coordinate government work plans for strengthening wildlife conservation.

the Wildlife Conservation Advisory Committee 野生動物保育諮詢委員會 shall review the classification of protected species at least once a year.

Enforcement of Wildlife Conservation Laws

The ROC government has redoubled its efforts to investigate and punish violators of the *Wildlife Conservation Law* and other conservation-related legislation. A six-member Wildlife Protection Unit 野生動物保護小組 (WPU), set up on November 26, 1993, is in charge of investigations. The WPU is assisted by more than 350 police officers who have completed special training in wildlife conservation.

The COA has continued to coordinate the implementation of the *Wildlife Conservation Law* at the local government level by maintaining frequent contact with local officials and organizing training workshops and conservation-related activities for them. All local governments have also established joint enforcement task forces, which coordinate affairs among different agencies at the county level and hold meetings to review and improve enforcement efforts.

In 1999, local governments investigated over 1,600 wildlife-related cases and found 206 violations of the *Wildlife Conservation Law*. Customs officials also uncovered 53 cases of wildlife product smuggling that year. In 2000, the WPU investigated 63 wildlife-related cases

2000 Wildlife Conservation Law Enforcement

Cases brought to trial	187
Persons involved	209
Persons sentenced	189
one to two years	9
six months to one year	103
two to six months	71
detention	4
Persons found innocent	19
Fines	2
Remitted	1

Source: Ministry of Justice

itself, while the eight district offices of the Taiwan Forestry Bureau made 504 investigations and seized 3,179 illegal pieces of hunting, trapping, and fishing gear.

The coastguard, local police officers, customs agents, and state investigators have ambitiously enforced the *Wildlife Conservation Law*, confiscating various smuggled wildlife and wildlife products at airports, harbors, coastal areas, and in open waters. For example, on May 5, 2000, customs officials at the port of Keelung seized 332 elephant tusks weighing 2.16 metric tons.

Wildlife Products in Traditional Chinese Medicine

Tiger parts and rhino horns have long been used in Chinese medicine, and their scarcity and aura of prestige have created a strong demand for them in the Chinese world. This has placed great pressure on these endangered species, and thus conservation groups and the ROC government have worked to eliminate this problem.

The ROC government has revised the *Wildlife Conservation Law*, strengthened enforcement, and established a registration system for rhino horn. By December 1994, a total of 458 kilograms of rhino horn had been accounted for and marked with tamper-proof identification labels. Photographs and other measurements were also taken, and all registration information was entered into a computer database to facilitate future reviews. This system has significantly strengthened the position of conservation officials. In March 1994, 6.5 percent of the traditional Chinese pharmacies investigated in Taiwan were found to have violated conservation laws; by August and September of that same year, this figure had dropped to nil.

In addition to the establishment of a computer database to better manage registered rhino horns and tiger parts, local governments also conduct regular and random checks for such products. In 1999, they conducted 211 re-checks of registered rhino horns and tiger parts. Local government authorities also inspected 288 traditional Chinese medicine shops and found no selling of rhino horns or tiger parts.

Despite recognizing the ROC government's overall effort to crack down on the illegal importation of endangered wildlife products, some US wildlife conservation institutions still list Taiwan as a major consumer of bear parts. All bear species, including American black bears, are now listed as protected species under the *Wildlife Conservation Law*. In 1998, customs officials uncovered five bear gall bladders and a total of 22.5 kg of suspected bear gall bladders in powder form. To boost public awareness of bear conservation, the Department of Health (DOH) 行政院衛生署, the COA, and the Government Information Office 行政院新聞局 employed various advertising means, including phone cards, post cards, magazines and newspapers, product packages, TV screens at the CKS International Airport, and rest stations along the freeway.

Habitat Protection

One of the best ways to protect wild animals is to preserve their natural habitat. Unfortunately, this is not easily done in Taiwan, since it contains roughly 612 persons per square kilometer and nearly as many motor vehicles as people, making it one of the most crowded places in the world. While the ROC government has been able to put a cap on serious pollution problems, the fact remains that much of Taiwan's unique habitat has suffered from human encroachment.

Taiwan's location between three major climatic zones and its diverse topography have endowed the area with a wide range of flora and fauna. Some 70 species of mammals, around 500 species of birds (40 percent of which reside on Taiwan year-round), 100 species of reptiles, 34 species of amphibians, nearly 2,500 species of fish, and 18,000 identified species of insects (including 400 butterfly species) are known to exist in the Taiwan area. With regard to plant species, Taiwan has 610 species of ferns, 28 species of gymnosperms, and 3,600 species of angiosperms. Moreover, because of the successful implementation of habitat conservation, species once thought to be extinct have been reappearing again in the Taiwan area. For example, on August 7, 2000, a flock of Chinese crested terns was found in the Matsu Islands tern refuge. The Chinese crested tern was first discovered in 1863 and thought to have become extinct during the past century. Its reappearance suggests that the ROC's wildlife protection policy has begun to enjoy some success.

The different land formations, climates, and forest types, not to mention the impact of large-scale human development, have combined to create ecological havens within the physical entity that is Taiwan. To protect these ecological havens, the ROC government has set aside 19.5 percent of Taiwan's total land area as part of a multitiered conservation system that comprises six national parks 國家公園, 19 nature reserves 自然保留區, 8 forest reserves 國有林自然保護區, 13 wildlife refuges 野生動物保護區, and 28 major wildlife habitats 野生動物重要棲息環境.

Three laws specifically authorize the designation and protection of natural areas and wildlife refuges: the *Cultural Heritage Preservation Law*, which authorizes the creation of nature reserves and identifies endangered species of flora and fauna; the *Wildlife Conservation Law*, which establishes wildlife refuges; and the *National Park Law* 國家公園法, which allows for the designation of national parks. The central government agencies that supervise Taiwan's protected areas are the Ministry of the Interior's Department of National Parks 內政部營建署國家公園組 and the Council of Agriculture. Answerable to the COA are the Taiwan Forestry Bureau 農委會林務局 and the Taiwan Forestry Research Institute 農委會林業試驗所; the Bureaus of Reconstruction 建設局 under the Taipei and Kaohsiung City governments; and the agriculture bureaus 農業局 of all city and county governments in the Taiwan area.

National Parks

The Republic of China has created a comprehensive national park system that balances conservation, recreation, and research. This has taken only ten years to implement, compared to over a hundred years for many other countries. Since the process has not begun until the island's population density was already quite high, park officials have faced a constant tug of war over land rights. Ownership of park land has been contested by businesses that previously occupied it, aborigines who claim it as ancestral land, investors who would like to develop hotels and other tourist facilities there, and even a veterans' agency that runs a farm in the middle of one of the parks.

The quick and continuous development of land did not give Taiwan the luxury of building its park system gradually. Instead, it has done the best it could, pushing through an ambitious park program that has placed 8.5 percent of its total land area under protection. Additional land acquisitions combined with the 52 existing protected nature and wildlife areas will eventually push the percentage of protected territory to over 12 percent of Taiwan's total area.

Taiwan's national park system was inaugurated in 1984 with the establishment of Kenting National Park 墾丁國家公園 at the southern tip of the island. In 1985 and 1986, Taiwan moved swiftly to set up Yushan National Park 玉山國家公園, Yangmingshan National Park 陽明山國家公園, and Taroko National Park 太魯閣國家公園 in central, northern, and eastern Taiwan, respectively. In 1992, Shei-Pa National Park 雪霸國家公園 was established in north-central Taiwan, and in October 1995, a sixth national park—Kinmen National Park 金門國家公園, occupying 25.5 percent of the Kinmen Islands—was opened to the public.

Each national park has a headquarters, which is supervised by the Department of National Parks. In fiscal 1999, the combined budget for all national park headquarters and the Department of National Parks exceeded US$104 million. Each national park has at least one visitor center and one nature display center. Most of the parks also have trailhead nature centers. Guided tours may be arranged by contacting the park headquarters in advance.

Taiwan's national parks received 12.4 million visitors in 1999. To minimize the impact of large crowds, all parks are divided into management zones. These zones identify the best use for each area within a park, classifying them as general protection areas, recreational areas, scenic areas, ecological protection areas, or cultural and historical sites.

Nature Reserves and Wildlife Refuges

The Council of Agriculture administers land protected under two designations: nature reserves and wildlife refuges. The COA has overseen the establishment of 19 nature reserves in Taiwan. These reserves range from a five-hectare plot to protect volcanic land forms in Kaohsiung to the 47,000 hectare forest reserve surrounding Mount Tawu 大武山. Altogether, 64,477 hectares of land have been designated as nature reserves. Twelve of these nature reserves are directly managed by the Taiwan Forestry Bureau under the Council

of Agriculture, while the rest are managed by such agencies as the Taipei City Government's Bureau of Reconstruction 臺北市建設局, the Penghu County Government 澎湖縣政府, the Lienchiang County Government 連江縣政府, and the Taiwan Forestry Research Institute. Each of these managing bodies must still report to the COA, though, and this ensures that all of the reserves are run in full accordance with the law.

In addition to nature reserves, 13 wildlife refuges encompassing 23,201 hectares of land have been established in the Taiwan area. The first to be established was the Cat Islets Seabird Refuge 貓嶼海鳥保護區, which is located in the southwestern corner of the Pescadores 澎湖群島 and encompasses both the Greater and Lesser Cat Islets. The refuge serves as a rookery and breeding ground for thousands of terns, and over 16 families and 26 kinds of sea birds—most of them migratory—have been sighted here. Designated as a seabird refuge in May 1991, the Cat Islets refuge is a little over 36 hectares in area.

Next to be established was the Nantzuhsien River Wildlife Refuge 楠梓仙溪野生動物保護區 in Kaohsiung County's Sanmin Township 高雄縣三民鄉. This refuge is home to 10 species of

Guandu Nature Park not only provides relief for Taipei residents from their bustling lives, its dense vegetation is also home to a great variety of water fowl and mud-dwelling fauna.

Nature Reserves

Taiwan Pleione Nature Reserve
臺灣一葉蘭自然保留區

Chatienshan Nature Reserve 插天山自然保留區

Chuyunshan Nature Reserve 出雲山自然保留區

Hapen Nature Reserve 哈盆自然保留區

Kenting Uplifted Coral Reef Nature Reserve
墾丁高位珊瑚礁自然保留區

Kuantu Nature Reserve 關渡自然保留區

Miaoli Sanyi Huoyenshan Nature Reserve
苗栗三義火炎山自然保留區

Nanao Broadleaved Forest Nature Reserve
南澳闊葉樹林自然保留區

Penghu Columnar Basalt Nature Reserve
澎湖玄武岩自然保留區

Pinglin Taiwan Keteleeria Nature Reserve
坪林臺灣油杉自然保留區

Taitung Hungyeh Village Taitung Cycas
Nature Reserve 臺東紅葉村臺東蘇鐵自然保留區

Tamsui River Mangrove Nature Reserve
淡水河紅樹林自然保留區

Tawu Taiwan Amentotaxus Nature Reserve
大武事業區臺灣穗花杉自然保留區

Tawushan Nature Reserve 大武山自然保留區

Watzuwei Nature Reserve 挖子尾自然保留區

Wushanting Mud Volcano Nature Reserve
烏山頂泥火山自然保留區

Wushihpi Coastal Nature Reserve
烏石鼻海岸自然保留區

Yuanyang Lake Nature Reserve
鴛鴦湖自然保留區

Chiuchiu Peak Nature Reserve
九九峰自然保留區

northeastern county of Ilan. Surrounded by diverse coastal forests, the 102 hectare site was designated as a bird refuge in September 1993 to protect its wetlands and bird habitats. Lakes, marshes, and streams within the site create an ideal environment for wildfowl such as the migratory ducks and geese that stop in Taiwan during the winter. According to one survey, close to 140 kinds of birds frequent the Wuwei Creek site. Every winter, from November to February, some 3,000 ducks and geese from 12 different species rest here.

The Taipei City Waterbird Refuge 臺北市野雁保護區 is home to 79 species of waterfowl and 41 species of plants. This 203 hectare wildlife refuge, set up in November 1993, serves as a natural classroom for Taipei citizens during the bird-watching season. Another urban area refuge is the Ssutsao Wildlife Refuge 四草野生動物保護區 in Tainan City. An important wetland site in southern Taiwan, this refuge is the permanent home to some 40 species of wild birds, and an additional 21 endangered and rare species of birds have been sighted here. Designated as a wildlife refuge in November 1994, the 515 hectare site also contains three kinds of rare mangroves.

In addition to the Cat Islets refuge, the Pescadores also contain the Wangan Island Green Turtle Refuge 望安島綠蠵龜產卵棲地保護區. Since the number of green turtles in the Taiwan area has fallen due to environmental degradation and poaching, the 23 hectare refuge was set aside in January 1995 to serve as a breeding ground and refuge for nesting green turtles. Wangan Island is one of the few green turtle habitats still largely untouched by human intrusion.

The Tatu River Mouth Wildlife Refuge 大肚溪口野生動物保護區, which straddles the border between Taichung County 臺中縣 and Changhua County 彰化縣, is a diverse collection of coastal waters, rivers, sandbanks, tidal flats, farmland, and fish farms. The refuge's wide plains and abundance of nourishing organisms brought in by the tides attract an enormous

freshwater fish and 80 species of birds, including the plumbeous water redstart, the little forktail, the gray-throated minivet, and the Formosan whistling thrush. The Nantzuhsien refuge covers 274 hectares and was set up in May 1993.

The Wuwei Harbor Waterbird Refuge 無尾港水鳥保護區 is located near Suao 蘇澳 in Taiwan's

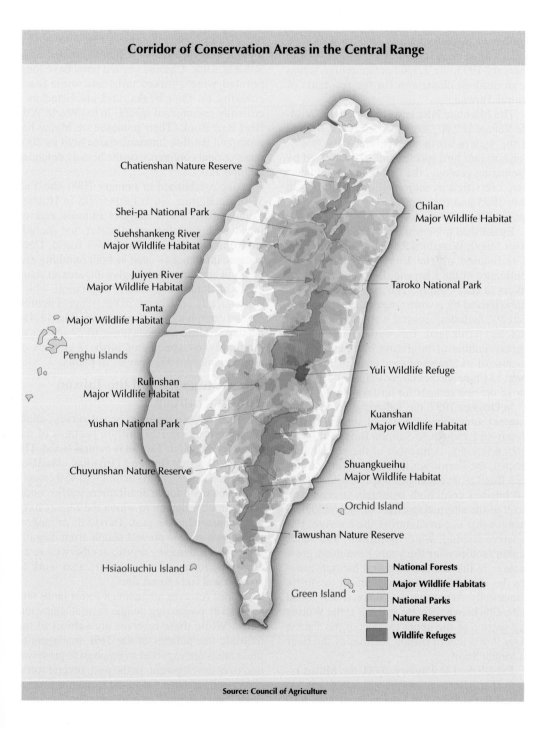

Corridor of Conservation Areas in the Central Range

Chatienshan Nature Reserve

Chilan
Major Wildlife Habitat

Shei-pa National Park

Suehshankeng River
Major Wildlife Habitat

Juiyen River
Major Wildlife Habitat

Taroko National Park

Tanta
Major Wildlife Habitat

Penghu Islands

Rulinshan
Major Wildlife Habitat

Yuli Wildlife Refuge

Yushan National Park

Kuanshan
Major Wildlife Habitat

Chuyunshan Nature Reserve

Shuangkueihu
Major Wildlife Habitat

Orchid Island

Tawushan Nature Reserve

Hsiaoliuchiu Island

Green Island

National Forests
Major Wildlife Habitats
National Parks
Nature Reserves
Wildlife Refuges

Source: Council of Agriculture

number of migratory birds, and 24 protected species have been sighted here. Established in February 1995, the 2,670 hectare refuge serves as an outdoor classroom for the residents of central Taiwan.

The Mienhua Islet and Huaping Islet Wildlife Refuge 棉花嶼花瓶嶼野生動物保護區 is located in the waters north of Keelung City 基隆市. Home to rare bird species and characterized by fascinating geology, the two uninhabited islets were classified as major wildlife habitats in June 1995 and then upgraded to wildlife refuges in March 1996.

Established in September 1996, the Lanyang River Mouth Waterbird Refuge 蘭陽溪口水鳥保護區 is located on the Lanyang Plain at the confluence of the Lanyang, Ilan, and Tungshan Rivers in Ilan County. The 206 hectare site is characterized by a wide range of topographical features, including coastal waters, rivers, sand bars, and fertile land. This wetland area attracts a great number of migratory birds every year because of its abundant food sources, and with some 231 bird species already sighted here, it is one of the best refuges for bird watching.

In October 1997, the Taichung County government announced the establishment of the Formosan Landlocked Salmon Refuge 櫻花鉤吻鮭野生動物保護區. A member of the glacial relic species, the Formosan landlocked salmon has been listed as an endangered species since 1989 and inhabits cold, high mountain streams as a result of the alternating effect of the geological changes that occurred during the Ice Age. Exhaustive fishing, water pollution, and other human factors over the years have done great damage to the salmon's natural habitat, causing the distribution and population to shrink dramatically. At present, the salmon is only found in the Chichiawan Stream 七家灣溪 at the Wuling 武陵 section of the upper reaches of the Tachia River 大甲溪 and in certain sections of the river on Mount Snow.

Established in January 2000, the Matsu Islands Tern Refuge 馬祖列島燕鷗保護區 has attracted the attention of international wild bird organizations and major news media to witness a great new discovery—Chinese crested terns 黑嘴端鳳頭燕鷗. Chinese crested terns have long, pointed wings, forked tails, and some black coloring on their beaks, and are listed as a critically endangered species in the World Wild Bird Red Book. Their presence on Matsu has prompted Birdlife International to hold its 2002 international conference on the heavily defended archipelago.

Also established in January 2000, the Yuli Wildlife Refuge 玉里野生動物保護區 in Hualien County boasts a wide range of altitudes, endowing it with multifarious climates that include subtropical, temperate, and even frigid. Deep oceanic influences—such as high humidity and plentiful amounts of rain—give this area an abundance of flourishing, diverse vegetation, which consequently contributes to the refuge's bountiful and complex biological species. The 11,414 hectare wildlife refuge is home to 29 species of mammals, 61 species of birds, 7 species of amphibians, and 372 species of plants.

Forest Reserves and the Taiwan Forestry Bureau

According to the most recent survey, about 72 percent of the 1.57 million hectares of national forestland in Taiwan is natural forest. The Taiwan Forestry Bureau (TFB) has classified the forests under its jurisdiction into 459 categories based upon forest distribution, traffic conditions, and the degree to which the forests have been damaged in the past. Two to three rangers patrol each zone to prevent people from illegally felling trees, dumping refuse, or otherwise damaging the forests. These rangers also work to prevent and fight forest fires.

Forest reserves are national forest lands recognized as possessing unique natural characteristics. While these reserves are subject to the multiple-use policies of the TFB, managers of these areas are expected to emphasize preservation over development. In the past, several forest reserves have been promoted to nature reserve status, and this practice is expected to continue.

In recent years, the people of Taiwan have placed greater emphasis on environmental protection, as can be seen from the planting of cypress trees pictured here.

The basic law regulating the preservation of forests in Taiwan is the *Forest Law* 森林法. In accordance with this law, the TFB began a forest conservation program in 1965. This program includes surveying and studying rare plants and animals, as well as drafting plans for long-term studies, experimentation, and educational tourism within protected nature areas. TFB workers are continuing to survey the forests of Taiwan to identify different kinds of representative ecosystems and rare flora and fauna. In addition to entering all data into a computer network and setting up management survey stations for researching and protecting wild plants and animals, the TFB also posts educational information along the perimeters of forest reserves.

Until 1989, the TFB was financed through logging operations; since then, however, forest management programs have not been tied to timber harvest receipts. The TFB operates a network of hostels in forest areas that are more than a day's journey from any city, increasing the accessibility of such isolated regions. Such hostels are open to the public for a fee that depends on the services available and the length of stay.

The COA has set up a website at *http://lovetree.forest.gov.tw* for people interested in sponsoring trees. After registering with the COA, people can then choose the areas of sponsorship that interest them and check online for updates on the trees they helped to plant. Officials are also encouraging companies to adopt trees on behalf of their employees, as well as cooperating with local hospitals to promote a parallel program for parents wishing to sponsor trees on behalf of their newborns.

Cultivating a Conservation Ethic

Many government agencies and private conservation groups are working to carry out a massive educational campaign aimed at cultivating a conservation ethic in Taiwan. At the forefront of conservation education is the COA, which sponsors research projects, hosts international symposia, and subsidizes publicity campaigns. The COA also commissions other government agencies to provide conservation-related publications. To help educate the public about conservation, the Ministry of Education 教育部 (MOE) trains teachers to teach courses on wildlife conservation and has introduced wildlife conservation into the public school curriculum. In 1998, 16 new textbooks introducing conservation concepts were published that are suitable for students of all ages.

Targeting the general public, the Government Information Office (GIO) has made wildlife conservation a major part of its own informational campaigns. In July 1995, the GIO went on the Internet (*http://www.gio.gov.tw*) with a new database—available in both Chinese and English—of facts and figures about Taiwan, including the island's efforts in the area of wildlife conservation.

The ROC has an established record of cooperation with international conservation organizations. In 2000, the COA and the Ministry of Foreign Affairs donated US$402,000 and US$74,000, respectively, to support international conservation activities and projects, such as the IUCN Species Survival Commission's project titled "Sustainable Trade in Medical Plants, Reptiles and Marine Organisms, the Role of the Precautionary Principle, and New Methods to Collect Species Status Information"; TRAFFIC (Trade Records Analysis of Flora and Fauna in Commerce) International's project titled "Assisting the Enforcement of CITES and Related National Legislation"; Bird Life International's project, Important Bird Areas of South Asia; and a project by the International Union of Forestry Research Organizations titled "Assisting the Development of the Chinese Version of Forest Terminology." The ROC government's donations toward international wildlife conservation efforts have continued into 2001.

Stray Dog Control

The *Animal Protection Law* 動物保護法, which was drafted by the COA with the assistance of both the Animal Protection Association of the ROC 中華民國保護動物協會 and the ROC Life Conservationist Association 中華民國關懷生命協會, was passed by the Legislative Yuan in October 1998. This bill ensures that all animals are given complete legal protection and devotes a specific section to the management of pets, providing the government with a legal instrument for handling matters related to pet owners. The regulations stipulated by the *Animal Protection Law* include:

• Certain pets must be registered and given IDs by local governments. Registration includes a complete record of the animal's birth, acquisition, transference, loss, and death. In addition, a program for sterilization and microchip implantation has been implemented to more effectively manage pets which, according to the Council of Agriculture, will focus on pet dogs and cats in its first stage.

• All animal keepers, including private pet owners, kennel owners, veterinarians, petstores, pounds, and shelters, must supply the animals in their care with sufficient quantities of food and water. Safe, sanitary, and adequate living space with proper ventilation, lighting, and temperature must also be given. Animal keepers shall not abuse, harass, torture, harm, or maltreat their animals.

• Animal keepers must provide proper medical care to their animals in the event of injury or illness. Any treatment or operation performed must be carried out by a qualified, licensed veterinarian.

• Pet owners who no longer wish to own their pets are required to send them to a licensed shelter, and can not simply abandon them.

• Whenever animals are being transported, proper attention must be given to their food, water, waste, environment, and safety. They should also be kept free from shock, pain, and harm during their journey.

• The euthanasia of animals must be carried out in a humane fashion by a veterinarian or under a veterinarian's supervision. Care should be taken to ensure minimal pain for the animal.

In the past, a lack of proper training and experience on the part of some kennel keepers employed by local governments led to occasional cases of inhumane treatment toward animals. These incidents triggered criticism by animal-rights groups and the public. The ROC government responded immediately, heeding the good advice contained in the investigative reports released by the ROC Life Conservationist Association and the UK-based World Society for the Protection of Animals (WSPA).

Since then, effective measures have been taken to improve the stray dog management of local governments. For example, in 1999 and 2000, the ROC government allocated nearly US$4 million to improve the equipment used in animal shelters and conduct an evaluation of 62 shelters. Up through December 2000, new shelters were constructed in Changhua, Nantou, Tainan, Pingtung, Taitung, Hualien, Ilan, Penghu and Kinmen counties, as well as the municipalities of Taipei and Tainan. In August 2001, the COA signed another three-year memorandum of understanding with the Humane Society of the United States (HSUS), America's largest animal protection organization. The two sides first entered an agreement in 1998, with the HSUS assisting Taiwan in stepping up efforts to enforce animal checkups and management of stray dogs.

At present, local governments are still in charge of handling the stray dog problem and are under the direct supervision of the central government's COA, which assists them by providing funds, training, and equipment. In addition, as the newly passed *Animal Protection Law* stipulates, an animal protection committee has been established under the COA in order to draw up animal protection policies and examine the enforcement of relevant regulations, especially those concerning the management of stray dogs.

In order to reduce the number of stray dogs in Taiwan, local governments have been aggressively promoting the adoption of stray dogs.

In 2000, the percentage of stray dogs adopted increased from 7 percent to 15 percent. Local government subsidies have also been given to veterinary research units so that they can offer sterilization operations at lower prices, thereby providing pet owners with an incentive to have their dogs sterilized. Furthermore, in an effort to more effectively identify dogs with their respective owners, the Council of Agriculture entrusted the Institute for Information Industry 財團法人資訊工業策進會 with the development of special radio-frequency microchips to be implanted into dogs for tracking purposes. This technique has been combined with new registration procedures for pets, and with the passing of the *Animal Protection Law*, the rights and safeguards regarding the well-being of animals in Taiwan have been strengthened even further.

Pet Registration

To resolve the problem of stray or lost dogs, the COA publicly proclaimed a "Pet Licensing Program," which took effect September 1, 1999. Under this regulation, all pet owners must apply for a pet license from a pet registration station in their residential area. The COA developed this pet licensing program in cooperation with the Institute for Information Industry, which developed the microchips to be implanted in dogs. Once the pet registration has been completed and the microchips implanted, the data is then sent to a central system and processed. Upon the report of a missing pet, this registration data is automatically transferred to the "Lost Pet Recovery Service." According to Article 31 of the *Animal Protection Law*, a pet owner who does not register or refuses to register their pet before September 2000 will be fined and reported to the authorities.

Related Websites
1. Environmental Protection Administration:
   http://www.epa.gov.tw
2. Council of Agriculture: *http://www.coa.gov.tw*

PROTECTING THE EARTH IS EVERYONE'S RESPONSIBILITY

Conservation is a global effort, and the Republic of China on Taiwan is doing its part to conserve nature's bounty. The government agency in charge of the nation's wildlife conservation program is the Council of Agriculture. We at the Council of Agriculture look forward to working with you to protect our planet.

COUNCIL OF AGRICULTURE EXECUTIVE YUAN

37 NANHAI RD.
TAIPEI, TIAWAN 100
REPUBLIC OF CHINA
TEL: 886-2-2312-4065
FAX: 886-2-2312-0337
E-mail: rc0000@mail.coa.gov.

TAIPEI 2002

INTERNATIONAL TRADE SHOWS

TAIPEI AUTOMAT	Taipei Int'l Automation & Precision Machinery Show	March 19-23
TaiSPO	Taipei Int'l Sporting Goods Show	April 3-6
TAIPEI CYCLE	Taipei Int'l Cycle Show	April 11-14
Giftionery Taipei	Taipei Int'l Gift & Stationery Spring Show	April 18-21
TaipeiOpto	Taipei Int'l Optoelectronics Show	April 25-29
TAITRONICS SPRING	Taipei Int'l Electronics Spring Show	April 25-29
AMPA	Taipei Int'l Auto/Motorcycle Parts & Accessories Show	May 24-27
COMPUTEX TAIPEI	Taipei Int'l Computer Show	June 3-7
FOOD TAIPEI	Taipei Int'l Food Show	June 12-15
FOODTECH TAIPEI	Taipei Int'l Food Machinery & Technology Show	June 19-23
TAIPEI PACK	Taipei Int'l Packaging Industry Show	June 19-23
INTERWOOD TAIPEI	Taipei Int'l Woodworking Machinery & Supplies Show	July 5-8
Taipei Telecom	Taipei Int'l Telecommunications and Networking Show	August 23-26
SEMICON Taiwan	Semiconductor Equipment and Materials	September 16-18
TITEX	Taipei Int'l Textile Machinery Show	September 25-29
TAITRONICS– Components & Equipment	Taipei Int'l Electronics Show	October 9-13
TAITRONICS– Finished Products	Taipei Int'l Electronics Show	October 16-20
Giftionery Taipei	Taipei Int'l Gift & Stationery Autumn Show	October 23-26
MEDIPHAR TAIPEI	Taipei Int'l Medical Equipment & Pharmaceuticals Show	November 9-12

*Subject to change without notice.

Make a date with the future

www.TaipeiTradeShows.com.tw

Organizer:
China External Trade Development Council (CETRA)
www.taiwantrade.com.tw

5 Hsin-yi Rd., Sec. 5, Taipei, Taiwan 110, R.O.C.
Tel: 886-2-2725-1111   Fax: 886-2-2725-1314

Sponsor:
Taipei World Trade Center

Venue:
Taipei World Trade Center Exhibition Hall

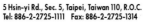

14
Transportation

The suspension bridge over the Kaoping River symbolizes Taiwan's recent economic progress and engineering achievements.
(Photo by Berlin Chi)

What's New

1. Figures updated
2. TRA's new sightseeing fleet service
3. Harbor-city merger plan

A well-developed transportation network is essential to the Republic of China's export-oriented economy. Therefore, transportation has always been an important priority in national development programs, from the Ten Major Construction Projects 十大建設 of the 1970s through the Six-year National Development Plan 國家建設六年計畫 and the Asia-Pacific Regional Operations Center Plan 亞太營運中心計畫 of the 1990s. The importance of having a good transportation infrastructure was extremely evident after the September 21, 1999 earthquake, as damaged roads and bridges hampered rescue efforts and threatened to paralyze the island's economy. Considerable resources are thus being devoted to ensuring that businesses in Taiwan enjoy the advantages of an extensive and efficient transportation network. At the beginning of this century, the ROC government is integrating advanced technologies with humanitarian concerns in construction, services, and equitable resource distribution.

Railways

Taiwan's modern railway system provides frequent and convenient passenger service between all major cities on the island. As of December 2000, Taiwan's railway network totaled 2,363 kilometers, an equivalent of 1.11 kilometers per 10,000 people, or 66 meters per square kilometer of land. This railway system transported 14.5 million tons of freight in 2000, 13.1 percent less than in 1999. The number of passengers carried increased 5.1 percent to a total of 192 million.

In 1945 when Taiwan was returned to the sovereignty of the Republic of China, the railway was in a desolate state with the majority of

tracks and trains damaged or destroyed during the World War II. After the initial reconstruction work was completed, the Taiwan railway system was thoroughly modernized over a period of five decades, and the locomotives were changed from steam diesel to electric. The North Link officially entered service in February 1980, and the South Link was completed in 1992. A complete railway network was in place that has assumed a significant role in providing inland transportation services for the country's economic development.

Several types of passenger train services are available. The fastest express class is the Tzuchiang express 自強號, which only stops at major stations. The next fastest express class, with more frequent stops at lesser, but still large

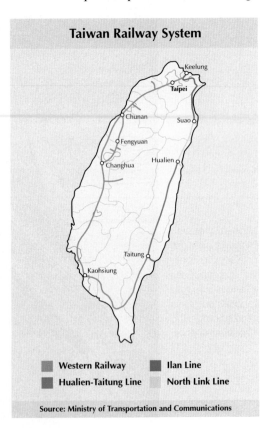

Taiwan Railway System

| Keelung |
| Taipei |
| Chunan |
| Suao |
| Fengyuan |
| Changhua | Hualien |
| Taitung |
| Kaohsiung |

- Western Railway
- Ilan Line
- Hualien-Taitung Line
- North Link Line

Source: Ministry of Transportation and Communications

Trains roll again on the Chichi rail line 16 months after the September 21, 1999 earthquake.

stations, is the Chukuang express 莒光號. The third class of trains, the Fuhsing express 復興號, includes stop at every station on a designated commuter routes. Finally, local trains serve mostly long routes, stopping at every station and generally yielding to higher-priority Tzuchiang, Chukuang, and Fuhsing trains.

The Taiwan Railway Administration (TRA) continues to upgrade both its equipment and facilities. It signed a modern optic fiber network investment agreement with EThome Telecom in January 2001, making it the most successful case of a state-run enterprise investing in the telecommunications business so far. In coordination with government's plan to promote domestic tourism and enhance the quality of railway tours, the TRA launched the sightseeing fleet service in 2001, with the first run between Taipei and Hualien.

The TRA has completed many major construction and business renovation projects in recent years, including the double tracking of the mountain line between Chunan 竹南 and Fengyuan 芬園 and the electrification of Kaohsiung-Pingtung Line 高屏線. Following projects include track structure renovation, beautification along the railroad routes, rail elevation and overhead crossings, level crossing protective equipment improvements, and train safety facilities improvements. The TRA also invested heavily in service improvements with the purchase of 810 Tzuchiang Express commuter cars which are now all in service. In the aspect of business renovation, the TRA has adjusted the pricing structure, received ISO 9000 certifications, upgraded ticketing services, strengthened inquiry services, improved the travel and transport facilities, built a barrier-free environment, and streamlined the services. The TRA has also diversified to invest in telecommunications business and land development to improve its financial structure.

The current construction and operation of the TRA has significantly changed. The renewal project is currently transforming the TRA into the hub of inland communications and transportation in Taiwan. Information on current fares can be obtained by calling the Taipei Railway Information Desk 臺灣鐵路局臺北站服務臺 (02-2371-3558, 02-2381-5226) or the Kaohsiung Railway Information Desk 臺灣鐵路局高雄站服務臺 (07-221-2376, 080-711-333).

217

High-speed Railway

The ROC government has begun the development of a high-speed railway (HSR) in Taiwan. The Bureau of Taiwan High Speed Rail 高速鐵路工程局 (BOTHSR) under the Ministry of Transportation and Communications 交通部 (MOTC) is responsible for the implementation of this project.

The planned 345-kilometer HSR route will pass through the western corridor of the island. Ten stations will be located in Taipei 臺北, Taoyuan 桃園, Hsinchu 新竹, Miaoli 苗栗, Taichung 臺中, Changhua 彰化, Yunlin 雲林, Chiayi 嘉義, Tainan 臺南, and Kaohsiung 高雄.

In May 1995, the Legislature approved construction of the HSR using the Build-Operate-Transfer (BOT) model—the first major infrastructure project in Taiwan to be constructed by the private sector under this model. The invitation to tender BOT bids for the HSR was officially announced on October 29, 1996. On July 23, 1998, the MOTC and the Taiwan High Speed Rail Consortium (THSRC) signed the "Taiwan South-North HSR Construction and Operation Contract" and the "Taiwan South-North HSR Station Development Contract," officially granting construction and operation concessions for the project to the THSRC.

The overall construction cost of the HSR project is estimated to be US$13.1 billion, of which 75.5 percent will come from private investment. In addition to these funds for the HSR itself, the MOTC has allocated an additional US$1.3 billion for the construction of roads connecting the train stations to neighboring commercial areas to improve accessibility. The government has already acquired 1,100 hectares of land for construction of the route, and the HSR is expected to begin operations in October 2005. Once operational, travel time from Taipei to Kaohsiung will be cut from 4.5 hours by existing train or highway vehicles to just 90 minutes.

The THSRC has signed a Core System Contract for Electrical and Mechanical Equipment with Taiwan Shinkansen Corporation (TSC), assuring that the Japan Shinkansen System will be adopted by Taiwan HSR. Bidding has been held for other civil engineering works, such as for station design, and all of the 12 major civil works contracts have already been awarded to local and international contractors. The THSRC has signed a Syndication Loan contract in the amount of US$10 billion with a syndicate of 25 local banks led by the Chiao Tung Bank 交通銀行.

Underground Railway Projects

To eliminate traffic jams, reduce noise interference, improve environmental quality, and integrate the Taipei Rapid Transit Systems, the High Speed Rail and the Taipei Railway Underground Project were initiated. Originally implemented as a three-stage project, the fourth stage

---

Transportation Administration

Transportation facilities are administered by several government agencies, including the national Ministry of Transportation and Communications (MOTC) and various municipal-level agencies. Each agency has different responsibilities depending on the type of transportation.

The MOTC has eight offices, departments, and divisions, three of which are devoted to various modes of transportation: Railways and Highways 路政司, Posts and Telecommunications 郵電司, and Navigation and Aviation 航政司. Numerous other MOTC committees are responsible for setting and administering transportation and communications policies. Local municipal units are primarily responsible for developing adequate municipal transportation facilities but have significant power over provincial and national transportation facilities located within their city limits.

The private sector participates in many areas of transportation, but it is especially prominent in the airline, airport, and shipping sectors. Private sector influence is certain to expand, as the government moves toward greater privatization and encourages increased private investment.

was added in 1998, and similar projects are currently being planned for other major cities.

The first and second stages of the Taipei Railway Underground Project connecting Wanhua 萬華 with Huashan 華山 (including Taipei Main Station) and Huashan with Sungshan 松山 are already operational. Construction of the third stage from Wanhua south to Panchiao began in September 1992 and is expected to be completed in October 2002. The fourth stage, the Nankang Extension Project, will extend the line further from Sungshan to Nankang 南港. Construction of this fourth section, which was coordinated with the development of the Nankang Economic and Trade Park, began on November 1, 1998, and is scheduled for completion by the end of 2009. The detailed design and peripheral construction works are now in process.

Underground railway projects for Kaohsiung, Taichung, and Tainan are currently in various stages. The integrated plan for the Kaohsiung Railway Underground Project was completed in November 1999, pending final approval by the Executive Yuan. This project is currently in the detailed design and in related construction work stages. The Taipei Railway Underground Project Office started overseeing the integrated planning of the Taichung and Tainan projects on August 23, 1999, and has completed the integrated planning. The MOTC has already submitted plans to the Executive Yuan for approval.

Upgrading Eastern Railways

Government plans to industrialize the east coast and balance urban and rural development requires considerable improvement in the region's railway facilities. In January 1991, the Executive Yuan approved the TRA's Eastern Railway Improvement Project 東部鐵路改善計畫 and made it a part of the Six-year National Development Plan. The project focuses on modernizing the 337 kilometers of railway consisting of the Ilan line, the North Link line, and the Hualien-Taitung line. Construction started in July 1991 and is scheduled to be completed in June 2003 at a total cost of US$1.57 billion. Improvements will include electrification, double tracks, heavy rails, a centralized traffic control system, new locomotives, repair facilities, and the relocation of the Hualien depot.

Harbors and Shipping

Maritime transportation is vital to Taiwan's trade-oriented economy. At the end of 2000, the ROC's 115 shipping lines had a fleet of 260 vessels that were over 100 gross tons each, or 5.3 million gross tons in total (8.3 million dead weight tons, DWT). The ROC's fleet of container ships was listed at the top of the world. The largest operator in Taiwan is the Evergreen Marine Corporation 長榮海運公司, which is the second largest container operator in the world. Another giant shipping line, the Yangming Marine Transport Corporation 陽明海運公司, now ranks as the world's sixteenth largest container operator.

For many years, people from Taiwan's southern and central regions have called for cultural and economic parity with their fellow citizens in the island's capital-city area. In response to this pressure, the ROC government approved a bill in 2001 granting certain city and county governments the right to manage adjacent harbors. The harbor-city merger plan applies to the international harbor facilities in Kaohsiung, Hualien, Taichung, and Keelung. The four local governments will each set up a port management committee to coordinate city planning, transportation, environmental protection, public safety, fire prevention, and health between the port and its host city or county. Each committee of 9 to 13 members will be composed of scholars as well as officials from local and central governments. The merger is expected to increase local revenue and therefore boost local development.

Taiwan has six international harbors: Keelung 基隆, Suao 蘇澳, Taichung 臺中, Hualien 花蓮, Anping 安平, and Kaohsiung 高雄. The total cargo handled by these ports totaled 181.7 million metric tons in 2000.

Kaohsiung Harbor

In 2000, Kaohsiung Harbor 高雄港 handled nearly 7.4 million TEUs (Twenty-foot Equivalent Units, a measurement for cargo equivalent to a standardized 20-foot container), making it the fourth largest container port in the world.

Kaohsiung Harbor has 118 operating berths, totaling 26.6 kilometers in length that can simultaneously accommodate up to 155 ships. The first and second harbor entrances are navigable by 30,000 metric tons and 100,000 metric tons ships, respectively. The port water area is approximately 12.42 square kilometers, and the inner harbor has a depth of 16 meters. Navigation channels for Kaohsiung Harbor are 18 kilometers long and have a 0.75 meter tidal range, a constant wind speed averaging 2.2 meters/second, and an average temperature of 25℃.

The harbor has five container terminals, 26 container wharves, 61 gantry cranes, and 293.5 hectares of container yards. It has also built one 80,000-metric-ton and one 100,000-metric-ton grain silo at the harbor. Container Terminal Number Five was completed at the end of 2000.

Kaohsiung Harbor's container terminals provide prompt, accurate, and comprehensive logistical services. The harbor effectively manages import, export, and transshipment containers and handles up to 10 million TEUs annually. Its strategic location makes it the ideal choice for a marine transportation hub in East Asia. Of the six leading ports in the Asia Pacific region (Kaohsiung, Singapore, Hong Kong, Pusan, Shanghai, and Tokyo), Kaohsiung Harbor's links are closer to the other five ports by an average of 53 hours of navigation time.

Anping Harbor

Anping Harbor 安平港, located on the western coast of southern Taiwan, is the sixth international harbor in Taiwan. Anping Harbor has a 7.5-meter deep channel navigable to ships up to 6,000 DWT. The harbor currently has a 320-meter wharf 3.5 meters deep, a 532-meter wharf 7.5 meters deep, and a 320-meter wharf 9 meters deep. The harbor is managed by the Anping Harbor Branch Bureau of the Kaohsiung Harbor Bureau. Anping Harbor is currently under Phase I expansion to accommodate 20,000-DWT vessels. It has developed into a multifunction harbor with routes covering Southeast Asia, Northeast Asia, Mainland China, Hong Kong, along with

Hundreds of cargo ships from around the world load and unload goods in Kaohsiung Harbor daily.

the ROC's offshore islands. With intensive development, Anping Harbor will help bring prosperity to southern Taiwan.

Keelung Harbor

Located near the northern tip of Taiwan, Keelung Harbor 基隆港 has 57 berths and 3 mooring docks capable of handling vessels in the 50,000 metric tons range (within the limits of a 14.5 meter draft). The harbor's two container terminals—with 15 berths measuring a total of 3,473 meters in length—and 27 container gantry cranes are capable of concurrently accommodating 15 container ships in the 30,000 metric tons range. Other facilities at Keelung Harbor include 190,183 square meters of marshaling yards (of which 84,046 square meters are for rent) capable of storing 5,592 TEUs and a 50,500 metric ton grain silo equipped with three vacuum loaders.

Total imports and exports handled by Keelung Harbor exceeded 88.34 million metric tons in 2000. To meet the requirements of global shipping and strengthen the harbor's competitiveness, a dredging project has widen its basin and channel, allowing it to accommodate 60,000-DWT conventional cargo ships and post-panamax type container ships. In addition, several conventional cargo berths are being converted into container piers. Lastly, to promote operational efficiency and improve the quality of service, the Keelung Harbor Bureau began allowing private companies to perform cargo handling and other services in the port on January 1, 1999.

Taichung Harbor

Taichung Harbor 臺中港 is a man-made port covering a total area of about 5,000 hectares. Located on the west coast of central Taiwan, the harbor was designed to help cope with the fast growing needs of national economic development. The port has not only relieved some of the shipping traffic from the heavily used Keelung and Kaohsiung Harbors, it has also aided in balancing the population and economic development of Taiwan itself.

Taichung Harbor's main channel and harbor basin are both 14 meters deep during low tide. The port has 40 deep-water wharves and eight container piers at the present time, and since the majority of its equipment is automated, Taichung Harbor is a very efficient port. In 2000, the harbor handled 1.13 million TEUs worth of cargo weighing 82 million metric tons.

Hualien Harbor

Located on Taiwan's east coast, Hualien Harbor 花蓮港 is a relatively small port with 25 deep-water berths totaling 4,742 meters in length. With the completion of a fourth extension in 1991, Hualien Harbor is now capable of simultaneously berthing one 100,000 metric tons class vessel in a special terminal for unloading coal, six 60,000 metric tons vessels, two 30,000 metric tons vessels, fourteen 5,000- to 15,000-metric-ton vessels, and two vessels under 5,000 metric tons. It also has several shallow water wharves with a total length of 504 meters for accommodating fishing boats and other small vessels. In 2000, the harbor handled 15.5 million metric tons of cargo.

Suao Harbor

Suao Harbor 蘇澳港 is situated on the northeast coast of Taiwan and serves as an auxiliary port for Keelung Harbor. The total water area of the harbor is about 2.9 square kilometers. The harbor currently has 13 operating berths with a total annual capacity of approximately ten million tons. Imports and exports passing through Suao Harbor in 2000 exceeded 5.64 million metric tons.

Affiliate Harbors

Makung Harbor

Makung Harbor 馬公港 is located southwest of Taiwan in the Pescadores Islands. It currently operates a 722-meter wharf for both passengers and cargo, and one harbor administration building. This harbor, capable of accommodating ships up to 5,000 DWT, will be expanded to include a commercial harbor area, fisheries areas, a shipyard, and a long-term commercial harbor area.

Putai Harbor

Putai Harbor 布袋港, on the western coast of Taiwan, has 7.6-meter navigable channels to accommodate ships up to 5,000 DWT. So far there are five 7.5-meter deep wharves to accommodate passenger-cargo ships serving offshore islands and domestic coastal shipping.

Taipei Harbor

Taipei Harbor 臺北港 serves as an auxiliary port for Keelung Harbor and is located on the south bank of the Tamsui River near Pali Township's Hsuntang Village in Taipei County. Since the primary purpose of the harbor is to relieve some of the heavy traffic burden confronting Keelung Harbor, Taipei Harbor has been undergoing a three-phase expansion of its facilities. The first phase of construction, which involved the construction of two nine-meter deep berths totaling 340 meters in length and a 70-hectare stacking yard, has already been completed. The second phase, the construction of an outer breakwater 3,810 meters in length, commenced in July 1997 and is scheduled for completion in February 2002. The third and final phase is set to be completed by 2011. Total imports and exports handled through Taipei Harbor exceeded 2.3 million metric tons in 2000. To enhance the port's competitiveness and comply with privatizing policies, plans are also being made to lease Taipei Harbor's facilities and open it to public and private investment.

Civil Aviation

In 2001, a total of 39 airlines including code-share airlines provided flight services to destinations in the ROC. Of these airlines, 33 foreign carriers and 6 ROC-based airlines (EVA Airways, Mandarin Airlines, China Airlines, Transasia Airways, UNI Airways, and Far Eastern Air Transport Corporation) are operating scheduled international air services to and from Taiwan, while the ROC-based U-Land Airlines was offering international charter services. Seven companies, including two helicopter operators, were offering domestic passenger flight services.

There are currently two international airports in the Taiwan area: Chiang Kai-shek (CKS) International Airport 中正國際機場 at Taoyuan in

---

Airlines Providing Scheduled International Services to/from Taiwan

Air Orient*	Malaysian Airlines*
Air Canada*	Mandarin Airlines*
Air Asia Sdn. Bhd.*	Martinair Holland
Air Macau*	Northwest Airlines*
Air Micronesia*	Pacific Airlines*
Air New Zealand*	Philippine Airlines*
Air Nippon*	Qantas Airways Ltd.*
British Asia Airlines*	Polar Air Cargo
Canadian Airlines International*	Royal Brunei Airways*
Cargolux Airlines International	Saudi Arabia Airlines
Cathay Pacific Airways*	Singapore Airlines*
China Airlines*	Swiss Air Asia*
Continental Micronesia*	Thai Airways International*
Dragon Airlines*	Transasia Airways*
EVA Airways*	UNI Airways*
Evergreen International Airlines	United Airlines*
Far Eastern Air Transport Corp.*	United Parcel Service
Federal Express Airways	Viet Air*
Japan Asia Airways*	
KLM Royal Dutch Airlines*	*Scheduled passenger service

northern Taiwan and Kaohsiung International Airport 高雄國際機場 in the south. In addition, there are fifteen domestic airports: Taipei, Hualien, Taitung, Taichung, Tainan, Chiayi, Pingtung 屏東, Makung 馬公, Chimei 七美, Orchid Island 蘭嶼, Green Island 綠島, Wangan 望安, Kinmen 金門, Matsu (Peikan 北竿), and Hsinchu. Since domestic air travel is expected to grow at an annual rate of about 10 percent for the next five years, work is currently under way to expand capacity at most of Taiwan's airports. Facilities have been enlarged at the Tainan, Hualien, Chiayi, Makung, Kinmen, and Orchid Island airports; navigational aids have been installed at the CKS, Kaohsiung, Taipei, Chiayi, and Pingtung airports; and new airports are being constructed on Matsu (Nankan 南竿) and at Hengchun in southern Taiwan.

In 2000, the number of inbound and outbound international passengers increased 11.2 percent to 19.8 million in comparison to 17.8 million in 1999. The total number of passengers, including international and domestic passengers, decreased 7.8 percent to 46.4 million, compared to 50.3 million in 1999. The air cargo handled increased from 1.45 million tons in 1999 to 1.62 million tons in 2000. Despite these increases, however, the number of flights decreased from 616,322 in 1999 to 586,560 in 2000.

Terminal I of CKS International Airport served a total number of 17 million passengers in 1999. The second terminal opened on July 28, 2000, also provides an annual handling capacity of 17 million inbound/outbound and transit passengers. To shuttle passengers and airport staff

between Terminal I and II, a people moving system connecting the two terminals is under construction and is expected to be in service by the middle of 2002. A mass rapid transit link is also being planned to connect the airport with Taipei City by 2006.

In addition to the CKS International Airport, the Kaohsiung International Airport also serves ROC's civil air transportation system. Since the opening of the new international passenger terminal on January 11, 1997, further expansions of airport facilities have continued so Kaohsiung can become a global business operations center. Completion of the planned construction and expansion projects at the airport are also expected to attract greater investment by transport businesses and international couriers, increasing airport operations and the city's offshore trans-shipment center.

ROC authorities have been negotiating additional air traffic rights for ROC carriers that operate international air services. In 2000 and the first half of 2001, ROC revised or renewed agreements with Vietnam, Netherlands, Macau, Brunei, and Germany. The ROC also plans to sign aviation accords with Brazil, India, Turkey, Spain, and other countries with market potential.

Highways and Freeways

In 2000, there were 17 million motor vehicles in Taiwan. The number of highway passengers for the year was 1.1 billion, down 3.9 percent from 1999. Cargo transported via Taiwan's

highways and freeways also decreased by 1.7 percent, to 343 million tons in 2000.

The Second Northern Freeway 北部第二高速公路 was opened to traffic in 1996. With a length of 99 kilometers, the main route stretches from the northern edge of Taipei to Hsinchu. In addition, it includes a 6-kilometer-long Taipei connecting route and a 12-kilometer-long inner beltway to the CKS International Airport.

Construction of the Extension to the Second Freeway was begun in 1993 and connects Keelung in the north with Pingtung in the south. The main route is 333 kilometers long, and it has four branches totaling 68 kilometers in length.

Sun Yat-sen Freeway

Inaugurated in 1978, the Sun Yat-sen Freeway 中山高速公路 (also called the North-South Freeway) was the ROC's first national freeway. The 373-kilometer-long route connects Kaohsiung in the south with both Taipei and Keelung in the north. The freeway is still the island's primary north-south thoroughfare, and the rapid rate at which the traffic load has grown since its opening has resulted in significant wear and tear. Thus, a number of recent transportation projects and plans focus on ensuring that the Sun Yat-sen Freeway remains a safe and efficient traffic corridor.

To relieve congestion along the section of the freeway running through Taipei, two 21-kilometer-long elevated viaducts have been constructed that run parallel with the Sun Yat-sen Freeway from the Hsichih 汐止 interchange in the north to the Wuku 五股 interchange in the south.

Several sections of the freeway running through northern and central Taiwan are becoming heavily congested. A 27.6-kilometer-long section of the four-lane freeway running from Yangmei 楊梅 to Hsinchu 新竹 is one such stretch. To alleviate this situation, an additional lane is being added to each side, and interchanges, toll stations, and service areas are being improved. Bidding for this project was held in March 1996, and the project is scheduled to be completed in January 2003 at a cost of US$175 million. An extra lane is also being added to each side of the heavily used 112-kilometer section from Hsinchu to Yuanlin 員林. This US$790 million project, which began in November 1994, is scheduled to be completed in December 2002.

The Sun Yat-sen Freeway is also becoming saturated in southern Taiwan, and preliminary plans were drawn up to widen the section between Yuanlin and Kaohsiung at the end of 1997. The US$1.39 billion project will begin at the Yuanlin interchange and run 158 kilometers to the Wuchia interchange 五甲交流道 in Kaohsiung. One lane will also be added to each side of the freeway, and two lanes are under consideration for a 4.3-kilometer stretch running through the Kaohsiung metropolitan area. For some sections, bidding and construction started at the beginning of 1997. The project will be completed in 2007.

Islandwide Parking Problem

The number of motorcycles and cars has continued to increase in recent years as strong overall economic growth and rising personal incomes have made the purchase of motor vehicles commonplace. In 2000, there were 17.02 million motor vehicles in the Taiwan area, more than 4.71 million of which were passenger cars. By comparison, there were only 10.05 million vehicles and 2.26 million passenger cars ten years ago. With such skyrocketing growth, parking has long been a serious problem. Accordingly, the MOTC has recommended in its revision of the *Highway Law* 公路法 (which has been submitted to the Legislature for approval) that every car buyer be required to have a personal parking space. Even so, alleviating the serious shortage of parking spaces in the ROC will take time. The Public Parking Lot Construction Plan 政府興建公共停車場五年投資計畫, which calls for building 303 new parking lots in major cities around the island, has also been implemented at an estimated cost of US$726 million.

Taiwan Highway Network

Legend:
- East-West Expressways
- Sun Yat-sen Freeway (North-South Freeway)
- Second Freeway
- Western Coastal Expressway
- Taipei-Ilan Freeway
- Central Cross-island Expressway
- Easten Expressway
- Southern Cross-island Expressway

The volume of traffic on the Sun Yat-sen Freeway has grown by an average of 11 percent annually since its opening. This heavy traffic load, combined with a hot climate, abundant rainfall, and overloaded trucks and trailers, has caused considerable damage to the freeway's surface. To maintain road quality, many five-year road surface repair projects have been completed since 1982.

In addition to expansion and maintenance projects, some major repair work is also being undertaken. The portion of the Sun Yat-sen Freeway crossing central Taiwan's Choshui River 濁水溪 at the Sino-Saudi Arabian Bridge 中沙大橋 is one such area. The riverbed has deepened over the years because of excessive gravel removal and flooding during typhoons, and thus work is being done to protect the pier and stabilize the riverbed.

New Freeways

With the rapid growth of traffic on the Sun Yat-sen Freeway, the Taiwan Expressway Network project was proposed in 1990 to alleviate some of the traffic load. This project included construction of the Second Freeway, the Taipei-Ilan Freeway, the Eastern Expressway, the Southern Cross-island Expressway, and the Central Cross-island Expressway.

The Second Freeway is generally divided into the Second Northern Freeway and its extension. The northern section, completed in August 1997, is 117 kilometers in length and includes a beltway linking the CKS International Airport with both the Sun Yat-sen Freeway in eastern Taipei and Hsinchu 新竹. The

388-kilometer extension, which has been under construction since 1993, will connect the Sun Yat-sen Freeway between central and southern Taiwan by branches. The 45-kilometer southern section between Tainan and Kaohsiung Counties was opened to traffic in early 2000. The Second Freeway is scheduled to be completed by 2003.

The Taipei-Ilan Freeway 北宜高速公路, which has been under construction since July 1992, will connect the Second Freeway in eastern Taipei with northern Ilan County. Most of the 31-kilometer freeway including 11 tunnels—the longest of which is 12.9 kilometers long—and 27 bridges have already been completed. Additional plans, however, call for extending the freeway another 24 kilometers past the Ilan Plain to Suao 蘇澳. The entire project is scheduled for completion by 2003. Once finished, the current three-hour drive from Taipei to Ilan will be shortened to a mere 40 minutes.

The remaining portions of Expressway Network Project, including the Eastern Expressway from Suao via Hualien 花蓮 to Taitung 臺東 (240 kilometers), the Southern Cross-island Expressway from Taitung to Pingtung 屏東 (76 kilometers), and the Central Cross-island Expressway from Taichung 臺中 to Hualien (127 kilometers), are all in the design or planning stages.

Freeway Traffic Control

During holidays, traffic volume is generally 30 to 50 percent above normal. Accordingly, the Taiwan Area National Freeway Bureau (TANFB) under the Ministry of Transportation and Communications 交通部臺灣區國道高速公路局 has adopted a ramp metering control system 匝道儀控管制系統 to maintain an acceptable flow of traffic. This system was introduced on four national holidays in 1993, and after proving to be fairly effective, was gradually extended to include long holidays, weekends, and normal weekdays. The TANFB has implemented a fully automated ramp metering control system over the entire Sun Yat-sen Freeway at a cost of US$14.1 million.

Traffic Control

Traffic control is the joint responsibility of the Traffic Division of the National Police Administration 內政部警政署交通組, the Highway Police Bureau 公路警察局, the Taiwan Provincial Highway Police Corps 公路警察大隊, and all local police departments. The Airborne Squadron 空中警察隊 assists when necessary.

Wild cherry and plum blossoms along No.14 Provincial Highway offer delightful mountain scenery at Wushe.
(Photo by Lin Shu-hua)

To increase the effectiveness of the ramp metering control system and smooth the flow of traffic on the freeway during long holidays, High Occupancy Vehicle Control 高乘載車輛專用通行時段管制 has been in force since the 1995 Chinese New Year holiday. This system involves allocating different time slots during which vehicles, depending on their number of passengers, can enter the freeways. High occupancy vehicles, such as buses and cars carrying at least four people, are given priority. As a result, congestion on the freeways during holidays has been significantly reduced.

Tolls

There are 14 toll stations: 10 along the Sun Yat-sen Freeway, 3 along the Northern Second Freeway in the north, and 1 in the south. Standard tolls are NT$40 (US$1.28) for cars, NT$50 (US$1.60) for buses and small trucks, and NT$65 (US$2.08) for trailer trucks. In 2000, a total of 433,179,721 vehicles passed toll stations and with the toll revenue of NT$17.7 billion (US$567 million).

To help vehicles pass through quickly, there are "No Change" toll lanes at every toll station. Drivers are also encouraged to use coupons, which can be conveniently purchased at post offices, gas and toll stations, and service areas.

Urban Traffic

Traffic in Taiwan's major cities is very congested. Urban planners in all of Taiwan's metropolitan areas must cope with a similar set of challenges: a soaring number of new motorcycles and cars, a limited number of streets, and the complexities of acquiring very scarce space for improvements. Fortunately, countermeasures such as mass rapid transit systems and swift and convenient bus services have alleviated some of the burdens.

Taipei's Traffic Challenge

The increased number of private vehicles has made traffic congestion and parking worse in the Taipei City. In 2000, there were 666,513 automobiles and 959,013 motorcycles, an

Taipei Metropolitan Area Mass Rapid Transit Systems Developing Network

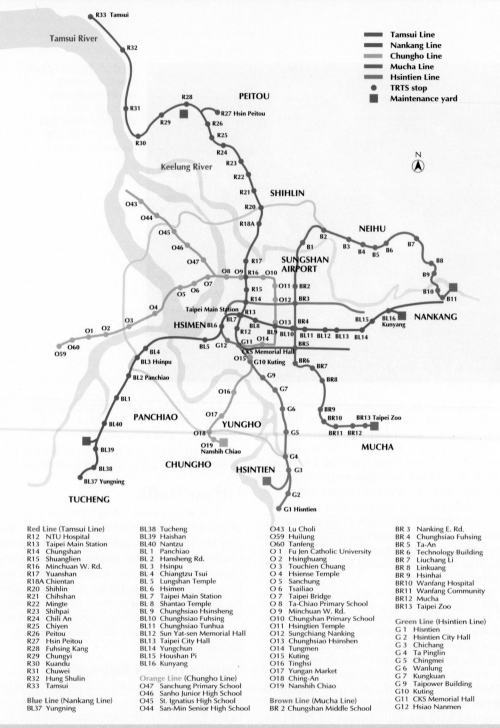

Red Line (Tamsui Line)
R12 NTU Hospital
R13 Taipei Main Station
R14 Chungshan
R15 Shuanglien
R16 Minchuan W. Rd.
R17 Yuanshan
R18A Chientan
R20 Shihlin
R21 Chihshan
R22 Mingte
R23 Shihpai
R24 Chili An
R25 Chiyen
R26 Peitou
R27 Hsin Peitou
R28 Fuhsing Kang
R29 Chungyi
R30 Kuandu
R31 Chuwei
R32 Hung Shulin
R33 Tamsui

Blue Line (Nankang Line)
BL37 Yungning

BL38 Tucheng
BL39 Haishan
BL40 Nantzu
BL 1 Panchiao
BL 2 Hansheng Rd.
BL 3 Hsinpu
BL 4 Chiangtzu Tsui
BL 5 Lungshan Temple
BL 6 Hsimen
BL 7 Taipei Main Station
BL 8 Shantao Temple
BL 9 Chunghsiao Hsinsheng
BL10 Chunghsiao Fuhsing
BL11 Chunghsiao Tunhua
BL12 Sun Yat-sen Memorial Hall
BL13 Taipei City Hall
BL14 Yungchun
BL15 Houshan Pi
BL16 Kunyang

Orange Line (Chungho Line)
O47 Sanchung Primary School
O46 Sanho Junior High School
O45 St. Ignatius High School
O44 San-Min Senior High School

O43 Lu Choli
O59 Huilung
O60 Linkou
O 1 Fu Jen Catholic University
O 2 Hsinghuang
O 3 Touchien Chuang
O 4 Hsiense Temple
O 5 Sanchung
O 6 Tsailiao
O 7 Taipei Bridge
O 8 Ta-Chiao Primary School
O 9 Minchuan W. Rd.
O10 Chungshan Primary School
O11 Hsingtien Temple
O12 Sungchiang Nanking
O13 Chunghsiao Hsinshen
O14 Tungmen
O15 Kuting
O16 Tinghsi
O17 Yungan Market
O18 Ching-An
O19 Nanshih Chiao

Brown Line (Mucha Line)
BR 2 Chungshan Middle School

BR 3 Nanking E. Rd.
BR 4 Chunghsiao Fuhsing
BR 5 Ta-An
BR 6 Technology Building
BR 7 Liuchang Li
BR 8 Linkuang
BR 9 Hsinhai
BR10 Wanfang Hospital
BR11 Wanfang Community
BR12 Mucha
BR13 Taipei Zoo

Green Line (Hsintien Line)
G 1 Hsintien
G 2 Hsintien City Hall
G 3 Chichang
G 4 Ta Pinglin
G 5 Chingmei
G 6 Wanlung
G 7 Kungkuan
G 9 Taipower Building
G10 Kuting
G11 CKS Memorial Hall
G12 Hsiao Nanmen

Source: Taipei Rapid Transit Corporation

Taipei Rapid Transit Systems Initial Network

Mucha Line 木柵線

Trains run on elevated tracks from the Taipei Zoo station 動物園站 in Mucha district, through Wanfang Community station 萬芳社區站 and then through tunnels in the Fuchou Hill Region 福州山地區 to Hoping East Road 和平東路, and along Fuhsing South & North Road 復興南、北路 to Chungshan Middle School station 中山國中站. Along the 10.9 km route are twelve stations and a maintenance depot.

Chungho Line 中和線

Chungho Line takes an underground route from Nanshih Chiao 南勢角 along Chingan Road 景安路, Chungho Road 中和路 and Yungho Road 永和路, and under the Hsintien River 新店溪 to Taipei City before joining the Hsintien Line at Kuting station 古亭站. Its 5.4 km route includes four stations and a stabling yard.

Hsintien Line 新店線

Hsintien Line joins the Tamshui Line at NTU Hospital station 台大醫院站 and runs south along Kungyuan Road 公園路, Roosevelt Road 羅斯福路, and Peihsin Road 北新路 to Hsintien station 新店站. Its 10.3 km route includes eleven underground stations and a stabling yard.

Tamsui Line 淡水線

Tamshui Line sets out on its southbound journey from Tamshui 淡水 along the right of way of the old Tamshui-Taipei railroad, and then at grade or elevated level through Peitou 北投, Shihlin 士林 and Yuanshan 圓山 before running underground to Taipei Main Station 台北車站. Along the 22.8 km route are twenty stations and the Peitou maintenance depot. Most of the stations along the Tamshui Line are built in traditional Chinese architectural style.

Nankang Line 南港線

Nankang Line runs underground from Kunyang station 昆陽站 in the east side of Taipei, passing Taipei City Hall station 市政府站 and Sun Yat-sen Memorial Hall station 國父紀念館站, and along Chunghsiao East Road 忠孝東路 and Chunghua Road 中華路 to Hsimen station 西門站. Its 10.3 km route includes eleven stations and a stabling yard.

Maintenance Line (Hsiao Nan Men Line) 小南門線

The TRTS network also includes a maintenance line that runs from Hsimen station to Chiang Kai-shek Memorial Hall station 中正紀念堂站. This line will facilitate trains serving the Nankang and Panchiao lines to transfer to the Peitou maintenance depot. The line is 1.6 km long and includes one station.

Panchiao Line & Tucheng Extension Line 板橋線及土城延伸線

Panchiao Line will take a subterranean route along Chunghua Road 中華路 to Hoping West Road 和平西路, under the Hsintien River 新店溪, and continue along Wenhua Road 文化路 to Fuchung station 府中站. An extension from this line will run along Nanya South Road 南雅南路 and Chungyang Road 中央路 to Tucheng 土城. Its 12.6 km route includes nine stations and a stabling yard.

Neihu Line 內湖線

Neihu Line is the extension of Mucha line and has been approved by the Executive Yuan as part of the TRTS Initial Network. It starts from the tail rail of Mucha Line just north of Chungshan Middle School station 中山國中站 and finally reaches Nankang Economic Trading Park Area 南港經貿園區. The total length is 14.8 km with twelve stations and an all-functional maintenance depot.

increase of 42,436 from the previous year. Therefore, the first priority for the transportation policy is to promote public transportation and to increase the share of public transportation to 50 percent.

Preparations for the Taipei Rapid Transit Systems 臺北都會區大眾捷運系統 (TRTS) began in early 1986, when the Executive Yuan 行政院 completed preliminary plans for the network and approved its implementation. The initial network, with a total length of 86.8 kilometers, was scheduled to be completed by the year 2005 at a cost of US$18 billion. The French contractor MATRA started work on the first TRTS line—the Mucha Line—in July 1988. The Mucha Line began service on March 28, 1996. The first section of the Tamsui Line opened on March 28, 1997, and by December 25 of that same year, the entire line was operational. The Chungho Line and the northern section of the Hsintien Line began service in December 1998, while the entire Hsintien Line and the Nankang Line from Taipei City Hall to Lungshan Temple opened at the end of 1999. The Panchiao Line from Lungshan Temple to Hsinpu Station began operation in September 2000. The entire Nankang Line was also operational at the end of 2000.

For Taipei's future development needs, the system has been planned to include the initial line, the Hsinchuang Line, the Luchou Line, the Hsinyi Line, the Sungshan Line, the Eastward Extension of the Nankang Line, the Tamhai Line, and the Orbital line, etc. Among these, the Hsinchuang, Luchou, Hsinyi, Sungshan Line and the Nankang Line Extension were approved by the Executive Yuan. The Orbital Line is scheduled to be built under a BOT contract. The corridor study of the Tamhai Line was completed as

---

Taipei Taxi Cabs

In May 2001, there were approximately 36,601 registered taxi cabs on the streets of Taipei City. Of these, 20,169 were operated by a total of 1,437 taxi companies. Another 8,111 were individually owned taxis, and 8,321 taxis belonged to 19 transportation cooperatives.

In December 2000, a slight fare increase was implemented. Although the base fare remained the same, the distance and time increments at which the meter changes was decreased. Many major hotels now record the number of the taxi cab on a card for their guests. This ensures that should there be any problem with a trip, the passenger has meaningful information with which to report to the passenger hotline listed below.

Effective Taipei Taxi Fares as of December 1, 2000

	Daytime (6 A.M.–11 P.M.)	Nighttime (11 P.M.–6 A.M.)
Base fare	NT$70 (1,500 m)	NT$70 (1,250 m)
Distance Increment	NT$5 (300 m)	NT$5 (250 m)
Time Increment	NT$5 every 2 min. under 5 km/hr.	NT$5 every 1.7 min. under 5 km/hr.

Regular additions to total fare:
      NT$10 for a dispatched cab
      NT$10 for each luggage placed in the taxi trunk

Complaints about Taxi Service

Passenger Hotline—Taipei City Police Headquarters 臺北市警察局 (02)2394-9007
Bureau of Transportation, Taipei City Government 臺北市交通局 (02)2725-6888
Office of Motor Vehicle Inspection, Taipei City Government 臺北市監理處 (02)2767-8217

Source: Bureau of Transportation, Taipei City Government

requested by the Ministry of the Interior and was handed to the Ministry of Transportation and Communications for approval.

The Taipei City Government improved the urban transportation by integrating bus and MRT connectivity with 48 feeder bus routes, providing one-way free bus transfers for MRT passengers, and unifying the pricing of bus operations. Countdown timing monitors have also been extensively installed at pedestrian crossings to improve safety. Lanes and parking bays exclusively for motorcycles have also been established. The Taipei City Government has authorized private operators to build parking lots and boosted parking fees to increase the number of parking spaces, raise the parking turnover rate, and reasonably reflect social costs. All of these efforts are designed to create a convenient transportation environment and improve Taipei's quality of life.

Kaohsiung Mass Rapid Transit System Development Plan (First Phase)

Kaohsiung, the second largest city in Taiwan, is also Taiwan's premier harbor and one of the busiest container ports in the world. Rapid industrial development and population growth have accentuated the need for efficient metropolitan transportation. Accordingly, the Kaohsiung City Government 高雄市政府 has planned the Kaohsiung Metropolitan Area Mass Rapid Transit System Development Plan (First Term) 高雄都會區大眾捷運系統第一期發展計畫, which was approved by the Executive Yuan in January 1994.

The Kaohsiung MRT system is designed to integrate high-speed and regular railways with the city bus system, thus providing a comprehensive mass transportation network.

The US$6 billion network will consist of a Red Line and an Orange Line with 37 stations and a total length of 42.7 kilometers. Two additional lines and extensions to both lines are currently in the planning stages. The Kaohsiung Mass Rapid Transit (KMRT) project will be constructed under the BOT approach and has been approved by the Executive Yuan and the Kaohsiung City Council. In 2000, the Kaohsiung Rapid Transit Corp. (KRTC) 高雄捷運股份有限公司 won the bid at US$5.38 billion. According to the requirements of contract, the KMRT project will be partially operational in December 2004. The operation of the northern section of the Red Line will begin in December 2005, and the full operation of the Red Line and Orange Line will begin in December 2006.

Rapid Transit in Other Cities

Following Taipei's lead, many other cities in Taiwan aside from Kaohsiung have also initiated plans for metropolitan rail transit systems. These cities include Taichung, Tainan, and Taoyuan. Private participation in the rapid transit systems projects for all of these cities is currently under study; however, the only project passing the planning stage so far is Kaohsiung's MRT.

Related website
Ministry of Transportation and Communications:
http://www.motc.gov.tw

China Airlines wins first prize for the world's best Service Efficienc

Even at 35,000 feet, no airline can escape the scrutiny of one of the leading aviati
quality advisors, SKYTRAX Research. The latest independent survey of 34 airlines
over 9000 passengers by U.K based SKYTRAX ranks China Airlines as the 5-St
winner of first class service efficiency.

Recognition of our successful "instant service" company philosophy is a great reward
but the satisfaction of our passengers is greater. We invite you to be our judg

CHINA AIRLINES

www.china-airlines.com   Reservations : 02-2715-1212

GLOBAL *e*-LOGISTICS SERVICE

Punctual, Speedy, Reliable and Economical

Saves you TIME... and that's MONEY

YANG MING GROUP
YANG MING MARINE TRANSPORT CORP.

http://www.yml.com.tw
Head Office 886-2-24559988 North America 1-201-2228899 Europe 49-40-320980

Taipei MRT Moving Forward

Taipei MRT Moving Forward

In the 21ˢᵗ century,
Taipei is continuing to develop a prosperous and thriving
metropolis with the completion of the Mucha, Tamshui,
Hsintien, Chungho and Panchiao-Nankang MRT Lines.
The MRT provides the people of Taipei with safe, fast,
comfortable and attractive transportation. It has
revolutionized transportation for commuters as well as
enhanced the quality of life for everyone in the city.
The completed routes of the Taipei MRT system presently
total 67.2km in length, while the Panchiao Line,
Tucheng Line, Hsinchuang Line, Luchou Line, Neihu Line,
Hsiao Pitan station, Sungshan Line, the Eastern Extension
of the Nankang Line, and the Hsinyi Line
are still under construction. Once the
ongoing construction work is completed,
the fully-formed Taipei MRT network
will provide the general public with a
state-of-the-art transportation system.

DEPARTMENT OF RAPID TRANSIT SYSTEMS, TCG.
7, Lane 48, Sec. 2 Chung-Shan North Road, Taipei Taiwan, R.O.C
Tel：(02)2521-5550   http://www.dorts.gov.tw

15
Public Health

Hepatitis B vaccinations of all newborns have significantly reduced the spread of this disease.
(Courtesy of the Department of Information, Taipei City Government)

What's New

1. Figures updated
2. Changes in the focus of public health policies, plans, and programs
3. The emergency medical care system
4. Health of ROC nationals
5. New measures of NHI

Shifting demographic patterns and changes in modern lifestyles have affected health care in Taiwan. The aging of the population has highlighted pension issues and long-term care for the elderly. The influx of 329,612 foreign laborers has exacerbated the problem of providing health care for foreign workers. Serious pollution and smoking problems have triggered a high rate of lung cancer, especially in the urban areas of Taipei, Kaohsiung, Keelung 基隆, and Tainan. Industrial development and the growth of urban traffic have resulted in an alarming rate of occupational and traffic accidents. Of the 10,515 fatal accidents recorded in 2000, 5,534 (or 52.63 percent) were transportation-related, constituting the leading cause of death for people under the age of 44 in this category. More than 97 percent of the fatalities (5,420 persons) were due to motorbike-related traffic accidents. A major youth health concern that has arisen is the unprecedented number of students using amphetamines, FM2, and MDMA. Health authorities are also concerned about the sanitation standards of Taiwan's many unregulated eateries, roadside stalls, lunch box caterers, and galleries of food vendors.

Overall, the control of infectious diseases in the ROC has greatly improved. Forty years ago, acute infectious diseases were the number one killer in the Taiwan area. Today, they are no longer among the top ten causes of death in Taiwan. Bubonic plague, smallpox, and cholera were all eradicated long ago and not a single case of rabies has been discovered since 1959. In 1965, the World Health Organization (WHO) of the United Nations declared malaria

Plans and Programs

The public health policies in the Taiwan area are mainly formulated by the Department of Health 衛生署 (DOH). In fiscal 2001, three primary plans and ten secondary programs were drawn up under the directions of the Executive Yuan and the Department of Health in order to improve the health conditions of the people and the efficiency of the public health care system. The three primary plans are: National Health Insurance IC Card 健保IC卡實施計畫, Fourth Phase Medical Care Network 醫療網第四期計畫, the Development of National Health Research Institute國家衛生研究院發展計畫. The ten programs, respectively, to be carried out according to schedule are: the Management Plan for the Control of Betel Nut Problem 檳榔問題管理方案, the Second Term Reinforcement Plan for the Control of TB 結核病防治第二期計畫, the Three-year Project for Long-term Care for the Old Age 老人長期護護三年計畫, the Second Term Program for the Control of AIDS 後天免疫缺乏症候群第二期計畫, the Project for Cancer Screening Community Service 癌症社區到點篩檢服務計畫, the Three-year Project for the Development of Community Health Care 社區健康營造三年計畫, and the Human-used Vaccines Production Project 人用疫苗自製計畫, Contagious Diseases Prevention Project 全國傳染病防治計畫, Third Term Project of New Family Planning 新家庭計畫三期計畫, Project of Medical Services in Mountain Areas and Offshore Islands 山地離島醫療服務計畫.

nonexistent in Taiwan. Other infectious diseases such as diphtheria, pertussis, neonatal tetanus, poliomyelitis, Japanese encephalitis, and tuberculosis are now under strict control. Major immunization drives in 1995 focused on eradicating poliomyelitis, measles, congenital rubella, and neonatal tetanus. In 1998, a pioneering plan was initiated that provided free flu vaccinations to senior citizens 65 years or older.

The economic prosperity of the Taiwan area has brought greater access to health care resources and enabled the government to launch the National Health Insurance 全民健康保險 (NHI) program, which officially began on March 1, 1995. By December 2000, over 96.16 percent of Taiwan's population, or 21.40 million persons, were insured under the program.

The health situation in Taiwan has made impressive gains over the past several decades. For example, average life expectancy from 1951 to 2000 has increased from 53.38 years to 72.63 years for males, and from 56.33 years to 78.30 years for females. The death rate dropped from 18.15 per 1,000 persons in 1947 to 5.61 per 1,000 persons in 2000, and the infant mortality rate also dropped from 44.71 per 1,000 live births in 1952 to a low of 4.8 per 1,000 in 1993. However, in 1996 infant mortality increased to 6.66 mainly due to the implementation of a new, more efficient nationwide registration system for reporting newborns. In 1999, the rate dropped again to 6.07, and then to 5.86 in 2000.

Medical Infrastructure

Manpower

At the end of 2000, there were 164,691 medical personnel in the Taiwan area. On average, there was one doctor of Western medicine for every 784 persons, one doctor of Chinese medicine for every 5,863 persons, and one dentist for every 2,591 persons. There are currently 11 medical schools, and 17 paramedical colleges and junior colleges in the ROC. Physicians may apply for a medical specialist license after being certified in such specialties as family medicine, internal medicine, pediatrics, obstetrics and gynecology, orthopedics, neurology, neurosurgery, urology, ENT, ophthalmology, dermatology, psychiatry, rehabilitation medicine, anesthesiology, radiology, pathology, nuclear medicine, plastic surgical medicine, emergency medicine, oral and maxillofacial surgery, oral pathology, and general surgical medicine. A specialist license is valid for five to six years, after which physicians must undergo a short period of retraining in new technology, systems, and equipment. After completion, physicians may extend their licenses for another term. This system was first set up in

1988, and by February 2000, 28,518 specialists had been certified.

Manpower imbalances pose major problems for the ROC's medical care system. A shortage of qualified nurses is especially serious, given the growing medical needs of an aging population. To improve the quality of medication and lower the doctor-patient ratio to 1:575, the DOH has proposed increasing medical student enrollments. The number of medical technicians capable of operating more sophisticated, advanced medical equipment has also been decreasing. The number of technicians and technologists in radiology and medicine, as well as dentists, have already exceeded the number of physicians.

Rural and remote areas are still short of qualified medical personnel. The government, therefore, offers incentives, such as increased pay and commuting subsidies to medical personnel serving in these areas. Beginning in 1999, medical school graduates who have studied on government scholarships are assigned to remote areas or

Medical Personnel in the Taiwan Area 2000

Type	Number in Service
Physicians	28,404
Doctors of Chinese Medicine	3,799
Dentists	8,596
Dental Assistants	71
Pharmacists	16,458
Pharmacist Assistants	7,660
Medical Technologists 醫檢師	6,630
Medical Technicians 醫檢生	380
Registered Professional Nurses	56,520
Registered Nurses	28,572
Midwives	653
Medical Radiography Technologists (Technicians) 醫用放射線技術師(士)	2,397
Physical Therapist & Assistants	2,714
Dieticians	1,108
Occupational Therapists & Assistants	690
Total	164,652

Source: Department of Health

special medical branches for one year. In accordance with the *Measures for the Improvement of Medicare in the Mountain and Remote Areas and Outlying Islands,* St. Paul's Hospital in Taoyuan City and 15 other medical institutions (hospitals, clinics, and health stations) provide medical services to 16 areas considered inaccessible. Twelve dental service groups have also been organized by dental associations at the national and local levels to provide services in 12 mountain areas. Transportation subsidies are also provided for patients who require transfer to cities.

Foreign nationals with licenses recognized by the ROC government may apply to take a written exam in Chinese which, if passed, will allow them to obtain a license to practice medicine in Taiwan. As of 2001, there were 744 physicians, 57 dentists, 17 medical assistants, and 31 pharmacists from overseas providing services in the ROC.

Medical Facilities

An extensive network of hospitals and clinics serves the people in the Taiwan area. Public medical care institutions consist of 96 hospitals and 481 clinics, including public hospitals, medical school hospitals, veterans hospitals and clinics, clinics affiliated with government institutions, and civil departments of military hospitals. Private medical care institutions consist of 573 hospitals and 11,382 clinics, including proprietary hospitals, hospitals affiliated with private medical schools, corporate hospitals and clinics, and private clinics. Medical institutions in the Taiwan area provide a total of 126,476 beds, averaging nearly 56.78 beds per 10,000 people. Sixty-five percent of these beds are provided by private medical institutions.

Teaching Hospitals 教學醫院 in Taiwan

Teaching hospitals are classified into five categories: medical centers 醫學中心, regional hospitals 區域醫院, district hospitals 地區醫院, specialty teaching hospitals 特殊功能醫院, and psychiatric teaching hospitals 精神專科教學醫院.

Accreditation and Licensing

A hospital accreditation system has been in operation since 1978 to assure quality hospital in-patient care and rank the service and quality of Taiwan area hospitals. Currently, hospitals are evaluated on the basis of the quality of personnel, facilities, hospital management, and community services, as well as the quality of medical care in various departments, such as internal medicine and surgery, radiological diagnosis and therapy, laboratory testing, nursing care, pharmaceutical service, ward management, infection control in hospitals, emergency care, and psychiatric care. The accreditation is valid for three years, after which a hospital must apply for reassessment. By the end of 2000, 497 hospitals had been qualified.

Clinics are not subject to accreditation procedures, but instead must apply to the local health station for an operating license. The requirements for obtaining such a license are set by each individual health station, which ensure that the clinics maintain high standards at all levels, ranging from the quality of the facilities to the credentials of the medical staff. Once clinics obtain their operating licenses, they are subject to periodic inspections by local health station personnel. Such routine checks help to maintain the high standards and must be passed in order for the clinics to renew their licenses.

Information Exchange

In 1991, the Department of Health commissioned the Institute for Information Industry 資訊工業策進會 to set up a computerized information exchange system in Hsinchu 新竹 between local medical institutions and hospitals. This Public Health Information Exchange was originally a three-year (1991-1993) experimental project to improve medical services in Hsinchu; however, owing to its success, the local project was extended in 1993 to cover the entire Taiwan area. By August 1995, regional centers had been established in Hsinchu, Taipei, Kaohsiung, and Taichung.

The Public Health Information Exchange incorporates three subsystems: the Health

Administration Information System (HAIS), the Administration System of General Affairs (ASGA), and the National Health Information Network (NHIN). The HAIS covers the exchange of medical affairs, pharmaceutical affairs, food sanitation, communicable disease control, and health promotion. The ASGA is primarily concerned with improving the administrative efficiency of public health. The NHIN provides the latest general profiles of national medical resources, shows the current certification for all medical personnel and management, displays information exchanges between medical institutions and medical administration units, and provides consulting services to the general public on relevant medical legislation through bulletin boards. This network was fully operational by the end of 1997, allowing all health stations to exchange information concerning medical records, insurance histories, medical personnel resumes, etc.

With the implementation of the National Health Insurance plan in 1995, the development of a more comprehensive, overall medical information network that would link NHI units with community dispensaries became one of the top priorities of the DOH.

Medical Care Network

Rapid industrialization and urbanization, as well as the aging population, have highlighted the need for better health care and more evenly distributed medical services. To balance medical resources, the DOH launched a 15-year project designated the Establishment of Medical Care Network 醫療保健計畫—籌建醫療網計畫 in the Taiwan area in July 1985. This three-phase project divides the Taiwan area into 17 medical care regions, each of which serves as the basic

---

Public Health Administration

Before July 1, 1999, public health administration in the ROC was organized at four levels: national, provincial/special municipality, county and city, as well as township. At the national level, the Department of Health under the Executive Yuan is the highest authority, and determines national health policies, formulates programs, and both supervises and coordinates health services at all levels. Beginning July 1, 1999, in coordination with reorganizing the government and streamlining of the Taiwan Provincial Government, the DOH established the Central Taiwan Office to replace the former provincial department of health. In July, 2001, the DOH made some adjustments in the organization of the central public health system, creating four bureaus to oversee medical affairs 醫政處, pharmaceutical affairs 藥政處, food sanitation 食品衛生處, and health planning 企劃處, respectively. The DOH has many subordinate agencies, including: the Center for Disease Control 疾病管制局, the Bureau of Health Promotion 國民健康局, the National Bureau of Controlled Drugs 管制藥品管理局. Other subordinate agencies are: the National Laboratories of Food & Drugs 藥物食品檢驗局, the National Health Insurance Supervisory Committee 全民健康保險監理委員會, the National Health Insurance Disputes Review Committee 全民健康保險爭議審議委員會, the Committee for the Negotiation of Medical Fees 全民健康保險醫療協定委員會, the Committee on Chinese Medicine & Pharmacy 中醫藥委員會, and the Bureau of National Health Insurance 中央健康保險局. There are also three DOH-affiliated organizations: the National Health Research Institute 國家衛生研究院, the Taiwan Joint Commission on Hospital Accreditation 醫院評鑑暨醫療品質策進會, and the Center for Drug Evaluation 醫藥品查驗中心.

At the special municipality government level are the Taipei City Bureau of Health 臺北市政府衛生局 and the Kaohsiung City Health Department 高雄市政府衛生局, along with their subordinate district health stations in each district within Taipei and Kaohsiung Cities. These agencies are responsible for implementing health and medical care programs in their respective administrative areas.

At the county and city level, health bureaus are the responsible health units, and health stations are located in each urban or rural township. In mountain areas and outlying islands, health rooms 衛生室 or small-scale health posts 保健站 have been set up to provide primary health services, improve health conditions, and raise the quality of medical care services at the grassroots level.

unit for developing medical manpower, facilities, and an emergency care network. These 17 medical regions are further subdivided into 63 subregions, based on population, geographic conditions, and transportation facilities. Each subregion is equipped with regional or district hospitals, as well as primary medical care units (i.e., private practitioners, group practice centers, and health stations). By December 1995, 174 group practice centers had already been established under the first phase of the 15-year project.

The second phase of the Establishment of Medical Care Network project also seeks to distribute medical resources more evenly by restricting the establishment or expansion of hospitals in regions with plentiful medical resources and setting up a Medical Care Development Fund to encourage the private sector to establish health care institutions in regions lacking sufficient medical facilities. The Medical Care Development Fund subsidized a total of 210 hospitals and 105 clinics between fiscal 1992 and 2000, making the 37 regions previously lacking medical facilities now sufficient.

The first phase of the Establishment of Medical Care Network was completed in 1990, and the second phase was completed in December 1996. The third phase, which started in January 1997, targets primary medical care in the mountain areas and offshore islands by expanding the emergency medical care network and developing health services for the chronically and mentally ill. In 1999, the Medical Care Network placed more emphasis on elderly care, emergency care, the prevention and control of mental illness, long-term medical care services, rehabilitation of the physically and mentally impaired, and health care in mountain areas and offshore islands.

The third phase was concluded in 2000. In 2001, the "New Century Health Care Network" was initiated, divided into two parts: the medical care services for the general group and for the particular group.

The new program focuses on setting up integrated medical care service regions, upgrading medical care quality, reforming the hospital accreditation system, enhancing skills of medical professionals, and consolidating medical resources, thereby increasing the efficiency of hospital operations.

Health Stations

Residents in mountain areas and offshore islands rely heavily on the medical services provided by local health stations 衛生所, which, along with health rooms 衛生室, provide general outpatient treatment and emergency medical care. Educational programs provided by the health stations include courses on maternal and child health, family planning, and the prevention and control of geriatric, acute, and chronic diseases. Surveys show that 70 to 90 percent of the visits to community health stations are for infant and child immunizations. In 1945, there were only 15 health stations in the entire Taiwan area. However, by the end of 2000, there were 368 health stations throughout the Taiwan area, with 12 district health stations in Taipei City, 11 in Kaohsiung City, and seven in both Kinmen and Lienchiang Counties. By the end of 1999, there were 503 health rooms in the Taiwan area, located in areas outside of Taipei City, Kaohsiung City, Kinmen and Lienchiang Counties.

Health stations are community-oriented and form the basis of primary health care in the Taiwan area. These health centers are staffed with physicians, dentists, pharmacists, nurses, and laboratory technicians. On the average, each health station has one to two doctors. Even health stations and health rooms in remote areas have basic medical equipment, such as regular and dental X-ray machines, and almost all group practice centers are equipped with automatic biochemical analyzers.

A health station with supporting hi-tech equipment to strengthen emergency care services has been set up in every township located in mountainous areas, outlying islands, and other areas with relatively limited medical resources. This includes 49 health stations established in 30 aboriginal townships scattered throughout 12 counties in Taiwan proper, the Pescadores, Liuchiu (in Pingtung County), and Green Island (off the coast of Taitung). Furthermore, approximately 200 health rooms have been set up to serve residents in inaccessible areas.

Since 1979, the government has been sending mobile medical teams to remote villages on a regular basis. In the Pescadores, a telecommunications medical care program was initiated in 1988 to provide emergency medical care for the island's residents. Later, 145 other points of service in various mountainous areas and other offshore islands also joined this telecommunications medical care network.

Since 1995, teaching hospitals, medical centers, and regional hospitals have joined the distance medical care network and provided services to health stations in remote areas. For example, by 1995, the National Taiwan University Hospital was linked with the Chinshan Health Station; the National Cheng Kung University Hospital with the Penghu Hospital; the Veterans General Hospital (Taipei) with the Military Kinmen Hospital and the Ilan County Health Station; and the Tri Service General Hospital (Taipei) with Matsu's Peikao Hospital, Lienchiang County Hospital, and the Military Matsu Hospital. Since 1999, the Tungchu, Peikan, and Tungying Health Stations on Matsu have also been linked with the Tri Service General Hospital, and the Kinmen County Hospital has been connected with the Veterans General Hospital.

Emergency Medical Care System

To improve the quality and efficiency of emergency medical services, the *Law on Emergency Medical Care* 緊急醫療救護法 was promulgated on August 9, 1995. The Department of Health has implemented a number of important measures in accordance with the law:
• Improving emergency medical care, installing emergency care facilities, and strengthening emergency departments. This includes establishing a system of specialists for emergency

Goals of DOH

The DOH provides all citizens a healthy living environment, an effective medical service system, and correct information regarding hygiene. The goals of the Department of Health are as follows:
• Health insurance:
  A special task force has been set up to monitor the national health insurance for the overall improvement measures to reduce costs of the NHI, and make it substainable.
• Health promotion:
  The promotion programs include cancer screening, prevention, and palliative care/hospice; anti-smoking campaign; new century medical care network; even distribution of medical resources; five-year project for emergency medical care; and better care for minorities, aborigines, and people in mountain areas and offshore islands.
• Epidemic prevention:
  Epidemic prevention is carried out at all levels, with professional staff and accessible information. In order to prevent epidemic after the establishment of the Three Small Links, the DOH is assisting the health bureaus of Kinmen and Lienchiang Counties in setting up epidemic prevention centers.
• Consumer protection:
  The use of antibiotics is further restricted. False advertisements are prohibited.
• International cooperation:
  The ROC has applied to the World Health Assembly (WHA) every May since 1997, to become an observer in the World Health Organization. In April 2001, Premier Chang Chun-hsiung ordered the formation of an inter-ministerial task force to promote Taiwan's bid to join the WHO. He also added that the task force should supervise various promotional projects and keep close contact with relevant private organizations. The premier further reminded the Mainland Affairs Council to include the WHO issues in dialogue between the two sides of the Taiwan Strait.

medical care, enhancing coordination in community hospital networks with emergency services, and purchasing well-equipped ambulances so that basic medical treatment can be provided. To alleviate the pressure of the large influx of emergency patients in big hospitals, the Bureau of National Health Insurance raised the level of medical payments for emergency care provided at other medical institutions.

- Supervision of key emergency service hospitals is provided at the regional level, so as to ensure the best medical treatment and services. As of May 1998, all check points had passed the DOH standard.
- By March 2000, a total of 253 emergency care doctors had been certified since the first specialist examinations were offered in August 1998.
- Key hospitals providing emergency services in remote areas have been subsidized and equipped.
- Hospitals that provide emergency medical care for toxic- or chemical-shock syndrome and nuclear accidents have been designated in northern, central, and southern Taiwan.
- The DOH monitors emergency services in different parts of the Taiwan area in accordance with the *Operational Points for Medical Institutions in Responding to the Emergency Needs of Large Number of Patients* 衛生機關及醫療機構大量傷病患緊急醫療救護作業要點.
- A nationwide communication network for emergency services has been established.
- The Five-year Plan for the Establishment of a Comprehensive Emergency Medical System is being implemented.
- Private sector medical resources are being integrated and organized to provide emergency services in the event of major disasters.
- Training is provided to emergency personnel affiliated with fire brigades.
- An interdepartmental operational network linking central and local emergency units has been established in order to provide efficient disaster rescue.

- In order to facilitate the mobilization of emergency medical resources, national and regional disaster medical assistant teams have been set up.

Long-Term Care

Elderly people, who are discharged from hospitals but still require some medical attention, or those who are chronically ill, usually require home health care. In 2000, this service was provided by 299 hospitals based in the Taiwan area. For less than US$58 per visit, elderly people can receive the medical care they need on a regular basis, usually twice per month. At the end of 2000, the DOH also commissioned 65 medical institutions to provide out-of-hospital services, as well as 19 day care centers. In 2000, there were 171 registered nursing homes caring for 7,917 elderly residents. Supportive services are also provided to families with members who are chronically ill. In addition, the Sun Yat-sen Cancer Center provides home care specifically for cancer patients. (Information on other welfare services for the elderly can be found in Chapter 19, Social Welfare.)

Health Insurance

Prior to March 1995, only 59 percent of Taiwan's population had health insurance, all under 13 public health insurance plans. In view of the rapidly growing medical care costs and the increasing number of the elderly, the ROC government launched the National Health Insurance program on March 1, 1995, to provide universal medical care. This system incorporated the medical insurance coverage provided by the original 13 public health insurance plans and further extended coverage to the 7.99 million citizens who were formerly uninsured, mainly the elderly, children, students, housewives, and the disabled. At the end of 2000, there were 21,400,826 people covered by the NHI program, representing 96.16 percent of the total 23 million population.

The benefits covered by NHI are very comprehensive. They cover inpatient care, ambulatory

National Health Insurance Premium Shares

Insured Status		Rate Shared %		
	Category	Insurant	Employer	Government
I	Civil servants, public-elected officials, and representatives	40	60	0
	Private school employees	40	30	30
	Wage earners of public and private firms	30	60	10
	Employers, self-employed, licensed professional practitioners, and technicians	100	0	0
II	Members of occupational associations, ROC sailors serving on foreign vessels	60	0	40
III	Farmers, fishermen, and members of irrigation associations	30	0	70
IV	Servicemen, military cadets, survivors of servicemen died in action, substitutive conscripts	0	0	100
V	Low-income households	0	0	100
VI	Veterans,	0	0	100
	survivors of deceased veterans,	30	0	70
	others	60	0	40

Source: Bureau of National Health Insurance, DOH

care, laboratory tests, X-ray examinations, pharmaceuticals, dental services, traditional Chinese medicine, day care for the mentally ill, and limited home health care. In addition, there are four preventive services, namely adult health examinations, pre-natal examinations, well-baby checkups, and pap smear examinations. Some of the expensive treatments are also included in the coverage such as the cocktail therapy for HIV positive patients and organ transplant.

Starting September 2001, the NHI carried out a five-disease treatment improvement project for cervix cancer, breast cancer, TB, diabetes, and asthma. The project encourages medical institutions to increase screening and to focus on long term follow-up treatment. For example, the more pap tests a medical institution performs, the higher pay it receives on each checkup. Also, medical institutions with higher survival rate and more completely cured patients will be rewarded with bonus in addition to the expenses paid for the treatment itself. It is estimated that the whole project would cost NT$2.9 billion. It was started with cervix cancer, and the other four will be subsequently implemented in different areas.

The NHI has benefited everyone, especially the 400,000 people suffering from serious or terminal illnesses who, in the past, had to pay expenses for medical care themselves or burden

their families with high medical costs. The NHI has also cushioned the high hospitalization expenses incurred from premature babies, thereby alleviating the huge financial stress normally placed on their families.

Under the *National Health Insurance Act* 全民健康保險法, participation in the NHI program is mandatory for all ROC citizens who have resided in Taiwan for more than four months, with the exception of prison inmates, who receive free medical care from the government. Foreign nationals, living in Taiwan with valid Alien Resident Certificates 外僑居留證 are also required to participate in the NHI.

As NHI is compulsory and an important part of social security, the Bureau of National Health Insurance 中央健康保險局 cross-checks the lists of uninsured persons with the government agencies overseeing household registration, internal revenue, and labor insurance to assist in locating and enrolling them in the NHI program.

By the end of 2000, 19,983 of the medical institutions in the Taiwan area had joined the NHI program, including 577 western medicine hospitals and 8,241 clinics, 52 Chinese medicine hospitals and 2,100 clinics, and 5,362 dentists. In addition, 3,061 community pharmacies, 230 medical labs, 304 nursing homes, 18 midwifery clinics, and 38 community rehabilitation centers for psychiatric patients are all providing services to participants under the NHI program.

Under the schedule for premiums and rates that was approved in July 1994, employees pay 30 percent of the premium, employers 60 percent, and the government 10 percent. Thus, a typical worker earning just over US$970 a month, with a spouse (non-working) and two children, would pay about US$49 a month. The law specifies a first-year premium rate of 4.25 percent of the monthly wage, which can be raised to no more than 6 percent thereafter.

Insured individuals consulted doctors an average of 14.8 times in 2000. And the average admission to the hospital was 12.7 persons per hundred. In order to make the beneficiaries cost-aware, a co-payment system of the outpatient

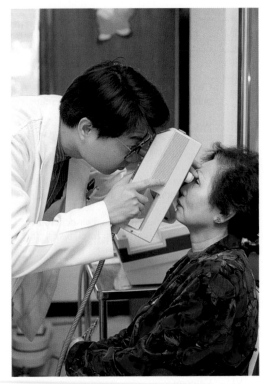

As of the end of 2000, 96.16 percent of ROC people were covered by the National Health Insurance program's effective medical care.

services based on pharmaceutical costs and use frequency was introduced on August 1, 1999 and revised on July 1, 2001. For example, after July 1, 2001, the maximum expenses of medication on the part of the insured increased from NT$100 to NT$200.

The global budget payment systems have been gradually applied since 1997. Currently, clinic outpatient services, dental services and Chinese medicine for outpatient services are all been reimbursed through respective global budget payment systems.

Integration with Existing Programs

Before the National Health Insurance program was implemented, there were 13 public health insurance plans that served as the primary sources of medical insurance. The majority of these plans were categorized under three main systems: labor insurance, government employees' insurance, and farmers' insurance. Although the medical coverage portions of these programs have been subsumed by the National Health Insurance program, the original programs still continue to provide benefits for various categories of extraordinary financial hardships.

The Labor Insurance program 勞工保險, for example, still provides benefits for workers, such as industrial workers, journalists, employees in nonprofit organizations, government employees and teachers not eligible for civil servants' or teachers' insurance, fishermen, and persons receiving vocational training in institutes registered with the government.

Labor insurance covers payments under two criteria: ordinary payments and compensation for occupational and industrial damage. Ordinary payments include cash benefits for maternity, subsidies for those who have no income during hospitalization, compensation for the disabled, lump-sum payments for old age, and funeral grants for survivors.

Since January 1999, an unemployment subsidy has been provided for those who are involuntarily unemployed. By April 2001, the total number of claims for unemployment benefit payments was about 240,000, and totalled more than US$118 million. Compensation for occupational injuries include medication and payments to workers during their hospitalization and compensation for workers killed or disabled on the job. After March 1995, the NHI program covered almost all health care services under one program. Labor insurance became supplementary in sharing part of the patients' out-of-pocket payments for hospital care. Supplemental health maintenance and treatment services are provided as a preventive measure on an annual basis for 23 health conditions to detect occupational diseases and injuries.

In order to simplify insurance regulations, improve the financial structure, and optimize the principle of risk sharing, the former nine insurance programs under the Government Employees' Insurance (GEI) 公務人員保險 were revised and consolidated into a new program, the Government Employee and School Staff Insurance (GESSI) 公教人員保險. The benefit packages remain unchanged and include cash benefits for disability, old age, and death, as well as funeral allowances for dependents.

On March 28, 1994, the *Statute of Health Insurance for Retired Government Employees* 退休公務人員疾病保險 was modified as the *Statute of Health Insurance for Retired Employees and Their Dependents of Government Organizations and Private Schools* 退休公教人員及其眷屬疾病保險. The revision combined the civil servant and private school staff health insurance programs. However, after the implementation of the National Health Insurance program in 1995, all health insurance programs related to the GEI were ended.

On May 31, 1999, the GESSI integrated the insurance program for private school teachers and administrative staff with the program for government employees. Non-profit private schools must meet the conditions stated in the *Private School Law* 私校法 to be covered by the insurance program. By June 2001, a total of 625,490 persons were covered under the GESSI. The Retired Government Employees' Insurance (RGEI) 退休人員保險 covers civil servants, who retired without receiving retirement benefits before July 1, 1985. The RGEI stopped enrollment on July 1, 1985. In June 2001, a total of 942 persons were covered by the program and the number has continued to decline.

All GEI programs are under the purview of the Examination Yuan's Ministry of Civil Service 考試院銓敘部 and are insured by the Central Trust of China 中央信託局, a government-owned financial enterprise.

At the end of 1999, the Comprehensive Farmers' Health Insurance program 農民健康保險 covered 1.8 million farmers. This insurance program is administered at the national level by the Ministry of the Interior 內政部, and at the local level by the respective provincial, county, and city governments. All farmers over 15 years of age, who engage in agricultural work for more than 90 days a year and are members of a farmers' association, are eligible for coverage under the Comprehensive Farmers' Health Insurance program. The coverage includes compensation in the event of illness and injury, and cash benefits for disability, maternity, and funeral expenses.

Health Promotion Programs

Maternal and Child Health Care

Since the first health care programs for mothers and children were begun in 1952, infant deaths caused by birth trauma and infection have been decreasing. The infant mortality rate was 5.86 per 1,000 live births in 2000. Unfortunately, the relative number of accidental injuries, premature births, and birth defects have increased since 1952. As estimated, about 8 to 10 percent of the 300,000 live births were premature; therefore, it is important that comprehensive health services cover all stages of development.

The current NHI program provides prenatal and postnatal care for early detection and treatment of pregnancy-related diseases, ensures safe deliveries, and maintains the health of both infants and mothers. Ten free prenatal checkups and a "handbook for pregnant women" are provided to record the health conditions of expectant mothers. On average, each pregnant woman in 2000 received 8.96 prenatal checkups. Breastfeeding is also encouraged. As a result, the health of mothers and children in the Taiwan area has greatly improved. In 1965, the number of women who died from childbirth was 75 per 100,000. This figure had dropped to 9.41 by 1986, and to 7.8 by 2000.

The infant mortality rate has also fallen. In 1965, it was 24 per 1,000; by 1994, the rate had decreased to 5.07 per 1,000. The figure rose to 5.86 per 1,000 in 2000, but this was mainly because of a flaw in the registration system in use prior to 1994, which resulted in infant and neonatal mortality rates being underestimated. This discrepancy has now been corrected through the implementation of a more efficient and accurate birth registration system.

Over 99.95 percent of all deliveries were assisted by qualified personnel in 2000, a marked improvement in health service over past years. A surprising 34.2 percent of all deliveries were done by Caesarean section (C-section). The reason for the increase in the number of C-sections is believed to be twofold. Although women who died of obstetric causes were at a low of 7.8 per 100,000 live births, women regularly asked for this procedure to secure the health of their babies. Furthermore, the expenses for this method of delivery are fully covered by the NHI program. Some critics have also suggested that hospitals were promoting C-sections out of a desire to increase their income.

A strong preventive health care program has been implemented in Taiwan with health stations around the island offering free vaccinations to infants and children for hepatitis B, poliomyelitis, measles, mumps, rubella, Japanese encephalitis, tuberculosis, diphtheria, pertussis, and tetanus. Comprehensive health programs and preventive health care services include six health examinations and a handbook on health for all infants and children up to three years of age. These examinations are conducted at clinics and hospitals islandwide. Growth and development norms, as well as recommended daily dietary allowances, are also charted; thus, health care information in kindergartens and nurseries is now available for preschool children to detect growth abnormalities at an early age.

Comprehensive measures have been taken to educate preschool teachers, parents, and expectant mothers on the importance and techniques of oral hygiene. Educational activities on the prevention of accidents and injuries are conducted every year on Children's Day (April 4).

To secure national health quality and to address health problems at an early age, the Ministry of Education 教育部 and the DOH decided that a complete health record for all elementary school students should be completed biannually, starting from the 1998 school year. The examination includes a record of the students' height and weight, eyesight, auditive and ENT conditions, oral hygiene, spine and chest, skin, cardiac and pulmonary system, and abdomen, as well as a check for eye diseases, parasites, diabetes, and other health problems. Parents and local health units will each receive a copy of the student's health records for follow-up inquiries and future reference.

Genetic Health Program

Congenital defects were one of the most common cause of neonatal and infant deaths in 2000, accounting for nearly 29.5 percent of all neonatal and infant mortalities. Although the infant mortality rate has declined as a result of improved health services, the percentage of babies born with congenital abnormalities has not fallen, with the percentage of newborns with congenital defects at 1.23 percent in 2000.

The government has long been aware of this problem, and in 1980 initiated the Congenital Malformation Registration and Follow-up Project 先天性缺陷兒登記追蹤計畫 to study the prevalence, causes, and care of birth defects. There are 285 medical institutions participating in the project to report cases of congenital abnormalities. Genetic health counseling centers have been set up at National Taiwan University Hospital, Tzu Chi Buddhist General Hospital (Hualien), the Taipei Veterans General Hospital, and the Kaohsiung Medical College Hospital. There are currently 24 certified cytogenetics laboratories operating in Taiwan, and, in 2000, approximately 99.1 percent of all newborns were screened for congenital metabolic disorders.

The Genetic Health Law 優生保健法 provides a legal basis for health services, such as premarital health examinations, prenatal diagnosis, neonatal screening for congenital metabolic disorders, and genetic counseling. In 2000, there were 722 institutions providing one or more of these services, and about 99.1 percent of all newborns were screened. The promotion of genetic health programs by the Medical Genetic Advisory Committee is also provided for under the Genetic Health Law.

In 2000, 30,021 pregnant women received cytogenetic examinations. Among these, 19,337 were over 34 years old, accounting for 75.5 percent of expectant mothers in the age group of 35 years old and over. Some 2.4 percent of the fetuses were found to have chromosome disorders through amniocentesis. To detect thalassemia major and other complications during pregnancy, screenings have been provided for pregnant women since July 1993. In 2000, 454 couples were found to be MCV abnormal, and among them, 207 couples were carriers of the same genes. Of the fetuses examined, 63 were found with thalassemia major. In 2000, 16,370 potential mothers received rubella vaccinations as a measure to prevent birth defects.

Family Planning

The use of contraceptives by married women between 22 and 39 years of age in the Taiwan area has increased from 24 percent in 1965 to 74.86 percent in 1998. Statistics also show that women are having fewer and fewer children. For example, a survey of women between the ages of 40 and 49 revealed that the average number of children per woman declined from 6.1 in 1975 to 2.79 in 1998. The percentage of women in this same age group having four or more children has declined from 18.8 percent in 1975 to 3.7 percent in 1997, and the number of women having only one or two children has increased from 61.8 percent to 80.5 percent during that same time period.

The proportion of women who married between the ages of 20 and 34 years has declined from 79 percent in 1965 to 45.6 percent in 2000. The average age at first marriage during this time period increased from 22.7 to 26.1 years for

women, and from 26.7 to 30.3 years for men. All of these factors have significantly lowered the birth rate in the Taiwan area. In 2000, the birth rate and death rate were 13.76 and 5.68 per 1,000 persons, respectively, with the natural population growth rate at 8.08 per 1,000 persons.

The aging of the population, the declining marriage rate among women between the ages of 20 and 34, and the falling birth rate have all raised concerns about a situation where the "dependent people are in the majority and the productive (young) people are in the minority" 食之者眾，生之者寡. Therefore, starting in 1990, the government adjusted its family planning policy to provide reproductive health services and education to married couples, potential mothers, and special groups (such as the disabled, infertile couples, youths, and residents in outlying areas).

Advanced developments in medical science and technology have enabled infertile couples to have their own babies through artificial means. The medical practices concerning artificial fertilization and implantation have been regulated very carefully in order to safeguard individual rights, as well as to ensure the quality and correct application of artificial reproductive technologies. Relevant legislation promulgated thus far includes the *Ethical Guidelines for Practicing Artificial Reproductive Technologies* 人工生殖技術倫理指導綱領, *Regulations Governing Artificial Reproductive Technologies* 人工協助生殖技術管理辦法, *Accreditation Standards for Institutions Providing Artificial Reproductive Technological Services* 施行人工協助生殖技術機構評估要點, and *Operational Explications to Data Concerning the Donation of Eggs and Sperm* 捐贈精卵資料作業說明. To date, 62 medical institutions have been accredited, enabling them to provide such services.

Teenage Pregnancy

The fertility rate among adolescents between the ages of 15 and 19 in the Taiwan area was 14 per 1,000 in 2000, higher than in some other Asian countries. The fertility rate for married teenagers in this age group was even higher than that of the United States: 899 per 1,000 in 2000.

Unexpected pregnancies and pregnant brides could help to explain this high rate. More than 13,000 children are born annually to teenage mothers in the Taiwan area. According to a study conducted by the Taiwan Provincial Government titled "Teenage Sexuality, Pregnancy and Abortion in Taiwan." A study comparing the results of a 1984 survey with the results of a survey conducted in 1994 showed a 264 percent increase in premarital sexual activities among teenagers. In 1994, approximately 10 percent of teenage girls in Taiwan had sexual experience. Two-thirds of those who had engaged in sex for the first time did not use any form of contraception, and 11 percent became pregnant. Eight percent of the pregnant girls chose to have an abortion, and the vast majority of the rest became teenage mothers. As social values and behavior change, the problem of unwed teenage mothers may grow.

The DOH has responded to this phenomenon by offering sex education and counseling services in schools, factories, and communities. In addition, civic organizations like the ROC Public Health Association 中華民國公共衛生學會, the School Health Association 中華民國學校衛生學會, the Mercy Memorial Foundation 財團法人杏陵醫學基金會, the Youth Guidance Foundation 中國青少年輔導基金會, Teacher Chang 張老師, and the Maternal and Child Health Association 中華民

Changes in the Nutrition and Health of ROC Nationals

The latest survey (1991-1996) on the nutrition and health conditions of ROC nationals by the Institute of Biomedical Sciences of the Academia Sinica found that people had taken in more protein and fat than required and were deficient in calcium. About 14.6 percent of males and 15.8 percent of females between the ages of 19 and 64 were considered obese in the survey. A new survey started in 1997 will extend through 2002 and focus on the nutrition and health conditions of people over 65 years old and children six to 12 years old.

Ten Leading Causes of Death by Illness in the Taiwan Area, 2000

Cause of Death	% of All Deaths	Mortality per 100,000
All Causes	100.00	561.12
Malignancies	25.35	142.23
Cerebrovascular Diseases	10.71	60.10
Heart Diseases	8.48	47.56
Accidents & Adverse Effects	8.45	47.40
Diabetes Mellitus	7.59	42.60
Chronic Liver Diseases & Cirrhosis	4.16	23.32
Nephrites, Nephrotic Syndrome & Nephrosis	3.11	17.45
Pneumonia	2.65	14.88
Suicide	1.99	11.14
Bronchitis, Emphysema and Asthma	1.29	7.23
Subtotal	73.78	413.91
Other Causes	26.22	147.21

Source: Department of Health

國婦幼衛生協會 have all cooperated with the DOH to develop educational materials, train professional counselors, and provide consultation services for teenagers. The Mercy Memorial Foundation and the Family Life and Sex Education Center 家庭生活與性教育中心 have gone one step further by providing sex education training to school administrators and teachers. At the end of 2001, 28 youth health promotion clinics 青少年保健門診 were established in both city medical centers and in teaching hospitals to provide counseling services and sex education for young people.

Adult and Geriatric Health

The aging population has increased the need for adult and geriatric health care. In 2000, persons aged 65 and over constituted 8.5 percent of the population, which according to United Nations standards qualifies the Taiwan area as an "aged society." Thus, geriatric health care will become more important in the future.

As the ratio of elderly people in society increases, chronic cardiovascular diseases have replaced infectious diseases as the major causes of death among adults. In 2000, for instance, cerebrovascular diseases, heart diseases, diabetes mellitus, and hypertensive diseases claimed 34,936 lives and were the second, third, fifth, and eleventh leading causes of death, respectively, representing 28.07 percent of all deaths that year.

Currently, persons over 65 are entitled to free blood pressure, blood sugar, and blood cholesterol tests at local health stations, and family health records are kept at all health stations for efficient follow-up. As a preventive measure, adults over 40 years of age are encouraged to take the three tests regularly. Cases of cardiac disease, diabetes, and hypertension are generally referred to adult or chronic disease clinics in public hospitals for treatment. After being discharged from public hospitals, patients are usually referred to local health stations for follow-up care. The primary health centers also provide home nursing services to persons aged 65 and over.

Local governments have appropriated special funds to subsidize medical expenditures for the aged. Guidelines on the control and

treatment of hypertension, diabetes, and hyperlipidemia have been established to provide standard treatment procedures for these medical groups in the Taiwan area. Likewise, a series of educational materials on the control of chronic diseases has been circulated among clinics. Finally, 61 education units for diabetes have been established in medical centers islandwide to provide comprehensive care for diabetic patients.

Health Control Programs

Myopia Control

For more than 10 years, Taiwan has had the world's leading prevalence of myopia. According to a survey in 2000, the prevalence of myopia in children entering elementary schools was 20.4 percent, and at graduation, was 55 percent. At senior high schools, the rate was 80 percent. Although the rate remained the same throughout senior high school, those students who already had myopia became more nearsighted. Vision screenings are now conducted in schools a month after school starts. By 2000, about 260 ophthalmologists were providing special outpatient services for students experiencing vision problems. The DOH has implemented a vision protection and screening program that includes preschool children and special occupational groups. Since 1995, visual screening has been conducted in every city and county, allowing the early detection of strabismus and amblyopia for preschool children by the age of five.

Cancer Control

Cancer has been the leading cause of death in the Taiwan area since 1982. In 2000, over 31,584 people died of cancer, accounting for 25.35 percent of all deaths. In Taiwan, the five most common forms of cancer for men are liver, lung, colorectal, stomach, and oral cancer, while women are mainly afflicted with lung, liver, colorectal, breast, and cervical cancer. The DOH has initiated cancer control programs targeting the prevention and control of the more common cancers, including cervical, liver, colorectal, oral cancer, and breast cancer.

The high incidence of oral and cervical cancer has been a serious problem for Taiwan residents. In 2000, 8.96 out of every 100,000 women had cervical cancer, resulting in 971 deaths that year. If detected and treated at an early stage, however, cervical cancer can be cured in 95 percent of the cases. Since July 1, 1995, National Health Insurance has covered cervical smear tests for women aged 30 and over, and in 2000, testing was conducted on about two million women, 34.3 percent of women in this age group, up from 28.6 percent in 1999. In 2000, oral cancer caused 1,375 deaths in men.

In 2000, breast cancer killed 1,149 people. Breast cancer programs focus on preventive measures, promoting self-examinations, and professional check-up once every year. Each year since 1993, approximately 400,000 women have learned how to conduct self-examinations.

To lower the death rate and strengthen early detection of cervical, breast, and oral cancer, the DOH formulated a community cancer-screening spot check plan. The goal of the plan is to provide free cervical smear tests to 5.87 million women over 30 years old, conduct breast palpation of up to 4.95 million women over 35 years old, and check 500,000 habitual betel nut chewers for oral cancer and precancerous lesions.

Occupational Disease Prevention

In Taiwan, the most common diseases or disorders attributable to work environment include blood poisoning by heavy metals, gas narcosis, black lung disease, skin disorders, trauma, and dysbarism. Between 1995 and 2000, there were 10,792 cases of occupational diseases. According to the Council of Labor Affairs, in 2000, labor insurance payments were made to 5.135 per 1,000 persons, including 4.251 for injury or illness, 0.801 for disability, and 0.083 for death.

Taiwan has six occupational health promotion and protection centers located in the following institutions: Tri-Service General Hospital, Chang

Gung Memorial Hospital, Changhua Christian Hospital, Kaohsiung Medical University Hospital, Chi-Mei Foundation Hospital, and Tzu-Chi Hospital. These occupational health promotion and protection centers provide diagnoses, treatments, follow-up assessments, and referrals. In addition, they offer consultation services at no charge to public and private enterprises. Another 37 medical institutions provide special outpatient services for occupational diseases. In 2000, some 428 medical institutions were qualified to detect black lung disease and to conduct ordinary and special health examinations for workers. The DOH also holds seminars on occupational diseases to improve the quality of medical services by increasing the knowledge of medical personnel.

Anti-Smoking Campaign

The smoking rate in Taiwan is high. In 1999, 11.33 percent and 3.16 percent of male and female youths, respectively, between the ages of 12 and 18 were smokers, including 3.31 percent and 1.56 percent of junior high school students and 16.76 percent and 4.46 percent of senior high school students. Categorized by gender, 47.29 percent of male adults and 5.23 percent of female adults smoked tobacco products regularly in 1999. On average, Taiwan's spending per capita on cigarettes was about US$100. A survey of public health in 1994 conducted by National Taiwan University (NTU) revealed that an average of over 10,000 Taiwan residents die each year from smoking related causes, including more than 4,490 who die of lung cancer. By sex, 12 percent of male deaths and 8 percent of female deaths in Taiwan were related to smoking. Economic loss due to sickness caused by tobacco products was estimated to exceed US$1.84 billion, and 148,186 years of potential life loss in 1994.

According to the NTU survey, 43.7 percent of the smokers consumed between half a pack and one pack each day, 37.4 percent smoked less than half a pack, and 15.3 percent smoked more than one pack. Since the government lifted the ban on the import of foreign cigarettes in 1987, the number of smokers has increased by 4.6 percent and includes a larger portion of the teenage and female populations.

With so many smokers in Taiwan, it should come as no surprise that more than 96 percent of the non-smoking female and child populations, including almost 75 percent of pregnant women, were frequently exposed to secondhand smoke. According to a survey conducted by Academia Sinica 中央研究院, 22 percent of non-smoking female lung cancer victims were frequently exposed to secondhand smoke.

In July 1990, the DOH launched an anti-smoking campaign. Under the project, free distribution of cigarettes to military personnel was terminated in July 1991, and more warnings against the health hazards of smoking have been printed on cigarette packs. Anti-smoking literature and films have also been distributed nationwide. By June 1995, all Taiwan-based airlines had prohibited smoking on both domestic and international flights.

Despite these government measures, concern over the hazards of smoking continued to increase in 1994. To speed up Taiwan's entry into the World Trade Organization, the Taiwan Tobacco and Wine Monopoly Bureau 臺灣省菸酒公賣局 lost its 40-year monopoly over alcohol and tobacco sales in June 1995, raising fears that the influx of foreign cigarettes would exacerbate an already serious health problem. On September 19, 1997, the *Tobacco Hazards Prevention Act* 菸害防制法 went into effect, outlawing the sale of cigarettes to minors under the age of 18, banning advertising and promotion by cigarette companies, and requiring the labeling of nicotine and tar contents on cigarette products.

The law was revised on May 23, 2000, to restrict smoking in public places, including schools (junior high and below), children's playgrounds, medical facilities, shared working places, and libraries. In addition, smoking is also prohibited in financial institutions, art galleries, public transportation vehicles, and places where highly flammable materials and products are manufactured, stored, or sold. Well-ventilated smoking rooms must be designated in places such as restaurants, department stores, government offices, etc.

Punishments for violators of this law vary according to the type of violation and the perpetrator of the crime. For instance, underage smokers could simply be made to attend smoking cessation courses. On the other hand, tobacco companies, newspapers, and magazines could be fined heavily for placing or carrying ads for tobacco products.

Such anti-smoking and consumer-interest groups as the John Tung Foundation 董氏基金會 have taken a more active role in increasing public awareness of the hazards of smoking. For example, the John Tung Foundation initiated a "Dear Legislator" campaign to ask lawmakers to support the revised version of the *Tobacco Hazards Prevention Act*. The Department of Health awarded the foundation a large grant for its anti-smoking campaign, which centers on a cartoon character named Hsu Tse-lin 徐則林 (a pun on Lin Tse-hsu 林則徐, the famous Ching dynasty official who fought the import of opium into China 160 years ago). The cartoon character is drawn as a "hip" guy sporting a ponytail reminiscent of the long braids Chinese men wore during the Ching dynasty. He can be spotted carrying an anti-smoking sign in made-for-TV videos, and on stickers, pamphlets, and placards in public places around Taiwan. The John Tung Foundation also came up with a new slogan to coincide with the implementation of the *Prevention Act*: "Take this opportunity to quit smoking, as the *Tobacco Hazards Prevention Act* is in force!" The lengthy revision process of this act took five years. Since smokers are reluctant to break this law for fear of being fined between US$32 and US$96, harm from secondhand smoke has been reduced.

The *Prevention Act* also stipulates that four years after its implementation, the nicotine and tar content of a single cigarette cannot exceed 1.5 mg and 15 mg, respectively. In 1999, more than 83 percent of the cigarettes produced in Taiwan met one or both of these standards. Ten years after the implementation of the *Tobacco Hazards Prevention Act*, the content will be further reduced to 1.2 mg and 12 mg, respectively. On March 28, 2000, the *Tobacco and Wine Taxation Law* was passed, attaching a heavy tax on wine and tobacco products to subsidize health care and discourage smoking. An amount of US$30 million was budgeted for anti-smoking campaigns.

The anti-smoking campaign by John Tung Foundation in year 2001 is "Strike Back Against Tobacco!"(不吸煙大自由) It features worldwide movie superstar Jackie Chan. Through collaborating with American Cancer Society, the campaign kicked off with an international press conference in New York on July 24, 2001, with Jackie Chan, Dr. Dileep Bal, president of ACS, and Senior Consultant of John Tung Foundation, Dr. Ming-liang Lee, Minister of Department of Health, in attendance.

The Betel Nut Problem

Betel nut, the seed of the areca palm, has long been used by Chinese doctors to treat parasitic infections and other intestinal disorders. It contains cytotoxocity and genotoxicity. Only when taken in excess does this pulpy nut have negative side effects; however, the betel nut widely chewed in Taiwan as a stimulant often contains unhealthy additives.

Experts estimate that 88 percent of oral cancer patients and 96 percent of mucous membrane fibrosis patients in the Taiwan area habitually chew betel nut. Statistically, the likelihood of contracting oral cancer is 28 times higher for people who chew betel nut than for those who do not, and the risk is 89 times higher for people who both chew betel nuts and smoke. Furthermore, those who chew, smoke, and drink heavily are 123 times more likely to contract oral cancer than those who do not indulge in any of these habits. Oral cancer deaths in the ROC have increased from 1.25 per 100,000 people per year in 1976 to 2.25 in 1991, and 6.73 in 2000. In 2000, there were an estimated three million betel nut chewers in the Taiwan area.

Especially worrisome to health officials is the increasing popularity of betel nuts and the changing demographics of the betel nut chewing population. In the past, most betel nut chewers were adult laborers in eastern and southern Taiwan. Today, young and educated urbanites and suburbanites are taking up the habit in unprecedented numbers. To cater to the demand of the chewers, betel nut farming has grown, becoming one of Taiwan's largest crops produced (about 170,000 metric tons in 2000) in Taiwan. In response to this shift, the government is now targeting anti-betel nut campaigns at the younger generation. The hazards of betel nut chewing are being publicized in the form of TV ads, video programs, and leaflets distributed to the general public and students.

Prevention of Unintentional Injury and Suicide

In 2000, there were 12,986 deaths from accidents and adverse effects, including suicide. This accounted for 10.44 percent of the total deaths reported that year, or an average of 58.54 per 100,000 people, making it the third largest cause of death in the Taiwan area.

In 1999, according to a survey covering the period from 1988 to 1996, about 60 percent of all skull injuries occurred in traffic accidents, with 72 percent motorbike accidents and 30 percent of the riders around the age of 20. Over the past few years, more than US$28 million has been spent on medical care for those who were left with brain damage from traffic accidents. According to the DOH, of the 10,515 fatal accidents recorded in 2000, 5,534 cases (or 52.63 percent) were transportation-related fatalities, constituting the leading cause of death for people under the age of 44 in this category. More than 97 percent of the fatalities (5,420 persons) were due to motorbike-related traffic accidents. Since a large number of accidents involving motorbikes resulted in death or permanent injury, the Ministry of Transportation and Communications 交通部 required helmets to be worn by all motorcyclists starting June 1, 1997.

To prevent the financial burden that often accompanies traffic accidents, third-person automobile liability insurance covering those injured or killed in car accidents became mandatory in 1998. In 1999, such insurance also became mandatory for motorbikes as well.

Suicide constituted the ninth leading cause of death in the ROC in 2000. Some 2,471 people took their own lives. According to DOH statistics, 156 youths between the ages of 15 and 24 killed themselves in 2000, making suicide the third major cause of death for this age group. The suicide mortality rate for this age group was 4 per 100,000 persons. Some 682 persons over the age of 65 committed suicide in 2000, making the elderly suicide mortality rate 35.49 per 100,000 persons. Compared with other countries, this rate is high. The mental health of the young and elderly is, in fact, a problem for society, and both age groups must be treated as equally important.

Communicable Diseases

An islandwide surveillance network of 468 physicians has been set up to report diseases. All the physicians involved are connected to the network and provide weekly updates by phone, fax, or mail. The latest information and medical updates are then made available to other physicians in the monthly *Epidemiology Bulletin* 疫情報導, which is circulated to medical centers islandwide. Currently, six disease surveillance centers and quarantine stations under the National Quarantine Service have been set up in Keelung, CKS International Airport, Taichung, Hualien, Kaohsiung, Hsiaokang International Airport. In the future, these six will be consolidated into four (the northern, central, southern, and eastern parts of the Taiwan area) to administer the control and prevention of communicable diseases.

The *Law of the Communicable Disease Control* 傳染病防治法 is a new piece of legislation governing the control of epidemics. In the past, communicable diseases that required being reported were divided into specified and unspecified communicable diseases. Under the new law, any cases involving the 38 infectious diseases listed must be reported, patients treated, and epidemic areas disinfected. Infectious diseases are now divided into four categories and are closely watched. The first category includes cholera, plague, yellow fever, rabies, and ebola marburg. The second category includes: a) typhus fever, diphtheria, meningoccal meningitis, typhoid, paratyphoid, and anthrax; and b) poliomymelitis, dysentery bacillary, amoebic dysentery, and open tuberculosis. The third category includes: a) dengue fever, malaria, measles, acute hepatitis A, enterohemorrhagic E. Coli, and enteroviral carditis (or meningitis); and b) tuberculosis (except open tuberculosis), Japanese encephalitis, leprosy, rubella, congenital rubella syndrome, pertussis, scarlet fever, tetanus, tsutsugamushi disease, acute hepatitis (except hepatitis A), mumps, smallpox, legionellosis, haemophilus influenza B, syphilis, gonorrhea, and influenza. The fourth category includes other infectious diseases not listed or newly discovered.

This new categorization is more inclusive of Taiwan's more prevalent infectious diseases, such as influenza and enterovirus, and also some diseases in the future, such as anthrax and legionellosis. Generally speaking, most of these diseases have been either eradicated or brought under control in the Taiwan area. However, in 2000 a total of 323 cases of amoebic dysentery, 321 cases of bacterial dysentery, 46 cases of typhoid and paratyphoid, 16 cases of meningococcal meningitis, 511 cases of scarlet fever, and eight cases of cholera were reported. In addition, an enterovirus complicated infections that occurred in 2000 and accounted for the deaths of 41 persons.

In 2000, about 15,000 cases of TB were reported, along with 29 cases of rubella. That same year, 3,870 cases of syphilis, 294 cases of acute hepatitis, and 139 cases of dengue fever were confirmed by the DOH. In addition, the DOH requires that any disease, parasitic infection, or unusual symptom related to pets be reported, especially in cases where both the owner and pet become ill.

Local health authorities routinely carry out vaccination programs for polio, measles, mumps, rubella, diphtheria-pertussis-tetanus (DPT), tuberculosis, Japanese encephalitis, and hepatitis B. The coverage rates for these vaccinations, with the exception of measles, have reached approximately 90 percent. In 1992, the DOH initiated the first stage (1992-1996) plan for the eradication of polio, neonatal tetanus (NNT), measles, and congenital rubella syndrome (CRS), with excellent results. No cases of polio, CRS, and NNT were reported in 2000, but there were sporadic occurrences of rubella (29 cases) and measles (5 cases) that year. There was a decrease in the occurrence of acute flaccid paralysis cases from 127 (1998) to 63 (2000). In order to eliminate polio by the year 2000 in accordance with World Health Organization policy, the DOH decided to continue with the second stage (1996-2001) of its plan, and attain vaccination coverage of 95 percent, strengthen the disease reporting network, and computerize vaccination records to minimize the likelihood that the diptheria-pertussis-tetanus (DPT) and oral polio vaccination series of shots would be discontinued. Other health measures include education on disease, and sanitation and vector control.

Enterovirus

In 1998, an outbreak of enterovirus infections killed 78 persons and put the whole preventive medicine system on alert. In order to prevent outbreaks of the disease, in April 1999, the DOH contracted 11 teaching hospitals in northern, central, southern, and eastern Taiwan to trace the infections of enterovirus that occurred in their respective areas. In 2000, there were 291 confirmed cases of enterovirus infections and 41 victims lost their lives. The disease reached its height during the period of May and

June then, decreasing gradually in the rest of the year. By July 2001, 357 cases had been discovered, 189 cases confirmed, and 28 deaths recorded. Under close supervision by the government and with the cooperation of parents, the disease has been brought under control.

Poliomyelitis

Free vaccinations against communicable diseases are available for infants and preschool children. In May 1994, the DOH launched the National Immunization Days (NIDs) as an islandwide campaign to administer Sabin oral polio vaccine to the estimated 1.8 million children under six years of age in Taiwan. All such children were required to be inoculated. No case of polio has been discovered since 1983. At the end of October 2000, the WHO declared that polio had been eradicated in the West Pacific region (including Taiwan).

AIDS

The *Acquired Immune Deficiency Syndrome (AIDS) Control Act* 後天免疫缺乏症候群防治條例 was promulgated in December 1990 to provide free screening and treatment for patients and to deal with those who are HIV-infected and yet knowingly transmit the disease to others. In order to battle AIDS, the DOH has initiated phases of prevention plans: the first phase was from 1994 to 1996, the second 1997 to 2001, and the third 2002 to 2006. The major measures include: (1) an immediate report system within 24 hours of discovering an HIV or AIDS patient, (2) free medical care to confirmed patients, (3) comprehensive blood screening system, (4) testing of HIV by blood centers after July 1, 1995, (5) more education on AIDS, (6) better training of physicians, nurses, and health administrators, and (7) research and development.

As of June 2001, over 25 million blood tests had been conducted to screen for the human immune deficiency virus (HIV) antibody. From 1984 to June 2001, a total of 3,552 people had been detected as HIV positive; among these, 3,252 (or 91.6 percent) were ROC nationals. In 1999 and 2000, the number of HIV positive

victims increased at an average of more than one case discovered per day. More than 89 percent were thought to have been infected through sexual contact with an HIV-infected person, and 115 married people were infected by their spouses. Among infected ROC nationals, 82.6 percent of the HIV-infections were in the 20 to 49 age group, 20.3 percent of the victims were unemployed, and 28.9 percent were businessmen or workers. Around 42.5 percent of HIV-positive cases in Taiwan were male heterosexuals, with 33.5 percent male homosexuals, and 13.4 percent bisexuals.

According to the DOH, the typical male HIV carrier in Taiwan is single, employed, around 33.7 years old, and has frequented prostitutes. Most female HIV carriers were between 30 to 39 years old. Many are housewives who have been infected by their husbands. By the end of 2001, HIV-infected males outnumbered females 8.3 to one. Among the 249 females infected with HIV, about one-fourth were foreign brides.

Despite its efficiency, the screening procedure has encountered setbacks. For fear of being discriminated against by hospital employees or having a positive HIV record in their hospital records, many people who suspected that they were HIV positive refused to be tested in a hospital. Instead, they turned to donating blood as a free and confidential method of testing, as health authorities would notify them if their blood test indicated the presence of the virus. As a result, the DOH called for legislation that would impose strict penalties on people who donate their blood for this purpose, because the DOH feared that infected blood may be donated when the virus is still undetectable. Since then, relevant legislation has been passed, and the results of blood tests from donated blood are no longer released to the donor.

People who suspect that they might be infected are now encouraged to go to public health centers across the island or to the 25 hospitals authorized by the DOH to conduct free HIV tests. Eight of them are both free and anonymous. DOH-authorized hospitals detected 67

percent of HIV positive cases, and 19.1 percent were detected at health stations or hospitals at the provincial level. HIV screening is required for all servicemen (military service is compulsory for almost all ROC men), inmates, and alien workers.

The DOH publishes pamphlets, booklets, and manuals on AIDS, which are distributed to medical personnel and the general public in selected areas. The government also produces TV programs and films to educate the public. To raise the survival rate of patients, free anti-retroviral therapy is provided by the DOH for all HIV-infected nationals.

Fifteen research projects on HIV infections in the Taiwan area have been contracted out during 2001. These projects focus on epidemiological investigations of specific groups, clinical research, and development of laboratory techniques to help formulate control policies.

Hepatitis

Around 90 percent of the people over 40 years of age in the Taiwan area are infected with the hepatitis B virus, and between 15 to 20 percent of the total population are estimated to be hepatitis B carriers. Therefore, liver cancer, which has been linked to hepatitis, has been the number one killer in the ROC for many years. An islandwide program to control the spread of hepatitis B was initiated in 1984. This immunization program covers all newborns, preschool children, elementary school children, young adults, medical personnel, and family members of carriers. For the rest of the population, vaccinations are available at a reasonable cost and are also offered at health stations and clinics islandwide.

In 1984, the Republic of China became the first country in the world to implement a hepatitis B immunization program, which has been a complete success. One study shows that hepatitis B carriers under six years of age are at an all-time low of 1.7 percent. Reduced incidents of liver cancer in children between six and 14 years of age has been another benefit of the immunization program. The incidence of liver cancer in

the six to 14 age group born between 1981 and 1986 was 0.7 in 100,000 persons, and the rate of the same age group born between 1990 and 1994 dropped to 0.36. Children between six and nine years of age who have been vaccinated have the lowest rate of liver cancer at 0.13 per 100,000 children. Before the implementation of the hepatitis B immunization program, the rate of liver cancer in the same age group was 0.52 per 100,000 children.

Hepatitis C, or post-transfusion hepatitis, is transmitted by bodily fluids , especially via blood or blood products, 80 percent of the time. It can also be transmitted as a result of sharing needles in tattooing or intravenous drug use. The hepatitis C anti-HCV prevalence rate in the Taiwan area was between 1 and 2 percent. The DOH requires that blood used for transfusions be tested for hepatitis C antibodies to prevent the transmission of the disease.

Poor sanitary conditions usually account for the transmission of hepatitis A. The infection rate in urban areas is low (less than 5 percent for preschool children), but in mountain areas the rate is 76 and 95 percent for elementary and junior high school students, respectively, due to poor living conditions and hygiene. Two immunization programs were instituted in mountain areas in 1995 and 1996, bringing the infection of hepatitis A under control. There were 851 cases of hepatitis A reported in 1995. This had dropped to 99 by 2000.

Tuberculosis

Tuberculosis (TB) was one of the leading causes of death in the 1950s. In 1947, the TB death rate was 294.44 per 100,000 people. Accordingly, a TB survey has been taken once every five years since 1957. That year, the prevalence rates of pulmonary tuberculosis and bacteriologically infectious tuberculosis were 5.15 and 1.02 percent, respectively, making TB the third leading cause of death by illness in Taiwan. By 1982, these rates had dropped to 0.88 and 0.15 percent, respectively. However, by the 1987 survey, the rate for pulmonary TB had increased to

1.29 percent, while bacteriologically infectious TB continued to fall to 0.11 percent. Although the TB death rate was only 6.91 per 100,000 in 2000, with 1,534 reported deaths, it was still high according to WHO standard, which was 2 per 1,000,000.

A five-year project running from 1994 to 1998 enhanced TB control by refurbishing treatment facilities, controlling chronically infectious cases, and implementing a surveillance system for TB risk groups, especially in the aboriginal communities, where TB was the eighth leading cause of death in 1998. Beginning in April 1995, the DOH implemented the Mountain Area TB Inpatient Subsidy Plan 山地鄉結核病人住院治療補助計畫 and the Chronic TB Patient Accommodation Plan 慢性開放性結核病人收容管理計畫, with 28 hospitals participating. Since 1996, a surveillance system to control TB, based on the data provided by the NHI medication record, has been in operation to locate those cases not reported. Since April, 1995, 181 patients of chronic infectious TB have received inpatient services.

In 2000, TB became the tenth death cause for men in Taiwan for the first time in the past five years. This was due to more frequent international travel, an increase number of foreign laborers, AIDS, and drug resistant strains.

A second term five-year project running from 1999 to 2003 has been implemented to strengthen the control of TB. The major two strategies are Directly-Observed Treatment Short-Course (DOTS) and upgrading the quality of screening mycobacterium-tuberculosis.

DOTS has been implemented since March 1997 at 31 mountain townships. Starting May 15, 2001, DOTS was expanded to all areas. The DOTS procedure requires a medical professional to watch a patient taking his medication in person each time, making sure the patient is following the right treatment.

At the same time, a complete network of phlegm screening for mycobacteriuim-tuberculosis has been established for TB patients as well as the general public.

On the other hand, X-ray is required for physical check-up of foreign employees of central government agencies and foreign laborers.

Dengue Fever

A center for the control of dengue fever, which is caused by a mosquito-borne virus, was set up in December 1988 by the DOH and the Environmental Protection Administration 環境保護署. The joint taskforce is responsible for the formulation and implementation of preventive measures, a surveillance system, vector surveying, insecticide spraying, and the elimination of mosquito breeding grounds. The taskforce provides medication to those infected and supervises the disease control measures of local governments.

In 1998, there were 238 indigenous cases. In 1999, there was a small scale outbreak of dengue fever in southern Taiwan, with 40 indigenous cases and 29 imported cases. In 2000, there were 113 indigenous cases, with most of the cases in Tainan City, and 27 imported cases. Although the number of cases increased from 1999, compared with the 4,389 cases in 1988, the disease has been brought under control. Every month, the results of a density index of vector mosquitoes and larvae are recorded and reported to the relevant units for evaluation. Frequent examination of the vector index and intensive environmental sanitation education after typhoons and floods are the most important jobs of the taskforce.

Quarantine

Quarantine procedures help to prevent the entry and spread of communicable diseases from abroad. Travelers, aircraft crew members, airport workers, and imported produce are scrutinized at ports of entry. International health regulations stipulate that all interference with modern transportation be minimized during such screening procedures, and the DOH makes every effort to comply while rendering efficient service.

The DOH consolidated the nation's seven quarantine stations and two substations into the National Quarantine Service in 1989. The service includes quarantine, port sanitation management, and disease surveillance divisions.

Since April 1995, travelers entering Taiwan from highly infected areas in Southeast Asia have been required to submit a Health Declaration Form to monitor infectious diseases. Travelers showing symptoms of the diseases are contacted by public health workers to identify cases for prompt treatment and to prevent further transmission. In 2000, some 2,266 suspected cases had been checked and one case confirmed.

Field Epidemiology

The DOH administers a two-year long field epidemiology instruction programs at the Center for Disease Control, in collaboration with the US Center for Disease Control and Emory University. Physicians, dentists, and researchers in related fields are chosen annually for on-site training in epidemiological investigations and long-term study projects. Since its inception, the program has trained 40 physicians, 25 dentists, and 10 veterinary and 75 public health specialist. Fifty-nine of these individuals now serve in public institutions, and 94 long-term projects have already been completed.

Food & Restaurant Regulation

Food Sanitation and Regulation

Revisions to the *Food Sanitation and Management Law* 食品衛生管理法 and the *Health Food Management Law* 健康食品管理法 (effective February 9, 2000 and August 3, 1999) increased the protection of consumer rights by clearly defining the responsibilities of manufacturers. In particular, health foods must be examined, approved, and registered, as well as categorized and labeled, before entering the ROC market.

An evaluation method for detecting genetically modified foods and ensuring their safety was drafted in 1998. The DOH has been working on developing a labeling and supervisory system for genetically engineered food products. Furthermore, the ROC has been referring to international agreements on the management of genetically modified foods (such as the Catagena Protocol on Biosafety of the Convention on Biological Diversity) as a guideline for its policy.

Restaurant Regulation

Since Chinese people love to eat out, the Department of Health monitors sanitary standards in eating places around the island to ensure safety. Local health authorities conduct routine spot checks of food establishments on a day-to-day basis using 13 basic diagnostic devices to test food. Educational materials are also distributed. In the year 2000, 505,371 spot checks were conducted, including restaurants, food stands, etc. After initial visual examination, 67,020 samples were sent to the lab with only 2,961 cases failing to meet the sanitary requirements. Those that fail are given a grace period to improve sanitary conditions. The establishments will be fined or have their licenses suspended, if they fail to meet the standards after being notified to improve.

The DOH, in collaboration with the Council of Labor Affairs, is also promoting a licensing system for food technicians. In 1994, the DOH released a new set of requirements for chefs at six types of restaurants to be licensed within the next five years to ensure better hygiene. The plan affected about 80 percent of the chefs at hotel restaurants, school cafeterias, banquet halls, catering services, airline caterers, and public cafeterias in the Taiwan area. At the end of 2000, there were 141,937 licensed chefs in Taiwan (5,299 B-grade licensed chefs and 136,638 C-grade licensed chefs).

Widespread sanitary practices have reduced the number of cases of food poisoning and hepatitis A. Disposable tableware is now available in many restaurants. Consumers can also purchase inspected processed-food products, which are clearly labeled as meeting the Chinese Agricultural Standard 中國農業標準 (CAS), or general food products, which have the seal of Food Good Manufacturing Practices 優良食品製造標準 (FGMP). By December 2000, 400 factories producing 3,543 food products had been authorized as Good Manufacturing Practices 優良製造標準 (GMP) factories. Similarly, 2,899 meat products and 175 food processing plants had qualified for the CAS label. Around 6,700 licenses were issued for imported food additives and over 1,700 licenses for domestically produced additives. Starting from July 1999, all processed food products are required to list nutrition facts.

The expanding food processing industry and international trade have complicated food safety, so current laws and regulations need to be strengthened to cope with the new situation. The DOH Bureau of Food Sanitation oversees the amendment of laws and related regulations and is also responsible for the review and approval of special dietary foods, the registration and premarket approval of food additives, and the inspection and management of domestically produced low-acid canned foods. By coordinating with the Council of Agriculture (COA) and the Ministry of Economic Affairs (MOEA), which oversees the importation of agricultural products, the DOH can respond quickly should a crisis arise. In June 1999, Belgium produce—including eggs, dairy products, and meat products—suspected of being contaminated were prohibited from entering Taiwan's market before investigation and evaluation had been made. Inspection, sampling, testing, supervision of foods, and food sanitation are handled by local health authorities.

Pharmaceutical Regulation

All medicines and medical devices, both imported and locally produced, must be registered and licensed by the DOH before they are marketed in the Taiwan area. Local health authorities conduct regular and unscheduled inspections, sampling medicines and cosmetics that are manufactured, imported, or sold in their areas. Manufacturers and purveyors of medicines and cosmetics that fail to pass inspections are punished according to the *Pharmaceutical Affairs Law* 藥事法 and the *Cosmetics Sanitary Control Law* 化妝品衛生管理條例.

Health authorities conduct routine spot checks of food establishments to ensure sanitary conditions.
(Courtesy of the Department of Information, Taipei City Government)

By 2001, the DOH and the Ministry of Economic Affairs 經濟部 had jointly issued the GMP seal to 229 certified pharmaceutical factories. An ongoing GMP monitoring program helps to maintain the integrity of the ROC pharmaceutical industry, as well as the quality of drug products in the market. All GMP drug manufacturers are inspected at least once every two years. Those which fail to make improvements may also be shut down by health authorities, and their applications for registration and market permits suspended during the probation period.

The DOH also monitors the safety of new medicinal products. During the monitoring period, manufacturers submit records of safety monitoring in designated teaching hospitals for their newly licensed drugs and immediately report any side effects observed. Test results of domestic clinical trials are also required. In July 1998, the Center for Drug Evaluation 財團法人醫藥查驗中心 was established to conduct research and develop standards on the safety, effectiveness, and labeling of all drug products, as well as review and evaluate applications for new drugs and medical devices before they reach the market. As of December 2000, 686 new pharmaceutical formulas were being monitored. On April 12, 1996, in preparation for entry into the World Trade Organization (WTO), the DOH promulgated ten basic standards for the registration and examination of imported medicines. Side effects from medicines would be reported through a monitoring system to safeguard patients' drug safety. For patients suffering from rare diseases and to ensure the supply of orphan drugs, the DOH encouraged the production of such drugs in Taiwan under the *Law of Rare Diseases Prevention and Orphan Drugs* 罕見疾病防治及藥物法, which was promulgated on February 9, 2000.

The DOH is currently conducting a truth-in-advertising campaign. The central and municipal health authorities strictly review applications for advertisements. According to the *Pharmaceutical Affairs Law*, media that run advertisements exaggerating the efficacy of medical products are subject to heavy fines.

The separation of the medical and pharmaceutical professions is one of the most important tasks in restructuring health services in Taiwan. On March 1, 1997, Taipei and Kaohsiung Cities were designated areas to first implement this separation. Gradually, the plan encompassed the entire Taiwan area. Effective August 2001, the separation policy covered most of Taiwan area except for Penghu county. About 3,000 community pharmacies that adhere to the "Good Dispensing Practice" were under contract with the Bureau of National Health Insurance as part of the health care delivery system. The DOH is also helping to upgrade the quality of pharmaceutical personnel through on-the-job training and by helping to set up computerized patient profiles, in order to prepare for the separation of the medical and pharmaceutical practice policy at the second phase.

Drug Injury Relief

The *Key Points for Drug Injury Relief* 藥害救濟要點 effective January 12, 1999, have been formulated to safeguard the interests of patients and pharmaceutical manufacturers. The *Law of Drug Injury Relief* 藥害救濟法 promulgated on May 31, 2000, extends the relief to cases related to Chinese medicinal products and practices. A drug injury review committee composed of experts has been set up under the Department of Health to examine and investigate all drug injury cases petitioned.

According to the *Law of Drug Injury Relief*, drug injury relief is based on no-fault liability insurance and covers drug injuries ranging from medical expenses for cases of reversible injury to compensation for fatal drug injuries. As stated, a maximum of US$64,040 in compensation can be given in a fatality.

In addition, a relief fund has been established. In order to operate the Drug Injury Relief Fund, the Foundation of Drug Injury Relief was established by the government in August 2001. The objective of the foundation is to assist the government in performing drug injury relief related tasks, such as fund collecting, fund disbursing, and research of adverse drug reaction prevention. The interests of consumers, medical facilities, and pharmaceutical firms are thus protected. Approximately 500 pharmaceutical companies have joined and contributed to the fund. According to the *Law of Drug Injury Relief*, around one-thousandth of the value of the company's annual domestic pharmaceutical sales is contributed. Thus far, the drug injury relief fund has raised US$2,657,700 and has given compensation in 53 cases involving drug injuries.

A special logo is provided to participating pharmaceutical manufacturers and sellers to inform consumers that they are covered by the relief fund in case of accidental drug injuries.

Substance Abuse

Until the last decade, Taiwan's drug problem was considered minor in comparison with its neighbors, such as Japan and Hong Kong, but that began to change in the early 1990s, as evidenced by the increasing number of drug-related criminal arrests. Previously, such arrests accounted for 5 percent or less of the total number of arrests made per year; however, this rate increased to 13 percent in 1991, climbed to 19 percent in 1992, and jumped to nearly 32 percent in 1993. By December 1994, drug offenders had replaced burglars as the largest group in Taiwan prisons, accounting for 63 percent of Taiwan's inmate population. The situation turned around in 1995, when there was a 7 percent decrease in drug-related criminal arrests, and this rate has continued to drop since then.

Substance and drug abuse in Taiwan appears to be heading toward harder drugs. In the 1970s, sporadic cases of glue sniffing were reported, and, in the 1980s, incidences of sedative abuse were occasionally uncovered. By the early 1990s, the drug of choice was amphetamines and heroin. Although there were fewer than 9,000 addicts in the Taiwan area in 2000, it is estimated that more than 200,000 people (or nearly 1 percent of the total population) are currently abusing at least one substance, primarily methamphetamine

or heroin. In contrast to the 956 kilograms of amphetamines (including raw materials and semi-products) seized in 2000, 370 kilograms of other illegal drugs were confiscated. A total of 73.98 kilograms of marijuana were also seized in 2000, almost double the seizure of 47.92 kilograms in 1999. Thus, amphetamines have moved to the forefront of current drug abuse concerns in Taiwan. In addition, incidents of the abuse of new substitutes, such as FM2 and MDMA (a type of methamphetamine), have been discovered in the past years. The abuse of FM2, or the "ecstasy pill," has become a serious problem among youths and is becoming especially popular in dancing parlors and pubs.

Currently, there are 147 hospitals which treat drug addicts in the Taiwan area. Convicted drug abusers are sent for treatment before serving their sentences. There are also five special jails for inmates sentenced for drug-related offenses. Following the US DAWN model, a network for surveying the prevalence of drug abuse and case reporting for the Taiwan area has been set up. However, these detoxification, rehabilitation, and medical care facilities are insufficient for the estimated 200,000 drug addicts in Taiwan and need to be expanded.

Traditional Chinese Medicine

Chinese medicine is just as valued today by Chinese people as it has been for thousands of years and is enjoying new-found respect from modern western medical researchers. In Taiwan, the main research body specializing in traditional Chinese medicine is the Committee on Chinese Medicine and Pharmacy (CCMP), whose members are selected from the nation's most distinguished practitioners of Chinese medicine. As of December 2000, there were 3,733 licensed doctors of Chinese medicine practicing in the Taiwan area. There were 2,513 Chinese medical hospitals and clinics, as well as 9,217 licensed dealers and 240 manufacturers of herbal medicines.

In Taiwan today, treatment through Chinese medicinal practices, including acupuncture,

moxibustion 艾灸 (burning of a medicinal plant close to acupuncture points 穴脈 to restore the body's "energy flow" 行氣 throughout what Chinese medicine refers to as the 12 meridians 經絡), and herbal remedies, is readily available. Treatment through Chinese medicine is also covered by the National Health Insurance program.

Chinese medicine is eliminating the stigma of being unscientific by combining age-old practices with modern technology. At the Foundation for East-West Medicine 國際醫學科學研究基金會 in Taipei, doctors are using an electrodermal screening device (ESD) to pinpoint the source of an illness. The ESD measures what traditional Chinese medicine refers to as the "energy flow" in a patient's body by probing the acupuncture points. Acupuncture is applied

in the dentistry department, for example, to locate problems by tracking the places of energy stasis in the mouth. Once the problem area is detected, dental instruments are used to pinpoint and treat the problem.

The ROC is the vanguard in research on Chinese medicines, acupuncture, and other Chinese medical practices. Many research projects have been conducted to evaluate the effects of Chinese medicine and acupuncture on various types of illnesses and diseases. The China Medical College 私立中國醫藥學院, for instance, has undertaken studies on the effects of Chinese medicine and acupuncture on hepatitis, sciatica, and other chronic diseases. Similar research studies have been done on the effects of Chinese medicine on nephrosis. Chinese herbal

---

Training in Chinese Medicine

Doctors of Chinese medicine can receive training at China Medical College Hospital 中國醫藥學院附設醫院, which offers a seven-year Chinese medicine program and a five-year post-baccalaureate Chinese medicine program to train modern Chinese medicine doctors. Since 1998, Chang Gung University 長庚大學 has offered a seven-year program of Chinese medicine. Candidates can then take the national examination offered by the Examination Yuan to qualify as Chinese medicine doctors, and those who pass the written examination can become qualified Chinese medicine practicioners. Non-Chinese Chinese medicine candidates must pass another special examination and receive eight months of training in basic medical sciences, followed by ten months of clinical practice, before they can be certified as doctors of Chinese medicine.

The Taipei Municipal Chinese Medical Hospital 臺北市立中醫醫院 and the Kaohsiung Municipal Chinese Medicine Hospital 高雄市立中醫醫院 were established to promote the development of Chinese medicine, and teaching hospitals are encouraged to set up affiliated departments of Chinese medicine. The advantages of the integration of western and Chinese medicine are thus cooperating to improve the health of people in the ROC. The 42 teaching hospitals with departments of Chinese medicine include the Chang Gung Memorial Hospital (Linkou, Keelung, Kaohsiung) 長庚紀念醫院, China Medical College Hospital (Taichung, Peikong)中國醫藥學院附設醫院, and Tzu Chi Buddhist General Hospital (Hualien) 慈濟綜合醫院, as well as the eight regional hospitals supervised by the DOH (Taipei Hospital 行政院衛生署臺北醫院, Keelung Hospital 行政院衛生署基隆醫院, Miaoli Hospital 行政院衛生署苗栗醫院, Yunlin Hospital 行政院衛生署雲林醫院, Chiayi Hospital 行政院衛生署嘉義醫院, Hsinying Hospital 行政院衛生署新營醫院, Hualien Hospital 行政院衛生署花蓮醫院, and Penghu Hospital 行政院衛生署澎湖醫院). Other hospitals with Chinese medicine programs include Taipei Municipal Chunghsiao Hospital 臺北市立忠孝醫院, Taipei Municipal Chungshing Hospital 臺北市立中興醫院, Taipei Municipal Jen-ai Hospital 臺北市立仁愛醫院, Taipei Municipal Yangming Hospital 臺北市立陽明醫院, Taipei Municipal Wanfang Hospital 臺北市立萬芳醫院, Taipei Municipal Women & Children Hospital 臺北市立婦幼綜合醫院, Tainan City Hospital 臺南市立醫院, Chi Mei Foundation Hospital (Tainan) 奇美醫院, Chenghsin Rehabilitation & Medical Center (Taipei) 振興醫院, Hsiu Chuan Memorial Hospital (Changhua) 秀傳紀念醫院, Cardinal Tien Center (Taipei) 耕莘醫院, Min-Shen General Hospital (Taoyuan) 敏盛綜合醫院, etc.

Chinese medicine is not only used to cure diseases, but also provides daily food supplements to prevent diseases.
(Courtesy of the Department of Information, Taipei City Government)

remedies have also been developed for diseases like systemic lupus erythematosus, intestinal ulcers, and bronchial asthma.

From 1996 to 2001, the CCMP sponsored 339 research projects on Chinese medicine. Twenty-five research projects were on acupuncture, 14 projects studied the Chinese medicine policies, 43 were clinical studies on Chinese medicinal practice, 33 were research projects on developing supportive devices for diagnosis, 131 studies examined the pharmacological efficacy of Chinese medicine, 75 projects involved quality control of Chinese drug products, 18 researched herbal medicine. Three books were

published as a result of this research: *The Quality Control of Chinese Medicine, A Compilation of Medical Fauna Used by Aborigines in Taiwan,* and *The Treatment of Osteoporosis with Chinese Medicine.* In addition, in pursuit of the Chinese medicine exchanges, ten exchange projects between the two sides of the Taiwan Strait have been subsidized.

Such efforts are helping to incorporate Chinese medicinal knowledge and techniques into modern mainstream medicine. Other projects include publishing research that uses modern scientific technologies to interpret important but abstruse classics on Chinese medicine. These

Number of Chinese Medicine Hospitals and Clinics, December 2000

	Hospitals	Clinics	Total
Taiwan Area	52	2,461	2,513
Taiwan Province	38	1,998	2,036
Taipei City	6	280	286
Kaohsiung City	8	183	191

Source: Department of Health

are compiled in the *Chinese Medicinal Yearbook* 中醫藥年報 published by the DOH. Information concerning Chinese medicine can be obtained on-line at *http://www.ccmp.gov.tw* or by sending an e-mail to *webmaster@ccmp.gov.tw*.

The Department of Health and the China Medical College study the distribution and cultivation of medicinal plants in the Taiwan area. With the assistance of agriculture and forestry agencies, some rare medicinal plants of high economic value have been cultivated on a trial basis. If the results of these trials are satisfactory, the plants will be farmed on a larger scale to safeguard the supply of raw materials. In the meantime, Kaohsiung Medical College and the China Medical College have been requested to evaluate and assess the efficacy of the available Taiwan-grown herbs to establish a data base on raw materials for Chinese medicine. A program to standardize some 337 Chinese medicine prescriptions was started in July 1990, and by June 2000, about 200 prescriptions had been standardized for use. The program also authorizes factories to produce Chinese medicine. In addition, the China Medical College is hosting a project to promote the cross-strait exchange of Chinese medicine doctors and pharmacists.

Related Websites
1. Department of Health: *http://www.doh.gov.tw*
2. Center for Disease Control: *http://www.cdc.gov.tw*
3. Bureau of National Health Insurance: *http://www.nhi.gov.tw*

16 Mass Media

The rapid development of the Internet has dramatically changed media markets in the Republic of China. Print media have gone online, with several newspapers bringing not just the daily printed news but also breaking news, while magazines try to lure readers with free access to selected articles in each issue. Book publishers and bookstores have established online bookstores to reduce overhead and offer round-the-clock service. Radio and television stations are also reaching out to the growing population of Netsurfers with streaming audio and video broadcasts of news and music programs, as well as drama series. This chapter discusses the most significant changes in the ROC media industry in recent years, including the proliferation of print media, the segmentation of the radio broadcast audience, competition between cable and over-the-air TV, and the liberalization of the telecommunications sector.

News Agencies

Taiwan's news agencies are concentrated in Taipei and are generally small, focusing on economic and financial news and developments in the stock market. They serve the print and electronic media, government agencies, financial organizations, the industrial and commercial sectors, and local schools.

The oldest and largest is the Central News Agency 中央通訊社 (CNA), which was established in Canton in 1924. It was relocated to Taiwan in 1949 and reorganized and incorporated in January 1996. As the first media organization in the ROC to be fully computerized in 1990, CNA has 15 departments that operate on a 24-hour basis. The agency maintains over 30 overseas offices, which file stories in both Chinese and English on Chinese and Asian affairs, political events, and economic news from major areas around the world.

CNA provides complete domestic, overseas Chinese, and international services, and provides a daily average of 280,000 words of general news to all newspapers, and radio and TV stations on Taiwan. Its economics and financial wire transmits another 2.5 million words daily to business-oriented clients. In its service to over 100 Chinese-language newspapers worldwide, CNA provides daily information on current Chinese affairs and feature stories, informing more than 22 million overseas Chinese of daily events in Taiwan, the Chinese mainland, and other parts of the world. CNA also offers general English-language news to foreign media and Spanish-language news to Latin American countries.

Among other CNA operations are a business news service offering up-to-the-minute global business and financial information, as well as a computerized newspaper-clipping data service for clients at home and abroad. CNA also conducts opinion polls on important issues. Since 1997, its website has become one of the most popular Internet portals, attracting millions of visitors from home and abroad seeking information about Taiwan.

Like CNA, the Overseas Chinese News Agency 華僑通訊社 provides information on overseas Chinese affairs to the domestic and international media. The agency is an affiliate of the Overseas Chinese Affairs Commission 會. The Military News Agency 軍事新聞通訊社 (MNA), which was founded in 1946 under the Ministry of National Defense 國防部, is the only domestic news agency that specializes in military news. MNA also provides video programs for television.

Another popular news source is the China Economic News Service 中國經濟通訊社 (CENS), founded in 1974 by the *United Daily News* 聯合報. With a 140-member staff, CENS provides domestic and foreign economic news in English on international finances and Taiwan's export industries. It also has two websites, one focusing on the latest developments in Taiwan's export sector, and the other providing daily coverage of Taiwan's economic, financial, and trade news.

Print Media

Newspapers

In the 1950s, Taiwan's newspaper industry faced the formidable situation of operating in an agrarian society with low purchasing power. By the 1960s, however, Taiwan's successful industrial transition had led to increased newspaper circulation and a doubling of the number of pages (although restricted by law to only eight pages). Competition began to intensify, not just within the newspaper industry itself, but also with the television media, which had just taken off in Taiwan. By the mid-1980s, newspapers had expanded to 12 pages. However, this was still insufficient to meet the needs of the public.

When restrictions were eased on newspaper licensing and publishing in January 1988, the papers continued to expand to 32 and even 40 pages per issue. News coverage became more professional and in-depth with specialized reporting. The recent economic slowdown, the rising costs of paper, the high penetration of cable television, and the rapid proliferation of the Internet, however, have stunted the growth of the newspaper industry. Advertising revenues, especially from the construction and automobile industry, decreased in 2000. The larger newspapers formed strategic alliances with other industries, cut salaries, laid off workers, or merged the previously independent editorial operations among affiliate publications. Smaller newspapers have closed and some publish fewer pages. Most of the newspapers are available online.

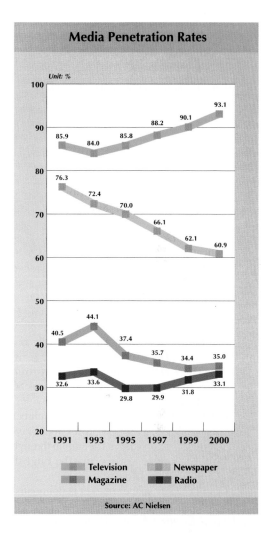

Media Penetration Rates

Unit: %

Television, Newspaper, Magazine, Radio

Source: AC Nielsen

What follows is a look at several Taipei-based, Chinese-language newspapers, which together show the diversity of the ROC newspaper industry.

Representative Publications

The Chinese-language morning newspaper market is dominated by three general-interest dailies, the *China Times* 中國時報, the *United Daily News* 聯合報, and the *Liberty Times* 自由時報.

The *China Times* is part of a chain of publications, including the *Commercial Times* 工商時報, the *China Times Express* 中時晚報, the *China Times Weekly* 時報週刊, the Taiwan edition of the French magazine *Marie Claire* 美麗佳人, *Q Girl* 愛女生, and *Art China* 新朝藝術. In September 1995, the enterprise went digital with the *China Times* website 中時電子報, providing daily news through the Internet to Chinese-language readers worldwide. Its strategic partners in online news services are mostly from the Internet and telecommunications sectors. Advertising accounts for 80 percent of its website revenue.

The *United Daily News (UDN)* is the flagship publication of another major family of publications, including the Taiwan-based *Economic Daily News* 經濟日報, *Min Sheng Daily* 民生報, *United Evening News* 聯合晚報, *Star* 星報, *Unitas* 聯合文學 literary monthly, *Historical Monthly* 歷史月刊, the *World Journal* 美洲世界日報 in New York, the *Europe Journal* 歐洲日報 in Paris, and the *Universal Daily News* 泰國世界日報 in Bangkok. The *UDN* website offers news from all its pages to readers worldwide and earns 50 percent of its revenue from advertising.

The *Liberty Times,* which has won a number of international awards for its professional layout in recent years, publishes a US edition through its Los Angeles branch office and the English daily *Taipei Times* in Taiwan.

The evening newspaper market is dominated by two dailies—the *China Times Express* and the *United Evening News*. These newspapers compete in their coverage of morning events, entertainment and recreational news, and stock market reports.

While Taipei's major papers provide extensive coverage of national issues and approach the news more objectively, local dailies based in Kaohsiung reflect a stronger sense of the local identity of the people in southern Taiwan. Aggressive and provocative, the Kaohsiung press places a heavy emphasis on political news as well as the culture, literature, and history of the southern region. Leading Kaohsiung papers, the *Commons Daily* 民眾日報 and the *Taiwan News* 台灣新聞報, are replete with expressions unique to the Taiwanese dialect.

In addition to these more traditional, general-interest newspapers, specialized dailies have also emerged to meet the widely varying needs of Taiwan's readers. Among the older publications that have shifted their orientation to appeal to targeted readership are the *Central Daily News* 中央日報, the official newspaper of the Kuomintang 中國國民黨, which focuses on education and culture rather than ROC politics; and the *Youth Daily News* 青年日報, which covers military news with a professional news approach. Newer entrants like the *Great News* 大成報 target younger age groups with colorful and more daring layouts styled after *USA Today* to attract consumers living or working in metropolitan areas.

Other specialized dailies include the *Wind Daily* 風報 and the *New Express* 捷運快報, both 16-page morning tabloids distributed for free at the Taipei mass rapid transit stations; the *Star* 星報, an affiliate tabloid of the *United Daily News* also distributed for free; and *Merit News* 人間福報, the first Buddhist newspaper to be issued in Taiwan. In addition, a number of community newspapers have sprung up in the September 21, 1999 earthquake disaster areas to provide local residents with up-to-date information on reconstruction projects and a public forum for discussion. While many of these newspapers were short-lived, some have continued to serve the local communities and to bring insightful reports and touching stories to people in unaffected areas. These include *Hsiang-chin Pao* (Local Community Newspaper) 鄉親報 distributed in Chungliao 中寮, Nantou County 南投縣; and *Shih-kang Jen* (The People of Shihkang) 石岡人 in Shihkang 石岡, Taichung County 臺中縣.

Regularly published children's papers include the *Mandarin Daily News* 國語日報 and the *Children's Daily News* 兒童日報. These carry news features and fictional stories written for elementary school students. Their texts feature Mandarin phonetic symbols as pronunciation guides for each Chinese character. The *Mandarin Daily News* operates the world's largest Chinese-language Internet portal for children.

Taiwan's English-language newspaper market is dominated by the *China Post*, the *Taiwan News*, and the *Taipei Times*. Although the *Asian Wall Street Journal* and the *International Herald Tribune* are currently printed in Taipei and delivered to Taiwan's readers eight hours earlier than before, they pose no threat to the local English dailies because their readership is segmented. The local newspapers are not only popular learning tools for students of the English language, but their increased economic and financial news coverage has allowed them to meet the growing needs of the expanding foreign business community in Taiwan.

The Government Information Office 行政院新聞局 (GIO) publishes the *Taipei Journal* (*TJ*) in English once a week, and a Spanish version every ten days. The *TJ* can also be accessed via the Internet.

Magazines

Despite the impact of the Internet and a continual decline of the magazines' penetration rate from 40.5 percent in 1991 to 33.6 percent in 1999, new periodicals such as *Easy Business Weekly* e週刊 and *Biznews* 商業新聞週刊 joined the already competitive market in Taiwan in 2000. Publishers attempted to boost sales by offering special promotional prices and expensive subscription gifts. Specialization and appeals to women readers and those with an advanced education continued.

A recent survey found an increase in readers aged between 15 and 29. Financial journals were becoming increasingly popular among women readers. In addition to offering Internet access to selected contents, a number of magazines have expanded into related services, such as the *ToGo* magazine 旅遊情報 with travel services, and *Smart* 理財生活 with financial information services.

General-interest Journals

General-interest magazines in Taiwan mainly cover current events and social and political issues. The *China Times Weekly*, *TVBS Weekly*, and the *Next* magazine, which publish insiders' stories and uncover the lesser-known ways of life of different social sectors and public figures, are highly popular among both male and female readers. Their generous use of color

National Press Council

The National Press Council of the ROC 中華民國新聞評議委員會 (NPC), founded in 1974, currently consists of eight news groups—the News Editors Association 中華民國新聞編輯人協會, the News Agency Association 中華民國新聞通訊事業協會, the National Association of Broadcasters, ROC 中華民國廣播電視事業協會, the ROC Television Association 中華民國電視學會, Taiwan Province Press Association 臺灣省報紙事業協會, Taipei Press Guild 臺北市報業公會, Kaohsiung City Press Association 高雄市報紙事業協會, and Taipei Journalists Association 臺北市新聞記者公會—and was established to safeguard press freedom, promote press discipline, and raise the standards of media ethics.

The NPC review board comprises veteran journalists, scholars of journalism, legal experts, and prominent civic figures. The panel regularly assesses the quality of media production in the Taiwan area in accordance with the Code of Ethics for Chinese Journalists 中國新聞記者信條, the Code of Ethics for the ROC Press 中華民國報業道德規範, the Code of Ethics for ROC Radio Broadcasting 中華民國無線電廣播道德規範, and the Code of Ethics for ROC Television 中華民國電視道德規範. The NPC reviews complaints raised by the public or other concerned parties and announces its conclusions after investigations and hearings. The NPC publishes a monthly magazine and numerous books exploring news issues. The council cooperates with the electronic and print media to promote the exchange of public views.

Foreign Media Represented in the ROC

As of November 2001, over a hundred correspondents and photographers representing 70 foreign mass media organizations from 14 countries and areas were stationed in the Republic of China. The accredited foreign correspondents were from the following:

News Agencies

- AFX-Asia Financial News (Hong Kong)
- Agence France-Presse (France)
- Associated Press (United States)
- Associated Press Television (United States)
- Black Star Photo Agency (United States)
- Bloomberg Financial News (United States)
- Dow Jones Newswires (United States)
- EFE News Agency (Spain)
- German Foreign Trade News (Germany)
- IDG News Service (United States)
- Jiji Press (Japan)
- Kyodo News (Japan)
- Laura Ronchi Photo Agency (Italy)
- Pan-Asia Newspaper Alliance (Japan)
- Reuters (United Kingdom)
- Reuters Television (United Kingdom)

Print Media

- *Asahi Shimbun* (Japan)
- *Asian Business* (Hong Kong)
- *Asian Today* (Australia)
- *The Asian Wall Street Journal* (Hong Kong)
- *Asiaweek* (Hong Kong)
- *The Australian* (Australia)
- *Bike Europe* (the Netherlands)
- *Business Times* (Singapore)
- *Business Traveler* (Hong Kong)
- *Cheng Ming Monthly* (Hong Kong)
- *The Chunichi Shimbun* (Japan)
- *Electronic Business Asia* (Hong Kong)
- *Electronic Engineering Times* (United States)
- *Emphasis Custom Media* (Hong Kong)
- *Emphasis Inflight* (Malaysia)
- *Euro Money* (United Kingdom)
- *Financial Times* (United Kingdom)
- *Gorilla Asia* (Hong Kong)
- *Jane's Defence Weekly* (United Kingdom)

- *Lianhe Zaobao* (Singapore)
- *Lonely Planet* (Australia)
- *Mainichi Shimbun* (Japan)
- *Ming Pao Daily News* (Hong Kong)
- *Moku* (Japan)
- *Nanyang Siang Pau* (Malaysia)
- *New Times* (Russia)
- *Nihon Keizai Shimbun* (Japan)
- *The Nishinippon* (Japan)
- *Oriental Press* (Hong Kong)
- *Ossietzky* (Germany)
- *San Francisco Chronicle* (United States)
- *Sankei Shimbun* (Japan)
- *Sin Chew Jit Poh* (Malaysia)
- *Sing Tao News* (Hong Kong)
- *South China Morning Post* (Hong Kong)
- *Straits Times* (Singapore)
- *Time* (United States)
- *Toronto Life Magazine* (Canada)
- *The Trend* (Hong Kong)
- *The Washington Post* (United States)
- *Yazhou Zhoukan* (Hong Kong)
- *Yomiuri Shimbun* (Japan)

Radio and Television

- Asahi Television (Japan)
- Bayerische Lokalradios (Germany)
- British Broadcasting Company (United Kingdom)
- Deutsche Welle (Germany)
- Hong Kong Commercial Broadcasting (Hong Kong)
- Media Corp News (Hong Kong)
- NHK (Japan)
- NNA Hong Kong Co., Ltd. (Hong Kong)
- NNN (Japan)
- Phoenix Satellite Television (Hong Kong)
- Radio Free Asia (United States)
- Telecom Asia (Hong Kong)
- Voice of America (United States)

and sensational choice of words have boosted their circulation and attracted advertisers in recent years.

Reader's Digest 讀者文摘 is widely read throughout Taiwan. The content of the Taiwan edition includes translations from the original English edition, supplemented by original Chinese-language essays of particular interest to Taiwan readers. *Global Views Monthly* 遠見雜誌 is another established general-interest magazine. Covering political, economic, social, and other domestic issues, this magazine helps to keep its readers well-informed on current developments in Taiwan.

Special-interest Magazines

Recent surveys have shown that the most widely read magazines in Taiwan are about science, computers, finance, leisure, and language learning, with the first three categories attaining the most newsstand sales. Over the past few decades, Taiwan's business-oriented society has shown a strong demand for financial magazines.

Among the most popular financial magazines is *CommonWealth* 天下雜誌. Established in 1981, it is highly respected for its attractive design, excellent business image, and concern for the welfare of society. Its coverage of macroeconomic trends and modern management concepts carries much prestige in the commercial sector. It is also distributed overseas, particularly in Southeast Asia, and is now accessible to Internet users throughout the world. *Wealth* 財訊, although the size of a thick paperback, is considered a "must read" by many stock investors, entrepreneurs, and politicians in Taiwan because of its insightful articles. Other popular magazines focusing on personal finance include *Money* 錢雜誌 and *Smart*.

Growing prosperity in Taiwan has led to a widespread interest in fitness and health. *Evergreen* 常春 offers extensive general information about common diseases and health conditions, as well as how to keep fit through exercise and proper diet. *Common Health* 康健 雜誌 covers a wide range of health and psychological issues, especially those related to working men and women. In contrast to these two magazines, the established periodical *Health World* 健康世界 offers in-depth coverage of diseases and detailed articles discussing medical and health issues.

In recent years, international women's magazines have launched Chinese editions on the island. *Harper's Bazaar* 哈潑時尚, *Cosmopolitan* 柯夢波丹, *Elle* 她, and *Vogue* 時尚雜誌 are among them. Despite the influx of foreign competition, locally owned women's journals, such as *Beauty* 美人誌 and *Non-no* 儂儂, remain the leaders in the domestic market.

The rise of the ROC computer industry and the Internet have made computer science magazines very popular among local readers. For instance, *PC Home* 電腦家庭, launched in February 1996, has quickly gained prominence. *The Third Wave* 第三波, published by the Acer Group 宏碁關係企業集團, Taiwan's computer giant, targets readers who are new to computers. *PC Magazine* 微電腦傳真 provides information on industrial computerization and also reviews new products and emerging technologies. *Amazing Computer Entertainment* 電腦玩家, a Chinese-language publication licensed by the US *PC Gamer* magazine, introduces and analyzes new computer games and software. A free CD-ROM is included with each issue.

English-language periodicals and magazines that juxtapose Chinese and English texts are an entertaining way for Taiwan readers to learn a foreign language. The more popular periodicals in this category include *Studio Classroom* 空中英語教室, with articles for senior high school and university students; and *Ez Talk* 美語會話誌 and *Let's Talk in English* 大家說英語, which target those eager to improve their spoken English. Some of these magazines are also available with audiocassettes or CD-ROMs.

Other English or bilingual magazines in Taiwan include the *Taipei Review* (available in English, French, German, Russian, and Spanish editions), *Sinorama* 光華 (available with English

or Japanese texts juxtaposed with Chinese), *Taiwan International Trade*, and *This Month in Taiwan*.

Books

In 2000, Taiwan's publishing industry continued to expand despite an economic depression. The number of book publishers increased to over 7,000, and about 30,000 titles were released. Literary and non-literary works accounted for the year's bestsellers in a three to seven ratio.

Most of the top-selling literary works were fiction novels, poetry, and essays. Poetry became more popular in Taiwan in 2000, partly due to an anthology of poems by renowned Chinese author Hsu Chih-mo 徐志摩 and a poetry contest sponsored by the Taipei City Department of Cultural Affairs 台北市文化局, from which winning entries were selected for posting on public buses and MRT trains. The successful sale of new fables led publishers to issue similar earlier works, including English/Chinese bilingual editions. Short, concise, easy to read, and containing a wealth of wisdom, fables often appeared on the reading lists of reading clubs and organizations on spiritual growth, which helped promote their sale.

The popularity of non-literary inspirational and psychological works reflects a desire for spiritual growth among Taiwan readers. Likewise, new categories that proved popular were also influenced by social trends. Books by well-known public figures on personal slimming experience, either through a controlled diet, exercise, or a combination of both, were widely read. Special history books discussing selected vegetables and fruits, such as olives, apples, and potatoes, and the evolution of their roles in the diets of different peoples presented Taiwan readers with a new choice. These topics, approached from the cultural standpoint, provided new information about diverse cultures around the world.

Books on overseas travel, popular in the past few years, were replaced on the bestsellers' lists by domestic travel books, as a result of the recent economic slowdown and implementation of the five-day workweek in Taiwan. Specialized publications on Taiwan's hot spring resorts, theme parks, and other outdoor activities, as well as maps and guides to rural communities catered to the different interests of consumers. Novels on which computer games were based also sold well in 2000.

Taiwan's social diversity and openness are reflected in the large variety of local and foreign magazines easily available on the newsstands.

Publications on language education retained their appeal by switching from conventional instructional materials to light and interesting content that incorporated everyday conversation. Readers preferred more practical language books, usually published by renowned teachers or successful men, promising swift mastery of the language. Just as convenience and efficiency influenced readers' choices, titles containing the word "easy" and offering guidance on anything from personal finance and Christmas

card-making to slimming and house purchasing maintained steady sales.

The inauguration of native Taiwanese Chen Shui-bian as ROC president in May 2000 also influenced the publishing industry. A well-known publishing company released books related to Taiwan's history, traditions, and customs. Taiwan literature and Mandarin-Taiwanese dictionaries were published. Biographies shifted focus from renowned and historical figures to the common people, such as a beggar boy and a

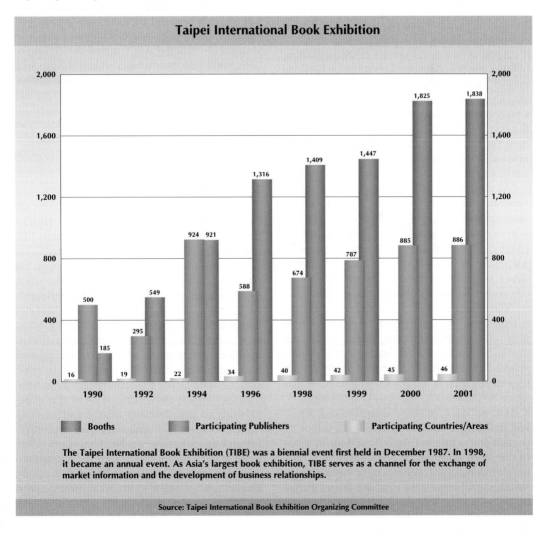

Taipei International Book Exhibition

The Taipei International Book Exhibition (TIBE) was a biennial event first held in December 1987. In 1998, it became an annual event. As Asia's largest book exhibition, TIBE serves as a channel for the exchange of market information and the development of business relationships.

Source: Taipei International Book Exhibition Organizing Committee

professor who once served time in prison. Their lives of struggle were more real and touching to the average reader.

Although color printing has been used for both text and illustrations in non-literary works over the past several years, it was not until 1999 that the practice became widely adopted, especially for travel, how-to, and women's books. These new visual effects marked an upgrading of Taiwan's publishing industry, but the additional printing costs did not translate into higher prices for books. The emergence of such publications has been interpreted as a result of intense competition among book publishers.

Another new development in the publishing industry has been increased cooperation between publishers and writers' workshops. Traditionally, a publisher would hire a writer to complete a book on an agreed topic and then release it. In the past three years, however, many publishers drew up plans for non-literary works and commissioned workshops to complete the books according to plan.

As the number of book categories increased, publishers and distributors have used various sales channels to target different groups of Taiwan readers. Different types of books are sold in chain bookstores, chain convenience stores, wholesale stores, supermarkets, traditional bookstores, stationery stores, and transportation centers such as airports and highway rest areas.

The introduction of e-commerce into Taiwan in recent years has led to the emergence of a new generation of writers creating works specifically for the Internet, but with little success. It also resulted in the establishment of many online bookstores, such as the Bookland Internet Bookstore 博客來網路書店, Silkbook 新絲路網路書店, Kingstone 金石堂網路書店, Yuanliou 遠流博識網, and San Min 三民網路書店. Although a lack of confidence in Internet security and the absence of a smooth information and commodity flow have hindered the development of online bookstores, the Chinese edition of the *Harry Potter* series sold very well online, especially since

consumers could pick up their copies at the convenience store of their choice.

Broadcasting

Taiwan's free media environment has resulted in the diverse and dynamic growth of radio and over-the-air, cable, and satellite television industries in recent years. To keep pace with these developments and coordinate with the government's liberalization policy, revisions have been made to related regulations on foreign investment, shareholding restrictions, market monopolies, and protection of consumers' rights. The newly revised *Cable Radio and Television Law* 有線廣播電視法 raised the ceiling of direct and indirect foreign shareholdings of a cable radio or television company to 60 percent. The programming business has also expanded rapidly in response to the growing demand for radio and television programs. As of December 2001, a total of 11,580 companies were supplying programs to the many broadcasting systems around Taiwan.

Radio

Prior to 1993, there were only 33 radio broadcasting companies in the Taiwan area. By December 2001, the number had increased to 142, and another 32 were under construction.

The radio broadcast industry in Taiwan has changed significantly since the 1950s, when dramatic, cultural, educational, and children's programs on the radio were the mainstays of household entertainment. TV broadcasting in Taiwan in the 1960s brought revolutionary change to local entertainment habits; however, another major change occurred in the 1980s, as radio stations specialized to secure target audiences. Currently, many radio stations focus almost exclusively on such specialty areas as current news, light music, traffic updates, stock market reports, or agricultural news. Throughout the 1990s, news stations have diversified their programming to include regular features and studio and telephone interviews. Also, newspapers, with their vast resources, are cooperating with radio stations to bring the latest news into local homes as quickly as possible.

The ROC's increasing social diversity and the public's growing assertiveness have led to a proliferation of radio call-in programs. Listeners are eager to express their views on the air about national developments and question government officials who visit the studios to answer inquiries about government policy. Call-in programs cover a wide range of topics from health care to traffic laws. Radio broadcasting in Taiwan includes regular domestic programming by medium-wave AM and VHF FM stations, medium- and shortwave broadcasts to the Chinese mainland, and specialized programming via shortwave transmissions to other countries. Programs in various Chinese dialects and English are also available.

Station Facilities and Services

The Broadcasting Corporation of China 中國廣播公司 (BCC), the pioneer of the ROC's broadcasting industry, was founded in Nanking in 1928 as the Central Broadcasting Station 中央廣播電臺 and reorganized under its present name in 1947. Two years later, it began international radio operations with its broadcast of the Voice of Free China 自由中國之聲 over short-wave channels. The BCC set up the ROC's first FM station in 1968 and was also the first to broadcast in stereo over AM channels in 1987.

The BCC operates its main station in Taipei, nine regional stations, and two professional stations that specialize in agricultural programs and traffic reports. The BCC has six national and five regional simulcast program streams. These networks offer popular music, national news, industrial and commercial services, educational and religious programs, stock market reports, and programs in the Southern Fujianese 閩南語 dialect. Its news and popular music broadcasts are also available via streaming audio on its website.

In January 1998, the Central Broadcasting System 中央廣播電臺 (CBS) was reorganized as the ROC's national radio station under the

Central Broadcasting System Establishment Statute 中央廣播電臺設置條例 by merging the CBS, formerly under the Ministry of National Defense, with the BCC's international department. The CBS operates a variety network and a news network in Mandarin Chinese; a dialect network that is broadcast in seven dialects, including Southern Fujianese, Cantonese, Hakka, Mongolian, and Tibetan; the Radio Taipei International 台北國際之聲, broadcast in 11 foreign languages; and the Voice of Asia 亞洲之聲, broadcast in English, Mandarin, Thai, and Indonesian. The CBS broadcasts news on ROC governmental policies, business activities, tourism, and education to the mainland and the global community.

Major Awards for the Media

- Golden Bell Awards 金鐘獎: Founded in 1965 to honor excellence in over-the-air broadcasting and presented annually, alternating each year between the radio and television industries.
- Golden Horse Awards 金馬獎: Presented annually since 1962 to advance motion picture art and recognize outstanding achievements in Chinese-language film production.
- Golden Melody Awards 金曲獎: Presented annually since 1990 to recognize outstanding performances in and contributions to pop, classical, and folk music.
- Golden Tripod Awards 金鼎獎: Founded in 1976 and presented annually since 1981 to individuals and publishers for outstanding achievements in four major categories—newspapers, magazines, books, and audio recordings.
- Golden Visual Awards 金視獎: Held annually since 1997 to recognize and encourage outstanding work in local cable television programming.
- Little Sun Awards 小太陽獎: Presented annually since 1996 to recognize writers' and publishers' efforts to produce outside reading books for elementary and junior high school students.

The Voice of Han Broadcasting Station 漢聲廣播電台 operates from its headquarters in Taipei and has five other stations and 15 transmission sites around Taiwan. It serves a wide variety of interests with programming that ranges from parent-child relationships and military life to Peking opera and popular trends of young working people. In addition to its AM and FM broadcasts in Taiwan, it also provides special programming to audiences on the Chinese mainland.

The UFO Network 飛碟聯播網 was established in 1996 and began a joint broadcast on seven FM frequencies around Taiwan a year later. In 1998, its broadcasts could be heard in major cities in the United States and New Zealand. Its programming is 30 percent news and related commentary, 50 percent music, and 20 percent variety programs. Programs are usually on public service and lifestyle and meet the interests of different occupation, gender, and age groups.

News98 is the only exclusive news station broadcasting on FM. It broadcasts news programs around the clock, with latest news updates every quarter hour. Its programming includes news forums on financial and political issues, world news, medical and health information, and literary developments. Based in Taipei, it also provides streaming audio online for listeners around Taiwan.

The government-run Public Radio System 警察廣播電臺 (PRS) specializes in traffic reports and social services. It operates three networks: a national traffic network 全國交通網, offering updates on traffic conditions on freeways and highways; a regional traffic network 地區交通網, consisting of five FM and two AM stations devoted to news on local traffic and weather conditions across the island; and an evergreen network 長青網 of five AM stations, which provides medical, health, travel, legal, and governmental policy information to the elderly, children, and women.

International Community Radio Taipei (ICRT), owned and operated by the Taipei International Community Cultural Foundation, is Taiwan's only predominantly English-language radio station. Its FM channels broadcast separate programming, including popular Western music, talk shows, and community service segments. ICRT is also available via streaming audio on its Internet website.

Television

The past decade has brought unprecedented challenges for Taiwan's television industry with the establishment of a public television system, the legalization of private cable operations, increased penetration of satellite broadcasting, and growing popularity of mainland Chinese, Korean, and Japanese drama series. In June 2000, digital television broadcasts began on a trial basis in Taiwan's northern metropolitan areas. Taiwan's five over-the-air TV stations expect to be fully digitized by the end of 2002. A digital TV environment will provide a greater number of channels, a wider variety of programs, and two-way interaction. Its multichannel capability will facilitate the reception of diverse opinions outside mainstream culture.

Commercial Television

ROC television began in February 1962, when the experimental National Education Television began broadcasting two hours of educational programming each day. This was followed by the establishment of Taiwan Television Enterprise 臺灣電視公司 (TTV) in 1962, China Television Company 中國電視公司 (CTV) in 1969, and Chinese Television System 中華電視臺 (CTS) in 1971. To meet growing demands for the liberalization of the electronic media, Formosa Television 民間全民電視臺 (FTV), affiliated with the Democratic Progressive Party, was inaugurated in 1997, and the Public Television Service channel was established in mid-1998.

Taiwan's over-the-air TV stations are being severely threatened as cable TV continues to gain viewers and advertising receipts. Intense pressure to preserve their market share requires over-the-air TV to improve programming and technical facilities. Regulated cable television operation arrived relatively late in Taiwan. When the *Cable Television Law* was passed in August 1993, illegal cable systems were already serving viewers throughout Taiwan, some improving reception of over-the-air television broadcasts in hilly areas and some offering a wide selection of satellite and videotape programming. These cable systems have since registered with the GIO and remain in temporary service until authorized cable systems under the *Cable Television Law* 有線電視法—which was revised and renamed the *Cable Radio and Television Law* in 1998—began to provide programming in the service areas concerned. As of December 2001, 11 of these cable systems were still in operation, while another 65 had already begun offering services under the *Cable Radio and Television Law*.

Taiwan's cable penetration rate ranges from 67 percent in Kinmen and Taitung to 89 percent in Kaohsiung. The cable systems usually offer subscribers a fixed package of over 70 channels at a fixed monthly rate of no more than US$20. These channels include news and information, Chinese and foreign movies, cartoons, religious programs, sports, music, and a variety of other entertainment programming, such as talk shows and home-shopping services. In December 2001, a total of 60 domestic and 16 foreign companies were offering 94 and 31 satellite channels, respectively, including a number of foreign channels like NHK from Japan; Home Box Office (HBO), Disney, and Discovery from the United States; as well as groups of specialized, satellite-based channels operated by local media conglomerates, such as Eastern Multimedia Group 東森媒體事業群, TVBS 無線衛星電視臺, Videoland 緯來電視臺, Sanlih Entertainment Television 三立電視臺, and Gala Television   .

The major news and information channels include TVBS-N 無線衛星電視新聞臺, FTV news, the Power TV (PTV) news channel 勁報電視新聞臺, the Eastern Television (ETTV) news channel 東森新聞臺, the Cable News Network (CNN), the Discovery Channel, and National Geographic. The more popular foreign movie channels are

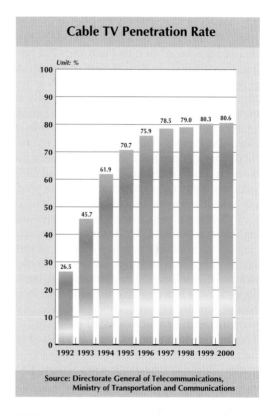

Cable TV Penetration Rate

Unit: %

Year	Rate
1992	26.5
1993	45.7
1994	61.9
1995	70.7
1996	75.9
1997	78.5
1998	79.0
1999	80.3
2000	80.6

Source: Directorate General of Telecommunications, Ministry of Transportation and Communications

HBO and Star Movie, both of which feature Chinese subtitles. For sports fans, live telecasts of Taiwan's professional baseball and basketball leagues along with a wide selection of other sports programming are available on several channels. A June 2000 survey showed that the most popular cable channels included HBO, TVBS-N, TVBS, ETTV news, Discovery, National Geographic, FTV news, and Star Chinese.

Public Television

The Public Television Service 公共電視臺 (PTS) was established on July 1, 1998, as an independent, non-profit station to serve the interests of the public, raise the standards of Taiwan's broadcast culture, safeguard the public's freedom of expression and access to knowledge, and enhance national education and culture. Under the *Public Television Law* 公共電

視法 passed in May 1997, PTS received a government subsidy of NT$1.2 billion (US$38.4 million) and raised its own funds of NT$3 million (US$96,000) in its first year of operation. However, with each passing year, PTS is becoming increasingly independent financially as the law mandates that government contribution be reduced by 10 percent annually until it falls to half of the first-year subsidy. PTS raises its own funds through program sponsorship from the business sector, individual donations, marketing videotaped programs and other peripheral products, and leasing studios and other facilities.

PTS offers a rich diversity of distinctive and high-quality programs for different age groups, ranging from children to senior citizens, as well as minority groups, including indigenous peoples and those with hearing impairments. It introduces Taiwan folk customs and traditional local operas; broadcasts music, dance, and theatrical performances; produces special programs on Taiwan's environment, ecology, and related issues; and records social changes and historical events. While emphasizing news issues, PTS also airs movies for children and young people and programs on politics, technology, economics, social sciences, and the arts. Its programming includes in-house productions as well as culturally diverse international programs that promote cultural exchange and expand the prospective of Taiwan audiences.

Motion Pictures

Taiwan's film industry has seriously declined since the mid-1990s, in part due to the aggressive marketing of Hollywood filmmakers and in part because of the ROC's continued relaxation of restrictions on film imports. Although liberalization has had a negative effect on domestic film production, it has also spurred the growth of cinema multiplexes in metropolitan areas. The excellent consumer services offered by multiplexes, such as their wide selection of available films in small screening halls, have forced many community theaters to merge into large complexes or improve their facilities in order to remain competitive.

The domestic film industry introduced 35 new films in the market in 2000, but only 17 in 2001. As in the past several years, the government's

Foreign movies dominate the Taiwan market, and accounted for 96 percent of all box office sales in 2001.

Domestic Film Guidance Fund 國片輔導金 continued to play the most important role of providing investment funding for high-quality domestic films. Budgeting for this fund has increased considerably since 1990, reaching US$2.6 million in 2001, with five films receiving funding of US$320,000, and another five receiving US$160,000.

Taiwan movies have captured the international spotlight in recent years by winning several awards at film festivals around the world. *Crouching Tiger, Hidden Dragon* 臥虎藏龍, directed by Lee Ang 李安, won the 2001 Academy Award for best foreign film, art direction, cinematography, and original score. Lin Cheng-sheng 林正盛 won the Silver Bear Award for best director for his work *Betelnut Beauty* 愛你愛我 at the 2001 Berlin International Film Festival. *Millennium Mambo* 千禧曼波, directed by Hou Hsiao-hsien 侯孝賢, captured the Silver Hugo at the 2001 Chicago International Film Festival and the award for best director at the Flanders International Film Festival in Belgium. *What Time Is It There?* 你那邊幾點, directed by Tsai Ming-liang 蔡明亮, won the Silver Hugo Grand Jury Prize, the Silver Hugo for best director, and the Special Jury Prize for cinematography at the 2001 Chicago International Film Festival; and the award for best film, director, and supporting actress at the Asia-Pacific Film Festival.

In order to promote domestic films in the global market, the GIO has worked with foreign film organizations to sponsor Taiwan Film Festivals overseas. These cultural activities have been held in many countries, including Canada, Japan, South Africa, Hungary, Senegal, Burkina Faso, France, and Denmark.

Domestically, the GIO works with the local film industry to plan exclusive screenings of domestic productions. Each year, it holds the Golden Horse Awards 金馬獎, which recognizes outstanding Chinese-language films in a number of categories, including features, shorts, documentaries, and animation. The Taipei Golden Horse International Film Festival 臺北金

馬國際影展 is held around the same time and features a non-competitive showcase of a wide range of foreign films.

Telecommunications

To comply with WTO requirements, the ROC has increasingly liberalized its telecommunications sector, established a mechanism for fair competition, and accelerated the development of broadband network infrastructure.

Mobile phone, radio paging, trunking radio, and mobile data services were open to the

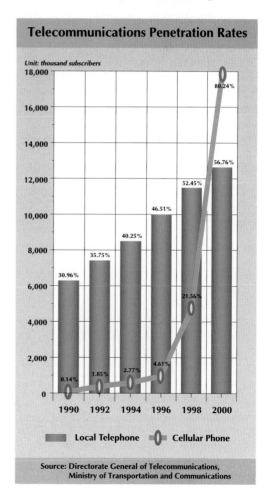

Telecommunications Penetration Rates

Unit: thousand subscribers

Local Telephone values:
- 1990: 30.96%
- 1992: 35.75%
- 1994: 40.25%
- 1996: 46.51%
- 1998: 52.45%
- 2000: 56.76%

Cellular Phone values:
- 1990: 0.14%
- 1992: 1.85%
- 1994: 2.77%
- 1996: 4.61%
- 1998: 21.56%
- 2000: 80.24%

Local Telephone • Cellular Phone

Source: Directorate General of Telecommunications, Ministry of Transportation and Communications

private sector in 1997; followed by satellite communications in 1998; cable leasing and 1900MHz digital low-power cordless phone services in 1999; fixed networking and international submarine cable leased-circuit services in 2000; and international simple resale (ISR) and third-generation mobile telecommunications services in 2001.

Local phone services are currently available via fixed networks throughout Taiwan. Chunghwa Telecom Co., Ltd. 中華電信股份有限公司 (CHT), which dominates Taiwan's telecommunications market, was joined by three private competitors in fixed networking in 2001. These networks are connected, facilitating dial-up connections to selected local phone service providers and a choice of other long-distance and international phone service providers.

Local phone and 0800 toll-free phone subscribers are also allowed to retain their phone numbers when they switched to new service providers. As of June 2001, local phone subscribers totaled 12.75 million, which pushed the penetration rate to 57 percent.

Since their liberalization at the end of 1997, mobile phone services have become more diverse, and the number of subscribers has increased. Four national and two regional operators provided services to 19.96 million subscribers at a penetration rate of 89.4 percent as of May 2001. The Ministry of Transportation and Communications 交通部 (MOTC) auctioned off five licenses for broadband wireless telecommunications service providers in February 2002.

Chunghwa Telecom currently employs fiber-in-the-loop technique to provide telecommunications services to some residential and commercial buildings, communities, and schools in remote areas, which together account for only 1 percent of its subscribers. Plans are underway to extend the use of this technique to serve government organizations, educational and medical institutions, commercial buildings, and industrial parks.

In compliance with the government's liberalization policy, local and long-distance cable leased-circuit services are open to public utility corporations employing cable transmission networks, in order to increase competition, lower operating costs, and facilitate faster network establishment by related service providers. The MOTC began accepting applications in June 1999 from electric power, mass transportation, petroleum, and cable radio and television systems; and by mid-2001, 12 licenses and 39 establishment permits had been issued.

As Taiwan's Internet penetration rate rose, e-commerce developed, and the demand for broadband networking expanded. Establishment permits were issued to three companies for international submarine cable leasing operations, expanding the international submarine cable traffic capacity, lowering related costs, and

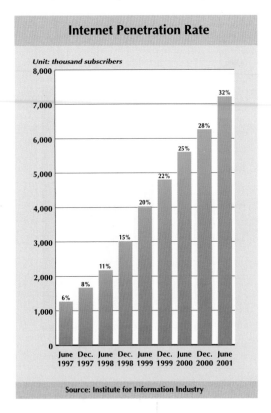

Internet Penetration Rate

Unit: thousand subscribers

June 1997	Dec. 1997	June 1998	Dec. 1998	June 1999	Dec. 1999	June 2000	Dec. 2000	June 2001
6%	8%	11%	15%	20%	22%	25%	28%	32%

Source: Institute for Information Industry

Heated competition amongst mobile phone companies have led to lower subscription rates, and consequently, made mobile phones a fad for young people in Taiwan.
(Photo by the Central News Agency)

enhancing Taiwan's competitive edge in the global telecommunications market.

As of December 2001, Taiwan's active Internet users totaled 7.82 million, representing a 25 percent growth from December 2000. Its online penetration rate was 35 percent. The steady increase in these figures is attributed to the availability of broadband services. In December 2001, ADSL and cable modem subscribers totaled 920,000 and 210,000, a respective increase of 700 percent and 89 percent from 2000. In contrast, narrowband and other comparably traditional Internet services users showed a decline, with dial-up, ISDN, and direct PC subscribers decreasing by 0.6 percent, 20 percent, and 28 percent, respectively. Leased-line subscribers, however, increased by 6 percent.

Related Websites
1. Government Information Office: *http://www.gio.gov.tw*
2. Central News Agency: *http://www.cna.gov.tw*
3. Taipei International Book Exhibition: *http://www.tibe.com*
4. Public Television Service: *http://www.pts.org.tw*
5. Taipei Golden Horse Film Festival: *http://www.goldenhorse.org.tw*
6. Directorate-General of Telecommunications: *http://www.dgt.gov.tw*

White Lucent
美・透・白

美白從 **透** 開始

清楚了就不會白忙一場。

紊亂的都市即使在清晨也顯得死氣沉沉，美白保養也是一樣，
膚紋搞亂了，美白再努力也是白搭；膚紋清楚了，美白才會長長久久，
全新的 美・透・白保養系列除了還原和抑制黑色素外，
還能調理膚紋，創造肌膚由內而外的透明感，呈現自然白皙，
透明的肌膚、清楚的美麗，這就是妳要的 美・透・白。

含有持續型美白維他命C、植物萃取精華的美白力量。

美・透・白系列
全新上市
清晢乳液(I)、(II)
淨透皂、美膚露、美膚調理組

中廣新聞網
NewsRadio
新聞快又廣

我的好鄰邊
中廣寶島廣播網
BCC FORMOSA NETWORK

WAVE.RADIO 96
中廣音樂網 BCC

中廣流行網
BCC POP NETWORK
生活好拍檔

中廣客家頻道
BCC CHANNEL HAKKA

中廣資訊網
BCC INFORMATION NETWORK

中廣鄉親網
BCC COUNTRY NETWORK

The radio station with largest listenership in Taiwan

BROADCASTING CORPORATION OF CHINA（BCC）

中廣中國廣播公司
BROADCASTING CORPORATION OF CHINA
ADDRESS: No. 375, Sung Chiang Road
Taipei, 104 Taiwan, R. O. C.
104臺北市松江路三七五號
http://www.bcc.com.tw
TEL: 886-2-25019688   FAX: 886-2-25018793

17 Education

Developing sound minds in healthy bodies is a priority of Taiwan's educational reform.

What's New

1. Figures updated
2. More about bilateral high schools
3. Comprehensive junior-senior high schools
4. New directives of educational policy
5. Multi-route promotion programs for entering senior high schools and for college-bound seniors
6. The nine-year comprehensive curriculum for elementary and junior high education
7. Continuing education outside of Taiwan

Education is strongly emphasized in the Republic of China, as it has been throughout Chinese history. Even the ROC Constitution requires an allocation of the national budget for educational purposes (Article 164). Over the last decade, the ROC's educational development focused on higher education. Some 22.86 percent of the education budget was allocated for 994,283 students (18.97 percent of the total student population) in the higher education system, whereas 39.76 percent was spent on the 2,884,388 elementary and junior high students (55.03 percent of the total student population) in the compulsory education system for the 1999 fiscal year. This uneven distribution caused the government to shift its focus and place greater emphasis on improving the quality of compulsory education. Civic educational organizations also advocated new legislation to remove the minimum requirement of the educational budget while still allocating a reasonable budget for educational purposes. In July 1997, the second session of the Third National Assembly passed a provision to Paragraph 10, Article 10, of the *Additional Articles of the Constitution of the Republic of China* (for a complete version of the ROC Constitution, see Appendix II) that states: "Priority shall be given to funding for education, science, and culture, and in particular funding for compulsory education, the restrictions in Article 164 of the Constitution notwithstanding."

Therefore, although this provision gives compulsory education higher priority funding within the education budget, it also removes the minimum expenditure requirements for different levels of the government as required in Article 164 of the ROC Constitution. Thus, after the implementation of the *Additional Articles*, the government was given more freedom to allocate budget resources for different government functions, improving past budget allocation problems a lot in the 2000 fiscal year. That year, some 24.32 percent of the education budget was allocated for 1,092,102 students (20.59 percent of the total student population) in the higher education system, while 51.32 percent was spent on 2,855,515 (53.85 percent of the total student population) students in the compulsory education system.

The draft *Law of Educational Budget Allocation and Management* 教育經費編列與管理法 passed the Legislative Yuan on November 28, 2000. Beginning in 2002, the educational budget shall not be less than 21.5 percent of the average of the three previous years.

For fiscal 2000, government spending for education exceeded US$17.1 billion, or about 5.5 percent of the GNP, with 4.13 percent for public schools and 1.37 percent for private ones. (The figures stated here are based on an exchange rate of one US dollar to 31.23 New Taiwan dollars.)

Nine years of education has been compulsory since 1968, and there is a wide range of other educational options for citizens of all ages. From August 1, 2000, to July 31, 2001, (hereafter, SY2000), some 99.94 percent of all elementary school-age children (age six to 11) were in school. The total enrollment rate of the population aged between six and 21 was 90.77 percent, and about 24 percent of the total population was attending an educational institution of some type—roughly 238.05 persons for every one thousand. In SY2000, there were 8,071 registered schools, with an average of 35.42 students per class and a student to teacher ratio of

Educational Tracks in the ROC

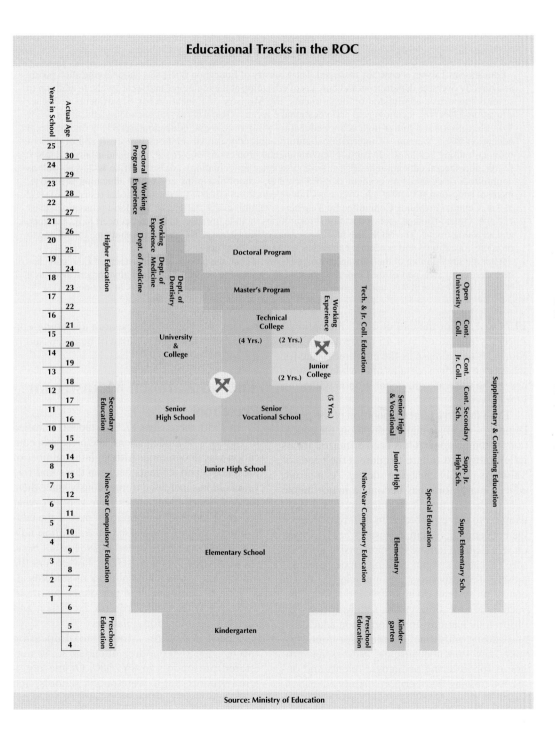

Source: Ministry of Education

289

Administrative Framework

Education in Taiwan is centrally managed. The Ministry of Education 教育部 sets national education policy and directly oversees departments and bureaus of education at the municipal and local levels. In addition to several supportive administration departments, the Ministry of Education has departments of higher education 高等教育司, technological and vocational education 技術及職業教育司, secondary education 中等教育司, elementary and junior high school education 國民教育司, social education 社會教育司, and physical education 體育司; bureaus of international cultural and educational relations 國際文教處 and of student military training 學生軍訓處; divisions of environmental protection 環境保護小組, mainland affairs 大陸事務工作小組, and special education 特殊教育工作小組; a science & technology advisory office 顧問室; as well as committees or councils on academics 學術審議委員會, school discipline and moral education 訓育委員會, medical education 醫學教育委員會, overseas Chinese education 僑民教育委員會, educational research 教育研究委員會, Central Grievance Committee for Teachers 中央教師申訴評議委員會, and Mandarin promotion 國語推行委員會. Other affiliated social educational institutions include libraries, museums, concert halls, theaters, and an acting troupe. The MOE also has 22 overseas offices to assist ROC students studying abroad and to promote educational and academic exchanges with other countries.

After the streamlining of the Taiwan Provincial Government, the provincial Department of Education has been restructured as part of the Central Regional Office 中部辦公室. Each municipal government also has a bureau of education 教育局, and county or city governments have education bureaus or sections 教育局.

19.74 to 1. As of the end of 2000, the national illiteracy rate stood at 4.45 percent. The rate continues to decrease as the enrollment rate for school-age children remains high while the number of the illiterate old generation is withering year by year.

Even though a larger proportion of the population now receives higher education, the education system in general has been criticized for its inflexibility and failure to address the needs of Taiwan's rapidly changing society. As a result, educational reform has become a major theme and, in the last few years, measures have been adopted to solve problems in different areas of the educational system. Measures have focused on establishing a more comprehensive compulsory education system; creating a more universal preschool education system; improving the higher education system; diversifying and refining the vocational education system; setting up a system of life-long learning and information education; and adding additional channels for continued study, new student counseling systems, and programs for fostering pedagogic talents and on-the-job training. Furthermore, family education, aboriginal education, special education, and

budget allocation and research are being emphasized. These measures will be discussed in the following sections.

The Educational Mainstream

Preschool

In 1950, there were 17,111 students enrolled in Taiwan's 28 kindergartens, and preschool education was uncommon. Although the number of preschools and students between three and five years old has increased tremendously since then, limited financial resources have kept two-year preschool education an optional part of the educational system. The *Preschool Education Law* 幼稚教育法 was promulgated in 1981 to set basic standards for preschools. This law covers the kindergarten system, the number of students allowed per class, required personnel qualifications, minimum standards for facilities, and financial penalties for violations.

According to the Ministry of Education (MOE), 243,090 children attended 3,150 registered preschools in SY2000. Of the registered schools, 1,230 were public schools, and the remaining 1,920 were private. Registered kindergartens accommodated one quarter of the three- to five-year-olds eligible for schooling. Another 309,716 children attended 3,345 crèche and nursery schools, raising the total enrollment to nearly 57 percent for this age group.

About 61 percent of registered kindergartens are private institutions, and therefore have higher tuition. Of Taiwan's kindergartens, 412 of them are in Taipei City (13 percent), and another 166 are in Kaohsiung City. Private kindergartens in metropolitan areas usually have fewer problems recruiting students, because most parents want their children to get a head start in the highly competitive educational system. Outside the larger cities, however, private preschool fees are often a burden for average-income families. By 2001, 49 public preschools had been set up in remote, mountainous, and outlying areas.

The MOE has recognized the widespread desire of parents to send their children to preschool, and it has tried to increase the number of these schools by affiliating them with existing elementary schools, often using the same school facilities. Public kindergartens set up by local governments are also encouraged. The central government hopes to increase preschool enrollment for five-year-old children to at least 80 percent.

In 1983, the MOE formulated the *Measures for Encouraging Private Preschool Development* 私立幼稚園獎勵辦法 to stimulate the growth of well-established preschools. This adjusted the preschool system in several ways, such as restricting the number of students per class, providing more on-the-job training programs for teachers, and improving the pupil-to-teacher ratio (12.09 pupils to one teacher in SY2000).

In 1995, the MOE promulgated the *Establishment Standard for Universities and Colleges Offering Teacher Education* 大學校院教育學程師資及設立標準, which created a regular channel for training teachers for the preschool system. In 2000, more than US$320,000 was spent on training kindergarten teachers.

In 1999, a mid-range plan for developing and improving preschool education was formulated to strengthen legislation, administration, teaching quality, evaluation, and supervision. The MOE is constantly reviewing preschool curricula to ensure that these schools fulfill the purposes stipulated in the *Preschool Education Law*, such as helping to foster good habits, promoting basic physical and mental development, and enriching children's living experiences.

Fundamental Education

The *ROC Constitution* entitles all children to at least six years of basic education. The *National Education Law* 國民教育法, promulgated in 1979, stipulates that all school-age children (between six and 15) must attend six years of public elementary school and three years of junior high school. Exceptions to this rule are children with special educational needs, students who spend time in supplementary education, and a small number of students in experimental schools (all discussed elsewhere in this chapter).

In 1982, the *Statute of Compulsory School Attendance* 強迫入學條例 was revised to state that parents or guardians of children between six and 15 are obliged to send them to school or be subjected to fines and other penalties. To enforce this statute, the Compulsory Attendance Committee 強迫入學委員會 was set up at different levels of local governments.

In SY2000, the net enrollment rate of elementary students eligible for universal public education was 99.94 percent. Almost all (99.71 percent) children eligible to begin the first year of elementary school were enrolled that year, as required by the ROC government, leaving only 1,061 children unenrolled. Also that year, 99.79 percent of all elementary school graduates went on to junior high, and 95.31 percent of all junior high school graduates continued their studies.

During the same school year, Taiwan had 1.93 million students attending 2,600 regular elementary schools, 929,534 students enrolled in 709 regular junior high schools, and a small

number attending experimental elementary and junior high schools. A larger percentage of students are now continuing their education. In 1950, about 94 percent of all students were in elementary or junior high schools, while only 3.7 percent were in high school programs or above. In SY2000, only 53.85 percent of all students were in elementary or junior high schools.

After taking exams that are open to all students, 95.31 percent of those who completed their compulsory education in SY2000 pursued further studies. Even though the remaining students entered the unskilled labor market or worked at marginal jobs, the MOE has designed a program to help these former students acquire more skills (see section on junior high school).

Elementary Education

Elementary schooling is the first formal education children receive, and the paramount aim is literacy. In 1952, about 42 percent of the Taiwan population could not read and write, and elementary school graduates accounted for 77.5 percent of the total number of all graduates. In the 15 years that followed, the population's general educational level improved as increasing numbers of children went on to secondary education. By the end of 2000, the illiteracy rate of ROC nationals was 4.45 percent, down from 5.08 percent from the previous year.

The implementation of universal elementary education has been a success. In 1967, about 97.52 percent of the students aged six to 12 were enrolled in school. By SY2000, the enrollment rate was 99.94 percent, with an average of less than 31 students per class.

In 1968, when the government introduced nine-year compulsory education, elementary school graduates accounted for 57.35 percent of Taiwan's total graduates. By SY1999, they accounted for 25.69 percent of the total, a strong indication that the general level of education had risen. In 2000, the government spent about US$2,714 on each elementary school student, roughly 4.75 times as much as was spent a decade ago. Of the 1,925,981 students in 2,600 elementary schools in SY2000, about 99.79 percent of those that graduated continued on to junior high.

Junior High School

The three-year junior high school program in the ROC educational system is similar to grades seven through nine in the United States. Before 1968, junior high school education was optional. Students at this level accounted for less than 15 percent of the total graduates in 1950, and less than one-quarter in 1968.

Junior high school, often referred to as "intermediate education" in Taiwan, is divided into academic and vocational tracks. The future of each child is profoundly affected by the decisions made by educational authorities during these years. After completing three years of junior high school courses, graduates of both tracks must pass open examinations in their respective tracks in order to enter senior high school or senior vocational school, both of which are three-year programs. It is no longer difficult for students to transfer from one track to the other. Junior high school graduates from both tracks can now choose to transfer to either

SY2000 Mainstream Primary and Secondary Educational Resources

	Kindergarten	Elementary School	Junior High	Senior High	Senior Vocational
Schools	3,150	2,600	709	277	188
Students	243,090	1,925,981	929,534	356,589	427,366
Teachers	20,099	101,581	49,394	30,471	18,812

Source: *Education Statistics of the ROC 2001,* Ministry of Education

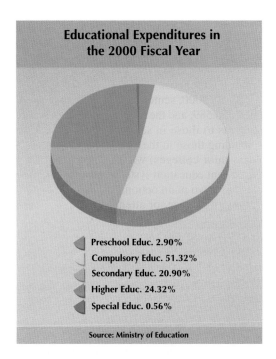

Educational Expenditures in the 2000 Fiscal Year

Preschool Educ. 2.90%
Compulsory Educ. 51.32%
Secondary Educ. 20.90%
Higher Educ. 24.32%
Special Educ. 0.56%

Source: Ministry of Education

senior high school, senior vocational school, or a five-year college.

According to the *National Education Law*, every ROC citizen between 12 and 15 years of age is eligible for public junior high school education and has the option of attending a private school. In SY2000, there were 929,534 students attending 709 junior high schools, with an average class size of 35.01 students. Only 86,109 students were registered in the seven private junior high schools around the island.

In SY2000, about 95.31 percent of all junior high graduates continued their studies in either senior high or vocational schools. As a part of educational reforms, the Joint Public Senior High School Entrance Examination was abolished in SY2001.

The junior high vocational program was abolished in 1970 after the implementation of nine-year compulsory education two years earlier. Some of the vocational courses were merged into the junior high curriculum, in accordance with Article 7 of the *National Education Law,* which states that junior high school curricula must meet both academic and vocational needs and technical courses should be included in junior high schools. Although specialized preparation for college or career usually begins at this level, specific vocational training is not particularly emphasized.

In 1992, the MOE implemented the Prolonged National Education Based Upon Vocational Education Program 延長以職業教育為主的國民教育. In 1993, the program became an extension of the nine-year compulsory education system. Technical training courses begin in the third year for junior high students who do not wish to continue in a general education curriculum. Upon graduation, they may also enroll in vocational schools that provide a minimum of one additional year of vocational training. In 1995, this program was transformed into the Practical Technical Program 實用技能班. In SY2000, 43,619 junior high graduates attended the program, and 9,990 students graduated from it in SY1999.

To reduce the pressures caused by the Joint Public Senior High School Entrance Examinations, the MOE is planning to introduce the Implementation Policies for Pedagogic Innovations at the Elementary and Secondary Levels 加強輔導中小學正常教學實施要點. These policies will set up alternatives to the entrance exams by establishing experimental bilateral (combined vocational and academic) high schools 綜合高中 and comprehensive junior-senior high schools 完全中學, as well as the Voluntary Promotion Scheme for Junior High School Graduates Entering Senior High Schools 國民中學畢業生自願就學輔導方案. These alternatives will give students different channels to complete junior high and senior high education.

Secondary Education

Secondary school in the ROC is a comprehensive system that provides students with various types of educational programs for their intellectual development and career interests. The system of schooling, which follows after the

nine-year compulsory curriculum, is a multilateral system in which students are assigned to different types of schools based on a range of factors. The majority of students in the mainstream educational system will enter one of three types of institutions after junior high school. Programs vary in length, though those oriented to college entrance are usually the longest and most difficult, terminating with rigorous examinations in the student's late teens.

Of the 336,893 junior high graduates in SY1999, 131,629 entered senior high schools, 118,583 went to three-year senior vocational schools, 24,461 studied at various supplementary schools, 32,093 went directly into five-year "junior colleges" 五專, which also cover a student's high-school years, and 14,323 attended the Practical Technical Program. Only 4.69 percent of the students who completed their nine years of compulsory education did not continue their schooling. Before SY2001, senior high schools focused primarily on training students to pass the Joint University Entrance Examination 大學聯考 (JUEE), which was a requirement for all students entering college. Entrance into all of these institutions, except for the Practical Technical Program and a few other experimental cases, was by competitive examination.

Senior High School

The three-year senior high school program prepares students aged 15 to 18 for specialized learning as well as for college study. In 1950, there were 62 senior high schools serving 18,866 students islandwide. Beginning in the 1970s, senior high schools entered a period of phenomenal growth. By 1972, there were 203 senior high schools with an enrollment of 197,151 students, more than ten times the number of students in 1950.

From 1971 to 1982, the number of students admitted into senior high schools gradually declined, while the number of students entering senior vocational schools increased to meet the growing demand for skilled workers in the rapidly growing economy. Later, when demand

for high-quality professionals increased, educational policies were reversed, reducing the number of senior vocational school students and increasing the number of students admitted into senior high schools.

By SY2000, senior high school students totaled 356,589, and the ratio of senior high school students to those in senior vocational schools (including those in the first three years of five-year junior colleges) was 45.5 to 54.5. Under the current education system, senior high graduates have two main options: either attend a university or college, or attend a two-year junior college after one year of work experience, provided that they have passed the relevant examinations. Some 68.74 percent of senior high school graduates chose to pursue higher education in SY2000.

To provide all students the opportunity for secondary education, the ROC has allowed all levels of training to be integrated, while maintaining enough variety to meet the different needs of students. The Voluntary Promotion Scheme for Junior High School Graduates Entering Senior High Schools calls for a unitary system, in which experimental classes or schools provide students with the option of attending a comprehensive junior-senior high school. This allows students to progress from the first year of junior high school through senior high school without having to take the competitive entrance examinations.

Senior Vocational School

The purpose of vocational school is to equip youths between the ages of 15 and 22 with vocational knowledge and skills. In 1950, there were 77 vocational schools enrolling a totall of 335,524 students: one senior vocational school, 44 junior vocational schools, and 32 junior-senior vocational schools. The number of junior vocational schools and students declined in the subsequent years, and by 1968, all junior vocational schools had stopped enrolling new students. With the termination of the junior high vocational program in 1970, only senior vocational schools now remain.

One of the major goals of vocational education is to prepare students for the job market.

In SY2000, a total of 427,366 students attended 188 senior vocational schools and 2,310 vocational classes offered by senior high schools. Specialized high schools include those for art, music, business, agriculture, specific trades, and industrial occupations, as well as paraprofessional occupations, such as nursing and midwifery. About 42 percent of vocational students majored in industry, 39.2 percent in commerce, 8.4 percent in home economics, 4.4 percent in nursing and midwifery, 3.6 percent in agriculture, 1.7 percent in marine products, and 0.7 percent in opera and arts.

Assuming they pass the relevant examinations, senior vocational school graduates may choose to either take a job or continue with studies at a four-year institute of technology, a university, an independent college, or a two-year junior college. In SY2000, about 38.43 percent of senior vocational school graduates entered an institution of advanced education or a noncollegiate post-secondary school.

Bilateral High School

Since 1996, several experimental bilateral high schools 綜合高中 have combined vocational and academic programs, enabling students to select from a much wider range of courses before deciding on either the academic or vocational tracks. This has broadened the knowledge base of students prior to selection between the two tracks and requires both minimum academic credits and years of attendance. Subjects covered in bilateral high schools, as part of the general education for junior high students, include: a first and second language, mathematics, social and natural sciences, the arts, domestic science, physical education, composite or extracurricular activities, and vocational education. Various technical courses are provided for students taking skilled trades and semiprofessional careers. Vocational training has been divided into different, optional levels. Preliminary college courses have been designated, and students who have graduated with 160 credits have a number of choices after graduation. They may go on to a university, four-year technical college, or two-year junior college by passing relevant examinations. Alternatively, they may leave school for work. In SY2000, there were 61,711 students enrolled in 121 high schools

Higher Education Institutional Growth SY1988/2000		
	1988	*2000*
Schools	109	150
Students	496,530	1,092,102
Source: Ministry of Education		

SY2000 Non-ROC Students in Taiwan

Overseas Chinese are offered places in Taiwan's educational system. There were 10,875 overseas Chinese at various levels in the system, including 299 elementary school, 660 junior high, 414 senior high, and 429 senior vocational school students. However, most of the overseas Chinese students came to Taiwan for higher education. There were 550 overseas Chinese in junior colleges and 6,529 in colleges and universities. (The remaining 1,994 overseas Chinese were in special preparatory, technical training classes, or supplementary schools.)

There were 7,524 foreign students in Taiwan, the overwhelming majority (6,579) of whom were studying Chinese language.

Source: Ministry of Education

(including 82 private schools) that had adopted the bilateral high school curricula system. Nevertheless, all students of such experimental bilateral schools must fulfill the same general requirements for graduation as other high school students.

Comprehensive Junior-Senior High School

A pilot program designed to relax the keen competition of the joint public senior high school entrance examination system and balance regional differences in educational resources between rural and urban areas has been conducted since 1996. Under the Comprehensive Junior-Senior High School System 完全中學, junior high students between 12 to 18 years of age involved in this program are directly promoted to senior high school without having to take the Joint Public Senior High School Entrance Examination. By SY2000, 61 high schools of this type had been established.

Higher Education

Higher education, also called post-secondary education or tertiary education, includes a variety of programs beyond secondary schools. In the ROC, such education is provided by junior colleges, colleges, universities, and graduate programs. College and university enrollment in SY2000 was 45.26 per 1,000 of the total population, and if the two open universities and continuing education are included, the percentage was 49.41, ranking the ROC as having one of the highest rates of enrollment in the world.

Junior colleges focus primarily on applied sciences, providing well-trained technicians for the labor market. Other than the five-year junior colleges, which usually enroll students directly from junior high school, there are also two-year junior colleges, technical and other colleges, and universities.

In theory, students can test into any of these institutions from either senior high or senior vocational schools. Moreover, students who complete any junior college program may take the relevant examinations to enter college or university as freshmen. If the college or university offers it, they may also transfer in by taking tests held by individual departments, entering as sophomores or juniors. Private medical colleges enroll transfer students through a joint entrance examination.

Finally, ROC universities and colleges offer a wide variety of master's and doctoral programs, which are also entered through either individual competitive examination or directly from college or university.

In 1950, seven institutions offered higher education programs to 6,665 students. One university had three graduate-level departments. Since then, the government has established additional colleges and universities and has also allowed the private sector to set up such institutions. By 1974, 13 public and 19 private higher education institutions had been opened. The number of higher education institutions in SY2000 reached 150, including 53 universities, 74 independent colleges, and 23 junior colleges. A total of 1,008,241 undergraduates were enrolled in these institutions, which also had 83,861 graduate students in 1,410 graduate programs.

Junior Colleges

Since 16 junior colleges were upgraded to technology colleges, there were only 23 junior colleges in SY2000. Nineteen of Taiwan's 23 junior colleges are private. Junior colleges are categorized according to their specialization, including industry and business, paraprofessional, commerce, industrial and business management, maritime affairs, pharmacy, medical care, foreign languages, and food catering.

Five-year Junior Colleges

A junior college under this category admits junior high school graduates for five years of specialized or paraprofessional training, except for those majoring in pharmacy, veterinary medicine, marine engineering, or navigation, who are required to take an additional year of training. In SY2000, 187,007 students were enrolled in 3,783 classes held at five-year junior colleges, with 35,848 students graduating in SY1999. Less than 13 percent of the total number of students studied in this type of public institution.

Three-year Junior Colleges

Three-year junior colleges, which have decreased in number and importance, stopped enrolling freshmen in SY1996. Most three-year junior colleges are being upgraded to independent colleges. In SY2000, only four students were still

in this category. After they graduate, there will be no more three-year junior colleges in operation.

Two-year Junior Colleges

This category admits senior vocational school graduates majoring in such subjects as business administration, engineering, math, computer science, medical care, agriculture, forestry, fishery, and home economics. Students with work experience can also seek admission. The architecture engineering program requires an additional year of training. In SY2000, there were 257,171 students studying in 4,930 classes. A total of 93,645 students graduated from two-year junior colleges in SY2000.

University, Graduate School, and Other Options

Most college and university programs last four years, with the exception of teacher training and architecture engineering, which require five years, and undergraduate law and medical programs, which last from five to seven years. In SY2000, 524,400 students were registered in 53 universities, including 25 national institutions. Another 74 independent colleges served the needs of 460,581 students.

Testing theories through experiments is an important task carried out by university science and technology departments.

Generally, institutes of technology recruit students through examinations, with two-year institutes of technology admitting junior college graduates and four-year institutes of technology admitting senior vocational school graduates.

A five-year post-bachelor's degree program of Chinese medicine recruits college graduates who have a minimum of four credits in each of the subjects of biology, organic chemistry, physics, and mathematics. Graduate programs usually admit students only after they have passed relevant examinations. Junior college graduates with relevant work experience are also allowed to take part in graduate school entrance exams.

Master's degree programs last one to four years. Doctorate programs admit master's degree holders or college graduates majoring in medicine. Such programs require two to seven years. In SY2000, there were 83,861 students studying in 1,410 graduate programs, including 13,822 studying for doctorates. In SY1999, 1,455 doctorates, 16,757 master's degrees, and 100,171 bachelor's degrees were awarded.

Alternatives to Mainstream Education

Special Education

This category includes programs and facilities for gifted children, as well as those with special needs due to handicaps or learning disabilities. There are special schools in the latter category for blind, deaf, physically handicapped, and mentally retarded students. Generally, these schools are operated by the government and run parallel to the mainstream educational system, extending from preschool through senior vocational school. In SY2000, there were 5,989 students in 23 such schools. In addition, 2,670 mainstream schools offered 4,783 classes for 92,492 special students (disabled or gifted).

In SY2000, three schools for the blind had an enrollment of 416 students, four schools for the deaf enrolled a total of 1,025 students, nine schools for mentally retarded pupils had

3,386 students, one school for the physically handicapped had 400 students, and six special schools for students with learning problems had 739 students.

In SY2000, the Resource Education Program 資源教育方案 helped establish 1061 resource rooms 資源班, providing facilities for 33,766 students with special needs at the elementary and high school levels.

In SY2000, a total of 143 schools offered classes for "gifted" students 資賦優異生, and another 408 schools provided classes for "talented" students 才藝優異生. Most gifted and talented children are educated in regular schools, but with special provisions to meet their needs. Gifted students are classified as those who have superior abilities in either mathematics or the sciences, whereas talented students are those who excel in such areas as music, fine art, dance, or sports.

Since the formulation of the *Special Education Law* 特殊教育法 in 1984, handicapped children or those with other health problems have been allowed to receive education at home. In SY2000, home study services were provided to 1,143 special students.

Social Education

The Ministry of Education supports a number of social education programs under the *Social Education Law* 社會教育法. These programs

Taiwan Area Libraries	
National Library	1
Public Libraries	562
College Libraries	161
Senior High & Vocational School Libraries	480
Junior High School Libraries	709
Elementary School Libraries	2,600
Professional Libraries	573
Total	5,086

Note: Branch libraries are not included.
Source: National Central Library

include support for supplementary education, adult education, and other services such as museums, libraries, exhibition centers, social education centers, and cultural centers. Social education programs include courses in Mandarin Chinese (for native speakers of regional dialects) and family education.

Supplementary Education

Supplementary schools may be private or public. Most students receive certificates upon completion, and some may receive diplomas equivalent in level to those in the mainstream system by passing examinations. The top schools in the supplementary system are open universities. National Open University 國立空中大學 has been in operation since 1987, while the new Open University of Kaohsiung 高雄市立空中大學 began enrolling undergraduates in 1997.

In SY2000, the two open universities provided education to 36,371 students. The male-female ratio was 1 to 2.2. Of all the age groups, female students aged between 35-39 ranked the highest. In SY1999, there were 2,431 graduates from these two universities.

Supplementary education can be divided into three types: compulsory, advanced, and short-term. Supplementary schools are attached to regular schools at their corresponding levels in the mainstream either as correspondence or night schools. Weekend classes are also offered.

Supplementary compulsory education, also known as fundamental supplementary education, is a formal educational activity for adults and includes elementary through junior high school level courses. Supplementary advanced education, or continuing education, enrolls students from four different areas: senior high school, senior vocational school, junior college, and college. After completing the prescribed courses of study and passing the qualification exams, graduates earn mainstream-equivalent diplomas. Those enrolled in short-term supplementary education usually do so in either general or technical educational courses.

In SY2000, 278,731 students attended 972 supplementary schools. Approximately 39,650 elementary and junior high students were in 677 schools; 5,600 senior high and 119,760 senior vocational students were in 236 schools; 72,249 junior college students were in 45 schools; 5,101 supplementary college students were in 14 schools; and 36,371 students were in the two open universities. There are two kinds of undergraduates in open universities: regular students and students of electives. To be admitted, regular students must be at least 20 years old and have senior high or equivalent qualifications. To graduate, regular students must acquire 128 credits. Students of electives must be at least 18 years of age, are not required to have senior-high equivalent qualifications, and need to get 40 credits before becoming regular students. If they choose to continue, they can get their bachelor's degree for another 88 credits.

In addition, 43,619 students participated in the Practical Technical Program offered by 159 schools. This program provides practical skills and craftsmanship for those who do not wish to continue academic studies.

Short-term Supplementary Classes

A large number of private supplementary schools 補習班 prepare students for the senior high school and university entrance examinations. Other cram schools specialize in such subjects as foreign languages, children's classes, civil service exams, TOEFL, and other exams required for study abroad. As of the end of May 2001, there were 8,666 such schools registered with the government; however, a much larger number operate without licenses. About 15.38 percent of Taiwan's registered cram schools are in Taipei City, 11.93 percent in Kaohsiung City, and 72.69 percent in other areas of Taiwan. Metropolitan areas have the largest market for short-term supplementary education.

A large number of students also attend review classes at such schools in order to gain academic assistance in general subjects and pass entrance examinations. Since cram schools fulfill a definite need in Taiwan's educational system, the government is exercising closer supervision of their safety and educational standards.

Continuing Education Outside of Taiwan

In August 2001, the Ministry of Education announced that universities in Taiwan would be able to open extension programs outside Taiwan. This change in policy was made to answer local universities' demands to offer extension programs for Taiwan businessmen in Southeast Asia and the Chinese mainland, as these two areas have the highest number of Taiwan businessmen.

Under this plan, credits earned in the extension programs will be applicable toward a bachelor's or master's degree. Current regulations will also be revised to accommodate the overseas education program.

International Exchanges

Cultural Exchanges

The Ministry of Education sponsors many activities to enhance international cultural and educational exchanges. For instance, in 2000, it offered grants to 71 international academic meetings and invited many outstanding foreign professionals to share their expertise with scholars and students in Taiwan.

In 2000, the MOE also subsidized 810 experts and scholars to attend international academic meetings overseas. In order to provide youngsters a chance to broaden their views and experience different cultures, various performing groups were organized for overseas exchanges by the MOE, which assisted some 102 performing groups from schools of different levels. Some 3,408 participants took part in these exchanges.

Scholastic Exchanges

Cultural exchange agreements have been signed with friendly nations to strengthen scholastic exchanges. Scholarships and donations of books and other publications have been offered. In SY2000, 7,524 foreign students from 83 countries studied in the ROC. About 74 percent of these students were from Asia, while 13 percent were from North and South America. Eighty-seven percent of them came to study the Chinese language.

Before 1989, government permission was required for all students to study abroad. According to official records, the number of ROC students studying abroad increased annually between 1973 and 1989. In 1988, 6,382 of the 7,122 ROC students going abroad went to the United States. ROC students applied for 31,054 overseas student visas in 2000.

Other Educational Options

Adult education classes are offered in such areas as writing skills, practical mathematics, and civics. Technical classes in basic job skills are also available at training centers. In addition, National Open University offers classes through radio and correspondence that can lead to a bachelor's degree. The Open University of Kaohsiung is the second university to offer such courses and is the first to be located in southern Taiwan. These open university programs are available to all senior high school graduates or equivalently qualified secondary education students. The Educational Broadcasting Station 教育廣播電臺, Chinese Television System 中華電視股份有限公司, and school-on-the-air 空中教學 also offer educational classes.

ROC Educational Reform

Mixed Success

The ROC educational system is, by many standards, a mixed success. On the one hand, literacy is high and educational opportunities are varied and widely accessible. A quarter of the total population is enrolled in some form of educational institution or program, and students generally emerge from the mainstream system skilled, well-informed, and self-disciplined.

On the other hand, calls for sweeping reform of the educational system are quite common. In particular, the Joint University Entrance Examination has come under frequent criticism.

In July 1994, the Seventh National Education Conference 第七屆全國教育會議 noted the need for diversified cultural development and improved education. Among the more important issues discussed were distributing educational resources, revising the structure and flexibility of the curriculum, improving teacher quality, life-long education, physical education, and promoting cross-strait academic exchanges.

The Commission on Educational Reform 教育改革審議委員會 (CER), headed by Nobel laureate Lee Yuan-tseh 李遠哲, was formed in late 1994. The commission was responsible for analyzing the problems of the education system and suggesting reforms. The commission's report was made public at the end of 1996 and included such suggestions as the implementation of multiple channels for students to advance to higher levels of education without relying solely on examinations. In the past, all junior high graduates were required to pass joint examinations in order to enter senior high schools; however, starting in SY1998, Taipei City became one of the first designated cities to allow junior high school students to advance to senior high school without passing an entrance exam (through a comprehensive junior-senior high school program). The report also suggested establishing a comprehensive six-year high school secondary education. The key concept underlying these reforms is flexibility. Other areas examined include the allocation of educational resources, adult education (including retraining), improved teacher training, innovative teaching techniques, and curriculum changes.

New directives in education have been formulated to enhance professionalism. Quality education will help meet world competition and sustain national growth. High-priority reforms include: lowering the number of students per class, increasing the number of professional personnel in compulsory education, improving professional education standards, strengthening preschool education, promoting computerization,

enhancing nine-year compulsory education, co-operating with enterprises, strengthening higher education, and caring for disadvantaged groups.

Inordinate Emphasis on Examinations

There is growing dissatisfaction with the emphasis on examinations, especially the university entrance exam system. Currently, students are required to take uniform national examinations depending upon the type of institution and the field of study they wish to enter.

This highly competitive system places tremendous stress on young people. A typical college-bound 17-year-old will devote at least a year to test preparation, often attending both regular senior high school and cram schools. Many students who fail to gain admission to the school or field of their choice will spend another full year preparing in cram schools to retake the examination.

Another main criticism is that the exams emphasize rote memorization of texts. Critics of the system, as well as many students, feel that exam-takers are forced to memorize vast amounts of disconnected trivia, which are regurgitated during the exams and then forgotten. The emphasis on preparation for examinations based on rote memorization is a problem that permeates the entire school system. Reformers say that students are denied the opportunity to develop creativity and independent thinking. They maintain that these skills, rather than the self-discipline for memorization and the deference to authority taught by the existing system, are more suited to contemporary needs.

Both the Joint Public Senior High School Entrance Examinations and the Joint University Entrance Examinations are under heavy criticism due to the fact that they dominate academic activities, twisting students into test-taking machines. Worst of all, this venue for pursuing higher education is only available to students once per year. After the multi-route promotion program has been implemented, however, students will have more choices and less stress from taking examinations.

Multi-route Promotion Programs

• Multi-route Promotion Program for Entering Senior High Schools 高中多元入學方案

Effective SY2001, the Joint Public Senior High School Entrance Examinations were eliminated, and a multi-route program to enter senior high school was implemented, allowing junior high graduates to enter senior high schools through assignment, application, or selection by recommendation. However, junior high graduates must still pass the Basic Achievement Test for Junior High Students 國中基本學力測驗.

The Basic Achievement Test (BAT), which takes place twice every year, covers Chinese, English, mathematics, natural science, and social science. The BAT is the primary index for admission into secondary institutions. After obtaining a BAT score, students can file applications, to be selected by recommendation, or get assigned based on their BAT score. Starting SY2002, all junior high school graduates planning on entering senior high schools, vocational schools, or five-year junior colleges will be required to submit a BAT score.

• Multi-route Promotion Program for College-bound Seniors 大學多元入學方案

The JUEE has been in use for 48 years. Starting SY2002, it will be replaced by a new system, which comprises application, selection by recommendation, or a new version of the JUEE. The application method will require students to first pass the general Scholastic Attainment Test for College-Bound Seniors 學科能力測驗, and then apply individually to the colleges they wish to attend.

The selection by recommendation method calls for recommendations by senior high schools on the student's behalf. Each senior high school will have a quota of students they can recommend. The student then takes the SAT and the College Testing of Proficiency for Selected Subjects of College-bound Seniors 指定項目甄試.

The new version of the JUEE is divided into three different models of examinations. Both model A and B will require SAT scores, but each will be on different subjects for the College Testing of Proficiency for Selected Subjects of College-bound Seniors 指定項目甄試, depending on the college. Model C is the same as the current JUEE.

To minimize the concerns of students, in SY2002, the application and selection by recommendation methods will only cover a quarter of the total students admitted into college, with the current JUEE (model C) accounting for 40 percent.

Shortage of Resources and Opportunities

Many of the problems facing Taiwan's educational system center around the inadequacy of resources, especially high student-to-teacher ratios and high student-to-classroom ratios. These ratios partially reflect the instruction quality, resources, and facilities of Taiwan's schools. By SY2000, the preschool student-to-teacher ratio was 12.09:1, 18.96:1 for elementary, 15.60:1 for junior high, and 19.69:1 for senior high.

The intense competition for entry into high schools and universities is the result of a demand for more places than currently exist in these institutions. In recent years, the government has allowed many colleges to expand and upgrade to university status in an effort to alleviate shortages. Moreover, plans are currently being discussed to restructure the ratio of students in senior high schools compared to those in senior vocational schools. Currently, the ratio is roughly 45.5:54.5. As the number of colleges gradually increases to accommodate more high-school graduates, the number of senior high school students is expected to be more than senior vocational schools in the future.

Reform Measures

New Paths for Advancement

A few experimental programs to provide alternative routes to higher education are now being tested. The experimental comprehensive junior-senior high schools and bilateral high schools are in many ways considered breakthroughs in secondary education. There are now a number of other experimental programs for senior high school entrance, such as by assignment in accordance with the Voluntary Promotion Scheme or by promotion within the same schools. Special education students may be recommended in accordance with the *Special Recommendation Measures of Advancement Governing the Age and Years of Study for Special Students* 特殊教育學生入學年齡修業年限及保送甄試升學辦法.

Senior high schools or high schools in the designated experimental districts are free to join experimental programs, and positions are available to junior high school graduates. In some experimental programs, advancement to successive levels is determined by either the student's in-school performance (cumulative grades at the rate of 20 percent for first-year grades and 40 percent for each of the next two years), achievement test scores, or assessment of early promotion test scores. Other experimental methods combine grades with examinations. Most of the experimental high schools are required to either set up a senior high school admission board or be placed under the district board.

The Nine-year Comprehensive Curriculum for Elementary and Junior High Education

Before educational reforms, incompatibilities between junior high and elementary curricula adversely affected the educational system. The Nine-year Comprehensive Curriculum for Elementary and Junior High Education 國民中小學九年一貫課程 is a more comprehensive and thorough curriculum designed for compulsory education. It is meant to foster well-rounded personalities within students, as well as respect for democracy and law, better judgement, humanitarian sentiment, creativity, and physical and mental aptitude. Five basic areas are emphasized in the nine-year comprehensive curriculum: developing a humanitarian attitude (self-understanding and respect for others and different cultures), harmonizing different human qualities (sense and sensibility, theory and practice, and human sciences and technology),

establishing a democratic attitude (self-expression, independent thinking, social communication, tolerance of different opinions, team work, social service, and a respect for law), fostering nationalist and nativist worldviews (both cultural and ecological), and creating a system of life-long learning.

There are seven courses of studies: languages, health and physical education, social studies, arts, mathematics, nature and technology, and composite activities. Language comprises 20 to 30 percent of the total curriculum; the other six areas are evenly distributed. In order to better prepare students for the world, English is compulsory from the fifth grade on, two years earlier than before. One of Taiwan's local dialects, i.e. Southern Fujianese, Hakka, or an aboriginal dialect, is required from first through sixth grade. When in junior high school, it becomes optional.

The Nine-year Comprehensive Curriculum began implementation in SY2001, following a test-run in 334 elementary and junior high schools. In order to smooth the path of adjustment, the curriculum was only implemented for first-grade students in SY2001, then to second, fourth, and seventh in SY2002; and finally to third, fifth, eighth, and sixth and ninth grades after SY2002. Revisions to the policy will be made after reviewing the results of this four-year term.

Curriculum Revisions

New teaching methods and textbooks are also being introduced. In 1992, the MOE introduced an experimental interactive teaching method for mathematics designed by a group of math teachers and other reform-minded educators. These methods were successful and are still being implemented today. Social science and history textbooks are being rewritten, and since SY1996, the MOE has given elementary school administrators the freedom to select their own textbooks. To achieve this, the ban on teaching materials was lifted and replaced by teaching outlines. Each school now has a curriculum development committee to review teaching materials in accordance with these teaching outlines

so as to best meet the demands of students in their particular area. Aside from the standardized elementary textbooks edited and published by the government, privately published texts, which are approved by competent authorities, are now also in use.

Greater Number of Choices

Students now have more opportunities to choose electives. Perhaps the clearest example of this increased flexibility is the MOE's experimental program, in which students do not have to define their major fields of study during their first year or two in college. This prevents students from being stuck with a major they chose while still a high school senior. This has made schools more responsive to market demands for various fields, making them better able to meet the needs of society.

The MOE is also continuing its policy, begun in 1993, of gradually reducing class sizes for all junior high and elementary schools to 35 students or fewer. All measures are subject to financial resources, teachers, and the land available for school construction. By SY1998, over 95 percent of all first grade classes had been reduced in size to 35 students or less.

Non-governmental reform efforts are also underway. Two well-known experimental elementary schools, the Forest School 森林小學 and the Caterpillar School 毛毛蟲學苑, have both been established with small class sizes, low student-teacher ratios, and a curriculum that stresses creativity, personal growth, dignity, independent thinking, and harmony with nature. Civic reform groups are also currently lobbying the government to make it easier to establish private educational institutions below the university level.

A Mixed Reform Outlook

The demand for increased educational resources will inevitably compete with other demands on the national budget, such as increased social welfare and environmental protection. Changes in the budgetary allocation for educational purposes are expected with the adoption of the new *Additional Articles of the Constitution of the Republic of China* in 1997. Even national universities must now raise part of their own funding, so that more resources can be allocated to fundamental (compulsory) education. In SY2001, 52 universities joined together in fund-raising activities. Although universities must now raise funds for 25 percent of their budgets, those that exceed this rate will not be penalized by cuts in government budgetary support. That is, 75 percent of all university budgets will still be provided for by the government as a stable source of financial support.

While alternative schools may provide ideal, flexible, humanitarian, and diversified education, they are very expensive. Moreover, despite the flaws of the exam system with its demands for rote memorization, its universality and uniformity is impartial. In SY2000, 60.11 percent of the people who took the JUEE passed, up from 59.83 percent from the previous year. The percentage increased to 64.46 in SY2001. An increase in the number of universities, colleges, and junior colleges to 150 in SY2000 has allowed more people to enter the higher education system.

Related Websites
1. Ministry of Education: *http://www.edu.tw*
2. National Central Library: *http://www.ncl.edu.tw*
3. College Entrance Examination Center: *http://www.ceec.edu.tw*

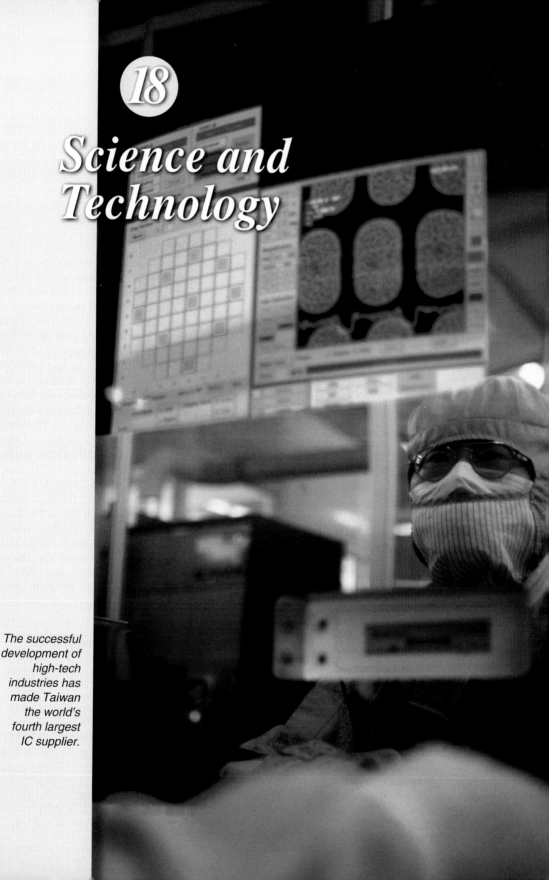

18

Science and Technology

The successful development of high-tech industries has made Taiwan the world's fourth largest IC supplier.

What's New

1. Expansion of public-private cooperation
2. Development of science-based industrial parks
3. Internet growth

The Republic of China is committed to scientific development and has allocated an ever-increasing portion of its budget and manpower to the research and development of new technologies. The government's education, national defense, and economic policies all emphasize the development of scientific expertise. The absolute and relative amounts of funding for R&D in both the public and private sectors have grown rapidly over the last decade. In 1999, national R&D expenditures totaled US$6.1 billion.

Because land and natural resources are limited in the Taiwan area and labor is becoming increasingly expensive, Taiwan must seek a comparative advantage in knowledge.

More people are now graduating with bachelor of science degrees, master of science degrees, or Ph.D.s in physics, chemistry, and biology. More ROC scientists are traveling abroad and more non-Chinese scientists are visiting Taiwan. There are more R&D institutes, more experiments, and more scientific publications in Taiwan than ever before.

Direct scientific research in Taiwan is motivated first by private-sector profit; and second, by the National Science Council 國家科學委員會 (NSC), the highest ROC government office charged with coordinating national science and technology policy, which closely coordinates all R&D activities, and funds public-sector scientific and technological research projects through grants and subsidies (see inset).

One major advance toward building Taiwan into a high-tech island is the Science and Technology White Paper 科技白皮書, issued by the government for the first time in June 1997. Intensified R&D will build Taiwan into a "green

silicon island." The legal foundation for facilitating science-technology development is the *Basic Law of Science and Technology* 科技基本法, promulgated in January 1999.

Public Sector Research

NSC-supported

The National Science Council's fiscal 2001 budget was US$613.29 million, a 6.67 percent increase over the previous year. The budgetary breakdown for the NSC and its subsidiary research centers is as follows: US$63.94 million for natural sciences and math, US$107 million for R&D in engineering and applied sciences, US$88.25 million for R&D in life sciences, US$39.26 million for R&D in humanities and social sciences, US$15.21 million for R&D in science education, US$54.4 million for the central processing department, US$28.79 million for the Synchrotron Radiation Research Center 同步輻射研究中心, US$4.13 million for the National Laboratory Animal Breeding and Research Center 國家實驗動物繁殖及研究中心, US$18.35 million for the National Center for High-performance Computing 國家高速電腦中心, US$3.8 million for the National Center for Research on Earthquake Engineering 國家地震工程研究中心, US$14.73 million for the National Nano-device Laboratories 國家毫微米元件實驗室, and US$55.46 million for the National Space Program Office 國家太空計畫室 (NSPO). Furthermore, the NSC

NSC Research Appropriations

	Support
Natural Sciences & Mathematics	19.95%
Engineering & Applied Sciences	33.39%
Life Sciences	27.54%
Humanities & Social Sciences	12.25%
Science Education	4.7%
Commission on Sustainable Development Research	2.17%

Source: National Science Council

Located in the highly seismic Pacific Rim, Taiwan conducts ongoing research on earthquake engineering and monitors ground motions with a strong-motion seismic network.
(Courtesy of the Ministry of Transportation and Communications)

appropriated US$25.81 million for the management of the Hsinchu Science-based Industrial Park 新竹科學工業園區, US$7.72 million for the management of science and technology information, US$7.68 million for the Precision Instrument Development Center 精密儀器發展中心, and US$6.28 million for the Tainan Science-based Industrial Park 臺南科學工業園區 development office. The remaining funds were deposited in a preparatory fund.

MOEA-supported

While a large portion of the NSC's annual budget finances academic research, the Ministry of Economic Affairs 經濟部 is committed to enhancing Taiwan's technology level in order to maintain continuous growth in manufacturing, expedite the transformation of traditional industries, and promote industrial development. In 2000, the MOEA allocated US$484.6 million to public and private nonprofit research institutes for applied industrial research as part of its broad-ranging Technology Development Program 科技研究發展專案計畫. The funds were primarily distributed among the Industrial Technology Research Institute 工業技術研究院

(see ITRI section), the Chungshan Institute of Science and Technology 中山科學研究院 (CIST, see also Chapter 8, National Defense), and the Institute for Information Industry 資訊工業策進會 (see inset on next page). The MOEA has entrusted research institutes to develop key technologies, conduct innovative research, and transfer necessary technology to the industrial sector. The MOEA also set up the Industrial Technology Information Services Office 產業技術資訊服務推廣計畫專案辦公室 in 1990 to provide a wide range of information covering products, technology, and companies in industries such as aerospace, electronics, mechanics, automation, food, metal, biochemistry, industrial materials, optoelectronics, chemistry, industrial safety, semiconductors, consumer electronics, information technology, shipbuilding, communications, measurement instrumentation, and textiles.

Close Public-private Sector R&D Cooperation

The close cooperation in R&D among public and private sectors has been a key factor in Taiwan's economic success. Publicly funded research in advanced technology has provided the

National Science Council

The National Science Council 國家科學委員會 (NSC) is the highest government organ responsible for promoting and planning overall scientific and technological development in the ROC; setting national science policies; recruiting experts in scientific fields; providing stipends and incentives for researchers; coordinating the scientific and technological research and development projects of other government ministries; reviewing the annual science and technology reports of these ministries; and developing science-based industrial parks.

The National Science Council consists of the heads of government offices that have science or technology projects, the ministers without portfolio 政務委員 in charge of reviewing scientific or technological development, the president of Academia Sinica 中央研究院, the secretary-general of the Executive Yuan 行政院, and noted scientists.

---

knowledge base and manpower to help new industries develop and prosper. This model has been applied to many areas and products, including the microelectronics and personal computer industries. As many of Taiwan's industries have become world-class in recent years, public-private cooperation in research has expanded in many ways. In an increasing number of projects, the government collaborates as a partner with major research institutions and private companies, rather than leader as in the past.

MOEA research funding, previously offered to only non-profit research institutions, is now available to private companies and academic institutions as well. The MOEA sponsors a special program to help small and medium-sized enterprises (SMEs) engage in R&D. Funding is also provided to support international cooperation.

These R&D programs have strengthened Taiwan's microelectronics-related lines. In 2000, Taiwan produced US$1.7 billion worth of CD-ROM drives, accounting for over 56 percent of world production. Innovation in heat-dissipation and other areas has bolstered its position in the notebook PC market. In 2000, over 52.5 percent of the world's notebook PCs—valued at US$13.5 billion—were produced in Taiwan. The island is also rapidly gaining ground in the market for digital cameras, personal digital assistants (PDAs), and other handheld devices.

After years of joint research with the Industrial Technology Research Institute (ITRI)

under the MOEA-funded "chemicals for electronics" project 電子化學專案計劃, several chemical companies have set up production lines for photo-resist and chemical-mechanical-planarization (CMP) materials used in the IC industry. This has strengthened the IC industry and opened a new avenue of growth for Taiwan's

---

Institute for Information Industry

Founded in 1979, the Institute for Information Industry (III) is a nonprofit organization under the sponsorship of the Ministry of Economic Affairs and the private sector. Its mission is to develop and promote the information industry as part of the overall process of spurring economic development in the ROC. With 1,235 employees (over 60 percent of whom have a master's degree or higher degree in a pertinent field), the III coordinates the efforts of the government, private, and academic sectors to build a sound base for the development of Taiwan's information industry. The significance of the III can be seen by the US$125 million in revenue it had generated by the end of 2000. The III is involved in various activities related to the development of Taiwan's IT industry, including policy-setting and planning, technology R&D, training, promotion, market intelligence, and IPR research. The III also provides a variety of training courses for IT professionals. In the past 20 years, over 250,000 people have benefited from the III's training programs.

Scientific Research Institutions and Agencies

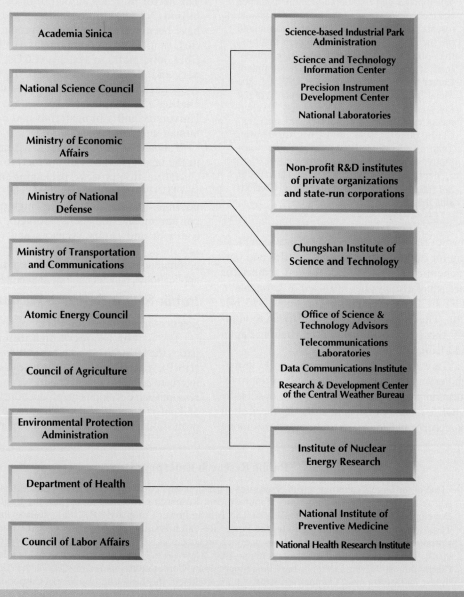

Sourse: Directorate-General of Budget, Accounting and Statistics

Private-sector Research Institutes

The numerous private research institutes in the Taiwan area focus mainly on experimental development and commercialization of science and technology. Some of the more active private research institutes in the Taiwan area include the Industrial Technology Research Institute, the Food Industry Research and Development Institute 食品工業發展研究所, the Development Center for Biotechnology 生物技術開發中心, the Metal Industries Development Center 金屬工業發展中心, the United Ship Design and Development Center 聯合船舶設計發展中心, the China Textile Institute 中國紡織工業研究中心, the Taiwan Textile Federation 紡織業外銷拓展會, the Automotive Research Testing Center 車輛研究測試中心, the Electronics Testing Center, Taiwan 臺灣電子檢驗中心, and the China Technical Consultants Institute 中國技術服務社.

---

mature chemical industry, which has been looking for opportunities beyond textiles and petrochemicals. The MOEA-funded project for flat-panel displays has attracted investments in TFT-LCD panels, totaling around US\$3 billion. This is expected to push Taiwan to number three in world production, behind Japan and Korea, in two years.

Taiwan is ranked sixth in the world in machinery and automation as a result of improvements in precision and versatility made possible by MOEA-funded projects at ITRI. IC-fabrication equipment and advanced tool centers are among the most promising growth areas. The most striking example, however, is the field of optoelectronics, which has been growing at an annual rate of over 30 percent for several years. The sector now has an output of over US\$12 billion (NT\$400 billion). Strong growth rates have been evident in all major product categories, ranging from components (LEDs, LDs, fiber optic parts) to systems (LCDs, 3D scanners and cameras, and DVDs). Taiwan also cooperates with leading institutions abroad, including a lower-power IC project at Stanford University and a biomaterials and computer-human interface project at MIT.

Taiwan has ongoing plans to assure its place in the next generation of microelectronics (IC Cu-fabrication process, packaging, materials, and DVD), chemicals (catalysts and advanced polymers), materials (batteries, high-density recording media, and energy storage), and environment and safety (sensors and recycling schemes). Priority areas of development include: communications (especially wireless and optical applications), nanotechnology, and biotechnology.

Public Sector Research Facilities

Science-based Industrial Parks

The first of a series of high-tech industrial parks, the Hsinchu Science-based Industrial Park (HSIP), was established in northwestern Taiwan to create an environment conducive to high-tech research and development, production, work, life, and entertainment, and which attracts high-tech professionals and technologies. The park, located

---

Public Research Enterprises

One of the largest government-run enterprises is the Chinese Petroleum Corporation 中國石油股份有限公司, which has set up the Refining and Manufacturing Research Center 煉製研究所 and the Exploration Development Research Institute 探採研究所. The Taiwan Power Company 臺灣電力公司, usually known as Taipower, has one research institute, the Power Research Institute 電力綜合研究所. The Taiwan Sugar Corporation 臺灣糖業股份有限公司 also has one such organization, the Taiwan Sugar Research Institute 臺糖研究所. The Taiwan Salt Industrial Corporation 臺鹽實業股份有限公司, the Taiwan Machinery Manufacturing Corporation 臺灣機械股份有限公司, the China Shipbuilding Corporation 中國造船股份有限公司, the Aerospace Industrial Development Corporation 漢翔航空工業股份有限公司, the Tang Eng Iron Works Corporation 唐榮公司, and the Taiwan Water Supply Corporation 臺灣自來水公司 all run research laboratories.

---

in Hsinchu County 新竹縣 and Hsinchu City 新竹市, is surrounded by a number of renowned science and engineering research institutes, such as ITRI, National Tsing Hua University 國立清華大學, and National Chiao Tung University 國立交通大學, which provide ample human resources for companies in the park. The park's excellent location and the rapid growth of its companies and products have made it the Silicon Valley of Asia.

The HSIP is a base for developing high-tech industries. Administered by a division of the National Science Council, the Science-based Industrial Park Administration 科學工業園區管理局, the park has made Taiwan a world leader in such high-tech industries as IC manufacturing and key information industry components. Since 1980, the ROC government has invested approximately US$783 million in the park's infrastructure and administration. As of December 2000, 289 high-tech companies, employing 102,840 workers, were located in the 605-hectare park. Turnover in 2000 totaled US$29.8 billion, a 46 percent increase over the previous year, while the total number of park employees grew 24 percent.

The 116 IC manufacturers in the park concentrate on producing DRAM and SRAM chips, as well as the development of Application Specific Electronic Module (ASEM) and Multichip Module (MCM) foundry services. IC manufacturing in the park is supported by a full range of industries that handle materials, design, testing, and packing. With an annual turnover of US$18.5 billion, these companies now account for 5 percent of the world's IC production value, making Taiwan the fourth largest supplier worldwide after the United States, Japan, and South Korea. The importance of computers and computer peripherals to Taiwan's foreign trade has risen over the past decade, and currently Taiwan ranks number one for global market share in six categories of information technology products, including notebook PC, mouse, scanner, monitor, interface card, and modem. (For more information on the economic aspects of the ROC's information industry, see Chapter 10, The Economy.)

As part of a global strategy to penetrate foreign markets, 64 of the park's companies have established branch offices overseas. Through international cooperation and strategic alliances, they are exploring international R&D resources to create an integrated technological production network. They have also used joint ventures and mergers to overcome growth limitations and globalize their operations.

The basic infrastructure of the HSIP has completed its third phase of expansion and companies have moved in. Given the rapid growth of high-tech industries, Chunan 竹南鎮 and Tungluo 銅鑼鄉 townships, 15 and 40 minutes' drive from Hsinchu, respectively, were chosen as the sites for the fourth phase of expansion. Groundbreaking was conducted in July 1999 for the 118-hectare Chunan base, which will house mainly companies developing intellectual biotechnology. Thirty-six hectares of land will be reserved for industrial use, half designated for biotechnology and half for optoelectronics and telecommunications. The 350-hectare Tungluo

---

ITRI Organizations

The ITRI includes the Union Chemical Laboratories 化學工業研究所 (UCL), the Mechanical Industrial Research Laboratories 機械工業研究所 (MIRL), the Electronics Research and Service Organization 電子工業研究所 (ERSO), the Computer and Communications Research Laboratories 電腦與通訊工業研究所 (CCL), the Energy and Resources Laboratory 能源與資源研究所 (ERL), the Materials Research Laboratories 工業材料研究所 (MRL), the Opto-electronics and System Laboratories 光電工業研究所 (OES), the Center for Measurement Standards 量測技術發展中心 (CMS), the Center for Environment, Safety and Health Technology 環境安全衛生技術發展中心 (CESH), the Center for Aviation and Space Technology 航空與太空工業技術發展中心 (CAST), and the Biomedical Engineering Center 生醫工程中心 (BMEC).

base will be used for diversified high-tech industries such as optoelectronics, telecommunications, microelectro-mechanics, as well as R&D for these three industries and others including semiconductor, biotechnology, computers, and peripherals.

To ensure that high-tech manufacturers have more room for expansion, the National Science Council designated a site in southern Taiwan for a second science-based industrial park. The Tainan Science-based Industrial Park (TSIP) 臺南科學工業園區 is located between Hsinshih rural township 新市鄉 and Shanhua urban township 善化鎮 in Tainan County. The location capitalizes on the agricultural resources of southern Taiwan and the technological support of institutions nearby, such as the Asian Vegetable Research and Development Center 亞洲蔬菜研究發展中心 and the Taiwan Sugar Research Institute 臺灣糖業研究所.

The core area of the TSIP covers 638 hectares of land, with a convenient transportation system and a high-quality residential complex, both equipped with state-of-the-art facilities such as public schools, hospitals, parks, museums, and sports complexes. The TSIP has signed cooperative agreements with 12 academic institutions to develop human resources, provide

training, and enhance the exchange of technology information so as to fully utilize the park's facilities.

The TSIP development office was officially set up in July 1997, and began operation a year later. The park represents part of the government's effort to build Taiwan into a "green silicon island." Current plans call for the park to initially serve companies from six major industries: semiconductors, computers and peripherals, telecommunications, optoelectronics, precision machinery, and biotechnology. As of June 2001, 64 firms had received approval to move into the park. By 2010, an estimated 200 companies located in the park are expected to produce an annual output of US$27 billion and create 77,000 jobs.

In addition to the Hsinchu and Tainan Science-based Industrial Parks, plans are under way to develop the Central Science-based Industrial Park 中部科學工業園區, and the three are expected to form a high-tech industrial cluster. Wireless communications and semiconductor equipment will be the core industries in the new park in central Taiwan.

Industrial Technology Research Institute

Headquartered in the Hsinchu Science-based Industrial Park area with branch offices

---

Internet Growth

With the rapid growth of the Internet, the ROC government adopted several measures to establish a safe and reliable environment for Internet application in August 2000. These include the formulation of a law governing electronic contracts; the extension of intellectual property rights protection to such Internet applications as linking, metatags, and framing; and the registration and management of domain names.

In addition, the government plans to establish a taxation system for e-commerce, and lay down regulations for monetary transfers and securities transactions via the Internet. Web-related offenses will be defined and penalties established. Meanwhile, the government is replacing traditional written documentation with electronic files and is working toward resource-sharing among the various agencies through an intranet that will provide the public with a "single window" service.

As of December 2001, Taiwan had 7.82 million active Internet subscribers and a penetration rate of 35 percent. Competition has intensified in the broadband services market, with the entry of private fixed networking companies. As of December 2001, ADSL and cable modem subscribers totaled 920,000 and 210,000, which reflected respective growth rate of 700 percent and 89 percent from 2000.

throughout Taiwan, the Industrial Technology Research Institute (ITRI) is the largest non-profit research organization in Taiwan, with a total workforce of 6,000 and a budget of US$503 million in 2000.

Founded in 1973 by the Ministry of Economic Affairs, ITRI is primarily responsible for developing industrial technologies and helping private enterprises enhance their competitiveness. ITRI's research projects cover a broad spectrum of industries, from traditional to emerging, and from labor-intensive to high-tech. A prominent example is the integrated circuit (IC) industry. During the mid-1970s, ITRI obtained access to CMOS technology from the United States. Over the following decade, ITRI led Taiwan's developing IC industry, providing both technology and human resources. The top two IC foundries in the world—Taiwan Semiconductor Manufacturing Company 臺灣積體電路製造股份有限公司 (TSMC) and United Microelectronics Company 聯華電子股份有限公司 (UMC), with revenues of US$5.2 billion and US$3.3 billion, respectively—both originated in ITRI.

Many other traditional industries have benefited from ITRI's R&D. Taiwan's textile industry has retained its competitive edge with the help of many ITRI innovations, such as microfibers, special polymers, water-repellent fabrics, and various surface-treatment methods. ITRI has helped in the transformation of mature chemical companies, by introducing various chemicals used in microelectronics production lines. Many industrial sectors, such as precision machinery and automation, energy and environment, and optoelectronics are also partners and beneficiaries of ITRI's projects.

ITRI receives about half of its funding from the government and half from industrial sources. In 2000, ITRI transferred technology in 314 items to 457 companies in Taiwan, hosted over 1,009 conferences and exhibitions, and published 605 reference papers and 583 conference papers. A total of 28,431 companies received services from ITRI.

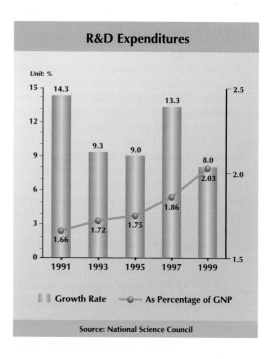

R&D Expenditures

Unit: %

Growth Rate — As Percentage of GNP

Source: National Science Council

Research Work Force

In 1999, a total of 136,323 people in Taiwan worked on R&D-related projects, of which 65.1 percent were researchers, 23.2 percent were technicians, and 11.7 percent were supporting personnel. About 88,700 of these were researchers, i.e., persons with a B.S., M.S., Ph.D., or associate degrees and more than three years of research experience outside the classroom.

ROC researchers in 1999 were assisted by 31,674 technicians, i.e., people who perform technical tasks under the supervision of researchers, and are typically high school, vocational school, or junior college graduates with less than three years of working experience. Both researchers and technicians rely heavily on supporting personnel (administrators, accountants, secretaries, and maintenance workers), nearly 16,000 of whom were employed at scientific or technical institutes.

Other Developments

Biotechnology

As part of the government's plan to build Taiwan into an Asia-Pacific manufacturing center, biotechnology and pharmaceuticals are being promoted as key industries. To encourage related research, the government plans to provide more subsidies for the development of biotechnology. Government R&D expenditures in the field of biotechnology in fiscal 2002 totaled US$288 million. Responsibility for basic research (including genetic engineering, gene therapy, transgenic animals and plants, enzyme engineering, protein engineering, and pharmaceutical development) lies with the National Science Council. The MOEA's Industrial Development Bureau 工業局 (IDB) is also involved in biotech R&D. In FY2000, IDB projects included the development of paclitaxel (an anticancer agent), diagnostics, and biopolymers (including gene chips).

Aeronautics and Space Technology

One of the primary objectives of the government's efforts to develop space technology is to upgrade Taiwan's overall competitiveness, as the versatile nature of space technology itself will inevitably further developments in other fields, including experimental research, communications, conservation, transportation, and agriculture. It was under such considerations that the National Space Program Office was initiated in October 1991. The NSPO is responsible for carrying out the ROC's 15-year space technology development program with a budget of US$631 million. In its initial stage, the NSPO is concentrating on a satellite project known as ROCSAT, which consists of three different satellite ventures. The first ROC satellite,

---

Science and Technology Advisory Group of the Executive Yuan

(行政院科技顧問組)

To actively promote comprehensive development of national science and technology, the Executive Yuan promulgated the "Science and Technology Development Program" in May 1979 as guideline for its ministries, councils, and agencies. This program also established the Advisory Board of Science and Technology in the Office of the Premier. A number of internationally prestigious leaders from various fields of science and technology were invited from abroad on the Advisory Board, which advises the premier and relevant members of his cabinet either collectively, or individually, on the government's science and technology options for future development. To ensure the effective operation of the advisory board, a mission-oriented organization called the Science and Technology Advisory Group (STAG) was established in December 1979.

In view of the considerable achievements made by the ROC in developing science and technology, and to promote Taiwan's science and technology, the Executive Yuan revised the Operational Guidelines of STAG in April 1998. In accordance with the revised guidelines, the premier is now able to invite a number of eminent local scientists, in addition to the overseas science and technology advisors, to serve on the advisory board. These advisors attend all of the science and technology meetings held by the Executive Yuan, and together form a consultative system for the entire cabinet.

The primary missions of STAG include: providing recommendations on national science and technological (S&T) development policy and important programs or projects for S&T development, sponsoring and organizing board meetings and various strategic review board meetings, steering the promotion of S&T development programs or projects designated by the cabinet, collecting important S&T development information, providing consultations, and other matters relevant to science and technology assigned by the premier.

STAG does not directly implement projects, but rather, coordinates different government agencies, industries, research institutes, and academia which implement them.

ROCSAT-3 is scheduled for launch in 2003 to collect distorted signals for weather prediction and ionosphere, climate, and gravity research.
(Courtesy of the National Space Program Office)

ROCSAT-1, was successfully launched on January 27, 1999, from Cape Canaveral, Florida. ROCSAT-1 was an experimental, low-earth orbit science satellite that contained three instruments on board: the Ionospheric Plasma Electrodynamics Instrument (IPEI), the Ocean Color Imager (OCI), and the Ka-band Experimental Communications Payload (ECP). Daily operations of ROCSAT-1 are being managed by the NSPO operations team, which controls the satellite from its NSPO Mission Operations Center located in Hsinchu.

ROCSAT-2 is a smaller satellite designed for remote sensing and contains an electron-optical imager and a Sprite imager to complete its tasks. The electron-optical imager can simultaneously capture four panchromatic, multispectrum images and then transmit this data to government agencies, private sector companies, and research organizations. The applications for such remote sensing include land management, agriculture, natural disaster assessment, environmental monitoring, scientific research, and educational activities. In addition to its remote sensing mission, ROCSAT-2 has the

scientific mission of investigating various lighting phenomena in the upper atmosphere. The launch date for ROCSAT-2 is currently scheduled for the middle of 2003. The ROCSAT-3 program is a collaboration project between the University Corporation of Atmospheric Research (UCAR) in the United States and the NSPO. The goal of ROCSAT-3 is to develop a constellation of low-earth orbiting microsatellites for operational weather prediction, space weather monitoring, and climate research. Each of the micro satellites will carry GPS/MET instrument to measure atmospheric refractivity through the use of GPS emitted signal passing through the earth's atmosphere. Scientists will then input global data collected from this constellation of satellites into a sophisticated model used for worldwide weather forecasting.

Related Websites
1. National Science Council: *http://www.nsc.gov.tw*
2. Science and Technology Advisory Group of the Executive Yuan: *http://www.stag.gov.tw*
3. Industrial Technology Research Institute: *http://www.itri.org.tw*
4. Institute for Information Industry: *http://www.iii.org.tw*

中油加油

加油

中油公司同時擁有遍佈全省的加油服務據點、專業的員工、
無以計數的微笑、以及一直在增加的熱忱………

**每天讓數以百萬計的車輛和車主得到更快、
更便捷的加油服務**

>>滿足e世代的實際需求，中油以專業、熱忱、提供更多元服務，讓中油不只是加油

92、95、98
無鉛汽油

汽車保養中心

各種費用代收服務

飲料、書報販售

50年專業經驗

心想事成

中國石油

National Health Insurance, Shortcut to Universal Care.

In everyday of your life, NHI will be there for you.

Bureau of National Health Insurance
140 Hsinyi Road, Section 3, Taipei 106, Taiwan,ROC
Toll-Free Call: 0800-212369   Fax: 886-2-2702-5834
http://www.nhi.gov.tw

Eternal life for NHI. Healthy life for all

19
Social Welfare

About 18.63
percent of Taiwan's
population consists
of children under
12 years of age,
and their well-being
is clearly defined
in the ROC's
Children's Welfare
Law first promulgated
in 1973.

What's New

1. Educational vouchers for five-year-old children attending private nurseries
2. The establishment of the Coast Guard Administration in February 2000
3. Sexual Violation Prevention Committee and Domestic Violence Prevention Committee
4. *Statute on Assisting the Families of Women in Difficult Circumstances*
5. Professional caretakers to provide in-house care for the elderly
6. The establishment of the Protection Committee for the Handicapped and Disabled in October 2000
7. The promulgation of the *Volunteer Service Law* in January 2001
8. Introduction on the private charity organization—the Buddhist Compassion Relief Tzu Chi Foundation

The vast majority of ROC citizens in the Taiwan area now enjoy a greater quality of life than ever before. Equal access to education, jobs, housing, medical care, travel, and the political system are the result of profound social and political changes accompanying the astounding economic success of recent years as Taiwan was transformed over the past five decades from traditional agriculture into a modern industrial economy. However, this restructuring of society has also generated new social ills.

Extended families were once the fundamental source of welfare services in Chinese society. However, the traditional concept of family-based support has changed in the post-agricultural economy in Taiwan. Currently, 50 percent of the population lives in the cities of Taipei, Taichung, Tainan, or Kaohsiung. It is now common for both parents to work full-time outside the home, and children are often cared for by the school system.

The transformation from extended farming families to nuclear urban families has resulted in growing numbers of children, women, handicapped, and senior citizens who require assistance from non-family sources. Coinciding with the need for outside assistance are two new phenomena: increased demand for government services and the proliferation of private organizations that provide welfare services. This chapter highlights services provided by the government and private sector to children, juveniles, women, the elderly, the handicapped, and the poor.

Welfare Sources

In fiscal 2002, the ROC central government allocated nearly US$8.55 billion, or 16.7 percent of its total expenditures, on what it broadly defined as "social welfare," a budget heading that includes social insurance expenses (9.2 percent), social relief expenses (0.4 percent), welfare services (6.1 percent), national employment expenses (0.1 percent), and medical care expenses (0.9 percent). The ROC government does not intend to be the sole source of welfare services in Taiwan despite its large allocated budget. Instead, the government sees its role as a facilitator and coordinator of welfare activities in local communities.

Communication between various government agencies, academic institutions, private charities, and care recipients is of crucial importance. In a typical scenario, the Department of Social Affairs 社會司 (DSA) under the Ministry of the Interior (MOI) 內政部 formulates welfare policies and drafts related legislation. The DSA then briefs local welfare offices on the latest policies. These offices commission universities or individual scholars to survey the actual demand for specific services in the local community. Once community demand has been assessed, local welfare officials invite representatives from private charities active in the area to attend seminars in which the new government guidelines are explained, community needs discussed, and responsibilities and priorities set. Special interest groups, charities, the media, and the more than 4,600 professional social workers in Taiwan provide feedback to policymakers at the highest levels of government.

Child Welfare

In 2000, about 18.63 percent of the people in Taiwan are children under 12 years of age, as defined in the *Children's Welfare Law* 兒童福利法. Children today have fewer siblings and less outdoor space for play, but face increased pressure from academic competition at an early age. More often than before, they are raised by a single parent, who must spend most of the time working outside the home.

The *Children's Welfare Law* was first promulgated in 1973, and revised in 1993 in light of the 1989 UN Convention on the Rights of the Child. Under the law, a pregnant woman may not smoke, drink, take drugs, chew betel nuts (see section on betel nuts, Chapter 15, Public Health), or engage in any other activity that might endanger her unborn child. The law also mandates subsidies for the medical care of premature babies and seriously ill children. Health care professionals, daycare workers, teachers, and the police are required to report cases of child abuse. The revised *Children's Welfare Law* also prohibits parents from leaving children who are under the age of six or who require special attention unattended. Parents violating this regulation must attend a minimum of four hours of parental responsibility training. Fines of US$38 to US$192 are charged for each refusal to attend the classes. Under the revision, courts are able to assign a child to another guardian if both parents are deemed incompetent. As an added measure, the revised *Children's Welfare Law* empowers authorities to make public the name of anyone who violates provisions of the law and to fine them up to US$3,842.

Child Protection

According to the Department of Social Affairs, reported cases of child abuse have increased steadily from 1,235 in 1993 to over 4,000 in 2000. Article 18 of the *Children's Welfare Law* requires that child abuse cases must be reported within 24 hours of discovery. In 2000, among the 4,093 children below the age of 18 protected by the Child and Youth Protection Center, physical abuse was the most common complaint (53.4 percent), followed by neglect (16 percent), and abandonment (8.2 percent).

According to the law, all reports of child abuse must be investigated. A social worker is dispatched to the site, sometimes accompanied by police. When a serious child abuse case is confirmed, and if the parents are unable to guarantee the safety of the child, the child is then removed and placed in a safe environment. According to the *Children's Welfare Law,* the protective custody may not exceed 72 hours without a direct court order. About 62 percent of the said 4,093 persons monitored by social workers received family counseling, of whom 10.3 percent were placed with relatives, temporary foster homes, or children's homes, and 13.5 percent in permanent foster care.

To further expedite the handling of child abuse cases, the government has set up a 24-hour "113" women's and children's protection hotline ——三婦幼保護專線 and a website 兒童保護網站 at *http://www.cbi.gov.tw* in 2001. In addition to accepting reports on child abuse cases and providing counseling on child protection, the hotline and website also offer information on foster homes, child adoption, parent-child relationships, missing children, and husband-wife relationships.

Childcare

The demand for childcare has risen rapidly in the ROC with the increase of single parent families and families with both parents working outside the home. The *Children's Welfare Law* and its enforcement rules, the *Nursery Establishment Measures* 托兒所設置辦法 and the *Foster Care Measures* 兒童寄養辦法 mandate the establishment of child welfare centers in all cities and counties in Taiwan. As of June 2001, 27 child welfare centers served the Taiwan area, while 43 homes for abandoned children and orphans cared for more than 2,400 children. In addition,

there were 295 public nurseries, approximately 2,995 private nurseries, and nearly 95 community nurseries serving nearly 310,000 children in the Taiwan area as of December 2000. Full-day childcare centers must meet legal standards for basic facilities, personnel qualifications, space, and number of staff. To accommodate children from low-income families in daycare centers, local governments pay all or part of the tuition fees for these children. In addition, a growing number of private corporations and government organizations now provide nurseries for the children of employees.

To relieve the financial burden of parents whose children attend private nurseries, the government began in September 2000 to grant educational vouchers 幼兒教育券 to children aged between five and six attending private nurseries for the last year in the pre-school education. Parents of such children are eligible to apply for US$160 for each child in each semester. Every child is entitled to apply for this subsidy twice in a lifetime for a total of US$320. By the end of September 2001, more than 170,000 children have been granted such a subsidy.

In view of the great number of parents who send their children under three years of age to babysitters, the central government has entrusted local governments and several colleges and universities to hold babysitter training programs. The skills of these trained babysitters are evaluated after the program is completed to further ensure the quality of their services. From March 1998 when the first skill evaluation was conducted through the end of 2000, a total of 15,874 babysitters have passed the evaluation and obtained the permits to work as qualified babysitters.

To match the schedules of working mothers, some elementary schools hold after-school classes for their students. In Taipei City, 76, or 51 percent, among the 140 public and ten private elementary schools held such classes in the second semester of school year 2000. In total, 645 classes were opened to 13,316 students after school.

Juvenile Services

As of December 2000, Taiwan's population aged 12 to 17 totaled 2.03 million. Most ROC citizens graduate from the nation's nine-year compulsory education system by age 15. These young people then have several options, such as entering senior high school or senior vocational school (see Chapter 17, Education) or looking for employment.

Juvenile delinquency is still a major problem in Taiwan, although both the number of juvenile crime suspects and the juvenile crime rate have been decreasing annually in the past decade. The MOI's National Police Administration 內政部警政署 (NPA) statistics indicate that 9.99 percent of all crime suspects in 2000 were juveniles between the ages of 12 and 17, down from 17.8 percent in 1992. Accordingly, the juvenile crime rate has also been reduced from 1,311 per 100,000 juveniles in 1992 to 883 per 100,000 in 2000. Burglary, violent crimes, and drug violations dominated juvenile delinquencies in 2000. In percentage terms, the arrests were 58.73, 8.76 and 10.47, respectively. The NPA reports that in 2000, police charged 49,797 people with drug violations, of which 30.17 percent were young people between the ages of 12 and 23.

Campaign Against Drug Abuse

To combat drug abuse and drug-related crimes, the government has mobilized the police and the military to protect the island from the influx of illegal drugs, as almost all drugs used on the island come from overseas. In addition to law enforcement agencies, customs authorities, and the judiciary, agencies working in such diverse areas as health, education, finance, and agriculture also attack this problem. Advertisements are run by the government to convince youngsters to stay away from drugs. Today, drug violations have gradually decreased in the ROC.

To curb drug-related crimes that are increasingly organized and high-tech, *Money Laundering Control Law* 洗錢防制法 was promulgated on October 23, 1996. *Narcotics Elimination Act* 肅

清煙毒條例 was also revised and renamed *Law for the Control of Narcotics* 毒品危害防制條例 in May 1998.

In an effort to effectively eradicate rampant smuggling, the Coast Guard Administration 海岸巡防署 was set up under the Executive Yuan on February 1, 2000. The administration is responsible for law enforcement at shore and coastal areas of Taiwan. In view of the worsening drug abuse problem at pubs and Internet cafes, the government has launched a "spring breeze campaign" 春風專案 to urge the young people to stay away from drugs and investigate the sources of such drugs as MDMA and FM2, which were frequently used by the youth.

After President Chen Shui-bian took office in May 2000, the Narcotics Endangerment Prevention Program 毒品危害防制方案 was applied to all levels of the government. Significant results have been achieved since then, and the ROC was deleted from the blacklist of drug transshipment countries by the US State Department in March 2000.

Youth Counseling and Guidance

Young people in need have readily available counseling and psychiatric services for youths at community health centers and psychiatric health clinics at major hospitals. Under the *Youth Welfare Law* 少年福利法, local governments have worked with private organizations to set up 24 counseling and educational centers, 35 youth welfare service centers, ten advice centers, 18 emergency short-term shelters, and three halfway schools around the island that provide youths with counseling, psychiatric advice, emergency aid, school and employment assistance, and recreational opportunities.

Hotlines in northern, central, and southern Taiwan also serve people in need. One such hotline, named "Teacher Chang" 張老師, was set up by the China Youth Corps (see inset) in 1969, as a free counseling service that recruits volunteers from all walks of life to provide phone counseling to youths.

Rewriting the Law

The *Law Governing the Disposition of Juvenile Cases* 少年事件處理法, first promulgated in 1962 and amended in 1980, was further amended in October 1997. The revised law strengthens the protective and counseling functions of the judicial system for juveniles and provides for juvenile courts. The law empowers judges to sentence parents or legal guardians of convicted juvenile offenders to between eight and 50 hours of parental counseling and instruction. The judges are also allowed to order juveniles to work or to remand them to the appropriate reformatory or welfare institutions after they are released from detention or parole. Juveniles who commit misdemeanors will have the offenses struck from their records two years after their sentences are served, after the completion of three years of probation, or when no trial is deemed necessary.

Teenage Prostitution

According to the *Criminal Code* 刑法, any person who has sexual intercourse with an individual aged 14 or under is guilty of statutory rape and is subject to a mandatory sentence of at least five years' imprisonment. A person who has sex with an adolescent aged 15 or 16 is also guilty of rape and must be sentenced to one to seven years in jail. But these provisions are based on the condition that a complaint must be filed either by the victim or the victim's guardian, not just by the public prosecutor.

In July 1995, the Legislative Yuan passed the *Child and Youth Sexual Transaction Prevention Act* 兒童及少年性交易防制條例. This law targets teenage prostitution, supplementing the *Criminal Code* with respect to sexual exploitation of adolescents. Pursuant to this law, public prosecutors can now independently press charges against pimps or patrons. The act stipulates that a sexual patron of a prostitute aged under 16 can be sentenced to a maximum of three years' imprisonment and a maximum fine of US$3,202. Patrons of prostitutes aged 16 or 17 are subject to the same fine but no imprisonment. Pimps can

be sentenced to life imprisonment and fined US$640,410.

Halfway houses provide rescued adolescent prostitutes with shelter, food, clothing, medical care, and counseling. In Taipei City, teenage prostitutes are sent to the Occupation Training Center for Women at the Taipei Municipal Kuangtzu Po Ai Institution 臺北市立廣慈博愛院. Its counterpart in Kaohsiung City and County is the 802 Military General Hospital 國軍802總醫院. In Taiwan Province, teenage prostitutes are cared for by the Taiwan Provincial Yunlin Institute 臺灣省立雲林教養院 and the Taiwan Provincial Jen Ai Vocational Training Center 臺灣省立仁愛習藝中心. In all, these public facilities can accommodate about 230 people. Their stay in these institutions ranges from 72 hours to one year, depending on the court decision.

Several halfway houses are operated by private foundations, such as the Good Shepherd Sisters 善牧基金會, a Catholic foundation, and the Garden of Hope Foundation 勵馨基金會. Their capacity totals 75 people. In addition to this, they also accept teenage girls who are victims of incest and sexual abuse.

Women

Over the last decade, women's roles have been re-defined as more Chinese women have received higher education, joined the work force, begun to compete with men, and become financially independent. In 2000, there were 10.88 million women in the Taiwan area, compared to a male population of 11.39 million. On average, first-time brides were 26.1 years old, up from 25.8 in 1990. Almost half of Taiwan's women are regular wage earners and help support their families.

Women's Education

In ancient China, few women were taught to read and write. However, at the end of 2000, 45 percent of junior college graduates, 50 percent of university and college graduates, and 29 percent of graduate school graduates were women. Two decades earlier, the figures were 37.6, 36, and 16 percent, respectively. Women now have better educational opportunities, with female graduates from university, college and graduate school having increased by 50 percent in 20 years.

Women's Service Networks

In the last 15 years, numerous women's organizations have been established to help women solve problems and clarify liberalized roles for both men and women. The government has adopted measures to protect women's welfare by setting up a "113" women's and children's

An increasing number of women nowadays choose to attend vocational training programs and seek a second career after their children reach school age.

Drug Seizure and Persons Arrested for Drug Abuse

Item	1991	1992	1993	1994	1995	1996	1997	1998	1999	2000
Narcotics (kg)*	154.52	90.82	814.18	526.99	105.58	47.69	110.08	624	550.1	929.16
Number of Cases	3,072	4,701	14,269	11,608	5,896	6,065	7,474	31,307	40,028	41,556
Number of People Charged	4,436	6,378	19,997	16,145	8,394	8,458	10,045	41,927	50,504	49,797
Age 12-17	156	214	614	523	258	243	218	2,805	2,726	1,899
Age 18-23	896	1,200	3,603	2,791	1,350	1,282	1,510	10,402	13,897	13,125

Note:*Includes opium, poppy and seed, marijuana, morphine, cocaine, heroin, codeine, other derivatives, and synthetic drugs.

Source: National Police Administration, Ministry of the Interior

protection hotline 一一三婦幼保護專線, Women's Rights Promotion Committee 婦女權益促進委員會 under the Executive Yuan, Sexual Violation Prevention Committee 性侵害防治委員會 and Domestic Violence Prevention Committee 家庭暴力防治委員會 under the MOI, and Women's Welfare Section 婦女福利科 under the MOI's Department of Social Affairs. City governments also allocate specific budget items for women services. Many local governments, under the supervision of the MOI, have organized regional coalitions to help women generate public awareness of gender issues, and provided medical, legal, psychological, educational, financial, and vocational assistance. With financial assistance from the MOI, a Foundation of Women Rights Promotion and Development 財團法人婦女權益促進發展基金會 was set up in 1998 to promote women's rights and interests. One of the main tasks of this foundation is to revise and research women-related laws and regulations for the reference of the government when making new laws. Since its establishment, this foundation has successfully served as a communication channel among women's welfare agencies in the government and the private sector.

In 2000, the Taiwan area had 40 comprehensive welfare centers offering counseling, vocational training, seminars, and other services to disadvantaged women. Halfway houses and shelters for women numbered 26 that year, up 11 from 1994. With a maximum capacity of 518 persons, they accommodated 226 in 2000.

On May 24, 2000, the government promulgated a *Statute on Assisting the Families of Women in Difficult Circumstances* 特殊境遇婦女家庭扶助條例. Financial assistance to these women includes emergency living allowances, medical stipends, and children's nursery school subsidies. Services are available at every level of the government to help women who need to file a lawsuit. In accordance with the statute, the Ministry of Education offers subsidies to senior high school children of the women who encounter difficult situations, and the Council of Labor Affairs also grants low-interest loans for these women to start their own businesses.

Female Employment Assistance

From January 2000 to May 2001, 2,628 women completed training courses at Taiwan's 13 vocational training centers as full-time students, and 7,263 as evening-class students. The government paid all school-related expenses for the full-time students and subsidized half the expenses for the evening-class students. During the same period, another 7,770 completed vocational programs organized by local county or city governments.

From January 2000 to May 2001, the Employment and Vocational Training Administration of the Council of Labor Affairs 行政院勞工委

Taipei Women's Services Network

Legal Consultation
The Taipei Citizen's Service Center 臺北市政府聯合服務中心 2725-6168
Taipei Women Center 臺北婦女中心 2832-1174

Domestic Violence and Child Abuse
Domestic Violence Prevention Hotline 0800-024995, 0800-000600, 113

Emergency Hotline
Suicide Prevention Center 生命線 2505-9595

Rape
Hotline 080-024995, 080-000600

Halfway Houses
The Garden of Hope Foundation 勵馨基金會 2550-9595
Home of Wisdom (for single mother family) 慧心家園 2701-1828
Good Shepherd Sisters Social Welfare Services 善牧基金會 2381-5402

Family Problems
Taipei Family Education Service Center 臺北市社會教育館家庭教育服務中心 2578-1885
Song San Women and Family Service Center 松山婦女暨家庭服務中心 2768-5256
Mackay Counseling Center 馬偕協談中心 2571-8427

Psychological Problems
Peace Line of the Mackay Counseling Center 馬偕協談中心平安線 2531-8595, 2531-0505
Christian Cosmic Light Holistic Care Organization 財團法人基督教宇宙光全人關懷機構 2362-7278, 2363-2107

Unwed Mothers
Cathwel Service 財團法人天主教未婚媽媽之家 2311-0223
The Garden of Hope Foundation 勵馨基金會 2550-9595
Christian Salvation Service 財團法人台北市基督徒救世會社會福利事業基金會 2729-0265

Forced Labor
ECPAT-Taiwan 終止童妓協會 2369-5255
Taipei Women's Rescue Foundation 婦女救援基金會 2700-9595

Job Counseling
Foreign Contract Workers Counseling Center, Taipei 外勞諮詢服務中心 2564-3157
Public Employment Service Center, Bureau of Labor Affairs, Taipei City Government
臺北市政府勞工局國民就業輔導中心 2594-2277

Vocational Training
Taiwan Women's Development Association 臺灣婦女展業協會 2369-8959
Vocational Training Center, Bureau of Labor Affairs, Taipei City Government
臺北市政府勞工局職業訓練中心 2872-1940

Divorcées and Widows
The Warm Life Association for Women 晚晴婦女協會 2708-0126
Song De Women Service Center 松德婦女服務中心 2759-9176
Single Parent Service Center 單親家庭服務中心 2558-0170

Foreign Brides
Pearl S. Buck Foundation 賽珍珠基金會 2704-1556
Rerum Novarum Center 新事社會服務中心 2397-1933
Taipei Pearl S. Buck Association 賽珍珠協會 2732-5349

Note: These telephone numbers are staffed by personnel who do not necessarily speak English.

Prevention of Sexual Assault and Domestic Violence

Under the provisions of the *Sexual Assault Prevention Law* 性侵害犯罪防治法 in January 1997, the Sexual Violation Prevention Committee 性侵害防治委員會 of the Ministry of the Interior has been working with hospitals, law firms, police stations, and private social welfare organizations to set up an integrated protection network for the victims of sexual assault. The services offered by the network include legal assistance, counseling, and emergency shelters. In 2000, the number of sexual assault cases handled by the police stations around the island was 2,219. In accordance with the *Regulations on the Use and Management of the Files on Sexual Assaulters* 性侵害加害人檔案資料管理及使用辦法, the government has set up a national DNA database of the offenders. In 2000, the files of 1,298 assaulters were established in the database.

In June 1998, the ROC government promulgated the *Domestic Violence Prevention Law* 家庭暴力防治法. To encourage domestic violence victims to seek professional assistance, the government enacted the civil protection order in June 1999. As of the end of 2000, a total of 13,691 petitions under the protection order had been filed, and 8,493 orders had been issued by the judicial departments at all levels of the government. A Domestic Violence Prevention Committee 家庭暴力防治委員會, established in April 1999, assists county/city governments to set up domestic violence prevention centers around the island. To better protect minors from domestic violence, special visitation centers have been set up in 25 county/city governments in order to supervise and arrange visits by the family members to minor victims. Resources, such as judicial, police, medical, educational, and volunteer service organizations, are integrated into an effective prevention system. Brochures on domestic violence and the civil protection orders were distributed to inform the public of available assistance provided by the government. In view of the increasing number of foreign and mainland brides, the Ministry of the Interior has solicited opinions from relevant government agencies and convened special meetings to formulate measures to solve the problem of domestic violence in families with intercultural marriages. Brochures on relevant information were also translated into Indonesian, Thai, and Vietnamese for the reference of the foreign brides from those countries.

員會職業訓練局 provided job placement assistance to 77,893 women, 3,751 people over 45, 2,900 handicapped, 3,754 aborigines, and 75 people from low-income households.

Divorce

During the 1980s, an increasing number of women in Taiwan began to earn their own paychecks. The experiences of women working outside the home have allowed them greater access to information and ideas about alternative lifestyles. Hence, their growing economic independence gives them more freedom to reject dysfunctional marriages. Data released by the Department of Population 戶政司 under the MOI indicate that the divorce rate in the Taiwan area has more than quadrupled in the last 25 years. The divorce rate was 2.38 couples per 1,000 people in 2000, compared to 0.37 in 1970, and 0.77 in 1980. However, the marriage rate showed only a slight overall increase, from 7.50 per

1,000 people in 1970 to 9.68 in 1980, and then back to 8.25 by 2000.

The Warm Life Association for Women 晚晴婦女協會 has been working to eliminate discrimination against divorced women and promoting their equality under the law. Founded in Taipei in 1988, Warm Life now has branches in Taichung and Kaohsiung. The organization provides professional legal advice, psychological counseling, and telephone hotlines in Taipei, Taichung, and Kaohsiung with emergency counseling for women in dysfunctional marriages or divorce.

Rewriting the Law

Many women's groups have lobbied lawmakers to change Book IV of the *Civil Code* 民法, which concerns family matters. This section of the *Civil Code* went into effect in May 1931 and was only partially revised in 1985. It covers divorce-related issues, such as child custody,

China Youth Corps

The China Youth Corps 中國青年救國團 (CYC) is a non-government organization which guides youth in their growth and development through various activities. Established in 1952, the CYC has a counseling hotline, and holds lectures and seminars to educate youth. Its most popular activities are the outdoor recreational programs during summer and winter vacations, designed for teenagers and young adults.

The organization also sponsors youth good will missions around the world to broaden young people's perspectives. Since July 1992, the CYC has organized youth cultural and education exchanges with the Chinese mainland. From November 2000 to July 2001, 86 ROC youths traveled to the mainland in four CYC groups, and 133 young mainlanders came to visit the ROC.

Young Chinese who were born overseas and foreign youth are included in CYC programs. During summer vacations, youth of Chinese descent can come to Taiwan to learn Chinese language, culture, and customs. In addition, young foreigners are invited to Taiwan for cultural and academic exchanges with their Chinese counterparts.

These cross-strait and intercultural exchanges are either partially or completely funded by such government agencies as the Ministry of Education 教育部, Overseas Chinese Affairs Commission 僑務委員會, Mainland Affairs Council 行政院大陸委員會, and Ministry of Foreign Affairs 外交部.

---

child support and alimony, and the division of property.

On September 6, 1996, several landmark revisions were made to Book IV by the Ministry of Justice 法務部. Article 1051, which automatically gave the father custody in the case of divorce by mutual consent, was struck from the books. Article 1055 was amended to stipulate that, when a court is ruling on a divorce, it must do so in the interest of any children involved, weigh all circumstances, and take into consideration all interview reports from social workers. Article 1089 was amended to give both parents equal priority in parental rights and obligations to minor children, and gave the court—rather than the father—final say in resolving disputes. This revision was crucial to filling in the legal void left after the Council of Grand Justices 大法官會議 ruled on September 23, 1994, that the original wording of Article 1089 giving fathers priority in the enforcement of parental rights violated the ROC Constitution.

Changes were also made with regard to property rights. Prior to the 1985 revision of the *Civil Code,* any property registered under a married woman's name belonged to her husband. The 1985 revision gave the wife full rights over property registered under her name, but these rights were extended only to women who married after the revision came into effect. The September 6, 1996, amendments extended this right retroactively to all married women, regardless of marriage date.

Since many social problems are generated by unhealthy families where unhappy married couples are kept together by the strict conditions required for getting a divorce, the Executive Yuan on November 7, 2001, passed the draft of several revisions in Book IV of the *Civil Code.* The revisions allow couples that do not live together for up to five years to file for a divorce, and grant the party mainly responsible for a broken marriage the right to apply for a divorce. According to current articles, only the party not at fault is allowed to plea for a divorce.

The Elderly

Welfare for the elderly is defined by the MOI as providing basic subsistence aid and health care to poor and helpless senior citizens. The government encourages elderly people to live with or near their children. In-home care is provided for senior citizens who live by themselves and have difficulties in performing everyday activities.

As the average life expectancy is 78.3 and 72.6 years in 2000 for women and men, respectively, elderly people comprise a growing proportion of the population. In December 2000, 8.62 percent of the population was over 65. With the aging population, there will be proportionally fewer wage earners to provide for the elderly (see Chapter 2, People, and Chapter 15, Public Health).

Elderly Pensions

Elderly residents of Keelung City, Ilan County, Hsinchu City and County, Miaoli County, Pingtung County, Hualien County, Kinmen County, and Lienchiang County benefit

A complete welfare system for the elderly in Taiwan has enabled older people to enjoy better life after retirement.

from organized pension systems. Residents of these areas who are 65 years of age or older and do not receive other forms of pension or subsidy from the government are entitled to a pension ranging from US$96 to US$192 per month, depending on the county or city of residence. This welfare policy is budgeted separately by each county or city government and is not universal throughout the Taiwan area.

Elderly Daycare

Daycare for the elderly has become more important as women enter the job market. In May 1988, the Taipei City Government 臺北市政府 established the Neihu District Elderly Service Center 內湖老人服務中心, Taiwan's first daycare center for people over 65. By the end of 2000, seven additional daycare centers similar to the Neihu center were set up in Taipei. Now, these centers and the Taipei Municipal Kuangtzu Po Ai Institution 臺北市立廣慈博愛院 together can accommodate 225 people per day. These centers conduct regular physical checkups and provide breakfast, lunch, and entertainment during working hours on weekdays and Saturdays. Similar institutions are now operating throughout the Taiwan area.

Nearly 4,500 senior-citizen recreation centers and organizations such as the Evergreen Academy 長青學苑, Community Longevity 社區長壽俱樂部, and Pine Clubs 老人文康中心 serve senior citizens and provide activities, such as folk dancing, Chinese "shadowboxing" 太極拳, folk music, opera, chess, and handicrafts. In 2000, 48,185 people were enrolled in classes provided by the 303 Evergreen Academies. Lung-shan Elderly Service Center 龍山老人服務中心, opened in Taipei in June 1996, is the first service center for the elderly operated by the private sector using government facilities. It is expected that future centers will follow this model.

For the elderly who are not able to leave the house, the Ministry of the Interior has provided subsidies to county/city governments and urban/rural township administrative offices to set up support centers for in-home care. As of the end

of 2000, a total of 105 support centers had been established around the island. To improve the quality of services to the elderly who are being attended at home, local governments have held nursing skill training programs for family members of the elderly. In addition, 196 medical skill training courses have also been held to train professional caretakers and relieve the burden of the families of the elderly. A total of 5,397 persons have attended these courses, and 5,342 are currently serving as in-home caretakers.

Independent Housing

Although Taiwan's 616 retirement and nursing homes accommodated over 28,376 elderly people by May 2001, there is a desperate shortage of housing for elderly people. The private Kaohsiung County Senior Citizens' Apartments 崧鶴樓, which began operating in July 1995, has set the example for residential complexes exclusively for senior citizens. This facility has a 350-person capacity. Other similar apartments include the Wuku Apartment Building for the Elderly in Taipei County 台北縣五股老人公寓 and the Evergreen Apartment in Tainan City 台南市長青公寓.

In Taipei City, the Yangming Apartment Building for the Elderly 陽明老人公寓 began operation in November 1998. The building provides living quarters for about 120 people, and includes small single- and double-occupancy residential units, indoor recreational facilities, and plenty of outdoor space. Only people who are over 65, healthy, and able to handle daily life qualify for residency. The planning of Chulun 朱崙, another similar building, is underway.

In addition, the self-paid nursing home in Taipei's Wenshan District 文山區 serves 370 old people who are able to care for themselves. Two other such facilities, one in Mucha 木柵 and one in Yangmingshan 陽明山, will serve an additional 1,168 elderly people.

The Disabled

As of 2000, a total of 711,064 people held Handicapped Certificates 身心障礙手冊 in the Taiwan

area, up 9.58 percent from the previous year's figure. In 2001, the ROC government allocated about US$52.58 million for welfare services for disabled people. This amount does not include the money spent by local governments on the handicapped. In 2000, the central government subsidized US$240.74 million to local governments to help the disabled by giving them a living allowance, nursing and medical stipends, and payments for supplementary instruments. Starting in 2001, local governments must collect this money themselves.

In accordance with the *Protection Law for the Handicapped and Disabled* 身心障礙者保護法, a Protection Committee for the Handicapped and Disabled 身心障礙者保護委員會 was set up under the MOI in October 2000. By April 2001, the committee had convened six regular meetings to promote the protection of rights and interests of the disabled. This protection law stipulates that welfare services must be provided for the autistic and for people with serious facial injuries or major organ malfunctions. The law also states that all private enterprises with more than 100 employees must hire at least one dis-

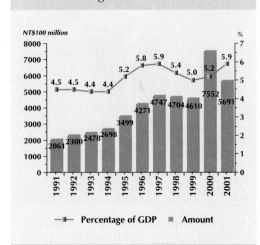

Social Welfare Expenditures
(Including Retirement Pension)

NT$100 million

Percentage of GDP: 4.5, 4.5, 4.4, 4.4, 5.2, 5.8, 5.9, 5.4, 5.0, 5.2, 5.9

Amount: 2061, 2300, 2478, 2698, 3499, 4271, 4747, 4704, 4610, 7552, 5691

(1991, 1992, 1993, 1994, 1995, 1996, 1997, 1998, 1999, 2000, 2001)

—■— Percentage of GDP   ■ Amount

Source: Directorate-General of Budget, Accounting and Statistics

abled worker. Government offices, public schools, and public enterprises with 50 or more employees must hire the disabled as 2 percent of their employees.

In 2000, the Department of Social Affairs of the MOI indicated that 8,388 private or government employers in Taiwan were subject to the provisions of the law. About 37,662 disabled people had been hired as of January 2001, with all employers having met or exceeded the minimum requirements.

Employers who do not meet the quota must pay US$507 every month for each handicapped person they have not yet hired into a Special Account for Handicapped Welfare 身心障礙者就業金專戶 set up and monitored by the Social Services Department 社會局 of the county or city where the employer is located. In January 2001, the Taipei City Special Account had a net balance of US$176 million. Employers who fail to pay the fine are prosecuted.

The money in this special account is used to make work places more accessible to disabled people, to pay the full salaries of disabled employees during their first three months of probationary employment, and to underwrite half the salary of each disabled employee who is hired after an employer has already met his quota.

Vocational Training

Several consulting service centers around Taiwan handle telephone consultations, correspondence management, one-on-one sessions, and interviews for disabled people who wish to take classes, receive special medical care, or seek employment. The centers also conduct seminars, recreational activities, and social gatherings. Thirty-eight public and private vocational training institutions for the disabled provide classes in practical skills to help disabled people lead independent lives.

The first civil service examination for disabled people took place in July 1996. The exam was open exclusively to disabled people between the ages of 18 and 55 with educational backgrounds from junior high school to graduate school. A total of 779 passed the exam and were admitted into the civil service.

Education of the Disabled

Disabled people are integrated into regular educational institutions as much as possible. Many regular schools, from the elementary to the senior high and senior vocational level, offer special classes for the disabled. In the 2000-2001 school year, the Taiwan area had 23 government-established special education schools exclusively for handicapped students (see Chapter 17, Education).

Indigenous Peoples

The welfare of Taiwan's various indigenous peoples, who numbered 413,519 in May 2001, is among the top priorities of the ROC social welfare system. Several new government organizations to serve the aborigine population were created in recent years. On March 16, 1996, the Taipei City Government established its Council of Aboriginal Affairs 原住民事務委員會. On December 10 of the same year, a cabinet-level Council of Indigenous Peoples 行政院原住民族委員會 was established under the Executive Yuan. On July 1, 1997, the Kaohsiung City Government also set up the Commission of Indigenous Affairs 原住民事務委員會. The *Additional Articles of the ROC Constitution* requires the government to protect the aborigines' rights and to assist and encourage them in many areas (see Chapter 2, People).

The government provides low-interest housing loans to aborigines. Under this program, aborigines can borrow up to US$70,445 at an annual interest of 5 percent, repayable over a 20-year period. Aborigines are accorded special status when taking entrance exams for high school and above. One percent of the total number of students recruited by these schools is reserved for aborigines. An extra 25 percent is added to the exam score of aborigines participating in the senior high school and senior vocational high school entrance examinations. Aboriginal students who participate in the college

and university entrance examinations receive an additional 25 percent on their final test scores. There are also scholarships for aborigines from low-income families, and tuition is waived for aborigines who take part in government-sponsored vocational training programs. They also receive a monthly US$384 living-expense stipend from the Council of Labor Affairs. The Council of Aboriginal Affairs also provides an additional US$96 monthly stipend to those who receive training for three months or more. A special civil-service examination for aborigines is administered biennially. By the end of 2000, the exam had been held a total of 20 times, with 1,856 aborigines passing.

Low-income Households

The ROC government provides special subsidies and assistance to low-income individuals and families, including job placement, educational aid for children, stipends during traditional festivals, and child and maternal nutrition programs, as well as other cash and noncash benefits. Most of the programs base eligibility on individual, household, or family income, and a few offer help on the basis of presumed need. To determine eligibility, the government sets the "monthly minimum expenses" based on the consumer price index and variations in regional income distribution each fiscal year. This figure differs from area to area: for example, for fiscal year 2002, the Taipei City monthly minimum expenses is US$415, Kaohsiung City is US$314, Taiwan Province is US$265, and Kinmen County is US$189. Families whose average monthly income is below this amount are classified as low-income families. In 2001, only 156,134 people (66,467 households), or 0.7 percent of the population, were considered members of low-income families.

Starting in July 1993, the ROC government began providing a monthly subsidy to the low-income elderly throughout the Taiwan area. The amount of this subsidy does not vary from locality to locality. All ROC citizens over the age of 65, whose average family income is less than or equal to 1.5 times the minimum monthly expenses, are qualified to receive a monthly subsidy of US$192. Elderly people whose average family income is between 1.5 and 2.5 times the minimum expense are eligible for a monthly relief subsidy of US$96. Through December 2000, approximately US$3.33 million had been distributed to more than 204,000 elderly people around the island.

Some low-income families with children qualify for an additional monthly subsidy, which varies depending on the locality. Children of families whose average monthly income does not exceed the minimum are entitled to a monthly subsidy. In Taiwan Province, the subsidy is US$58 per child, with each household limited to subsidies for two children. In Kaohsiung City, each child also qualifies for a monthly payment of US$58. In Taipei City, households with children under the age of 18 are eligible for a monthly subsidy of US$186 for each child if the average monthly income for the family is between US$62 and US$248. That same subsidy is decreased to US$168 if the family monthly income totals between US$248 and US$341, and to US$32 if the income ranges between US$341 and US$416.

The disabled from low-income families are eligible to a monthly subsidy ranging from US$64 to US$192 according to the financial condition of the family and the severity of the handicapped condition. In the latter half of 1999 and in 2000, the government distributed nearly US$191 million to more than 3.2 million disabled people.

Volunteer Services

Volunteers play an extremely important role in the ROC's social service system. On January 20, 2001, the ROC government promulgated the *Volunteer Service Law* 志願服務法 to better integrate available manpower at all levels of society and make the best use of all social resources.

Beginning July 1997, the National Youth Commission (NYC) under the Executive Yuan 行政院青年輔導委員會 initiated a program to recruit people from 15 to 45 years of age for volunteer services. Schools, communities, enterprises, and social service organizations are also encouraged to recruit volunteers within their own institutions to be organized into volunteer service groups with at least 30 persons in each group. These groups in the same district were then further combined into volunteer centers. As of June 2001, three such volunteer centers have been set up in eastern, central, and northern Taiwan respectively.

To encourage the participation of more youth to participate in volunteer service, the NYC held a Youth Volunteer Day 青年志工日 in March 2000. More than 100 volunteer service organizations were invited to present the results of their work. In 2000, the NYC invited more than 31,000 students from over 900 volunteer service clubs at colleges and universities to visit communities in remote and aboriginal residence areas. In the same year, approximately 40,000 volunteers from more than 200 volunteer service organizations were also invited by the NYC to render services in such areas as environmental protection, youth counseling, aboriginal welfare, and community development. As an effort to continue its care for the victims of the major earthquake in 1999, the NYC sent more than 1,000 volunteers to the earthquake-stricken areas and visited over 100,000 victims in March 2000.

The ROC's complete network of volunteer services is a joint effort of the government and the private sector. One of the largest charity organizations in Taiwan today is the Buddhist Compassion Relief Tzu Chi Foundation 佛教慈濟基金會. Established in 1966 by Master Cheng Yen 證嚴法師, the organization has been involved in charity, medicine, education, culture, international relief, bone marrow donation, environmental protection, and community services. This non-profit organization now has offices in 28 countries and four million supporters around the world. In the United States, there are seven Tzu Chi Chapters with a total of 48 offices across the country.

Related Websites

1. Ministry of the Interior: *http://www.moi.gov.tw*
2. Children's protection website: *http://www.cbi.gov.tw*
3. Ministry of Education: *http://www.edu.tw*
4. Taipei City Government: *http://www.taipei.gov.tw*
5. National Police Administration: *http://www.npa.gov.tw*
6. Coast Guard Administration: *http://www.cga.gov.tw*
7. China Youth Corps: *http://www.cyc.org.tw*
8. Ministry of Justice: *http://www.moj.gov.tw*
9. Council of Labor Affairs: *http://www.cola.gov.tw*
10. Council of Indigenous Peoples: *http://www.apc.gov.tw*
11. National Youth Commission: *http://www.nyc.gov.tw*
12. Buddhist Compassion Relief Tzu Chi Foundation: *http://www.tzuchi.org.tw*
13. Foundation of Women Rights Promotion and Development: *http://www.wrp.org.tw*

With a joint effort, Taipower and the people of Republic of China are continuing to develop our land into a place of vigor, brightness, and prosperity.

TAIWAN POWER COMPANY
REPUBLIC OF CHINA
242 Roosevelt Rd., Sec. 3, Taipei, Taiwan
TEL:886-2-23651234/ FAX:886-2-23650037
h t t p : / / w w w . t a i p o w e r . c o m . t w

拒絕仿冒

DON'T COUNTERFEIT ; PROTECT INVENTIONS

Protecting Intellectual
Property Rigths
is Promoting National
Economic Strength.

保護創作

中華民國全國工業總會保護智慧財產權委員會
INTELLECTUAL PROPERTY PROTECTION COMMITTEE, R.O.C.
台北市復興南路一段390號12樓 TEL:886-2-27060223 FAX:886-2-2704-2477
12TH FL., 390 FU HSING S. RD., SEC. 1, TAIPEI, TAIWAN, R.O.C.
http://www.cnfi.org.tw   e-mail:intell@cnfi.org.tw

20 Labor

The rights and interests of Taiwan's skilled and productive workforce are well protected by several labor laws.

What's New

1. Emphasis on occupational safety
2. New policy on foreign workers
3. EDAC conclusions on employment issues

The ROC's economy over the past 50 years has benefitted from a well-educated and highly motivated work force, especially in the areas of science, technology, and high value-added manufacturing. The ROC has a diversified and skilled work force of roughly 9.8 million people. Approximately 6.7 million are employees and the rest are either self-employed or have some other working status.

The government has sought to maintain a productive and qualified work force, so legislative priorities have focused on the rights of workers, workers' welfare, gender equality, labor-management relations, safety and health, and appropriate quotas for foreign workers. The minimum monthly wage is currently US$507.

Labor Rights

Legal Framework

The basis of workers' welfare is prescribed in Article 153 of the Constitution: "The State, in order to improve the livelihood of laborers and farmers and to improve their productive skill, shall enact laws and carry out policies for their protection." Under this constitutional provision, several significant laws have been passed to guarantee workers' rights.

Labor Standards Law

The key labor law in the ROC, the 1984 *Labor Standards Law* 勞動基準法, defines such terms as worker, employer, wages, and contract. It delineates the rights and obligations of workers and employers; prescribes the minimum requirements for labor contracts; and has provisions on wages, work hours, leave, and the employment of women and children. Since December 1998, the

law has been extended to cover all employer-employee relationships, except in a few selected work categories such as private school teachers and workers, athletes and coaches of professional sports, lawyers, and accountants.

The *Labor Standards Law* also prohibits unreasonable work hours and forced labor and grants workers the right to receive compensation for occupational injuries and layoffs, as well as a pension upon retirement. Effective January 1, 2001, the maximum number of work hours is 44 regular hours per week, and no more than 84 hours every two weeks.

Employment Services Act

The *Employment Services Act* 就業服務法, promulgated on May 8, 1992, guarantees equal job opportunities and access to employment services, with the objective of balancing manpower supply and demand, efficiently using human resources, and establishing an employment information network. To protect workers' rights during times of economic slowdown, the act stipulates that the central government should encourage management, labor unions, and workers to negotiate work hour reductions, wage adjustments, and in-service training to avoid layoffs.

Labor Force Participation Rate in Major Countries and Areas

Countries/Areas	1997	Unit: % 2000
ROC	58.3	57.7
Canada	64.9	65.9
Germany	57.4	57.5*
Hong Kong	61.2	60.7
Japan	63.7	62.4
South Korea	62.2	60.7
Singapore	64.2	68.6
United Kingdom	62.6	62.9*
United States	67.1	67.2

* 1999 figures

Source: Directorate-General of Budget, Accounting and Statistics

Work Hours and Salaries		
	Industrial Sector	*Service Sector*
Employees on Payroll	2,959,800	2,867,100
Average Monthly Earnings	US$1,263	US$1,421
Average Monthly Hours	196.9	183.3

Source: Directorate-General of Budget, Accounting and Statistics, 2000

The *Employment Services Act* also regulates public and private employment service agencies, and encourages employment guidance for the handicapped, indigenous peoples, low-income families, female heads of households, the elderly, and the unemployed. Public agencies compile and analyze labor market information on wage fluctuations and manpower supply and demand, offer advice on professional training programs, and recommend jobs or training for the unemployed. These service agencies achieved a placement rate of 36.12 percent for job-seekers in 2000 and 34.21 percent in the first five months of 2001.

As of mid-2001, employment discrimination evaluation committees 就業歧視評議委員會 have been established under the *Employment Services Act* in Taipei, Kaohsiung, and 17 of Taiwan's 21 counties and cities. These committees, formed by government, labor, management representatives, scholars, and experts, ensure equal employment opportunities and determine whether discriminatory actions have been taken by an employer against an employee.

Protecting Labor Rights

Labor Insurance

The *Labor Insurance Act* 勞工保險條例 was promulgated in 1958 to provide insurance coverage

EDAC Conclusions on Employment Issues

A two-week Economic Development Advisory Conference 經濟發展諮詢委員會 was convened in August 2001 to resolve domestic issues arising from the global economic recession and the structural transformation of Taiwan's industry. Panel discussions were held on five different areas: cross-strait relations, employment, finance, investment environment, and industrial competitiveness. The panel on employment issues reached a consensus on the following:

- Flexible adjustment of work hours to allow for the effective utilization of human resources
- Relaxed work-hour restrictions on women
- Relaxed restrictions on wage arrears repayment for workers affected by company shutdowns
- Establishment of a personal account or annuity insurance system to replace the existing retirement system
- Establishment of a labor-management consultation and negotiation mechanism
- Formulation of a law to protect employees against mass dismissal and establishment of a mechanism for handling labor-management disputes
- Reasonable adjustment of the foreign workers' wages to reduce production costs
- Review of the foreign-labor policy to meet the demands of the business sector while considering job opportunities for domestic workers
- Strengthening of employment services measures
- Integration of vocational training resources and expansion of related programs
- Formulation of a single law on unemployment insurance
- Provision of relief aid in exchange for work by the unemployed
- Increase of job opportunities through the development of the tourism industry and information infrastructure projects
- Formulation of strategies to counter the unemployment problem that may arise after Taiwan's WTO accession

to workers in the private sector, including industrial workers, journalists, employees of nonprofit organizations, fishermen, persons receiving vocational training in institutes registered with the government, and members of unions. Teachers and employees working in government agencies who are not eligible for teachers' or civil servants' insurance are also covered under this law. When the labor insurance program was first launched in 1950 under provincial regulations, there were 554 insured units, with a total of 128,625 insured laborers in Taiwan. By April 2001, there were about 398,500 insured units, and the number of workers covered by the program had grown to approximately 7.85 million.

Labor insurance coverage consists of two types: ordinary labor insurance, with six kinds of benefits—maternity, injury and sickness, disability, old-age, death, and unemployment; and occupational injury insurance, with four kinds of benefits—injury and sickness, medical care, disability, and death. The *Labor Insurance Act* was revised in February 1995, with the transfer of medical care coverage to the National Health Insurance 全民健康保險 program (see section on

---

Duration of Paid Leave

Unit: working days, unless otherwise noted
Annual
  7 (1-3 years)
  10 (3-5 years)
  14 (5-10 years)
  14 plus 1 additional day for every additional year over 10 years to a maximum of 30 days
Maternity (weeks)
  8 (childbirth)
  4 (miscarriage)
Funeral
  3-8 (length of leave depends on worker's relationship to the deceased)
Wedding
  8

Health Insurance in Chapter 15, Public Health). Unemployment benefits, now available to selected categories of insured ROC workers, were incorporated in the labor insurance program in January 1999.

In 2000, the premium rate for ordinary labor insurance was 6.12 percent of the beneficiary's reported monthly insurance salary, which was

Women's rights in the workplace are better protected under the Gender Equality Employment Law *enacted in March 2002.*

limited to US$1,345 for the purpose of premium calculations. For insured persons not covered under the unemployment benefits program, the premium rate is 5.5 percent. The responsibility of paying for the premium is generally shared by employees, employers, and the government in the proportion 2:7:1. Occupational injury insurance premiums are paid by employers. The rates differ among the 52 categories of businesses covered, ranging from 0.08 percent to 3 percent of reported wages and averaging 0.34 percent. In May 2001, the labor insurance fund totaled US$14.3 billion, of which US$672 million was reserved for the occupational injury fund.

Occupational Safety and Health

The *Labor Safety and Health Law* 勞工安全衛生法 was revised and promulgated in 1991 to cover workers in mining and quarrying; manufacturing; construction; electricity, gas, and water; transportation; and other industries designated by the central authorities, including agriculture, forestry, fishery, and animal husbandry; restaurants and hotels; machinery and equipment rental and leasing; mass media services; and repair services. The amendments included many new requirements on the installation of safety and health equipment in work places, particularly at dockyards and fireworks factories. It also prohibited women and employees under the age of 16 from working in dangerous or harmful environments. Businesses with more than 300 workers at the same site are required to set up a medical center. For businesses engaged in potentially hazardous operations, the same requirement applies when the number of workers reaches 100. The Council of Labor Affairs is currently drafting a law to enhance measures to prevent occupational accidents and related diseases.

In 2000, the occupational accident rate in the ROC stood at 5.135 per 1,000 workers, with a mortality rate of 0.083 per 1,000 persons, up 0.354 percentage points from 1998. To prevent occupational diseases, 484 hospitals islandwide are authorized by the government to offer annual medical checkups for workers. In 2000, 88 percent of the 66,500 workers engaged in hazardous employment received medical examinations.

In 1992, the Council of Labor Affairs established the Institute of Occupational Safety and Health 勞工安全衛生研究所. The institute consists of five divisions: Occupational Safety, Occupational Hygiene, Method Development and Analysis, Occupational Medicine, and Occupational Safety and Health Exhibition. It surveys the work environment and conditions, evaluates occupational injuries and diseases, offers advice on their prevention, and conducts technological research on occupational safety and health management and personal protective equipment. The institute has seven domestic and foreign patents for the safety and protective equipment for workers, including items for the handicapped and a brakes-failure warning system. The institute also holds mobile exhibitions on occupational safety and health at vocational schools and industrial zones, which attracted over 700,000 visitors between May 2000 and June 2001.

Labor Inspections

The *Labor Inspection Law* 勞動檢查法 was promulgated on March 1993, to replace the *Factory Law* 工廠法. Labor inspections are conducted by the CLA and the Taipei and Kaohsiung city governments to guarantee workers' safety, rights, and interests in accordance with related labor laws.

These inspections cover health, safety, and insurance. The approval of labor inspectors is required before workers are allowed to work at potentially dangerous sites, including petroleum cracking plants; agrochemical, firework, and gunpowder manufacturing sites; designated locations with steam boilers and containers holding gas under high pressure; dangerous and

---

Vocational Training and Occupational Skill Testing

The ROC government encourages the development of skilled manpower in Taiwan through the Employment and Vocational Training Administration (EVTA). The EVTA plans and provides vocational training, skill testing, and employment services. It also trains supervisors and technical personnel for public and private training institutions. Each year, its 13 government-funded training centers offer entry-level and advanced courses to about 23,000 trainees in over one hundred occupational categories. The number of trainees totaled 417,600 between 1981 and 2000.

The EVTA assists large enterprises to set up training centers and helps trade associations establish on-the-job training programs for small and medium-sized enterprises. Its training service teams also assist the business sector in technical services, subsidies, tax exemptions, and other incentives. In addition, the EVTA offers vocational training to foreign workers employed by investors based overseas.

The CLA recently formulated a sustainable employment plan to counter the global economic recession and Taiwan's rising unemployment rate. The plan calls for the integration of public and private resources to create job opportunities and upgrade employment skills to meet the needs of economic development. By mid-June 2001, a total of 305 proposals from non-governmental and non-profit organizations throughout Taiwan had been approved, benefiting 7,000 people.

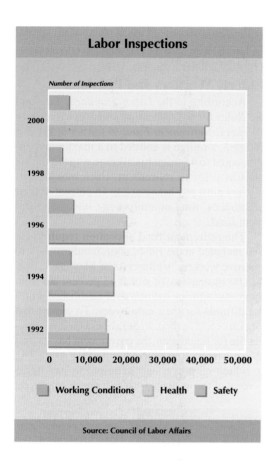

Labor Inspections

Number of Inspections

2000

1998

1996

1994

1992

0   10,000 20,000 30,000 40,000 50,000

■ Working Conditions   ■ Health   ■ Safety

Source: Council of Labor Affairs

In 2000, the CLA implemented a new policy of reducing the number of occupational fatalities by 40 percent over a four-year period. It also called for more frequent inspections of worksites where hazardous working conditions are prevalent and assistance for the businesses to establish a self-inspection mechanism. Its success has been reflected in the 11.3 percent decrease of occupational fatalities from 477 persons in 1999 to 423 in 2000.

Labor Unions and Industrial Relations

As of March 2001, a total of 1,128 industrial unions and 2,631 craft guilds had been formed, representing 2.87 million employees in Taiwan. Under the CLA's efforts to improve labor-management relations, 16,854 enterprises had established work rules as of March 2001. Of these, 1,150 had implemented stock option plans for their employees.

A revision of the *Labor Union Law* 工會法, the *Collective Agreement Law* 團體協約法, and the *Settlement of Labor Disputes Law* 勞資爭議處理法 are now awaiting legislative approval. The *Collective Agreement Law* will designate the labor union as the sole labor representative in the signing of labor-management agreement, which will promote cooperation and cover wages,

hazardous materials manufacturing and handling sites; and construction sites designated by the central authorities.

In 2000, Taiwan's 253 labor inspectors conducted nearly 39,000 inspections at 8.2 percent of the 276,700 enterprises on the CLA's inspection list. The CLA effectively utilizes its limited manpower by annually assessing the overall labor conditions and the occurrence of occupational accidents in its planning of special inspections for highly and potentially dangerous sites. Inspections are strengthened for workplaces where there is a potential occurrence of serious disasters, as well as locations where a fire, explosion, or leakage of hazardous materials has previously occurred.

Average Monthly Income per Industry in 2000	
	US$
Mining and Quarrying	1,394
Manufacturing	1,242
Electricity, Gas, and Water	2,869
Construction	1,245
Trade and Restaurants	1,211
Transportation, Storage, and Communications	1,671
Finance, Insurance, and Real Estate	1,844
Business Services	1,660
Social and Personal Services	1,356

Source: Directorate-General of Budget, Accounting and Statistics

Information and Service Centers

An islandwide network of 29 employee service centers offers career counseling, information on labor-management disputes, labor welfare, career planning, insurance, pensions, and labor education services to workers in the Taiwan area. Over 114,000 employees were served in 2000. Every city and county government in Taiwan also has a regional Labor Education Promotion Committee 勞工教育推行委員會 to offer labor training courses.

The CLA has a labor issues hotline for the Taiwan area [(02) 8770-1860, or toll free, 0800-211-459].

work hours, layoffs, pensions, compensation for occupational injuries, and procedures for labor complaints and disputes. As of March 2001, a total of 301 government and private businesses had entered into collective bargaining agreements with employees, and 2,057 companies had labor-management committees.

There were 2,321 labor disputes in the first quarter of 2001, a 33 percent increase compared to the same period of 2000. A total of 18,380 workers were involved, up 35.6 percent over the same period in 2000.

Elderly Workers and Pensions

According to the *Labor Standards Law* and the *Rules for the Allocation and Management of Workers' Retirement Fund* 勞工退休準備金提撥及管理辦法, a retiree is entitled to a maximum pension equal to 45 times his average wage in the six months prior to retirement. Each month, employers must pay between 2 to 15 percent of their employees' total monthly wage into the retirement fund.

The retirement fund allocation requirement was included in the 1984 *Labor Standards Law* to improve workers' welfare. As of May 2001, over 47,100 businesses, of which 43 percent are from the manufacturing industry, had established retirement funds for their employees. To ensure that workers receive their wages should their employers file for liquidation, the government has set up a Wage Arrears Repayment Fund 積欠工資墊償基金, to which employers are required to pay 0.025 percent of the insurance wages for each employee.

Counseling and service centers have been established around the island to offer legal information and mediate disputes for Taiwan's foreign workers.

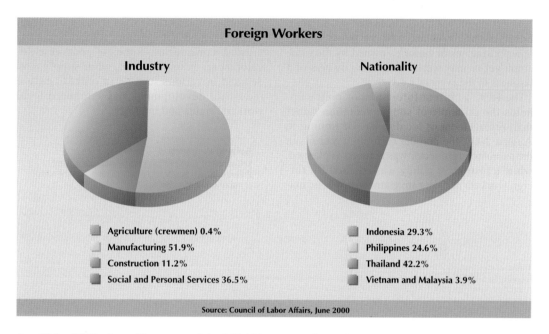

Foreign Workers

Industry

- Agriculture (crewmen) 0.4%
- Manufacturing 51.9%
- Construction 11.2%
- Social and Personal Services 36.5%

Nationality

- Indonesia 29.3%
- Philippines 24.6%
- Thailand 42.2%
- Vietnam and Malaysia 3.9%

Source: Council of Labor Affairs, June 2000

As of May 2001, about 93 percent of the 360,000 eligible firms in the Taiwan area were contributing to the fund and had set aside a total of US$126.8 million.

Foreign Workers

In 1990, the ROC liberalized its foreign labor policy to remedy a labor shortage. About 326,500 foreign workers were employed in Taiwan in 2000. As of May 2001, approximately 54 percent of these workers were employed in the manufacturing industry, and 11 percent were working in construction. Approximately 141,300 were from Thailand. About 104,000 foreign workers, mostly from Indonesia and the Philippines, were employed as nurses and care-providers. Another 8,700, mostly from the Philippines, were employed as domestic helpers in families with dependents under six or over 75 years of age.

The *Employment Services Act* covers the employment of foreign workers in nine occupational categories. Foreign workers can stay in Taiwan for a maximum period of two years. Employers may apply for a one-year extension of the work permits only once. An additional six months' extension is available under special circumstances for foreign workers engaged in major construction projects.

To protect the rights of legal foreign workers and help them adjust to life in Taiwan, 20 foreign worker counseling and service centers have been established islandwide. These centers offer information on pertinent laws and regulations, provide psychological counseling, and mediate disputes. Hotlines have also been set up to offer guidance and other services.

Almost all enterprises provide programs and services for foreign employees, such as insurance coverage under the government's labor insurance program and through private group insurance. Other programs and forms of assistance include recreational activities on weekends, cultural and recreation centers, counseling sessions, weekend religious activities, and Chinese language training.

With the recent slowdown in economic growth, the CLA now allows foreign workers to apply for a change of employer in the event that a company shuts down, suspends production, lays off employees, or automates production. Foreign employees may also be transferred to other businesses or factories owned by the same employer or may work for the new owners of a business in the event of a takeover.

The ROC's current foreign-labor policy upholds the principle of supplementation rather than replacement of local labor. Beginning in August 2000, the number of foreign recruits in the manufacturing sector was reduced as planned, while a restrictive policy was adopted for foreign workers in major investment projects, major public construction projects, and caretaking. When deemed appropriate, the policy is reviewed, considering domestic economic development, unemployment, labor supply, and demand in various sectors, in order to ensure industrial development and safeguard local workers' rights and interests.

Related Websites
1. Council of Labor Affairs: *http://www.cla.gov.tw*
2. Employment and Vocational Training Administration: *http://www.evta.gov.tw*

21
The Arts

Folk art by Taiwan's indigenous Ami people is displayed in the gallery of Asian artists at the Yingko Ceramics Museum.

What's New
1. Information updated
2. National Award for Arts
3. International art festivals

Traditional and contemporary, Eastern and Western, local and international—Taiwan's artists in both visual and performing arts are exploring styles across the spectrum, combining elements from different periods and traditions. In fact, one characteristic that marks the art of Taiwan today is an increasingly sophisticated and successful blending of seemingly incompatible genres.

Aboriginal Arts

While the culture of Han Chinese is dominant on Taiwan, the island is also enriched by the cultures of ten aboriginal peoples—the Atayal 泰雅族, Saisiyat 賽夏族, Ami 阿美族, Bunun 布農族, Tsou 鄒族, Rukai 魯凱族, Puyuma 卑南族, Paiwan 排灣族, Yami 雅美族, and Shao 邵族—whose ancestors arrived perhaps 15,000 years ago. Arts such as woodcarving, weaving, basketry, as well as ceremonial dances and songs, have long played a central role in aboriginal life, with each people developing their own distinct artistic style.

Recent years have seen a growing interest in preserving and developing the aboriginal arts. Tribal members themselves have been involved in a number of projects, such as recording their songs and dances, as have researchers and individuals in the Han Chinese community. The government is also making efforts to promote tribal culture. In the last few years, the Council for Cultural Affairs' annual National Festival of Culture and Arts 中華民國全國文藝季 has included performances, exhibitions and seminars on aboriginal arts.

A major contribution was made in 1994 by businessman Safe C.F. Lin 林清富, who established the Shung Ye Museum of Formosan Aborigines 順益臺灣原住民博物館 across the street from the National Palace Museum 國立故宮博物院. Housing a private collection, the four-floor museum is the first to be dedicated solely to Taiwan's native cultures. In addition to its displays of artifacts, costumes, musical instruments, household utensils, and weapons, the museum provides extensive information on aboriginal history, lifestyles, social relationships, religious beliefs, and customs.

The museum has also helped to promote research of Taiwan's indigenous peoples, including grants to Academia Sinica and to writers and filmmakers involved in recording aboriginal culture. It has also funded research projects at the University of California, Berkeley, and the University of Tokyo. In addition, the museum has provided money for university scholarships for aboriginal students.

Another museum introducing aboriginal civilization is the National Museum of Prehistory 國立臺灣史前博物館, situated adjacent to the Puyuma archeological site in Taitung County. Officially opened on July 10, 2001, the museum contains 14 exhibition rooms displaying Neolithic artifacts related to the natural history and prehistory of Taiwan, as well as the island's Austronesian-speaking people, who were closely connected to the island's aboriginal population. It is also devoted to conducting research that focuses on Taiwan's cultural past.

The collections at the Shung Ye Museum, the National Taiwan Museum 國立臺灣博物館, the museum of Academia Sinica's Institute of Ethnology 中央研究院民族學研究所博物館, the National Museum of Prehistory, and the National Museum of Natural Science 國立自然科學博物館 in Taichung provide good introductions to the artistic traditions of the various peoples.

Woodcarving

The Paiwan and Rukai, which may have once been a single people, are especially known for their woodcarvings. The homes of important members of the people, for example, are decorated with relief carvings of stylized human figures, zigzag or triangular patterns, and the hundred-pacer snake with its menacing diamond-shaped head. The snake is particularly prominent in Paiwan and Rukai art, being revered as the incarnation of tribal ancestors.

Woodcarving skills are also highly developed among the Yami, who live primarily on Orchid Island, off the southern coast of Taiwan. The Yami are best known for their sturdy handbuilt canoes, which can carry ten or more people and are made without nails or glue. They are decorated in delicately carved relief designs that feature a concentric sun-like motif and stylized human figures accented with spiral formations. The canoes are then painted white, red, and black, before undergoing an elaborate launching ceremony.

Weaving

Another art form central to aboriginal culture is weaving, which is especially well-developed among the Atayal. Using simple back-strap looms, Atayal women create rectilinear patterns of squares, diamonds, and triangles, using mostly red, blue, black, and white. Some designs also incorporate strings of thin shell beads or rows of small bronze bells.

Architecture

The aboriginal peoples also have unique architectural traditions. Two of the best places to view these traditions are at the privately run Formosan Aboriginal Cultural Village 九族文化村 located near Sun Moon Lake 日月潭 in central Taiwan, and the Taiwan Aboriginal Culture Park 臺灣原住民文化園區 in Pingtung County. Although commercialized and intended for tourists, both have sections that have carefully reproduced traditional homes of the different aboriginal peoples. Among the most interesting are Rukai houses, traditionally made of stacked slate, and Yami houses, which are situated partly underground as protection against typhoons.

Music and Dance

Dance and music are perhaps the richest legacies of Taiwan's native peoples. Communal dances, performed at regular ceremonies and rituals, consist mostly of simple but harmonious walking and foot-stomping movements, often performed in unison and accompanied by melodic choruses. The sound of small bells or other metal ornaments attached to the dancers' colorful costumes or to ankle bracelets add to the celebratory atmosphere.

Aboriginal dance rituals usually go on for several days and are performed in connection with specific customs or legends. The *Ilisin* spring festival of the Ami, for example, involves the annual rite of passage of the members of various age groups. The three-day *Pastáai* ceremony of the Saisiyat (the Ceremony of the Dwarfs 矮人祭), held every other year in the tenth lunar month, is performed to appease the legendary race of dwarfs who are said to have taught the Saisiyat people farming. The Yami on Orchid Island perform rituals every year to mark the launching of new boats and to celebrate the season of the flying fish, one of their staple foods. The latter ritual includes an impressive "hair dance," in which women swing their long hair back and forth.

Even more than dance, aboriginal music is intimately connected to nearly every aspect of tribal life, from daily chores to religious rites, and has been studied by ethnomusicologists and other scholars from around the world. The songs have been divided into four groups, according to theme: harvests, daily work, love, and tribal legends.

There are four types of aboriginal musical instruments: drums, simple stringed instruments, woodwind instruments (such as flutes), and other percussion instruments (rattles, wooden mortars and pestles). One interesting example is a kind of Jew's harp used by the Atayal, which consists of a piece of bamboo with one or more small metal strips that are played by moving a thread back and forth with the mouth. The Paiwan have a unique double-piped nose flute.

A number of efforts have been made in recent years to preserve tribal dance and music and introduce it to general audiences. The success of such efforts was evident at the 11th Golden

Melody Awards 金曲獎, the local equivalent of the US Grammy Awards, where aboriginal music stole the spotlight. Chen Chien-nien 陳建年, whose tribal name is Purdur, was selected best composer and best male performer at Taiwan's 2000 Golden Melody Awards, while the award for best new-comer went to 22-year-old Chih Hsiao-chun 紀曉君, whose Puyuma name is Samingad. The honor for the top folk album also went to an aborigine, the internationally known Ami singer, who uses his tribal name Difang.

Many aboriginal peoples have also been in-volved in re-enacting their dance and song ritu-als on stage. The Taipei National University of the Arts 國立臺北藝術大學, working in conjunc-tion with the Institute of Ethnology at Academia Sinica, has already recorded dances of several tribes in Labanotation (an internationally rec-ognized way of depicting dance movements on paper) and has reconstructed these for staged performances. Some private groups, including the Cloud Gate Dance Theatre Foundation 財團法人雲門舞集文教基金會, have produced high-quality cassettes and CD recordings of authen-tic aboriginal singing.

One of the most important developments has been the creation of the Formosa Aboriginal Dance Troupe 原舞者 in April 1991. The troupe is made up of young people from several differ-ent tribes who work directly with elder tribe members to learn the dances and songs of a particular ritual, often doing their fieldwork in conjunction with qualified ethnologists. The troupe has undertaken several overseas tours, including performances in the United States, France, Spain, and Hungary.

Folk Arts

While handicrafts such as paper cutting, knot-ting, and dough sculpture continue to be fairly common in Taiwan, other apprentice-oriented folk arts are struggling to survive. In addition to the challenge of competing with inexpensive machine-made goods, folk crafts are finding it difficult to attract young people to the profes-sions of woodcarving, lantern making, and other crafts. Few are willing to endure the lengthy period of training, which results in only modest financial rewards. Traditional performing arts—such as puppetry, dragon and lion dances, folk dance, folk opera, and traditional acrobatics—have had an even tougher time competing with TV, movies, and karaoke (see sections on Pup-petry, Dance, and Drama).

Still, many folk arts have benefited from a revival of interest in the past two decades, with government, scholars, artists, and private indi-viduals joining in preservation and promotion. One of the first steps in government support came in 1980, when the Ministry of Education sponsored a survey of the island's folk arts. The survey discovered 70 types of crafts and 56 types of traditional performing arts still being prac-ticed by some 4,000 artists. In 1981, the Council for Cultural Affairs (CCA) 行政院文化建設委員會 was set up to give equal attention to fine arts and folk arts. It has sponsored a number of folk arts festivals, publications, and other projects.

Preserving Folk Arts

The *Cultural Heritage Preservation Law* 文化資產保存法, passed in 1982, committed the government to preserve and promote folk arts. The Folk Art Heritage Awards 民族藝術薪傳獎 were set up in 1985 to honor outstanding folk art masters. The prestigious title of Folk Arts Master 重要民族藝術藝師, established in 1989, has provided leading woodcarvers, puppeteers, traditional musicians, and other craftspeople and performers with a monthly stipend and helped them recruit and subsidize apprentices and training programs to pass on their skills. Other government efforts have included record-ing performances on videotape and transcribing dialogues of traditional puppet plays.

One of the most extensive efforts to preserve, promote, and reintroduce folk arts has been the CCA's National Festival of Culture and Arts. In recent years, the annual festival has focused primarily on traditional arts, working in con-junction with private organizations and county cultural centers to organize folk art exhibitions and performances around the island. Festival events have included everything from paper umbrellas and lanterns, to Hakka yodeling songs, drum dances, and carnival skits. Such activities as temple preservation seminars, tea-picking festivals, and folk operas have also been on the festival agenda.

Private organizations such as the Chinese Folk Art Foundation 中華民俗藝術基金會 have also been promoting traditional crafts and performing arts. Besides its many local activities, the foundation promotes Taiwan folk arts overseas. In 1999, for example, it sponsored the International Yunlin Puppet Theatre Festival and several other international seminars.

Other private efforts include the Taiwan Folk Arts Museum 臺灣民俗北投文物館 in Peitou 北投, which houses an extensive collection of folk arts, Chinese clothing, and embroidery; and the Tzuoyang Art Workshop 左羊藝術工作坊 in Lukang 鹿港, which increases public appreciation of the island's folk arts.

To revive and innovate folk arts, the Council for Cultural Affairs founded the Preparatory Office for the National Center of Traditional Arts (NCTA) 國立傳統藝術中心籌備處 in 1996. The NCTA promotes, preserves, exhibits, and researches in various fields of traditional arts, such as traditional drama, music, crafts, dance, and folk acrobatics. It also holds an annual Traditional Crafts Awards 傳統工藝獎 ceremony, sponsors several national seminars, and works on projects to preserve folk arts. Moreover, through cooperation with colleges and local artists, it has developed a means for promoting, preserving, and extending traditional arts to ordinary people.

Temple Arts

Not only have temples been a traditional venue for many folk art displays and performances—particularly lantern-making competitions, puppet shows, and folk operas—but some of the buildings themselves are a repository of some of the most important folk crafts on the island. Examples of traditional stone-carving,

colorful ceramic figurines (known as *chien-nien* 剪黏), and embroidered banners of legendary scenes are just some of the many arts that can be viewed at a well-preserved temple.

The most predominant form of temple craftsmanship, however, is woodcarving. From the entranceway to the back altar, nearly every beam, lintel, and other wooden support structure is covered with elaborate carvings of legendary figures and stories from history, literature, and folklore. Also common are symbolic animals, including birds, dragons, and other mythical creatures. The subject matter chosen is often not directly related to the religious function of the temple but tends to promote traditional ethical values such as loyalty, chastity, filial piety, and patriotism.

Like most traditional crafts, exquisite hand-carvings are in danger of being replaced by simpler, machine-tooled decorations. Woodcarving, as well as other temple crafts, have gotten a boost, however, through several temple reconstruction projects. One of the most significant has been the 200-year-old Tsushih Temple 祖師廟 in Sanhsia 三峽, which has been undergoing extensive renovation for 50 years and has employed some of the island's top craftspeople.

Among those who have worked on the Tsushih Temple was Huang Kwei-li 黃龜理, who died in 1996 at the age of 94. A woodcarver for 75 years and a national Folk Arts Master, he created thousands of carvings for more than 80 temples around the island, with many of his works depicting complex battle scenes from history or literature.

Another woodcarver well known for his temple figurines is Lee Sung-lin 李松林, who died in 1999 at the age of 93. His works can be seen at the Tsushih Temple and the Tienhou Temple 天后宮 in Lukang. Among the younger generation of carvers is Chen Cheng-hsiung 陳正雄, who has worked on the Tsushih reconstruction for nearly two decades.

Woodblock Printing

Another folk art that has benefited from renewed interest is woodblock printing 版畫, which is used to make colorful Chinese New Year hangings. Traditional woodcut prints in Taiwan are of a simple, rural style brought by early immigrants from Fujian Province in mainland China. Common images are the God of Wealth 財神, the Kitchen God 灶神, and Door Gods 門神, who often appear in the form of elaborately dressed and fierce-looking generals. These images are usually printed on red or orange paper in prominent black outlines and then filled in with several colors.

Among the handful of woodcut artists left is Pan Yuan-shih 潘元石, who has been a key figure in passing on the art form to children, university students, and teachers. Exhibitions and annual competitions sponsored by the Council for Cultural Affairs also help to keep the art of New Year printmaking alive. These events promote both traditional and modern methods—including lithography, silkscreening, and etching—as well as a wider variety of subject matter.

Puppetry

Before television arrived in Taiwan in the early 1960s, puppet shows were one of the primary forms of entertainment. Nearly every festive occasion, whether a wedding, holiday, or temple festival, called for a puppet performance. Numerous troupes were active throughout the island, and in the early days they often traveled from village to village by foot, carrying their stage, musical instruments, and trunks full of puppets on poles over their shoulders.

The styles of puppetry common in Taiwan—glove puppets 布袋戲, shadow puppets 皮影戲, and marionettes 傀儡戲—were brought here by immigrants from southeastern China in the early 19th century. Although the forms have evolved into distinct local styles and have also adopted modern innovations, they still retain many of their original characteristics, especially in their similarities to Chinese opera. As in opera, a puppet's costume and facial "makeup" indicate the type of character portrayed. Specific roles, such as the young scholar, the refined woman, or the fierce general, are also drawn from opera.

In glove puppetry, the stage is covered with intricate carvings that are painted gold, resembling the entrance to a traditional Chinese temple. The elaborate setting is ideal for presenting the finely embroidered costumes, exquisite headdresses, and delicately carved faces

The four protagonists from the Chinese classic "Journey to the West" come to life in this shadow puppet show. From left to right are: Friar Sand, the Buddhist monk Hsuan Tsang, Pigsy (a pig spirit), and Sun Wukung (the Monkey King).

of the puppets, which stand nearly a foot high. Shadow puppets, which stand one to two feet, are expertly cut out of leather, then engraved, dyed, and painted in bright colors. With joints to allow movement, the puppet characters are pressed against a white screen lit from behind, thus creating a colorful and lively performance for audiences. Marionette puppets, about two feet high and manipulated by 11 to 14 strings, are usually presented in front of a simple backdrop. As in Chinese opera, many of the stories used in puppet shows are adapted from classical literature or ancient legends. Some popular examples are *The Tale of the White Serpent* 白蛇傳 and *Journey to the West* 西遊記. As in opera, traditional puppet performances are always accompanied by live music.

Master Puppeteers

In the hands of several masters, puppetry in Taiwan developed along its own lines into a regional style distinct from puppetry in mainland China. This is especially true of glove puppetry. However, among the 200 plus puppet troupes still active around the island, only a handful continue to work primarily in the traditional regional style. One of the most popular was the late Lee Tien-lu 李天祿, whose life was immortalized in Hou Hsiao-hsien's 侯孝賢 award-winning film *The Puppetmaster* 戲夢人生 (1993, see section on Film). Lee, a national Folk Arts Master, first became famous in the 1950s and 1960s for his serial dramas based on kungfu novels. Lee was especially popular for his innovative martial arts sequences, acrobatic stunts, and use of modern slang mixed with classical Chinese. Along with his two sons, Lee helped set up two children's puppet troupes, the Wei Wan Jan 微宛然 and the Cheau Wan Jan 巧宛然, both of which have been highly praised. In addition, Lee's own troupe, I Wan Jan 亦宛然, performed throughout Asia, the United States, and Europe, winning awards at puppetry festivals in New York and France. The beloved puppet master passed away on August 13, 1998, at the age of 90.

Another key figure in glove puppetry is Hsu Wang 許王, whose Hsiao Hsi Yuan 小西園 troupe has also toured mainland China, Japan, Canada, and the United States. Hsu keeps a busy local schedule, often performing about twice a month. The Chinese Folk Art Foundation also frequently invites Hsu to perform at temples and other venues around the island.

One more acknowledged master is Huang Hai-tai 黃海岱, whose melodramatic tales of ancient swordsmen full of action-filled battle scenes are highlighted by elegant and highly literary dialogue. Huang's son, Huang Chun-hsiung 黃俊雄, was at the forefront of the 1960s trend to modernize puppet theater for television. Using his father's chivalry repertoire, he added popular music and fantastic lighting and other visual effects to create *chin-kuang* 金光, or gold light puppetry. The Huang family now runs its own cable TV channel, devoted exclusively to puppet shows.

The less common forms of shadow and marionette puppetry have had a much harder time surviving than glove puppetry. Among the more prominent representatives of shadow puppetry still performing today is the family of Chang Te-cheng 張德成. Chang, who died in 1996, was a national Folk Arts Master. Chang's son, Chang Fu-gwo 張榑國, represents the sixth generation in carrying on the family puppet troupe. Shadow puppeteer Hsu Fu-neng 許福能, whose group Fu Hsing Ko 復興閣皮影劇團 has earned two Folk Art Heritage Awards and has toured in Asia, Europe, and North America, has been highly active in efforts to pass on his art, regularly giving lessons and demonstrations to students around the island.

Painting

Only a limited amount of traditional Chinese painting was practiced in 18th and 19th century Taiwan. Works produced at the time were mostly amateur paintings of landscapes and flowers by scholars or government officials sent from the mainland. This art would have little influence on later artistic developments.

Western-style Oil Painting and Impressionism of the Japanese Era

During the Japanese occupation (1895-1945), few cultural influences from mainland China affected Taiwan. Painters such as Chen Cheng-po 陳澄波, Li Shih-chiao 李石樵, Li Mei-shu 李梅樹, and Yang San-lang 楊三郎 studied Western oil painting in Japan, mainly at the Tokyo Fine Arts Institute, where they learned fixed perspective and a naturalistic rendering of light and shade. Strongly influenced by French Impressionism (filtered through Japan), these artists were eager to capture and depict the flavor and hues of the Taiwan landscape. Their subject matter often centered on common, daily scenes of the island's villages, farms, and rural areas. These oil painters had an important influence on Taiwan's artistic developments, as many of them became influential teachers and leading figures in art circles. They also dominated the two most important annual exhibitions at the time, the Taiwan Fine Arts Exhibition 臺灣美術展覽會, first held in 1927, and the Taiyang Arts Show 臺陽美展, which began in 1934. Through their influence at these exhibitions, the Taiwan impressionists ensured the importance of Western-style painting in the future development of Taiwan art.

The works of this group became known as nativist art 鄉土藝術, which also had a parallel development in literature. Characterized by a conscious desire to depict images that evoked Taiwan's unique identity, the nativist art had a long-lasting influence. It would surface again in the 1970s, in both art and literature, and subsequently in music and film.

1950s: Traditional Chinese Painting

While many of the nativist impressionists were reaching their prime, an influx of traditional Chinese ink painters arrived with the ROC government from the mainland. With the government eager to reintroduce Chinese culture to Taiwan, landscape artists such as Huang Chun-pi 黃君璧 and Fu Chuan-fu 傅狷夫 enjoyed official backing, and by the early 1950s, their genre of painting had replaced Western styles at official art exhibitions, competitions and in school curricula.

The most important figure to emerge from the mainland emigre artists was Chang Dai-chien 張大千, who went far beyond the conventional precepts of Chinese painting. Before arriving in Taiwan, he had already made a significant contribution to the Chinese art world with his more than 200 detailed copies of the ancient Buddhist murals in China's Dunhuang Caves 敦煌石窟, which he painted in the early 1940s. Chang's mature paintings, which earned international recognition, were marked by his unique splash-ink technique. Using broad strokes and deliberate blotches of color—particularly deep greens and blues—he created powerful landscapes that were often monumental in size.

1960s: Abstract Art

By the late 1950s and early 1960s, many younger artists were beginning to feel disillusioned with traditional Chinese painting, but were unable to identify with the Japanese-trained impressionists. Social changes of the post-war era were begging for a new vehicle of expression. These younger artists, most of them also of mainland origin, were drawn to contemporary Western trends, especially abstract art. The rising young modernists were very outspoken in their criticism of the older traditionalists. They banded together in private art groups, the most prominent of which were the Eastern Art Group 東方畫會 and the Fifth Moon Group 五月畫會, both formed in the mid-1950s. The most influential of the Taiwan abstract art pioneers was Li Chun-shan 李仲生. Once established, some of the more prominent artists of this generation sought to find a synthesis between modern abstraction and traditional painting. Liu Kuo-sung 劉國松 and Chuang Che 莊喆, for example, sought to create a new, modern form of Chinese landscape art.

By the late 1960s, artists were working in a much greater variety of modernist styles as more Western movements filtered into Taiwan.

"Abstract 526" (1978). Watercolor by Li Chun-shan, a pioneering master of Taiwan's avant-garde art.
(Courtesy of the Lee Chun-shan Foundation of Contemporary Painting)

American trends, such as pop art, minimalism, and optical art, all had their local followers. European trends, such as surrealism and especially dada art, also found avid supporters. Many modernist painters of the 1960s emigrated to the United States and Europe in order to fully develop their Western-oriented art skills.

1970s: New Nativist Art

Artists in the late 1960s and 1970s began rejecting the idolization of Western-style art in search of something that was more in touch with their own environment and culture. What emerged was a new nativist movement in Taiwan art.

The new movement found its expression most among those who had been trained in Western-style oil painting and those with backgrounds in Chinese ink painting. A number of artists who had left Taiwan to find inspiration in America or Europe returned at this time. Among this group was Hsi Te-chin 席德進, who gave up his earlier devotion to abstraction and in 1966 began sketching and painting local scenery and architecture, exploring the island's folk art traditions. His

change in direction had significant influence on younger artists of the time.

Another influential artist of this time was Wu Hao 吳昊, whose folk-like woodblock prints were often colorful and nostalgic renditions of the Taiwan countryside. At the same time, Cheng Shan-hsi 鄭善禧 was providing a new direction to traditional ink painting. He focused on local landscape scenes rather than idealized memories of mainland scenery, rejecting the refined brushstrokes of old in exchange for a more colorful and down-to-earth vitality. In the calligraphic inscriptions on his works, he replaced classical poetic lines with vernacular descriptions.

Important inspiration was also found in the work of "native" artists like Ju Ming 朱銘 (see section on Sculpture) and Hung Tung 洪通. The latter had no training as a painter, but possessed a rich imagination nurtured on Taiwanese folk traditions. His intriguing, childlike paintings, full of colorful patterns and simplistic figures and animals, became the talk of the art world, especially after the influential *Hsiung Shih Art Monthly* 雄獅美術 published a special issue on Hung Tung in 1973.

Contemporary Trends

During the 1980s and 1990s, artists displayed a much greater variety of styles and subject matter than previously.

Taiwan consciousness was an important starting point for the influential 101 Modern Art Group 一〇一現代藝術群 founded in 1982. These artists often expressed their sense of local identity with symbolic or metaphorical images. Wu Tien-chang 吳天章 and Yang Mao-lin 楊茂林, for example, filled their canvases with primitive-looking images that often suggested social events. Often working in monumental scale with a harsh black and white palette, Wu has produced works commemorating the February 28 Incident 二二八事件 and commented on other events and figures from Taiwan's past. By comparison, Yang's *Made in Taiwan* 臺灣製造 series presents a quieter juxtaposition of subjects native to the island, such as sweet potatoes, sea shells, images of Taiwan's aboriginal peoples, and references to the 17th century Dutch occupation of Taiwan. His approach presents a more subtle vision of Taiwan history and society.

Chinese ink painting has continued its solid standing in Taiwan. Many artists, such as Chiang Chao-shen 江兆申, the late deputy director of the National Palace Museum, remain fairly well-grounded in the traditional style, although many incorporate subtle innovations. Yu Cheng-yao 余承堯, who only began painting after retiring from a long military career, ignores the traditional brushstroke lexicon and instead works over his mountains and trees with closely knit, interwoven strokes that create a richly textured surface.

Other painters have departed from tradition not only in their brushstrokes but in their subject matter. Lo Ching 羅青, for example, in his *Palm Tree Boulevard* 棕櫚大道, replaces the standard pine or willow trees with palm trees, and mountains or waterfalls with an asphalt road. In his inscriptions, he replaces traditional metaphors with modern-day references. Lo and other ink painters have also embraced the exploration of a Taiwan consciousness, drawing much of their inspiration from local reality rather than from distant memories of mainland China.

Plastic Art

Sculpture

There was no strong formal tradition of sculpture brought from mainland China. Before the 1920s, temple and folk sculpture were the only sculptural forms thriving in Taiwan, and it was not until the 1970s that sculpture was widely accepted as a fine-art genre.

Taiwan's first fine-art sculptor was Huang Tu-shui 黃土水, born in 1906. Like many painters of his generation, he studied Western-style techniques at the Tokyo Fine Arts Institute. His most celebrated works are of water buffaloes, an animal that symbolizes the heart of the Taiwan countryside. The most renowned sculptor after Huang was Chen Hsia-yu 陳夏雨, who was also trained in Japan and returned to Taiwan after World War II to create realistic portraits and figures, often of women in pensive poses.

The tide of Western-oriented abstraction that swept through the local art world in the 1960s produced the first Taiwan sculptor to gain worldwide attention. Yuyu Yang (also known as Yang Ying-feng 楊英風), who died in 1997, was most famous for his stainless steel sculptures, which often converted traditional Chinese symbols like the phoenix and dragon into fluid abstract forms. His works, which were sometimes monumental in size, have been erected in cities around the world. His *East West Gate* 東西門 (1973) stands on Wall Street in Manhattan, and the 23-foot *Advent of the Phoenix* 鳳凰來儀 (1970) can be found in Osaka. In 1996, Yang held a major retrospective of his work in England, at the invitation of the Royal Society of British Sculptors.

The back-to-roots movement of the 1970s (see section on Painting) is exemplified by Ju Ming, who was initially trained as a folk sculptor but later studied with Yuyu Yang. Ju was initially admired for his rustic, simple figures carved from wood, especially his monumental *Tai Chi Series* 太極系列. In recent years, he has explored a variety of materials, including painted bronze and rolled stainless steel sheets, creating abstract figures of athletes, ballerinas, and people in everyday poses. Like Yuyu Yang, Ju has exhibited worldwide, in Hong Kong, England, New York, and elsewhere.

Ceramics

Taiwan is also known for its high-quality reproduction ceramics, an industry that got its start in the late 1940s. Several talented figures, such as Lin Te-wen 林德文 and Tsai Hsiao-fang 蔡曉芳, became known for their skill at imitating ancient porcelain. Today, there are a number of kilns in the north-central city of Miaoli 苗栗 and in Yingko 鶯歌鎮, a small town southwest of Taipei, that are known worldwide for their reproductions of Ming and Ching dynasty ceramics. In the early 1950s, several ceramists, including primarily Lin Pao-chia 林葆家, Wu Jang-nung 吳讓農, and Wang Hsiu-kung 王修功, made their first efforts to develop Taiwan's ceramics into a contemporary art form. These men began their careers by working in ceramics factories, helping to revive the industry after its decline during the Japanese occupation. Eventually, they broke away to pursue their own creative ideas and to establish teaching studios. Although they remained within the traditional framework of functional ceramics, making vases, bowls, and pots, their works represented a creative venture into unusual shapes and experimental glaze effects.

It was not until the late 1960s, however, that creative ceramists began to gain widespread recognition, thanks in large part to exhibitions at the National Museum of History 國立歷史博物館, which continues to play a central role in promoting the art form. In 1968, the museum held the island's first major solo ceramics show, featuring Wu Jang-nung. In the following decade, ceramic exhibitions at private galleries gradually became more common. A key figure during this era was Chiu Huan-tang 邱煥堂, who

studied ceramics in Hawaii and returned to Taiwan to introduce the contemporary ideas he had learned abroad. Ceramist Sun Chao 孫超 also gained recognition during this time for his crystalline glazes 結晶釉. After a career in the National Palace Museum, Sun began applying his experiments with ancient glazing techniques to his own work. In recent years, he has moved from making decorative crystal patterns on vases and bowls to large, flat glaze "paintings" that combine Chinese ink landscapes with abstract expressionism.

After 1981, ceramic art quickly came into its own, boosted by the 1983 opening of the Taipei Fine Arts Museum 臺北市立美術館, which included ceramics in its opening show. In 1986, the National Museum of History held its first biennial ceramic show. The Chinese Ceramics Association 中華民國陶藝協會 was formed in 1992, and the following year held its first festival, which featured indoor and outdoor exhibitions, demonstrations, and lectures by prominent ceramic artists. Taiwan's first ceramics museum, the Yingko Ceramics Museum 鶯歌陶瓷博物館, opened in November 2000. It presents Taiwan's ceramic development and promotes cultural exchange between local and overseas ceramic artists.

Seal Carving

Carving name chops, or Chinese seals, with names or other calligraphic inscriptions was once a necessary skill, along with painting and calligraphy, for any well-rounded literati artist. Although machine-carved name chops are commonly used for most business transactions today, only a handful of artists specialize in the art of engraving name chops by hand. Among them are Wang Pei-yueh 王北岳, who teaches seal carving at the art department of National Taiwan Normal University. Among the younger generation of chopmakers is Huang Ming-hsiu 黃明修, who was recognized in the 1994 Provincial Art Contest for his work. Name chops are made of wood, jade, or soft precious stones, such as *tienhuang* 田黃, or "field yellow." The body of the chop may be a plain rectangle, or it may be sculpted into a lion, dragon, or other symbolic image. Besides their use in business transactions, name chops are also stamped on traditional paintings and calligraphy, both to identify the artist and to add an aesthetic touch.

Museums and the Art Market

Art Museums

Taiwan's best-known museum is the National Palace Museum in Taipei, a repository for traditional art from mainland China. In 1933, the numerous treasures in the museum's collection started traveling from Beijing to Taiwan in a harrowing 12,000-kilometer journey around China over the course of 16 years, evading both the Japanese army and the Chinese communists. In 1965, the museum finally opened in Taipei and is recognized for having the world's best collection of Chinese art, from ancient bronze castings, calligraphy, scroll paintings, porcelains, jade, and rare books. The museum's current collection numbers over 640,000 items, a collection so large that only about 1 percent can be accommodated for display at any one time, while the rest is kept in storage.

In 1996, the National Palace Museum greatly enhanced its international image with a spectacular US tour of 452 of its finest works of art. The "Splendors of Imperial China" ran from March 1996 through April 1997, with stops at the Metropolitan Museum of Art in New York City, the Art Institute of Chicago, the Asian Art Museum of San Francisco, and the National Gallery of Art in Washington, D.C. Curators and scholars in the United States hailed the exhibition, which attracted 900,000 visitors, as a once-in-a-lifetime experience that could very well give new impetus to the study of Chinese art, just as a smaller-scale 1961 exhibition inspired many of today's Chinese art scholars. In 1999, the National Palace Museum held a special joint exhibition with the Guanghan Sanxingdui Museum 廣漢三星堆博物館 in Sichuan province of the Chinese mainland, providing a better understanding

The newly-opened Yingko Ceramics Museum greets visitors with cascading waterfalls and installation artworks.

of the lifestyles prevalent during the prehistoric Chinese kingdom of Shu 古蜀王國.

In 2000, some of the important exhibitions held by the National Palace Museum included "China at the Inception of the Second Millennium A.D.—Art and Culture of the Sung Dynasty, 960-1279"; an "Exhibition of Buddhist Sculpture Through the Dynasties"; the "Development of Porcelain in China"; and "Chinese Jades." While continuing to be a major venue for displaying classical Chinese and Asian art, the National Palace Museum also offered local audiences a chance to appreciate Western art by hosting the "Dali—A Genius of the 20th Century" 魔幻達利 exhibition from January 20 to April 20, 2001. Eighty-five works (38 oil paintings and 47 water colors and sketches) by the surrealist master on loan from the Gala-Salvador Dali Foundation in Spain were exhibited, attracting large crowds.

The National Museum of History, also located in Taipei, is best known for its impressive collection of ancient bronzes, pottery, and ceramic burial figurines. The museum regularly exhibits the works of major Chinese artists of the 20th century. In 1999, the museum held five exhibitions introducing Taiwanese artists in Estonia, the US, and Latvia. In 2000, the museum held important exhibitions of Han dynasty artifacts, tea culture, fan art, and the paintings of Hsia Yi-fu 夏一夫. As part of cross-strait cultural exchanges, the National Museum of History presented the "Terra Cotta Warriors and Horses of China's First Emperor Special Exhibit" 兵馬俑秦文化特展 from January to March 2001, drawing an unprecedented number of visitors that exceeded all other museum exhibitions on the island. Designed as a simulation of Pit Number One, one of the three pits discovered to contain terra cotta warriors and horses, the exhibit was an excellent display of cultural and technological achievements in ancient China. The museum also held the "La Mesopotamie" exhibition 美索不達米亞羅浮宮兩河流域珍藏展 between March and July of 2001. A total of 299 artifacts, including the Code of Hammurabi on loan from the Louvre, were displayed.

Since its opening in 1983, the Taipei Fine Arts Museum has been a major catalyst for the development of modern art. It has featured many local artists and important foreign exhibitions, including the 1999 "Outdoor Sculpture of the 20th Century," which was supported by Paris Musees and held in the newly opened Taipei Art Park. It also hosts annual and biennial competitions, as well as invitational exhibitions. From November 9 to December 3, 2000, it hosted the biennial exhibition 臺北雙年展 entitled "The Sky Is the Limit" 無法無天, with the works of 31 artists from 18 countries. The museum has also been commissioned for the Taiwan Pavilion at the Venice Biennial 威尼斯雙年展 since 1995, providing a channel for Taiwanese contemporary art to communicate with the global art world. The Taiwan Pavilion at the 49th Venice Biennial held from July to November 2001 featured the works of five Taiwanese artists with the theme of "Living Cell" 活性因子.

The Institute of Contemporary Arts, Taipei, 臺北當代藝術館 located in the refurbished old city hall, officially opened in May 2001. The opening exhibition, entitled "The Gravity of the Immaterial" 輕且重的震撼, presented the contemporary world art scene by inviting 26 artists from both Taiwan and abroad to display their works. As the second fine arts museum in Taipei, it promises to further invigorate the city with new cultural energy while keeping step with a quickly changing society.

Modern art museums have also been established in Taichung and Kaohsiung. The Taiwan Museum of Art 國立臺灣美術館, located in Taichung, opened in 1988, concentrating on Taiwan's artistic development. Items in its collection range from the Ming and Ching dynasties to contemporary works. The museum hosts both research exhibitions and planned exhibitions. Besides presenting the works of local artists, the museum also introduces works by foreign artists of worldwide fame and hosts international exchange exhibitions. The museum sponsored a touring exhibition entitled "Chinese New Year Prints" to Central America; the action art exhibition "No Destruction, No Construction"; the "Life City" exhibition at the Seventh International Exhibition of Architecture in Venice; and the Yuen Shui-long exhibition in Paris. The Kaohsiung Museum of Fine Arts 高雄市立美術館, which opened in 1993, is one of the largest fine arts museums in Asia.

The Chang Foundation Museum 鴻禧美術館, which opened in 1991, is the island's first private Chinese art museum. Although relatively small, with only about 16,000 square feet of exhibition space, it has an impressive collection that features traditional painting, exquisite porcelain, and other ceramics. This museum also holds exhibitions in cooperation with museums on the Chinese mainland.

The Juming Art Museum 朱銘美術館, which opened on September 19, 1999, boasts a full collection of Ju Ming's works done at different stages in his life, including around 500 pieces of sculpture in wood, mud, stone, bronze, and stainless steel, as well as 500 paintings in oil, ink, pastel, and multimedia. Works by world-renowned masters, such as Picasso, Henry Moore, and Andy Warhol, are also on display in the galleries.

Galleries

The number of galleries in Taiwan has grown tremendously from a single enterprise, the Lungmen Gallery 龍門畫廊 in 1975, to about 150 galleries today. Lungmen Gallery has retained its prominence among the galleries and shows works by artists from both Taiwan and overseas. The Hanart Gallery 漢雅軒, which has a home gallery in Hong Kong, has also played an important role in promoting Taiwan's younger generation of artists.

Other prominent galleries include the Galerie Elegance 愛力根畫廊; the Eslite Gallery 誠品畫廊; the Taiwan Gallery 臺灣畫廊, and Home Gallery 家畫廊, which focus on contemporary art; and the Caves Art Center 敦煌藝術中心 and the

Pristine Harmony Art Center 清韻藝術中心, which focus on Chinese ink paintings by both traditional and contemporary artists. IT Park 伊通公園 is an alternative gallery for non-commercial artists and provides a much-needed venue for installation and performing artists.

Several galleries in central and southern Taiwan have established themselves in the art market. Some of the best known include Gallery Pierre 臻品藝術中心, East Gallery 東之畫廊, and Modern Art Gallery 現代藝術空間 in Taichung; New Phase Art Space 新生態藝術環境 in Tainan; the Up Gallery 阿普畫廊 and Duchamp Gallery 杜象藝術中心 in Kaohsiung; and Gallery Venus 維納斯藝廊 in Hualien 花蓮.

The increase in art galleries around the island has been partly due to the great expansion of art collecting in the 1980s, which in turn has been driven by growth of the stock and real estate markets. Taiwan collectors are also active in the art markets in Hong Kong and New York, prompting such high-profile auction houses as Sotheby's and Christie's to provide previews of their Hong Kong and New York auctions in Taiwan. Both houses have held auctions in Taiwan beginning in the early 1990s, with varying degrees of success. Both have focused primarily on traditional Chinese painting and works by Taiwan's Japanese-trained impressionists, such as Chen Cheng-po, whose 1931 painting *Sunset at Tamsui* 黃昏淡水 (see section on Painting) was sold by Sotheby's for US$380,000 in 1993, a record-breaking price for a contemporary Chinese painting.

Another major development has been the annual Taipei Art Fair International 臺北國際藝術博覽會, which began in 1992 and promotes the local art market both regionally and internationally. The event gives local art collectors a chance to appreciate and bid for masterpieces by world renowned artists, drawing around 70,000 to 80,000 visitors each year. Organized by the ROC Art Galleries Association 中華民國畫廊協會, the 2000 fair was held December 14-18 with the theme of "Awakening" and an exhibition on Gao Xingjian 高行健, the first Chinese Nobel

Laureate for Literature. The fair celebrated its tenth anniversary in November 2001 with the participation of over 28 local galleries and Japanese art dealers.

Music

Taiwan has a very active music scene, in both the traditional Chinese and classical Western styles—and sometimes a combination of the two. The great variety and rich tradition of music in Taiwan has been featured in such events as the "100 Years of Taiwanese Music" 臺灣音樂一百年, a major festival and conference held in 1995 that had performances of Taiwanese folk songs, Fujian and Hakka music, and contemporary compositions by some of Taiwan's leading composers (see section below on Composers).

Recent years also saw more international music events taking place in Taiwan. The 1996 Taipei International Music Festival 臺北國際樂展 and the 1998 Asian Composers' League Conference and Festival 亞洲作曲家聯盟大會暨音樂節 covered a wide range of music, both traditional and contemporary, Chinese and Western. With violin soloist Lin Cho-liang 林昭亮 as music director, the second Taipei International Music Festival 國際巨星音樂節 held in May 2000 invited world-renown musicians and received great support from music fans.

Taiwan's first World Music Festival 世界音樂節 was staged from May 28 to June 2, 2000. Embracing the spirit of WOMAD (world of music, arts, and dance, an organization founded by Peter Gabriel), the event gathered music groups from Spain, Greece, Belgium, Hungary, Australia, and Serbia and gave local residents a chance to enjoy the global rhythms of non-mainstream music. The 2001 Taiwan World Music Festival took place in Ta An Forest Park between May 19 and 24. Taipei citizens again relished diverse world folk music brought by 10 music groups from 9 countries, which included performers from Argentina, Mongolia, and several African countries.

Two of the world famous "Three Tenors" visited Taiwan in 2001. The first, Placido

Domingo, charmed a Taipei audience at a packed National Concert Hall 國家音樂廳 on June 10, 2001, accompanied by the National Symphony Orchestra 國家交響樂團. On his fifth visit to the island, José Carreras, the second tenor, gave recitals in Kaohsiung and Taipei in October and Taichung in November.

Traditional Chinese Music

The four professional groups primarily performing Chinese music in Taiwan are the Taipei Municipal Chinese Classical Orchestra (TMCCO) 臺北市立國樂團, the National Chinese Orchestra 國立實驗國樂團, the Kaohsiung Chinese Orchestra 高雄市國樂團, and the Chinese Orchestra of the Broadcasting Corporation of China 中國廣播公司國樂團. In addition, 10 smaller ensembles perform regularly around the island. The Ensemble Orientalia of Taipei 臺北民族樂團, which has performed in the United States and Australia, conducts fieldwork, including researching and transcribing traditional music from throughout Taiwan.

While the musicians in these groups play mostly traditional Chinese instruments, they sometimes perform Western compositions or Chinese works that incorporate Western-style rhythms or harmonies.

Increased cultural contacts with mainland China have brought new ideas to Chinese music in Taiwan. Since the late 1980s, a number of groups from the mainland (representing both Western-style and traditional music) including major orchestras—such as the Shanghai National Music Orchestra and the China Central Ensemble of National Music—as well as smaller ensembles, such as the Shanghai Quartet and the Shanghai Chinese Traditional Folk Music Ensemble, have performed in Taiwan.

Pei-kuan and Nan-kuan

While many traditional Chinese musicians are drawing on Western influences, others have shown a renewed interest in preserving the traditional quality of several types of ancient music—including *pei-kuan* 北管, a fast-tempo music that commonly accompanied operas and traditional puppet shows, and *nan-kuan* 南管, which has a more delicate and soothing sound. The interest in nan-kuan music has been especially prominent, as this musical form is thought to have flourished in southern China during the Tang dynasty and first appeared in Taiwan during the 16th century. The Han Tang Classical Music Institute 漢唐樂府, which was founded in 1983 by Chen Mei-o 陳美娥, has performed nan-kuan in the United States, Europe, and Asia, and released a number of CDs. The group later established the Liyuan Dance Studio 梨園舞坊, which was inspired by "The Musical Theater of the Pear Orchard" 梨園戲, a form that flourished during the eighth century and was brought to Taiwan in the 18th century. The two groups often perform together at Han Tang's own theater in Taipei, which offers a small, traditional teahouse-like setting.

Other main figures in nan-kuan music are singer Wu Su-ching 吳素慶 and musician Lee Hsiang-shih 李祥石. Lee was honored with the Folk Arts Master Award (see section on Folk Arts) for his work. Both Wu and Lee were invited to teach in a special Nan-kuan Performance Program set up in 1988 at the Taipei National University of the Arts. The Changhua County Cultural Center 彰化縣立文化中心 has also maintained a Nan-kuan and Pei-kuan Center 南北管音樂劇曲館 since 1990.

Western Classical Music

While traditional Chinese music has an important position in Taiwan, Western classical music still predominates. In fact, many more musicians are trained in Western music than in Chinese music. Young classical musicians from Taiwan, along with their counterparts elsewhere in Asia, have succeeded in international music circles. Violinists Lin Cho-liang, Hu Nai-yuan 胡乃元, and Edith Chen 陳毓襄 are among the many Taiwan-born musicians who have attended elite music schools abroad, won prestigious competitions, and become prominent internationally. Conductor Lu Shao-chia 呂紹嘉, a graduate of the Vienna Conservatory, is now the music director of Germany's leading opera house, Niedersachsische Staatstheater Hannover (NSH), the highest post ever held by an ethnic Chinese conductor. While many young musicians often have successful careers abroad, many more are now returning to Taiwan, both as visiting musicians and as regular members of orchestras and chamber groups.

Taiwan's main Western-style orchestras are the National Symphony Orchestra, now under the direction of Chien Wen-pin 簡文彬, and the Taipei Symphony Orchestra 臺北市立交響樂團, under Chen Chiu-sen 陳秋盛. The National Taiwan Symphony Orchestra 國立臺灣交響樂團, based in Taichung, is conducted by Chen Cheng-hsiung 陳澄雄. The Kaohsiung City Symphony Orchestra 高雄市交響樂團 is a semi-professional group.

The largest private orchestra is the Taipei Sinfonietta and Philharmonic Orchestra 臺北愛樂室內及管弦樂團, founded in 1985 by conductor Henry Mazer. With some of the island's most talented musicians among its members, the group has toured the United States, Canada, and Europe.

Perhaps the busiest ensemble on the island is the Ju Percussion Group, directed by Ju Tzong-ching 朱宗慶. This group performs more than 100 times every year—at concert halls, schools, and outdoor venues, and holds many educational demonstrations for teachers and the general public. The group's music is often a hybrid of Western and Chinese, and its instruments are both traditional and experimental, ranging from drums, gongs, and xylophones to empty beer bottles, sawed-off steel pipes, and even bursting balloons. The affiliated Ju Percussion Foundation 財團法人擊樂文教基金會 oversees a research center for traditional Chinese percussion music and operates educational centers for children around the island. In 1996, the foundation organized the second International Percussion Convention. The group has performed in major cities of the United States, France, South Korea, and the Chinese mainland.

Western Opera

The Taipei Opera Theater 臺北歌劇劇場, under Tseng Tao-hsiung 曾道雄, and the Taiwan

Metropolitan Opera 首都歌劇團, directed by internationally known tenor William Wu 吳文修, has performed Western opera in Taiwan, performing such works as Gounod's *Faust*, Mozart's *Magic Flute*, and Verdi's *Rigoletto*. The Taiwan Metropolitan Opera has presented Puccini's *Madame Butterfly*; Leoncavallo's *Cavalleria Rusticana* and *I Pagliacci*; and *The Great Wall* 萬里長城, a Western-style opera sung in Chinese that narrates a Chinese story. Another active opera promoter is the Taipei Symphony Orchestra, which presented Verdi's *Aida* in 1995, Wagner's *The Flying Dutchman* in January 1997, both featuring international casts, and Puccini's *Turandot* in 2000.

Composers

Taiwan hosted the annual conference and festival of the Asian Composers' League (ACL) most recently in 1998. Hsu Chang-hui 許常惠, considered by many to be the pioneer local composer, was one of the founders of the ACL in 1973. Hsu, who studied in France, founded the Music Creative Group 製樂小集, which promoted the development of local music composition in the 1960s. He also introduced new, experimental developments from the West, such as Arnold Schoenberg's serialism. For many years, Hsu conducted extensive research of Taiwan folk music. His passing away in January 2001 is a great loss to the local music scene.

Other composers known regionally and internationally include Ma Shui-long 馬水龍, whose works have been performed in Europe, the United States, South Africa, and Southeast Asia; and Pan Huang-lung 潘皇龍, who has introduced avant-garde composition to local audiences.

Drama

Chinese Opera

Chinese opera is one of Taiwan's premier art forms. Although performances are not as frequent as they once were, they can still be seen on a weekly basis at opera schools, community theaters and temples, and on television, as well as in major seasonal productions at the National Theater 國家戲劇院. While opera includes many regional styles, the most common in Taiwan are Peking opera, which first reached maturity in the Ching dynasty, and Taiwanese opera (see section on Taiwanese Opera below), which was influenced by the operatic forms of southern China. Most regional forms of Chinese opera are sung in the dialect of their region of origin, hence Taiwanese opera is performed by speaking and singing in Southern Fujianese. Peking opera is an exception, however. Dialogue is in the Beijing dialect, but the arias are recited or sung in an artificial phonetic stage dialect.

Peking Opera

Peking opera is a colorful and lively form of drama. Plots are adapted from Chinese history and classical literature and reflect traditional Chinese Confucian moral values, such as loyalty, filial piety, and patriotism. Human foibles are also well represented, and usually there is at least one exciting battle scene or acrobatic display per performance. All characters are developed within the confines of traditional roles, with each actor specializing in a specific type of character, such as the *hsiao-sheng* 小生, a handsome young scholar, the *wu-tan* 武旦, a beautiful female warrior, or the *chou* 丑, a clown. Each role is limited by a specific range of gestures and makeup. Singing is stylized, with some characters requiring a high-pitched falsetto (since traditionally, only men appeared on stage, even in female roles). Live musical accompaniment is closely integrated with the action, with the conductor regulating the pace of performance and cueing actors through his control of the beat. Traditional string and wind instruments accompany the singing, while percussion instruments comment on stage movements, including stage entrances and exits, fight scenes, and acrobatic scenes.

Taiwan's major Peking opera troupes are the National Kuo Kuang Chinese Opera Company 國立國光劇團 and the Chinese Opera Troupe of the National Taiwan Junior College of Performing

Arts 國立臺灣戲曲專科學校附設國劇團, formerly the National Fu-Hsing Chinese Opera Theater 復興國劇團. The former, established in 1995, is funded by the Ministry of Education, while the latter is affiliated with the National Taiwan Junior College of Performing Arts 國立臺灣戲曲專科學校. The Kuo Kuang Company maintains a traditional repertoire, while the Chinese Opera Troupe of the National Taiwan Junior College of Performing Arts is more adventuresome in its productions, performing new scripts that often combine traditional and modern ideas.

On July 1, 1999, the National Kuo Kuang Academy of Arts 國光藝校 and the National Fu-Hsing Dramatic Arts Academy 國立復興劇藝實驗學校 were merged into the National Taiwan Junior College of Performing Arts. In the near future, both opera troupes are scheduled to merge with other performing groups into one "National Dramatic Arts Center" (NDAC) 國立戲劇藝術中心. Five major performing groups will be formed within the NDAC: Peking Opera Troupe I 京劇一團, Peking Opera Troupe II 京劇二團, Yuchu Troupe 豫劇團, Performing Troupe 綜藝團, and Taiwanese Opera Troupe 歌仔戲. Each performance group will have its own distinct roles and functions.

Peking opera has undergone a degree of experimentation in Taiwan, and one important innovator has been the Contemporary Legend Theater 當代傳奇劇場, founded by opera actor Wu Hsing-kuo 吳興國 in 1984. This internationally acclaimed group is best known for its Peking opera adaptations of Western classics, such as Shakespeare's *Macbeth* and Euripides' *Medea*, which incorporate elements of Western drama, including dramatic stage and costume designs, as well as greater psychological character development than is generally found in traditional Chinese opera. Using tragic stories to raise moral questions rather than providing conventional answers is also a distinct departure from tradition. Due to financial difficulties, however, the group stopped performing in late 1998.

Taiwanese Opera

Taiwanese opera 歌仔戲 was once performed on nearly every auspicious occasion, including weddings, birthdays, and temple festivals. By tradition, the form is said to have its origin in short songs from Ilan County 宜蘭縣. These songs were purportedly influenced by the narrative music of Taiwan's aboriginal peoples and later evolved into a more powerful musical form. These "Ilan folk songs" are accompanied by an orchestra consisting of the *san-hsien* 三絃, a three-stringed Chinese banjo; the *pipa* 琵琶, a four-stringed vertical lute; the *tung-hsiao* 洞簫, a vertical flute; the *sona* 哨吶, a trumpet-belled, double-reeded horn; and various percussion instruments, including gongs and drums. Various regional Chinese music theater forms, particularly the *pei-kuan* and *nan-kuan* music theater brought to Taiwan by early immigrants from southern China, have clearly influenced Taiwanese opera. This is evident from the colorful makeup and costumes, stage props, and stylized gestures used in Taiwanese opera, which had become a complete musical genre by the 1930s.

The role of Ilan in the development of Taiwanese opera continues to be important today. Several major troupes are based there, including one sponsored by the Ilan County Cultural Center 宜蘭縣立文化中心, which also houses a Taiwanese opera museum. Today, there are nearly 200 troupes performing around the island, but only a few of professional calibre. The best-known is the Ming Hwa Yuan Theater Troupe 明華園歌劇團, established in 1929. Like other Taiwanese opera troupes, it began performing on outdoor stages, often set up in front of temples, but today it also performs at such prestigious venues as the National Theater. The troupe has also toured overseas, performing in Paris and mainland China. Other important companies include the Ho Lo Taiwanese Opera Troupe 河洛歌仔戲團, the Han Yang Troupe 漢陽歌劇團, and the Lan Yang Troupe 蘭陽戲劇團.

Taiwanese opera's most celebrated actress is Yang Li-hua 楊麗花. With a career spanning over 30 years, she continues to periodically present her own productions. Like many Taiwanese opera actresses, Yang is known for playing only male roles.

Television performances of Taiwanese opera have also been important to its development since the 1960s. Although many TV troupes have a soap opera mentality, with electronic music and pop songs, the Yeh Ching Taiwanese Opera Troupe 葉青歌仔戲團 is one of the few that retained the basic traditional form. Its founder, actress Yeh Ching, has developed an islandwide following through her TV performances and has won numerous awards.

Other Regional Opera Forms

The Kuo Kuang company has a section for Henan opera 河南梆子, which is sung in a natural voice rather than the falsetto common to Peking opera. Taiwan audiences have also been introduced to Hakka opera, which incorporates traditional tea-farming folk songs, through the Rom-shing Hakka Teapicker Opera Troupe 榮興客家採茶劇團. In keeping with tradition, the majority of its productions are presented outdoors, although it also performs at major venues such as the National Theater.

Another opera form found in Taiwan is Pei-kuan opera. The Hsin Mei Yuan Troupe 新美園劇團 is the only professional Pei-kuan opera group on the island to ever win the Heritage Award.

An opera form that has been regaining attention in recent years is Kun opera 崑曲, which preserves late Ching dynasty musical scores and singing techniques from the longest extant tradition of Chinese music theater, possibly dating back to the late 12th or early 13th century. Compared to Peking opera, Kun opera features more delicate and complex music and singing, and also employs more poetic language. Although there are currently only two amateur groups performing Kun opera in Taiwan, a major project is under way to establish a professional troupe. Under the sponsorship of the Kuo Kuang opera school and the private Chinese Folk Arts Foundation, 20 students have been chosen for a three-year program in which

the group will train under Kun masters from the Chinese mainland.

Taipei hosted the Chinese Drama Festival 華文戲劇節 in 2000, which was organized by performing groups from Chinese speaking areas (mainland China, Taiwan, Hong Kong, Macau, and Singapore). The biennial Chinese Drama Festival, which began in Beijing in August 1996, was held in Hong Kong in November 1998. The Third Chinese Drama Festival, which was co-organized by the National Chiang Kai-shek Cultural Center 國立中正文化中心 and Chinese Taipei Theatre Association 中華戲劇學會, was held in Taipei in 2000. Beginning July 22, 2000, seven opera troupes held two weeks of opera performances and seminars at the National Concert Hall, the Taipei Municipal Social Educational Hall 臺北市立社會教育館, and Novel Hall 新舞臺. Ten Kun opera troupes also performed in Taiwan from the end of December 1999 to early January 2000.

Spoken Drama

Non-musical Theater

The first Western drama in Taiwan was based on 19th and early 20th century playwrights, such as Ibsen, Chekhov, and O'Neill. The only plays produced, however, were dull and didactic performances by government-sponsored troupes that attracted little attention.

The theater scene began in the 1960s, with what is known as the Little Theater Movement 小劇場運動. Thanks to the enthusiasm and talent of several new dramatists, including Li Man-kuei 李曼瑰 and Yao Yi-wei 姚一葦, the repertoire of locally written plays expanded in a more creative direction. Li, alone, wrote more than 50 plays, including full-length dramas, one-act plays, and children's performances, which have been compiled into a volume entitled *Collection of Chinese Plays* 中華戲劇集.

The first professional stage play produced by an independent (rather than government-sponsored) troupe was Yao Yi-wei's *Red Nose* 紅鼻子, which became a classic among local plays and was later staged in both Beijing and Japan. The 1970 debut of *Red Nose* initiated the prolific era of the 1970s, when private mini-theaters proliferated and directors began experimenting more freely with stage techniques and imaginative interpretations of both local and Western plays.

Early Innovators

The Lan-ling Drama Workshop 蘭陵劇坊, founded in 1977 by Wu Ching-chi 吳靜吉, was the first theater group to recast a Chinese opera into modern colloquial language. This involved an experimental approach that emphasized strong physical movement and the importance of body language. Lan-ling's groundbreaking 1977 production *Ho-chu's New Match* 荷珠新配, adapted from a well-known Peking opera story, was a contemporary social satire on the new bourgeoisie. This play began a new theatrical genre in Taiwan, with future theater groups staging contemporary adaptations of other Peking operas. Other Lan-ling avant-garde productions included the 1986 adaptation of the ancient Chinese poetry anthology *Nine Songs* 九歌, which dispensed with both plot and dialogue in favor of improvisation, rhythmic movements, chanting, and other elements of ritualism. Although Lan-ling is no longer active, it continues to have an influence on theater in Taiwan.

Another theater pioneer was the New Aspect Art Center 新象藝術中心, established in 1978. Although New Aspect never maintained an actual theater group, it has produced a number of major plays and presented some new dramatic forms to the local theater world. In 1982, it introduced a new multimedia approach associated with epic theater in the landmark production of *Wandering in the Garden and Waking from a Dream* 遊園驚夢. Taiwan's first locally produced musical, *The Chess King* 棋王, was also a New Aspect production. Today, New Aspect is an arts agency, bringing a wide variety of performing arts to Taiwan from abroad.

The Performance Workshop

The early efforts of Lan-ling and New Aspect helped set the stage for the mid-1980s,

when several leading theater companies were established. Most prominent is the Performance Workshop 表演工作坊, set up in 1984 by Stan Lai 賴聲川, who introduced collective improvisational theater, which was heavily influenced by Shireen Strooker's Amsterdam Werkteater.

The group's first production to attract more than just a student audience was *The Night We Became Hsiang-sheng Comedians* 那一夜我們說相聲. The play marked the first time that the highly stylized *hsiang-sheng* 相聲, a traditional form of fast-paced comic dialogue (cross-talk), was expanded into a full-length play.

Performance Workshop's other productions reflect on modern Taiwan society. *The Island and the Other Shore* 回頭是彼岸 (1989) and *Look Who's Cross-talking Tonight* 這一夜誰來說相聲 both examine the island's complex and controversial relationship with mainland China. In the 1994 play *Red Sky* 紅色的天空, the troupe revealed the experiences of Taiwan's elderly population. The two week performance of *The Complete History of Chinese Thought—Cross-Talk Version* 又一夜, 他們說相聲 in 1997 at the National Theater again ran to capacity audiences. Performance Workshop director Stan Lai has also ventured into filmmaking, with one of his movies based on his play *The Peach Blossom Land* 暗戀桃花源 (see section on Film, The Second New Wave). The workshop's latest productions include *Millennium Teahouse* 千禧夜我們說相聲 in 2000 and *The Comedy of Sex and Politics* 一婦五夫 and *Waiting for Godot* 等待狗頭 in 2001.

The Pin-Fong Acting Troupe 屏風表演班, organized in 1986, has also become popular among local audiences. Directed by Li Kuo-hsiu 李國修, who formerly worked with the Lan-ling as well as the Performance Workshop, the troupe often presents slapstick comedies. Underneath the pranks and wisecracks, however, are satirical comments on Taiwan society.

The Godot Theater Company 果陀劇場, set up in 1988, often combines theater, music, and dance. The company has staged local adaptations of such works as *Our Town* and Shakespeare's *The Taming of the Shrew*. In 1996, Godot produced a martial arts drama called *Chiao Feng, the End of Destiny* 天龍八部之喬峰, adapted from a Chinese novel written by Chin Yung 金庸 about a beggar king. Godot's 1998 musical *The Angel Never Sleeps* 天使不夜城, about a prostitute in search for real love, was a big success. In 2001, the company presented two plays by Peter Shaffer, *Black Comedy* 黑色喜劇, 白色幽默 and *Amadeus* 莫札特謀殺案, and a new musical, *Looking Up the Golden Sun* 看見太陽.

Another unusual group is the U Theater 優劇場, founded by Liu Ching-min 劉靜敏 and dedicated to creating a form of contemporary theater that expresses a unique Taiwanese identity. To absorb the traditions of Taiwanese culture, the actors and actresses participate in a strict physical training program that includes martial arts. They work with a variety of folk artists, Taiwanese opera performers, and traditional drummers.

Theater companies, based in central and southern Taiwan, include the Tainan Jen Theater Troupe 臺南人劇團 in Tainan, the Taitung Theater Troupe 臺東劇團 in Taitung, and the Nan Feng Theater Troupe 南風劇團 in Kaohsiung.

Dance

Dance in Taiwan has become especially diverse since the late 1960s. Early pioneers of modern dance in Taiwan include Tsai Jui-yueh 蔡瑞月 and Lee Tsai-o 李彩娥, who studied European-influenced modern dance in Japan and began performing in the 1940s. After the ROC government moved to Taiwan in 1949, Chinese folk dance was encouraged as a means of promoting traditional Chinese culture on the island. However, modern dance revived in the 1960s, as local dancers and audiences experienced new styles following tours by American companies such as Alvin Ailey and Paul Taylor.

The Revival of Modern Dance

One of the first to introduce modern dance to Taiwan was Liu Feng-shueh 劉鳳學, whom many today consider the matriarch of Taiwan dance. With dancers from her own studio, which was established in 1967, as well as students from the Department of Physical Education at National Taiwan Normal University, Liu presented modern choreography. In 1976, she formed the Neo-Classic Dance Company 新古典舞團, which continues to perform today. Her choreographic style is heavily influenced by Rudolf Laban, whose famous system of dance notation she studied in Germany in the 1970s. As a result, many of her works, such as *Carmina Burana* 布蘭詩歌 (1993), emphasize structural concepts of space and group formation.

The Cloud Gate Dance Theatre

In the early 1970s, Lin Hwai-min 林懷民 formed the Cloud Gate Dance Theatre 雲門舞集, which later became Taiwan's premier dance company, gaining a devoted local audience as well as an international reputation in numerous overseas tours. After studying under Martha Graham, Lin returned to Taiwan in 1973 and began using modern techniques along with Chinese opera concepts. His early works had strong Chinese themes, as in *The Tale of the White Serpent*, an updated version of a classic story.

Like the nativist artists and writers (see section on Painting, and Chapter 24, Literature) of the 1970s, Lin was eager to express a local identity. Cloud Gate's signature work, *Legacy* 薪傳 (1978), told the dramatic story of the first Chinese pioneers in Taiwan. Later works featured more contemporary concerns. *The Rite of Spring* 春之祭 (1983), for example, examined the plight of urban existence. The 1984 *Dreamscape* 夢土, and its reproduction in 1995, explored the Chinese conflict between modern life and traditional culture.

The 90-minute *Nine Songs* 九歌 (1993), which was re-staged at New York's Kennedy Center in 1995, draws on the work of ancient Chinese poet Chu Yuan 屈原 and contains many references to gods and goddesses, as well as movements from Indian and Javanese dance and Chinese opera. *Songs of the Wanderers* 流浪者之歌 (1994) depicts the pilgrimage of the spirit for peace and harmony. The work is deeply rooted in the religions, mysticism, meditation, and philosophies of Asia, especially Hinduism, Buddhism, and Zen. In 1997, the troupe performed *Songs of the Wanderers* in Paris, Copenhagen, and Hamburg.

Portrait of the Families 家族合唱 (1997), is an epic saga of Taiwanese under Japanese colonial rule and the martial law era of the Nationalist government. The work portrays the universal theme of human suffering and hardship at the hands of oppressors, and the fortitude to survive and heal.

Moon Water 水月 (1998), hailed as one of Cloud Gate's best works so far, integrates movements of tai chi and meditative philosophy into dances that portray themes of "nothingness."

Cloud Gate's more recent works include the millennium production *Burning the Juniper Branches* 焚松 (2000), based on Tibetan religious rituals, and *Green* 年輕 (2000), which incorporates dynamic movements and dazzling street dance. *Bamboo Dream* 竹夢, which premiered on April 21, 2001, uses the poetic image of bamboo groves to evoke serene Buddhist meditations and lofty classical ink paintings. *Cursive* 行草, which is Cloud Gate's latest work, incorporates masterpieces of classical Chinese calligraphy and premiered on December 1, 2001. It is scheduled to tour France, Australia, Germany, Norway, and the United States.

Cloud Gate has made dozens of overseas tours throughout Europe, Asia, Australia, North America, and South America, including engagements at the New York Next Wave Festival, the Sydney 2000 Olympic Arts Festival, the Lyon Biennial Dance Festival, the Adelaide Festival, the festival celebrating the 25th anniversary of Pina Bausch's Tanztheatre Wuppertal, Sadler's Wells Theatre London, Deutsche Opera Berlin, and the Kennedy Center. It was also the only Asian group invited to perform in the 2000 Sydney Olympic Games.

Cloud Gate Dance Theatre II was founded in 1999 to encourage young choreographers, touring campuses and local communities in Taiwan.

Diverse Dance Styles

Since the 1980s, a number of smaller dance companies have started up, many of them founded by former Cloud Gate members. Among them the most prominent is Lin Hsiu-wei's 林秀偉 Taigu Tales Dance Theater 太古踏舞團, known for its meditative dances based on Asian philosophy. With an emphasis on poetic expression and soul-searching, her works are stirring and cathartic, often with a primitive quality similar to the modern Japanese dance form Butoh.

Another former Cloud Gate dancer Liu Shao-lu 劉紹爐 also studied with Liu Feng-shueh early in his career and started his own group, the Taipei Dance Circle 光環舞集. Liu's best known work, *Olympics* 奧林匹克, is based on an innovative technique in which dancers with oiled bodies spin and slide on an oiled floor to create a surprisingly poetic display of motion. In 1996, the play received the Ludwig Foundation's Award in the performing arts for innovative choreography.

The Dance Forum Taipei 舞蹈空間, founded in 1989 by Ping Heng 平珩, presents a wide mixture of styles, but is best known for works that combine postmodernism with a Chinese or Asian frame of reference.

Although ballet has held a less prominent position in Taiwan, there are several ballet schools and small companies. One of the better known is the Taipei Chamber Ballet 臺北室內芭蕾舞團, which presents annual summer performances choreographed by Yu Neng-sheng 余能盛, the artistic director of Landestheater Coburg in Germany.

The works of Legend Lin Dance Theater 無垢舞蹈劇場, founded and directed by Lin Li-chen 林麗珍, are inspired by Taiwan's folk tradition. Its *Mirrors of Life* 醮, performed at France's Avignon Art Festival in July and August 1998, has a strong local flavor and features the vivacity of Taiwan's folk culture, while brilliantly demonstrating Taiwan's originality in choreography. Inspired by Taiwan's folk rituals, especially the sacrificial feasts of the Ghost Festival, the highly stylistic *Mirrors of Life* transcends the limits of culture and convention and attains universality through its enticing quietude, harmony, mystery, and wildness. Lin's latest work, *Anthem for Fading Flowers* 花神祭 (2000), is slow moving but measured as it equates the four seasons with the life cycle. The work was well received at the 2000 French Lyon Biennial Dance Festival 法國里昂雙年舞蹈節.

Several children's folk dance troupes have also introduced Chinese culture abroad. The best-known internationally is the Lan Yang Dancers 天主教蘭陽舞蹈團. Established in 1966 by Catholic missionary Gian Carlo Michelini, the troupe has been received by Vatican popes on six occasions and has made over 30 tours to Europe, America, Asia, Africa, and mainland China.

For the first time, Taiwan was invited to perform at the French Lyon Biennial Dance Festival (Biennale de la Danse, Lyon), which opened on June 26, 2000. Besides Cloud Gate and the Legend Lin Dance Theater, other performing groups that were invited include the Han Tang Classical Music Institute, the U Theater, and the performance troupe of the National Taiwan Junior College of Performing Arts 臺灣戲曲專科學校綜藝團, as well as artists Chen Chieh-jen 陳界仁 and Mai Ting-yen 梅丁衍.

The first Taipei International Dance Camp 臺北國際舞蹈營, co-hosted by the Taipei Arts International Association 臺北藝術推廣協會 and the Taipei National University of the Arts, took place between July 16 and August 5, 2000. Following its success, the 2001 Taiwan Dance Festival held from July 8 to 28 assembled 17 contemporary international dance masters to instruct in over 15 different types of dance and participate in panel discussions.

Cinema

Since the late 1980s, Taiwan films have been honored at film festivals and award ceremonies around the world. The prizes attained include the prestigious Golden Lion for best film awarded by the Venice International Film Festival to Hou Hsiao-hsien's *City of Sadness* 悲情城市 (1989), and Tsai Ming-liang's 蔡明亮 *Vive l'Amour* 愛情萬歲 (1994); the Golden Bear awarded by the Berlin International Film Festival to Ang Lee's 李安 *The Wedding Banquet* 囍宴 (1993); the Jury Prize awarded by the Cannes Festival to Hou

Hsiao-hsien's *The Puppetmaster* (1993); and a nomination of *The Wedding Banquet* for best foreign film at the 1994 Academy Awards.

In 1996, Taiwan cinema made a particularly impressive showing at the Asia-Pacific Film Festival: best director to Hou Hsiao-hsien for *Good Men, Good Women* 好男好女, best screenplay to Lee Khan 李崗 and Sylvia Chang 張艾嘉 for *Tonight, Nobody Goes Home* 今天不回家, and special juror award for *Ah Chung* 忠仔, directed by Chang Tso-chi 張作驥. In 1997, *The River* 河流, directed by Tsai Ming-liang, won a special jury prize at the Golden Bear in Berlin. In 1998, Hou Hsiao-hsien's *Flowers of Shanghai* 海上花 and Tsai Ming-liang's *The Hole* 洞 were among the Features in Competition at the Cannes Festival. In November 1999, *Darkness and Light* 黑暗之光, a film by Chang Tso-chi was awarded the prize for best picture at the 12th Tokyo International Film Festival. On November 26, Rene Liu 劉若英 was named best actress at the 1999 Asia-Pacific Film Festival for her performance in *The Personals* 徵婚啟事. On May 21, 2000, Edward Yang 楊德昌 won a Golden Palm award for best director at the Cannes Film Festival for *A One and A Two* 一一.

On February 18, 2001, *Betelnut Beauty* 愛你愛我, directed by Lin Cheng-sheng 林正盛, walked away from the Berlin International Film Festival with the Silver Bear for Best Director, and the movie's star, Lee Sinjie 李心潔, captured the Piper Heidsieck New Talent award for Best Young Actress. Later in March, Ang Lee's *Crouching Tiger, Hidden Dragon* 臥虎藏龍 won four Oscars at the 73rd Annual Academy Awards: Best Foreign Language Film, Best Art Direction, Best Cinematography, and Best Music (Score). It was also the highest grossing foreign language film in the US. In May 2001, Taiwanese sound engineer Tu Duu-chih 杜篤之 was awarded the Technical Prize at the 54th Cannes Film Festival for two films, *What Time Is It There?* 你那邊幾點? (by director Tsai Ming-liang) and *Millennium Mambo* 千禧曼波 (by director Hou Hsiao-hsien). Tsai Ming-liang's *What Time Is It There?* was also a big winner in the 46th Asia-Pacific Film

Festival held in October 2001, winning the prizes for Best Picture, Best Director, and Best Supporting Actress.

It has only been in the last dozen years, however, that Taiwan cinema has come into its own. Although during the late 1960s and early 1970s the island's film industry was one of the strongest in Asia, the scene was dominated by syrupy romances, grade-B kungfu movies, and moralistic or propaganda-oriented dramas. In time, the public and the media grew weary of the limited variety of domestically produced films. People were also exposed to high-quality foreign

Ang Lee's Oscar-winning epic "Crouching Tiger, Hidden Dragon" successfully introduces Eastern philosophy and the Wuxia genre to mainstream Western audiences.
(Courtesy of the Buena Vista Films)

movies through film festivals held by the National Film Archives 電影資料館 (originally the Motion Picture Library 電影圖書館), set up in 1977, and through the increasing availability of movies on videotape. Opportunities for scholarships and awards for young filmmakers and scriptwriters through the Motion Picture Development Fund 中華民國電影事業發展基金, established in 1975, helped create a better environment for quality cinema. Another plus was the Golden Horse Awards 金馬獎, Taiwan's version of the Oscars. Established in 1962, the awards first attracted world attention in 1980, and since then have become a prestigious affair for Taiwan film.

The Government Information Office 行政院新聞局 set up the Guidance Fund for Domestically Produced Films 國片製作輔導金 in 1990 to assist filmmakers in producing high-quality domestic films and thus promote the development of Taiwan's film industry. Over 80 films supported by the fund have represented the ROC in international film festivals and been recipients of major awards, raising the global status of Taiwan's film industry and contributing to the world recognition of many talented directors, screenwriters, and actors.

New Wave Cinema

The real breakthrough for Taiwan cinema came in 1982 with *In Our Time* 光陰的故事, a four-part film produced by the Central Motion Picture Corporation 中央電影公司 that featured four talented young directors: Edward Yang, Tao Te-chen 陶德辰, Ko I-cheng 柯一正, and Chang Yi 張毅. The film won over audiences by replacing melodrama and escapism with a realistic look at life in Taiwan.

This new approach paved the way for New Cinema, or New Wave Cinema, which has been compared stylistically to the Italian neo-realism. Initially inspired by Taiwan's nativist literature of the 1960s and 1970s (see also Chapter 24, Literature), New Wave directors, such as Hou Hsiao-hsien, Edward Yang, and Wang Tung 王童, created a cinema with a unique Taiwanese flavor by focusing on realistic and sympathetic portrayals of both rural and urban life.

Many New Cinema films were actually based on famous nativist novels. This was in fact the continuation of an established tradition of adapting literary works to the screen. From 1965 to 1983, for example, a total of 50 films were adapted from the romance novels of Chiung Yao 瓊瑤. However, the New Wave directors were not only interested in the stories of these novels, but also in their realistic, down-to-earth style and spirit. They wanted to give a genuine local flavor to their films. Like the nativist writers, they also critically reviewed some of the central issues facing Taiwan society, such as the struggle against poverty, conflicts with political authority, and the growing pains of urbanization and industrialization.

One of the first films in this mode was *The Sandwich Man* 兒子的大玩偶 (1983), a three-part movie by directors Hou Hsiao-hsien, Tseng Chuang-hsiang 曾壯祥, and Wan Jen 萬仁, and adapted from several short stories by the famous writer Huang Chun-ming 黃春明 dealing with the struggles of working class people in 1960s Taiwan.

New Cinema directors took a highly introspective approach in examining the effects of the political, social, and economic changes that Taiwan had experienced in the past five decades. Their works thus offer a fascinating chronicle of the island's social transformation in modern times. For example, Wang Tung's *The Strawman* 稻草人 (1987) and *Hill of No Return* 無言的山丘 (1992) portray the tragic, work-burdened lives of rural Taiwanese during the Japanese occupation. Wang's latest work, *The Red Persimmon* 紅柿子 (1996), tells the story of a mainland family that escaped to Taiwan in 1949. Hou Hsiao-hsien's *The City of Sadness* takes place just after the Japanese occupation and focuses on the conflicts between the local Taiwanese and the newly arrived Nationalist government, which came to a climax in the February 28 Incident of 1947 (for historical details, see section concerning the ROC on Taiwan in Chapter 4, History). Another of Hou's films, *A Time to Live and a Time to Die* 童年往事 (1985), examines life in rural Taiwan in the 1950s and

1960s. His more recent *Good Men, Good Women* covers political developments from the end of World War II to the present day. In contrast, the works of Edward Yang, such as *Taipei Story* 青梅竹馬 (1985), *The Terrorizers* 恐怖份子 (1986), and *Confucian Confusion* 獨立時代 (1994), reflect the clash of traditional values and modern materialism among young urbanites of the 1980s and 1990s.

Second New Wave

While New Wave films have continued to win critical acclaim, the initial enthusiasm of local audiences began to wear off in the late 1980s. The genre soon gave rise to many low-quality imitations, and viewers, growing tired of New Wave seriousness, were drawn to the escapist, entertainment-oriented films from Hong Kong, which soon began to dominate the market. Local directors found it increasingly difficult to secure financing for their films, which were not big box-office draws.

Nevertheless, during the lean years of the late 1980s and early 1990s, a number of talented new filmmakers started to create a "Second New Wave" for Taiwan cinema. Compared with the older generation, these new directors offer a much greater variety, in both content and style, although they still appear strongly committed to portraying a uniquely Taiwan perspective. They also tend to reject the nostalgic, historical approach of older filmmakers, being drawn instead toward exploring the pain and absurdities of contemporary life.

One of the major figures of the Second New Wave is Tsai Ming-liang, whose films *Rebels of the Neon God* 青少年哪吒 (1992) and the 1994 Venice winner *Vive l'Amour* take an existentialist approach to the plight of urban teenagers and young adults who are on the margins of today's affluent society. The latter also won praise for its unique style of filmmaking: it has no music or soundtrack, only the background noises of the city, and a minimal amount of dialogue, relying instead on the power of simple but ambiguous images.

Second New Wave director Stan Lai, also a key figure in Taiwan's stage theater (see section on The Performance Workshop), has also brought an experimental and light-hearted touch to his films. *The Peach Blossom Land* (1992), which won prizes at the Tokyo and Berlin film festivals, is an adaptation of one of Lai's stage productions. It is a tragic comedy involving two groups of actors who take turns rehearsing two very different plays on the same stage. His 1994 film, *The Red Lotus Society* 飛俠阿達, juxtaposes a fantastic story about a young man who is determined to fly like the martial arts masters of ancient China against the realistic setting of modern-day Taipei.

The films of Ang Lee, another Second New Wave director, take a more realistic approach to contemporary life. *Pushing Hands* 推手 (1991), *The Wedding Banquet* (1993), and *Eat Drink Man Woman* 飲食男女 (1994) look at the generational and cultural conflicts confronting modern Chinese families.

In 1994, Wu Nien-chen 吳念真, who already had a solid reputation as one of the island's top screenwriters before making his debut as a director, produced *A Borrowed Life* 多桑, which was awarded best film at the Turin International Film Festival, and *Buddha Bless America* 太平天國 (1996), which was shown at the Venice Festival. Chen Yu-hsun 陳玉勳 was awarded the Blue Leopard Prize at Switzerland's Locarno Film Festival for *Tropical Fish* 熱帶魚 (1995). Hsu Hsiao-ming 徐小明, Steve Wang 王獻篪, and Lin Cheng-sheng are also among Taiwan's new directors whose works have been shown at prestigious film festivals around the world.

Cross-Strait Collaboration

The film world has benefitted from the ROC government's relaxation on contacts with mainland China in recent years. The first contacts were at international film festivals in the mid-1980s, and in 1991, the ROC allowed actors from Taiwan to attend the Golden Rooster awards 金雞獎 in Beijing. Mainland directors Chen Kaige 陳凱歌 and Peng Xiaolian 彭小蓮 attended the Golden Horse awards 金馬獎 in

Taipei. Soon after, actors and directors from both sides were regularly exchanging visits, and Taiwan directors began shooting footage, or even entire films, on the mainland. Two recent examples are Wang Shau-di's 王小棣 *Accidental Legend* 飛天 (1996), shot in China, and Hou Hsiao-hsien's *Good Men, Good Women*, which includes several mainland scenes.

Perhaps the most significant cross-strait development in cinema has been Taiwan financing of mainland films. Mainland director Chen Kaige's *Farewell to My Concubine* 霸王別姬, which won the Golden Palm at Cannes in 1994 and was nominated (along with *The Wedding Banquet*) for an Academy Award, was financed by Taiwan actress-turned-producer Hsu Feng 徐楓. Hsu also backed Chen's 1996 production, *Temperance Moon* 風月.

ERA International 年代影視 is another Taiwan company that has supported mainland directors. ERA collaborations include two highly successful films by Zhang Yimou 張藝謀: *Raise the Red Lantern* 大紅燈籠高高掛, which won the 1992 Silver Lion Award in Venice and received an Academy Award nomination; and *To Live* 活著, winner of the Grand Jury Prize at Cannes in 1994. More recent Taiwan-backed mainland films include Huang Jianxin's 黃建新 *Wooden Man's Bride* 驗身 (1995) and Wu Ziniu's 吳子牛 *Don't Cry Nanking* 南京一九三七 (1995), both produced by Long Shong International 龍祥影視, and *Beijing Bicycles* 十七歲的單車 (2000), which won the Grand Jury Prize at the 2001 Berlin International Film Festival.

Public Art

"Public art" is a rather new concept in Taiwan. In 1992, the *Statute on Encouraging and Rewarding Cultural and Art Enterprises* 文化藝術獎助條例 began a new era in the development of Taiwan's public art. Article 9 of the statute stipulates that "the owner of public buildings should set up artworks with an expenditure of no less than one percent of that for such buildings in order to beautify the buildings and environment," and that "large-scale government projects of public construction should include the installment of artworks for a more beautiful environment." In accordance with this regulation, the *Public Art Establishment Measures* 公共藝術設置辦法, drafted by the Council for Cultural Affairs were promulgated and implemented in January 1998.

In 1994, the Council for Cultural Affairs began work on the Public Art Exhibition (Experimental) Establishment Project 公共藝術示範(實驗)計劃, with nine sites chosen for the exhibition of public art.

The Taipei City government designated 1997 as the Year of Public Art. Public buildings in Taipei that occupy more than 1,500 square meters or have construction expenditures of over US$14.7 million must allocate one percent of the cost to public art. Rewards are offered to encourage private enterprises that are exempt from this rule but are still willing to place public art. Public buildings or construction projects that are required to set up public art, but fail to do so, are unable to receive construction licenses from the Taipei City government.

Promoting the Arts

National Award for Arts

Following passage of the *Statutes on the Establishment of the National Culture and Arts Foundation* 國家文藝基金會設置條例, the National Culture and Arts Foundation 國家文化藝術基金 was founded in January 1996 as a non-profit organization whose goals include providing a locale for cultural-artistic endeavors, encouraging cultural-artistic work, and improving cultural-artistic levels. Since 1997, the foundation has been granting cultural awards to honor outstanding artists. In 2001, the award was renamed "National Award for Arts" 國家文藝獎 and divided for the first time into three categories: literature, fine art, and performing arts. The 2001 winners for the National Award for Arts were Yeh Shih-tao 葉石濤 in literature, Wang Pan-yuan 王攀元 in the fine arts, and Stan Lai and Hsu Wang in the performing arts.

International Art Festivals

In recent years, the Council for Cultural Affairs has vigorously promoted international cultural exchanges and the rejuvenation of local culture. It has helped various counties and cities hold small-scale international cultural and artistic events in the hope that these activities will take root in communities and become local features. In 2001, 19 cities and counties organized events that celebrated folk arts like masks, performance arts like puppet theater and woodwind orchestras, fine arts like glass works, crafts like kite-making and weaving, and even art in the largest sense with festivals of "container art" and "land art." Taipei City also hosted the 2001 Cultural City of Asia-Pacific 亞太文化之都 from July to November. The event included seven series of cultural activities co-organized by other local governments under the theme of "Crossing Over" 跨越. A total of 90 mayors and cultural leaders from 41 Asia-Pacific cities also attended the 2001 Asia-Pacific Cultural Cooperation Conference 亞太文化合作會議 in Taipei to enhance cultural exchanges and cooperation in the Asia-Pacific region.

Further Reading

(in Chinese unless otherwise noted):

The Art of Classical Chinese Flower Arrangement (in English). The Women's Garden and Art Club of the Republic of China, ed. Taipei: Council for Cultural Affairs, Executive Yuan, 1986.

Chang Shao-tsai 張少載. *Chinese Architecture* (Chung-kuo te chien-chu yi-shu 中國的建築藝術). Taipei: Grand East Enterprise, 1979.

Chen Chi-lu 陳奇祿. *Woodcarving of the Paiwan Tribe of Taiwan* (Pai-wan-tsu mu-tiao wen-wu-chan 排灣族木雕文物展). Taipei: Council of Chinese Culture Renaissance, 1992.

Lydia Chen 陳夏生. *Chinese Knotting* (in English). Taipei: Echo Publishing Co., Ltd., 1982.

Chiu Kun-liang 邱坤良. *Music in Traditional Chinese Opera* (Chung-kuo te chuan-tung hsi-chu yin-yueh 中國的傳統戲曲音樂). Taipei: Yuan Liu Publishing Co., 1981.

Contemporary Ceramics from the Republic of China (Chung-hua min-kuo tang-tai tao-tzu-chan 中華民國當代陶瓷展; Chinese-English bilingual). Taipei: Council for Cultural Affairs, Executive Yuan, 1988.

Contemporary Sculpture Exhibition: ROC, 1991 (Yi-chiuchiu-yi chung-hua min-kuo tang-tai tiao-su-chan 一九九一中華民國當代雕塑展; Chinese-English bilingual). Taipei: Taipei Fine Arts Museum, 1991.

Chuang Po-ho 莊伯和. *Chinese Sculpture* (Chung-kuo te tiao-ke yi-shu 中國的雕刻藝術). Taipei: Council for Cultural Affairs, Executive Yuan, 1988.

Current Concerns: Humanistic Focus in Modern Taiwan Clay (Tang-hsia-kuan-chu: Tai-wan-tao te jen-wen hsin-ching 當下關注：臺灣陶的人文新境; Chinese-English bilingual). Taipei: Taipei Fine Arts Museum, 1995.

The Development of Modern Art in Taiwan (Tai-wan ti-chu hsien-tai mei-shu te fa-chan 臺灣地區現代美術的發展). Taipei: Taipei Fine Arts Museum, 1990.

A Guide to the Taiwan Folk Arts Museum (Tai-wan min-chien yi-shu hsin-shang 臺灣民間藝術欣賞; Chinese-English bilingual). Taipei: Taiwan Folk Arts Museum, 1989.

International Conference, China: Modernity and Art (Chung-kuo hsien-tai mei-shu kuo-chi hsüeh-shu yen-tao-hui lun-wen-chi 中國現代美術國際學術研討會論文集; Chinese-English bilingual). Taipei: Taipei Fine Arts Museum, 1991.

International Print Exhibition: 1983 ROC (Chung-hua min-kuo kuo-chi pan-hua-chan 中華民國國際版畫展). Taipei: Council for Cultural Affairs, Executive Yuan, 1983.

Ju Ming Sculptures (Chu-ming tiao-ke 朱銘雕刻; Chinese-English bilingual). Singapore: Ministry of Community Development, 1986.

Juan Chang-jui 阮昌銳. *The Sculptural Art of Taiwan's Ab-origines* (Tai-wan shan-pao tiao-ke yi-shu 臺灣山胞雕刻藝術). Nantou: Department of Education, Taiwan Provincial Government, 1991.

T.C. Lai, *Chinese Seals* (in English). Seattle: University of Washington Press, 1976.

Lin Hsing-yüeh 林惺嶽. *The Vicissitudes of Taiwanese Art Over 40 Years* (Tai-wan mei-shu feng-yun ssu-shih nien 臺灣美術風雲四十年). Taipei: *The Independence Evening Post*, 1991.

Liu Liang-yu 劉良佑. *Chinese Handicrafts* (Chung-kuo chi-wu yi-shu 中國器物藝術). Taipei: Hsiung Shih Art Books Company, 1972.

Local Folk Arts (Hsiang-tu te min-tsu yi-shu 鄉土的民族藝術). Taipei: Council for Cultural Affairs, Executive Yuan, 1988.

The Origins and Development of Chinese Calligraphy

(Chung-hua shu-fa yuan-liu 中華書法源流). Yunlin: Association for the Promotion of the Welfare of the Hearing and Speaking Impaired in Taiwan Province, 1972.

An Overview of the Chinese Film Industry (in English). Taipei: Kwang Hwa Publishing Company, 1991.

So Yu-ming 索予明. *The Best of Classical Chinese Handicrafts* (Ku-tien kung-yi ching-hua 古典工藝精華). Taipei: Council for Cultural Affairs, Executive Yuan, 1984.

Sung Lung-fei 宋龍飛. *The Exquisite Art of Chinese Porcelain* (Ching-ya chüeh-lun chung-kuo tzu-chi 精雅絕倫中國瓷器). Taipei: Council for Cultural Affairs, Executive Yuan, 1988.

Taipei Biennial: The Quest for Identity (Yi-chiu-chiu-liu shuang-nien-chan: tai-wan yi-shu chu-ti-hsing 一九九六雙年展：臺灣藝術主體性; Chinese-English bilingual). Taipei: Taipei Fine Arts Museum, 1996.

Talks on Dance and the Cloud Gate Dance Company (Yun-men wu-hua 雲門舞話). Taipei: Yuan Liu Publishing Co., 1976.

Teng Sui-ning 鄧綏寧. *Chinese Drama* (Chung-kuo te hsi-chu 中國的戲劇). Nantou: Department of Information, Taiwan Provincial Government, 1969.

Tu Yun-chih 杜雲之. *Chinese Cinema* (Chung-kuo te tien-ying 中國的電影). Taipei: Crown Publishing Co., 1978.

Yearbook of the Performing Arts (Piao-yen yi-shu nien-chien 表演藝術年鑑). Taipei: National Chiang Kai-shek Cultural Center, 2001.

"Yu Peng and the Postwar Generation of Chinese Painters in Taiwan," *Yu Peng a Contemporary Chinese Painter* (in English). Towson, Maryland: Asian Arts Center, Towson State University, 1991.

Yuyu Yang in Stainless Steel (Yang Ying-feng pu-hsiu-kang tiao-su 楊英風不鏽鋼雕塑; Chinese-English bilingual). Singapore: The Ministry of Information and the Arts, 1991.

100 Years of Taiwanese Music: 1895–1995 (Tai-wan yin-yueh yi-pai-nien 臺灣音樂一百年). Taipei: The Egret Cultural and Educational Foundation, 1995.

Related Website
Council for Cultural Affairs: *http://www.cca.gov.tw*

NRS™
NO RESONANCE SYSTEM

GIANT BICYCLES®

ULTIMATE SUSPENSION

Giant uses Formula One racing technology to develop first no-power loss suspension system. Computer monitoring shows significant performance improvements.

For the details, go & check our web.

w.giant-bicycles.com

The Beauty of Taiwan Crafts

CRAFTS EXHIBITION CENTER
573, Chung-Cheng Rd., Tsao-Tuen, Nantou
9AM-5PM, Tuesday-Sunday, Closed on National Holidays
TEL: 886-49-367805   FAX: 886-49-356593
E-mail add: exhibit@ntcri.gov.tw

TAIWAN CRAFTS CENTER
9F. 20 Nan Hai Rood, Taipei, Taiwan, ROC
9AM-5PM, Tuesday-Sunday, Closed on National Holidays
TEL: 886-2-23563880   FAX: 886-2-23563882
E-mail add: tphritpe@ms17.hinet.net

 國立台灣工藝研究所
NATIONAL TAIWAN CRAFT RESEARCH INSTITUTE
http://www.tpg.gov.tw/ntcri

A Proven
Track Record

ow 17 years since the Howard
aza Hotel Taipei's 1984
ening and still leading the field.
aiwan's first five star hotel chain,
e group has expanded to
siness hotels in Taipei,
sinchu, Taichung and
aohsiung and luxury resorts in
cific Green Bay, Shihmen Dam
d Kenting. Well established
and-wide our state of the art
rvices mean we've got all the
gles covered. At work or at play,
herever you are, giving you
e choice.

Howard
OTELS · RESORTS · SUITES

porate Sales Office
, Jen Ai Road, Sec. 3,
ei, Taiwan 106, R.O.C.
: 886-2-23267527
: 886-2-27082376
ail : howard@ howard-hotels.com
: http ://www.howard-hotels.com

22
Tourism

Resort areas in central Taiwan devastated by the 921 earthquake, such as Sun Moon Lake in Nantou County, have received government funding to rebuild. (Photo by Chen Chih-ming)

Exotic culture, breathtaking scenery, priceless art, the entire range of Chinese cuisine, and friendly people make the Republic of China an excellent destination for tourists. Travelers to the ROC can enjoy themselves in comfort with fast and convenient transportation, excellent hotels, and clean restaurants. Unfortunately, many visitors to Taiwan never go far beyond Taipei, and thus deprive themselves of rich cultural experiences and the island's scenic wonders.

Northern Taiwan: Where Ancient and Modern Coexist

The ROC's "economic miracle" has modernized Taipei, but the city still maintains traditional lifestyles, making it a fascinating destination for visitors.

Taipei's National Palace Museum 國立故宮博物院 has the world's largest collection of oriental art treasures, spanning over five millennia of Chinese history. Much of the immense collection of jade, porcelain, paintings, and bronzes is regularly rotated, so each visit is unique. The museum has regular guided tours in several foreign languages, including English and French. English-language tours begin daily at 10:00 A.M. and 3:00 P.M., and self-guided tape tours in English and Japanese are also available.

The Chiang Kai-shek Memorial Hall 中正紀念堂 in Taipei is the island's most impressive monument to the late president. The massive marble memorial hall dominates beautiful gardens, graceful pavilions, and placid ponds. A Ming-style arch at the main entrance is flanked by two buildings: the National Theater 國家劇院 and the National Concert Hall 國家音樂廳.

To appreciate the vitality of Chinese temples, Lungshan Temple 龍山寺—one of the city's oldest and most famous, with striking ornamentation—is highly recommended. Stone columns, with figures dancing on the backs of intricately carved dragons, support a heavily-ornamented roof.

The World of Yesterday 昨日世界 offers visitors displays of mythology, ancient toys, games, and handicrafts. Chinese opera and demonstrations of crafts and folk arts are presented on Sundays and holidays. The World of Yesterday is located on Chung Shan North Road across from the Taipei Fine Arts Museum 臺北市立美術館, which hosts exhibitions by both international and domestic artists.

The Lin Family Garden 林本源園邸 is Taiwan's best example of Ching dynasty Chinese architecture and gardens. Originally a Fujian merchant's house, the garden is landscaped with exquisite pavilions, towers, cottages, bridges, artificial mountains, and placid pools, offering views of distant mountains.

North of Taipei is Yangmingshan National Park 陽明山國家公園, where visitors can find waterfalls, volcanic craters, lakes, steaming hot springs, and springtime cherry and azalea blossoms. Well-maintained walkways and trails lead to the park's main scenic spots, which offer picnic and recreation areas.

Other areas of northern Taiwan beyond the borders of Taipei City are rich in country beauty. At Yehliu 野柳, or "wild willows," on the northern coast west of Keelung 基隆, wind and water have carved the rocks into a variety of unusual shapes.

The coastline east of Keelung, set aside as the Northeast Coast National Scenic Area 東北角海岸國家風景區, is one of the loveliest regions on the island. A notable feature of this area is the magnificent sandstone promontory that rises from the sea at Lungtung 龍洞. Farther down the coast, pure white sand and azure waters make the Fulung Seaside Park 福隆海濱公園 one of Taiwan's best beaches. Next to Fulung is the Yenliao Seaside Park 鹽寮海濱公園, whose wooden pavilions and walkways lend a Chinese character to the park. The scenic area maintains a Ching dynasty footpath. Sailing, surfing, camping, and fishing equipment can also be rented.

Taiwan's largest camping area was opened in 1991 at the most beautiful part of the Northeast Coast National Scenic Area. Lungmen Riverside Camping Resort 龍門露營渡假基地, a short distance from Yenliao and Fulung, provides sightseeing, water sports, camping, and bicycling.

Tourist boats now take visitors on the "blue highway" connecting Ilan County and Taipei County.

A historical fort, fresh seafood, and beautiful sunsets make the quaint seaside town of Tamsui 淡水 a popular day trip from Taipei. Old-fashioned shops along the main road give visitors a feel for the town's history. Oxford College and Mackay Hospital, which were both built in the late 1800s by Western missionaries, are still operating. Fort San Domingo, known as the "Red-haired Fort" 紅毛城, was built by the Spanish in

1629, occupied by the Dutch in 1642, leased to the British in 1867, and bombarded by the French in 1884.

Tamsui has many seafood restaurants, with large selections of fresh delicacies on display. Some of the restaurants are built along the Tamsui River to provide diners with a riverside view of Tamsui's sunset.

Wulai 烏來, just south of Taipei, is an aboriginal enclave where visitors can enjoy hot springs, witness the traditional dances and ceremonies of Taiwan's Atayal tribe, and view a powerful waterfall cascading through lush vegetation.

Just an hour south of Taipei, visitors can take a one-stop tour of China's Great Wall, Beijing's Forbidden City, and the Temple of Heaven. Window on China 小人國 displays 130 of the best-known structures in both Taiwan and the Chinese mainland in miniature, and a recently added section features famous buildings from all over the world. With careful attention to detail, thousands of living trees and shrubs are shaped and grown to sizes proportional to the various buildings. Window on China also has a classical Chinese garden, restaurants, snack bars, a tea house, an amusement park, and souvenir shops.

Buddhist temples, shrines, and monasteries reminiscent of ancient China are perched on the cool, verdant hills of Lion's Head Mountain 獅頭山, which is located about halfway between Taipei and Taichung.

A short trip through the lush countryside southwest of Taipei brings visitors to the small town of Yingke 鶯歌, which produces hand-painted replicas of elegant Ming (1368-1644) and Ching (1644-1911) vases. Yingke is Taiwan's ceramics center, and the narrow streets are lined with shops selling an endless variety, ranging from simple earthenware tea sets to delicate statues. Some of the factories provide tours, allowing visitors to watch potters working the clay and artists painting vases. The information desk at the Yingke Town Hall can help arrange such tours.

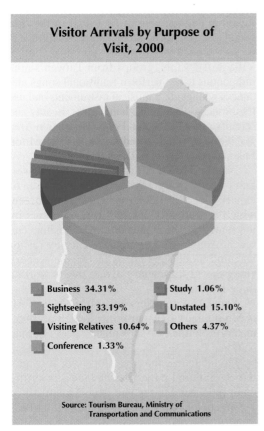

Visitor Arrivals by Purpose of Visit, 2000

Business 34.31%
Sightseeing 33.19%
Visiting Relatives 10.64%
Conference 1.33%
Study 1.06%
Unstated 15.10%
Others 4.37%

Source: Tourism Bureau, Ministry of Transportation and Communications

For those who enjoy shopping, night markets offer fun and a lot of local color. Products include casual clothes, fruits, snacks, and novelty items. The night markets with the best bargains in food, fashions, and curios in the Taipei area include the Shihlin 士林 night market, located north of the Grand Hotel; the Kungkuan 公館 night market, near National Taiwan University; the Shihta 師大 night market, on Shih Ta Road off of Hoping East Road; the Hua Hsi Street 華西街 night market; the Tung Hua Street 通化街 night market, near the World Trade Center; the Jao Ho Street 饒河街 night market, in the Sungshan district; and the Chingkuang 晴光 market, which is off of Chung Shan North Road.

Central Taiwan: Enchanting Cascades and Snowy Peaks

Central Taiwan displays the full range of the island's beauty: mountain lakes and shining seas, roaring rivers and steaming hot springs, lofty snow-capped peaks and lush tropical valleys, and emerald forests and craggy ravines.

Taichung is the major city in this region and is one of Taiwan's main business centers. Taichung's location, quality hotels, museums, cafes, and convenient transportation make it a good starting point for trips to many of the island's tourist sites.

Encore Garden 亞哥花園, a masterpiece of landscape gardening, is located just ten kilometers northeast of Taichung. In addition to a tremendous variety of flowering plants, the garden also has snack bars, a children's playground, hiking trails, and camping and barbecue sites. In the evenings, a fountain lit by multicolored lights pulses to the rhythm of music.

A giant Buddha statue sits on Pakua Hill 八卦山 overlooking Changhua City 彰化, southwest of Taichung. Inside the hollow statue are dioramas illustrating Buddhist teachings, and visitors can also view the surrounding area through the statue's eyes. South of Changhua is the quaint old town of Lukang 鹿港, or "deer harbor," one of Taiwan's most important historical and cultural centers. Lukang is noted for its impressive Matsu and Lungshan temples, as well as for the annual four-day Lukang Folk Arts Festival, which begins usually three days before the Dragon Boat Festival.

The Central Cross-island Highway 中橫公路, Asia's most beautiful mountain road, winds its way from just outside of Taichung, over the Central Mountain Range, through Taroko National Park 太魯閣國家公園, and down to the island's east coast. The route offers travellers broad vistas across cloud-filled valleys, mist-shrouded peaks, starry skies, beautiful sunrises, delightful forest walks, rushing mountain streams, and hot springs.

Southeast of Taichung lie some of the region's most popular scenic spots. Emerald waters, jade mountains, temples, hiking, boating, and a picturesque pagoda can all be found in the Sun Moon Lake National Scenic Area 日月潭國家風景區. At the nearby Formosan Aboriginal Culture Village 九族文化村, groups from Taiwan's nine indigenous tribes perform traditional songs and dances with ancient musical instruments and use traditional tools to make handicrafts. Beauty and serenity make the Hsitou Forest Recreation Area 臺大溪頭實驗林場, located south of Sun Moon Lake, another favorite getaway.

Nearby Mount Ali (Alishan) 阿里山 is well known for its view of the sunrise over a sea of clouds. Blue peaks rise from a fleecy gray ocean, which is gradually painted in vivid colors by the sunrise as the clouds dissipate. Visitors can reach Mount Ali from Chiayi City by rail or bus, and though the bus is faster, the scenery along the 72-kilometer railway ride is worth a three-hour trip.

Some 15 kilometers away from Mount Ali is Mount Jade (Yushan) 玉山, which at 3,952 meters is Northeast Asia's highest peak. Yushan National Park 玉山國家公園, which is dominated by Mount Jade's massive slopes, is Taiwan's largest national park. Mount Jade's towering main peak can be reached from Mount Ali or via an ancient trail known as the Patung Pass Road 八通關古道.

Southern Taiwan: Bucolic Scenes from the Past

Southern Taiwan is a study in contrasts. Bustling modern cities with all the latest amenities are surrounded by the pastoral panorama of old Taiwan.

Tainan, the island's oldest and fourth largest city, has the unhurried atmosphere of a small country town. Famous today for its unusual snacks, it is also filled with reminders of the city's past: gates, memorial arches, remnants of forts, and temples that date back three centuries or more.

Visa Information

Tourist visas for the Republic of China can be obtained from the ROC Ministry of Foreign Affairs and ROC embassies, consulates, and designated representative offices in foreign countries (see Appendix, Directory of ROC Representatives Abroad).

Foreign nationals may obtain a visitor visa if they hold a foreign passport or travel document valid for more than six months and wish to stay less than six months in the Republic of China for business, sightseeing, family visits, study or training, visits by invitation (with letter of invitation), transit, technical assistance, medical treatment, or other legitimate activities.

Visa requirements include one completed application form, incoming and outgoing travel tickets (or a letter of confirmation from a travel agency), three photos, documents verifying the purpose of the visit (except for transit or sightseeing), and, in some cases, a letter of guarantee.

Foreign nationals coming to the ROC for tourism purposes are issued a visitor visa valid for between two weeks and 60 days, and unless restricted to two weeks, may apply for a maximum of two extensions of 60 days each for a total of six months. The visa may be either single- or multiple-entry and valid for up to one year (or up to five years for citizens of those countries that have signed reciprocal agreements with the ROC) for stays of up to six months. Holders of a visitor visa for tourism are not permitted to assume employment in the ROC.

Participants in major international meetings and guests of the ROC government can get visas upon arrival, if their names are on an approved list.

Citizens of 20 countries—Australia, Austria, Belgium, Canada, Costa Rica, France, Germany, Greece, Italy, Japan, Luxembourg, the Netherlands, New Zealand, Portugal, Singapore, Spain, Sweden, Switzerland, the United Kingdom, and the United States—may enter the ROC visa-free for stays of up to 14 days, so long as their passports are valid for at least six months from the date of entry, and they possess onward or return tickets with confirmed seats.

Complete information on ROC visas can be obtained from:

Bureau of Consular Affairs
Ministry of Foreign Affairs
3rd Floor, 2-2 Chi Nan Road, Section 1
Taipei 103, Taiwan, ROC
Phone: 886-2-2343-2888

More than 200 temples in Tainan provide some of the best remaining examples of southern Chinese architecture in Taiwan. They range from the serene Confucian Temple 孔廟 built in 1666 to the elaborate new Temple of the Goddess of the Sea 聖母廟 at Luerhmen 鹿耳門, a complex built by some of Taiwan's finest artisans.

Tainan's other major historical sites include Fort Zeelandia 安平古堡 and Fort Provintia 赤崁樓, both originally built during the Dutch occupation in the 1600s, and the "new" Eternal Fortress 億載金城, built by the Chinese in 1876.

Directly south of Tainan is Kaohsiung, Taiwan's second largest city, foremost industrial center, and largest international port. In addition to offering excellent shopping, dining, and night life, Kaohsiung is also close to many notable tourist attractions. One such attraction is Mount Longevity 壽山, whose hillside temples, pavilions, shaded terraces, and city view make it worth a stop. Cheng Ching Lake 澄清湖, just north of Kaohsiung, features a pagoda, islands, pavilions, tree-lined pathways, and a variety of recreational facilities. Both the graceful Spring and Autumn Pavilions 春秋閣 and the nearby Dragon and Tiger Pagodas 龍虎塔, all of which stand in the placid waters of Lotus Lake 蓮池潭, are also worth a view. Beside the lake are temples dedicated to Confucius and the God of War.

About an hour's drive northeast of Kaohsiung is the island's tallest image of a Buddha, which gazes over the surrounding rice paddies in the countryside. The huge, 120-meter-tall gilded statue is surrounded by 480 life-size, gold-colored Buddha images near the entrance to the Light of Buddha Mountain (Mt. Fokuang) 佛光山, home to one of Taiwan's largest temple complexes and the island's center of Buddhist scholarship.

Moon World 月世界, an area of banana and jujube orchards, bamboo groves, and fish ponds, is named for its lunar landscape of sharp-peaked clay hills with steep, deeply eroded slopes and sawtooth ridges. One of the most interesting sights here is the unpredictable "mud volcano,"

a small crater filled with thin, cold mud through which gas bubbles occasionally rise to the surface. A deep rumble gives a warning just before the gas bursts through, whipping the mud into a bubbling gray mass that spills out of the crater.

The southernmost point of Taiwan, which is a two-hour drive from Kaohsiung, forms a crescent known as the Hengchun, or "eternal spring," Peninsula 恆春半島. Kenting National Park 墾丁國家公園, the ROC's first national park, encompasses much of the peninsula and offers spectacular shorelines with both coral and rock formations. Kenting also has some of Taiwan's best beaches, with clean white sand and many types of water sports. Pleasant wooded paths

Pertinent Customs Regulations for Inbound Passengers

All adults aged 20 or over, may bring into the ROC one liter of alcoholic beverages, 25 cigars, 200 cigarettes, or one pound of tobacco products duty-free.

A written declaration is required when bringing dutiable articles into the ROC. Passengers may bring in any amount of gold, but must declare it to Customs. If the total value of gold exceeds US$10,000, an import permit issued by the Board of Foreign Trade (Ministry of Economic Affairs), is needed at the port of entry. No more than NT$40,000 in notes can be brought in by each passenger unless a permit from the Central Bank of China is obtained in advance. Any amount of foreign currency may be brought in, but amounts in excess of US$5,000 must be declared.

There are severe penalties for the importation, use, possession, or sale of the following prohibited articles:
• Counterfeit currency or forging equipment;
• Gambling apparatus or foreign lottery tickets;
• Obscene or indecent materials;
• Publications or other articles propagating Communism;
• Articles produced, manufactured, processed, originated or published on the Chinese mainland not including those products within the scope of limitation;
• All arms (including shotguns, fishing-guns, and airguns) whether real or toy, gun-shaped appliances, ammunition, cartridges, explosives, posionous gas, assault knives, and other weapons of war;
• Opium, poppy seeds, cannabis seeds, cocaine seeds, or narcotics drugs that are listed in the *Law for the Control of Narcotics,* as well as their derivatives and products;
• All restricted substances or drugs that are non-prescription or non-medicinal in nature (including marijuana);
• Articles infringing on the patents, designs, trademarks, or copyrights of another person or entity;
• Contraband articles, as specified by other laws, e.g., soil, plants, and their products brought in from districts affected with injurious pests and diseases, and/or animals and their products from an infected area. No fruit can be brought in by passengers. All aquatic products (excluding dried, canned, and vacuum-packed ones) shall be destroyed or returned abroad;
• Any wild animals, endangered species of wildlife, or products made from such are not allowed to be imported, unless a permit is obtained from the authority concerned in advance.

Source: Directorate General of Customs, Ministry of Finance

wind through a large botanical garden containing a variety of exotic plant life. Visitors can also wander through unusual dryland coral formations or rest at pavilions and enjoy the view by the sea. Facilities include an international-class resort hotel, as well as economical lodgings.

The Penghu Archipelago 澎湖群島, also known as the Pescadores, consists of 64 separate islands in the Taiwan Strait roughly midway between Taiwan and the Chinese mainland. Fishing is the major source of income, and a meal of fresh seafood is a must for visitors. The islands offer fascinating sightseeing opportunities, with ancient temples, picturesque farms, windswept fishing villages, friendly people, fine beaches, and rugged coastlines. Fishing, swimming, snorkeling, scuba diving, wind surfing, and boating are the major recreational activities in the archipelago. In July 1995, the government established the Penghu National Scenic Area 澎湖國家風景區.

Eastern Taiwan: Unspoiled Natural Beauty

Eastern Taiwan has some of the island's most beautiful and accessible attractions, notably Taroko Gorge, the East Coast National Scenic Area 東部海岸國家風景區, and the East Rift Valley National Scenic Area 花東縱谷國家風景區.

Taroko Gorge, a spectacular marble-walled cleft that runs for 19 kilometers through the mountains near the east coast, is the focus of Taroko National Park. At the head of the gorge is the village of Tienhsiang 天祥, which is known for its suspension bridge, pagoda, and new five-star hotel.

Located at the eastern end of the Central Cross-island Highway, the city of Hualien 花蓮 is renowned for producing the best marble products on the island. The vast marble deposits in the area are sculpted into an amazing range of products, such as animal figures, chess sets, wine and coffee sets, bookends, ash trays, kitchen utensils, and furniture.

Hualien is also popular for performances of song and dance by the island's indigenous people. Nearly 80,000 aborigines, mostly from the Ami tribe 阿美族, reside in the area. The annual Ami harvest festivals, which are held in more than 20 villages in Hualien and Taitung Counties on various days in July and August, are elaborate spectacles of colorful, costumes, music, and dance. Tribal dances are also performed regularly at the Ami Culture Village 阿美文化村, which is about a 15-minute drive from Hualien.

The Yami don their traditional costumes only during certain ceremonies and rituals. The hand-carved canoes often serve as a central focus of such events.

Most of the coastal road from Hualien to Taitung runs through the East Coast National Scenic Area, an isolated, unspoiled region where development is strictly controlled to preserve the area's natural beauty. The coastal highway's attractions include picturesque temples inside mountain caves, ancient banyan trees, coral reefs, fantastic rock formations, and deserted beaches that stretch for miles.

The East Rift Valley National Scenic Area covers the inter-mountain valley in Hualien and Taitung Counties, with the exception of the nine urban planning areas of the National Dong Hwa University 國立東華大學 special district. The total area is 138,368 hectares. The East Rift Valley National Scenic Area Administration 花東縱谷國家風景區管理處 was established on April 15, 1997, to develop the area. A total of NT$370 million will have been invested in this area by the end of fiscal year 2001.

Just south of Taitung is the Chihpen Hot Springs 知本溫泉 resort, which offers several interesting sites for tourists. First is the Chihpen Hot Springs itself, which has public bathing facilities. Nearby hotels provide more private bathing. A short distance from the hotels, a path leads to the beautiful White Jade Waterfall 白玉瀑布. Inner Hot Spring, two kilometers down the main road from Chihpen Hot Spring, has newer hotels and a mineral water swimming pool. On a lane off the main road from Chihpen to the Inner Hot Spring 內溫泉 is Chingchueh Temple 清覺寺, which has two large Buddha images: one of bronze from Thailand and the other of jade from Burma. A suspension bridge leads to the Chihpen Forest Recreation Area 知本森林遊樂區, which is located on a mountainside covered with bamboo groves and dense forests. The recreation area offers a riverside picnic spot, campground, bonfire area,

---

Customs Regulations for Outbound Passengers

A written declaration is only required for outbound passengers carrying the following:
- Gold, over US$5,000 in foreign currencies or over NT$40,000 in New Taiwan Dollar notes;
- Commercial samples or dutiable items such as a personal computer (PC), professional photography equipment and cameras, etc., that are beyond the duty exemption limit in value but are intended to be brought back into the country.

Each passenger is allowed to take out of the country:
- Up to US$5,000 in cash or its equivalent in other foreign currencies (Higher amounts must be declared to and recorded by Customs, if not, they will be subject to confiscation);
- Up to NT$40,000 in cash (Higher amounts are allowed if a permit from the Central Bank of China is obtained in advance, if not, the excess cannot be brought out);
- Any amount of gold, but passengers must first declare it to Customs (If the total value of gold exceeds US$20,000, an export permit issued by the Board of Foreign Trade, Ministry of Economic Affairs, is needed at the port of departure).

Articles that may not be taken out of the country include unauthorized reprints or copies of books, records, and videotapes; genuine Chinese antiques, ancient coins, and paintings; and items prohibited from entry, such as firearms, drugs, counterfeit currency, and contraband.

For further Customs information, please contact:

Directorate General of Customs
Ministry of Finance
13 Ta Cheng Street
Taipei 103, Taiwan, ROC
Phone: 886-2-2550-5500

flower garden, and a footpath to a waterfall. Near the top is a huge banyan tree, whose long, gnarled roots surround half of a restful pavilion.

Green Island 綠島, located just off the Pacific coast of Taiwan, is now a part of the East Coast National Scenic Area. The island is known for its saltwater hot spring (one of only three in the world), coral reefs, and spectacular coastal scenery. The island's reefs, waters, and beaches are great for fishing, swimming, snorkeling, and scuba diving.

Just south of Green Island lies Orchid Island 蘭嶼, which takes its name from the wild orchids that grow in the hills. Orchid Island is inhabited by the Yami, Taiwan's indigenous tribe, who do some farming but rely primarily on fishing for a living. The intricately painted wooden boats used by the tribe are built entirely by hand and are joined together by wooden pegs (for more about the Yami, see Chapter 2, People).

Chinese Festivals

All Chinese lunar festivals are celebrated with verve and color throughout Taiwan (see Appendix, National Holidays and Festivals).

The first major festival of the year, Chinese New Year or Lunar New Year 春節, is the most important of the annual festivals. It is followed by the Lantern Festival 元宵節 on the first full moon of the lunar calendar (usually during the month of February on the solar calendar). Next on the calendar is the birthday of Matsu, Goddess of the Sea, which is celebrated with elaborate rites at Matsu temples throughout Taiwan. Tourists should visit Peikang 北港, or the "northern harbor," to see the annual pilgrimage and elaborate celebrations. After Matsu's birthday is the Dragon Boat Festival 端午節. At this time, dragon boat races are held and rice dumplings wrapped in bamboo leaves 粽子 are eaten to commemorate the drowned poet-statesman Chu Yuan. The Ghost Festival 中元節, which comes next, is the time when the gates of Hell are opened and spirits visit the land of the living. It is marked by elaborate temple ceremonies, feasts for wandering ghosts, and other activities. The Mid-Autumn or Moon Festival 中秋節, usually held in September, celebrates the harvest moon with family reunions, barbecues, gazing at the full moon,

The sky lanterns of Pinghsi in Taipei County is a serene affair, which attracts thousands of people each year.

Visitor Information Sources

• *The Tourism Bureau*
  Ministry of Transportation and Communications (MOTC)
  9th Floor, 280 Chung Hsiao E. Road, Section 4, Taipei 106
  Phone: 886-2-2349-1635
  Internet Address: *http://www. tbroc. gov. tw*
  E-mail: *tbroc@tbroc.gov.tw*

• *Taiwan Visitors Association*
  5th Floor, 9 Min Chuan E. Road, Section 2
  Taipei 104
  Phone: 886-2-2594-3261

The Tourism Bureau's Tourist Information Hot Line (886-2-2717-3737) provides a wide range of assistance and information in Chinese and English (and other languages as needed) to callers from anywhere in the world. The hot line operates every day of the year from 8 A.M. to 7 P.M., local time (UTC +8 hours).

• *Travel Information Service Centers*
  The Tourism Bureau's Travel Information Service Centers provide information to inbound and outbound tourists. There are service centers at the Chiang Kai-shek International Airport in Taoyuan, as well as these other locations:

Taipei:
345 Chung Hsiao E. Road, Section 4
Phone: 886-2-2717-3737

Taichung:
4th Floor, 216 Min Chuan Road
Phone: 886-4-227-0421

Tainan:
10th Floor, 243 Min Chuan Road, Section 1
Phone: 886-6-226-5681

Kaohsiung:
5th Floor-1, 235 Chung Cheng 4th Road
Phone: 886-7-281-1513

and eating special rich pastries known as "moon cakes" 月餅. Confucius's Birthday, also celebrated as Teachers' Day 教師節, is also in September and features an ancient dawn ceremony of dance, costume, music, and rites.

The last major festival of the year is Double Ten National Day 雙十節, which commemorates the anniversary of the October 10, 1911, revolution that led to the overthrow of the Ching dynasty and the founding of the Republic of China. Huge parades in front of Taipei's Office of the President, displays of martial arts, folk dances, and other cultural activities attract enormous crowds of well-wishers on this day.

Cuisine

China's widely diverse geography allowed each region to develop its own distinctive cuisine, and all of them found their way to Taiwan from the Chinese mainland during the major waves of immigration following World War II. At Taipei's top restaurants, visitors can savor the true taste of Chinese cuisine.

Sichuan cuisine 川菜, which along with its cousin, Hunan cuisine 湘菜, favors the liberal use of garlic, scallions, and chilies. Sichuan food is distinguished by its hot peppery taste, while Hunan food is richer and either spicy and hot or sweet and sour. Chicken, pork, river fish, and shellfish are all common ingredients for both cuisines.

Jiangsu-Zhejiang cuisine 江浙菜 is the best known branch of the eastern Chinese style. Because of the area's proximity to the ocean, major lakes, and rivers, this culinary style is renowned for superb seafood. For the most part, these dishes are lightly spiced and fairly oily, with rich and slightly sweet sauces.

Beijing (Peking) cuisine 北京菜 was developed in the area of the imperial palace and uses wheat rather than rice as a basic staple. Generally mild in flavor, noodles, steamed breads, buns, and dumplings are the distinguishing features of this cuisine.

Cantonese cuisine 粵菜, probably the best known Chinese cuisine in the West, tends to be more colorful and less spicy. It is usually stir-fried to preserve both texture and flavor. A noon meal of dim sum 點心, featuring snack-sized servings, is a great way to pick and choose a wide variety of items.

Taiwanese cuisine 臺菜 is a branch of the eastern Chinese style: light, simple, easy to prepare, and often liberally spiced with ginger. Like its Shanghai cousin, Taiwanese cuisine features a lot of seafood.

ROC Tourism in 2000-2001

Taiwan's visitor arrivals increased 8.82 percent to 2,624,037 in 2000, primarily because of international promotions made by the Tourism Bureau. This high growth rate is expected to continue, since the number of countries whose citizens are allowed visa-free 14-day stays was increased to 20 countries in 2001.

The Tourism Bureau promotes Taiwan through its Internet homepage and the efforts of its overseas branches. The Seoul branch, which was closed following the rupture of diplomatic ties with South Korea, was reopened in 1995, and a Hong Kong branch was inaugurated in June 1996. This brought the Tourism Bureau's total number of overseas offices to nine.

In 2000, Japan still contributed the largest number of visitors to the ROC with 916,301, an increase of 10.90 percent from 1999. Hong Kong became Taiwan's second-largest source of visitors, totaling 361,308, an increase of 12.97 percent from 1999. The United States was Taiwan's third largest source of visitors, totaling 359,533, an increase of 13.13 percent from 1999.

Visitors from Singapore increased by 10.55 percent to 94,897. Arrivals from Indonesia (107,332) and the Philippines (84,088) consisted largely of contract workers. Visitors from Thailand, another major source of contract workers, totaled 133,185, a decrease of 3.47 percent; and arrivals from Malaysia rose 10.14 percent to 58,017.

Visitors from Europe decreased by 0.49 percent in 2000, with the Netherlands having the largest decrease of 11.55 percent to 12,603. Germany was the largest source of European visitors to the ROC, with 34,829, a 1.87 percent

decline; followed by the United Kingdom at 35,519, an increase of 6.89 percent. France ranked third with 23,720, followed by the Netherlands (12,603) and then Italy (12,073).

Visitors from Australia and New Zealand increased 6.56 percent in 2000, with arrivals from Australia totaling 31,842 and New Zealand totaling 6,020. The number of visitors from Canada also increased 8.91 percent to 38,399, while visitors from South Africa increased 22.17 percent to 4,948. Korean visitors increased by 9.96 percent to 83,729, while visitors from India increased by 14.51 percent to 13,233.

The final destinations of outbound travelers is not completely clear, since ROC citizens going abroad are no longer required to fill out departure cards stating their destination. In

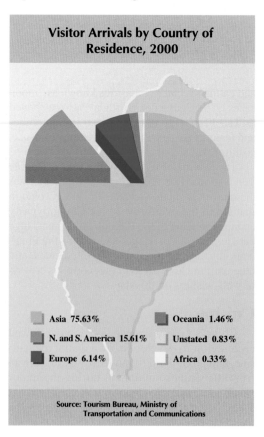

Visitor Arrivals by Country of Residence, 2000

Asia 75.63%	Oceania 1.46%
N. and S. America 15.61%	Unstated 0.83%
Europe 6.14%	Africa 0.33%

Source: Tourism Bureau, Ministry of Transportation and Communications

compiling destination figures, therefore, officials must rely on the first landing point of the flights on which travelers leave Taiwan, leaving much latitude for inaccuracy. It is clear, however, that most passengers travel to destinations within Asia, especially Hong Kong, Macao, and Japan, where most transit to their final destinations on the Chinese mainland. Taiwan residents traveling to Hong Kong numbered 2,311,095 in 2000, up 17.98 percent, visitors to Macao rose by 31.09 percent to 1,032,638, and visitors to Japan rose by 12.55 percent to 811,388. Travel within Asia as a whole totaled 5,853,619, up 17.82 percent.

The United States attracted the fourth largest group of outbound travelers in 2000, totaling 651,134, up 15.45 percent from the previous year. Travel to Canada rose by 6.78 percent to 181,409. Trips to Europe as a whole increased by 21.05 percent for the year to 272,449, with the greatest number traveling to the Netherlands (137,021), followed by the United Kingdom (40,277). Travel to New Zealand was up 75.51 percent to 50,779, while trips to Australia decreased 10.71 percent to 51,874.

To attract more foreign tourists and provide local residents with more cultural and recreational activities, the Tourism Bureau sponsored two major annual events in 2001: the Kaohsiung Lantern Festival 高雄燈會 and the Taipei Chinese Food Festival.

The Lantern Festival is held two weeks after the Chinese New Year on the first full moon of the lunar year, usually in February. This cultural extravaganza features displays of traditional and modern decorative lanterns, folk arts performances, handicraft demonstrations, and religious processions. The 2001 Kaohsiung Lantern Festival was held February 7-14.

In association with the Taiwan Visitors Association 財團法人臺灣觀光協會, the Tourism Bureau sponsored the 2001 Taipei Chinese Food Festival August 23-26, attracting more than 100,000 visitors. The festival focuses on Chinese cuisine in all its regional variations but is becoming more international in scope every year. In addition to the display and sale of a vast number of artistically presented dishes, the festival also offers demonstrations, contests, workshops, and other activities, all designed to advance the art and appreciation of Chinese cuisine.

New Attractions

The Tourism Bureau designated 2001 as "Tourism Action Year" 觀光行動年 with the ultimate objective of building Taiwan into an "island of tourism." To attain this objective, the bureau has striven to carry out the various measures included in the Action Program for Implementation of Taiwan's New Tourism Development Strategy for the 21st Century 二十一世紀臺灣發展觀光新戰略行動執行方案, which seeks to achieve "tourism on the minds of all the people" while "working together to build an internationalized Taiwan." Thus far, all of the bureau's actions have been wholeheartedly supported by the general public.

To keep tourism growing and provide a wider range of recreational choices, the Tourism Bureau has been promoting a large number of other attractions and activities. Various brochures have been published, mostly in Chinese, English and Japanese. These brochures are not only for general tourists, but also for business travelers who might have spare time during their stay in Taiwan. A CD-ROM entitled "Taiwan" has also been published.

In order to offer local residents and foreign visitors alike an opportunity to learn more about Taiwan's festivals and culture, the Tourism Bureau chose 12 characteristic Taiwanese festival activities from different areas of the island for intensified promotion. These activities were packaged and introduced, one each month, for the entertainment and edification of the public. The activities chosen for the year 2001 were the Lantern Festival (February), Sung Chiang Battle Array 宋江陣 (March), Matsu Culture Festival 媽祖文化節 (April), Sanyi Wood Carving Festival 三義木雕節 (May), Dragon Boat Festival (June), Ilan International Children's Folklore & Folkgame Festival 宜蘭國際童玩藝術節 (July), Taipei Chinese Food Festival 臺北中華美食展

(August), Keelung Ghost Festival 基隆中元祭 (September), Hualien International Stone Sculpture Festival and Yingko Pottery Exposition 花蓮 國際石雕藝術季, 鶯歌陶瓷嘉年華 (October), Asian Windsurfing Tour and Penghu Pro-Am 亞洲杯國 際風浪板巡迴展 (November), and the Oceanic Art Festival 南禹文化節 (December).

Among the Tourism Bureau's newest initiatives is a joint effort with the tourism promotion units of the Keelung City, Taipei County, and Ilan County governments to package and market the tourism resources of Taiwan's greater Northeast Coast area. These resources include Keelung's night scene and ancient fortresses, the gold-mining history of Chiufen 九份 and Chinkuashih 金瓜石, the rural scenery of Pinghsi 平溪 and Shuanghsi 雙溪, the bays and capes of the Northeast Coast National Scenic Area, the hot-spring baths of Chiaohsi 礁溪, and Ilan's sculpted riverside park on the Tungshan River 冬山河.

In response to the impending opening of Taiwan to tourists from the Chinese mainland, and to integrate the tourism resources of the southern part of the island, the Tourism Bureau—together with the governments of seven cities and counties (Kaohsiung City and County, Pingtung County, Tainan City and County, and Chiayi City and County)—called together private tourism associations and operators to work out tourism promotion programs for southern Taiwan. A decision was made to have the Kaohsiung City Bureau of Reconstruction and the Kaohsiung Tourism Association take charge of integrating the tourist sites of the different cities and counties, carry out the planning of unique tourism resources, and package and promote of those resources with the aim of featuring the local characteristics of the tourist industry in southern Taiwan. A number of southern Taiwan itineraries have already been introduced for tourists to choose from.

Among the bureau's other responsibilities are the development and management of national scenic areas and the construction of parking lots, pavilions, beach facilities, hiking trails, toilets, marinas, food and beverage outlets, visitor centers, and display halls. Once the infrastructure is completed, the private sector is then encouraged to invest in hotels, restaurants, and recreational facilities in the national scenic areas.

There are currently ten national scenic areas in Taiwan: the Northeast Coast, East Coast,

The older homes in Kinmen are classic examples of traditional Fujian architecture, a remnant of former ties with the mainland.

Penghu (Pescadore) Islands, Tapeng Bay 大鵬灣 in southwestern Taiwan, East Rift Valley that runs between Hualien and Taitung 花東縱谷 in eastern Taiwan, Matsu 馬祖, Sun Moon Lake, Tri-Mountain 參山, Alishan, and Maolin 茂林. The latter two national scenic areas are the newest and were only recently approved by the Executive Yuan.

The fortress island of Kinmen (Quemoy), situated less than two kilometers (at low tide) off the coast of the Chinese mainland, was opened to tourism in 1992. Kinmen was the focus of fierce attacks by Chinese Communist forces in 1949 and artillery battles in the late 1950s, the failure of which discouraged the communists from attempting to invade Taiwan. In addition to its historical significance, Kinmen is also a fascinating repository of traditional Chinese architecture and culture. Granite "wind lion" 風獅爺 statues and remarkably preserved houses built in the old Fujianese style attract many visitors, while the island's renowned pottery and *kaoliang* 高粱—a fiery sorghum liquor—make popular souvenirs. The ROC's newest national park, which serves as both a war memorial and a nature reserve, was established on Kinmen in 1995.

In addition to tourism, a growing number of foreign visitors are coming to Taiwan for international meetings and conventions. The Taipei International Convention Center 台北國際會議中心 (TICC), opened in 1991, is one of the best such facilities in the world. The TICC is managed by the China External Trade Development Council, which is also in charge of the adjoining Taipei World Trade Center Exhibition Hall.

Yamay Resort 月眉育樂世界, Taiwan's largest theme park at 198 hectares, began operating in July 2000 by opening its water amusement park as the first stage of its development. Completion of the third and final stage of the Disneyland-type park with an Oriental flavor is set for 2006.

Travel Services

Services for Inbound Tourists

The CKS International Airport Tourist Service Center maintains two travel service counters, one in each of the main lobbies at Terminal 1 and Terminal 2. Personnel offer a variety of services in several different languages. Travel information is also provided around the clock on 25 display racks at the two service counters, transit lounge, inbound arrivals area, Terminal 2, and bus waiting area. There is also an interactive, multimedia travel information inquiry system for travelers in the main lobby. The Kaohsiung International Airport Tourist Service Center was established on January 15, 1997, with the opening of the new airport's terminal, and provides travel information and related inquiry services to international travelers arriving in southern Taiwan.

Accommodations

Hotels in Taiwan were once rated by a plum blossom system analogous to the star system used internationally. The Tourism Bureau had long planned to revise this system to provide a clearer ranking of the island's hotels. However, many hoteliers resisted the change, fearing downgrading, and the plum-blossom system was eventually abandoned. Tourist hotels in Taiwan today are officially classified in just two categories, each of which encompasses a vast range of properties: tourist class and international tourist class.

In addition to the officially rated hotels recognized by the Tourism Bureau, there are also large numbers of unrated ones, some of which are quite luxurious and expensive. Others are inexpensive hostels and youth activity centers, which vary widely in facilities, services, and price.

In addition to the usual guest rooms, shopping arcades, swimming and exercise facilities, entertainment systems, and business centers, Taiwan's hotels also offer fine dining. While most of the best Chinese restaurants on the island are independent establishments, some are also found in international tourist-class hotels. Top hotels frequently offer the best quality Western cuisine.

Transportation

Surface travel in the ROC is both convenient and reasonably priced. Express buses link all cities, towns, and scenic spots, and the railway line reaches all the way around the island. Rental cars are widely available, though the major international car rental agencies have yet to succeed in setting up their own operations in the local market. Renting a car in Taiwan requires an international or ROC driver's license, plus a major credit card or a sizable deposit.

Major cities have comprehensive and convenient public bus services. Taxis are plentiful, but few drivers speak any non-Chinese language. The third line of Taipei's mass rapid transit system (MRT), Panchiao-Nankang Line from Hsinpu to Kunyang, began operation on December 30, 2000. Additional lines are under construction in Taipei, and more MRT systems are being planned for other large cities. Convenient local and international air services are provided by more than 50 domestic and international airlines (for additional information see Chapter 14, Transportation).

Related Websites
1. Tourism Bureau: *http://www.tbroc.gov.tw*
2. Directorate General of Customs: *http://www.dgoc.gov.tw*

23
Sports and Recreation

Spending on sports and recreation by ROC citizens has increased by an average of 10 percent each year over the last decade.

What's New

1. Figures and information updated
2. International competition
3. Surveys on recreation

Since entering the 21st century, aside from continuing to give impetus to educational reform and scientific development, placing stress on the humanities, and turning Taiwan into a Green Silicon Island, the government has also actively promoted sports development so that people in Taiwan can be healthier and happier.

The National Council on Physical Fitness and Sports (NCPFS), the highest sports organization of the ROC, continues to promote "sports for all people" so as to improve people's physical fitness and increase sports strength.

Healthy habits of proper exercise acquired early in life by students, and plentiful, well-equipped recreational facilities readily accessible to old and young alike, have both become more prominent goals in educational reform proposals and government plans. The growing value placed on exercise and leisure is also apparent at the individual consumer level. According to the Directorate-General of Budget, Accounting and Statistics 行政院主計處 (DGBAS), spending on sports and recreation by ROC citizens has increased by an average of 10 percent each year over the last decade. This chapter provides a balanced overview of the ROC's sports and recreation programs by giving a brief introduction of all of the options available to the public.

Sports Facilities

In densely populated Taiwan, it takes time, money, and determination to participate in a sport. Just finding a place to play tennis or go jogging is often a major undertaking. The government, therefore, places a high priority on providing sports facilities. The Taiwan area has 46 major public stadiums with artificial tracks at various locations. Each county and major city in Taiwan also

Number of Sports Facilities in Taiwan

Type of Sport	Number of Facilities	
	Number	%
Total	63,409	100.0
Track & Field	3,526	5.6
Swimming	1,850	2.9
Judo	175	0.3
Taekwondo	385	0.6
Cycling	87	0.1
Croquet	257	0.4
Basketball (standard)	3,181	5.0
Basketball (simple)	4,156	6.6
Volleyball	1,413	2.2
Soccer	500	0.8
Baseball or softball (standard)	124	0.2
Baseball or softball (simple)	600	0.8
Table tennis	3,967	6.3
Handball	324	0.5
Tchoukball	114	0.2
Tennis	1,420	2.2
Gymnastics	747	1.2
Kendo	64	0.1
Dance (including yoga, folk dance)	2,487	3.9
Weightlifting	169	0.3
Boxing	29	0.0
Shooting	24	0.0
Crossbow	36	0.1
Gymnasiums (county)	11	0.0
Gymnasiums (township)	4	0.0
Volleyball (beach)	2	0.0
Horsemanship	25	0.0
Bowling	657	1.0
Billiard rooms	3,131	4.9
Golf	83	0.1
Golf (driving range)	209	0.3
Beach	26	0.0
Sports park	15,251	24.1
Ice skating	717	1.1
Roller skating	14	0.0
Beach	26	0.0
Badminton	1,870	2.9
Football	30	0.0
Karate	141	0.2
Outdoor multi-purpose sports grounds	4,358	6.9
Indoor multi-purpose sports grounds	2,208	3.5
Rock-climbing	40	0.1
Dodge ball	18	0.0
Fitness	259	0.4
Physical strength and game playing	1,075	1.7
Field events	59	0.1
Ball game practice	62	0.1
Tai chi chuan	85	0.2

has school playgrounds and a network of base-ball parks.

Under the "sports for all people" 全民運動 campaign begun in 1979, a total of 72 public sports centers have been built around the island, each with a track, swimming pool, gymnasium, and tennis courts. An additional 4,000 elementary schools, 2,000 junior high schools, 400 senior high schools, and 130 colleges open their sports facilities to the public for at least a few hours each day.

One facility available for serious athletes in Taiwan is the first-class living and training facilities at the Tsoying National Athletes' Training Center 國家選手運動訓練中心. Taiwan has one stadium for soccer in Taipei, Chungshan Soccer Stadium 中山足球場, and two major competition arenas for track and field, Taipei Municipal Stadium 臺北市立體育館 and Kaohsiung Municipal Stadium 高雄市立體育館. The island's largest competition-level indoor facility for basketball, Chunghua Stadium中華體育館, burned down in 1988 and was replaced by a much improved facility constructed at the National College of Physical Education and Sports 國立體育學院 in Linkou, a suburb of Taipei.

In early November 2001, a groundbreaking ceremony was held at the site of the Taipei City Baseball Stadium 臺北市立棒球場 for a multifunctional stadium, Taipei Sports Dome 巨蛋體育場, which is scheduled to be completed in 2004. The 15,000-seat stadium, costing around US$1 billion, will be also used for concerts, band performances, and art exhibitions. In 2000, the central government provided US$31.29 million in assistance to local governments for building 246 sports grounds, including 20 county and city sports grounds, 15 township sports grounds, 17 township swimming pools, six sports parks, 733 community sports grounds, lighting facilities for 55 sports grounds, and other projects. A survey conducted in 1999 found that Taiwan had a total of 63,409 sports grounds. The majority of these facilities are sports parks (see chart on previous page). Sports facilities damaged during the September 21, 1999, earthquake were repaired with a government subsidy of US$5.33 million.

A smaller outdoor stadium was opened to the public in June 2000, in Tienmu 天母 on the outskirts of Taipei. This 16-hectare sports stadium includes a baseball stadium, track and field, swimming pools, and tennis courts.

During the 1999 winter vacation, around 7,300 recreational sports activities were held on weekends and holidays for teenagers and youths, as well as 120 winter sports and recreation camp activities, 14 activities that included foreign visits for recreation and sports, and 11 activities that provided various recreational and sports services.

Sports in the Schools

Physical education is a required subject in every elementary school, secondary school, college, and university. However, in reality, physical education instruction programs in schools have traditionally been kept to a minimum in order to allow students more time to prepare for the all-important high school and college entrance exams. In practice, junior and senior high school students are only required to take two hours of P.E. class per week. Although they can also choose athletics for their two hours of weekly electives, most students use this time to study. In order to alter this situation, it has been suggested that physical fitness be included in the entrance evaluations to senior high schools and colleges.

Regular P.E. courses cover physical hygiene and sports physiology. The courses are also de-signed to cultivate skills in a wide variety of sports, including tennis, track and field, baseball, and the martial arts. In practice,although the limited time available does not allow many students to become proficient at any particular sport, they do, however, get a good introduction to a variety of sports skills and games.

Currently less than 20 percent of Taiwan's population regularly engages in sports or exercise. This is low when compared to the US and European rates of 40 to 50 percent. To improve this situation, the ROC government enacted a Five Year Medium-term Plan for Physical Education (1998-2002) to cultivate the concept of lifelong sports and exercise into Taiwan students. It is expected that the percentage of students engaging in regular exercise will increase from the current 25 percent to 35 percent in the year 2002. The total budget for this plan is US$180 million.

The government has had more success with programs that focus on physical health. It is currently reviewing the physical education curriculum and revising physical education textbooks. As part of its push to promote student health, the government established

In addition to educational reform and scientific development, the government is also actively promoting sports development to improve fitness and broaden leisure activities

New Steps for Developing Athletic Talent

To discover potentially outstanding athletes and begin their training at an earlier age, the government has set up athletic aptitude classes in elementary and high schools throughout Taiwan. National sports foundations are responsible for selecting and training youths with superior athletic talent for participation in large-scale international competitions, such as the Olympics and the Asian Games. The ROC government rewards successful athletes with either the Chungcheng Physical Education Award 中正體育獎章 or the Kuokuang Physical Education Award 國光體育獎章, and provides these athletes with educational or vocational guidance. In fiscal 1999-2000, some US$30.6 million was awarded to local athletes through these prestigious awards.

Increased funding from the Ministry of Education for school athletic teams made it possible to maintain 570 primary school baseball teams in 1996. The ministry's plan also includes selecting various primary and junior high schools to specialize in a specific sport. For example, the Keelung Girls' High School 基隆女中 is building its taekwondo team while Taipei's Yucheng Elementary School 玉成國小 is expanding its swimming program. Starting in 1998, Taitung's Hsinsheng Junior High School 臺東縣新生國中 began developing a baseball program. The ministry hopes to foster cooperation between these selected schools and the various national sports associations with regard to developing new athletic talent.

a student health checkup system and supplied elementary school students around the island with healthier lunches.

Baseball is the most popular extracurricular activity. Little League baseball is now offered to both boys and girls in about 47 percent of elementary and junior high schools, 16 percent of high schools, and a small fraction of colleges.

Basketball is also popular. In 1997, nearly 60 percent of junior high schools and 42 percent of high schools participated in basketball league matches. Other extracurricular sports range from softball, volleyball, table tennis, and badminton to judo, taekwondo, and kendo. Most schools also have their own dance clubs, marching bands, drill teams, and table tennis clubs.

Sports After Graduation

After graduating from high school, most athletes have little chance to continue their sporting careers, with the more dedicated athletes having to choose between taking exams or continuing their training. Since 1992, the best players have been able to attend one of nine colleges specializing in sports. Other universities and colleges can also recruit outstanding athletes as needed. In practice, this option has remained limited since athletes are only admitted if they happen to meet the needs of the school's sports teams.

Most athletes end up majoring in physical education at one of the sports colleges.

Many in Taiwan believe that creating more options for athletes would make individual competitors happier and would also speed the development of Taiwan's college sports by spreading the best athletes throughout the school system. The result would be a more equal development of sports and a more competitive field for athletes.

In June 2001, a total of 317 students graduated from the National College of Physical Education and Sports 國立體育學院. For the majority of them, however, the end of school meant the end of their athletic careers.

Amateur Sports in the ROC

The ROC Sports Federation

The Republic of China Sports Federation 中華民國體育運動總會 is the primary body in charge of amateur sports in the ROC. The federation is under the jurisdiction of and receives funding from the National Council on Physical Fitness and Sports.

The primary functions of the Sports Federation are to provide its member sports associations with technical and administrative assistance, raise their sports standards and administrative efficiency, increase participation in international competitions, and train good athletes. The following 53 sports are represented by national sports associations that belong to the federation: aikido, airsports, alpine sports, archery, badminton, baseball, basketball, billiards, bodybuilding, bowling, boxing, canoeing and kayaking, crossbow, cycling, dancing sports, equestrian, fencing, folk sports, football (soccer), gateball, golf, gymnastics, handball, hockey, judo, karate, kendo, korfball, kuoshu, luge and bobsledding, pentathlon and biathlon, powerlifting, roller skating, rowing, rugby, shooting, skating, skiing, softball, soft tennis, swimming, table tennis, taekwondo, tai chi chuan 太極拳, tchoukball, tennis, tug-of-war, volleyball, water skiing, track and field, weightlifting, wrestling, and yachting. Sports associations serving the armed forces, district sporting associations (Taiwan Province, Taipei, Kaohsiung, and Kinmen 金門), and associations of athletic trainers and the disabled are also members of the federation.

The Sports Federation operates the Tsoying National Sports Training Center and the Northern National Sports Training Center to train national team members preparing for international competition. These centers provide accommodations, coaching, training facilities, and pocket money for athletes, as well as academic tutoring when necessary.

The Sports Federation is also engaged in sports science research aimed at furthering athletic performance and the prevention and care of injuries. The federation also participates in international sports exchanges and has signed official sports exchange agreements with Hungary, Korea, Germany, Peru, Guatemala, Paraguay, Argentina, Italy, Costa Rica, Nicaragua, Uruguay, and Vietnam.

To encourage athletes, the ROC government gives outstanding athletes special medals and monetary awards for excelling in athletics, such as through the Kuokuang and Chungcheng award programs. So far, the government has awarded 1,636 Kuokuang medals and money awards of US$18.5 million, and 358 Chungcheng medals and accompanying money awards of

---

Promotion of Sports in the Schools

Since the late 1980s, the Ministry of Education has taken several significant steps to promote sports in schools. The ministry launched a US$740 million National Physical Education Development Medium-Range Plan 國家體育建設中程計畫 from 1989 to 1993 that called for the construction of 100 athletic facilities at schools islandwide and 36 basic recreation centers and parks in various counties and cities. To date, 100 stadiums have been constructed at elementary and secondary schools.

In an effort to establish an integrated system for the training of athletes, the government set up the National Taitung Experimental Senior High School of Physical Education 國立臺東體育實驗高級中學 in 1995. To better guide and reward highly-gifted athletes, government education units revised the *Regulations for the Counseling and Academic Advancement of Athletically Gifted Students at the Secondary School Level* 中等學校運動成績優良學生升學輔導辦法.

US$415,000. The NCPFS has recently revised the regulations on the issurance of Kuokuang medals and money awards for outstanding athletes. Furthermore, to encourage such athletes to concentrate on their training, the government has formulated and sent to the Executive Yuan for approval a set of guidance regulations for the employment of outstanding athletes.

International Competition

Since the 1984 Olympics, the Republic of China has competed in international competitions under the banner of "Chinese Taipei."

From July 2000 to June 2001, 1,191 ROC athletes participated in international tournaments and competitions. Among them, 649 athletes attended 92 international championships in 40 sports. In total, ROC athletes took home 89 gold, 86 silver, and 62 bronze medals from these events.

The 2001 World University Games were held in Beijing, China, between August 21 and September 1, with 167 countries participating. The

ROC delegation had 106 athletes competing in eight areas: tennis, table tennis, track and field, gymnastics, swimming, basketball, volleyball, and judo. They returned to Taipei with three silver and five bronze medals.

Other International Championships

In the area of international sports exchanges, the ROC took part in the III Open Summer Games "Olympic Hopes" held May 11-13, 2001, in Bulgaria. ROC athletes participated in five areas of competition, including swimming, and won 21 gold, 17 silver, and 6 bronze medals.

Between May 18 and May 28, 2001, the ROC delegation participated in the Third East Asian Games held in Osaka, Japan, winning 6 gold, 16 silver, and 31 bronze medals. Overall, the ROC team ranked fifth, after Japan, the Chinese mainland, South Korea, and Kazakhstan.

ROC athletes also competed in several events sponsored by the International School Sport Federation in 2001, including swimming, basketball, track and field, and gymnastics. They returned with a gold medal in men's group competition swimming, a silver medal in women's

group competition swimming, a silver medal in gymnastics for men's floor, a bronze medal in gymnastics for men's horse-vaulting, and a bronze medal in men's group competition track and field. Overall, the ROC delegation ranked fifth of all competing teams.

The 10th World Police and Fire Games were held in Indiana, USA, in July 2001. Competition areas included judo, track and field, billiards, bowling, swimming, tennis, and badminton. The 36 ROC athletes participating won 16 gold, 10 silver, and 10 bronze medals.

The ROC delegation participated in the Fourth Taekwondo Opens held in the United Kingdom in July, winning 19 gold, 9 silver, and 8 bronze medals. The ROC team won first place overall out of the 12 countries participating.

Following its success in the 2001 Taipei International Dragon Boat Race Championship held in June, the Taipei Physical Education College scored a victory at the 2001 Long Beach World Cup Dragon Boat Championships in Los Angeles. Rowing under the title of the Chunghua team, the group garnered its title at 2 minutes 5.12 seconds, defeating 72 contestants from the United States, the Chinese mainland, the Philippines, and Canada.

Four ROC billiard players went to Connecticut, USA, to compete in the 2001 International Challenge of Champions in July. Chao Fengpang from the ROC won the 2001 WPA World Pool Champion and US$50,000.

During the Sixth World Games held in Akita, Japan, between August 16 and August 26, the ROC delegation of 65 athletes won three gold, three silver, and five bronze medals, placing the ROC team in 14th place out of 92 countries.

Dragon Boat Racing

Dragon boat racing originally started out as a festival to commemorate the death of the patriotic poet Chu Yuan 屈原, who committed suicide on the fifth day of the fifth lunar month in 277 B.C. (see Chinese Festivals in Tourism). Today, dragon boat racing is one of the most popular sports worldwide.

Training Facilities

The facilities at the three sports colleges and in university sports departments vary widely. At the National Taiwan College of Physical Education 國立臺灣體育學院 and the Taipei Physical Education College 臺北市立體育學院, much of the equipment is older. In contrast, the nine-year-old National College of Physical Education and Sports is equipped with international-class training facilities. Located on a 66-hectare site near the northern town of Linkou, this school is considered Taiwan's best sports institution. Students can earn undergraduate degrees in health, physical education, or sports technique, and graduate degrees in physical education or sports science. Entrance into the undergraduate health program is by written examination, but applicants must also be top athletes for admission to the physical education and sports science programs.

In June 2001, 12 counties and cities held 15 dragon boat races and related activities during the Dragon Boat Festival. In addition, the international dragon boat races held in Taipei attracted 116 local and foreign teams between June 23 and June 25, 2001. After three days of competition, the Taipei Physical Educational College won both men's and women's first place.

World Sports Events in the ROC

The ROC hosts a growing number of international competitions in Taiwan, furthering international exchanges and providing top-notch competition for Taiwan sports fans. In 2001, the world sports events held in Taiwan included the 21st Asian Cycling Championships and the 8th Asian Youth Cycling Championships in July, the 1st Asian Junior Taekwondo Championship in August, the 4th Junior Baseball Championship in September, the 34th World Cup Baseball Tournament in November, and the 13th Asian Women's Football Championship in December.

In addition, the ROC was awarded the right to hold the 44th International Council for Health,

Physical Education, Recreation, Sports and Dance (ICHPER.SD) World Congress in June 2002, the International School Children's Games between August 30 and September 3, 2002, and the World Table Tennis Championship for the Disabled in October 2002.

34th Baseball World Cup

The Republic of China hosted the 34th Baseball World Cup in November 2001. The 13-day tournament, with 16 countries participating, helped win back the hearts of the island's baseball fans and injected life into the once popular baseball sport. Cuba beat the United States 5-3 at the packed Tienmu Stadium in Taipei to win the championship for the seventh time in a row. The ROC team beat Japan to clinch the third place. Panama ranked fifth; South Korea, sixth; the Netherlands, seventh; and the Dominican Republic, eighth.

National Games

In 1998 it was decided that beginning in 1999, the Taiwan Area Games 臺灣區運動會, with a history of 25 years, would be replaced by the

During the 34th Baseball World Cup in November 2001, 16 countries participated in the 13-day tournament held in Taipei. The ROC team beat Japan to win third place and Cuba won the championship for the seventh consecutive year.
(Photo by Hou Yung-Chuan, *Min Sheng Daily*)

ROC Track and Field National Records

Men's Events

Sports	Record	Units	Athlete	Date
100M	10.37	sec	Cheng Hsin-fu 鄭新福	6/28/86
200M	20.93	sec	Tao Wu-hsun 陶武訓	10/16/94
400M	46.72	sec	Chang Po-chih 張博智	10/26/98
800M	1:47.24	min/sec	Wang Jung-hua 王榮華	5/3/80
1,500M	3:46.4	min/sec	Huang Wen-chen 黃文成	6/11/83
5,000M	14:04.0	min/sec	Chang Chin-chuan 張金全	6/13/75
10,000M	29:12.10	min/sec	Hsu Chi-sheng 許續勝	11/28/93
110M hurdle	13.90	sec	Wu Ching-Chin 吳清錦	11/5/83
400M hurdle	48.63	sec	Chen Tien-wen 陳天文	8/31/01
3,000M steeplechase	8:43.61	min/sec	Huang Wen-chen 黃文成	9/18/82
400M relay	39.27	sec	Lai Cheng-chuan 賴正全	10/3/90
			Cheng Hsin-fu 鄭新福	
			Lin Chin-hsiung 林金雄	
			Hsieh Chung-tse 謝宗澤	
1,600M relay	3:07.61	min/sec	Chen Tien-wen 陳天文	12/19/98
			Chang Po-chih 張博智	
			Lin Chin-fu 林進福	
			Lee Ching-yen 李清言	
high jump	2.22	meters	Liu Chin-chiang 劉金鎗	10/29/82
long jump	8.34	meters	Nai Hui-fang 乃慧芳	5/14/93
pole vault	5.30	meters	Lee Fu-en 李福恩	10/29/90
triple jump	16.65	meters	Nai Hui-fang 乃慧芳	11/17/89
shot put	18.02	meters	Lu Ching-i 呂景義	4/29/94
discus	53.68	meters	Lin Chung-cheng 林宗正	8/10/85
hammer	65.62	meters	Hou Chin-hsien 侯金賢	4/30/97
javelin	72.92	meters	Lin I-shun 林義順	3/17/90
decathlon	8,009	pts	Yang Chuan-kwang 楊傳廣	4/27-4/28/63

National Games 全民運動會 and held every two years. It was also decided that the competition categories would be limited to those at the Asian and Olympic Games. The purpose of this change was to internationalize, professionalize, and standardize the National Games. The last Taiwan Area Games were held in Tainan County in southern Taiwan in 1998. The first National Games were held in December 1999 in Taoyuan County in northern Taiwan. The second National Games were held in Kaohsiung in December 2001 in the southern part of Taiwan. Twenty-five counties and cities participated in 30 categories of competition at the games.

Beginning in 2000, the National College Games were renamed the ROC National College Games. The Minghsing Institute of Technology in Hsinchu held the ROC National College Games between April 23 and April 28, 2000, with 242 competitions. All told, 117 universities and colleges participated, with 4,772 athletes and team members. The games are held each year between March and May, and last from four to six days.

Kuoshu

The development of traditional Chinese sports is vital to the preservation of Chinese culture.

ROC Track and Field National Records (continued)

Women's Events

Sports	Record	Units	Athlete	Date
100M	11.22	sec	Chi Cheng 紀政	7/18/70
200M	22.56	sec	Wang Huei-chen 王惠珍	10/30/92
400M	52.74	sec	Chi Cheng 紀政	7/29/70
800M	2:04.74	min/sec	Lee Ya-huei 李雅惠	7/21/98
1,500M	4:22.80	min/sec	Lee Chiu-hsia 李秋霞	5/17/75
3,000M	9:37.68	min/sec	Lee Su-mei 李素梅	6/24/79
5,000M	17:28.64	min/sec	Chiang Chiu-ting 江秋婷	11/22/96
10,000M	36:29.75	min/sec	Su Tzu-ning 蘇子寧	10/22/93
100M hurdle	12.93	sec	Chi Cheng 紀政	7/12/70
400M hurdle	55.71	sec	Hsu Pei-ching 徐佩菁	10/14/98
400M relay	44.58	sec	Gao Yu-juan 高玉娟	10/16/94
			Hsu Pei-ching 徐佩菁	
			Chen Shu-chen 陳淑珍	
			Wang Huei-chen 王惠珍	
1,600M relay	3:39.88	min/sec	Hsu Ai-lin 徐愛齡	9/29/85
			Shen Shu-feng 沈淑鳳	
			Cheng Fei-ju 鄭妃汝	
			Lai Li-chiao 賴利嬌	
high jump	1.86	meters	Su Chiung-Yueh 蘇瓊月	4/23/89
triple jump	13.51	meters	Wang Kuo-hui 王國慧	4/29/98
long jump	6.56	meters	Wang Kuo-hui 王國慧	11/5/97
pole vault	3.71	meters	Chang Ko-hsin 張可欣	3/29/99
shot put	14.89	meters	Tsai Mei-ling 蔡美玲	5/12/98
discus	48.48	meters	Fang En-hua 方恩華	10/3/93
javelin	55.02	meters	Fang En-hua 方恩華	4/25/95
hammer	54.76	meters	Huang Chih-feng 黃芝鳳	3/30/99
heptathlon	5,786	pts	Ma Chun-ping 馬君萍	10/11/94

Kuoshu 國術, or "Chinese martial arts," is a collective name for more than 20 different styles of martial arts, including the better known tai chi chuan. Kuoshu is a recognized sport in the Asian Games. Reflective of Taiwan's commitment to kuoshu, the Chinese Taipei Kuoshu Federation 中華國術總會 receives funding directly from the National Council on Physical Fitness and Sports, and the ROC is the headquarters of the International Chinese Kuoshu Federation 中華民國國術國際聯盟總會. During the Third East Asian Games held in Osaka, Japan, between May 18 and May 28, 2001, the ROC Kuoshu delegation won one silver and two bronze medals. The ROC team won four silver and three bronze medals during the First Asian Youth Kuoshu Championship held in Vietnam in 2001, and attended the Sixth World Kuoshu Championship held in Armenia in October 2001.

Training Amateur Athletes

To seek out and cultivate potential athletes and develop new sports with distinctive features, the central government continues to assist and guide county and city governments in establishing basic-level training centers, which are under sports and recreation centers. Efforts are also made to establish training centers for outstanding athletes who can compete in important international sports events such as the Olympic Games or Asian Games.

The Tsoying National Athletes' Training Center continues to be responsible for cultivating and training outstanding athletes in the military. In 2001, there were four coaches and 55 athletes at the center.

In 2001, around 17 universities and colleges, such as the Taipei Physcal Education College, continued to train outstanding athletes, including 59 sports teams, 93 coaches, and 695 athletes.

Aboriginal Athletes

Without a doubt, the most famous athlete in ROC history is Yang Chuan-kwang 楊傳廣. Yang, of the Ami indigenous tribe, won the silver medal in the decathlon at the 1960 Rome Olympics. In recognition of his achievement and that of the Ami team from Taitung County 臺東縣, which won the ROC's first World Little League Baseball Championship, the ROC Sports Federation organizes special programs to help cultivate the talents of aboriginal athletes. One of these programs, supported by the Chinese Taipei Amateur Baseball Association 中華民國棒球協會, is the Pacific League, which started in 1993. With the participation of aboriginal professional baseball players, the Pacific League organizes baseball games and clinics for children in Ilan, Hualien, and Taitung Counties.

The 2001 Aboriginal Sports Meet was held in Pingtung County between March 22 and March 24. The items of competition included track and field, marathon, eight-people tug-of-war, boxing, traditional dance, traditional archery, traditional wrestling, a race performed while carrying a heavy load on the back, table tennis, and judo. About 96 people broke records on 30 events. Pingtung County won the championship. The 2003 Aboriginal Sports Meet will be held in Miaoli County.

In addition, 23 aboriginal organizations, such as the Tali Bay Sustainable Development Association, held 27 sports activities for the indigenous people.

Coaching

One of the biggest obstacles facing local athletes is the lack of a comprehensive professional coaching system. Coaching school athletes has only recently become a full-time job and permanent career. In 1989, the MOE established a full-time school-coach training system wherein recruits receive three months of training before being assigned full-time coaching positions at a school, sports association, or the Tsoying National Sports Training Center. Since coaches still receive lower salaries and have less job security than teachers, most prefer teaching positions instead. Consequently, most school teams are coached on a volunteer basis by teachers who enjoy sports. Many national associations choose to hire coaches on a part-time or contractual basis. These coaches hold short-term contracts and go back to their positions as P.E. teachers or coaches of professional teams after a particular event is over.

Most national associations and their athletes, however, cannot afford coaching. Therefore, athletes must rely on coaches willing to volunteer their time. In order to help alleviate the shortage of coaches, the ROC Sports Federation has invited distinguished coaches and athletic trainers to Taiwan from Australia, the Chinese mainland, Germany, Hungary, Japan, Russia, South Korea, the Philippines, and the United States to provide instruction in swimming, weightlifting, archery, shooting, diving, judo, taekwondo, track and field, equestrian, golf, table tennis, gymnastics, softball, boxing, baseball, badminton, kuoshu, fencing, basketball, and soccer.

The National Council on Physical Fitness and Sports is actively studying the implementation of a system for certifying and rewarding coaches. Besides revising the "implementation guidelines on training and supervising full-time

Chinese Taipei Olympic Committee

Officially recognized by the International Olympic Committee, the Chinese Taipei Olympic Committee 中華奧林匹克委員會(CTOC) is the sole sports organization with exclusive powers to organize and field representative delegations from the ROC at the Olympic Games, the Asian Games, and other international sports competitions recognized by the International Olympic Committee.

The mission of the Chinese Taipei Olympic Committee is to promote the Olympic Movement in the Republic of China in accordance with the Olympic Charter. CTOC members are approved by the CTOC Executive Board upon recommendation from the CTOC president. Currently, there are 58 members, the majority of whom are presidents of national sports associations.

The CTOC works closely with the International Olympic Committee, the Olympic Council of Asia, the Association of National Olympic Committees, the General Association of International Sports Federations, and the Asian, Pacific and Oceania Sports Assembly. It also maintains close relations with other national Olympic committees worldwide.

school coaches," the NCPFS also issued the "reward and punishment standards for full-time school coaches" in September 1999 and held related seminars for coaches. In addition, the government held the 1999 Coach Training Seminar for International Games to raise the standards of coaches working with sports basics, and 420 coaches participated.

Sports for Disabled People

In order to create a comprehensive plan for promoting sports for disabled people, the National Council on Physical Fitness and Sports established the Sports for the Disabled Committee. The 2002 National Sports Games for the Mentally and Physically Disabled will be held in Pingtung County.

The National Council on Physical Fitness and Sports issued NT$22.8 million (US$730,000) to outstanding athletes who attended the 2000

Sydney Paralympic Games and the Sixth Asian Games for the Deaf.

At the 2001 World Games for the Deaf in Rome, Italy, held between July 22 and August 1, the ROC delegation won one gold medal in the men's decathlon by An Ching-lung, one silver medal in bowling by Chang Li-hsiao, and one bronze in the women's discus by Kuo Chia-mi.

A seven-member ROC team also participated in the Czech Open 2001 Table Tennis Tournament for the Disabled and returned to Taipei with one gold, one silver, and two bronze medals. The ROC has won the right to host the 2003 World Deaf Bowling Championship.

In addition, 28 organizations, including the ROC General Committee on Sports Games for the Mentally Disabled, held more than 50 sports activities, seminars, and recreational activities for the mentally disabled.

The Chinese Taipei Sports Federation for the Disabled 中華民國殘障體育運動協會 assists with athletic training for disabled athletes and sponsors many of their competitions. The association is a member of the International Paralympic Committee and other international sports federations for the disabled.

Special Olympics

Between March 4 and March 11, 2001, the ROC delegation participated in the 2001 Winter Paralympic Games held in Alaska, USA, and won 9 gold, 7 silver, and 5 bronze medals in such events as speed skating, figure skating, and floor hockey.

Professional Sports

Professional Golf

At the 23rd Queen Sirikit Cup Amateur Ladies Asian Invitational Golf Team Championship held in Hong Kong in April, the ROC team won second place. In May, ROC delegations went to Malaysia to compete in the 2001 Pan West Malaysia Amateur Open Golf Championship and the 23rd Asia-Pacific Junior Golf Championship, and won first place in both events. ROC teams also placed second in both the 34th

Junior World Golf Championship held in the United States and the 54th Singapore Open Amateur Golf Championship.

Professional Baseball

Taiwan fans pack local stadiums each season to watch the four teams in the Chinese Professional Baseball League中華職棒聯盟: the Brother Elephants兄弟象, President Lions 統一 獅, Sinon Bulls興農牛, and China Trust Whales 和信鯨. In the 2001 season, from March to October, each team played more than 180 games. Fans island-wide can see the action, with games held in Hsinchuang, Hsinchu, Taichung, Chiayi, Tainan, and Kaohsiung. In the 2001 season, the Brother Elephants outperformed the other teams.

The ROC, following an early loss against Japan during the preliminaries, got its revenge and took first place by defeating Japan 2-0 on September 4, 2001, in the finals of the Fourth Asian Youth Baseball Championship in Taipei. South Korea won third place and Australia fourth. The tournament began on August 30 and brought together eight teams representing Japan, South Korea, Australia, India, Thailand, Indonesia, the Philippines, and the Republic of China.

Taiwan Major League Professional Baseball 臺灣大聯盟 made its debut in 1997 with four teams: Gida 太陽隊, Agan 金剛隊, Luka 勇士隊, and Fala 雷公隊, all of which are taken from aboriginal languages. In the 2001 seasons, Agan outplayed the other three teams to win the championship after 196 games.

Professional Basketball

The 24th R. William Jones Cup International Basketball Tournament was held in Kaohsiung, southern Taiwan, in August 2001. Teams from eight countries participated in the eight-day competitions. The ROC team won the championship, with Korea second, Russia taking third, and the Philippines taking fourth. The victory marked the first time in the tournament's 24-year history that Taipei has won the cup.

During the 21st Asian Basketball Championship for Men held in Shanghai in July 2001, the ROC team placed seventh.

The ROC basketball team won second place during the 3rd East Asian Games 2001 held in Osaka, Japan, in May.

Cross-Strait Sports Exchanges

The government has assisted and guided local associations and organizations to proceed with sports exchanges with the Chinese mainland. Exchanges have included sending athletes from Taiwan's various colleges of physical education and sports to visit the Chinese mainland, as well as attending cross-strait sports terminology seminars and seminars on sports and leisure culture. Athletes from the Chinese mainland coming to Taiwan to compete are allowed to apply for entry upon arrival. Between January 1999 and May 2001, 1,761 mainland athletes were allowed into Taiwan, including table tennis players, and judoists. Since January 1997, the China Olympic Committee (COC) of the Chinese mainland and the Chinese Taipei Olympic Committee (CTOC) have been taking turns in hosting the Cross-strait Olympic Committees Conference on Sports Exchanges 兩岸奧會體育交 流座談會. The fourth and latest conference was held in Taipei on May 7, 2001. Chairman Yuan Weimin of the COC led an 11-person delegation to attend the conference.

To support Beijing's bid to host the 2008 Olympic Games, the cross-strait running activity that had been suspended for three years was resumed on June 16, 2001. Ten major cities in Taiwan and the Chinese mainland joined the long-distance relay run. The mainland's 23-member team included several Olympic gold medal winners and nine journalists. The Taiwan team included Yang Chuankwang, silver medal winner in the decathlon at the 1960 Rome Olympics; Chi Cheng, women's track and field Olympic bronze medallist; and several other outstanding athletes. The activity lasted for 15 days.

In addition, the ROC sent 12 bowlers to participate in the 9th China Open between

July 29 and August 4. Four ROC martial artists also participated in the Chinese Martial Arts Championship held in Beijing on July 17, with Li Yi-yuan from Taiwan winning the championship.

Recreation

A 1999 survey performed by National Taiwan Normal University's Department of Physical Education revealed that 91.61 percent of the 15,360 respondents participated in at least some form of recreational activity, with the most popular activities being walking, bicycling, basketball, jogging, and hiking. About 25 percent of the respondents spent a regular amount of time on sports and recreation.

A survey released by Roper Starch Worldwide in June 2001 reported that the people in Taiwan spent on average 53.4 hours per week working, ranking the ROC fourth out of the 32 countries participating in the survey. In first place were the South Koreans, spending 55.1 hours. Americans worked 42.4 hours a week.

Another survey performed in August 2001 on six Asian countries was made by Asia Market Intelligence in Hong Kong. This survey revealed that 51 percent of the people in Taiwan felt great pressure from their work, ranking the island in second place after the Chinese mainland's 53 percent. Of the Taiwan respondents, 78 percent of those between 31 and 40 years old were worried about job security and 73 percent were worried about the unstable political situation. Only 26 percent of those surveyed had sought out relaxation methods.

Between 1995 and 1999, the people in Taiwan spent on average US$7.9 billion per year making outbound trips. In 1997 and 1998, the expenses for outbound tourism even exceeded Taiwan's trade surplus. In 2001, though the island experienced economic recession and a rising unemployment rate, outbound tourism from January to April still grew 4.7 percent in comparison with the same period for 2000.

Therefore, to encourage domestic tourism, the government established centers for promoting local sports and recreation in 25 counties and cities, including the major metropolises of Taipei and Kaohsiung.

Since group activities hold a strong appeal to Chinese, many local corporations, government agencies, and schools have intramural sports teams and activity clubs. Table tennis, basketball, softball, badminton, and tennis give office workers a chance to get some moderate exercise. To encourage tourist consumption within Taiwan so as to boost the economy, the government is giving a US$500 subsidy to all government functionaries who spend their two weeks of mandatory, paid vacation within Taiwan.

The Council of Agriculture under the Executive Yuan allocated a subsidy of US$26 million to promote the plan of "one county, one recreational farm." In August 2001, the council selected 50 qualified counties around the island to proceed with the plan, which was aimed at uniting ecology, scenery, life, agricultural development, and community culture by building farm villages that possessed both regional assets and characteristics.

A survey released by the King Car Education Foundation on February 13, 2001, revealed that on two-day weekends, around 60 percent of teenage respondents did not have any planned activities. Of those teenagers, roughly 30 percent spent their weekends studying while the other 70 percent ended up watching TV. Only 6 percent of all respondents actively took part in sports activities in order to improve their physical fitness. The survey also disclosed that only 45 percent of the families surveyed were able to enjoy two-day weekends together.

Another survey revealed that more than half of Taiwan's teenagers had frequented one or more of the 5,000 Internet cafes settled around the island, either playing games, doing online chats, or simply surfing the web. For primary school students, multipurpose summer camps focusing on native culture, ecology, and sports, have become a popular way to learn and relax. More and more parents are sending their children to such summer camps in the United States.

It is also becoming popular for both high school and college students to study English in summer programs held in the United States, Canada, or the United Kingdom.

In September 2001, the Taipei City Government set up a website to provide information on recreation for city residents and tourists. The website includes information on art groups, museums, art galleries, writers, restaurants, and related departments of the Taipei City Government, as well as data on the arts, performances, outdoor recreation, health, food, and TV and cinema.

Outdoor Recreation

"Adventure sports" such as surfing, scuba diving, and sailboarding are gaining popularity around the island as a result of interest generated by classes, rental shops, and clubs. Even gutsier activities such as paragliding and bungee jumping are also attracting brave souls not scared off by the danger or expense. A less thrilling but equally trendy sport that has become a lure to children and adults alike is roller blading. People, particularly children, wearing roller blades and skating to their heart's content is now a common scene in parks and playgrounds. A variety of

fishing activities have also gained in popularity. In addition to seaside fishing, there are also many private ponds where people can fish for a small fee. Sea parks and aquariums have also been set up around the island in Kenting, Taipei, and Penghu.

In 1993, the National Taiwan College of Physical Education 國立臺灣體育學院 located in Taichung established the first and only Department of Recreational Sports in Taiwan. The department's goal is to train specialists in recreational sports coaching, planning, management, and promotion. Students choose from a variety of courses, including diving, bowling, skiing, surfing, and yachting, while working in local recreational businesses. Private associations have also been formed to conduct research on leisure-related topics and promote outdoor recreation through seminars, lectures, and group activities. In 1988, the Outdoor Recreation Association of the ROC 中華民國戶外遊憩學會 was founded. This association has sponsored hiking lectures led by botanists, geologists, and other nature specialists, allowing participants to learn as they picnic or hike.

Organized recreational activities are offered all year round by groups like the China Youth

The Council of Agriculture has selected 50 qualified counties and cities around the island to carry the "one county, one recreational farm" project, which is aimed at uniting ecology, scenery, livelihood, agricultural development, and community culture. (Photo by Chen Yi-yu)

Corps 中國青年救國團. On weekends and holidays and during summer and winter vacations, the corps offers young people diverse outdoor activities like parachuting, rafting, skiing, and mountaineering. Each year it also organizes mock military exercises, back country hiking and camping, talent camps, and safari-style adventures for teenagers and young adults alike. For those who prefer indoor activities, the corps arranges arts and craft courses, such as guitar workshops, knitting courses, and painting classes. There are also self-improvement programs, including management courses, vocational workshops, and psychological counseling.

The China Youth Corps holds activities throughout the Taiwan area—in major cities, the countryside, and even on the offshore island of Penghu 澎湖. Altogether, the corps has 23 youth activity centers and hostels, complete with recreational, educational, and camping facilities. One of its largest centers, the Chientan Overseas Youth Activity Center 劍潭海外青年活動中心, even provides services and programs especially for foreign youth traveling or studying in the Taipei area.

For those who are able to get away from the city for a whole afternoon, golf is yet another tremendously popular form of recreation in Taiwan. There are currently 25 registered golf courses in the Taiwan area, all of which are up to international standards. While the price of membership in one of Taiwan's more prestigious golf clubs can be very high, people still flock to the greens on the weekends. The basic cost for playing 18 holes, not including rentals, caddie fees, and gratuities, ranges from US$50 to US$100.

Ultimately, however, the Chinese city park still provides the best idea of how Chinese people seek exercise and relaxation. If one strolls through any park in Taipei early in the morning, one will witness people dancing folk dances, practicing kung fu, playing Chinese chess, doing aerobics, jogging, stretching, singing, and even taking their birds "for a walk." After spending a few minutes in this peaceful environment, one gains a better understanding of the traditional Chinese concept of health through harmony.

For a change of atmosphere, many people retire to one of the numerous traditional teahouses or "tea art" shops all over Taiwan. Chinese teahouses are a blend of contemplative serenity and bustling activities. A casual afternoon at a teahouse will bring one to the heart of the social, artistic, intellectual, and political activities brewing in Taiwan. A number of such teahouses have been local trend setters for art and culture, hosting art exhibitions, ceramic displays, antique shows, and teapot collections.

Many of these teahouses are set in elegant cultured gardens, making them ideal hideaways for tea drinkers to relax while sampling a wide selection of first-class teas. Tea drinking in Taiwan is akin to the high art of wine tasting in the west, and tea drinkers will gladly pay between US$40 and US$80 for a half kilogram of good tea. On weekends, mountainside tea-art shops and restaurants offering open-air tea drinking, dining, and scenic views have become favorite destinations for Taipei residents. Perhaps the most notable of these are the teahouses in the Mucha 木柵 district of Taipei.

Related Websites
1. National Council on Physical Fitness and Sports: *http://www.ncpfs.gov.tw*
2. Taipei City Government: *http://www.taipei.gov.tw* *http://letsgo.taipei-elife.net*

24

Literature

Traditional Chinese literati, such as Chao Meng-fu (1254-1322), expressed themselves through poetry, creative writing, painting, and calligraphy.

What's New

1. The discipline of Taiwanese literature
2. Nobel Laureate Gao Xingjian in Taiwan
3. Taiwanese literature in translation
4. Poetry contest for foreign workers
5. Taipei International Poetry Festival

To recognize the rich legacy of Chinese Literature and its significant impact on Taiwan's literary consciousness, a description of Chinese Literature before 1949 will follow that of Taiwanese literature per se.

Early Taiwanese Literature

Aboriginal Traditions

The aboriginal peoples settled on the island of Taiwan thousands of years ago and developed distinct oral narratives, languages, customs, and cultures. For centuries, aborigines on Taiwan have been marginalized in the expression of Taiwanese culture. As each tribe has its own language and customs, intertribal communication or coordination is weak. Only recently was some progress made for such intertribal purposes, and the major event that drew different tribes together was the 1985 Wu Feng Incident 吳鳳事件, in which the statue of Wu Feng, a fictional deity invented by the Han 漢 Chinese to domesticate the "barbaric" aborigines, was crushed. Quite a few aboriginal intellectuals joined their people in the demonstration, urging the government to drop the ethnocentric Wu Feng mythology in the primary school textbooks and to pay more attention to the crisis the aboriginal population was facing.

Since 1980, aboriginal intellectuals have tried to recreate their own past by reexpressing their peoples' oral traditions. A large body of oral narratives about creation myths and tribal heroes have been transcribed and circulated in the form of parallel texts, in which the original aboriginal languages are spelled out in romanization and accompanied by Chinese translation. The texts are not only intended for Chinese-speaking audiences, but are also primarily used as textbooks for the younger generations in the aboriginal population. For many aboriginal intellectuals, such texts literally constitute the last utopian hope for their traditions to be transmitted in the struggle for cultural survival, fully aware of the brutal fact that even their children are resisting the use of the native tongue. As a result, indigenous languages and literatures are on the verge of disappearance.

Chinese Immigrant Literature

Between 1612 and 1844, quite a few Chinese intellectuals visited or stayed in Taiwan, most notably the Ming poet Shen Kuang-wen 沈光文, who was forced to land on the island by a typhoon in 1662 and afterward played an important role in forming a Taiwanese poets society under the name of *Tung-yin* 東吟. Like Koxinga 鄭成功, who came with his soldiers and conquered the island in 1661, Shen was loyal to the Ming emperors, even though China had by then been taken over by the Ching rulers. His poetry was mostly composed in regulated verse, expressing his patriotic feelings and nostalgia for the empire lost. Shen was thus instrumental in planting the seeds of classical Chinese literature on the island. Students were trained to familiarize themselves with the grand Chinese literary tradition. The lyric subjects were often on exotic landscapes or the poet's own inscapes of consciousness that had little to do with the social reality of Taiwan. As a consequence, for more than two hundred years, there were only a few memorable pieces composed in prose narrative by high officials who happened to be in Taiwan for a brief period. Examples are *Chu-lo-hsien chih* 諸羅縣志 by Chen Meng-lin 陳夢林 (who arrived in Taiwan in 1716) and *Hsiao-liu-chiu man-chih* 小琉球漫誌 by Chu Shih-chieh 朱士玠 (who stayed from June 1763 until August 1764).

Several local Taiwanese poets began to make their names known during the mid-19th century, among them Tsai Ting-lan 蔡廷蘭, Chen Chao 陳肇, Huang Ching 黃敬, Cheng Yung-hsi 鄭用錫, and Lin Chan-mei 林占梅. They were literati and cultural elites writing in the mode of classical

Chinese lyric, and as intellectuals who played important roles in Taiwan's history, their influence on local culture remains strong. In response to the colonial world of the late Ching period and in reaction to their precursors, Taiwanese poets of the next two decades became more devoted to everyday subjects and were often committed to expressing nationalist sentiment. Tang Ching-sung 唐景崧 and Chiu Feng-chia 丘逢甲 were two prominent officials and poets who got deeply involved in establishing the Taiwan Republic 臺灣民主國 on May 25, 1895, upon hearing the news that the Ching court had ceded Taiwan to Japan. Other major poets of this generation, such as Chen Wei-ying 陳維英 and Wang Kai-tai 王凱泰, were equally interested in describing ordinary people and popular culture. In many ways, they opened paths toward a more dynamic era of literary production, the period of Taiwanese literature under Japanese rule (1895-1945).

Early Colonial Literature

On April 17, 1895, in the Treaty of Shimonoseki, which put an end to the first Sino-Japanese War, the Ching empire ceded Taiwan and the nearby Pescadores to Japan. Subsequently, the Japanese army landed on Taiwan on May 29, 1895, but met fierce resistance from the Taiwanese, who had proclaimed independence. The Taiwan Republic established by a group of cultural elite and local people lasted only ten days; however, the Taiwanese fought the Japanese troops for four months before surrendering Tainan City in October 1895. Sporadic guerrilla resistance to the colonizer continued for some 20 years. The casualties on both sides were quite heavy; more than 10,000 Taiwanese died. As a result, the Japanese gradually modified their policies to seek the acquiescence of the Taiwanese elite and began to introduce modern technology and social reforms, instead of resorting to military or political force.

Between 1895 and 1913, a minor group of national elite, mostly poets writing in the classical Chinese tradition, returned to China, thinking that they could not survive colonialism. The remaining local elite tried, on the other hand, to preserve their cultural heritage, retain ties with other provinces, and develop their distinctive arts of improvisation in the midst of colonial banality and brutality. Hung Chi-sheng 洪棄生 was probably the most famous writer of the period. He refused to cut off his queue, withdrew from public life, and wrote in classical Chinese, to make the point that he was identifying himself with the Ching. In his poetical and prose works, Hung constantly referred to the society and culture of Taiwan of the time to reveal his patriotism and nationalism. However, the most important literary event in the first 20 years under Japanese occupation was the establishment of the Li Poetry Society 櫟社, of which the key members included Lien Ya-tang 連雅堂, Lin Chih-hsien 林痴仙, Lin Hsien-tang 林獻堂, and many others. The society was responsible for publishing an influential journal on poetry and poetics, *Taiwan Wen-i Chiu-chih* 臺灣文藝舊誌; it was also instrumental in supporting nationalist movements. Lien's monumental work on Taiwan's history, *A Comprehensive History of Taiwan* 臺灣通史, remains a classic in the field.

In 1911, Liang Chi-chao 梁啟超 visited Taiwan and brought with him ideas of Western enlightenment and experimental literature. Even though Taiwanese writers of the time were versed in the classical Chinese tradition, they were forced to confront the colonial reality and to work in more realistic modes of literary expression. This made a shift toward modern literature inevitable.

Taiwanese New Literature

The Colonial Context

Whereas most literature in Taiwan prior to 1920 was written in the style of the classical Chinese tradition, a new strand of modern Taiwanese literature emerged in the early 1920s in a process commonly referred to as the Taiwanese New Literature (TNL) movement 臺灣新文學運動. Compared with its mainland counterpart, TNL displayed two distinctive features that universally characterized colonial cultural products: its multi-linguisticity and its overriding political import. In addition to Chinese-language works, many of the literary products of this movement—especially in the later stage—were written in Japanese. There was also a viable Taiwanese Language movement 臺灣話運動 in the early 1930s, advocating the use of a new written language based on spoken Taiwanese, which is a version of the southern Fujianese dialect used by the majority of the population in Taiwan.

From the beginning, TNL was an integral part of a new phase of sociopolitical resistance by the Taiwanese people against Japanese colonial rule. In the 1920s, the Taiwanese intelligentsia, revolving around the Taiwanese Cultural Association 臺灣文化協會 (1921-1931), launched a large-scale cultural reform program full of various political agendas, in lieu of the futile and often brutally suppressed armed revolts in the first two decades of the Japanese period. Key figures of the early stage of the movement, such as Lai Ho 賴和 (1894-1943), frequently regarded as the "Father of Taiwanese New Literature," Chen Hsu-ku 陳虛谷, and Tsai Chiu-tung 蔡秋桐, were also active members of the Association, participating in its well-known islandwide mass education lecture tours. Not surprisingly, nationalistic sentiments were expressed through their literary works. Even after 1931, when a harsh crackdown by the colonial government put an end to the lively resistance activities of the previous decade, the New Literature movement, nourished by the sociopolitical movements of the 1920s, continued to grow among the increasingly bilingual intellectual class of Taiwan. The legacy of resistance to colonialism, too, persisted, in either overt or covert forms, until the very end of the Japanese period.

However, the broadly defined political nature of TNL refers not only to explicit criticism of the colonizers, in works by such undaunted anti-imperialist fighters as Lai Ho and Yang Kui 楊逵, but also to the cultural hybridity in later works of the TNL movement written in the colonizer's language, which was by definition a political product and carries with it imprints of an unjust power relationship. Whereas the first generation of TNL writers, most of whom were born after the Japanese takeover, still exhibited a characteristically Chinese cultural and artistic outlook, there was a notable shift in the second generation of TNL writers. The overall increase in the degree of hybridity in Taiwanese culture in the second half of the Japanese period may be explained by changes in the colonizer's governing policies.

Beginning in 1918-1919, the Japanese adopted an effective assimilation policy 內地延長主義 ("the principle of treating Taiwan as an extension of

The Father of Taiwanese New Literature, Lai Ho, was one of the active members of the Taiwanese Cultural Association that launched a large-scale cultural reform program against Japanese suppression. (Courtesy of Lai Ho Memorial)

Japan proper"), which shifted from high-handed police control and differential treatment of the Taiwanese to more enlightened civil governing, emphasis on education, and cultivation of a more congenial relationship between Japanese and Taiwanese. As the new colonial situation steadily took shape and Japanese language education became more effectively implemented, a greater number of students in the colony went to study in Japan. Those among them who enrolled in college literary departments and had contact with famous Japanese writers later played influential roles in the literary scene of Taiwan. An even more drastic change was that, during the last phase of the Japanese period (1937-1945), as Japan declared war with China, the colonial government mobilized huge amounts of social resources to enforce an intensified Japanization program 皇民化運動 (literally, "the movement of converting Taiwanese into loyal subjects of the Japanese Emperor"), which included a ban on Chinese-language publications.

The hybrid nature of this colonial literature reflects Taiwan's colonial past and its relatively unusual experience as a Japanese colony. A territory of Han settlers since the 17th century and a province of the Manchurian-governed China since 1885, Taiwan was incorporated by Japan into a different geopolitical and economic system in the early part of the 20th century, and as a result went through the initial stages of modernization via its East Asian colonizer, which had itself recently modernized after the Western model. The kind of society produced in Taiwan by this process was inevitably of a hybrid nature, with modern and traditional institutions of different ethnic origins coexisting side by side. Taiwan occupied a strategic position in Japan's imperialist project, serving as a base for Japan's further advancement into South China and Southeast Asia. For this reason, it is said to have received relatively benign treatment from the Japanese (as compared to Japan's other colonies, such as Korea), considerably mitigating the hostility between colonizer and colonized. The colonial condition in Taiwan is thus a product of the extremely intricate political and cultural negotiations between the colonial government and the local elite, articulated by progressive intellectuals who often served as spokesmen for the elite. Fine Taiwanese writers of the later period, such as Chang Wen-huan 張文環, Lu Ho-jo 呂赫若, Yang Kui, and Lung Ying-tsung 龍瑛宗, achieved their distinctive art under the influence of Western artistic trends through Japanese literary institutions.

Taiwanese New Literature Movement

As stated earlier, the TNL movement began as part of a larger cultural reform movement during the 1920s. A brief introduction of this cultural movement, sometimes called the Taiwanese New Culture movement 臺灣新文化運動, may be in order. The first events of this movement took place in 1920, when some Taiwanese expatriates in Tokyo organized the New People Association 新民會, followed by a student-based Taiwanese Youth Association 臺灣青年會. The two organizations published a journal called *Taiwanese Youth* 臺灣青年 to propagate progressive ideas and voice opinions about the current state of affairs in Taiwan.

The zeal for cultural reform soon spread to the island itself and was carried on by the Taiwanese Cultural Association. There are significant parallels between the Taiwanese New Culture movement and the Chinese mainland's May Fourth movement 五四運動. First of all, intellectuals in both societies, faced with the imperative to modernize, identified the cultural sediments of Neo-Confucian moralism and the feudalist social order as reactionary forces obstructing progress. Inspired by democratic ideals of modern Western society, both groups had come to associate the "old" with the conservative mentality of the gentry class, and the "new" with ways of the "modern citizen"—and sought to transform the masses through popular education and cultural enlightenment 文化啓蒙. The popular idea of social Darwinism, which equated rejuvenation of national culture with survival of the people, added to the urgency of the task of cultural reform as a means of national self-preservation. Secondly, the new intellectuals of both societies were influenced by the dynamics of progressive discourse on national emancipation and socialist revolution in the years following the First World War. Such currents of thought created an imaginary alliance among the "weak and oppressed" nations of the world and provided a powerful rationale for nationalistic resistance by victims of imperialist aggression, as obviously the Chinese mainland and Taiwan both were. Thus, a patriotic discourse combining the two components of sociocultural modernization (cultural enlightenment) and anti-imperialism (national salvation and anti-colonialism) was developed in the 1920s and shared by the new intellectuals on both the Chinese mainland and Taiwan.

Although in the first two issues of *Taiwanese Youth* there were already articles on language reform and the need for rejuvenating contemporary Taiwanese literature, it was not until the heated New Versus Old Literary Debate 新舊文學論戰, which began with Chang Wo-chun's 張我軍 attack on traditional poets in 1924 and lasted until 1926, that the TNL movement was formally launched. In this debate, new literary concepts—mainly those centering around the advantage of adopting the vernacular as a new literary medium and the social functions of literature in a modern age—were introduced, criticized, and defended. Traditional poets were castigated for using literature to incur social gains and political favor, their literary style criticized as hackneyed and insincere. Advocates of new literature, on the other hand, were branded as shallow and ignorant charlatans, their literary views ungrounded in solid learning. As in the case of many literary debates in modern times, the heated antagonism between opposite camps prevented a meaningful exchange of ideas. Rather, the debate performed an important ritualistic function: after the debate, traditional literary activities were increasingly confined to poetry clubs that continued to thrive but with limited social reach, while New Literature was legitimized as a

powerful social institution. Through this institution, the new intellectuals denounced their Chinese cultural heritage—partly by taking traditional men of letters and their world views as scapegoats—and endorsed a vision of "modern civilization." These denouncements and this new vision constituted the major content of TNL for at least a decade.

If the two New Culture movements on the Chinese mainland and Taiwan were analogous but separate, the relationship between the Chinese and Taiwanese New Literature movements was actually much closer. In the early stages, literary reform in the TNL movement virtually mirrored its slightly earlier Chinese counterpart (1917-1925). When Chang Wo-chun wrote the polemical essays that triggered the New Versus Old Literary Debate, he was a student of Beijing Normal University. During the debate, the major tenets for the May Fourth literary revolution, such as Hu Shih's 胡適 "Principle of Eight Don'ts" 八不主義 from his "Preliminary Suggestions for Literary Reform" were introduced with slight modifications. Even the harsh style of the way Chang Wo-chun castigated the traditional poets was immediately reminiscent of the radical Chinese reformist Chen Tu-hsiu 陳獨秀. Furthermore, throughout the decade of the 1920s, creative works by Chinese New Literature writers, such as Lu Hsun 魯迅, Hu Shih, Kuo Mo-jo 郭沫若, Ping Hsin 冰心, Wang Lu-yen 王魯彥, and Ling Shu-hua 凌淑華, were reprinted in Taiwanese journals and undoubtedly served as models for literary practice.

However, within a decade, this dependent relationship began to change. Apparently, during this time the deepening of Japanese colonization had begun to structurally transform Taiwan society and steer it further away from the cultural orbit of the Chinese mainland. Consciousness of this new reality among the Taiwanese intellectuals manifested itself in two consecutive literary debates in 1931-32, the Nativist Literature Debate 鄉土文學論戰 and the Taiwanese Language Debate 臺灣語文論戰, and represented a turning point in the TNL movement.

The Nativist Literature Debate testified to the prominent leftist presence in Taiwan's literary circles. The literary program proposed by its chief advocate Huang Shih-hui 黃石輝, who suggested that writers target their creative works at the masses in the working class, was clearly modeled upon the leftist concept of proletarian literature. The split of the Taiwanese Cultural Association in 1927 was primarily a result of disagreement in resistance strategies between the nationalist right wing and the socialist left wing. After the split, the association was controlled by the left-wing members Lien Wen-ching 連溫卿 and Wang Min-chuan 王敏川. The more moderate members formed the Taiwanese People's Party 臺灣民眾黨 and continued to fight for greater constitutional rights for the Taiwanese people. However, the political climate in the colony was so disillusioning by that time that even the Taiwanese People's Party began to display a leftward leaning tendency. Consequently, it was forced to dissolve by the colonial government in 1931.

Initially, the Taiwanese New Culture movement focused on cultural enlightenment to address the society's internal needs to modernize, and the main targets of its attack were old Chinese customs and lingering social ills of feudalism. As Taiwan proceeded along the course of modernization, however, the worldwide economic depression of the late 1920s exacerbated social problems, such as unemployment and class exploitation, thus leading to a rise in support for socialist ideology and Taiwan nativism.

Primarily concerned with internal social problems and conflicts between classes, leftist intellectuals called for a Taiwan-centered view in literary creation. Aside from his class-oriented literary view, Huang Shih-hui was also known for forcefully arguing that Taiwanese writers should only write in their own language about things on their own homeland. Termed by historians as following the direction of "self-improvement based on one province (Taiwan)" 一島改良主義, advocates of the nativist literature clearly envisioned a "Taiwanese consciousness" as something to be distinguished from the more inclusive "Chinese consciousness," or the ethnic consciousness of the Han race 漢民族意識.

This Taiwanese consciousness was the core spirit of Kuo Chiu-sheng's 郭秋生 campaign for the Taiwanese language. The Taiwanese Language Debate, with the literary journal *Nan-yin* 南音 as its major forum, revealed the anxieties and ambivalent feelings of a colonized people in their attempts to develop a national language. In an effort to assert Taiwanese subjectivity, the movement had effectively severed the Taiwanese intellectuals' emotional ties with China. First and foremost, the movement called attention to the fact that early advocates of the TNL movement had followed the Chinese model of the May Fourth movement too closely. They had thus unwittingly mistaken the latter's problems and strategies for their own, without giving proper attention to the objective circumstances of Taiwan.

To facilitate popular education in a country with an extremely high illiteracy rate, advocates of the May Fourth movement proposed to replace the difficult, obsolete classical Chinese language with modern Chinese vernacular as the official written language. The basic theoretical assumption was that since there would be a close correspondence between the spoken and written versions of modern Chinese, as reflected in the famous slogan "我手寫我心" (My hand writes what my heart feels), the efforts required to become literate in Chinese would be greatly lessened. In reality, however, a standard Chinese vernacular had yet to be popularized within the country; people from different regions were still predominantly using dialects, some of which were even mutually unintelligible, for daily communication (see section Dialects, Chapter 3, Language). There was, to be sure, a considerable disparity between the standard Chinese vernacular and the southern Fujianese dialect used by the majority of Taiwanese. Moreover, as Taiwan had already been politically separated from China for over two decades, its people had far fewer channels for learning the standard

Chinese vernacular through public institutions, such as an education system, publications, or a state bureaucracy.

Nevertheless, early advocates of the TNL movement still favored the adoption of Chinese vernacular as the medium for TNL. The fact that this position was uncontested at the time shows that by then the ethnic-cultural identity of Taiwanese intellectuals was still predominantly Chinese. One popular argument they espoused was that since most of the Taiwanese gentry class members were still tutored in the written language of classical Chinese in their childhood, minimal additional efforts would be needed to enable them to use the Chinese vernacular as a literary medium. The advantage of this was that it would facilitate the circulation of Taiwanese literary works in the larger Chinese community, since obviously Chinese recognition was still highly regarded by Taiwanese intellectuals. In practice, however, despite the goodwill on the part of most TNL writers, the disadvantages are by no means negligible. It is said that Lai Ho had to write his works in classical Chinese first, then translate it into the Chinese vernacular, and finally revise it with more lifelike Taiwanese colloquialisms. Yang Shou-yu 楊守愚, a writer well-versed in the Chinese vernacular because of his background, had to regularly rewrite works submitted for publication when he served as the editor for the literary section of the *Taiwanese People's Newspaper* 臺灣民報. Such a cumbersome and laborious process work against the fundamental principle of realistic literary writing, which explain why the kind of reevaluation offered by the Taiwanese Language movement was well-received even by Lai Ho, a writer with ostensible Chinese consciousness.

Without political enforcement, however, the goals of the Taiwanese Language movement were very difficult to materialize. The fact that many words in the Taiwanese spoken language are not believed to have corresponding Chinese characters made the development of a new writing system an enormous project beyond the reach of private groups. It is said that Lai Ho, after extensively using the Taiwanese language in writing his short story "A Letter of Criticism from a Comrade" 一個同志的批評信 (1935), was so frustrated with the experiment that he completely stopped writing fiction in the New Literature style. The colonial government, not surprisingly, only tried to hinder such a nationalistically motivated project and viewed it as an obstacle to the implementation of Japanese as the official language in Taiwan. The Taiwanese Language Debate thus reveals a typical dilemma facing colonized people: as the effort to develop a new national language based on the native tongue was seen by the Japanese colonial rulers as mainly a linguistic strategy of resistance and a means to assert one's own subjectivity, it was not likely to gain the political support required for its success. Despite failure, however, the Taiwanese Language movement must be regarded as a significant turning point in the TNL movement. There was a marked decline in the number of works by Chinese New Literature writers reprinted in Taiwanese journals after 1931. From this point on, the development of TNL began to consciously depart from the Chinese model, embarking on a path of its own.

Maturation and Growth

A crackdown of leftist organizations and the general suppression of sociopolitical movements in 1931 ironically heralded a period of maturation and growth for TNL, which lasted for over a decade. Various literary organizations were formed and new literary journals mushroomed. Having passed its initial, experimental stage, the evolution of the new literary form, particularly in the technical respect, made impressive progress during this period. Whereas the first generation of TNL writers continued to be productive, a group of young talents also joined the ranks. There was, however, a notable gap between the two generations of TNL writers in such respects as cultural outlook, aesthetic preference, and vocational orientation. This apparent disjuncture in the relatively brief history of TNL is particularly noteworthy, as it points to a rapidly changing cultural landscape in the second half of Taiwan's Japanese colonial period.

It has been argued that by the time the New Literature movement began, the cultural identity of Taiwanese intellectuals was still predominantly Chinese, despite the fact that Taiwan had already been colonized by the Japanese for more than two decades. Members of an ordinary Taiwanese gentry family were still sufficiently exposed to the Chinese cultural tradition, as children were still sent to private tutorial classes, or *shufang* 書房, to study classical Chinese. Most of the first generation of TNL writers, being members of the traditional gentry class, were well-versed in classical Chinese and competent in traditional Chinese poetry writing, a practice to which some of them returned after Chinese publications were banned in 1937. The fact that there were no substantial changes in society in the ethnic content of cultural production or reproduction is attributable to the special kind of colonial policies that were applied to Taiwan during the first two decades of the Japanese colonial period. Acknowledging that the colony had a separate history of its own, the Japanese were primarily concerned with maintaining social stability, rather than culturally assimilating the Taiwanese people. The cultural upbringing and community imagination of Taiwanese writers whose formative years fell into the first half of the colonial period were therefore not fundamentally transformed by colonial rule, even though most of them also received formal education in Japanese and were equipped with modern knowledge. Lai Ho, for example, went to a modern-style medical school and knew the Japanese language well, but he never used it in his creative writing. More importantly, as evidenced by both his writing and the role he played in the literary community, he was in many ways an exemplary traditional Chinese intellectual.

Significantly influenced by the Chinese May Fourth movement and its reformist ideology, the historical role played by this generation of Taiwanese writers was primarily that of new intellectuals in a premodern society struggling to break away from the past and to usher in progressive social visions. The past, however, was still very much with them. It can be easily demonstrated that, compared to their younger followers, this generation of Taiwanese writers carried over a considerable cultural legacy from the Chinese tradition in their New Literature-style works. Many of their works criticized a "spiritual disease" of Taiwanese society directly reflecting the Neo-Confucian moralist world view. The formal dimension of literary works by writers of this generation also displays a characteristically transitional character. The omniscient narrative point of view and episodic plot structure were obvious traits inherited from Chinese vernacular fiction. Since the modern short story, the novel, and free verse were essentially forms imported from the West, this generation of Taiwanese writers' assimilation of Western literary techniques and artistic conceptions was largely superficial.

The situation, however, was very different with writers born at later dates (Yang Kui was born in 1906; Weng Nao 翁鬧, 1908; Chang Wen-huan, 1909; Lung Ying-tsung, 1911; and Lu Ho-jo, 1914). In their formative years, the colonial cultural institutions were increasingly consolidated, and there was consequently a marked decrease in the value of Chinese learning as cultural capital. Generally speaking, unlike their immediate predecessors, the generation of Taiwanese writers active in the 1930s and 1940s lacked a solid background in traditional Chinese learning and demonstrated a more characteristically hybrid cultural identity. (Hsu Chun-ya 許俊雅, a researcher from the Taiwanese Literature Studies workshop, points out that the use of Japanese in literary creation gradually began to increase around 1933, and by around 1936 to 1937, there were actually very few works written in Chinese.) At the same time, rapid social change, already a norm in 20th-century non-Western countries, was greatly accelerated by Taiwan's colonial authorities.

The gap between the social visions of the two generations of writers was even more remarkable, as the younger writers were raised in a society at a considerably more advanced stage of modernization than their predecessors. Several critics have pointed out that Lai Ho seemed to be obsessed with the abusive power of laws and regulations enforced by the colonial government and its agents. These critics often justified Lai Ho's criticism with the fact that police control was notoriously harsh in Taiwan during the Japanese colonial period. Nevertheless, judging from the many passages in Lai Ho's fiction in which he meditated on the demarcation line between justice and law from various philosophical points of view, one gets the impression that his ideals and framework of reference were still derived from a premodern, Confucianist world view. The fact that younger writers tended to present both the evil and the benign sides of the law indicates that these writers held a more realistic view of the modern judicial system, despite discriminatory practices in the colonial context. Thus, in many ways these two generations of Taiwanese writers perceived the relationship between the individual and society quite differently.

Another significant factor is that the younger generation of writers were oriented to the literary profession in an entirely different manner from their predecessors. The 1930s saw the emergence of a new cohort of writers who had studied in Japan, a group that constituted the majority of second-generation TNL writers. While in Japan, these aspiring young Taiwanese writers found themselves on the periphery of an entirely different system of cultural production, and many of them began to earnestly seek membership in Japanese literary institutions. They enrolled in university literary classes, attended salons revolving around famous writers, and, above all, joined literary contests, which seemed to be an effective way of earning recognition from mainstream Japanese literary circles (often referred to as *Chung-yang wen-tan* 中央文壇). Yang Kui, Lu Ho-jo, and Lung Ying-tsung were winners of literary prizes in the mid-1930s.

As Japanese assimilation of the West surpassed that of the Chinese in the same period, the Taiwanese writers' knowledge of Japanese seemed to have enabled them to have a firmer grasp of Western artistic concepts, and, more importantly, of the kind of vocational vision that artists in a modern society often take for granted. These writers soon came to perceive themselves as professional artists with their own technical expertise and individualistic aesthetic visions, and thus it was less conceivable that they would ever become spiritual leaders like Lu Hsun or Lai Ho, whose status as major writers was derived from personal charisma and outstanding moral character in addition to literary talent.

Apparently, the younger writers enjoyed access to a wide range of literary models, mainly from the West, as evidenced by the remarkable diversity their works have shown in both artistic mode and ideological outlook. To give a few better known examples: Yang Kui adhered to a more orthodox leftism and dedicated his literary works to humanitarian criticisms of class exploitation, imperialism, and general evils in a capitalist society. Chang Wen-huan's approach was more humanistic in a liberal vein. His interest in the mystic power of the individual's inner self, projected onto Nature, resulted in some beautifully written lyrical pieces. Lu Ho-jo successfully emulated naturalism, offering realistic portraits of Taiwan's degenerated gentry class through "typical characters." Lung Ying-tsung's works showed influences of symbolism: delicately aesthetic but with visible touches of decadence.

It is perhaps ironic that, whereas early advocates of the TNL movement insisted on using the Chinese vernacular to ensure a place in the Chinese literary world, two out of three Taiwanese stories first collected in anthologies published in China—"The Newspaper Man" 送報夫 by Yang Kui and "The Ox Cart" 牛車 by Lu Ho-jo (the third story selected was the Chinese language "The Ill-fated" 薄命, by Yang Hua 楊華)—were translated from Japanese. Furthermore, the high reputation enjoyed by these two stories was clearly derived from the fact that they had won prizes in literary contests sponsored by important Japanese magazines. Hu Feng 胡風,

the editor of the Chinese collections in which these stories were found, *Mountain Spirit: Short Stories from Korea and Taiwan* 山靈: 朝鮮臺灣短篇小說集 and *Anthology of Stories from Weak and Small Nations in the World* 世界弱小民族小說選, was a renowned leftist literary theorist. The fact that Hu selected Yang and Lu's stories in recognition of their anti-imperialist spirit points to an extremely complex relationship between the Taiwanese authors and their Japanese colonizers, who were simultaneously oppressors and bestowers of cultural prestige. Such facts speak eloquently of the profoundly ambivalent cultural positions in which the second-generation TNL writers found themselves in the 1930s.

End of an Era

After the Sino-Japanese War broke out in 1937, the colonial government in Taiwan started an intensive Japanization program and banned the Chinese-language sections in newspapers and magazines. The impact of the harsh reality of war was not, however, fully felt until 1941, when Japan launched the Pacific War. The year 1937, for example, still saw the publication of the literary magazine *Wind and Moon* 風月報, the only Chinese-language magazine of this period. *Wind and Moon* featured popular types of literati writings, such as pulp romance, familiar essays, and occasional pieces of traditional scholarship, and enjoyed wide circulation.

In 1940, a literary organization consisting mainly of Japanese writers published the aesthetically-oriented journal *Literary Taiwan* 文藝臺灣. With the onslaught of the Pacific War, however, the Japanese stepped up their war campaign efforts and began to actively mobilize people in the colony to make a contribution to the "Great East Asian War" 大東亞戰爭. Between 1941 and 1942, *Literary Taiwan* chimed in with the colonial government's call for arms and published such stories as Chou Chin-po's 周金波 "Volunteer Conscript" 志願兵 and other unabashedly propagandist poems and plays. Several well-known second-generation writers of TNL, disapproving of both the political stance and artistic orientation of *Literary Taiwan*,

formed their own literary organization and began to publish *Taiwanese Literature* 臺灣文學 in 1941. Before the two journals were forced to merge by the government under the new name of *Taiwanese Literature and Art* 臺灣文藝 in 1944, *Taiwanese Literature* published perhaps the most important works of second-generation TNL writers: "Capon" 閹雞 and "Night Monkeys" 夜猿 by Chang Wen-huan; "Wealth, Offspring, and Longevity" 財子壽, "Peace for the Entire Family" 閤家平安, and "Guava" 石榴 by Lu Ho-jo; "A Village Without Doctors" 無醫村 by Yang Kui; and "Rapid Torrents" 奔流 by Wang Chang-hsiung 王昶雄.

The contention between *Literary Taiwan* and *Taiwanese Literature* between 1941 and 1944 represented a significant turn of events, as second-generation TNL writers began to directly confront oppressive relationships within the colonial structure. For these writers, who had been partially nourished by Japanese culture in their formative years and to which they held various degrees of allegiance, this experience must have been simultaneously disillusioning and educating. Above all, it became clear to them that artistic approaches were not ideologically innocent.

One thing that the Taiwanese writers objected to was the Japan-centered, typically colonist point of view of *Literary Taiwan*, which treated Taiwan as an exotic "foreign" place to be romanticized for the connoisseurship of readers in Japan. To the Taiwanese writers, such a literary approach was obviously complicitous in the colonial government's effort to involve culture in the process of political domination by way of diverting people from sociopolitical concerns to purely aesthetic ones. Such realizations were undoubtedly behind the tactics used by writers of *Taiwanese Literature* in their endeavors to champion realism as opposed to the exquisite aestheticism and romanticism of *Literary Taiwan*. Aside from works directly informed by leftist ideology, such as those by Yang Kui, it is said that some writers of the *Taiwanese Literature* group consciously shifted to more detailed depictions of local customs, rural life, and folk traditions of Chinese/Taiwanese origin in order to register their resentment of the Japanization program.

The nationalistic orientation of *Taiwanese Literature*, however, failed to attract some of the ardent writers of an even younger generation, such as Yeh Shih-tao 葉石濤 and Chou Chin-po, who published their works in *Literary Taiwan* and expressed either aestheticism or political loyalty to the colonizer. Yeh even wrote the controversial essay "Shit Realism" 糞寫實主義, which provoked a heated response from colleagues at *Taiwanese Literature*. However, it was not until the next period that some of this younger generation of writers began to deeply reflect upon the complicated issues surrounding colonial subjectivity.

The unusually convoluted trajectory traveled by TNL writers may also be illuminated by a brief examination of their intriguingly different attitudes toward the issue of modernity. The wholehearted embrace by many first-generation writers of modernity as an advanced stage of civilization was expressed in vacant terms, for essentially they never had any real experience of a truly modernized society. Most of the second generation, pressured by wartime literary policies, engaged in indirect resistance by means of asserting nativism, to the effect of notably decreasing their criticism of traditional, feudalistic traits in Taiwanese society. However, if some of them consciously denigrated modern urban civilization, symbolically represented by the Japanese metropolis, still others held exactly the opposite stance. In the works of Chen Huo-chuan 陳火泉 and the younger writer Chou Chin-po, both of whom opted to side with progress, a prominent theme was the urgency to modernize in view of the obvious benefits that modernity could bring to the Taiwanese people. As Japan was equated with civilization, they ardently supported Japanization, albeit not without doubts from time to time.

In artistic terms, the modern literary form of the TNL movement significantly departed from the classical Chinese tradition, but its evolution was brought to an abrupt cessation at the end of the Second World War when Taiwan was returned to China. Several years later, the Nationalists, having lost the Chinese mainland to the communists in the civil war, relocated to Taiwan and started an entirely new era. The drastic changes such historical events brought to Taiwanese society caused most of the TNL writers to halt their creative activities. Thus, many artists were never allowed to develop to their fullest potential, and the movement ended before any genuinely masterful works of art could ever appear.

The legacy of the TNL movement was suppressed in the postwar years, as the dominant culture now consisted of the mainland Chinese tradition. However, there were still some significant works written and published under the TNL movement, and the exploration of colonial subjectivity continued to be the dominant concern of works written by writers directly nourished by the TNL of the Japanese colonial period, such as *The Orphan of Asia* 亞細亞孤兒 by Wu Cho-liu 吳濁流, *The Oleander Flowers* 夾竹桃 by Chung Li-ho 鍾理和, *The Man Who Rolls On the Ground* 滾地郎 by Chang Wen-huan, and later works by Yeh Shih-tao. Despite their largely marginal position, these writers would play a crucial role in Taiwan's postwar literary history by offering alternative visions to the dominant culture, and their impact was increasingly felt in the nativist 本土化 movement of the last two to three decades.

Post-1949 Literature in Taiwan

Shifting Literary Trends

Taiwan's post-1949 era began when China's Nationalist government, led by Chiang Kai-shek, settled on the offshore island of Taiwan after the mainland fell to the Chinese communists. The 40-year period under the rule of two presidents from the Chiang family was characterized by remarkable social, political, and cultural continuity and homogeneity. Drastic structural changes have been occurring at all levels of society since the mid-1980s as direct consequences of the lifting of martial law, the recognition of opposition parties, the removal of the ban on establishing newspapers, and the resumption of communication with mainland China at the nonofficial level. New intellectual and artistic currents have emerged, many with the explicit or implicit motive of reexamining existing orders. Nonetheless, it is undeniable that the literary accomplishments of writers from the earlier post-1949 decades laid solid groundwork for Taiwan's vital and pluralistic cultural development in the 1990s.

As China split into two political entities with different sociopolitical systems after 1949, the tradition of Chinese New Literature 新文學 traveled along divergent paths in these two Chinese societies. Writers in post-1949 Taiwan were selective in developing their literary heritage; whereas revolutionary literature and "critical realism" were suppressed, the more inoffensive, lyrical-sentimental strand enjoyed great popularity. From the anticommunist propaganda of the Cold War decade of the 1950s, through the modernist and nativist literary movements of the 1960s and 1970s, to the expression of today's pluralism and the burgeoning of market-oriented mass culture, literary currents in post-1949 Taiwan have closely mirrored the country's larger sociopolitical transitions.

The Western-influenced modernist literary movement of the 1960s and the popular nativist literary movement of the 1970s may appropriately be regarded as "alternative" and "oppositional" cultural formations in Taiwan during this period. As the modernists adopted literary concepts developed in Western capitalist society, they simultaneously longed for an ideological transformation, taking such bourgeois social values as individualism, liberalism, and rationalism as correctives for the oppressive social relations derived from a traditional system of values. The nativist literary movement, by contrast, with its use of literature as a pretext to challenge the dominant sociopolitical order, may be properly considered as counterhegemonic.

The movement was triggered by the nation's diplomatic setbacks in the international arena during the 1970s, and provided a forum for native Taiwanese intellectuals to vent their discontent with the socioeconomic problems that have accompanied the country's accelerated process of industrialization since the 1960s.

For different reasons, both movements dominated Taiwan's literary scene only for a relatively brief period of time. By the late 1970s and early 1980s, the influence of both the modernists and the nativists had sharply declined, and some of their inherent shortcomings had become obvious with the passage of time. As most of the modernist writers advocated artistic autonomy and were politically disengaged, the subversive elements of their works were easily co-opted by more powerful cultural forces and their critical impact was consequently diluted. The more radical adherence to aestheticism by certain writers, moreover, was deeply at odds with the predominantly lyrical sensibility of ordinary Chinese readers. Even though the essential dynamics of the modernist movement were not entirely exhausted by the loss of popular favor, both critics and general readers received the movement's most mature output in the 1980s with nonchalance.

In the meantime, the militant political agenda of the nativists both threatened and bored middle-class readers. The resistant activities of the more radical nativists, moreover, were increasingly channeled into direct political involvement. The subsiding of these contending literary voices paved the way for the rise of a "serious" literature that was more popular in nature and a resurgence of the lyrical and sentimental strain of the 1980s. Thus, the younger generation of writers of this decade assimilated the technical sophistication of the modernists while displaying a social awareness as a result of nativist influence. Their vocational visions, however, significantly departed from those of their mentors and were much more deeply conditioned by the market logic of Taiwan's increasingly commercialized cultural setting.

Mainland Emigre Literature: 1950s

After Taiwan was returned to rule by a Chinese government in 1945, Mandarin Chinese replaced both the Taiwanese dialect and Japanese as the official spoken language of the island. The creative activities of middle-aged native Taiwanese writers were greatly hampered by this language barrier. Political fear is another factor that silenced native Taiwanese writers, as many Taiwanese intellectuals were persecuted during and after the February 28 Incident in 1947 (see pertinent section of Chapter 4, History). The literary scene in Taiwan during the 1950s was therefore virtually dominated by mainland writers who followed the Nationalists to Taiwan around 1949. These emigre writers were frequently mobilized in the state-sponsored cultural programs and produced a literature that has often been characterized as anticommunist.

In addition to political propaganda, writers of the 1950s have been frequently faulted for their amateurism, which is partly the product of a special institution in Taiwan, the *fu-kan* 副刊, or literary supplement to newspapers. The *fu-kan* undeniably has been the most significant sponsor of literary activities in Taiwan before the new millennium; nevertheless, with its large demand for works of immediate popular appeal, it at the same time fostered casual, lightweight writing and pandered to middlebrow literary tastes. As literary writing became less professional, the distinction between artistic and journalistic genres was often blurred.

Although the general climate of the 1950s was not conducive to the production of serious art, works of considerable artistic merit by a number of writers deserve greater critical attention than is usually given to them. Two broad categories of writings, traditionalist prose and realistic fiction, are considered to be representative of the literature in this decade.

Traditionalist Prose

Contrary to the situation in the People's Republic of China, where gentry literature of China's feudal past was sometimes renounced for ideological reasons and where numerous political idioms designed to mobilize the masses were added to the vocabulary, the prose style in post-1949 Taiwan tended to be more literary, retaining a great many more archaic expressions and allusions to classical literature. The proliferation of traditionalist prose 散文 in Taiwan during the 1950s, in the form of familiar essays and the hybrid genre of essay-fiction, was apparently a continuation of an earlier trend on the mainland during and following the Sino-Japanese war. The decade's best-known essayists—Chang Hsiu-ya 張秀亞, Chung Mei-yin 鍾梅音, Hsu Chung-pei 徐鍾珮, Liang Hsuan 亮軒, and Chi-chun 琦君—were therefore all mainland emigre writers.

Realistic Fiction

Having been exposed to the works of Lu Hsun, Mao Tun 茅盾, Pa Chin 巴金, and Lao She 老舍 in their formative years, mainland emigre writers active in the 1950s and 1960s by and large carried on the Chinese "realist" tradition—a somewhat atrophied version of 19th-century European realism—established during the May Fourth era and the 1930s. For political reasons, however, they consciously or unconsciously modified those realistic conventions that might have been offensive to the dominant culture of post-1949 Taiwan: revolutionary and proletarian themes were taboo, and references to class consciousness were avoided. Nevertheless, the nature of literary conventions is such that their suppression can never be as complete as it appears on the surface.

The 1960s saw the publication of several well-written, "anticommunist" realistic novels, such as *Rice-sprout Song* 秧歌, *The Whirlwind* 旋風, and *The Ti Village* 荻村傳. Although important in their own right, these stories were set exclusively in pre-Revolutionary China, and their authors either never resided in Taiwan (e.g., Eileen Chang 張愛玲, 1921-95), or were marginal to Taiwan's literary scene (e.g., Chiang Kui 姜貴 and Chen Chi-ying 陳紀瀅), thus diminishing their significance in Taiwan's post-1949 literary history. Far more relevant were such writers as Wang Lan 王藍, Meng Yao 孟瑤, Pan Jen-mu 潘人木, Lin Hai-yin 林海音, Nieh Hua-ling 聶華苓, Peng Ko 彭歌, Chu Hsi-ning 朱西寧, Tuan Tsai-hua 段彩華, Ssu-ma Chung-yuan 司馬中原, and Chung Chau-cheng 鍾肇政, who had established their literary reputations around the mid-1950s and who continued to play prominent roles in Taiwan's literary scene for some time.

Although the fiction of these writers is also filled with nostalgic recollections of the mainland past, their works are nevertheless unique products of the contemporary cultural and political environment. Unmistakably, the emancipation ethos, a legacy of pre-1949 realist literature, has informed a number of their writings set in the past on subjects such as the oppression of women, the repressive nature of the traditional Chinese family system, and the condition of working-class people and domestic servants. In addition, the realistic codes were rewritten and the critical messages mitigated or displaced: rightist political convictions and active support of the present government frequently caused these writers to domesticate the revolutionary spirit with counterdevices and to shift the thematic focus from the sociohistorical to private domains. The rise of the young modernists, with their liberalism and new aesthetic conceptions, challenged not only these older writers' artistic visions, but also the dominant culture's ideological control over creative writers. The changes brought forth by the modernists in the artistic realm formed the basis for more radical cultural critiques found in later decades.

Modernist Literary Movement: 1960s

The dominant culture in post-1949 Taiwan carries on many traditions established in China during the Republican era (1911-1949). The modernist literary movement is an expression of the predilection by Chinese intellectuals of the time to emulate Western high culture. Ever since the end of the 19th century when China was shocked to devastating effect by its encounters with Western culture, modern Chinese intellectuals have attempted various kinds of cultural rejuvenation, the most potent formula of which has been the assimilation of Western cultural products. Taiwan's modernist literary movement, as one of the latest in a series of such efforts, inevitably displays some of Western culture's essential characteristics.

Second, an important link can be perceived between this movement and the liberal strand of thought in China's pre-Revolutionary era, especially that of the Anglo-American wing of intellectuals. It is readily observable that the ideas of important literary figures of post-1949 Taiwan, such as Liang Shih-chiu 梁實秋, former member of the Crescent Moon Society 新月社, Hsia Chi-an 夏濟安, mentor of a core group of modernists, and Yen Yuan-shu 顏元叔, leading critic of the 1960s who introduced New Criticism to Taiwan, are all fundamentally rooted in Western liberal-humanist traditions. Yen Yuanshu's proposition that "literature has the dual function of being the dramatization and criticism of life," in particular, closely echoes both Matthew Arnold and the Literary Studies Association's famous tenet, "art for life's sake."

Taiwan's modernists especially stressed the principle of artistic autonomy, among other liberal conceptions of literature, and, by and large, have more thoroughly adhered to this principle than their pre-1949 liberal predecessors. From the point of view of literary history, however, the epoch-making significance of Taiwan's modernist literary movement rests primarily in terms of its generation of new dynamics among contemporary writers and its redirecting of their artistic mode of expression.

New Thematic Conventions

In terms of theme and subject matter, writers of Taiwan's modernist fiction endeavored to explore new spheres of human experience beyond the confines of traditional literature. In doing so, they continued the efforts of their early-20th century May Fourth movement predecessors and even surpassed them in depth. To comprehend and analyze the complexity of human experience in the modern world, they generally favored rationalism, scientism, and serious, if at times immature, philosophical contemplation. We have thus witnessed the establishment of a set of thematic conventions that supposedly incorporate advanced knowledge of human behavior made available by the modern sciences. For example, apparently influenced by popular versions of Freudian psychoanalysis, young writers at the early stage of the modernist literary movement were particularly fascinated with nontraditional or even abnormal interpersonal relationships. These writers included Wang Wen-hsing 王文興, Pai Hsien-yung 白先勇, Ou-yang Tzu 歐陽子, Chen Jo-hsi 陳若曦, Shui Ching 水晶, Chen Ying-chen 陳映真, to name just a few. Their sincerity and bold, honest self-analysis broke new ground in Taiwan's cultural context and redefined the boundaries of normality in human behavior, thus presenting challenges to the conservative middle-class mentality that has been the backbone of the dominant culture in post-1949 Taiwan.

Some truly radical cultural examinations are found in the movement's later more mature stages. For example, with a common theme of father-son conflict, two of Taiwan's most significant modernist novels, Pai Hsien-yung's *Crystal Boys* 孽子 (1983) and Wang Wen-hsing's *Family Catastrophe* 家變 (1973), offer bitter protests against the traditional ethical norms that are crystallized in the Confucianist notions of loyalty 忠 and filial piety 孝, and thus call into question fundamental underpinnings of the superstructure of contemporary Taiwan society. Notably, in both works, the battle against the social retention of traditional values is waged with the aid of Western conceptual frames.

Family Catastrophe features as its central theme the conflict of bourgeois individualism with the concept of filial piety in a financially strapped modern Chinese family. That the hero is portrayed as a fanatic rationalist shows the degree to which the author is skeptical of the real efficacy of such an ideological transfer. *Crystal Boys*, on the other hand, projects a more idealistic vision influenced by the countercultural movement of the 1960s in the United States, with its anarchic assertion of the emancipatory power of the Dionysian impulse, its celebration of youth and beauty in their ephemeral physical forms, and its romantic affirmation of the redeeming virtue of love. The author further enriched the symbolic level of this book by infusing this vision with mythical themes from the Chinese classic *Dream of the Red Chamber* 紅樓夢. The underground homosexual community of New Park 新公園 in *Crystal Boys,* like residents of the Garden of the Grand Vision 大觀園 in the famous traditional novel, is ruled by the supreme order of sentimentality 情 and the heart 心, which can be both salvational and damning. This microcosm, however, is extremely vulnerable, as it is forever overshadowed by the law of the father—the dominant order of the patriarchal, Confucianist society outside the garden. The prominence of the father-quest motif in both *Family Catastrophe* and *Crystal Boys*—heroes in both novels are constantly searching for paternal surrogates—betrays their authors' anxiety over the general corruption of the terms governing human relationships in contemporary Taiwan society, terms that in history were solidly built on the patriarchal order.

Formal Innovations

Particularly eye-catching in the initial stages of the modernist literary movement was the temporary surge of an avant-garde trend. One prominent feature of the self-styled avant-garde writers of the 1960s was their infatuation with the intellectual current of existentialism. As Franz Kafka was introduced early in the movement, the use of obscure plots and bizarre language quickly became a fad, and the basic tenor of works by many young writers—Chi-teng Sheng 七等生, Tsung Su 叢甦, and Shih Shu-ching 施叔青 among them—seemed to be dominated by nihilism, agonism, and an anxiety over the absurdity of existence.

The upsurge of aesthetic iconoclasm in the 1960s represented a significant moment in postwar Taiwan's literary history. The vigorous dynamics of newly introduced artistic conceptions associated with modernism called into question conventional forms and criteria of literary excellence. The more enduring efforts generated by this initial enthusiasm eventually ushered in a new era of modern Chinese literary history.

Most modernist fiction writers in Taiwan stayed within the general confines of realism, but they were no less experimental. Their conscious explorations of language and voice brought forth fundamental changes in rhetorical conventions of modern Chinese narrative. Since, as some scholars have observed, the attempts of earlier modern Chinese writers to offer realistic portraits of life were frequently hampered by the dominance of the subjective voice in the work's rhetorical structure, the modernists tried to redress this deficiency by introducing a new "objective form." They strove to present an "impartial" picture of reality so that readers could be given the privilege of forming their own opinions and moral judgments. To be sure, these ideas are more reminiscent of the realists' concept of literary representation than the modernist view of literature as self-referential discursive practice. Throughout the 1960s, in fact, the majority of critical writings introducing Western literary concepts focused on basic technical rules and critical criteria that have long been naturalized and taken for granted in the West. Authoritative US-trained scholars and critics, such as Yen Yuan-shu, Chu Li-min 朱立民, and Wai-lim Yip 葉維廉, systematically expounded the fundamentals of a whole set of Western literary codes, and their influence on creative writing and practical criticism in Taiwan was immeasurable. Such a phenomenon is actually not very difficult to understand, given that the literary genres of the short story and the novel (in the strict sense) were both imported from the West during this century.

It is also true, however, that the appropriation of foreign literary codes necessarily involved larger, more complicated networks of artistic and ideological systems. Given that the most noteworthy formal feature popularized by the modernists was the widened distance between author and text, their efforts may be seen as having continued the general trend in modern Chinese literary history away from the traditional expressive view toward the mimetic or imitative means of representation. With their denunciation of sentimentalism and express interest in the hidden complexities of the human psyche, personal emotions were no longer treated as the source or origin of literature, but rather as objects for detached observation.

It is arguable that, despite the fact that Taiwan's modernist literary movement took place in a "postmodern" period from the standpoint of the West—in the 1960s and 1970s—and despite the fact that many newer artistic trends and techniques were incorporated by the modernist writers into their work, the dominant tendency of this movement nevertheless was closest to the early phase of Western modernism in the late 19th century and early 20th century. In other words, in the extremely compressed timetable of Taiwan's modernist literary movement, one nevertheless discerns features such as the reversal of the conventional content-form hierarchy and the radical rejection of traditional writing techniques that could only be the result of a burgeoning skepticism about language and meaning. Most of the modernists' explorations of language unmistakably reflect Western influences. However, more original experiments were also made, which resulted from a new awareness of the unstable relationship between language and its referents, as well as of a reawakened sensitivity toward the ideographic nature of the Chinese language. These experiments—especially those found in Wang Wen-hsing's two novels *Family Catastrophe* and *Backed Against the Sea* 背海的人 (1981), and Li Yung-ping's story series *Chronicle of Chi-ling* 吉陵春秋 (1986)—marked the apex of the development of modernist aestheticism in contemporary Chinese literature.

Nativist Literary Debate: 1970s

As the modernist fiction writers began to mature artistically in the late 1960s and early 1970s, so too did the resistance to modernism's dominance of Taiwan's literary scene begin. The precursor to a large-scale denunciation of the modernist literary movement was the 1972 Modern Poetry Debate 現代詩論戰, which involved a number of academic critics and modernist poets who discussed specific Western-influenced features in contemporary Taiwan poetry. The consensus reached in this debate seemed to be that, despite its other merits, the currently practiced modern poetry suffered from such unhealthy qualities as semantic obscurity, excessive use of foreign imagery and Europeanized syntax, and evasion of contemporary social reality. These features, furthermore, were considered symptomatic of the faulty style generally promoted in Taiwan's modernist literary movement.

While it may not be unusual in literary history for critics and writers to periodically reexamine and revolt against the current dominant style, the Modern Poetry Debate bore a special social implication in that it was closely tied to the Taiwan intellectuals' growing consciousness of their endangered Chinese/Taiwanese cultural identity. In what was later known as the "return to native roots" 回歸鄉土 trend around the 1970s, progressive intellectuals criticized the blind admiration and slavish imitation of Western cultural models, and exhorted their compatriots to show more respect for their indigenous cultural heritage, as well as greater concern for domestic social issues. Many liberal scholars, especially those who had just returned from the United States, played important roles in igniting this new trend, which at first revolved around several universities and intellectual magazines.

Shortly after the Modern Poetry Debate, a group of critics began to publicly renounce the foreign-influenced modernist work and to advocate a nativist, socially responsible literature. This trend reached its apex with the outbreak of two virulent Nativist Literature Debates in 1977 and 1978, and suddenly declined when, in 1979, several key figures of the nativist camp exited from the literary scene and became directly involved in political protests. The tradition of nativist literature as a creative genre—of which the main features were the use of the Taiwanese dialect, depiction of the plight of country folk or small-town dwellers caught up in economic difficulty, and resistance to the imperialist presence in Taiwan—can be traced back to the nativist literary trend during the Japanese colonial period. While inheriting the dominant nationalist spirit from this earlier trend, the nativist literature champions of the 1970s had their own political agenda as well.

Viewed retrospectively, the nativist camp was the first oppositional formation at a critical juncture in Taiwan's post-1949 history. After two decades of political stability and steady economic growth, the country suffered a series of diplomatic setbacks at the turn of the decade—beginning with its expulsion from the United Nations in 1971, followed by Richard Nixon's visit to the Chinese mainland and the termination of the ROC's diplomatic relations with Japan in 1972—which caused not only international isolation, but also a confidence crisis among Taiwan intellectuals.

Unlike the majority of the country's liberal intellectuals, who demanded democratization while supporting capitalist-style economic modernization, the nativists believed that the socioeconomic system of Taiwan must be changed. They fiercely attacked the ROC government's economic dependence on Western countries (especially the United States), deplored the infiltration of "decadent" capitalist culture into the ordinary lives of Taiwan's people, expressed indignance on behalf of Taiwan's farmers and workers who paid a high economic price for the nation's urban expansion, and attempted to draw public attention to the adverse effects of the country's overall economic development.

The regionalist sentiment implied in the nativist project immediately touched on an extremely sensitive issue, the "provincial heritage problem" 省籍問題. Tensions between native Taiwanese and mainlanders had always existed, especially given the perceptions of an unbalanced distribution of political power at the time. As a consequence, even though some of the leading nativist critics were socialists or nationalists rather than separatists promoting Taiwan independence, the nativist critical discourse as a whole could not but be part of the ongoing political strife.

It is therefore undeniable that literary nativism was used by a special group of people at a particular historical moment to challenge the existing sociopolitical order. However, it appears that ideological debates in modern Chinese society inevitably generate widespread polemics around literature, as evidenced by the numerous such disputes held during the May Fourth period in the 1930s, and during the entire communist reign on the mainland. The traditional Chinese pragmatic view of literature and the legacy of a gentry ideology, which assigns to intellectuals, especially writers, lofty social missions, combined to make literary discourse a genuine political space. As a result, the attacks launched by the nativists on the modernist writers, whose literary ideology was conspicuously apolitical, largely centered on the latter's default of their social responsibilities as members of the intelligentsia.

The home base for the anti-modernist critics was the journal *Literary Quarterly* 文季, founded in 1966. With Yu Tien-tsung 尉天聰 as the central mover, the journal's founding members included several writers already known for their modernist works, such as Chen Ying-chen, Liu Ta-jen 劉大任, Shih Shu-ching, and Chi-teng Sheng. Furthermore, the journal had discovered two important writers, Huang Chun-ming 黃春明 and Wang Chen-ho 王禎和, whose fiction significantly departed from the current modernist fads and depicted rural life with unaffected realism. Although both writers refused to label their works as "nativist," the literary reformers on the journal's editorial board were ready to use them as weapons in their fight against the modernist hegemony.

In 1973, Tang Wen-piao 唐文標, a visiting math professor closely associated with the *Literary Quarterly*, criticized the modernists' elitist tendencies and neglect of the masses. The straightforward accusations so startled the liberal critics that Yen Yuan-shu referred to this critical attack as the "Tang Wen-piao Incident." However, even more vehement militancy was to be seen when the nativist critics chose individual writers as targets. Almost simultaneously with the Tang Wen-piao Incident, the *Literary Quarterly* organized a series of seminars to examine the thematic implications of Ou-yang Tzu's fiction, and branded it "corrupt and immoral." By the mid-1970s, Taiwan's literary writers were already deeply split into opposing camps.

The literary climate in this decade became truly unpleasant with the increasing politicization of critical discourse. With the founding of the radical magazine *Summer Tide* 夏潮 in 1976 and its provocative use of such taboo terms as "proletarian literature" and "class consciousness," the deep-seated anticommunist sentiments of the liberals were incited. In the summer of 1977, the country's leading modernist poet Yu Kuang-chung 余光中 wrote a short essay entitled "The Wolf Is Here" 狼來了 openly accusing the nativists of being leftists. This fatal charge ignited highly emotional responses and retaliations from all sides, and polemical writings about literature and politics began to flood the country's newspapers and literary magazines. This so-called Nativist Literary Debate was finally brought to an end in the middle of 1978 as a result of threatened government intervention.

Placed within a larger historical context, the modernist-nativist split was part of the continual struggle in modern Chinese history between liberal and radical intellectuals with different reform programs and different views of literature's social function. The new paradigm of ideological writing as established in the mid-1970s moved in a direction diametrically opposed to that of the introspective, humanist, and

431

universalist approach of the modernists and deliberately focused on the historical specificity of contemporary Taiwan society. In addition to later works by Huang Chun-ming on imperialism, such writers as Yang Ching-chu 楊青矗 and Wang To 王拓 explored capitalist exploitation as it affected urban factory workers and fishermen. These literary efforts were also backed by some serious theoretical thinking, although most of the Nativist Literary Debate itself was virtually divorced from contemporary literary practice.

Wang To's 1977 essay, "It Should Be 'Literature of the Here and Now,' Not 'Nativist Literature'" 是現實主義文學, 不是鄉土文學 stood out among numerous polemical writings precisely because of its accurate representation of the reality of recent literary practice. The main argument that Wang proposed in this essay was that, instead of writing about rural regions and country people, nativist literature should be concerned with the "here and now" of Taiwan society, which embraces a wide range of social environments and people. Thus, nativist literature should be defined as a literature rooted in the land of Taiwan, one that reflects the social reality and the material and psychological aspirations of its people. By using the term *hsien shih* 現實 (contemporary reality, the "here and now") rather than *hsieh shih* 寫實 (realism), and by enlarging the scope of nativist literature to include all levels of social reality in Taiwan, Wang stressed high-priority nativist issues. The essay, therefore, represented an important step in the nativists' process of self-definition.

The critical evaluation of nativist works produced in the 1970s, however, was in general not very positive. Although the change in thematic conventions since the 1970s met the approval of most critics, excessive ideological concern was considered to have detracted from their literary achievement. Even Huang Chun-ming, who was often regarded as an exception, has been criticized by many who felt that his art, too, deteriorated in direct proportion to the increase in social commentary in his later works. However, just as modernist literature continued to evolve after the rise of nativist literature, the practice of nativist literature did not come to an end even though the Nativist Literary Debate folded toward the end of the 1970s. In the continuing efforts made by such nativist ideological writers as Chen Ying-chen, Sung Tse-lai 宋澤萊, Li Chiao 李喬, and Wu Chin-fa 吳錦發 in the 1980s, one can discern a sharp increase in formal consciousness, as well as attempts to experiment with innovative techniques.

Pluralism: 1980s

In a sense, the articulation of dissident views during the Nativist Literary Debate paved the way for more intense struggles toward democratization, which rapidly gained momentum in the early 1980s. Eventually, with the formation in 1987 of an opposition party, the Democratic Progressive Party, literature was largely relieved of its function as a pretext for political contestation. At the same time, however, it became even more inextricably involved in the country's booming mass media. Most notably, the two competing media giants, the *United Daily News* 聯合報 and *China Times* 中國時報—with each claiming the loyalty of a group of writers—invested heavily in their literary pages for marketing purposes. The annual fiction contests they sponsored between the mid-1970s and mid-1980s gave creative writing a solid boost—an overwhelming majority of the writers of the baby-boom generation rose to literary prominence by winning one of these contests.

The nativist theorists may have felt both frustrated and vindicated in the 1980s, as the "spiritual corruption" of capitalist society, which they had predicted, appeared along with the ascendancy of materialism and a sharp rise in the crime rate. The overall cultural environment also became heavily consumer-oriented. Not without a touch of irony, even the nativist literature itself was largely co-opted by the cultural establishment, especially between the late 1970s and early 1980s. Newspaper supplements and literary magazines were inundated by pseudo-nativist works, which displayed an abundance of Taiwanese local color but contained little ideological content.

As public fervor for both the modernist and the nativist causes subsided, the literary scene of the 1980s became largely dominated by the baby-boom generation, whose vocational visions were drastically different from those of their predecessors. Rather than treating creative writing as an intellectual project or a political quest, they were more concerned with popularity and with various problems affecting Taiwan's middle-class urbanites, especially the new social affluence and the relaxation of moral standards. Some writers with a cynical intellectual pose, such as Huang Fan 黃凡 and Li Ang 李昂, offered critiques of materialism and the cultural impoverishment it caused; while others with down-to-earth pragmatism, such as Hsiao Sa 蕭颯 and Liao Hui-ying 廖輝英, examined the new social factors that had changed ordinary people's way of life, showing particular interest in liberated sexual views and the problem of extramarital relationships; and still others, such as Yuan Chiung-chiung 袁瓊瓊, Chu Tien-wen 朱天文, and Su Wei-chen 蘇偉貞, fell back on the sentimental-lyrical tradition and focused their attention on subjective, private sentiment with a posture of complacency in regard to sociopolitical issues.

Whether progressively or conservatively inclined, the new generation of writers seemed to share a common response to the emergence of new political situations. As knowledge about the Chinese on the other side of the Taiwan Strait suddenly became available, and with the public debate over the nature and pace of unification with the Chinese mainland intensifying on a daily basis, many of the writers of the baby-boom generation tended to deliberately stress their unique cultural identity, rooted in the specific sociohistorical realities of Taiwan's post-1949 era.

Writers' approaches to literature in this decade were certainly pluralist. While writers of the modernist generation published their more mature works during this decade, literary products of the younger generation were marked by a rich diversity— *chuan tsun* 眷村 (residential military community) literature, works about life in business corporations, political fiction (with a special sub-genre on the February 28 Incident), neo-nativist literature, resistance literature, feminist works, and science fiction—a phenomenon that may be aptly characterized as the orchestration of a multitude of discordant "voices."

The broadly defined trend of "returning to one's native roots" carried over into the early 1980s beyond the modernist-nativist contention. After the Nativist Literary Debate, new interest in an indigenous literary heritage fostered a trend of cultural nostalgia. Several former modernist writers made notable contributions to this trend. Shih Shu-ching and Li Ang, for example, consciously turned to folk traditions and native subject matter in their writing. Lin Huai-min 林懷民, a former modernist writer who had studied under Martha Graham while in the US, founded the first Chinese modern dance troupe and produced the well-received "Cloud Gate Dance Ensemble" 雲門舞集, which incorporated both classical Chinese and folk Taiwanese elements in its choreography (see section, Dance, in Chapter 21, The Arts). All of these accomplishments set the tone for creative endeavors in the new decade, even while encouraging commercial exploitation of traditional and native cultural signs.

As the indigenous began to replace the foreign as the primary source of exotic imagination, and "Chinese/Taiwanese cultural identity" began to occupy a prominent place in the public consciousness, "postmodernism" became vogue after the mid-1980s and again raised issues about Western influences on contemporary Chinese/Taiwanese literature. In a pattern closely resembling that by which such earlier Western literary trends as romanticism, realism, and modernism were appropriated by writers of Taiwan, the postmodern mode of writing became a new fad and its surface markers, such as double endings, juxtaposition of the factual and the fictional, and the technique of pastiche, among others, appeared profusely in works by both greater and lesser writers. Such imitative literary products cannot but recall works written during the earliest phase of the modernist literary movement, and not surprisingly, are considered to be of dubious value by some veteran modernists.

The younger writers of the 1990s consciously subscribed to the more cynical, "postmodern" ideology—as evidenced by their emphasis on difference, tolerance of pluralistic coexistence of the incommensurable, and, above all, their appetite for the indeterminacy that is uncongenial to the modernist temperament. However, there were also similarities between the two generations of writers: their intellectual disposition, their globalism, and the way they looked to the West—or Western-influenced literary traditions, such as those of Eastern Europe and Latin America—for literary models. As prescribed by "postmodern" ideology, however, the younger writers were more keenly aware of the self/other dichotomy, and thus did not endorse universalism as the modernists did.

Multiculturalism and Postidentity Politics: 1990s

Taiwan has undergone an interpretive turn in terms of national identity and critical multiculturalism in the 1990s. Taiwanese literature of the 1990s tends to use mixed genres and multilingual devices, drawing on a wide range of both global and local cultural codes, idioms, and traditions, to express the fluid, albeit disoriented, structure of feelings.

In the 1990s, Chu Tien-wen and Chang Ta-chun 張大春 were still prominent figures in the field of political fiction, especially for their nostalgic narratives on the dissolution of a certain culture within government housing compounds. Chang was reputed for his technique of intermixing various genres—including history, dream text, diary, and news reports—and voices. As a writer appropriating all news and media events, Chang gradually moved from writing cynical diaries and "factual fiction" based on the tragic death of a navy officer to producing public TV programs and increasingly becoming a media person. Chu's *Notes of a Desolate Man* 荒人手記 won the 1994 *China Times* best fiction award. Although the second-generation mainlanders who serve as the subjects of this novel reappear repeatedly, Chu's sensitivity to the ethnic tensions, rupture of tradition, and societal psychopathologies is nicely matched by her literary style and narrative coherence.

In between Chu and Chang was Yang Chao 楊照, a young talent who successfully blended romance with saga, collapsing the distinctions between public and private and the personal and the social. Yang is currently a cultural critic, political activist, and novelist. His multiple roles in contemporary Taiwanese public culture, as well as his impressive talent in fusing personal and interpersonal histories, are self-evident in one of his trilogies, *A Dark Alley on a Confusing Night* 暗巷迷夜.

In contrast to Li Ang, who severely criticized the patriarchal system of domination, younger women writers emerging in the 1990s, such as Lo Yi-chun 駱以軍 or Cheng Ying-shu 成英姝, were more playful in their treatment of sexual liaisons in bars (often gay or lesbian), of the object-choice "medial woman," and of the fantasies and frustrations of the so-called "New Human Species" 新新人類 in relation to the new, unsettling social milieu that had thus far failed to take shape. Writers like Cheng were on their way to expressing postidentity politics, celebrating postmodern flexibility and unpredictability in the global cyberspace of easy accessibility. Their counterpart in the field of poetry was the late Lin Yao-te 林燿德, who employed the language of the fax machine and computer terminal to describe the fluid human relations in a transnational capitalistic society. Lin was very active in the 1980s in promoting postmodern poetry about urban culture and cityscapes, following poets like Lo Men 羅門, Lo Ching 羅青, and others. These poets differed greatly from the humanist traditions set up by Lo Fu 洛夫, Wai-lim Yip, and Ya Hsien 亞弦, as well as from the traditions revised by Chien Cheng-chen 簡政珍, Hsu Hui-chih 許悔之, and Chiao Tung 焦侗, who added phenomenological, psychoanalytical, and even poststructuralist twists.

To question Chinese nationalism, quite a few writers tried to highlight issues associated with the Taiwan independence movement, minority discourse, political feminism, and environmental protection. Reportage, science fiction, and biography were the most popular modes of literary expression and ethnographic exploration of everyday political subjects among these writers. Ku Ling 苦苓 was a most celebrated political satirist who never failed to make fun of statesmen, as Yu Fu 魚夫 did in his political cartoons. A prolific poet who also wrote on such subjects was Li Min-yung 李敏勇. However, it was in the mini theater 小劇場 that serious political satires truly intermingled with comic relief. The stages for mini plays took on many forms, and could be found in the theater, on the street, in city hall, or even in front of the Legislature. Some differing and milder versions of post-avant-garde theater, on the other hand, were offered by playwrights like Stan Lai 賴聲川, Li Kuo-hsiu 李國修, and Chung Ming-te 鍾明德, who drew their inspiration from a range of Chinese and Western dramas—both ancient and modern. (see Spoken Drama and Traditional Music Theater sections, Chapter 21, The Arts)

An important trend in the 1990s was the revival of the local vernacular tradition. As the localization process took root, Taiwanese (southern Fujianese) and Hakka came to be looked upon as the preferred linguistic mediums for literary expression. In this regard, Chang Chun-huang 張春凰 was hailed, since the publication of her pioneering prose work *Paths to Youth* 青春 ê 路途 in 1995 made her the first prose writer to write in Taiwanese. The work represents a crucial step in rearticulating one's literary tradition toward a more promising future, in which linguistic nuances and cultural differences are appreciated and cherished. After all, it is the diversity of languages and customs on the island that has enriched the literary expressions of the people of Taiwan.

Online Literature

The proliferation and dissemination of information technology in Taiwan has led to the emergence of new literary vehicles unique to the computer era. Electronic bulletin boards (BBS), the Internet, and electronic mail (e-mail) have not only diversified the means by which literary works are circulated, but also created a new aesthetic dimension for literature arising from the manipulation of on-line techniques, such as animation, multimedia, hyperlinking, and interactive writing. Works probing into the virtual reality of cyberspace, categorized as hypertext literature, are distinguished by their creative form from those appearing in the traditional print-based media (and from those works going on-line without hypertextual elements). They illustrate an "organized stream of consciousness," as one of the supportive statements for hypertext literature goes. The Garden of Forking Paths 歧路花園 (*benz.nchu.edu.tw/~garden*) is one of the sites devoted to the creation and promotion of hypertext literature.

The recent developments of on-line literature in Taiwan include the establishment of online bookstores, professional literary sites, and intermedia sites (e.g., the literary supplements of newspapers, such as the *China Times* and the *Central Daily News,* are now on-line). Another phenomenon is the appearance of literary sites, organizational and personal, on the WWW, changing the scene of on-line literature formerly dominated by the BBS.

One of the most significant characteristics of on-line literature is its immediacy, as well as its expansion across social, racial, sexual, and other hierarchical boundaries. For one thing, the writer can bypass both publishers and editors to reach readers directly through the ideally indiscriminate world of cyberspace, without joining in the marketing system of popular culture. According to some literary theorists, the free flow and easy access of on-line literary resources have vigorously challenged the "cultural hegemony" of traditional media.

While there are still considerable controversies and even anxieties over the would-be paradise of cyber literature (the overflow of online works, the infringement of copyrights, and the intervention of commercialism have posed problems or complications), the function of digital archives on the Internet makes an indisputable contribution, as the availability of literary materials will surely aid in literary research and appreciation. One such effort is the Contemporary Authors Full-Text & Image System 當代文學史料影像全文系統 established by the National Central Library 國家圖書館, which collects personal information, brief biographies, manuscripts, photos, chronicles of works, critical sources, translation sources, famous words, and records of literary awards of around 1,000 modern writers in Taiwan. Another example is the "Way of Poetry" 詩路 project by the Council for Cultural Affairs (CCA) and the Online Alliance of Taiwan's Modern Poetry 臺灣現代詩網路聯盟, which gathers the works, translations, and multimedia materials of Taiwan's most important modern poets.

The New Millennium

At the end of the 20th century, literature was reaching readers not only from newspaper supplements but also the Internet. On June 20, 2001, Taiwan's two major Internet bookstores, Book4u 華文網 and Silkbook.com 新絲路, announced their merger. A "print on demand" service has been made available to readers on the Chinese mainland as part of its goal to dominate all Chinese publication markets, including Taiwan, the Chinese mainland, Singapore, and Malaysia. The intense competition in the Chinese publication industry is not only for market share, but also for cultural influence, and is expected to become even more severe after both sides of the Taiwan Strait join the WTO.

The nativist literary movement of the 1970s continued after the Nativist Literary Debate ended and became well established in the 1990s. Many tertiary education institutes formed new departments specializing in Taiwanese literature. Aletheia University opened the first Taiwanese Literature Department and National Cheng Kung University the first Graduate Institute of Taiwanese Literature in 1997 and 1999 respectively. In May 2001, the first class of students with a degree in Taiwanese Literature graduated from the Aletheia University.

To further strengthen academic research in Taiwanese literature, National Cheng Kung University will open its Taiwanese Literature Department and offer doctoral courses in 2002, providing Taiwan's first complete academic program in the field. The National Tsing Hua University's Graduate Institute of Taiwanese Literature and National Chung Hsing University's Taiwanese Literature Department will open in 2002 as well. Furthermore, Academia Sinica has approved a three-year research project, commencing in 2002, on Taiwanese literature proposed by the Preparatory Office of the Institute of Chinese Literature and Philosophy.

The nativist sentiment has been enhanced by Hakka writers in the 1990s. The *Hakka Magazine* 客家雜誌 was launched in January 1990, followed by many works and events that focused on Hakka ethnic awareness, such as the *Taiwanese Literature of Hakka* 客家台灣文學論 in 1993, the first Hakka film *Regretless Youth* 青春無悔 in the same year, *An Anthology of Taiwanese Literature* 台灣文學選 in 1994 (focusing on Hakka writers), a collection of Hakka language poetry in 1995, and the history of Hakka Taiwanese literature in 1998.

The history of local literature compiled during this period recorded the experiences of the people. Moreover, National Hualien Teachers' College 國立花蓮師範大學 established the first Graduate School of Folk Literature in 1998, and National Penghu Institute of Technology 國立澎湖技術學院 held a conference on folk literature and oral narratives between May 18 and 21,

2001. Thirty papers were presented in the conference, covering seven hundred years of local history. All these efforts enhanced and consolidated community spirit and preserved local history through literature.

The nativist movement helped to develop the local literature, various county/city cultural centers published collections from their regions, awarded local writers, and held such conferences as the Hualien Literature Conference and Chiayi's Taocheng Literary Award 桃城文學獎.

Nobel Laureate Gao Xingjian in Taiwan

In addition to local awards, the most influential and noteworthy event in the literary field was the Nobel Prize for Literature awarded to Gao Xingjian 高行健, a Chinese writer, playwright, and painter, in October 2000. The first Chinese Nobel Laureate in Literature Gao was honored as an artist-in-residence by the Cultural Affairs Bureau of Taipei 台北市文化局, during one of his previous visits to Taiwan. His visit between February 1 and 14, 2001, focused on the globalization of literature. During his stay, Gao attended the book release reception for his three new books: a work of esthetic criticism, *Another Kind of Estheticism* 另一種美學, a play, *Weekend Quartet* 週末四重奏, and a literary criticism. He also enjoyed a local production of his drama *August Snow* 八月雪. Gao delivered a speech on the future of Chinese literature and discussed such phenomena as literature translation and Nobel Prize, the foreign land and homeland dichotomy in literature, and the interrelation of literature and culture in contemporary literary works. This event was a focus of excitement for the local literary circle and provided impetus for literature translation projects.

Taiwanese Literature in Translation

On November 13, 2000, the CCA and the Institute de France jointly presented the ROC-France Cultural Award to French Sinologist and translator Andre Levy, who has translated Chinese classics *Journey to the West* 西遊記, *Golden Lotus* 金瓶梅, *Strange Stories from a Chinese Studio* 聊齋誌異, and *The Peony Pavilion* 牡丹亭.

His translation of *Crystal Boys* and *Tales of Taipei Characters* 台北人 by contemporary writer Pai Hsien-yung were also translated into Spanish and Portuguese. Moreover, the Institut Francais de Taipei and the CCA cosponsored the "Taiwan Literature in Translation" project in 2001 to promote cultural exchanges for better world recognition and to sustain cultural traditions in second and third generation overseas Taiwanese. The CCA has also funded the translation into Western languages of the "Modern Taiwanese Fiction" series and the "Japanese Translations of Modern Taiwanese Literature," a three-year project. The Chiang Ching-kuo Foundation for International Scholarly Exchange has subsidized many translation projects of Chinese classics and reference books into English, Russian, Czech, and Polish.

A conference on five Taiwanese poets was held at the Chinese Information and Culture Center in New York on July 16, 2001, to promote the English translation of *Modern Poets of Taiwan* 台灣現代詩人, which includes "Drifting" 漂泊 by Chang Tsuo 張錯, "Across the Darkness of the River" 在黑暗的河流上 by Hsi Mujung 席慕蓉, "Erotic Recipes: A Complete Menu for Male Enhancement" 完全壯陽食譜 by Chiao Tung, "The Mysterious Hualien" 神祕的花蓮 by Chen Yi-chih 陳義芝, and "Book of Reincarnation" 轉世之書 by Hsu Hui-chih. Poems were recited in both Chinese and English to show different temperaments and highlight cultural contrasts. Another similar attempt was the publication of *Frontier Taiwan: An Anthology of Modern Chinese Poetry* 二十世紀台灣詩選, which contains works from fifty contemporary Taiwanese poets published by the Columbia University Press. The chief editor Michelle Yeh 奚密 quoted poet Chen Li 陳黎 that the *Anthology* portrays the unique "characteristic of Taiwan: a vitality stimulated by constant assimilation and tolerance."

International Poetry Contest and Festival

In August 2001, the Foreign Labor Information Center 外勞資訊中心 of the Taipei Bureau of

Labor Affairs 台北市勞工局 hosted the first poetry contest for the approximately 36,000 foreign workers in the city, while the "Cultural City of Asia-Pacific" was held in Taipei between July and October. The Center received a total of 213 entries, consisting of 118 from Indonesians, 74 from Filipinos, 17 from Vietnamese, and four from Thais. The winning poems, "Glove Puppets," "Tears of a Foreign Maid," "Kuang Fu Road," "Foreigners' Hopes," "Thanks to Taiwan," and "Grandma and Baby," not only present a vivid portrayal of their lives in Taiwan, but also expressed their loneliness, aspirations, and appreciation.

The Cultural Affairs Bureau of Taipei and *UNITAS* 聯合文學, a literary magazine affiliated to the *United Daily* newspapers group, co-hosted the Taipei 2001 International Poetry Festival in September. The 1992 Nobel Laureate Derek A. Walcott, born in the Caribbean island nation St. Lucia, was the Festival's guest of honor. Other world-renowned poets invited were: Arthur Sze 施家彭 from the U.S.,

Jaan Kaplinski from Estonia, Marc Delouze from France, Dieter M. Graf from Germany, Ramakanta Rath from India, Gozo Yoshinasu from Japan, Lim Swee Tin 林天英 from Malaysia, Bavuugiin Lkhagvasuren from Mongolia, Erik Lindner from the Netherlands, J. Neil C. Garcia from Sweden, Naowarat Pongaiboon from Thailand, and Dao Kim Hoa from Vietnam. Around 300 local poets also participated in this grand occasion. Professor Michelle Yeh of the University of California, Davis, translated and edited *Iconography of the Sea* 海的聖像學, containing Mr. Walcott's masterpieces, as a memento of the Festival for Taiwan's readers.

Earliest Chinese Literary Traditions

The beginnings of Chinese literature go back thousands of years, with the earliest pieces in the *Book of Songs* 詩經 dating back to the 12th century B.C. A number of scholars believe that writings in the *Book of History* 書經 (or 尚書) tradition should be classified as history rather

The Council for Cultural Affairs sponsored various translation projects to introduce the outstanding works of various Taiwan-based authors to the rest of the world and promote cultural exchanges.
(Courtesy of the Council for Cultural Affairs)

than literature. Furthermore, private accounts, as opposed to government archives, have since the time of Confucius been classified as expositions of thought. Official archives were relegated to the realm of history and private writings to that of philosophy, leaving only works belonging to the *Book of Songs* tradition as being classified as literature. Because the *Book of Songs* is an anthology of poetry, Chinese literature came to be regarded as a basically lyrical tradition.

The prevalence of this way of thinking has led some scholars to insist that China has no epic traditions, no fiction until the seventh century A.D., and no drama until the 13th century. This ignores the fact that public and private writings "recording words and events" have been produced in China without interruption since the *Book of History*, and that they have always enjoyed the status of fine literature. They often disregard the narrative traditions contained in the numerous fables that appeared in histories after the *Book of History*, in philosophical works —such as *Chuang Tzu* 莊子, *Mencius* 孟子, *Han Fei Tzu* 韓非子, the *Spring and Autumn Annals of Mr. Lu* 呂氏春秋, and *Lieh Tzu* 列子, all written after the fourth century B.C.—and in myths from earlier ages that were preserved in these and similar works.

The earliest fiction in China—be it in the form of a continuation of mythical narrative or an imitation of official history called *yeh-shih* 野史 ("unofficial history")—was created in the spirit of the fable. The narrative tradition—comprising history, myth, fable, and fiction—balanced and supplemented the lyrical traditions of poetry produced after the *Book of Songs*.

"Recording words," the other expressed feature of the *Book of History*, in turn influenced philosophical works and *san-wen* 散文 (essay-type prose). Philosophical works, like *The Analects of Confucius* 論語, have been produced since the sixth century B.C., and are basically collections of quotations or records of a master's sayings, inseparable in content and style from the personalities, speech habits, and biographical experiences of the masters themselves. This style of writing, which fuses reason and emotion, served as a model for the essay in later ages. The essay thus became the most important genre in Chinese literature, and *san-wen* even became a synonym for literature itself, while poetry was considered a specialized branch of literature.

In contrast to the personalism of the essay, Chinese poetry gradually departed from the spoken language and came to stress formalistic rules. Poetry thus became relatively objective and impersonal and, while still lyrical in nature, was often more symbolic and constructive than prose.

The Literary-Vernacular Split

Related to the division of Chinese literature into the traditions of the *Book of Songs* and the *Book of History* is the fact that the spoken and written Chinese language are actually two independent representational systems. Chinese writing, having evolved from pictographs, is an ideographic script that expresses meaning directly through the forms of the characters themselves. The Chinese system stands in contrast to the phonetic alphabets and syllabaries of Japan, Korea, and the West, which express meaning through phonetic representation. As a result, Chinese writing constitutes a notational system that is partially independent of the phonemic nature of the Chinese spoken language; and the relative independence of this notational system has had a major effect on Chinese literature.

One example of this effect can be seen in the *Book of Songs* tradition, which during the several centuries of its evolution gradually broke away from music in pursuit of its own metrical form. The combination of an independent writing system with the Chinese spoken language—which in early times was mainly monosyllabic—produced neat lines of four, five, or seven characters, and sometimes three or six. Tonal theory evolved in the fifth and sixth centuries, based on a new apprehension that Middle Chinese syllables had tonal or pitch distinctions that affected meaning. Thus, "even" 平 and "deflected" 仄 tones were matched and contrasted, and words of parallel or anti-thetical meaning were aligned. Literary forms almost completely divorced from the spoken language developed, such as parallel prose 駢文 and regulated verse 律詩. This formalistic beauty, which derived from a neat matching of written characters, became an important aesthetic characteristic of traditional Chinese poetry.

Following territorial expansion and the establishment of a unified empire encompassing a large number of local dialects, the maintenance of the *Book of History* tradition depended increasingly on scholars and officials learning a form of written communication called *ku-wen* 古文 (classical prose). In early antiquity, the classical prose style may have reflected the contemporary spoken language, but it eventually evolved into a purely literary style that allowed the literary language to experience no major syntactic changes for 2,000 years.

Around the fifth century A.D., the spoken language began to gradually evolve from being mainly monosyllabic in nature toward bi-syllabicity or polysyllabicity, as the Old Chinese consonant clusters were gradually lost and originally distinct vowels merged. The unchanging stability of the literary language, or *wen-yen* 文言, thus led to a gradual split with the vernacular language, or *pai-hua* 白話.

The vernacular literature of the common people, consisting for the most part of fiction and drama, developed parallel to the literature of the scholars, which was composed mainly of poetry and essays written in classical Chinese. Literature written in the classical language received official sanction by becoming the testing material for the examination system, while vernacular literature owed its increasing popularity mainly to growth in the popular entertainment industry.

An Outline of Traditional Chinese Literature

Traditional Chinese literature can be divided into four periods: early antiquity, from the 12th century B.C. to 206 B.C.; middle antiquity, from 206 B.C. to A.D. 618; late antiquity, from 618 to 1279; and the premodern era, from 1279 to 1911.

Early Antiquity

The literature of early antiquity includes the classics preserved from the Chou 周 dynasty and organized by Confucian scholars; the works of philosophers from the Spring and Autumn 春秋 period and the Warring States 戰國 period; the *Songs of the South* (*Chu*) 楚辭; and the early myths, which were compiled from various sources. Together, these works laid the spiritual foundation of Chinese literature and culture. Both the *Book of Songs* from northern China and the *Songs of the South* represent the fundamental dichotomy of Chinese poetry: realism and lyricism versus romanticism and imagination.

The early myths are scattered among a number of works: chiefly, *Chuang Tzu*, the *Mountain and Sea Classic* 山海經, and the poem "Heavenly Questions" 天問 in the *Songs of the South*. These works had a fundamental influence on the way the Chinese people view the universe, mankind, nature, and civilization.

From the *Book of History* tradition of recording the words of the early kings developed both the narratives of the historians and the speculative works of the philosophers. The most important works of history are the *Spring and Autumn Annals of Mr. Lu*, the *Tso Commentary* 左傳, and the *Conversations from the States* 國語. Corresponding to the recording of words in the *Book of History* is the recording of deeds in the *Spring and Autumn Annals*. This work records in concise language—often only a single sentence—major historical events in chronological order. It uses the method of "according praise or censure in a single word" to make penetrating ethical judgments about the events it relates. It is with the *Tso Commentary* and the *Conversations from the States* that narrative literature in China became fully mature, fusing the twin traditions of recording words and recording deeds. These works used the techniques of recording deeds and rendering ethical appraisals from the *Spring* and *Autumn Annals* as models for their treatment of narrative and subject matter. They also applied the technique of recording words from the *Book of History* in creating dialogs that illumined the psychology and motivations of characters to thereby depict and morally judge historical events.

Thinkers of the ancient era prior to the third century B.C. not only made major contributions to the development of Chinese thought, but also had a lasting effect on Chinese aesthetics and literature. The effect of the Confucian thinkers is reflected in an emphasis on ethical, social, and political concerns. Taoist influence can be seen in a striving for transcendental, universal meaning, and in an awareness of an eternal, metaphysical significance of life beyond history and society, achieved through an appreciation and description of one's natural surroundings.

The works of these ancient philosophers, through their method of illustrating morals through fables, established narrative models for characterization and plot development, which was a break from the recording of words and deeds of outstanding historical figures used in historical narrative. The various styles that evolved along these lines subsequently influenced the development of Chinese prose. *The Analects of Confucius* and Lao Tzu's *Classic of the Way and Its Power* 道德經 made terseness and profundity the foremost criteria of prose style. *Mo Tzu* 墨子 advanced the methods of logical exposition, while *Chuang Tzu* established the model of an exuberantly imaginative composite form that defied classification. *Mencius* made full use of the expressive powers of the spoken language in forging an eloquent verbal style. Hsun Tzu 荀子, in addition to being the first writer of Chinese *fu* 賦 (prose-poems), made full use of the isolating character of the Chinese writing system to develop a regulated aesthetic of parallelism and antithesis. All these works became sources and models for later literature, both spoken and written.

Middle Antiquity

The major political development during the middle antiquity period was the conclusion of the feudal system of the Chou 周 dynasty and the establishment of a stable, unified empire under the Han 漢. In the area of philosophical thought, the effect of this development was the triumph of Confucianism; in literature, it was the independence of literature from philosophy, and a striving for formal aesthetics and emotional experience. Its first literary product was the *Songs of the South*, which was written as a prose-poem.

The prose-poem is a literary form that is recited rather than sung. Tied less to musical form than poetry, the prose-poem combined visual and aural elements in its attention to formal rules and euphony. As its development came in response to the preferences and patronage of the emperor, its earliest subjects were invariably praise and glorification of the splendor of the imperial palace, the capital, parks, and hunting grounds. Out of this arose a tradition of exhaustive description, often accompanied by the coining of new Chinese characters, which catered specifically to the ruler's consciousness of possessing the empire, the world, the universe, and everything in it. Works of this type, which were presented to the emperor, are called *ta-fu* 大賦 (greater prose-poems).

As writers came to realize that a consciousness of totality must be connected with a sense of individuality to have value and meaning, they began to experience anxiety over individual existence. Thus, "the scholar born out of his time" became a basic theme of the *hsiao-fu* 小賦 (lesser prose-poem). Chia I 賈誼 and Szu-ma Hsiang-ju 司馬相如 in the second century B.C., and Chang Heng 張衡 and Wang Tsan 王粲 in the second century A.D., were the most important writers of prose-poems, a genre that would continue to develop right up until the end of the 19th century.

Shih 詩, or poetry of lines of equal length, was still identified with song when the *Yueh-fu* 樂府 (Music Bureau) was established during the reign of Emperor Wu Ti 武帝 (140-86 B.C.) in the

441

Han dynasty. The amalgams of song and poetry produced then were generally referred to as *Yueh-fu shih* (Music Bureau ballads). Often originating from the common people, these pieces were rich in narrative content and filled with laments over social issues, especially the gap between the rich and poor, the posting of soldiers to distant regions, the plight of widows and orphans, and the vicissitudes of life and time. Poems that reflected social realities and contained a sharp consciousness of moral crisis continued to be created under the name of *yueh-fu* in later times. Although they were no longer set to music, they preserved the external form of early *yueh-fu*, with its lines of unequal length.

Another literary development during the nearly 400 years of the Han dynasty era was the appearance of poems written in neat five- or seven-character lines that were unbound to music. It later became the universally acknowledged fundamental poetic form. The rules for matching and balancing characters in parallel constructions became increasingly refined, and ultimately resulted in the regulated verse of the seventh century onward. Middle antiquity can be considered the period of formalization of Chinese literary aesthetics. From the third century onward, the method of writing prose-poems was extended to the writing of essays, culminating in the blossoming of parallel prose in the sixth century.

The five-character line 五言詩 form of poetry emerged after the period of the lesser prose-poem. Anxiety over life and death became a basic theme for this new poetic form as well. Representative examples are found in the *Nineteen Ancient Poems* 古詩十九首 collection of the first century, the most important work in this genre at the time. Finding consolation in Taoist thinking to dispel the cares of existence, poets gradually turned to the subject of fields, gardens, hills, and streams, discovering and reveling in the natural beauty of landscapes. The most important poets of this period were Tsao Chih 曹植, Juan Chi 阮籍, Tao Chien 陶潛, and Hsieh Ling-yun 謝靈運.

Middle antiquity was also a fruitful period for the narrative tradition. First and foremost of the works in this genre was Szu-ma Chien's 司馬遷 *Records of the Grand Historian* 史記. *Records*, written during the first century B.C., was the first comprehensive work to recount China's ancient and recent history. It also established a model for historical writing centered around biography. Szu-ma Chien shifted the focus from unity of plot evident in the *Tso Commentary* and the *Conversations from the States* to a unity of character. His writing helped pave the way for the *chuan-chi* 傳奇 (classical tales) of the eighth and ninth centuries.

Pan Ku's 班固 *History of the Former Han Dynasty* 漢書 was the first history devoted to a single dynasty. Pan Ku's work, together with Fan Yeh's 范曄 *History of the Later Han Dynasty* 後漢書, Chen Shou's 陳壽 *Records of the Three Kingdoms* 三國志, and *Records of the Grand Historian*, are traditionally considered the pillars of Chinese historical writing.

Although its narrative roots can be traced back to *Chuang Tzu*, *Hsun Tzu*, and the *Tso Commentary*, Chinese fiction is often said to have begun its development under the influence of the romantic and supernatural adventures related in the biographies of diviners and imperial concubines in the *Records of the Grand Historian*. This genre, consisting of depictions of courtly affairs and supernatural occurrences, was referred to as *chih-kuai* 志怪 ("recording the strange") fiction. Among the earlier examples of this sort of fiction were the *Private Life of Lady Fei-yan* 飛燕外傳 and the *Intimate Biography of Han Emperor Wu* 漢武內傳, both written during the fourth century.

Late Antiquity

A milestone in the development of Chinese society was the establishment of the bureaucratic examination system in the seventh century. This system produced a new class of officials who played a leading role in society both politically and culturally. The literature of late antiquity was the activity and expression of this new class.

Unlike the old aristocracy, the members of the new class owed their entrance to officialdom to success in the examinations. They had to form factions to avoid isolation, and when policies changed or power alliances shifted, they had to worry about demotion or exile. The effect of this situation was twofold. On the one hand, the new officials felt a strong sense of self-awareness as individuals, and did not identify solely with the family; on the other, they traveled widely throughout the country, whether in exile or in official service. As a result, the literature of late antiquity was characterized by a high degree of mobility, autobiography, and sense of regionalism.

During the seventh through ninth centuries, examination candidates were tested in poetry, which led to the widespread development of that genre, whereas during the tenth through 12th centuries, they were tested in essays on public policy, which led to a flourishing of the literary language. The seventh century saw the refinement of regulated verse, in response to the needs of the examination system. Seventh through ninth century poetry generally strived for a consciousness of human existence through descriptions of natural beauty. Wang Wei 王維, Li Pai 李白, Tu Fu 杜甫, Pai Chu-i 白居易, Han Yu 韓愈, and Li Shang-yin 李商隱 were the most important poets of the Tang dynasty (which spanned the seventh through ninth centuries) and were also major figures in the history of Chinese poetry. The Sung dynasty poets of the 11th and 12th centuries introduced philosophy into poetry, and discourse and reasoning became important characteristics of their works. Tang and Sung poetry became the twin paradigms of Chinese poetry in later ages. Ou-yang Hsiu 歐陽修, Wang An-shih 王安石, Su Shih (Su Tung-po 蘇東坡), Huang Ting-chien 黃庭堅, and Lu Yu 陸游 were the major representatives of Sung poetry.

The medieval era of the seventh through ninth centuries was a time of cultural fusion. Not only was there a melding of the contrasting cultures of earlier dynasties from the fourth through sixth centuries when China was politically divided, but the administration of the western regions and the reopening of the Silk Road led to the absorption and popularity of music and dance from Central Asia.

The lyric 詞, a poem with lines of unequal length originally set to music, became the dominant poetic genre. Poems (shih) of the literati had by this time moved toward strict regulation (both in formal "neatness" and in tonal contraposition) due to the examination system, and had become increasingly alienated from the spoken language. The art of the lyric, on the other hand, was cultivated at banquets and entertainment activities among merchants and the common people.

The lyric genre began to attract the attention of the literati during the ninth and tenth centuries, and by the 11th century, had become the second most important poetic genre among the literati. Due to the differing lengths of its lines and its origins among the common people, it preserved characteristics of the spoken language to a considerable degree.

For poets of the Sung dynasty, the poem came to express the rational and public aspect of the writer's spirit, and the lyric, his emotional and private side. The most important lyricists were Wen Ting-yun 溫庭筠, Wei Chuang 韋莊, Feng Yen-szu 馮延巳, Li Yu 李煜, Liu Yung 柳永, Su Shih, Chou Pang-yen 周邦彥, Hsin Chi-chi 辛棄疾 and Chiang Kuei 姜夔.

Another major literary development of late antiquity was the revival of the classical literary language, or ku-wen 古文. Pien-wen 駢文, or parallel prose, had been criticized as being beautiful in form but shallow in substance ever since the late sixth century. The reform of prose writing, however, did not occur until the mid-eighth century, when Han Yu and Liu Tsung-yuan 柳宗元 began to promote the classical literary language. Their models were Mencius and the Records of the Grand Historian. They ultimately succeeded in developing a new, more comprehensive style of writing that reflected the life of people outside the class of officials and returned to the tenets of Confucian thought as a main theme.

This type of writing emphasized narration and argument, both of which became autobiographical and lyrical vehicles of expression by lending prominence to the writer as a subjective entity. The classical literary language achieved unprecedented success during the 11th century and became the main form of prose writing in China thereafter. Major writers in this genre during the Sung dynasty were Ouyang Hsiu, Wang An-shih, Su Hsun 蘇洵, Su Shih, Su Che 蘇轍, and Tseng Kung 曾鞏.

The career ups and downs experienced by the new class of officials inspired a narrative form that conveyed change. The form gradually encompassed social realities and human life, but was at the same time influenced by the *chih-kuai* genre of fiction of the fourth century onward, and the *Records of the Grand Historian* tradition that emphasized outstanding individuals. By the eighth century, this type of fiction was called the *chuan-chi* 傳奇. These stories often added elements of the mysterious and fantastic to everyday occurrences. Representative classical tales include *Chen-chung Chi* 枕中記 by Shen Chi-chi 沈既濟, *Nan-ko Tai-shou Chuan* 南柯太守傳 by Li Kung-tso 李公佐, *Ying-ying Chuan* 鶯鶯傳 by Yuan Chen 元稹, and *Chang-hen-ko Chuan* 長恨歌傳 by Chen Hung 陳鴻.

The Premodern Era

The Mongolian invasion represented the end not only of the Sung dynasty, but also of the cultural patterns of late antiquity, which centered on a class of officials selected through the examination system. The imperial examinations were halted for some 80 years during the Great Mongol Empire, known in China as the Yuan dynasty, and the social status of the Confucianists plummeted. Commerce and world-class cities, on the other hand, thrived in this age. This led to the growth of the entertainment industry and an unprecedented flourishing of vernacular literature aimed at the petty bourgeoisie. A vernacular narrative genre called *pien-wen* 變文 ("changed writing"), which was partly recited and partly sung, arose from the reciting of Buddhist sermons in temples from the seventh century onward. At the start of the 12th century, a form of *chantefable* involving a medley of tunes called the *chu-kung-tiao* 諸宮調 ("all keys and modes") was created. It was designed to be sung and narrated, and so was structurally organized around suites of poetic songs sung to popular tunes of the age. A work of oral storytelling, it was part of a professional storytelling tradition that developed around the ninth century, and was already highly popular in Pienliang and other cities during the 11th and 12th centuries. The most complete surviving example of this genre is available in English translation under the title *Master Tung's Romance of the Western Chamber* 西廂記諸宮調.

The musical influence on plot structure inherited from the *chantefable*, combined with the verbal repartee of the *yuan-pen* 院本 genre of dramatic skits of the 11th century, formed the basis for the earliest known form of completely developed music drama in China, the *Yuan tsa-chu* 元雜劇, or Yuan Music Drama of the 13th century. Less than 170 complete examples of this genre have survived, with plots ranging from melodrama and crime to comedy and spiritual redemption. Among these theatrical works are intensely melodramatic works, such as Kuan Han-ching's 關漢卿 *Injustice to Tou O* 竇娥冤, Pai Pu's 白樸 *Rain on the Wu Tung Tree* 梧桐雨, Ma Chih-yuan's 馬志遠 *Autumn in the Han Palace* 漢宮秋, and Chi Chun-hsiang's 紀君祥 *Orphan of Chao* 趙氏孤兒. Most of the musical comedies were social satires, such as fantasies about scholars climbing the bureaucratic ladder, often through love and at the expense of merchants. One of the most influential romantic music comedies from the 14th centuries was the *Romance of the Western Chamber* 西廂記, traditionally attributed to Wang Shih-fu 王實甫, which had an enormous impact on the plot structure of later music drama and fiction with its popularization of the *chia-jen tsai-tzu* 佳人才子 ("Beauty-Scholar") motif.

The literary heart and soul of all three of these theatrical forms—the *chantefable*, *yuan-pen*, and Yuan Music Drama—was a new kind of poetry called the *chu* 曲 (ditty), based on a new song form that appeared in northern China during the 12th and 13th centuries. The lyrics of the ditty also became an independent poetic form in their own right, originally sung to the tune of the ditty in a manner like the *lieder* settings of 18th and 19th century German poetry by Franz Schubert and other contemporary Viennese composers. The major difference was that these composers created music to match an already existing poetic text, while the 12th and 13th century Chinese ditty poets created text to match an already existing ditty melody. By the 14th century, the original northern ditty melodies were gradually lost, yet ditty lyrics were still successfully set to what succeeding generations preserved as their original tune matrix, and new music from southern China was ultimately created to again allow musical performance.

A special characteristic of the ditty was that filler words could be freely added outside the fixed metrical pattern for euphonic effect. The metrical pattern itself was flexible within certain musically proscribed limits. This freedom gave the ditty a strikingly colloquial nature. Furthermore, several or even a score of ditties in the same mode could be combined into a ditty sequence 套數. Ditty writers in either music dramas or independent verses often flirted with the comic and risqué, although nostalgic and angry ditties were also written. In addition to the Yuan playwrights who frequently wrote ditties outside the context of music dramas, major ditty poets included Chang Yang-hao 張養浩 and Chiao Chi 喬吉.

Earlier kinds of poetry, such as the *shih* and lyric, were part of the fabric of vernacular fiction in its earliest manifestations, prompt books 底本, or *hua-pen* 話本. These seem to have arisen, either directly or indirectly, through the imitation of the oral storytelling tradition, whose roots extended back to the 11th or 12th centuries of the Sung dynasty. All three kinds of poetry played an integral role in short, medium, and full-length vernacular fiction until the 19th century. The

vernacular fiction genre flourished in the 14th through 16th centuries of the Ming 明 dynasty, thanks to the expansion of commercial printing.

The most outstanding extant examples of short story collections from this period are Feng Meng-lung's 馮夢龍 *Three Collections of Words [to Awaken the World]* 三言 and Ling Meng-chu's 凌濛初 *Two Collections of Striking the Table [in Amazement]* 二拍. There are four great works of extended fiction, major editions of which date from the 15th and 16th centuries of the Ming: *The Romance of the Three Kingdoms* 三國演義; *Water Margin*, also translated as *All Men are Brothers* 水滸傳; *Journey to the West*, also translated as *Monkey*; and *Golden Lotus*.

Unlike earlier ninth through 12th century classical literary tales written in the literary language about scholars, courtesans, semi-mythical characters, fox-spirits, and ghosts, the vernacular short story generally featured characters in an urban, middle-class setting. Money, marriage, social and business ethics, and the vagaries of fortune often constituted the principal plot concern. Of the four great works of

The Romance of the Three Kingdoms is one of the four great works of extended fiction in Chinese history that was revised and embellished by storytellers over the centuries until the Ming dynasty.

extended fiction, *The Romance of the Three Kingdoms, Water Margin,* and *Journey to the West* were all products of a long and gradual process of revision and embellishment by storytellers and editors over the centuries leading up to the Ming dynasty, so they can be considered collective national creations, even if their later Ming versions primarily reflect a single literary mind. This process of collective revision could even be said of *Golden Lotus,* which circulated in manuscript form among various Ming literati prior to appearing in several different editions. In their Ming manifestations, all four of these great works of extended fiction reflect a growing sense of literary irony in their retelling of the traditional story plot. This may have been an expression of growing literati dissatisfaction with the moral and political climate of the Ming court and society.

The Ming also witnessed the flourishing of a new kind of literati music drama called *chuanchi* 傳奇 (Grand Music Drama), the same Chinese name as the literary tales of the eighth century onward, but otherwise a completely separate literary genre. Unlike Yuan Music Drama, which continued to be written during the Ming, albeit in increasingly modified form, Grand Music Drama evolved from an early popular form of music drama in southern China known as *nan-hsi* 南戲 (Southern Music Drama) into a highly sophisticated theatrical genre that came to rival the prevailing Yuan Music Drama in literary quality. Grand Music Drama plots were more complex and expansive than the neat, highly structured Yuan Music Drama, which organized acts around suites of ditties in the same key or mode. Instead of being dominated by musical considerations, the structure of Grand Music Drama plots often became bipolar, with two major strands of plot development interwoven through the length of the play. The dominant plot strand was almost always a variation on the "Beauty-Scholar" theme so prevalent in both drama and fiction throughout the Ming. Various actors on the stage could also have singing roles at the same time, unlike the northern Yuan Music Drama, which restricted the singing role to a single star throughout the drama.

The most influential early example of Grand Music Drama was *The Lute* 琵琶記 by Kao Ming 高明, which has even appeared in a highly modified version on the Broadway stage as *The Lute Song.* The 14th century Ming original used more extensive imagery and poetic diction than had ever been used before, setting a new standard for the Southern Music Drama tradition and lifting it beyond the ken of casual theater-goers. As a result, Grand Music Drama after *The Lute* gradually evolved into a new, highly complex musical tradition that took its name and some of its characteristics from the music of Kun-shan 崑山. *Kunqu* (Kun Music Drama), as Grand Music Drama had then come to be called, reached its peak of popularity during the 16th century when Tang Hsien-tsu 湯顯祖 wrote his cycle of four dream plays, including *The Peony Pavilion.* Although a famous scene from *The Peony Pavilion* is often performed today as one of the few remaining examples of Kun Music Drama, Tang Hsien-tzu was in fact less concerned for musical effect than for achieving highly theatrical effects through the lyrical intensity and figural density of his poetic imagery.

The genre had reached the climax of its literary development in Hung Sheng's 洪昇 *Palace of Eternal Sorrow* 長生殿. Appropriately, it took as its plot a well-known narrative poem by the ninth century poet Pai Chu-i 白居易 titled "Song of Eternal Sorrow" 長恨歌, depicting the story of the eighth century Emperor Hsuan-tsung 唐玄宗 and the loss of his favorite imperial consort, Yang Kuei-fei 楊貴妃. Thus, 17th and 18th century Kun Music Drama achieved a literary richness beyond that of its predecessors, but in its greatest works also conveyed a sense of despair and irrevocable loss indicative of the age. The fall of the Ming dynasty and the ultimate consolidation of political power under the Manchus in the 17th century are reflected in the plot of the most famous 17th century Kun Music Drama, *Peach Blossom Fan* 桃花扇 by Kung Shang-jen 孔尚任. *Peach Blossom Fan* bore witness to the increasing distance between the musical and literary dimensions of Kun Music Drama, which culminated in the virtual demise of the form by the 18th century.

This same mixture of literary qualities can be found in increasing intensity among the majority of 17th through 19th century works of extended fiction, such as Wu Ching-tzu's 吳敬梓 *The Scholars* 儒林外史, Li Ju-chen's 李汝珍 *Flowers in the Mirror* 鏡花緣, and Tsao Hsueh-chin's 曹雪芹 *Dream of the Red Chamber* 紅樓夢, or as it is alternatively known, *The Story of the Stone* 石頭記. The extended fiction of the 19th and early 20th centuries generally displayed a growing sense of despair at the moral lethargy of contemporary society. Among them were Wu Yen-jen's 吳趼人 *Strange Events Witnessed in the Past Twenty Years* 二十年目睹之怪現狀, Li Po-yuan's 李伯元 *Bureaucracy Exposed* 官場現形記, and Liu O's 劉鶚 *The Travels of Lao Tsan* 老殘遊記.

Although fiction became increasingly popular from the 13th century onward, this was mainly as leisure reading among the literati and merchant class. After the Mongols were driven out in the 14th century and Han Chinese rule reestablished, efforts were made to return to the views and values of two earlier great periods of Han Chinese rule, the Han and Tang dynasties. The formalistic eight-legged essay 八股文 (so named because it was divided into eight parts) also got its start at this time. The eight-legged essay was the form adopted for the explication of the Confucian classics, which formed the basis for a reinstatement of the examination system. Thus, the eight-legged essay and imitations of the classical literary language of the earlier eras of Chinese cultural greatness became the major written genres of the time. There were no further breakthroughs in literary writing, except for a style of artistically heightened descriptions of everyday life experiences, called *hsiao-pin* 小品 ("little sketches"), which emerged in the 15th and 16th centuries.

Fiction, in the form of jottings 筆記 that were written in the literary language, also regained popularity at this time. The most important collections in this genre were Pu Sung-ling's 蒲松齡 *Strange Stories from a Chinese Studio* and Chi Hsiao-lan's 紀曉嵐 *Jottings from the Thatched Hall of Close Observations* 閱微草堂筆記. Although vernacular literature developed greatly during the 14th through 19th centuries, literature written in the classical literary language by scholars still constituted the cultural mainstream, given that literacy was still primarily their specialized province. This situation remained essentially unchanged up until the emergence of the New Literature movement.

Modern Chinese Literature

The New Literature Movement

After attempts by the Western powers, Japan, and Russia to carve up or annex China in the late 19th and early 20th century, several professors at Peking University initiated the New Culture movement with the founding of the monthly magazine *Hsin Ching-nien* 新青年 *(La Jeunesse; New Youth)*. *New Youth* criticized traditional culture and welcomed the arrival of "Mr. Democracy" and "Mr. Science" from the West.

The new literature heralded social reform. Hu Shih 胡適 raised the curtain for the literary revolution with his 1917 essay, "A Modest Proposal for the Reform of Literature." In another essay, "On a Constructive Literary Revolution," Chen Tu-hsiu, Chien Hsuan-tung 錢玄同, and Hu Shih advocated "...a literature in the national language, and a national language of literary quality." They hoped that a nation with more than 2,000 different dialects could adopt a unified "national language" 國語 and that the written literary language of the scholarly class could be discarded in favor of this national language as the basis for writing (see section The National Language, Chapter 3, Language). In his *History of Vernacular Literature* 白話文學史, Hu Shih reevaluated the Chinese literary tradition and attempted to raise the vernacular literature of the people from its previous position as a subbranch of literature to the mainstream. His goal was for vernacular literature to replace the classical literature of the scholars, which he pronounced "dead writing."

The early period of new literature was fraught with contradiction: individual freedom was encouraged so as to oppose traditional society, but was at the same time to be abandoned in the name of social justice, social concern, and the building of modern organizations. Rejecting the traditional culture and literature of the scholars, the reformers insisted that vernacular literature was the only living literature. Yet, because vernacular literature grew out of the professional storytelling tradition, they also viewed it as backward and primitive. With the exception of a few great works rich in cultural criticism, they also adopted a largely negative attitude towards the vernacular tradition because it had originated as popular entertainment.

Chou Tso-jen 周作人 and others faced the dilemma of advocating a vernacular literature while being unable to identify with either the form or content of traditional Chinese vernacular literature. To solve this dilemma, Hu Shih, Chen Tu-hsiu, and others proposed using the genres, forms, and spiritual consciousness of Western literature as models for imitation. Translation became a required intermediary in the creation of the new literature. The first translators had no scruples about remolding the Chinese language along European lines, and the foreign flavor of their writing became one of its major characteristics. Thus, a deliberate "horizontal transfer" of literature was advocated as part of the movement to modernize China. Actual literary works of the time, however, were not simply imitations of foreign models. Lu Hsun's 魯迅 story, *Diary of a Madman* 狂人日記, for example, was obviously influenced by Gogol, but the thrust of its content—such as its denunciation of the overly severe and demanding ethics of traditional culture—was an expression of a uniquely Chinese situation. Its style approached that of the fables of Chuang Tzu, Lieh Tzu, Han Yu, and Liu Tsung-yuan.

The Early Period of the New Literature

The new literature experimented with different genres and drew on varied sources, and as a result was eclectic and multifaceted in nature. Works such as Lu Hsun's novella *The True Story of Ah Q* 阿Q正傳 and Lao She's novel *Rickshaw Boy* 駱駝祥子 were told in a satirical tone filled with sorrow and pity. Both of these works recalled stories from the early vernacular short story tradition and described the fickle fate of the lower classes, in contrast to the entertainment-oriented themes of the "Beauty-Scholar," itinerant swordsman, or detective-officials fictional works popular in the 17th and 18th centuries. These early works of modern fiction were also influenced to a certain degree by left-wing Western thinking and the tradition of Confucian scholars of pleading to the emperor on behalf of the people.

The neat five- and seven-syllable lines of traditional poetry were replaced in this period by the cadences of spoken Chinese, modeled after the line patterns of Western poems. Even more notable was the discord that resulted from the introduction of intellectual argumentation and the search for meaning and freedom into the traditional themes of love and natural scenery. Whether through ardent passion or cold critique, these poems signaled an end to gentleness and ingenuousness, to the fusion of emotion and scenery, and to the original harmony of man and nature; and announced the beginning of an aesthetics of bitterness and anguish.

Prose writers such as Lin Yu-tang 林語堂 and Liang Shih-chiu 梁實秋, who were intimately acquainted with the Western tradition, wrote informal essays in the style of Montaigne and Lamb. Except for their use of the colloquial language, they generally followed the classical prose style of the ninth through 12th centuries, mixing reason with emotion, and musing on minor events of daily life. Chu Tzu-ching 朱自清, Hsia Mien-tsun 夏丏尊, Feng Tzu-kai 豐子愷, and Hsu Chih-mo 徐志摩 were all masters of this genre of writing.

The impassioned critiques of Liang Chi-chao, the cogent lucidity of Hu Shih, and the caustic wit of Lu Hsun were often expressed in "wars of the pen." Standing in contrast to this high level of social involvement were writers such as Chou Tso-jen and Lin Yu-tang, who rediscovered the informal essays of the 16th and 17th centuries. They advocated an easygoing humor and the *savoir-vivre* of sipping tea and copying old books; but were at the same time conversant with Freud and D.H. Lawrence. Although both types of essays were written in the colloquial language, their spirit was still rooted in the old culture of the scholar. The writers themselves, however, were not government officials, but college professors, publishing house editors, journalists, and high school teachers.

Leftism in the New Literature

Owing to continued internal turbulence and constant power struggles among the warlords, a number of writers (mainly members of the Creation Society 創造社 literary group) followed up the literary revolution with a call for a "revolutionary literature," advocating that literature should serve the revolution. The Chinese Communist Party (CCP) set up the League of Leftist Writers 左聯. By the eve of the War of Resistance against Japan, the CCP had, through the power of organized party struggle, effectively stifled creativity and freedom of expression in many writers. Following the Japanese invasion, literature became totally subservient to the war effort, and the vigor and diversity of the early period of modern literature drew to a halt.

In the process of fanning the flames of patriotism and nationalistic fervor during the War of Resistance, a higher reassessment was made of traditional Chinese culture and literature. Many writers began adopting methods from folk drama and storytelling in their propaganda campaigns, presaging the literature of workers, peasants, and soldiers later espoused by the Chinese communists. Immediately following the Japanese surrender, China was plunged into all-out civil war. After the Chinese mainland fell into Chinese communist hands, socialist realism and Mao Zedong's talks on art and literature at Yen'an set the narrow confines within which writers on the mainland could operate. At the same time, the withdrawal of the ROC government to Taiwan began a new chapter in modern Chinese literature.

Further Reading

(in English unless otherwise indicated):

Birch, Cyril, ed. *Anthology of Chinese Literature*. New York: Grove Press, 1965.

—tr. *Stories From a Ming Collection*. New York: Grove Press, 1958.

Chang Chien 張健, ed. *Chung-kuo wen-hsueh pi-ping lun-chi* 中國文學批評論集 (A Collection of Chinese Literary Criticism; in Chinese). Taipei: Heavenly Lotus Publishing Company, 1979.

Chen Jo-hsi 陳若曦. *Spirit Calling: Tales about Taiwan*. Taipei: Heritage Press, 1962.

—*The Execution of Mayor Yin* 尹縣長 *and Other Stories from the Great Cultural Revolution*. Bloomington: Indiana University Press, 1978.

—[Chen Ruoxi]. *The Old Man* 老人 *and Other Stories*. Renditions paperback. Hong Kong: Chinese University of Hong Kong, Research Centre for Translation, 1986.

Chen Ying-chen. *Exiles at Home: Stories by Chen Ying-chen*. Trans. Lucien Miller. Ann Arbor: University of Michigan, Center for Chinese Studies, 1986.

Chi Pang-yuan 齊邦媛, ed. *An Anthology of Contemporary Chinese Literature*. Seattle: University of Washington Press, 1989.

Chung-kuo ku-tien wen-hsueh lun-tsung: tse-erh, wen-hsueh pi-ping yu hsi-chu chih pu 中國古典文學論叢：冊二，文學批評與戲劇之部 (Essays on Chinese Literature: Vol. 2, Literary Criticism and Drama; in Chinese). Taipei: Chung Wai Literary Monthly, 1976.

Chung-kuo ku-tien wen-hsueh yen-chiu tsung-kan: san-wen yu lun-ping chih pu 中國古典文學研究叢刊：散文與論評之部 (Essays on Classical Chinese Literature: Prose and Criticism; in Chinese). Taipei: Chu Liu Book Company, 1979.

Chung-kuo wen-hsueh chiang-hua 中國文學講話 (On Chinese Literature; in Chinese). Taipei: Chu Liu Book Company, 1982. 6 vols.

Crump, J.I. *Chinese Theater in the Days of Kublai Khan*. Tucson: The University of Arizona Press, 1980.

Ho Chi-peng 何寄澎, ed. *Chan-hou wu-shih nian tai-wan wen-hsueh kuo-chi hsueh-shu yan-tao-hui lun-wen-chi: wen-hua, jen-tung, she-hui pian-chien* 戰後五十年臺灣文學國際學術研討會論文集：文化、認同、社會變遷 (Essays from the International Conference on Postwar Taiwan Literature: Culture-Identity-Social Change; in Chinese). Taipei: Council for Cultural Affairs, 2000.

Hsieh Wu-liang 謝無量. *Chung-kuo fu-nu wen-hsueh shih* 中

國婦女文學史 (History of Chinese Women's Literature; in Chinese). Taipei: Chung Hwa Book Company, 1973.

Hu Min-hsiang 胡民祥. *Tai-wan wen-hsueh ju-men wen-hsuan* 台灣文學入門文選 (An Introductory Anthology of Taiwanese Literature; in Chinese). Taiwanese Literature Series 台灣文學叢書. Taipei: Avanguard 前衛出版社, 1989.

Hu Shih. *Pai-hua wen-hsueh shih* 白話文學史 (A History of Chinese Vernacular Literature; in Chinese). Tainan: Tunghai Publishing Company, 1981.

Hu Yu-huan 胡毓寰. *Chung-kuo wen-hsueh yuan-liu* 中國文學源流 (The Origins of Chinese Literature; in Chinese). Taipei: Commercial Press, 1967.

Huang Chun-ming 黃春明. *The Drowning of an Old Cat* 溺死一隻老貓 *and Other Stories*. Trans. Howard Goldblatt. Bloomington: Indiana University Press, 1980.

Hwa Yen 華嚴. *Lamp of Wisdom* 智慧的燈. Taipei: *Woman Magazine*, 1974.

Ke Ching-ming 柯慶明, Lin Ming-te 林明德, ed. *Chung-kuo ku-tien wen-hsueh yen-chiu tsung-kan: hsiao-shuo chih pu* 中國古典文學研究叢刊：小說之部 (Essays on Classical Chinese Literature: Novels; in Chinese). Taipei: Chu Liu Book Company, 1979.

Kuo, Gloria Liang-hui 郭良蕙. *Taipei Women*. Hong Kong: New Enterprise Company, 1983.

Lau, Joseph S.M., ed. *Chinese Stories from Taiwan, 1960-1970*. New York: Columbia University Press, 1976.

Li Ang. *The Butcher's Wife* 殺夫: *A Novel by Li Ang*. Trans. Howard Goldblatt and Ellen Yeung. San Francisco: North Point Press, 1986.

Lin Hai-yin 林海音. *Green Seaweed and Salted Eggs* 綠藻與鹹蛋. Taipei: Heritage Press, 1963.

Lin Wen-keng 林文庚. *Chung-kuo wen-hsueh fa-chan Shih* 中國文學發展史 (The History of the Development of Chinese Literature; in Chinese). Taipei: Ching Liu Publishing Company, 1976.

Liu Chen-lu 劉振魯, ed. *Tang-chien Tai-wan so-chien ke-sheng hsi-chu hsuan-chi* 當前臺灣所見各省戲曲選集 (Selected Local Drama from Various Provinces Still Performed in Taiwan Today; in Chinese). Taichung: Taiwan Provincial Historical Commission, 1982. 2 vols.

Liu Wu-chi, ed. *An Introduction to Chinese Literature*. Bloomington: Indiana University Press, 1966.

—ed. *Sunflower Splendor: Three Thousand Years of Chinese Poetry*. Bloomington: Indiana University Press, 1975.

Lo Lien-tien 羅聯添, ed. *Chung-kuo wen-hsueh shih lun-wen hsuan-chi* 中國文學史論文選集 (Essays on the History of Chinese Literature; in Chinese). Taipei: Student Book Company, 1985. 5 vols.

Lu Hsing-chang 呂興昌. *Tai-wan shih-jen yan-chiu lun-wen chi* 台灣詩人研究論文集 (Research Essays on Taiwanese Poets; in Chinese). Tainan: Cultural Center of Tainan City, 1995.

Ma, Y.W. and Joseph S.M. Lau, eds. *Traditional Chinese Stories, Themes and Variations*. New York: Columbia University Press, 1978.

McNaughton, William, ed. *Chinese Literature: An Anthology from the Earliest Times to the Present*. Rutland: Charles E. Tuttle Company, 1974.

Mulligan, Jean, tr. *The Lute, Kao Ming's Pi-pa chi*. New York: Columbia University Press, 1980.

Nieh Hua-ling 聶華苓, ed. *Eight Stories by Chinese Women*. Taipei: Heritage Press, 1962.

—*Mulberry and Peach* 桑青與桃紅: *Two Women of China*. London: Women's Press, 1986, c1981.

Nienhauser, William H., ed. *The Indiana Companion to Traditional Chinese Literature*. Bloomington: Indiana University Press, 1986.

Pai Hsien-yung. *Wandering in the Garden, Waking from a Dream* 遊園驚夢: *Tales of Taipei Characters*. Trans. Pai Hsien-yung and Patia Yasin. Ed. George Kao. Bloomington: Indiana University Press, 1982.

—*Crystal Boys*: *A Novel by Pai Hsien-yung* Trans. Howard Goldblatt. San Francisco: Gay Sunshine Press, 1990.

Peng Ko 彭歌. *Black Tears* 黑色的淚, *Stories of War-Torn China*. Trans. Nancy Ing. Taipei: Chinese Materials Center Publications, 1986.

Shih Shu-ching. *The Barren Years* 那些不毛的日子 *and Other Short Stories and Plays*. Trans. John M. Mclellan. San Francisco: Chinese Materials Center, 1975.

Tseng Yung-i 曾永義. *Shuo hsi-chu* 說戲曲 (On Drama; in Chinese). Taipei: Linking Publishing Company, 1976.

Wang Chiu-kuei 王秋桂, ed. *Chung-kuo wen-hsueh lun-chu yi-tsung* 中國文學論著譯叢 (Essays on Chinese Literature; in Chinese). Taipei: Student Book Company, 1985.

Wang Wen-hsing. *Family Catastrophe*. Trans. Susan Dolling. Honolulu: University of Hawaii Press, 1995.

—*Backed Against the Sea*. Trans. Edward Gunn. Ithaca: Cornell East Asia Program, 1993.

Wu Chin-fa 吳錦發. *Yuan chia shan-ti lang: tai-wan shan-ti san-wen hsuan* 願嫁山地郎:台灣山地散文選 (An Anthology of Taiwan Aboriginal Prose; in Chinese). Taiwan Aboriginal Literature Series 台灣原住民文學. Taichung: Christian Literature Center 晨星出版社, 1989.

Wu Chun-chieh 吳俊傑. *Yung-yuan te pu-luo: tai-ya pi-chi* 永遠的部落:泰雅筆記 (The Eternal Tribe: Notes on Ataya; in Chinese). Taiwan Aboriginal Literature Series 台灣原住民文學. Taichung: Christian Literature Center 晨星出版社, 1993.

Yeh Ching-ping 葉慶炳. *Chung-kuo wen-hsueh shih* 中國文學史 (The History of Chinese Literature; in Chinese). Taipei: Student Book Company, 1987. 2 vols.

Yip Wai-lim, ed. *Chung-kuo hsien-tai wen-hsueh pi-ping hsuan-chi* 中國現代文學批評選集 (An Anthology of Contemporary Chinese Literary Criticism; in Chinese). Taipei: Linking Publishing Company, 1976.

25
Religion

Meditation, an important practice of Buddhists, is used to discipline and concentrate believers' minds so that they may achieve spiritual enlightenment.

What's New
1. Figures updated
2. Cross-strait religious activities
3. The Dalai Lama's second visit to Taiwan
4. Commemoration of Dr. Mackay

Age-old religious customs, icons, and beliefs permeate all levels of Taiwan's Chinese culture. Almost all adults in Taiwan, even those not formally subscribing to a religious belief or worshiping regularly at a particular temple, engage in religious practices stemming from one or a combination of traditional Chinese folk religions. It is very common in Taiwan to see homes and shops include a lighted shrine with incense burning to honor a deity, hero, or ancestor. Most families perform the filial duty of ancestral worship; and on important occasions, as when a son or daughter takes the university entrance examination, a visit to the temple is made to present petitions and solicit divine assistance. Many taxi drivers in Taiwan decorate their cars with charms, amulets, statuettes, and religious slogans for protection against accidents and harm. Yet strictly speaking, these people are not necessarily Buddhist, Taoist, officially affiliated with any certain temple, or registered with a religious organization.

The latest figures released by the Ministry of the Interior 內政部 (MOI) in December 2000 indicate that about 10.8 million people in Taiwan— almost half of the population—are religious believers (see chart, next page). Altogether, 21,181 temples and churches dot the island serving the spiritual needs of the people on Taiwan.

Polytheistic and syncretic, Chinese society is dominated by ancestor worship, Taoism, and Buddhism, but has never excluded the addition and development of other indigenous and foreign religions. Although each religion may appear to postulate an independent doctrine, some cannot be strictly differentiated. For example, the Taiwan folk deity Matsu 媽祖, Goddess of the Sea, and Kuanyin 觀音, the Buddhist Goddess of Mercy, are often worshiped together in the same temple. This reveals the special character of the Chinese religious outlook, which can accommodate seemingly contradictory beliefs simultaneously.

Another important factor influencing religion in Taiwan is the extremely eclectic nature of the Chinese religious view. The religions currently practiced in Taiwan are for the most part combinations of elements from several religions. Even Taoism, which is rooted in traditional Chinese philosophy, has absorbed many aspects of non-Chinese dogmas. Unlike Christianity, Islam, and Judaism, which require that believers adhere only to their particular doctrines, the Chinese have seldom felt it necessary to exclude aspects of other faiths from their personal or collective religious beliefs.

Freedom of religion is a fundamental right of every citizen in the ROC: "The people shall have freedom of religious belief," states Article 13 of the ROC Constitution. People of all recognized religions can publicly proselytize, evangelize, and congregate as long as they do not violate ROC laws and regulations, public morals, and social systems. To be recognized, however, these groups must apply and register with the Civil Affairs Department of the MOI 內政部民政司 after meeting stipulated requirements, including a minimum number of local believers, organizations, and sufficient funds. Currently, there are 16 religions recognized by the government: Taoism, Buddhism, Catholicism, Protestantism, Islam, Hsuan-yuan Chiao 軒轅教, Li-ism 理教, Tenrikyo 天理教, the Baha'i faith 巴哈伊教, the Lord of Universe Church (Tien Dih Chiao) 天帝教, Tien Te Chiao 天德教, I-kuan Tao 一貫道, Mahikarikyo 真光教, Confucianism 儒教, Ta Yi Chiao 大易教, and Hai Tse Tao 亥子道.

Concerted Efforts to Help Humanity

In August 2000, the United Nations (UN) held a four-day summit dubbed "The Millennium World Peace Summit of Religious and Spiritual Leaders (WPS)." Around 1,000 world religious and spiritual leaders worked together

Statistics on Religions in Taiwan

Items	Temples & Churches	Believers	Universities & Colleges	Hospitals	Publishing Houses
Religions					
Taoism	8,604	4,546,000	1	2	9
Buddhism	4,010	3,673,000	8	3	35
I-kuan Tao	3,124	845,000	--	21	30
Protestant	3,875	593,000	7	14	78
Catholicism	1,193	298,000	4	11	9
Lord of the Universe Church	47	213,000	1	--	2
Tien Te Chiao	5	200,000	--	--	1
Li-ism	131	187,000	--	--	1
Hsuan-yuan Chiao	21	150,000	--	--	1
Islam	6	54,000	--	--	1
Tenrikyo	150	24,000	--	--	--
Baha'i	7	16,000	--	--	1
Mahikarikyo	9	1,000	--	--	--
Total (by Dec. 2000)	21,182	10,800,000	21	51	168

Source: Civil Affairs Department, Ministry of the Interior

to tackle peace, poverty, and environmental issues as interfaith allies with the UN. Among the world religious leaders joining the summit were Master Sheng Yen 聖嚴法師 of the Association of Dharma Drum Mountain Cultural and Educational Organization 法鼓山文教組織協會 and Master Hsin Tao 心道法師 of the Ling Jiou Mountain Buddhist Society 靈鷲山佛教教團 from Taiwan. They joined hundreds of religious leaders in signing the "Commitment to Global Peace," which condemns violence in the name of religion and appeals for respect for the right of religious freedom. The WPS is also developing "Peace Initiatives for Regions of Conflict," which focuses on the roles of the religious leaders in reducing regional conflicts, something religious leaders in Taiwan could take up.

Religious groups have traditionally been the backbone of community services in Taiwan. As of December 2000, religious groups were operating 51 hospitals, 62 clinics, 29 retirement homes, 31 centers for the mentally retarded, 12 handicapped welfare institutions, nine rehabilitation centers, 18 orphanages, and 37 nurseries in Taiwan. These groups have also established 390 kindergartens, 11 primary schools, 37 high schools, six colleges, 15 universities, and 84 monasteries and seminaries. They have also set up 166 libraries, 168 publishing houses, and 300 publications.

Immediately following the 921 Earthquake on September 21, 1999, the religious community contributed immensely to relief efforts with great compassion and efficiency. They were among the first to reach out to victims in the disaster areas, bringing hope, comfort, food, materials, and monetary assistance. Particularly noteworthy were the Buddhist Compassion Tzu Chi Relief Foundation 佛教慈濟慈善事業基金會; Fo Guang Shan 佛光山 (FGS) and its affiliate, the Buddha's Light International Association 國際佛光會, which formed a 921 Earthquake United Relief Fund/Center 佛光山國際佛光會聯合救災基金/中心; the Association of Dharma Drum Mountain Cultural and Educational Organizations; the Catholic 921 Earthquake Relief Center 台灣

天主教九二一賑災救助中心; and the Taiwan Christian United Rescue Action for the 921 Earthquake 九二一地震救助行動 set up by Chinese Christian Relief Association of Taiwan 中華基督教救助協會.

Another concerted effort made by the religious groups in Taiwan was to assist the families of the 82 passengers and crew members of Singapore Airlines flight SQ006, which crashed on October 31, 2000, at the Chiang Kai-Shek (CKS) International Airport in Taoyuan. Around 300 Taiwanese and 100 relatives of the victims from Britain, India, Indonesia, Malaysia, Singapore, and the United States participated in the religious ceremonies held by local Buddhist, Muslim, Protestant, Catholic, and Taoist communities.

Aside from sharing a common concern for the poor and disaster victims, religious organizations have also diversified into medical services, free health checkups, community projects, and visitations to homes and hospitals. Churches in Taiwan have also taken the lead in organizing cultural and recreational activities. Whereas the Protestant church has focused on promoting youth activities, Taoist organizations have channeled much of their efforts into preserving and staging traditional Chinese dramas, and Buddhist groups have offered a wide range of self-improvement seminars.

Government and Private Organizations and Institutions

Taiwan's first religious association, the Taiwan Association for Religious Studies, was established on April 18, 1999, by a group of scholars and academics. The association researches mainstream and folk religions in Taiwan and publishes a monthly newsletter. In addition, National Chengchi University 國立政治大學 established a graduate school in religious studies in 2000, the only university unaffiliated with religious groups to set up a graduate program in religion. Other universities provide religious studies under the laws governing private schools that prevent discrimination on religious grounds include Aletheia University 真理大學, Chung Yuan

Christian University 中原大學, Fu Jen Catholic University 輔仁大學, and Hsuan Chuang University 玄奘大學. The Department of Higher Education under the Ministry of Education (MOE) is also inspecting existing theological seminaries and Buddhist studies schools that are registered under the MOI as "research institutes of religious teachings," attempting to incorporate them into the former educational system while maintaining proper tertiary education standards.

Although nearly half of Taiwan's residents practice the 16 religions recognized by the government, many religious groups are legally registered as organizations. Therefore, former Minister of the Interior Chang Po-ya 張博雅 ordered the Religion Section of the Civil Affairs Department 民政司宗教輔導科, currently staffed by only six civil servants, to be expanded and upgraded into a Religious Affairs Department in the near future. The MOI sent to the Legislative Yuan a reorganization draft in June 2000, under which the new department would have 53 staff members.

The Ministry also established a Religious Affairs Counseling Committee 宗教事務諮詢委員會 on October 2, 2000. Vice Minister Lee Yiyang 李逸洋 serves as the convener, and the committee members consist of six Buddhist, five Catholic, one Hai Tse Tao, three I-kuan Tao, one Muslim, five Protestant, one Tien Te Chiao, one Tenrikyo, one Tien Dih Chiao, and six Taoist representatives, four academics, and two officials. Out of these 37 members, one Buddhist, one Taoist, two Presbyterians, one Catholic, and one academic were selected to draft the *Law Governing Religious Groups* 宗教團體法, which was submitted to the Executive Yuan in March 2001 for deliberation. The law was intended to solve problems such as requiring a secular manager in addition to a religious leader in order to formally register a temple, a system that was first established during the Japanese occupation. However, articles related to tax exemption, property ownership, and construction regulations have ignited fierce debates.

Alternative Military Service

In coordination with the implementation of alternative military service beginning in July 2000, the MOI agreed that conscripts inducted into the military in 1999 could apply for a one year postponement due to religious reasons, but must produce a certificate of proof from a legitimate religious group.

In 2000, a total of 28 Jehovah's Witnesses and three Buddhists had applied for the 33-month alternative to military service, which is 11 months longer than ordinary military service. All were assigned to do social work in the Taichung area by the 921 Earthquake Post-Disaster Recovery Commission, Executive Yuan 行政院九二一震災災後重建推動委員.

Cross-Strait Religious Exchanges

Invited by the Nanhua Management College of Fo Guang University 佛光大學南華管理學院 and the Straits Exchange Foundation 海峽交流基金會, five officials from mainland China's Bureau of Religious Affairs 宗教局 arrived in Taiwan on July 28, 1998, for a twelve-day visit. The group toured various religious centers, temples and churches of the Buddhist, I-kuan Tao, Catholic and Protestant religions. The purpose of the visit was to promote exchanges and research on Taiwan's religious development.

After the Legislature passed the *Offshore Islands Development Act* 離島開發條例 in March 2000, the issue of direct cross-strait religious visits via the offshore islands was thoroughly discussed and debated. Several religious groups applied for direct sea travel to the Chinese mainland in order to save energy, time, and money for pilgrims, especially the elderly. However, due to political considerations, the Chenlan Temple 鎮瀾宮 in Tachia, Taichung County, arranged for more than 2,000 pilgrims, Taiwan's largest group ever, to fly to Fujian Province via Hong Kong for celebrations held July 16-20, 2000.

Immediately after the "three small links" was formally implemented on January 1, 2001, allowing direct links between Matsu 馬祖 and Kinmen islands with the Chinese mainland, 500 Matsu residents took a two-hour crossing to Fuzhou City on the Chinese mainland for pilgrimage. Another 190 pilgrims from Kinmen took a 30-minute voyage to Meizhou, a Fujian Province islet, for a six-day tour in March 2001. The pilgrims escorted three statues that were brought to Kinmen more than 300 years ago back to the Tienhou Temple at Meizhou, the first time in five decades. Nevertheless, until the political climate changes, pilgrims from Taiwan proper will still need to take indirect routes for their annual journeys.

In 2001, the Wuchi Sanching Taoist Temple 無極三清總道院 of Taichung County held a summer camp dubbed "Shaolin Martial Arts and Zen Meditation for Spiritual Reform" and invited 19 monks, the youngest of whom was only four years old, from the Buddhist Shaolin Temple in mainland China's Henan Province. The purpose of this camp was to show the youth of Taiwan who spent most of their holidays studying how to train their bodies and spirit, and give adults a chance to regenerate their energy through meditation. This summer camp featured not only cross-strait interactions, but also interfaith cooperation.

Confucianism

Confucianism is a philosophy with a religious function. It is named after Confucius, whose discourses on ethical behavior have been passed down from generation to generation to become the definitive marker of things Chinese. It embraces some elements of traditional Chinese religion, such as a reverence toward heaven and the worship of ancestors, but is primarily concerned with the moral cultivation of the individual in order to establish harmonious relationships with others and society. It does not assert or deny the existence of a deity.

Most Chinese do not identify Confucianism as a religion, but rather view it as a philosophy. They regard Confucian temples more as halls to honor Confucius rather than places of worship. Visitors may witness an elaborate ceremony to honor Confucius at Taipei's Confucian Temple

every year on his birthday, September 28, which is also designated as Teachers' Day in the ROC.

Folk Religion

Chinese folk religion is a faith whose theology, rituals, and officiants are widely diffused into other secular and social institutions. Taiwan's difficult pioneer environment of the 17th and 18th centuries created a strong need for religion, and folk religion was the choice of many Chinese immigrants to the island. They brought from the mainland images of gods and traditional religious beliefs. While transplanting their religion, they adapted it functionally to

Despite having no official number of registered followers, Chinese folk religion has some of the most energetic believers and is one of the most celebrated religions in Taiwan.

their new society, sometimes even creating new gods and rituals to meet their needs for security and survival. The resulting mixture of beliefs is called folk religion for the sake of convenience.

Like Taoism, folk religion has a broad pantheon of gods and goddesses. Relations between gods and people, and between gods and gods, are of paramount importance. Like Buddhism, folk religion offers salvation, or at least temporary aid, for true believers. Although folk religion has been influenced significantly by Buddhism and Taoism, it is neither Buddhist nor Taoist. People associated with Taoism often place folk religion in the same category as Taoism; however, they concede that folk religion includes a number of gods that Taoism does not recognize.

In folk religion, the supreme deity is the God of Heaven 天公, who is recognized as a personification of justice. Below this supreme deity are hundreds of lesser gods. Almost every neighborhood in Taiwan has a temple for the Earth God 土地公, and many families make offerings to the House God 地基主 when they move into a house.

One of the most popular deities is Matsu, the patron goddess of the sea and fishermen. Meizhou in Fujian Province is where worship for the Meizhou Matsu originated. In 1987, worshipers celebrated the 1,000th anniversary of Matsu's ascent to heaven with a round-the-island parade of her image. Her birthday on the 23rd day of the third lunar month is regularly celebrated with great pomp as worshipers carry her image in a procession through cities around Taiwan.

On April 7, 2001, ten Yuan Hsiang Matsu Temples in Tainan, one of the oldest Han Chinese settlements in southern Taiwan, jointly held a festival, instead of holding their own events individually. Statues from the temples were paraded through the streets of Tainan together to show the characteristics of each temple. To promote the event as a tourist attraction in addition to a religious ceremony, the Tainan City Government provided free bus rides to visitors during the festivities.

Some deities in Taiwan folk religion were originally people who, through their actions or accomplishments in life, later became gods. The brave warrior Kuan Yu 關羽 from the Period of the Three Kingdoms; General Koxinga 鄭成功, who drove the Dutch colonists off Taiwan in the 17th century; and the renowned healer Hua Tuo 華陀, who lived sometime between the first and third century A.D., all have faithful followings in Taiwan. Their birthdays are celebrated following the traditional rituals similar to those of Confucius' birthday. For example, on August 13, 2001, the Hsingtien Temple 行天宮 in Taipei City and the Hsiehtien Temple 協天廟 in Chiaohsi, Ilan County held grand, yet frugal, celebrations for Kuan Yu.

Taiwan's Wang Yeh 王爺 deities are believed to be celestial emissaries sent by the heavens to ensure the safety of mankind by driving away evil spirits and eradicating epidemics. There are said to be 360 Wang Yeh in Taiwan, but the religious practices surrounding each of these celestial lords are different, depending on the locality and the time of year. Wang Yeh are often worshiped together in groups of three or five.

While the Wang Yeh are worshiped mainly by those originally from Fujian Province, the San Shan Kuo-wang 三山國王, literally, the Three Kings of the Mountains, are revered by Chinese of Hakka descent (an ethnic and linguistic subset of Han Chinese culture). Legendary stories surrounding the two groups of deities are similar, the only difference being that the San Shan Kuo-wang originated from the worship of mountains. With the outward spread of Hakka Chinese from the Hsinchu and Miaoli areas throughout Taiwan, the three gods have been separated and are often worshiped individually instead of as a group.

Meanwhile, traditional magical calculations such as geomancy 風水 and physiognomy 看相, are not only still in fashion, they are also changing with the times. For example, some stock market speculators consult fortune-tellers to make decisions, and pregnant women and their families occasionally demand Cesarean sections at auspicious times.

Taoism

Taoism developed from the philosophy of Lao Tzu 老子, who lived in the sixth century B.C. He and his disciples emphasized individual freedom, laissez-faire government, human spontaneity, and mystical experience. Taoist philosophy takes *The Way and Its Power* 道德經 as its central text.

The themes of Taoism as a religion coalesced in the third century B.C., but Taoism itself did not become an organized religious movement until the second century A.D. The fundamental aim of religious Taoism was the attainment of immortality. Accordingly, people who lived in harmony with nature were said to become "immortals" 仙. Lao Tzu, founder of the philosophy of Taoism, eventually was deified as a Taoist god at the head of a huge pantheon of "immortal" folk heroes. Famous generals and sages made up the rest of the pantheon once they had ascended to immortal status. The Taoist pursuit of everlasting life ultimately led to a search for immortality pills or potions. Medieval Taoist rituals to some extent mirrored alchemical research in Europe during the same period.

Taoism was adopted as the religion of the imperial court during the seventh through the ninth centuries, and Taoist mystical elements were codified. In the ensuing centuries, the Taoist religious community was increasingly fractionalized. Taoism became interlaced with elements of Buddhism, Confucianism, and folk religion. The particular forms of Taoist religion brought to Taiwan (then regarded as an outlying frontier area) some 300 years ago are considered typical of the fragmented Taoist traditions. The most distinctive feature of the present practice is the worship of one's forebears alongside Taoist deities.

During the period of Japanese occupation (1895-1945), the Japanese colonial government implemented a policy of suppressing Taoism in Taiwan, because it was associated with Chinese patriotism. Many religious images in Taoist temples were burned, and various repressive measures were directed against Taoist followers.

After Taiwan's retrocession to China in 1945, Taoist temples that had been registered as Buddhist under pressure from the Japanese colonial government returned to the Taoist fold. Taoist priests from the Chinese mainland, including Chang En-pu 張恩溥, a 63rd generation Taoist priest of the Cheng I 正一 sect of Lung Hu Mountain 龍虎山, began moving to Taiwan in increasing numbers. In 1950, Chang En-pu established a Taoist fellowship in Taiwan, assuming the position of director. This was the beginning of organized Taoism in Taiwan.

In the past, much emphasis was put on constructing luxurious temples and holding frequent, lavish festivals. Today, adherents and priests pay more attention to preaching through the mass media. Some Taoist leaders have turned to the strategy of using temple associations to unite the various "generic" temples under the umbrella of a common main deity, while at the same time trying to win over temple diviners from small local or home temples 神壇 and offering them guidance.

As of 2000, a total of 8,604 Taoist temples and 33,850 Taoist clergy were meeting the spiritual needs of some 4.55 million Taoist faithful living in Taiwan. Six Taoist seminaries and 24 institutes for proselytizing provided instruction in Taoist doctrine and rites. There were also one college, 59 kindergartens, three retirement homes, two hospitals, 19 clinics, 16 libraries, nine publishing houses, and 172 publications.

Buddhism

Chinese Buddhism

Buddhism is a pan-Asian religion originated in India and was brought to China sometime before the sixth century. Buddha was an Indian prince named Siddhartha Gautama who renounced his royal family and luxurious lifestyle to search for religious understanding and release from the human condition. It is said that he achieved enlightenment through self-denial and meditation, and thereafter instructed his followers on the nature of dharma, the true way.

Buddha preached a doctrine envisioned in the "Four Noble Truths": life is fundamentally difficult and disappointing; suffering is the result of one's desires; to stop disappointment one must control one's desires; and the way to stop desire is through right views, intention, speech, conduct, livelihood, effort, mindfulness, and concentration.

Buddhism spread south to Ceylon, Cambodia, and Laos to become Theravada or Hinayana (Little Vehicle 小乘) and north to China, Korea, and Japan, where it developed into Mahayana (Great Vehicle 大乘). Hinayana is concerned more with individual salvation through contemplation and self-purification, while Mahayana teaches compassion and universal salvation.

Mahayana adherents believe in powerful godlike bodhisattvas, enlightened individuals

Buddhism, as the second largest religion in Taiwan, has been known to attract more than 10,000 participants to its public ceremonies.

who are capable of saving all sentient beings and transporting them to a state of release (nirvana) from the human condition. Bodhisattvas possess the natural disposition to attain enlightenment and become Buddhas, a potential which is inherent in all people. Mahayana adherents also believe in a cycle of lives which continues until one attains nirvana and becomes a Buddha.

Several Mahayana concepts, such as a life of suffering, many powerful godlike figures, and possible transcendence to a higher state of being, meshed well with similar ideas in Taoism and folk religion already widely accepted in China. As a result, Mahayana Buddhism became the most popular form of Buddhism in China, and indeed, in all of Northeast Asia.

Although Buddhism originated in India, it has undergone thorough Sinification since its introduction to China. In terms of thought system, canons, and ceremonies, the Buddhism practiced in China today is distinctly Chinese, and few Chinese people consider it a foreign religion.

Buddhism in Taiwan

Buddhism was introduced into Taiwan in the late 16th century. By the time Ming loyalist Koxinga escaped to Taiwan and drove out the Dutch, Buddhist monks were already coming to Taiwan with official sanction. Buddhist temples were built with the support of Koxinga and his followers. By the 17th century, several Buddhist temples had been erected by officials, the gentry, and local people; however, Buddhist missionary work at the time seems to have been limited in scope. Some Buddhist temples were used as temples of folk religion by the people, and thus received popular support.

Japanese Buddhism was introduced into Taiwan during the Japanese colonial period (1895-1945). Eight Buddhist sects, namely, the Tendai 天臺, the Shingon 真元, the Pure Land 淨土, the Soto 曹洞宗, the Rinzai 臨濟宗, the Shin 真, the Nichiren 日蓮, the Hokke 法華, and the Agon 阿含, came to Taiwan to proselytize. Buddhist sects already established in Taiwan responded to the incursion by accommodating the newcomers.

By 1925, a large number of Japanese monks were in leading positions in Taiwan's established Buddhist temples. Buddhism in Taiwan gradually took on a Japanese cast, particularly in the areas of moral and disciplinary codes and education.

During the Japanese occupation, Buddhist groups in Taiwan separated into the northern, central, and southern schools. The monk Shan-hui 善慧 founded the Yueh-mei Mountain 月眉山 school of Keelung (the northern school), and the monk Chueh-li 覺立 established the Fa-yun Szu 法雲寺 school of Miaoli (the central school) and the Kai-yuan Szu 開元寺 school of Tainan (the southern school). Most Buddhist temples of this era belonged to one of these three schools. Towards the end of the Japanese occupation, many monks actively engaged in proselytizing activities and established Buddhist organizations.

Postwar Buddhism in Taiwan has witnessed the reestablishment of the Chinese Mahayana tradition, renewed stress on moral and disciplinary codes and the ceremony of ordination 傳戒大典, emphasis on Buddhist education and the establishment of Buddhist institutes, and active proselytizing. In 1947, Master Chang-chia 章嘉 established the Buddhist Association of the ROC 中國佛教會 in Nanjing. Large numbers of Chinese monks followed the Chinese Nationalist government to Taiwan and established the Taiwan provincial chapter of the Buddhist Association of the ROC. Monks from the Chinese mainland headed the association at first, and temples throughout the island became association members. Since the 1950s, the Buddhist Association of the ROC has held ordination ceremonies for Buddhist monks, nuns, and lay people. Temples recognized by the association hold an annual third-level ordination ceremony 三壇大戒, with monks and nuns receiving one month of stringent training before ordination. Since then, thousands of monks and nuns have been ordained in this ceremony at various temples and monasteries around the island.

The Museum of World Religions 世界宗教博物館 located in Yungho City, Taipei County was

459

opened on November 9, 2001. Hosted by Ling Jiou Mountain's Master Hsin Tao, 180 religious leaders and Museum experts from nearly 40 countries participated the inaugural ceremony. The Museum collects Buddhist art from the Chinese mainland, Tibet, Nepal, Myanmar, Cambodia, India, and Thailand. Artifacts of Taoist and Taiwanese folk religions are also featured in its main collections.

As of 2000, Buddhists in the ROC had registered 4,010 temples, 35 seminaries, five universities, three colleges, four high schools, 46 kindergartens, 32 nurseries, six orphanages, five retirement homes, one center for the mentally retarded, 64 institutions for proselytizing, three hospitals, three clinics, 118 libraries, and 35 publishing houses with 25 publications. There were also around 9,300 Buddhist clergy serving the 3.67 million Buddhists of Taiwan.

Tantric Buddhism

Since 1980, Tantric Buddhism, an esoteric sect that developed between the second and fourth centuries A.D. in India, has become increasingly popular in Taiwan. In recent years, exiled Tibetan monks of the Tantric sect have come to Taiwan, rapidly attracting a large following and thereby exercising a significant effect on Taiwan's religious culture.

On March 22, 1997, the Nobel Prize winning religious and political leader of Tibet, the Dalai Lama, set foot again on Chinese soil for the first time in 38 years, ever since his exile in 1959. Invited by Master Ching Hsin 淨心長老 of the Buddhist Association of the ROC, the 14th Dalai Lama held two public talks and a Buddhist consecration ceremony, met with religious leaders, and ended his five-day visit to Taiwan on March 27 by meeting with former President Lee Teng-hui. On April 16, 1998, the Tibet Religious Foundation of His Holiness the Dalai Lama 財團法人達賴喇嘛西藏宗教基金會 was formally established. Although religious in name, the Foundation serves as a de facto Tibetan representative office in Taiwan.

The Dalai Lama visited Taiwan a second time in April 2001. More than 20,000 people attended the two-day ceremony where he preached the Buddha's teachings. Although the trip was classified as "strictly religious," the Dalai Lama met with not only religious leaders, such as Master Cheng Yen 證嚴法師 of the Buddhist Tzu Chi Compassion Relief Foundation, Master Sheng Yen of the Dharma Drum Mountain, and Master Hsin Tao of the Ling Jiou Mountain Buddhist Foundation and the Museum of World Religions during the 10-day trip, he also conversed with President Chen Shuibian, Vice President Lu Hsiu-lien, former President Lee Teng-hui, and other influential political figures. His appeal for permits to allow more Tibetans to study Mandarin, receive vocational training, and obtain employment in Taiwan received a positive response. The Dalai Lama also donated US$150,000 for post-quake reconstruction works.

Education

The road traveled by Buddhist education has not been a smooth one. Its beginning in post-retrocession Taiwan dates from the invitation by the Buddhist Master Miao-kuo 妙果 of the Yuan-kuang Temple 圓光寺 in Chungli to the Buddhist Master Tzu-hang 慈航 from the Chinese mainland to establish a Buddhist institute in Taiwan. Master Tzu-hang later founded a Maitreya monastery in Hsichih, Taipei County. Next, Master Yin-shun 印順 assumed the directorship of a Buddhist institute in Hsinchu. Subsequently, over 50 Buddhist institutes were founded islandwide. Many of these institutes functioned intermittently; only a portion of them were able to maintain unbroken operations. One explanation for this is that Buddhist and other religious institutes were not officially recognized by the MOE. Another is that many Buddhist figures founded independent educational institutes instead of uniting to establish one large institute.

Nonetheless, the Buddhist-sponsored Tzu Chi Junior College of Nursing 慈濟護理專科學校 opened in 1989, the Huafan College of Humanities and Technology 華梵人文科技學院 opened the following year, and the Tzu Chi Medical

College 慈濟醫學院 began enrolling students in 1994. The Nanhua Management College of Fo Guang University 佛光大學南華管理學院, located in Chiayi, which began enrolling students in October 1996, was renamed in 1999 as Nanhua University 南華大學.

Missionary and Humanitarian Works Abroad

Buddhists are becoming more missionary-oriented. Over the past decade, television proselytizing has gained popularity, and lectures on Buddhism have begun to draw large crowds. Intellectuals have been drawn to Buddhism from the beginning, for both academic and religious reasons, and some have become renowned monks and nuns. By stressing "Buddhism for this world," Buddhist leaders have also managed to attract people outside of academia who have contributed significant amounts of financial and spiritual support to Buddhist organizations.

Some of Taiwan's leading figures in Buddhism have expanded their missions overseas. For example, after the January 14, 2001, earthquake in El Salvador, the Buddhist Tzu Chi Compassion Relief Foundation dispatched medical teams from the United States to provide food and build prefabricated houses for victims. It has also opened three relief distribution stations at New York's Pier 94 and Chinatown and Liberty State Park in New Jersey since the collapse of the World Trade Center on Spetember 11, 2001, and provided a total of US$950,000 relief funds within two months of the incident. The Foundation cooperated with Knightsbridge International to provide food, blankets, medicine, and US$5 per household to the Afghan refugees. The two organizations have collaborated to provide medicine for the Afghans from February to May 1998 and various relief materials for Kosovo refugees in 1999.

I-kuan Tao

The Chinese words I-kuan Tao can be roughly translated as the "Religion of One Unity." The name belies I-kuan Tao's nature as a religious doctrine that draws upon both traditional Chinese teachings and each of the world's major religions. I-kuan Tao is a modern, syncretic faith, and the third most popular religion in Taiwan.

According to I-kuan Tao adherents, this religion attempts to identify common principles underlying Taoism, Buddhism, Christianity, Islam, Judaism, and Hinduism. I-kuan Tao faithful believe that by uncovering a single set of universal truths, the "increasing chaos" of modern times can be defeated and the world can live peacefully in harmony. They believe in a God beyond all other gods, called Ming-ming Shang-ti 明明上帝 (the God of Clarity).

I-kuan Tao evolved from Hsien-tien Tao 先天道, which was founded by Huang Te-hui 黃德輝 in the 17th century. Huang combined the three main belief systems of China with a belief in the Wu-sheng Lao-mu 無生老母 deity to form Hsien-tien Tao.

One reason for its rapid spread throughout China over the years was that, although I-kuan Tao claimed to be a universal religion, its basic writings, forms of religious observance, and moral precepts were all couched in traditional Chinese terms. By drawing heavily on Confucian, Buddhist, Taoist, and folk religious terminology, I-kuan Tao was readily understandable in traditional Chinese religious terms.

I-kuan Tao adherents follow many of the rituals of Confucianism and engage in ancestor worship. Services are usually held at family shrines and are aimed at both cultivating personal character and regulating family relations—two key concepts in Chinese culture. Proselytism of I-kuan Tao has not always been such an open matter. Indeed, I-kuan Tao teachings incorporate a tradition of secrecy inherited from the various clandestine religious sects that have thrived during periods of chaos in Chinese history. In their day-to-day lives, I-kuan Tao followers strive to uphold the precepts of not killing, stealing, committing adultery, lying, or drinking alcohol, while putting into practice the I-kuan Tao ideals of benevolence, righteousness, courtesy, wisdom, and faith.

461

By 2000, there were 3,124 large or medium-sized I-kuan Tao temples in Taiwan with 2,281 temple priests serving approximately 845,000 believers. By increasing the number of I-kuan Tao temples, the faithful believe they are bringing the Buddhist "Western Paradise" to earth and creating a world of brotherhood and universal love as envisioned by Confucian teachings.

Personal sublimation and a life of service are key tenets in the I-kuan Tao moral philosophy, and adherents devote a great deal of resources to social work. In Taiwan, there are four I-kuan Tao seminaries, 34 kindergartens, one nursery, one orphanage, four retirement homes, 21 hospitals, eight clinics, 20 libraries, 30 publishing houses, and 32 publications. The service ethic is closely related to the order's tradition that believers should "give their hearts to the universe and contribute their lives to humanity."

Since it was brought to Taiwan, I-kuan Tao has established many cultural and educational units. These units train an average of 10,000 I-kuan Tao devotees each year. Over half of the vegetarian restaurants around the island are run by I-kuan Tao adherents, who are required to follow a strict vegetarian diet.

Christianity

Before 1945

Christianity came to Taiwan with the Dutch in 1624. The first missionary in Taiwan was Georgius Candidius of the Reformed Church of Holland. Six Pingpu 平埔 aborigine communities near modern day Tainan were the center of his mission activities. (The Pingpu tribe was later assimilated by Han settlers.) Robert Bunius continued Candidius's mission work in southern Taiwan, where he lived for 14 years. By 1643, over 6,000 aborigines have been converted to Christianity. Mass conversions were typical of his evangelistic style.

In 1626, a Spaniard, Father Martinez, in the company of Spanish troops, brought with him four Dominican missionaries from the Philippines to the Keelung and Tamsui areas to do mission work. The Spanish army occupied a portion of northern Taiwan, and ruled there for 16 years. Missionaries actively spread Roman Catholicism at this time, during which they won approximately 4,000 aborigines over to their faith.

In 1642, the Dutch forces occupying southern Taiwan pushed northward to rout the Spaniards, arresting them and driving them out of Taiwan. It is not known what became of the Roman Catholic converts, since no trace of them was to be found. All that remains from this period of Roman Catholic missionary activity are a few historical records. By the time the Chinese general Koxinga drove the Dutch off the island, this scantily documented page in the history of Christianity in Taiwan had more or less come to an end. By 1714, when the Roman Catholic Jesuits came to Taiwan for map-making, they found a few descendants of these early Christians who had still preserved some remnants of their forebears' beliefs.

In 1859, the Spanish Dominican Father Fernando Sainz and Father Angel Bofurull arrived in Kaohsiung from the Philippines via Amoy, and founded the first Roman Catholic church in Kaohsiung, the Holy Rosary Church. Father Sainz later conducted mission work in the Kaohsiung, Tainan, and Pingtung areas. In 1861, he founded the Immaculate Conception Church in what today is Wanchin Village 萬金村 in Wanluan. This is the oldest extant Roman Catholic church in Taiwan.

In 1860, British missionaries Reverend Carstairs Douglas and Reverend H.L. Mackenzie came to Tamsui and Mengchia 艋舺 (present-day Wanhua in Taipei) to preach the gospel. In 1864, Dr. James L. Maxwell was officially sent to Taiwan by the English Presbyterian Mission to preach Christianity. With Tainan as his base, he concentrated his efforts in southern Taiwan. In 1872, the Canadian Presbyterian Church dispatched George L. Mackay to northern Taiwan to do mission work, choosing Tamsui as his center.

Prior to the Japanese occupation of Taiwan in 1895, there were 97 Protestant churches, 4,854 believers, about 90 mission workers, and

13 foreign missionaries in Taiwan. During the period of Japanese occupation, the colonial government exercised control over churches and had them absorb Japanese Christian groups. The Japanese also strictly forbade Christian mission work among the aborigines. When the Japanese left in 1945, Taiwan had about 238 Protestant churches and 60,000 believers.

Roman Catholicism also experienced a relatively slow development during the Japanese occupation. Some theorize that this was due to suppression by the Japanese colonial government; however, there is no concrete evidence to support this. By 1945, there were only about 10,000 Roman Catholics (some records report 8,000), 52 churches or missions, and 20 missionaries in Taiwan.

Protestant Church

Christianity in Taiwan developed in a new direction after the mainland fell to communism and the central government relocated to Taiwan in 1949. Churches of numerous denominations flocked to Taiwan, and the number of Christian denominations active in Taiwan went from just three in 1945 to approximately 40 in 1955.

Taiwan's Protestant churches experienced rapid growth between 1950 and 1964, but after the mid-1960s, they entered a phase of sluggish and even negative growth. By 2000, the congregation had expanded to approximately 593,000 with 3,875 churches, 2,554 ministers and 1,109 foreign ministers. Although the tradition of foreign Protestant missionary work can be traced back for centuries in Taiwan, the means of spreading the teachings has moved from providing relief goods in the 1950s, offering social services in the 60s and 70s, to a revived focus on the Biblical message. Deeming the traditional Chinese practice of ancestral worship incompatible with the Gospel, Protestants suggest the followers to pray "for" their ancestors instead of "to" them, while emphasizing the Fifth Commandment: "Honor thy father and mother."

On June 1, 2001, the 100th anniversary of George L. Mackay's death, a commemorative stamp was issued in his honor. His diary was also translated into Chinese and published in 12 volumes the same month. Dr. Mackay's collection of aboriginal artifacts, which was considered the finest of the pre-Japanese colonial era, was loaned by the Royal Ontario Museum for exhibition at the Shung Ye Museum of Formosan Aborigines 順益台灣原住民博物館 between June 2 and September 13, 2001. Mackay's degree of assimilation and marriage to a local Chinese, to the shock of his contemporary Westerners, has distinguished him from many other missionaries in Taiwan and his influence on his wife's relatives has resulted in the Chen family's participation

The Tamsui Presbyterian Church was built in 1933, 60 years after Dr. George L. Mackay, a Canadian missionary, first established the Presbyterian denomination in northern Taiwan.

463

in the development of the Presbyterian Church on the island. To honor his contributions and dedication to Taiwan, a street in Tamsui is named after Mackay, one of the only three foreigners commemorated in this way on the island besides President Roosevelt and General MacArthur of the US.

Roman Catholic Church

Roman Catholicism made a remarkable comeback in Taiwan after the island was returned to the Republic of China. In 1948, the number of believers stood at 13,000. When the central government moved to Taiwan in 1949, multitudes of Roman Catholic clergy and believers followed, infusing Roman Catholicism in Taiwan with new strength and vigor. The number of converts grew rapidly in the 1953-1963 period, from 27,000 to 300,000. The number of practicing Roman Catholics peaked in 1969, when the total reached nearly 306,000, and seven dioceses were formed: the Taipei archdiocese, and the Hsinchu, Taichung, Chiayi, Tainan, Kaohsiung, and Hualien dioceses. Since then, the Roman Catholic church of Taiwan has faced a period of slow growth. As of 2000, there were 1,193 Catholic churches, 693 clergymen, and 664 foreign missionaries in Taiwan serving about 298,000 believers.

On January 18, 1998, Bishop Paul Shan 單國璽 of the Catholic diocese in Kaohsiung was appointed to the status of cardinal by Pope John Paul II. Shan officially assumed this position on February 21, when the College of Cardinals congregated at the Vatican. He is the only Taiwanese to be conferred the title of cardinal in the past 20 years and is the fifth Chinese cardinal in the history of the Roman Catholic Church. The last cardinal from Taiwan was Cardinal Yu Pin 于斌, who was elevated to cardinal status in Nanjing before he relocated to Taiwan in 1950.

Among the leading schools founded by the Catholic church in Taiwan are Fu Jen Catholic University, the Cardinal Tien School of Nursing & Midwifery 耕莘高級護理助產職業學校, the Blessed Imelda's School 靜修女子高級中學, the Kuang Jen

Refurbished in 1928, the Holy Rosary Church was built in 1863 by the Spanish Dominican Father Fernando Sainz and Father Angel Bofurull, both of whom arrived in Kaohsiung via Amoy in 1859.

Middle School 光仁中學 and Kuang Jen Primary School 光仁小學, Providence University 靜宜大學, Taichung Viator High School 台中市私立衛道高級中學, and the Wentsao Ursuline College of Modern Languages 文藻外國語文學院.

Independent Churches

While mainstream Protestant churches and the Roman Catholic Church have enjoyed a head start in their evangelical work, independent churches are also growing consistently by emphasizing fundamentalist theology, flexible administration, and self-supporting financial power. Popular independent churches include the True Jesus Church, the Mandarin Church, and the Ling Leung Church.

The first missionaries from the Church of Jesus Christ of Latter-day Saints, also known as the Mormon Church, arrived in Taiwan in 1956. By 1963, the book of the Mormon Church had been translated from English into Chinese by Hu Wei-I 胡唯一, and a branch of the Mormon Church had been established locally. Since then, the Mormon gospel has been spread to the most remote reaches of Taiwan. In most areas, foreign missionaries also offer free English conversation classes to the public, and a handful of full-time church workers provide assistance to those in need. Although assisted by a steady rotation of foreign missionaries, all Mormon churches in Taiwan are headed by local Chinese leaders.

The Jehovah's Witnesses came to Taiwan in 1950 and registered with the MOI in 1964. In the past 50 years, many foreign missionaries have come to Taiwan to preach the doctrines of the Jehovah's Witnesses. Though a relatively small group of only around 4,000 followers, the faithful have remained true in carrying out their religion's teachings, including the doctrine of opposing war and violence. As a result, many conscripts of Jehovah's Witnesses have chosen to serve prison terms instead of complying with mandatory ROC military service laws. Promulgation of the *Alternative Military Service Act* 替代役實施條例 has provided a solution to this problem and on December 10, 2000, President Chen pardoned 19 conscientious objectors.

The Unification Church, registered as the Holy Spirit Association for the Unification of World Christianity, came to Taiwan in 1971. Mass weddings are a special tradition of the Unification Church. "Blessing '98," in which 120 million married couples reaffirmed their marriage vows, was held on June 13, 1998, at Madison Square Garden in New York City with the Rev. Sun Myung Moon and several world religious leaders presiding. Six hundred and twenty-three unwed youths from Taiwan participated in this event.

Social Services

Various international Christian organizations have established branches in Taiwan. Working with local groups that have sprung up, these organizations provide a network of welfare and social services to various target groups in society. World Vision of Taiwan has been instrumental in providing aboriginal and child welfare; Campus Crusade and Navigators are active on college campuses; the Garden of Hope Foundation 勵馨基金會 runs halfway houses for teenage prostitutes; Mackay Counseling Center 馬偕協談中心 offers family and psychological counseling services; and Cathwel Service 財團法人天主教未婚媽媽之家 and Christian Salvation Service provide assistance for unwed mothers.

With the increasing number of foreign workers in Taiwan, there have been occasional disputes with their local employers. As there were 88,773 Filipinos and 10,519 Vietnamese working in Taiwan by July 2001, eight temporary shelters have been set up by church groups to accommodate and assist them in emergency situations. The Catholic Church has set up one shelter in Taoyuan, Chungli, Hsinchu, Taichung, and Taipei City each, as well as one in Miaoli County. The Council of Labor Affairs intended to subsidize their expenses, but it is constrained by a limited budget. Two shelters were also set up in Kaohsiung City to serve 6,105 Filipinos and 480 Vietnamese workers in the area, and one of them currently receives a subsidy from the Kaohsiung City government.

Christian missions, along with their evangelical intent, have contributed to Taiwan's education and social work as well. As of 2000, the Roman Catholic Church operated one seminary, three universities, one junior college, 25 high schools, 10 elementary schools, 202 kindergartens, four orphanages, 14 retirement homes, six rehabilitation centers, 26 centers for the

465

mentally retarded, six handicapped welfare institutions, one institute for spreading church teachings, 11 hospitals, 11 clinics, and nine publishing houses.

Protestants are involved with 29 seminaries, six universities, one junior college, eight high schools, one elementary school, 46 kindergartens, four nurseries, seven orphanages, three retirement homes, three rehabilitation centers, four centers for the mentally retarded, six handicapped welfare institutes, one institute for evangelizing, 14 hospitals, 15 clinics, four libraries, and 78 publishing houses producing 52 publications.

Islam

Chinese Muslim History

The spread of Islam among the Chinese is one of many examples that follow the Islamic teaching "no compulsion in religion." (Qur'an 2:256) The first Muslim envoys to China were officially recorded in A.D. 651, proving that the Chinese royalty of the Tang dynasty (618-907) was introduced and invited to Islam more than 1,000 years ago. The messengers were well received and the Chingchiao Mosque 清教寺 was built in the capital city Changan as a gesture of goodwill.

Between A.D. 651 and 798, a total of 39 Muslim delegations visited China. However, it was the constant flow of merchants who came eastward from the Islamic world through the Silk Road and Spice Road, married local Chinese, and eventually formed a new ethnic group —Hui 回族, that truly carried out the mission of spreading the Islamic teachings. According to an official chronicle, around 4,000 Muslims had been living in Changan for more than 40 years by A.D. 787.

Quanzhou, now named Jinjiang, a coastal city in the southeastern Fujian Province, was one of the four ports open to foreign merchants in the Tang dynasty. Mosques built in Guangzhou, Quanzhou, and Hangzhou (all coastal cities) can be traced back to as early as the eighth century. Around 1350, a Ting Muslim clan 丁氏 migrated to Chendai 陳埭 to escape ethnic violence. The Ting descendents were almost completely sinicized by 17th century, including the families that came to Taiwan.

In 1376, a Kuo Muslim clan 郭氏 escaped from Quanzhou to the remote Baiqi 百崎 in Huian County near Quanzhou. They maintained their religion for five generations until another social unrest destroyed their mosques and faith. Nevertheless, more than one hundred of the seventh to 10th generations Baiqi Kuo's reverted to Islam. Their offspring joined the troops that Koxinga led to Taiwan in the mid-17th century, among other Muslims and non-Muslims. Some of these soldiers made Taiwan their permanent home, leaving historical traces that are still visible in Lukang, Tamsui, and other places. By the time of Taiwan's retrocession to China in 1945, however, most of the descendants of these Muslims no longer embraced Islam; at best, only a few Islamic burial traditions were still observed.

Muslims in Taiwan

Approximately 20,000 Muslims accompanied the central government to Taiwan in 1949; most were soldiers, civil servants, or food service workers. Two Muslim organizations reestablished themselves in Taiwan: the Chinese Muslim Association (CMA) 中國回教協會 and the Chinese Muslim Youth League 中國回教青年會.

Differences in everyday habits and customs—such as food and drink or religious ceremonies and activities—limited contacts between Muslims and the mainstream Taiwanese during the 1950s. Believers in Islam depended to a large extent on a liaison network that regularly met in a house on Lishui Street 麗水街 in Taipei. By the 1960s, realizing that return to the mainland would not be likely in the immediate future, Muslims in Taiwan began to engage in permanent occupations. Although there was still a considerable degree of interdependence in the community, Muslims began, primarily out of professional need, to have increasingly frequent contact with the mainstream society. In the past five decades, the first generation of these Muslim immigrants to Taiwan has gradually passed away. Many of the second and third generations Muslims married converts. Ethnic background does not pose any obstacle when new converts join the family of Islam.

Taiwan's busy urban lifestyle has been a trial to both converts and hereditary Muslims. Only a few Muslim women have adopted the traditional veil; and a handful of halal butchers and restaurants prepare meat according to the strict Islamic food observances. Attending prayer services every Friday is another test for Muslim employees. In addition, all prayers are conducted in Arabic, which means that every adherent must learn the language despite linguistic constraints.

Since the 1980s, thousands of Muslims from Indochina came to Taiwan in search of a better life. Many of them are descendents of the nationalist soldiers who fled to Myanmar and northern Thailand after the communists took over their homeland—Yunnan Province. Three out of the six mosques in Taiwan are currently lead by imams from this part of the world.

Three Arabian-style mosques, constructed in Kaohsiung, Taichung, and Lungkang, have joined Taipei's two mosques in meeting the needs of Muslim faithful during the 1980s. These three mosques cost a total of US$2.7 million, half of which was funded by overseas donations, predominantly from the Middle East. In addition, a four-story apartment building financed by Muslims in the Tainan and Kaohsiung areas has been built on a piece of donated land in Tainan to serve as a mosque. The Taipei Grand Mosque, on the verge of being demolished several times because of disputes over land deeds, was recognized as a Taipei City religious heritage site in 1999 after being surveyed by academics and scholars. The four-decade old mosque will be protected on its present site.

The CMA has been sending Muslim students overseas to receive formal Islamic education for decades and the Taiwan Muslim community retained weekend classes for their young since World War II. The new generation of the scattered Muslim population are not merely working to preserve their faith and identity, but also actively introducing their religion to the people on Taiwan. For instance, the Association has developed a plan to "educate the secular educators" and obtained approval from the Taipei City Bureau of Education 臺北市教育局 to hold introductory courses for primary and secondary school teachers during summer vacations. Providing authentic Islamic information to public school teachers is intended to eliminate stereotyping and misunderstanding.

Like all members of the international Muslim community, Muslims in Taiwan must observe their five basic duties, including the pilgrimage to Mecca. On February 17, 2001, a total of 24 Muslims from Taiwan began their religious journey and returned on March 12. As the number of Muslims traveling to and through Taiwan increased, the Kaohsiung International Airport administration has accepted the CMA's suggestion and set up a prayer room for Muslims in its terminal in July 2001, and the CKS International Airport followed suit in August.

As of 2000, Taiwan was home to approximately 54,000 Muslims. It also had 34 mullahs, six mosques, five libraries, and one publishing house with six publications. Nearly 88,500 Indonesian and 90 Malaysian workers also resided in Taiwan by July 2001 and many of them participated in the activities of the local congregation. The mosques liaise with the local authorities on behalf of these Muslims in emergency situations to provide timely assistance.

Other Independent Religions

There are several other independent religions in Taiwan that generally fall into one of the following four categories: religions brought to Taiwan from the Chinese mainland; religions brought in from foreign countries; new religions developed from existing ones; and new religions created in Taiwan.

Religions from the Chinese Mainland

Included in the first category are Chai Chiao 齋教, Hsia Chiao 夏教 (neither is recognized by the ROC government as a religion), Li-ism, and Tien Te Chiao. Chai Chiao entered Taiwan during the 17th century, and is divided into three major schools: Lung Hua 龍華, Chin Chuang 金幢, and Hsien Tien 先天 (a forerunner to I-kuan Tao). It is a modified form of Buddhism combined with elements of Confucianism, Taoism, and folk beliefs. Chai Chiao adherents worship Buddha and the goddess Kuanyin. As vegetarians who neither shave their heads nor don the monk's robes, they worship in the home, thus giving Chai Chiao the common title "Lay Buddhism." During the Japanese occupation of Taiwan, the group joined the Soto sect of Buddhism to escape Japanese suppression, and the religion greatly declined as a result.

Hsia Chiao was founded by Lin Chao-en 林兆恩 in the 16th century, and was brought to Taiwan during the Japanese occupation. When praying, adherents burn four incense sticks—instead of the usual folk practice of burning three—to venerate Confucius, Lao Tzu, the Buddha, and the founder of the religion.

Li-ism (Doctrine of Order) was founded by Yang Lai-ju 楊來如 in the 17th century. Its creed stresses traditional Chinese morals and ethics, such as the loyalty and filial piety of Confucianism, the world salvation and forgiveness of Buddhism, and the natural way and inaction of Taoism. It is, in fact, the synthesis of Confucianism, Buddhism, and Taoism given a new dimension by the worship of Kuanyin. Though Li-ists worship Kuanyin, they do not reject deities of other religions. They believe the providence may be revealed in the form of other deities and prophets. Li-ists abide by the great law of Li-ism called *Fapao Tiehwen* 法寶牒文 (The Precious and Official Decrees), written by Yang.

Some Li-ist clergy came to Taiwan from the Chinese mainland in 1949. The Association of Li-ism 中華理教總會 was officially reestablished in Taiwan in 1950, with headquarters in Taipei. Today, Li-ism has spread to Korea, the United States, Hong Kong, Japan, and the Philippines. In 1952, Sheng-li College 聖理書院 was established for Li-ists to study the classics. Today, there are 638 Li-ist clergy in 131 temples islandwide serving about 187,000 adherents. There are also five Li-ist seminaries, three kindergartens, 15 institutes for Li-ist proselytizing, six clinics and one publishing house. Adherents enthusiastically provide relief, free medicine, and scholarships to the needy.

Tien Te Chiao was founded in 1923 in China by a young shaman, Hsiao Chang-ming 蕭昌明, now known to his followers as the "celestial worthy." Tien Te Chiao is a synthesis of the two major religio-philosophical traditions of China, Confucianism and Taoism, and three world religions—Buddhism, Christianity, and Islam. Adherents are required to strictly follow 20 principles: loyalty, forbearance, honesty, openness, virtue, uprightness, righteousness, faith, endurance, fairness, universal love, filial piety, benevolence, kindness, consciousness, moral integrity, frugality, truth, courtesy, and harmony. Tien Te Chiao adherents also practice various methods of self-cultivation, health preservation, and psychic healing. They are trained to tap acupuncture points to cure ailments. Believers learn to meditate under the guidance of their masters in order to search for their original being, which is free and untainted from worldly ties and yearnings.

Since Tien Te Chiao was introduced into Taiwan in 1953, worship and medical service centers have been set up throughout Taiwan. Tien Te Chiao was officially recognized by the government in 1989. By 2000, there were five Tien Te Chiao temples and 31 masters for its 200,000 believers in Taiwan. Members must be at least 20 years of age. There are also 23 institutes for Tien Te Chiao proselytizing, two Tien Te Chiao libraries, one publishing house, and four publications.

Religions from Abroad

This category of comparatively less believers in Taiwan includes foreign religious groups such as Baha'i, Judaism, Tenrikyo, and Mahikarikyo.

The first Taiwan convert to the Baha'i faith was an overseas student in the United States in 1949. An Iranian husband-wife team came from mainland China in 1954 to do pioneer work and established Taiwan's first Baha'i center in Tainan. There are currently seven Baha'i places of worship, one foreign missionaries, one institute for Baha'i theology, one publishing house, and eight publications to help serve the 16,000 Baha'i faithful in Taiwan. The local Baha'i headquarter, the National Spiritual Assembly of the Baha'is of Taiwan 財團法人巴哈伊教台灣總靈體會, is located in Taipei.

Baha'i communities all over the world target urgent social issues in each region. In Taiwan, the local Baha'i assemblies have singled out environmental protection as their main area of social concern. Since 1990, the Baha'i community has launched joint projects with government organizations to promote environmental education amongst kindergarten and elementary school teachers around the country. Baha'i teams visit schools all over Taiwan, organizing simulation games designed to teach basic environmental principles. The Baha'i community has produced 30-odd radio programs and a videotape on environmental issues, as well as published a book on environmental education in collaboration with the Homemakers's Union and Foundation 主婦聯盟環保基金會.

Jews from Persia and other areas began to settle in China about 1,000 years ago during the Tang dynasty. Thriving communities developed in many large cities, but particularly in Kaifeng, which became the center of Chinese Jewish life. Due to gradual assimilation, however, these communities had virtually disappeared by the middle of the 19th century. During the 20th century, China again received an influx of Jews, this time refugees from persecution in Europe—first from Russia, and later from eastern European countries taken over by the Nazis. The largest groups of Jews settled in Harbin in Manchuria and in Shanghai; however, after World War II, most of this population moved to the West due to the communist threat in China.

Taiwan's small Jewish community consists of expatriates (mainly Americans, but also Israelis and Europeans) who are either long-term residents or assigned to Taiwan on tours of duty by multinational corporations, academic institutions, or international organizations. The community is affiliated with the Asia-Pacific Jewish Association based in Australia. Activities include religious observances, religious instruction for children, holiday celebrations, and cultural events. Most activities are held in a community center maintained in the Tienmu district of Taipei.

Tenrikyo was founded in Japan in 1838 by a farm woman, Miki Nakayama. The religion was first introduced into Taiwan during the period of Japanese occupation. The doctrine of Tenrikyo stresses respect for ancestors, filial piety, self-cultivation, and service to mankind, and thus resembles traditional Chinese ethics and the concept of universal brotherhood. The religion was therefore readily accepted in Taiwan, continued to develop, and was formally recognized by the MOI in 1973. As of 2000, there were 150 Tenrikyo temples and 32 foreign clergymen serving 24,000 believers in Taiwan.

Mahikarikyo was founded in 1959 by Yosikazu Okata, a former Japanese army officer. It was registered with the MOI on April 8, 1996, under the title of Foundation Corporation Taiwan General Meeting of Funds for Mahikari Organization 財團法人真光教團台灣總會基金會. Supervised by the above organization, as of 2000, Mahikarikyo had ten clergymen and seven foreign clergymen, nine temples for worship, and 1,000 believers in Taiwan. Mahikarikyo advocates respect for nature, love among human beings, and spiritual purification through religious teachings.

New Extensions

A large number of new religions in Taiwan were developed on the basis of previously existing ones. The main representative of this group is the Lord of Universe Church, which was founded by Lee Yu-chieh 李玉階 in the mid-1980s after he split with Tien Te Chiao. The

doctrines of this new religion emphasize the cultivation of one's moral self, and it has "20 True Words" 二十字真言 that serve as "required daily homework" for its followers. Believers are especially concerned about nuclear war. Since its founding, the Lord of the Universe Church has established 47 temples with 127 clergymen. These temples are concentrated mainly in Taipei, Taichung, Tainan, Pingtung and Hualien. It currently claims a following of 213,000 believers in Taiwan. The religious group has one foreign clergy, two seminaries, one university, one library, two publishing houses, and 44 institutes for proselytizing.

Religions Founded in Taiwan

Few religions fall into the fourth category of new religions founded in Taiwan. A typical example is Hsuan-yuan Chiao, which was formally founded in Taiwan in 1957 by 82-year-old legislator Wang Han-sheng 王寒生. Hsuan-yuan Chiao attempts to raise people's sense of nationalism and to organize and unite the religious thoughts of China over the ages, including Confucianism, Taoism, and Mohism 墨家. Its main creed is respect for heaven and ancestors. Hsuan-yuan Chiao is named after the ancient legendary founder of the Chinese nation.

The religion was inspired by Wang's grief over the loss of the Chinese mainland to the Chinese communists. Wang attributed the loss primarily to the absence of national spirit, which could only be restored by a renewal of Chinese culture. Adherents abide by the principles set forth in the Hsuan-yuan Chiao scriptures, the *Huang Ti Ching* 黃帝經.

Hsuan-yuan Chiao affirms the existence of a creator who can be identified as the "Tao" or Way. Hsuan-yuan Chiao holds that man can become divine through self-cultivation and enlightenment in the Tao. The highest state attainable in the new religion is "the union of heaven and man" where "the self is denied and yet is omnipresent." This progress can only be accomplished through self-purification, cultivation of illustrious virtues, and helping others to achieve salvation. As of 2000, Hsuan-yuan Chiao had 21 temples and 150 clergy serving 150,000 believers, one seminary, 21 institutes for proselytizing, and one publishing house with one publication.

Further Reading

(in Chinese unless otherwise noted):

Chen Pao-liang 陳寶良. *Shang-ti te shih-tu: ming mo ching chu te ye-su hui-shih* 上帝的使徒:明末清初的耶穌會士 (God's Missionaries: The Jesuits of the Late Ming and Early Ching Dynasties). Taipei: Wanjuan 萬卷樓, 2001.

Cheng Chih-ming 鄭志明. *Tai-wan te tsung-chiao yu mi-mi chiao-pai* 台灣的宗教與祕密教派 (Religions and Clandestine Religious Sects of Taiwan). Taipei: Tai-yuan Publishing Co., 1990.

—*Liang-an tsung-chiao chiao-liu chih hsien-kuang yu chan-wang* 兩岸宗教交流之現況與展望 (The Current Situation and Future Prospects of Cross-Strait Religious Exchanges). Religious and Cultural Research Center Series. Chiayi: Religious and Cultural Research Center of Nanhua Management College, 1997.

—*Tai-wan hsin-hsing tsung-chiao hsien-hsiang: chuan-tung hsin-yang pian* 台灣新興宗教現象:傳統信仰篇 (Taiwan's New Religious Phenomena: The Traditional Religions). Chiayi: Nanhua University Press, 1999.

Chiang I-cheng 姜義鎮, comp. *Tai-wan te min-chien hsin-yang* 台灣的民間信仰 (Folk Beliefs of Taiwan). 3rd ed. Taipei: Woolin Publishing Co., Ltd., 1990.

Chien-lung Chu-shih 潛龍居士. *Chung-kuo min-chien chu-shen chuan* 中國民間諸神傳 (Stories of the Chinese Folk Gods). Taipei: Chuan Yuan Publishing Co., 1992.

Chu Hai-yuan 瞿海源. *Tai-wan ti-chu min-chung te tsung-chiao hsin-yang yu tsung-chiao tai-tu* 台灣地區民眾的宗教信仰與宗教態度 (Religious Beliefs and Religious Attitudes of People in the Taiwan Area). Taipei: Institute of Ethnology, Academia Sinica, 1987.

—*Pien-chien-chung te tai-wan she-hui* 變遷中的台灣社會 (Taiwan Society in Transition) ed. by Yang Kuo-shu 楊國樞 and Chu Hai-yuan. Taipei: Institute of Ethnology, Academia Sinica, 1987.

Chuang Chia-ching 莊嘉慶. *Tsung-chiao chiao-tan te chi-chu* 宗教交談的基礎 (The Foundation of Religious Dialogue). Religion and Peace Series 宗教與和平叢書. Taipei: Yako 雅歌, 1997.

Fang Li-tien 方立天. *Chung-kuo fo-chiao yu chuan-tung wen-hua* 中國佛教與傳統文化 (Chinese Buddhism and Traditional Culture). Taipei: Laureate Book Co., Ltd., 1990.

Fu Tung-hsien 傅統先. *Chung-kuo hui-chiao chih* 中國回教史 (Chinese Islamic History). 2nd ed. Taipei: Taiwan Business Publishing Co., Ltd., 1996.

Heirakawa, Akira 平川彰 (Hsu Ming-yin 許明銀, tr.). *Fo-chiao yen-chiu ju-men* 佛教研究入門 (An Introduction to the Study of Buddhism). Taipei: Dharma-tatha, 1990.

Ho Shih-chung 何世忠, Hsieh Chin-yan 謝進炎. *Ma-tzu hsin-yang*

yu shen-chi 媽祖信仰與神蹟 (Matzu: Beliefs and Miracles). The Religious Belief Series 宗教信仰叢書. Tainan: Shihfeng 世峰, 2000.

I-kuan Tao chien-chieh 一貫道簡介 (Introduction to I-kuan Tao). Tainan: Tien Jiuh Book Store, 1988.

Kung Peng-cheng 龔鵬程. *Tao-chiao hsin lun* 道教新論 (New Commentaries on Taoism). Religious Series 宗教叢書. Chiayi: Nanhua Management College, 1998.

Nan Huai-chin 南懷瑾. *Tao-chiao mi-tsung yu tung-fang shen-mi-hsueh* 道教密宗與東方神祕學 (Tantric Religions of Taoism and Oriental Mysticism). Vols. I & II, 7th ed. Taipei: Lao Ku Cultural Foundation Inc., 1990.

Tsung-chiao chien-chieh 宗教簡介 (Introduction to Religion). Taipei: Ministry of the Interior, 2000.

Yang Sen-fu 楊森富. *Chung-kuo chi-tu-chiao shih* 中國基督教史 (The History of Chinese Christianity). Taipei: The Commercial Press Ltd., 1991.

Yao Li-hsiang 姚麗香. *Tai-wan te tzu-szu yu tsung-chiao* 台灣的祠祀與宗教 (Worship and Religion in Taiwan). 2nd ed. Taipei: Taiwan Publishing Co., 1990.

中國輸出入銀行

The Export-Import Bank
of the Republic of China
A SPECIALIZED BANK
THAT OFFERS

Medium-And Long-Term Loan For Purchase of Machinery, Equipment And Turnkey Plants From The ROC

Our low-interest loans with repayment periods of up to seven years make it easy for overseas buyers to procure machinery, equipment and turnkey plants from the ROC.

Head Office	8th Fl., 3 Nan Hai Road. Taipei, Taiwan, R.O.C. Tel: (02)2321-0511　　Fax: (02)2394-0630　　Tlx: (02)26044
Kaohsiung Branch	8th Fl., 74, Chung Cheng 2nd Road, Kaohsiung, R.O.C. Tel: (07)224-1921　　Fax: (07)224-1928
Taichung Branch	5th Fl., 1-18, Sec. 2, Tai Chung Kan Road, Taichung, R.O.C. Tel: (04)2322-5756　　Fax: (04)2322-5755
Taipei Branch	2F-2A15, 5 Hsinyi Rd., Sec. 5, Taipei, R.O.C. Tel: (02)8780-0181　　Fax: (02)2723-5131
Representative Office in Jakarta	Wisma Dharmala Sakti 11th Fl., Ji Jendral Sudirman No. 32 Jarkarta Indonesia Tel: 6621-5704320, 6621-5701136　　Fax: 6621-5704321
Representative Office in Warsaw	Neptune Building ul. Domaniewska 41 02-672 Warszawa, Poland Tel: (48-22)874-3582　　Fax: (48-22)874-3583
Representative Office in Sao Paulo	Alameda Santos, 234, 6 andar, CEP 01418-000 Sao Paulo-SP Brazil Tel: (5511)283-3392, 288-4550　　Fax: (5511)3253-4802

Appendices

 Treasuring the earth's resources is the common
responsibility of all inhabitants of the global village.

ROC Chronology: January 1911—December 2001

(The following chronology details the major events in the Republic of China from its founding, through the relocation of the central government to Taiwan, to the ROC on Taiwan today. The first half of the chronology deals with events on the Chinese mainland, and the latter half is devoted to Taiwan.)

1911
Oct. 10 — A revolt against the Manchu (Ching) dynasty erupts in Wuchang and is followed by revolutionary activities throughout China.

1912
Jan.   1 — The Republic of China is founded, with Dr. Sun Yat-sen as the first provisional president.

    28 — A provisional senate is established in Nanjing.

Feb. 12 — Henry Pu Yi abdicates as emperor, ending the rule of the Manchu dynasty.

    13 — Dr. Sun tenders his resignation to the provisional senate.

    15 — Yuan Shih-kai is elected provisional president by the provisional senate.

Mar. 11 — A provisional constitution is promulgated.

Apr.   2 — The provisional senate resolves to move the seat of the government to Peking (Beijing).

Aug. 25 — The Tung-meng Hui (Revolutionary Alliance) is reorganized as the Kuomintang (Nationalist Party).

1913
Apr.   6 — The provisional senate is dissolved.

    8 — The Republic's first congress is organized.

May   2 — The United States recognizes the Republic of China.

July 12 — Li Lieh-chun of the Kuomintang starts the second revolution against Yuan's dictatorial rule.

Oct.   6 — Yuan forces the congress to elect him president.

    10 — Yuan formally assumes the presidency.

1914
May   1 — Yuan annuls the provisional constitution.

June 23 — The Kuomintang is reorganized as the Chung-hua Ke-ming Tang (Chinese Revolutionary Party) in Tokyo. Dr. Sun is elected director-general.

Aug.   6 — Yuan declares China's neutrality in World War I.

1915
Jan. 18 — Japan presents the notorious 21 Demands to the Peking government.

May   15 — Yuan signs the "*Sino-Japanese Agreement*" (the 21 Demands).

Dec. 12 — Yuan proclaims himself emperor.

    25 — Tsai O, Tang Chi-yao, and Li Lieh-chun revolt against Yuan in Yunnan Province.

1916
June   6 — Yuan dies, and the republican form of government is restored.

    7 — Li Yuan-hung becomes president of the Peking government.

1917
July 12 — An attempted coup d'état by Chang Hsun to restore the Manchu dynasty fails.

Aug. 14 — The Peking government declares war on Germany and Austro-Hungary.

    25 — Dr. Sun forms a military government in Canton.

Sept. 1 — The congress elects Dr. Sun Yat-sen as grand marshal of the Army and Navy of the Chinese Military Government.

1918
Sept. 4 — The "Militarists' Parliament" in the north elects Hsu Shih-chang president.

Nov. 23 — The Ministry of Education adopts the National Phonetic Symbols.

1919
Apr. 30 — The Paris Peace Conference allows Japan to take over Germany's prewar rights in Shandong Province.

May   4 — More than 3,000 students demonstrate in Peking against the Paris Peace Conference decision.

June   28 — China refuses to sign the *Versailles Treaty* on grounds that German rights in Shantung were given to Japan.

Oct.   10 — The Chung-hua Ke-ming Tang (Chinese Revolutionary Party) is reorganized as the Chung-kuo Kuo-min Tang (abbreviated as Kuomintang, or Nationalist Party).

1920
June   29 — China joins the League of Nations.

1921
May   5 — Dr. Sun Yat-sen assumes the presidency of the newly formed southern government in Canton.

1922
Feb.   4 — China signs an agreement with Japan in Washington to settle the Shandong dispute.
June   2 — Hsu Shih-chang resigns as president of the Peking government.
      11 — Li Yuan-hung resumes the presidency in Peking.
      16 — Chen Chiung-ming revolts against Dr. Sun.
Aug.   15 — Dr. Sun issues a manifesto urging the unification of China by peaceful means.

1923
Jan.   26 — Dr. Sun and Adolf Joffe, representative of the Soviet Communist Party, issue a joint statement declaring that neither the communist social order nor the Soviet system is suitable for China.

1924
Jan.   20 — The first National Congress of the Kuomintang in Canton adopts a policy of cooperation with the Soviet Union and the Chinese Communist Party.
May   3 — Chiang Kai-shek is appointed superintendent of the Whampoa Military Academy.
Nov.   10 — Dr. Sun, in a manifesto, calls for the early convocation of a national people's convention and the abolition of unequal treaties.
      24 — Tuan Chi-jui becomes provisional chief executive in Peking.

1925
Mar.   12 — Dr. Sun dies in Peking at the age of 59.
July   1 — The national government is established in Canton.
Nov.   3 — The Kuomintang proposes disciplinary measures to restrict communist activities.

1926
Apr.   9 — Tuan Chi-jui resigns as provisional chief executive.
June   5 — Chiang Kai-shek becomes commander-in-chief of the National Revolutionary Forces.
      27 — Chiang Kai-shek launches the Northern Expedition from Canton.

1927
Apr.   12 — The Kuomintang starts a "purification" movement by expelling communist members.
      18 — The national government is established in Nanjing by the Kuomintang.
Aug.   1 — The Chinese communists stage the Nanchang Uprising against the national government.
      13 — Commander-in-chief of the National Revolutionary Forces, Chiang Kai-shek, resigns in order to unify the Nanjing and Hankou factions of the Kuomintang.

1928
May   3 — Japanese troops attack the Northern Expeditionary Forces in Jinan, touching off the May 3 (Jinan) Incident.
June   4 — Chang Tso-lin is killed on a train by a bomb explosion. His son, Chang Hsueh-liang, succeeds him as ruler of Manchuria.
      29 — Peking is renamed Peiping.
Oct.   8 — Chiang Kai-shek is elected chairman of the national government of the Republic of China.

Dec.   5 — The Legislative Yuan is formally established.

       29 — Chang Hsueh-liang pledges allegiance to the national government, which leads to the unification of China.

1929

May   20 — Japanese troops withdraw from Jinan.

July   23 — The national government severs diplomatic relations with the Soviet Union.

Dec.   30 — The Ministry of Foreign Affairs proclaims the nullification of consular jurisdiction in China to rid China of foreign privileges.

1930

Jan.   6 — The Examination Yuan is formally established.

July   13 — Rebels set up a government in Peking under the leadership of Wang Ching-wei.

1931

Feb.   16 — The Control Yuan is formally established.

May   5 — The National People's Convention is held in Nanjing under the chairmanship of Chiang Kai-shek.

June   1 — The Provisional Constitution for the Period of Political Tutelage is promulgated.

July   4 — Korean immigrants occupy Wanpaoshan in Jilin Province at the instigation of Japanese militarists.

Sept. 18 — Japanese troops occupy Shenyang (Mukden) in a surprise attack. Important cities in Liaoning and Jilin Provinces fall to the Japanese.

Oct.   24 — The Council of the League of Nations adopts a resolution urging Japan to withdraw its troops from Northeast China by November 16.

       26 — Japan turns down the League's resolution.

       27 — Nanjing and Canton representatives meet in Shanghai for peace negotiations.

Dec.   15 — Chiang Kai-shek retires in the interest of party unity.

       28 — The national government is reorganized, with Lin Sen as chairman.

1932

Jan.   3 — The Chinese communists set up a Soviet regime in Ganxian, Jiangxi.

        8 — US Secretary of State Henry Stimson declares that the United States will not recognize any treaty that violates the Open Door Policy.

       28 — Japanese naval forces attack Shanghai. The 19th Army Corps puts up stiff resistance.

Feb.   6 — The National Military Council is established.

       19 — The United States refuses to recognize Japanese puppet state of "Manchukuo" (State of Manchuria).

Mar.   14 — The League of Nations' Lytton Commission arrives in China to investigate the Shenyang (Mukden) Incident.

       18 — Chiang Kai-shek becomes chairman of the National Military Council.

May   5 — China and Japan sign an armistice in Shanghai.

June   28 — Chiang Kai-shek arrives in Hankou from Lushan to direct the campaign against the Chinese communists.

Dec.   12 — China resumes diplomatic relations with the Soviet Union.

1933

Feb.   14 — The League of Nations refuses to recognize "Manchukuo."

Apr.   18 — Fighting spreads in North China. Several strategic passes along the Great Wall fall to the Japanese.

May   31 — The *Sino-Japanese Tangku Armistice Agreement* is signed, ending hostilities in North China.

Nov.   20 — Leaders of the 19th Army Corps form a "people's government" in Fujian.

1934

Feb.   19 — Chiang Kai-shek launches the "New Life Movement" in Nanchang.

Mar.   1 — Henry Pu Yi is enthroned as "Emperor of Manchukuo" in Changchun by the Japanese militarists.

Oct.   10 — The main forces of the Chinese communist troops flee their bases in Jiangxi to the northwest, launching the "Long March."

21 — Government troops capture Juichin, the communist capital in Jiangxi.

1935
Oct.   2 — Chiang Kai-shek is appointed commander-in-chief of the Northwestern Communist Suppression Army and Chang Hsueh-liang, deputy commander-in-chief, with headquarters in Xian.

Nov.   4 — The national government proclaims the nationalization of all silver, making notes issued by the Central Bank of China and the Bank of Communications legal tender.

1936
May   5 — The government promulgates the May 5 Draft Constitution.

Dec.   12 — Chang Hsueh-liang's troops mutiny in Xian and hold Chiang Kai-shek and other ranking government officials hostage.

22 — Mme. Chiang, accompanied by W.H. Donald and T.V. Soong (Sung Tzu-wen), fly to Xian.

25 — Chang Hsueh-liang accompanies Generalissimo Chiang Kai-shek and Mme. Chiang to Loyang, en route to Nanjing.

1937
July   7 — Japanese troops near Lugouqiao (Marco Polo Bridge), southwest of Peking, attack Wanping city at night, formally starting the war between China and Japan.

17 — Chiang Kai-shek lays down four conditions for settlement of the Lugouqiao Incident.

Aug.   21 — China and the Soviet Union sign a non-aggression treaty in Nanjing.

Sept. 28 — The League of Nations adopts a resolution denouncing Japan's aggression in China.

Oct.   6 — The US State Department condemns Japan's invasion of China.

7 — The League of Nations adopts a resolution pledging moral support for China.

30 — The national government decides to move the capital from Nanjing to Chongqing.

Nov.   3 — China presents her case at The Nine-Power Conference in Brussels.

Dec.   13 — Japanese troops occupy Nanjing. During the following two months, the aggressors rape and kill some 300,000 defenseless Chinese.

1938
Mar.   28 — The Ministry of Foreign Affairs issues a statement denouncing the "Reform Government of China," a puppet regime set up by the Japanese in Nanjing.

Apr.   1 — The Emergency National Congress of the Kuomintang in Wuchang elects Chiang Kai-shek as its director-general and decides to organize a People's Political Council and a San-min-chu-i Youth Corps.

July   6 — The first session of the People's Political Council opens in Hankou and adopts a program of armed resistance and national reconstruction.

7 — Chinese troops win a victory in Taierzhuang.

9 — The San-min-chu-i Youth Corps is established with Chiang Kai-shek as head.

Oct.   25 — Chinese troops evacuate Wuchang and Hankou.

Dec.   22 — The Japanese prime minister, Prince Konoye, lays down three points as guiding principles for the settlement of the Sino-Japanese conflict and the establishment of the "New Order in East Asia."

26 — Chiang Kai-shek reiterates China's determination to carry on the war of resistance against Japan and charges that Konoye's statement clearly reveals Japan's intention to conquer China.

1939
Jan.   28 — The fifth plenary session of the Fifth Central Committee of the Kuomintang decides to create a Supreme National Defense Council with Chiang Kai-shek as chairman.

Nov.   20 — Chairman Chiang Kai-shek is appointed to the concurrent post of president of the Executive Yuan.

1940

Mar. 29 — Wang Ching-wei establishes a puppet regime in Nanjing which is recognized by Japan on November 19.

30 — The Ministry of Foreign Affairs declares the Nanjing puppet organization illegal.

Sept. 6 — Chongqing is proclaimed provisional capital of China.

1941

Jan. 4 — The Communist New Fourth Army revolts against the national government.

14 — The revolt of the New Fourth Communist Army is suppressed.

Apr. 14 — Condemning the *Soviet-Japanese Neutrality Pact*, Foreign Minister Wang Chung-hui declares that Outer Mongolia and the northeastern provinces are Chinese territory and that the Soviet-Japanese statement is not binding on China.

17 — US President Roosevelt approves the first military aid program of US$45 million for China.

Sept. 30 — Chinese troops win the second battle of Changsha.

Dec. 9 — China formally declares war on Japan.

1942

Jan. 2 — Chinese Expeditionary Forces enter Burma.

— Generalissimo Chiang assumes office as supreme commander of the China Theater of War.

15 — Chinese troops win the third battle of Changsha.

Mar. 4 — General Joseph Stilwell arrives in Chongqing to assume duties as chief of staff of the China Theater of War and also to take command of all American armed forces in China, Burma, and India.

Apr. 19 — Chinese Expeditionary Forces capture Yenangyuang, rescuing more than 7,000 British and Burmese troops from Japanese encirclement.

June 2 — Foreign Minister T.V. Soong and US Secretary of State Cordell Hull sign the *Sino-American Lend-Lease Agreement* in Washington.

Oct. 10 — The US and UK governments announce their intention to relinquish extraterritoriality and related rights in China.

1943

Jan. 11 — China signs the new *Sino-American Treaty* in Washington and the new *Sino-British Treaty* in Chongqing.

Oct. 10 — Chiang Kai-shek is sworn in as chairman of the national government.

Nov. 23 — Chiang Kai-shek, US President Franklin D. Roosevelt, and UK Prime Minister Winston Churchill confer in Cairo.

Dec. 3 — The Joint Declaration of the Cairo Conference is issued simultaneously in Chongqing, Washington, and London.

1944

June 16 — Chinese Expeditionary Forces capture Kaimaing in northern Burma.

18 — US Vice President Henry Wallace visits China.

25 — Chinese Expeditionary Forces capture Magaung in northern Burma.

Sept. 29 — The Chinese-American-British phase of the Dumbarton Oaks Conference begins.

Oct. 9 — China, the US, the UK, and the USSR promulgate the draft for the *Charter of the United Nations*.

29 — US General Albert C. Wedemeyer is appointed chief of staff of the China Theater of War.

1945

Feb. 4 — The US, the UK, and the USSR hold a conference in Yalta. A secret agreement, among other conclusions, is reached on February 11 by the three that the USSR shall enter the war against Japan on condition that its former rights (in China) plundered by Japan in 1904 shall be restored.

Mar. 5 — China, the US, the UK, and the USSR issue joint invitations to the United Nations Conference in San Francisco on April 25.

June 26 — Representatives of 50 nations, including China, sign the UN Charter in San Francisco.

July 26 — Chiang Kai-shek, US President Truman, and UK Prime Minister Churchill issue a joint ultimatum, calling for Japan's unconditional surrender.

Aug. 9 — Soviet troops enter Manchuria.

11 — The Chinese communist headquarters in Yenan order communist troops to launch an all-out revolt against the government.

14 — Japan surrenders.

— The *Sino-Soviet Treaty of Friendship and Alliance* is signed in Moscow.

— Chiang Kai-shek invites Mao Tse-tung to come to Chongqing for a conference.

15 — The Legislative Yuan unanimously approves the *Charter of the United Nations*.

23 — Soviet troops occupy Manchuria.

Sept. 2 — Japan's surrender is signed on the USS Missouri, with General Hsu Yung-chang signing for China.

9 — General Ho Ying-chin receives the formal surrender of Japanese forces in China from General Okamura in Nanjing.

Oct. 25 — Taiwan is formally retroceded to China after 50 years of Japanese occupation.

Dec. 20 — Soviet troops move an estimated US$2 billion worth of machinery from Manchuria to the Soviet Union.

22 — General George C. Marshall arrives in Chongqing as US President Truman's special envoy.

28 — The Big Three Foreign Ministers' Conference in Moscow announces agreements on a commission and allied council for Japan, the ultimate establishment of a free Korea, and the withdrawal of Soviet and US troops from China.

1946

Jan. 7 — Government and communist representatives hold their first truce meeting with General Marshall as mediator.

10 — The government issues a cease-fire order.

— The Political Consultative Conference opens.

13 — The UN Security Council is created, with China as one of the five permanent members.

Feb. 11 — US Secretary of State James Byrnes makes public the *Yalta Secret Agreement*.

20 — The Ministry of Foreign Affairs declares the *Yalta Secret Agreement* not binding on China.

22 — More than 20,000 students demonstrate against the *Yalta Secret Agreement* and call for the Soviet Union to withdraw its forces from China.

Mar. 5 — The Ministry of Foreign Affairs announces that China has rejected the Soviet claim to all Japanese military enterprises in Manchuria.

13 — Government forces enter Mukden following the evacuation of Soviet troops.

Apr. 17 — Communist troops enter Changchun.

26 — Communist troops take over Harbin and Qiqihar as the Soviet forces evacuate.

May 5 — The national government moves back to Nanjing.

23 — Government troops recapture Changchun.

June 6 — Chiang Kai-shek accepts General Marshall's proposal to issue a second cease-fire order during the 15-day armistice.

July 3 — The Supreme National Defense Council votes to convene the National Assembly on November 12, 1946.

Aug. 17 — Yenan issues a second mobilization order instructing all communist forces to launch full-scale war against the government.

Sept. 3 — Chiang Kai-shek agrees to create a committee of five headed by US Ambassador J. Leighton Stuart to pave the way for a coalition government.

Oct. 16 — Chiang Kai-shek presents the communists with eight conditions for a nationwide cease-fire.

18 — The communists reject the government's latest peace offer.

Nov. 4 — China and the United States sign a five-year *Treaty of Friendship, Commerce, and Navigation*.

8 — Chiang Kai-shek issues a third cease-fire.

15 — The National Assembly officially opens. Chiang Kai-shek announces termination of Kuomintang tutelage.

Dec. 25 — The National Assembly completes drafting the new Constitution.

1947

Jan. 1 — The government promulgates the Constitution.

29 — The US State Department announces abandonment of efforts to mediate between the national government and the communists.

Feb. 28 — Rioting breaks out in Taipei, following an incident between police and a peddler who violated the tobacco monopoly.

Mar. 19 — Government troops capture Yenan.

May 26 — The third plenary session of the Fourth People's Political Council adopts a resolution to invite communist members to attend.

June 25 — The Ministry of Foreign Affairs reveals repeated Soviet Union attempts to block Chinese troops from entering Dairen and Port Arthur.

July 22 — General Albert C. Wedemeyer, US President Truman's special representative, arrives in Nanjing.

Nov. 21 — The first general elections in China are held.

Dec. 25 — The government adopts the Constitution.

1948

Mar. 29 — China's first National Assembly under the Constitution opens with 1,629 delegates attending.

Apr. 18 — The first National Assembly approves, by a two-thirds majority, temporary provisions granting emergency powers to the president during the period of the anti-communist campaign.

19 — The first National Assembly elects Chiang Kai-shek as China's first president under the new Constitution by 2,430 out of 2,704 votes.

21 — Government troops evacuate Yenan.

May 20 — President Chiang Kai-shek and Vice President Li Tsung-jen are sworn in.

1949

Jan. 5 — General Chen Cheng is sworn in as governor of Taiwan.

15 — Tianjin falls.

21 — President Chiang announces his retirement from the presidency. Vice President Li Tsung-jen is empowered to exercise presidential powers temporarily.

Apr. 5 — The national government begins talks with the Chinese communists.

12 — The Farm Rental Reduction Program goes into effect in Taiwan.

21 — The communists resume their all-out offensive and cross the Yangtze River.

23 — Government forces evacuate Nanjing.

May 15 — Government forces evacuate Hankou and Wuchang.

27 — Shanghai is evacuated.

June 15 — Taiwan adopts a new currency.

July 10 — At the invitation of Philippine President Elpidio Quirino, President Chiang flies to Baguio to discuss formation of a Far Eastern anti-communist alliance.

Aug. 6 — At the invitation of Korean President Syngman Rhee, President Chiang flies to Chinhae, Korea, to discuss formation of a Pacific alliance.

15 — The Southeast China Governor's Office is established in Taipei, with General Chen Cheng as governor.

Sept. 27 — China files a complaint with the UN General Assembly against the Soviet Union's aid to the Chinese communists and violation of the *Sino-Soviet Treaty* of 1945 and the *UN Charter*.

Oct. 1 — The communists set up a regime in Peking with Mao Tse-tung as "chairman," which is recognized by the Soviet Union the next day.

3 — The ROC severs diplomatic relations with the USSR.

— The US State Department reaffirms US recognition of the national government as the only legal government of China.

13 — Government troops evacuate Canton.

25 — Government troops win a victory at Kinmen (Quemoy) against a communist attack.

Dec. 7 — The government moves its seat to Taipei.

10 — President Chiang flies from Chengdu to Taipei.

15 — The Executive Yuan names Wu Kuo-chen governor of Taiwan.

1950

Jan. 6 — The Republic of China severs diplomatic relations with Britain following Britain's recognition of the communist regime.

11 — The UN Security Council rejects a Soviet proposal for the immediate expulsion of the ROC delegation.

28 — The Ministry of Foreign Affairs declares that the Republic of China will not be bound by any agreement signed between the Chinese communist regime and the Soviet Union.

Mar. 1 — President Chiang Kai-shek resumes office in Taipei.

7 — President Chiang nominates General Chen Cheng as president of the Executive Yuan (premier).

Apr. 5 — The Executive Yuan grants Taiwan authority to carry out self-government by popular election in counties and cities within two months.

June 27 — US President Truman orders the US Seventh Fleet to prevent a communist attack on Taiwan and asks the ROC government to cease air and sea operations against the mainland.

July 2 — A popular election for a Hualien county council is held, marking the beginning of self-government in Taiwan.

31 — General Douglas MacArthur arrives in Taipei to confer with President Chiang.

Aug. 10 — Karl L. Rankin arrives in Taipei as chargé d'affaires of the US embassy.

16 — Taiwan, formerly consisting of eight counties and nine cities, is redivided into 16 counties and five cities.

Nov. 1 — The Chinese communists announce aid to the Korean communists in the fight against UN forces in Korea.

30 — The UN Security Council orders the Chinese communist forces to leave Korea.

1951

Feb. 1 — The UN General Assembly condemns the Chinese communists as aggressors in Korea.

May 1 — US Major General William C. Chase arrives in Taipei as the first chief of the Military Assistance Advisory Group (MAAG) in Taiwan.

18 — The UN General Assembly approves a global embargo on shipments of arms and war material to the Chinese and North Korean communists.

25 — The Legislative Yuan adopts the *37.5 Percent Farm Rental Reduction Act.*

30 — The government announces plans to sell arable public land to tenant farmers on easy payment terms.

Dec. 11 — The Taiwan Provincial Assembly is established.

1952

Feb. 1 — The UN General Assembly finds the Soviet Union guilty of violation of the 1945 *Sino-Soviet Treaty of Friendship and Alliance.*

Apr. 28 — The *Treaty of Peace between the Republic of China and Japan* is signed in Taipei.

Oct. 22 — The first worldwide Overseas Chinese Conference opens in Taipei.

31 — The China Youth Corps is organized.

1953

Jan. 10 — The Legislative Yuan adopts the *Land-to-the-Tiller Act.*

25 — President Chiang announces abrogation of the *Sino-Soviet Treaty of Friendship and Alliance* of 1945 and its related documents.

Apr. 2 — Karl L. Rankin becomes the American ambassador to the ROC.

12 — The Legislative Yuan passes a bill submitted by President Chiang, extending the term of office for legislators another year, i.e., to May 7, 1954.

July　17 — Guerrillas on Kinmen conduct a successful raid against the communist-held Tungshan Island off the southern coast of Fujian.

Sept.　27 — President Chiang recommends an extension of the term of office of the delegates to the first National Assembly, elected in 1947, until the second National Assembly can be elected.

Nov.　24 — The government protests to the United States against the proposed American transfer of the Amami Oshima Islands to Japan.

　27 — Korean President Syngman Rhee arrives in Taipei.

1954

Jan.　23 — More than 14,000 Chinese communist POW's in Korea, who refused to return to the Chinese mainland, arrive in Taiwan.

Mar.　11 — The second session of the first National Assembly approves indefinite extension of the *Temporary Provisions Effective During the Period of Communist Rebellion.*

　22 — Chiang Kai-shek is reelected president for a second six-year term.

　24 — Chen Cheng is elected vice president.

May　20 — President Chiang nominates O.K. Yu to be president of the Executive Yuan (premier).

June　4 — President Chiang appoints Yen Chia-kan governor of Taiwan.

Dec.　3 — The *Sino-American Mutual Defense Treaty* is signed in Washington.

1955

Jan.　26 — The US House of Representatives approves a resolution authorizing President Eisenhower to employ American armed forces to defend Taiwan, the Pescadores, and "related positions and territories."

Feb.　7 — Government troops begin to evacuate the Tachen Islands.

Mar.　3 — Foreign Minister George K.C. Yeh and US Secretary of State John Foster Dulles exchange instruments of ratification of the *Sino-American Mutual Defense Treaty* in Taipei.

1956

Jan.　12 — The Taiwan Provincial Government promulgates the *Rules for the Enforcement of the Statute on Urban Land Reform.*

May　28 — Foreign Minister George K.C. Yeh informs Philippine Ambassador Narciso Ramos that the ROC has full sovereignty over the Nansha Islands.

July　7 — Ground is broken for the construction of the Central Cross-island Highway.

1957

Apr.　21 — Taiwan voters go to the polls for the third time to elect county magistrates, city mayors, and provincial assemblymen.

May　3 — The Council of Grand Justices of the Judicial Yuan rules that the nation's three top representative organs—the Legislative Yuan, the Control Yuan, and the National Assembly—shall collectively represent the Chinese parliament in all international parliamentary organizations.

Aug.　8 — General Chow Chih-jou is appointed governor of Taiwan, succeeding C.K. Yen.

Sept.　26 — The first council meeting of the Asian Peoples' Anti-Communist League opens in Taipei.

Oct.　20 — President Chiang is reelected Tsungtsai (director-general) of the Kuomintang.

1958

May　14 — Mohammed Reza Pahlevi, the Shah of Iran, arrives in Taipei for a five-day state visit.

Aug.　1 — An insurance program covering 180,000 government employees is put into effect.

　23 — The Battle of the Taiwan Strait begins with the Chinese communists firing on the Kinmen Islands.

Oct.　23 — President Chiang and US Secretary of State John Foster Dulles issue a joint communiqué reaffirming solidarity between the two countries and stating that Quemoy and the Matsu Islands are "closely related" to the defense of Taiwan and the Pescadores under present conditions.

1959

Mar. 6 — The Faith (36,000 tons), the first tanker built in the ROC, is launched at Keelung.

9 — King Hussein of Jordan arrives in Taipei for an eight-day state visit.

July 21 — The Legislative Yuan revises the *Conscription Law*, stipulating that 19-year-old men are to be drafted for two years' service in the army or three years in the navy or air force.

Aug. 15 — The ROC Army receives Nike-Hercules ground-to-air guided missiles from the United States under a military aid program.

Sept. 1 — The *Law on Compensation for Wrongful Detentions and Convictions*, designed to compensate people in cases of miscarriages of justice, goes into effect.

1960

Feb. 2 — The Council of Grand Justices of the Judicial Yuan announces that the total membership of the National Assembly, under the present period of national emergency, shall be 1,576.

23 — The ROC establishes diplomatic relations with Cameroon.

Mar. 11 — The third session of the first National Assembly adopts an amendment to the *Temporary Provisions Effective During the Period of Communist Rebellion*.

19 — The third session of the first National Assembly decides to set up a committee to study the exercise of initiative and referendum by the National Assembly.

22 — Chiang Kai-shek is reelected to a third term as president, and Chen Cheng, to a second term as vice president.

May 2 — Philippine President and Mrs. Carlos Garcia arrive in Taipei for a six-day state visit.

9 — The Central Cross-island Highway is opened to traffic.

June 18 — US President Eisenhower arrives in Taipei for a state visit.

19 — President Chiang and US President Eisenhower issue a joint communiqué pledging that their governments will continue to stand solidly behind the *Sino-US Mutual Defense Treaty* against the Chinese communists in this area.

— The Chinese communists hit Kinmen, and the ROC artillery units retaliated.

Aug. 15 — The Council of Grand Justices of the Judicial Yuan rules that, courts of all levels shall be placed under the jurisdiction of the Judicial Yuan.

— The ROC recognizes the Congo (Brazzaville) Republic.

25 — The ROC Olympic Team in the opening procession of the Olympic Games in Rome protests the International Olympic Committee's ruling compelling ROC athletes to compete under the name of "Taiwan" instead of the "Republic of China."

Sept. 6 — Yang Chuan-kuang, the ROC's decathlon champion, wins the ROC's first Olympic silver medal.

1961

May 14 — US Vice President and Mrs. Lyndon B. Johnson visit the ROC.

Oct. 7 — Two defecting Chinese communist pilots, Shao Hsi-yen and Kao Yu-tsung, arrive in Taipei from South Korea.

27 — The 16th UN General Assembly votes for the admission of Outer Mongolia. The Republic of China abstains.

Dec. 1 — The first nuclear reactor in the ROC, installed by Chinese scientists at the National Tsinghua University campus in Hsinchu, is put into operation.

18 — The ROC establishes diplomatic ties with Upper Volta.

1962

Mar. 14 — Foreign Minister Shen Chang-huan declares that the ROC does not recognize Japan's so-called "residual sovereignty" over the Ryukyu Islands.

Apr. 3 — President and Mme. Philbert Tsiranana of the Malagasy Republic arrive for a six-day state visit.

Oct. 30 — The ROC rejects the McMahon Line as the boundary between China and India.

Nov. 22 — General Huang Chieh is appointed governor of Taiwan, succeeding General Chow Chih-jou.

Dec. 28 — The Ministry of Foreign Affairs declares border agreements signed between the Beijing regime and Outer Mongolia and Pakistan illegal and not binding on the ROC.

1963

June 5 — King Bhumibol Adulyadej and Queen Sirikit of Thailand arrive in the ROC for a state visit.

Aug. 4 — The Ministry of Foreign Affairs declares that the ROC does not recognize the border treaty signed between the Beijing regime and Afghanistan.

23 — Ambassador to the United States Tsiang Ting-fu signs the nuclear test ban treaty on behalf of the ROC.

Sept. 1 — The Council for International Economic Cooperation and Development is inaugurated to replace the Council for US Aid.

Oct. 6 — Dahomey President and Mme. Hubert Maga arrive for a six-day state visit.

Nov. 16 — The new premier, Yen Chia-kan, assumes office.

1964

Feb. 12 — Japanese Premier Shigeru Yoshida arrives in the ROC to confer with President Chiang Kai-shek.

June 14 — The NT$3,200 million multipurpose Shihmen Dam is dedicated.

Oct. 27 — The ROC and Korea sign a treaty of amity in Seoul.

1965

Apr. 9 — The ROC and the United States conclude in Taipei an accord to establish a Sino-American fund for economic and social development in Taiwan.

25 — The ROC and the United States sign in Taipei an inventory of atomic equipment and materials to be reported to the International Atomic Energy Agency.

July 1 — The United States phases out economic aid to the ROC.

31 — The ROC and the United States sign an agreement in Taipei on the status of US forces in China.

Nov. 11 — Malagasy President Tsiranana arrives for a four-day visit.

23 — US warships return to the ROC 102 cases of rare books that were sent to the United States for safekeeping during World War II.

1966

Jan. 1 — US Vice President Hubert H. Humphrey arrives in the ROC to confer with government leaders.

Feb. 15 — Korean President Park Chung Hee arrives for a four-day state visit.

Mar. 21 — The National Assembly elects President Chiang Kai-shek to a fourth term as president of the Republic.

22 — The National Assembly elects Premier Yen Chia-kan the third vice president of the Republic.

26 — The Ministry of Foreign Affairs announces the ROC's opposition to US recognition of Outer Mongolia.

July 3 — US Secretary of State Dean Rusk arrives in Taipei to confer with ROC government leaders.

6 — The Legislative Yuan approves the *Sino-Haitian Treaty of Amity* signed in Port-au-Prince on February 15, 1966.

1967

Feb. 1 — The National Security Council is established by President Chiang Kai-shek with Vice Premier Huang Shao-ku as secretary-general and Ku Shu-tung as his deputy.

Apr. 4 — Australian Prime Minister Harold E. Holt arrives for a three-day visit.

July 1 — Taipei becomes a special municipality, with Kao Yu-shu as its mayor.

28 — The Chinese Cultural Renaissance Movement is officially organized, with President Chiang Kai-shek as its head.

Aug.   3 — The Executive Yuan decides to extend the period of compulsory education from six to nine years beginning in 1968.

       4 — Malawi President Dr. H. Kamuzu Banda arrives for an eight-day state visit.

Sept. 25 — The first conference of the World Anti-Communist League opens in Taipei, with more than 200 leaders from 72 nations and areas attending.

Nov. 24 — The Chinese Economic Development Research Institute is inaugurated in Taipei.

1968

Aug. 24 — Taichung's Golden Dragons baseball team wins the 23rd Little League World Championship.

     25 — Lesotho Premier Leabua Jonathan arrives in the ROC for an official visit.

Oct. 23 — Nigerian President Hamani Diori arrives in the ROC for an official visit.

Dec. 17 — The Chinese National Committee of the International Press Institute is established in Taipei.

     20 — The nation chooses 26 new members to the National Assembly and the Legislative Yuan.

1969

May 26 — Sierra Leone Premier Siaka P. Stevens arrives in Taipei to confer with ROC leaders.

1970

July 12 — ROC athlete Chi Cheng breaks the women's 200-meter record in West Germany, with a time of 22.44 seconds.

1971

Aug. 14 — Ground for the construction of the North-South Freeway is broken near Linkou.

Oct. 25 — The Republic of China withdraws from the United Nations.

1972

Mar. 21 — President Chiang Kai-shek is reelected to a fifth six-year term.

May 26 — Former Vice Premier Chiang Ching-kuo becomes premier after approval by the Legislative Yuan.

Aug. 20 — The ROC Mei Ho baseball team wins the Senior League world title.

     27 — The Taipei Little League baseball team wins the world title.

Sept. 29 — The Republic of China severs diplomatic relations with Japan.

Oct. 16 — President Dawda Kairba Jawara of Gambia arrives for an eight-day visit.

Nov. 12 — The Republic of China wins the World Cup Golf Championship in Melbourne.

Dec. 23 — An election of additional members to the National Assembly, Legislative Yuan, the Taiwan Provincial Assembly, and of mayors and county magistrates is held in Taiwan, Kinmen, and Matsu.

1973

Jan. 22 — H.R.H. Prince Tuipelehake, C.B.E., prime minister of the Kingdom of Tonga, arrives for a one-week visit.

Oct. 30 — Tsengwen Dam and Reservoir, the largest in Taiwan, are completed.

Dec. 25 — Construction of the Suao-Hualien railroad is launched.

1974

Jan. 26 — Premier Chiang Ching-kuo announces an across-the-board price adjustment to help stabilize the economy.

Apr. 20 — The ROC announces the termination of Taiwan-Japan flights by China Airlines and Japan Airlines.

May 14 — Chen Te-nien, director of the Taiwan Railway Administration, and Peter Godwin, representing Lazard Brothers Co., sign an agreement under which a British consortium will loan £575 million to TRA's railway electrification project.

Oct. 30 — The first F5E Freedom jet fighter made in the Republic of China rolls off the assembly line.

1975

Feb. 17 — The China Steel Corp., the Continental Illinois National Bank, and the Trust

Company of Chicago sign a US$200 million loan contract to help finance construction of a steel mill in Kaohsiung.

Mar. 21 — Chinese officials stationed in Phnom Penh return to Taipei.

Apr. 5 — President Chiang Kai-shek passes away.

6 — Yen Chia-kan, vice president of the Republic of China since 1966, takes the oath of office as the nation's second constitutional president.

26 — The Embassy of the Republic of China in Saigon suspends operations.

28 — Premier Chiang Ching-kuo is elected chairman of the Central Committee of the ruling Kuomintang.

June 9 — The Republic of China terminates diplomatic relations with the Republic of the Philippines.

July 1 — The ROC terminates diplomatic relations with Thailand.

9 — The Republic of China and Japan sign a private aviation agreement that restores the Taiwan-Japan services of China Airlines and a Japanese airline.

Oct. 21 — The second naphtha cracking plant of the Chinese Petroleum Corp. begins production.

1976

Mar. 26 — Dr. Lin Yu-tang, 81, one of the best known Chinese writers in English, dies in Hong Kong.

July 17 — The ROC team withdraws from the Montreal Games to protest competing under the name of "Taiwan."

Aug. 21 — Prince Maphevu Harry Dlamini, prime minister of the Kingdom of Swaziland, accompanied by Mme. Dlamini and a party of eight, arrives for a seven-day visit.

Oct. 31 — Taichung Port in west central Taiwan is formally opened.

1977

Mar. 26 — The Chinese research vessel Hai Kung returns to Keelung after a 115-day exploratory expedition to the Antarctic.

May 18 — China Airlines' new Boeing 747SP begins nonstop service between Taipei and the US West Coast.

June 3 — The 445,000-ton tanker Burmah Endeavour, built by the China Shipbuilding Corp. for US Gatx Oswego, is launched at Kaohsiung. It is the world's third largest vessel.

July 9 — President Yen Chia-kan leaves for a three-day state visit to Saudi Arabia, at the invitation of King Khaled Bib Abdul Aziz Al-Saud.

Sept. 19 — King Taufa'ahau Tupou IV and Queen Halaevalu Mata'aho of the Kingdom of Tonga arrive for a week's state visit at the invitation of President and Mme. Yen Chia-kan.

Oct. 17 — Akira Nishiyama, former Japanese ambassador to South Korea, arrives to assume his duties as director of the Japan Interchange Association's Taipei office.

1978

Mar. 21 — Premier Chiang Ching-kuo is elected by the National Assembly as president for the sixth constitutional presidential term of the Republic of China.

30 — The first generator of Taiwan's first nuclear power plant begins its full capacity operation of 636,000 kilowatts.

May 26 — The Legislative Yuan endorses President Chiang's appointment of Sun Yun-suan, former minister of economic affairs, as the new premier.

June 20 — The Republic of China is listed the 25th largest trading country in the world by the International Monetary Fund.

Oct. 31 — The Taiwan Area Freeway, with a total length of 377 km, is opened to traffic.

Dec. 8 — The Legislative Yuan passes the revised *Foreign Exchange Management Regulations* under which the New Taiwan dollar is no longer pegged to the US dollar.

16 — President Chiang Ching-kuo strongly condemns the US decision to sever diplomatic relations with the Republic of China in favor of the Beijing regime.

1979

Mar. 1 — The US embassy in Taipei formally closes, to be succeeded by the American Institute in Taiwan.

— The Washington Office of the Coordination Council for North American Affairs of the Republic of China opens.

Apr. 10 — US President Jimmy Carter signs legislation permitting continued commercial and cultural relations between the US government and the ROC following the break in diplomatic ties.

July 1 — The electrification of Taiwan's 1,153-km-long west coast trunk line railway between Keelung and Kaohsiung is completed.

— Kaohsiung becomes a special municipality under the direct jurisdiction of the Executive Yuan.

Sept. 6 — The Cabinet announces the extension of the ROC's territorial waters to 12 nautical miles, and the establishment of a 200-mile economic zone.

Nov. 16 — The Republic of China and the United States conclude 40 days of talks on the revision of their air transportation agreement. Under the memorandum issued by the two parties, the ROC will open civil air services to four new US stops: Guam, Seattle, New York, and Dallas-Fort Worth.

Dec. 10 — A demonstration organized by opposition politicians and the *Formosa Magazine* to commemorate Human Rights Day, turns into the bloody riot known as the "Kaohsiung Incident," in which scores of demonstrators and policemen were injured.

1980

Jan. 3 — The US government informs the ROC government that it will resume arms sales to the ROC after a one-year suspension.

Dec. 27 — Twenty-two supplementary members are elected to the Control Yuan from among 54 candidates by members of the Taiwan Provincial Assembly, the Taipei City Council, and the Kaohsiung City Council.

1981

Apr. 2 — President Chiang Ching-kuo is reelected chairman of the Kuomintang by acclamation at the 12th National Congress in Taipei.

May 4 — The first European Trade Fair in the Republic of China is held at the Taipei World Trade Center with some 293 companies from 13 Western European countries participating.

1982

May 12 — The Council for Agricultural Planning and Development (CAPD) reveals the second phase of the land reform program.

20 — The Cabinet approves the draft of a *Genetic Health Law* to legalize abortion and prevent couples with known genetic diseases from having children.

June 20 — The Directorate General of Telecommunications (DGT) opens the first public data switching service in the ROC.

Oct. 16 — Aleksandr I. Solzhenitsyn, 1970 Nobel Literature Prize winner, arrives in Taiwan from Tokyo at the invitation of Wu San-lien Awards Foundation of the ROC.

1983

Jan. 14 — The Legislative Yuan passes a revision of the *Trademark Law* to impose prison terms for infringement of trademarks.

Feb. 16 — The Dutch airline Martinair inaugurates flight service to Taiwan, marking the opening of air service between the Netherlands and the Republic of China.

Apr. 12 — China Airlines inaugurates regular flight service to Amsterdam as the first step toward establishing a world-girdling commercial air service.

June 7 — The Legislative Yuan passes the *Firearms Control Law*, placing the manufacture, possession, and use of firearms and other weapons under stricter control.

Oct. 31 — Taipei's 809-m-long Kuantu Bridge, the first multi-arch steel bridge in East Asia, is opened to traffic.

1984

Jan. 12 — The Cabinet approves a plan to build a synchrotron research center within five years.

Mar. 1 — The Republic of China's first domestically developed jet trainer AT-3 rolls off the assembly line. The twin-seat trainer, fitted with two Garrett TFE 731-2-2L engines, each with a thrust of 1,590 kg, was developed by the Aeronautical Institute of Science and Technology.

21 — President Chiang Ching-kuo is reelected for a second six-year term.

May 20 — President Chiang Ching-kuo nominates Yu Kuo-hwa, chairman of the Council for Economic Planning and Development and governor of the Central Bank of China, as the new premier.

June 29 — The Legislative Yuan approves the long-awaited and controversial *Genetic Health Law.*

July 20 — The Legislative Yuan passes the *Labor Standards Law.*

Sept. 20 — The ROC Council of Agriculture is formally established.

Oct. 12 — The ROC-Australia Trade Association and the Chinese-New Zealand Business Council are formally inaugurated in Taipei.

1985

Jan. 8 — The Hong Kong Affairs Task Force under the Executive Yuan decides to simplify exit and entry application procedures, relax controls on foreign exchange, and adopt incentive measures to encourage large enterprises and monetary institutions in Hong Kong to move to Taiwan.

Apr. 16 — The first test tube baby in the Republic of China is born at Veterans General Hospital in Taipei.

July 9 — The last part of a transoceanic telecommunication cable system, which will link Taiwan, Hong Kong, and Singapore, is hauled ashore in Toucheng, Ilan.

19 — The Ministry of National Defense announces that a domestically developed surface-to-air missile named "Sky Bow" made a successful debut in a test firing.

Sept. 29 — ROC decathlon athletes Ku Chin-shui and Li Fu-en win a gold and silver medal respectively in the sixth Asian Track and Field Championships in Jakarta, Indonesia.

1986

Apr. 23 — National Taiwan University Hospital separates a pair of 14-day-old Siamese twins, saving one of the baby girls' life and setting a world record for separating the youngest Siamese twins.

24 — ROC Minister of Foreign Affairs Chu Fu-sung and Paraguayan Foreign Minister Carlos Augusto Saldivar sign an extradition treaty in Taipei on behalf of their respective governments.

May 18 — The Ministry of National Defense announces that an air-to-air "Sky Sword" missile has been successfully tested by shooting down a Hawk missile.

Aug. 3 — Construction of the Synchronous Radiation Research Center is started at the Hsinchu Science-based Industrial Park.

Sept. 25 — The Republic of China, after withdrawing 13 years ago, is readmitted to the Olympic Council of Asia (OCA).

Oct. 15 — Lee Yuan-tseh, a member of the Academia Sinica, wins the 1986 Nobel Prize in chemistry.

Nov. 6 — The Democratic Progressive Party (DPP) holds its first Representative Assembly and releases a draft of its charter and platform.

1987

June 23 — The Legislative Yuan passes the *National Security Law during the Period of National Mobilization for Suppression of the Communist Rebellion.* After the law becomes effective, the *Emergency Decree* in Taiwan and the Pescadores (Penghu) will be lifted.

July 15 — The *Emergency Decree* is lifted in the Taiwan area, the *National Security Law* is promulgated, and foreign exchange controls are relaxed.

Aug. 1 — The Council of Labor Affairs is formally established under the Executive Yuan.

Nov. 2 — The ROC Red Cross Society begins accepting applications from local residents wishing to visit relatives in the Chinese mainland.

10 — ROC-US talks on intellectual property rights begin in Taipei.

1988

Jan. 1 — Registrations for new newspapers are opened, and restrictions on the number of pages per issue are relaxed.

11 — The Legislative Yuan passes the *Law on Assembly and Parades during the Period of National Mobilization for Suppression of the Communist Rebellion*, which outlines three fundamental principles and specifies areas that will be off-limits to demonstrators.

13 — President Chiang Ching-kuo passes away of heart failure and hemorrhage at 3:50 p.m.

— Vice President Lee Teng-hui is sworn in as president of the Republic of China to complete the late President Chiang's second six-year term, which runs from 1984 to 1990.

Mar. 3 — The Council for Economic Planning and Development approves the establishment of a US$11 billion International Economic Cooperation and Development Fund to assist developing countries.

24 — The Government Information Office and the Ministry of National Defense reiterate that the ROC has never engaged in the development of nuclear weapons. This is confirmed by the US government.

Apr. 18 — The ROC Red Cross Society begins forwarding mail from Taiwan residents to the Chinese mainland.

28 — An ROC delegation attends the annual convention of the Asian Development Bank (ADB) in Manila.

July 8 — Acting Chairman Lee Teng-hui is elected chairman of the Kuomintang at the ruling party's 13th National Congress.

28 — The Executive Yuan approves regulations governing the import of publications, films, and radio and television programs from communist-controlled areas.

Aug. 18 — The Mainland Affairs Task Force is established under the Executive Yuan.

30 — ROC-US talks on finance and banking open in Washington. The ROC negotiators agree to open the Taiwan market to credit card companies and to expand credit for foreign banks.

Oct. 25 — A comprehensive farmer health insurance is initiated.

Nov. 3 — The Mainland Affairs Task Force revises regulations to allow mainland compatriots to visit sick relatives or attend their funerals in Taiwan.

17 — The Executive Yuan approves the private installation of small satellite dish antennas, which will allow viewers to tune into the KU-band and receive television programming from Japan's NHK station.

Dec. 1 — The Executive Yuan announces guidelines governing unofficial participation in international academic conferences and cultural and athletic activities held on the mainland, as well as regulations governing visits to Taiwan by overseas mainland scholars and students.

1989

Jan. 10 — The ROC and the Commonwealth of the Bahamas establish diplomatic relations.

20 — The Legislative Yuan passes the *Law on Civic Organizations*.

26 — The Legislative Yuan passes the *Law on the Voluntary Retirement of Senior Parliamentarians*.

Mar. 6 — President and Mme. Lee Teng-hui arrive in Singapore for a four-day visit.

Apr. 7 — The Chinese Taipei Olympic Committee announces that ROC athletic teams and organizations will participate in international sports events held on the mainland under the name "Chinese Taipei."

17 — The Mainland Affairs Task Force

passes the proposal to allow teachers and staff of public schools to travel to the Chinese mainland for family visits. On the 18th, the council decides to permit newsgathering and filmmaking on the mainland.

30 — Finance Minister Shirley Kuo leads an ROC delegation to the 22nd annual Asian Development Bank meeting in Beijing.

May 28 — Ching Kuo, the first ROC-developed and manufactured indigenous defense fighter, successfully completes its first test flight.

31 — One million students participate in a "Hand in Hand, Heart to Heart" rally in support of the mainland democracy movement.

June 1 — Lee Huan is sworn in as premier of the ROC.

4 — President Lee Teng-hui issues a statement condemning the Tienanmen Massacre.

10 — Direct telephone links are opened between the two sides of the Taiwan Strait.

19 — The Hong Kong and Macau Affairs Task Force announces the government's plan to simplify procedures for the relocation of Hong Kong and Macao compatriots in Taiwan and to provide assistance for their emigration to a third country.

July 11 — The Legislative Yuan approves a partial revision of the *Banking Law* which completely abolishes interest rate controls and deregulates entry into the banking system. The law goes into effect on July 19.

20 — The ROC establishes formal diplomatic ties with Grenada.

Aug. 1 — A foreign currency call loan market is established in Taipei, designed to make the metropolis an international financial center.

Sept. 4 — Guatemalan President Marco Vincicio Cerezo Arevalo and President Lee Teng-hui sign a joint communiqué in Taipei calling for closer bilateral relations.

15 — Prime Minister Mary Eugenia Charles of the Commonwealth of Dominica arrives in Taipei for a six-day visit.

25 — The Sky Bow Weapons System, developed and manufactured by the ROC, is added to the nation's military defense system.

26 — The Executive Yuan permits pro-democracy supporters from the mainland to settle in Taiwan.

Oct. 2 — The ROC and Liberia re-establish diplomatic relations. Beijing severs formal ties with Liberia in protest.

12 — The ROC and Belize announce the establishment of diplomatic relations.

— King Mswati III of Swaziland arrives for a five-day visit.

Dec. 2 — Elections for the Legislative Yuan, Taiwan Provincial Assembly, Taipei and Kaohsiung city councils, county magistrates, and provincial-level city mayors are held.

1990

Jan. 14 — President Lee Teng-hui and President Prosper Avril of Haiti sign a joint communiqué calling for stronger bilateral cooperation.

16 — Low-ranking government employees are permitted to visit relatives across the strait, and native Taiwanese who moved to the mainland before 1949 are allowed to visit relatives in Taiwan.

Feb. 13 — The Mainland Affairs Task Force permits Taiwan's performing artists to stage commercial performances on the mainland and to participate in activities sponsored by the Chinese communists.

26 — President Lee Teng-hui and El Salvadoran President Alfredo Felix Cristiani Burkard sign a joint communiqué for closer bilateral cooperation.

Mar. 1 — The Executive Yuan approves direct trade between the ROC and the Soviet Union and Albania.

17 — Thousands of university students stage a sit-down protest at the Chiang Kai-shek Memorial Hall Plaza to express opposition to the National Assembly's attempt to expand its authority.

21 — Lee Teng-hui is elected the eighth-term president of the ROC.

22 — Li Yuan-zu is elected vice president of the ROC.

27 — The eighth plenum of the National Assembly approves a motion to force members who failed to attend the plenary session to retire by the end of July 1990.

Apr. 5 — The ROC re-establishes diplomatic relations with the Kingdom of Lesotho. Beijing severs ties with Lesotho two days later.

8 — Economics Minister Chen Li-an and Singaporean Minister of Trade and Industries, Lee Hsien Loong, preside over the first ministerial-level conference between the two countries on economic cooperation.

30 — Elected officials of all levels are permitted to make private visits to the mainland during recesses. Veterans who were stranded on the mainland after the national government moved to Taiwan in 1949 are allowed to apply for resettlement in Taiwan.

May 16 — The KMT Central Standing Committee accepts the resignation of Premier Lee Huan and his Cabinet ministers.

20 — Lee Teng-hui and Li Yuan-zu are inaugurated as president and vice president of the ROC.

— President Lee Teng-hui announces a special amnesty, which includes the pardoning of dissidents Hsu Hsin-liang and Shih Ming-teh.

26 — The ROC establishes diplomatic relations with Guinea Bissau.

29 — Premier nominee Hau Pei-tsun is approved by the Legislative Yuan, and is immediately appointed premier by President Lee Teng-hui.

June 17 — President Andres Rodriguez of Paraguay arrives in Taipei to sign a joint communiqué calling for closer bilateral relations with the ROC.

21 — The Council of Grand Justices announces that senior parliamentarians should terminate their responsibilities by December 31, 1991.

25 — Reporters from the mainland are permitted to visit Taiwan for newsgathering purposes, and government employees from Taiwan are allowed to visit sick relatives or attend funerals on the mainland.

July 4 — The National Affairs Conference concludes in Taipei, after six days of discussions on parliamentary reforms, the central and local government systems, the Constitution, and mainland policy.

22 — The ROC severs diplomatic relations with Saudi Arabia, after the latter switches formal recognition to communist China.

Aug. 10 — The ROC government declares its support of a United Nations call for world sanctions against Iraq over its invasion of Kuwait.

31 — Premier Hau Pei-tsun advises the Legislative Yuan that ROC relations with the mainland will operate under the concept of "one country, two areas."

Sept. 1 — Premier Hau Pei-tsun announces the objectives of the Six-Year National Development Plan, which includes public construction projects affecting economics, culture, education, and medicine.

17 — A team of 200 athletes and coaches flies to the Chinese mainland for the ROC's first attendance of the Asian Games in 20 years.

19 — The Red Cross societies of the ROC and the mainland reach agreement on procedures for the repatriation of illegal mainland entrants to Taiwan.

Oct. 7 — The National Unification Council is established under the Office of the President to help plan the policy framework for national unification, and to integrate various opinions about the issue at all levels of society.

11 — The Ministry of the Interior reiterates that the Tiaoyutai Islets belong to the ROC. The chain of eight uninhabited islets, located in the East China Sea, also is claimed by Japan and communist China.

18 — The Mainland Affairs Council is established under the Executive Yuan to

formulate and implement mainland policy.

27 — Moscow City Mayor Gavriil H. Popov arrives for a formal visit to the ROC to discuss the strengthening of ROC-Soviet trade relations.

Nov. 1 — President Lee Teng-hui receives an Outstanding International Alumnus Citation from Cornell University.

15 — The Ministry of Foreign Affairs announces the ROC-Canadian agreement to exchange aviation rights and establish Taipei economic and cultural offices in major Canadian cities.

20 — The first ROC-USSR fishery cooperation conference is held in Tokyo for discussions on technological exchanges and expansion of fishing zones.

21 — The Straits Exchange Foundation, a private intermediary organization financially supported by the government, is established to handle technical affairs arising from people-to-people contacts between Taiwan and the mainland.

1991

Jan. 6 — A memorandum is signed between the ROC and Saudi Arabia for the mutual establishment of representative offices in their capital cities.

7 — French Minister of Industry and Territorial Development Roger Fauroux participates in the seventh ROC-France Economic Cooperation Conference in Taipei.

31 — The Executive Yuan approves a budget of about US$303 billion for the Six-Year National Development Plan.

Mar. 14 — The Executive Yuan passes the *Guidelines for National Unification*, which are now the highest directives governing ROC mainland policy. Its long-term goal is to establish a democratic, free, and equitably prosperous China.

Apr. 22 — The second extraordinary session of the First National Assembly passes, at its sixth plenary meeting, the *Additional Articles of the Constitution of the ROC* and approves the abolishment of the *Tem-*

porary Provisions Effective During the Period of National Mobilization for Suppression of the Communist Rebellion.

30 — President Lee Teng-hui declares the termination of the Period of National Mobilization for Suppression of the Communist Rebellion, effective on May 1. He abolishes the *Temporary Provisions* and promulgates the *Additional Articles of the Constitution*, also effective on May 1.

May 24 — The Legislative Yuan approves the abolishment of the *Statutes for the Purging of Communist Agents*.

June 26 — Approval is given to 15 of the 19 applications to set up private commercial banks.

27 — Government Spokesman Shaw Yu-ming announces that mainland journalists will no longer have to renounce their membership in the Chinese Communist Party when applying to visit Taiwan.

July 4 — The ROC and Czechoslovakia agree to exchange representative offices.

8 — The ROC and the Central African Republic resume diplomatic relations.

Aug. 5 — President Lee Teng-hui receives Fijian Prime Minister Ratu Sir Kamisese Mara; an ROC-Fiji technological cooperation agreement is signed on August 6.

12 — Two mainland journalists arrive in Taipei, marking the first-ever visit by the mainland Chinese press.

18 — Vice President Li Yuan-zu leaves for a state visit to Costa Rica, Nicaragua, and Honduras, and to attend the 23rd Plenary Meeting of the World League for Freedom and Democracy at San José, Costa Rica.

Oct. 11 — Direct air service begins between Australia and the ROC.

Nov. 6 — The ROC and Latvia sign memoranda for economic cooperation and the exchange of trade offices.

13 — The ROC joins the Asia-Pacific Economic Cooperation (APEC) along with Hong Kong and the Chinese mainland.

15 — South African President Frederik Willem de Klerk signs a joint communiqué with

President Lee Teng-hui for closer relations between the two countries.

Dec. 21 — The ruling Kuomintang wins 71 percent of the vote and 254 of the 325
seats in the election for the Second
National Assembly.

22 — Dissident mainland Chinese astrophysi-
cist Fang Li-chih visits Taipei.

31 — All senior delegates to the First National
Assembly, Control Yuan, and Legislative Yuan retire from office.

1992

Jan. 20 — The French Secretary of State for Foreign Trade Jean-Noël Jeanneney visits
Taipei to discuss participation in the Six-
Year National Development Plan and
further economic cooperation between
the ROC and France.

27 — The Fair Trade Commission is established under the Executive Yuan.

29 — The ROC and Latvia announce the establishment of relations at the consulate-
general level.

Feb. 4 — The *Fair Trade Law* goes into effect.

18 — A delegation from the US President's
Export Council arrives to promote ROC-
US trade.

28 — The ROC and the Philippines sign an official investment guarantee agreement to protect investments by Taiwan businessmen.

Mar. 7 — Nicaraguan President Violeta Barrios de
Chamorro and President Lee Teng-hui
sign a joint communiqué in Taipei for
stronger bilateral relations.

23 — The first-ever meeting convenes in Beijing
between the Straits Exchange Foundation
and the mainland's Association for Relations Across the Taiwan Straits, to discuss
issues related to document verification
and indirect registered mail services.

27 — The ROC and Bulgaria agree to establish
direct air links between Taipei and Sofia.

Apr. 17 — Legislative proceedings are completed
for the *National Employment Act*, which
will serve as the basis for the employment of foreign nationals in the ROC.

19 — Minister of Foreign Trade Yvonne C.M.T.
van Rooy of the Netherlands visits Taipei
to seek stronger bilateral relations.

29 — Bolivian Vice President Luis Ossio
Sanjines officiates the inauguration of
the Bolivian Commercial and Financial
Representative Office in Taipei.

May 10 — Swedish Minister of Transport and Communications, Mats Odell, visits Taipei to
discuss closer cooperation and future
exchanges with the ROC.

11 — President Andre Kolingba of the Central
African Republic visits Taipei.

17 — Wu Ta-you, president of Academia
Sinica, attends academic conferences in
Beijing and Tianjin.

30 — The Additional Articles 11 through 18 of
the Constitution go into effect.

31 — The Mainland Affairs Council allows
Chinese mainlanders to come to Taiwan
and care for their old or sick relatives.

June 10 — A revised *Copyright Law* goes into effect, providing explicit legal protection
for intellectual property rights and im-
posing heavier penalties for infringement
of copyright.

14 — Ronald Freeman, Vice President of the European Bank for Reconstruction and Development, visits the ROC to discuss Sino-
European trade and financial relations.

19 — The ROC resumes diplomatic relations
with Niger.

— The Legislative Yuan approves the *Law
on Foreign Futures Contracts*, which
will take effect in January 1993.

July 3 — The Legislative Yuan passes a revision
of the *Law on Civic Organizations*, which
calls for a Political Party Review Committee to be formed under the Ministry of
the Interior.

7 — The Legislative Yuan passes a revision
of the *National Security Law*, which
would reduce the number of black-listed
persona non grata from 282 to five.

9 — The Argentine Trade and Cultural Office
is opened in Taipei after a 20-year break
in diplomatic relations.

16 — The Legislative Yuan passes the *Statute Governing Relations Between People of the Taiwan Area and the Mainland Area.*

19 — The ROC's five-year lease of three Knox-class frigates from the United States is approved by US President George Bush.

23 — Former French Premier Michel Rocard visits the ROC to strengthen friendship between the two countries.

Aug. 1 — The National Unification Council defines "one China" as "one country and two areas separately ruled by two political entities."

— Taiwan Garrison General Headquarters, the ROC's highest security institution in the Taiwan area, is disbanded; and the Coastal Patrol General Headquarters is established under the Ministry of National Defense.

18 — The Department of Anti-Corruption is established under the Ministry of Justice.

23 — The ROC severs diplomatic relations with South Korea.

25 — Niger's Prime Minister Amadou Cheiffou arrives in Taipei to advance mutual understanding between the two countries.

30 — Former British Prime Minister Margaret Thatcher expresses support for the ROC's entry into the GATT during her visit to Taipei.

Sept. 2 — President Lee Teng-hui and Guatemalan President Jorge Antonio Serrano sign a joint communiqué calling for closer bilateral cooperation in Taipei.

— Canadian International Trade Minister Michael Wilson visits Taipei to boost ROC-Canada trade ties; he is the first ministerial official to visit the ROC since bilateral ties were severed in 1970.

— The Bureau of Entry and Exit announces that members of the Chinese People's Political Consultative Conference in mainland China may apply to visit Taiwan for cultural and academic exchanges.

6 — Direct air service between the ROC and Vietnam resumes for the second time in 13 months.

13 — Latvian Prime Minister Ivars Godmanis visits Taipei to seek mutually beneficial cooperation; an ROC-Latvia investment guarantee agreement is signed on September 17.

21 — The US Department of Defense decides to sell 12 SH-2F light airborne multipurpose system helicopters to the ROC.

22 — Political Vice Foreign Minister John Chang and Oleg Lobov, chairman of the Export Council to the Russian President Boris Yeltsin, sign two diplomatic memoranda and a document of state protocol pledging the promotion of trade, tourism, investment, cultural, and scientific and technological exchanges.

24 — Foreign Minister Fredrick Chien and his Vanuatu counterpart Serge Vohor sign a joint communiqué pledging reciprocal recognition.

29 — The ROC is granted observer status in the GATT, which also resolves to accept the ROC's application into GATT under the name, the "Separate Customs Territory of Taiwan, Penghu, Kinmen and Matsu."

Oct. 11 — President Lee Teng-hui and Panamanian President Guillermo Endara sign a joint communiqué to expand bilateral cooperation.

12 — Premier Hau Pei-tsun receives Austrian Minister for Economic Affairs Wolfgang Schüssel.

22 — Belgian Foreign Trade Minister Robert Urbain visits Taipei to relay a message of welcome to Taiwan businessmen intending to invest in Belgium and pledges support for the ROC's bid to join GATT.

27 — Australian Tourism and Resources Minister Alan Griffiths visits Taipei to promote closer bilateral trade relations. Mr. Griffiths is the first Australian Minister visiting Taipei since 1972.

Nov. 3 — Indonesian Minister of Research and Technology Bacharuddin Habibie leads a 30-member delegation to Taiwan.

4 — Vice Minister of Economic Affairs Chiang Pin-kung heads an observer delegation to the Geneva meeting of GATT Council of Representatives after the ROC's absence of 21 years.

7 — After more than three decades of military administration, Quemoy (Kinmen) and Matsu revert to civilian rule as the *Statute Governing the Security and Guidance of the Kinmen, Matsu, Tungsha, and Nansha Areas* goes into effect.

9 — Saint Lucia's Prime Minister John George · Melvin Compton visits Taipei.

10 — The Nigerian Trade Office is set up in Taipei to promote economic relations with the ROC.

12 — ROC and US defense representatives sign a letter of offer and acceptance for the ROC's purchase of 150 F-16A and F-16B jet fighters from the United States.

18 — German Vice Chancellor Jürgen Möllemann and Economics Minister Vincent C. Siew reach an agreement on the establishment of direct air links and channels of communication on trade between the ROC and Germany.

19 — The Council of Agriculture bans all import, export, and trade of rhino-horn products.

30 — United States Trade Representative Carla A. Hills visits Taipei.

Dec. 19 — The Kuomintang wins 53.02 percent and the Democratic Progressive Party 31.03 percent of the popular vote in the election for the Second Legislative Yuan.

1993

Jan. 14 — The Legislative Yuan approves a US$12.47 billion budget for the purchase of 150 F-16 jet fighters from the United States and 60 Mirage 2000-5s from France.

15 — ROC and Philippine officials sign an agreement in Manila, setting the guidelines for transforming the former US naval facility at Subic Bay into an industrial complex.

Feb. 22 — Taiwan-made film *The Wedding Banquet* wins a Golden Bear Award for Best Picture at the 43rd annual Berlin International Film Festival.

26 — Two mainland Chinese basketball teams arrive in Taiwan to play exhibition matches against local teams; this marks the first time in four decades that athletes from Taiwan and the mainland will compete in Taiwan.

27 — Taiwan Provincial Governor Lien Chan succeeds Hau Pei-tsun as premier of the ROC following his confirmation by the Legislative Yuan.

Mar. 21 — Republic of Nauru President Bernard Dowiyogo visits Taipei.

26 — In an interview with the US Cable News Network, President Lee Teng-hui stresses the ROC's willingness to form a regional collective security system with Asia-Pacific countries.

29 — Direct air service between the ROC and the United Kingdom begins.

— New Zealand's minister of customs and associate minister of tourism, Murray McCully, leads a nine-member delegation to Taipei. Mr. McCully is New Zealand's first minister to visit Taipei since 1972.

Apr. 22 — The Legislative Yuan ratifies the 1989 ROC-US copyright agreement and passes amendments to the *Copyright Law*, which go into effect on April 26.

— Tonga's Prime Minister Vaea and Mme. Vaea visit the ROC.

29 — Representatives of the Straits Exchange Foundation and its mainland counterpart, the Association for Relations Across the Taiwan Straits, sign three agreements and a joint accord at a historic meeting in Singapore; the agreements and accord go into effect on May 29.

May 1 — The Taipei Economic and Trade Office in Tel Aviv begins operation.

7 — The first ROC-made PFG-2 missile frigate, the Cheng-kung, goes into service.

8 — A 186-member team from the ROC

participates in the first East Asian Games in Shanghai.

13 — Former US Secretary of Defense Dick Cheney visits Taipei.

15 — Tuvalu's Prime Minister Bikenibeu Paeniu and Mme. Paeniu visit the ROC.

June 11 — President Lee Teng-hui receives former Philippine President Corazon Aquino.

29 — President Lee Teng-hui receives former US Vice President Dan Quayle.

30 — The Executive Yuan approves an Economic Stimulus Package to accelerate industrial upgrading and to develop Taiwan into an Asia-Pacific Regional Operations Center.

July 2 — The *Public Functionary Assets Disclosure Law* goes into effect.

8 — The ROC and Nicaragua sign a joint communiqué pledging bilateral cooperation.

10 — Vietnam's Economic and Cultural Office in Taipei opens.

12 — The Taipei-Moscow Economic and Cultural Coordination Commission begins operation in Moscow.

Aug. 10 — The New KMT Alliance breaks with the ruling Kuomintang and forms the New Party.

11 — The *Cable Television Law* goes into effect.

16 — The 14th National Congress of the KMT opens. President Lee Teng-hui is re-elected chairman of the KMT; while Vice President Li Yuan-zu, former Premier Hau Pei-tsun, Judicial Yuan President Lin Yang-kang, and Premier Lien Chan are elected vice chairmen on August 18.

17 — The ROC and Australia sign two memoranda on the protection of industrial property rights and on investment promotion and technical cooperation.

Sept. 2 — The Executive Yuan passes an administrative reform package to eradicate corruption and inefficiency in the government.

23 — The ROC and Belgium sign three investment cooperation agreements to boost economic and technological ties.

Oct. 26 — The ROC and Mexico sign a pact to promote investment and technology transfer.

Nov. 19 — Vincent C. Siew, chairman of the Council for Economic Planning and Development, represents President Lee Teng-hui at the APEC leaders economic conference in Seattle.

25 — South Korea opens its Korean Mission in Taipei to replace the embassy closed after South Korea and the ROC broke off diplomatic relations.

30 — The ROC signs an investment promotion and protection pact with Argentina to strengthen economic ties with South America.

Dec. 9 — The Government Information Office lifts the ban on radio stations and approves the applications of 13 broadcasting companies for operation licenses.

15 — The Legislative Yuan approves a revision of the *University Law*, which gives more autonomy to colleges and allows students to participate in meetings related to school affairs.

1994

Jan. 11 — The *Consumer Protection Law* goes into effect; manufacturers are held responsible for harming consumers even when negligence or intent to do harm are not found to be factors.

12 — The ROC and Lesotho sever diplomatic relations.

15 — Lee Yuan-tseh succeeds Wu Ta-you as president of Academia Sinica.

Feb. 9 — President Lee leaves for the Philippines, Indonesia, and Thailand on an eight-day visit.

Mar. 2 — The ROC and Belize sign a joint communiqué pledging bilateral cooperation.

23 — The Legislative Yuan increases the annual number of permanent residency permits for mainland spouses from 300 to 600.

25 — The SEF and the ARATS hold talks in Beijing on fishery disputes and the repatriation of illegal entrants and hijackers.

28 — The ROC and the Central African

Republic sign a joint communiqué pledging further cooperation.

Apr.　12 — The Mainland Affairs Council decides to suspend all cultural and educational exchanges with the mainland before the Chinese communists provide reasonable and satisfactory explanations of the Qiandao Lake tragedy on March 31 in which 24 Taiwan tourists were killed.

May　2 — The ROC and Grenada sign a joint communiqué pledging bilateral cooperation.

　　4 — President Lee Teng-hui leaves for Nicaragua, Costa Rica, South Africa, and Swaziland on a 13-day official visit.

June　6 — Premier Lien Chan pays the first visit of a high-ranking ROC official to Mexico in 23 years after the two severed diplomatic ties.

　　29 — The Peruvian Trade Office opens in Taipei.

July　7 — The Legislative Yuan passes the *Self-governance Law for Provinces and Counties*, explicitly stipulating that provincial governors be chosen by direct election. The *Self-governance Law for Special Municipalities* is passed the next day.

　　13 — Seven foreign ministers and representatives from Central American countries come to Taiwan to participate in the Third Mixed Commission Conference of Central American Nations, and sign a joint declaration with the ROC supporting the ROC's bid for UN participation.

　　30 — The SEF and the ARATS start talks in Taipei. This is the first high-level dialogue between the two organizations since the Qiandao Lake incident on March 31, 1994.

Aug.　8 — The SEF and the ARATS sign and make public a joint press release confirming the results of the second round of Chiao-Tang talks.

　　9 — The US government announces trade sanctions against the ROC under the Pelly Amendment, placing a ban on imports of Taiwan wildlife products effective from August 19, 1994.

Sept.　7 — US Assistant Secretary of State Winston Lord formally notifies the ROC representative in Washington, Ding Mou-shih, of the result from the Clinton administration's policy discussions about Taiwan: The US agrees to the ROC representative office changing its name to the Taipei Economic and Cultural Representative Office in the United States, and to ROC officials visiting all US government offices except the White House and the Department of State on official business.

　　19 — On behalf of their respective governments, the ROC representative in Washington, Ding Mou-shih, and the chairman of the American Institute in Taiwan, Natale Bellocchi, sign a *Trade and Investment Framework Agreement*.

　　22 — The chairman of the UN General Committee drops the proposal on the ROC's UN membership from the agenda after a 90-minute debate in which seven nations support the ROC and 20 oppose the proposal.

Oct.　27 — The Legislative Yuan passes revisions to the *Wildlife Conservation Law*, greatly toughening penalties against violators and stipulating that the breeding in captivity of endangered animals must cease within three years.

Dec.　3 — The first popular elections for the governor of Taiwan Province and mayors of Taipei and Kaohsiung municipalities are held. James C.Y. Soong is elected governor of Taiwan. Chen Shui-bian and Wu Den-yih win the mayor seats of Taipei and Kaohsiung, respectively.

　　4 — US Secretary of Transportation Federico Pena visits the ROC, becoming the first US cabinet member to carry out the new US policy governing high-ranking official visits to Taipei.

　　12 — The Lien Cabinet is re-organized and new cabinet members are sworn in on December 15.

　　29 — The first squadron of Ching-kuo indigenous defense fighters is officially commissioned, upgrading the combat

ability of the ROC Air Force and demonstrating initial results of research and development.

1995

Jan.   5 — The Executive Yuan Council approves the plan for developing Taiwan into an Asia-Pacific Regional Operations Center.

    30 — Mainland Chinese President Jiang Zemin offers an eight-point proposal, urging Taiwan to hold talks with the mainland to officially end the hostile standoff between the two sides.

Feb. 28 — President Lee expresses an apology to families of the victims of the February 28 Incident of 1947 at the Taipei New Park, where a monument commemorating the tragedy was built with government sponsorship.

Mar.   1 — The National Health Insurance program is formally inaugurated.

    6 — A Coordination and Service Office for the Asia-Pacific Regional Operations Center (also known as the APROC Window) is established in the Council for Economic Planning and Development to ensure that the Asia-Pacific Regional Operations Center plan is faithfully implemented.

  20 — Sheu Yuan-dong replaces Liang Kuo-shu as governor of the Central Bank of China.

  23 — *Regulations Governing the Management and Compensation for Victims of the February 28 Incident* passes the Legislative Yuan. According to the regulations, a foundation will be established to manage affairs concerned, and February 28 will be designated a national commemoration day.

Apr.   1 — President Lee starts his four-day visit to the United Arab Emirates and Jordan.

    8 — At the meeting of the National Unification Council, President Lee offers a six-point proposal for Taiwan-mainland relations.

  19 — Malawi President Bakili Muluzi pays a state visit to Taipei.

May 19 — The Legislative Yuan approves the tem-

porary statute on welfare payments for elderly farmers, granting them a monthly stipend of NT$3,000.

  22 — The ROC and Papua New Guinea sign a joint communiqué in Taipei and establish mutual recognition in order to improve cooperation on the basis of reciprocal benefits.

June   7 — President Lee arrives in the United States for a reunion at his alma mater, Cornell University.

  15 — Premier Lien Chan launches a six-day visit to three European countries: Austria, Hungary, and Czechoslovakia. He is the highest ROC official to visit Europe since the ROC government moved to Taipei in 1949.

  30 — The US government officially announces cancellation of the sanctions against Taiwan issued under the Pelly Amendment.

July   1 — The ROC resumes full diplomatic relations with Gambia after a 21-year hiatus.

  19 — The Legislature approves the *Presidential and Vice Presidential Election and Recall Law*, setting ground rules for the March 23, 1996, popular election of the ROC president and vice president.

  21 — The Chinese mainland begins eight days of firing surface-to-surface missiles into the East China Sea about 140 kilometers north of Taiwan.

  26 — The US Congress honors Mme. Chiang Kai-shek at a Capitol Hill reception in recognition of her contribution to Allied efforts during World War II.

Aug. 15 — The Chinese mainland begins 11 days of firing tactical guided missiles and live artillery shells into the sea 136 kilometers north of Taiwan.

  17 — Control Yuan President Chen Li-an announces his candidacy for president and, on the following day, renounces his 42-year KMT membership.

  19 — The Foreign Ministry issues a position paper entitled "Why the UN Resolution No. 2758 Adopted in 1971 Should Be Reexamined Today." The paper stressed

that UN Resolution 2758, which excluded the ROC from the UN system and its activities, is obsolete and unjust and ought to be reexamined.

22 — The KMT convenes its 14th National Congress and Lee Teng-hui, party chairman, announces he will seek the party's presidential nomination. Lin Yang-kang, a KMT vice chairman, declares his intention not to seek the nomination but to run as an independent.

24 — President Juan Carlos Wasmosy of Paraguay leads a delegation to Taipei for a four-day visit.

31 — The KMT nominates incumbent President Lee as its presidential candidate; the next day President Lee names Premier Lien as his running mate.

Sept. 7 — The ROC and Singapore initial an agreement to cooperate on a project to launch a telecommunications satellite.

17 — An exhibition of 71 landscape paintings from the collection of the Louvre in Paris opens at the National Palace Museum in Taipei.

21 — Economics Minister Chiang Pin-kung leads a delegation to the 19th Joint Conference of ROC-USA and USA-ROC Economic Councils in Anchorage, Alaska.

25 — The DPP nominates Peng Ming-min, a former political science professor and a long-time dissident in exile, as its presidential candidate after a 15-week primary; Peng later names Legislator Frank Chang-ting Hsieh as his running mate.

— Rodrigo Oreamuno, vice president of Costa Rica, arrives in Taipei for a weeklong visit.

27 — Jeffrey Koo, chairman of the Chinese National Association of Industry and Commerce, leads a delegation to the Pacific Economic Cooperation Council meeting in Beijing.

Oct. 3 — Manuel Saturnino da Costa, prime minister of Guinea-Bissau, arrives in Taipei for a six-day visit.

17 — The ROC and Macau establish a five-year renewable air pact allowing Eva Airways, Transasia Airways, and Air Macau to fly routes between Taiwan and Macau.

21 — Independent presidential candidate Chen Li-an names Wang Ching-feng, a Control Yuan member, as his running mate.

Nov. 15 — Independent presidential hopeful Lin Yang-kang names former Premier Hau Pei-tsun as his running mate.

17 — Koo Chen-fu, a senior adviser to the ROC president, arrives in Osaka, Japan, to attend the Asia-Pacific Economic Cooperation forum summit in place of President Lee.

21 — The ROC and Australia sign a memorandum of understanding to permit temporary duty-free entry of certain goods as a means of increasing two-way trade.

25 — The ROC and Poland, to boost economic ties, initial an agreement to avoid double taxation and prevent tax evasion by investors.

Dec. 2 — The Republic of China elects 164 lawmakers to the Third Legislative Yuan.

1996

Jan. 3 — The ROC and the Republic of Senegal resume full diplomatic relations.

11 — Vice President Li Yuan-zu leaves for the Republic of Guatemala to attend the inaugural ceremony of President Alvaro Enrique Arzu Irigoyen, traveling via Los Angeles, USA.

16 — The Legislature passes three telecommunications laws—the *Telecommunications Act*, the *Organizational Statute of the Directorate General of Telecommunications, Ministry of Transportation and Communications*, and the *Statute of Chunghwa Telecom Co., Ltd.* These laws relieve the DGT of the function of providing telecommunications services, making it a regulatory agency only; open the telecommunications sector to private and foreign investment; and strengthen controls on transmission frequencies.

23 — An ROC Ministry of Education ad hoc committee decides that 452 works of art from the National Palace Museum in

Taipei will be allowed to go on a 13-month exhibition trip to the United States. This is one of the largest bodies of national treasures ever to tour overseas.

Feb. 12 — Faced with threatening military maneuvers undertaken by Beijing, the Executive Yuan sets up a temporary policy-making task force to closely follow developments and coordinate the actions of various agencies to respond to the situation.

Mar. 8 — The Chinese mainland begins eight days of test-firing surface-to-surface missiles in waters close to major ports in northeastern and southwestern Taiwan.

12 — The Chinese mainland commences nine days of naval and air military exercises in an area of the Taiwan Strait only 53 kilometers from Kinmen and 70 kilometers from the Penghu Islands.

18 — The Chinese mainland begins eight days of war games involving ground, air, and naval forces in an area of the sea located 85 kilometers northwest of Taiwan proper.

23 — Four pairs of candidates compete in the first-ever direct election of the ROC president and vice president. The Lee-Lien ticket wins, garnering 54 percent of the vote. At the same time, 334 members of the Third National Assembly are also elected.

28 — After eight years of construction, the Mucha Line of the Taipei Mass Rapid Transit Systems officially commences operations.

Apr. 28 — The Ministry of Economic Affairs announces that starting July 1, 1996, imports of another 1,609 categories of industrial commodities will be allowed from the Chinese mainland, marking the ROC government's largest-scale relaxation of restrictions on mainland imports.

May 20 — Lee Teng-hui and Lien Chan are sworn in as ROC president and vice president, respectively.

In his inaugural address, President Lee emphasizes that it is neither necessary nor possible to adopt a so-called "Taiwan independence" line. He expresses his hope that the two sides will counter animosity with peace and forgiveness and turn to the important task of ending the enmity across the strait. President Lee also indicates his willingness to make a "journey of peace" to the Chinese mainland. He says that in order to bring forth a new era of communication and cooperation between the two sides, he is willing to meet and directly exchange opinions with the top mainland leadership.

June 5 — President Lee Teng-hui appoints Vice President Lien Chan to serve concurrently as ROC premier. A cabinet reshuffle is passed three days later.

7 — At his first press conference as vice president/premier, Lien Chan indicates that the ROC has not ruled out the possibility of the two sides exchanging visits by high-ranking officials. He also emphasizes the need to reopen channels for cross-strait talks.

28 — The ROC exchanges economic and trade representative office with the Republic of Belarus. Belarus is the second (Russia being the first) member of the Commonwealth of Independent States to establish such a level of relations with the ROC.

30 — South African Foreign Minister Alfred Nzo arrives for a three-day visit.

July 4 — The National Assembly convenes and subsequently elects Fredrick Chien speaker and Shieh Lung-sheng deputy speaker.

11 — Paraguayan President Juan Carlos Wasmosy visits the ROC.

15 — Honduran President Carlos Roberto Reina arrives in Taipei for a five-day visit.

18 — The European Parliament passes a resolution supporting ROC efforts to be represented in international organizations.

24 — The Foreign Ministry protests Japan's decision to include the Tiaoyutai Islets in its 200-nautical-mile exclusive economic zone.

30 — Chen Jing wins a silver medal in women's table tennis singles at the Olympics in Atlanta.

Aug. 12 — Vice President and Premier Lien Chan departs for the Dominican Republic to attend the August 16 inauguration of President Leonel Fernandez.

19 — Vice President and Premier Lien Chan visits Ukraine.

— Niger switches diplomatic ties from Taipei to Beijing.

24 — The ROC wins the 1996 Little League World Series in the US city of Williamsport, Pennsylvania.

28 — El Salvador President Armando Calderon Sol visits the ROC.

Sept. 11 — The US removes the ROC from a wildlife conservation watchlist in recognition of its progress in protecting endangered species.

12 — The ROC states a four-point position in the Tiaoyutai Islets dispute with Japan: the ROC's absolute sovereignty, a rational attitude, no cooperation with Beijing, and the protection of Taiwan's fishing rights.

24 — The US House of Representatives endorses a July 18 European Parliament resolution supporting ROC efforts to participate in the international community.

Oct. 31 — Former Polish President Lech Walesa visits the ROC.

Nov. 20 — Gambian President Yahya Jammeh visits the ROC.

27 — South Africa announces it will switch full diplomatic recognition from Taipei to Beijing on January 1, 1998.

Dec. 2 — Foreign Minister John Chang departs for South Africa.

6 — The Legislature revises the *Labor Standards Law* so that employees in nearly all industries will be covered by the end of 1998.

10 — The cabinet-level Council of Aboriginal Affairs is established.

— The Taiwan Independence Party (TAIP), a DPP splinter group, is established.

23 — The five-day National Development Conference begins. Discussion focuses on three major topics: enhancing constitutional system of government and multiparty politics; economic development; and cross-strait relations.

31 — Taiwan Provincial Governor James Soong submits his resignation to Premier Lien Chan.

1997

Jan. 7 — Vice President and Premier Lien Chan departs for Nicaragua to attend the January 10 inauguration of President Arnoldo Aleman.

14 — Vice President and Premier Lien Chan meets with Pope John Paul II and shares with him views on world peace and humanitarian pursuits.

16 — Vice President and Premier Lien Chan pays an academic visit to Ireland.

Feb. 23 — The Legislative Yuan passes the amendment to the fourth article of the *February 28 Incident Disposition and Compensation Act*, stipulating that February 28, also named "Peace Memorial Day," be a national holiday.

Mar. 17 — Former Chairman of the US Joint Chiefs of Staff General Colin L. Powell visits the ROC.

22 — Tibetan spiritual leader Dalai Lama pays a six-day visit to the ROC.

Apr. 2 — US House of Representatives Speaker Newt Gingrich meets with President Lee Teng-hui during his four-hour visit to the ROC, praising Taiwan's political progress and economic achievement.

— The *Statute Governing Relations with Hong Kong and Macau* is promulgated by President Lee Teng-hui and will go partially into effect on July 1 of this year for Hong Kong, and 1999 for Macau.

May 5 — The second session of the Third National Assembly begins to amend the *Constitution*. The focus of the session is to streamline the local government;

reform the election process for the president and members of the National Assembly; and clarify the president's relations with the Executive Yuan and the Legislature.

6 — The ROC establishes formal diplomatic relations with the Democratic Republic of São Tomé e Príncipe in western Africa.

18 — The Ministry of Foreign Affairs announces the ROC's decision to immediately terminate its diplomatic ties with the Bahamas.

31 — The Legislative Yuan passes the third reading of the *Public Television Bill*, which will enable the public television station to begin broadcasting in 1998.

June 21 — Koo Chen-fu, chairman of the Straits Exchange Foundation, is invited by mainland's Association for Relations Across the Taiwan Straits to attend the ceremony marking the transfer of Hong Kong's sovereignty to the Chinese mainland on June 30.

July 1 — The Mainland Affairs Council sets up the Hong Kong Affairs Bureau to handle ties between Taipei and Hong Kong after Hong Kong is reverted to the Chinese mainland.

27 — The Ministry of Foreign Affairs announces the closure of the Taipei Economic and Cultural Representative Office in Phnom Penh, Cambodia.

Aug. 1 — The Council of Grand Justice rules that legislators who engage in violence during legislative sessions will no longer be immune from arrest and prosecution.

6 — Nicaragua President Arnoldo Alemán Lacayo arrives in Taipei for a five-day visit.

10 — The ROC and Costa Rica sign a media cooperation agreement.

12 — The Republic of Chad resumes official ties with the ROC after a 25-year hiatus.

21 — Vice President and Premier Lien Chan heads the Cabinet and tenders resignation to the president. Legislator Vincent C. Siew will succeed him to be the new premier of the ROC.

26 — President Lee Teng-hui is re-elected chairman of the ruling Kuomintang with 93 percent of the votes cast by over 2,000 party representatives of KMT's 15th National Congress.

28 — KMT's 15th Central Committee elects 17 members to the enlarged Central Standing Committee, along with 16 appointed by the chairman, immediately following conclusion of National Congress.

Sept. 1 — The ROC swears in a new Cabinet with Vincent C. Siew as the premier. At a press conference after his inauguration, Premier Siew vows to improve law and order, further develop the economy, raise people's quality of life, and normalize cross-strait relations.

4 — President Lee Teng-hui leaves for Latin America via the US to attend the World Congress on the Panama Canal in Panama City, where he will meet with heads of state of ROC allies including Panama, Nicaragua and Honduras.

Oct. 3 — Swaziland King Mswati III visits the ROC through October 5. During his trip to Taipei, the King and the ROC President Lee Teng-hui will sign a joint communiqué to further strengthen bilateral relations.

5 — Vice President Lien Chan embarks on a 12-day visit to Iceland and Austria to strengthen ROC's substantive ties with the two nations.

9 — Taiwan film *Such a Life* wins the Best Picture Award at the 42nd Asia-Pacific Film Festival.

15 — Steven Chu, member of the ROC Academia Sinica, wins the 1997 Nobel Prize for physics.

26 — Chad President Idriss Deby visits the ROC through October 30.

Nov. 5 — Liberian President Charles Ghankay Taylor, accompanied by his wife and a 43-member delegation, arrives in Taipei for a seven-day state visit.

22 — The ROC signs a letter of intent with Hungary on cooperation in customs affairs.

25 — Koo Chen-fu, chairman of the Straits Exchange Foundation, represents President Lee Teng-hui to attend the APEC summit in Vancouver.

26 — Stricter regulations on firearms go into effect as part of the ROC government's efforts to strengthen and stabilize social order.

29 — In the election for county magistrates and city mayors, the ruling KMT takes eight seats out of the 23 seats at stake. The Democratic Progressive Party doubles its number of seats from six of the last election to 12. The remaining three seats go to the hands of independents.

Dec.   2 — The *Asian Wall Street Journal*, the first multinational newspaper to set up a printing site in Taipei, launches printing operations.

31 — The ROC severs its official ties with South Africa, thereby putting an end to diplomatic relations between the two nations established in 1976.

1998

Jan.   1 — Vice President Lien Chan and his wife start a four-day private visit to Singapore. Discussions over financial turmoil in the Asia-Pacific with high-ranking officials of the host nation stand high on his agenda.

12 — Premier Vincent C. Siew arrives in Manila for an unofficial visit.

20 — Premier Vincent C. Siew arrives in Jakarta, where he is scheduled to meet with Indonesian President Suharto to discuss over the possibility of establishing a financial cooperative mechanism in the Asia-Pacific region.

21 — Bishop Shan Kuo-hsi of the Catholic diocese in Kaohsiung is formally appointed one of only three cardinals representing the world's Chinese communities by Pope John Paul II.

24 — The Republic of China elects local-level county and city councilmen, and rural and urban township chiefs. The ruling KMT wins a landslide victory.

29 — The ROC suspends relations with the Central African Republic.

Feb.   11 — Malaysian Deputy Prime Minister Anwar Ibrahim pays a visit to the ROC as part of his government's drive to seek cooperative measures to stabilize the region's troubled financial sector.

14 — Foreign Minister Jason C. Hu launches a 12-day visit to ROC allies in Africa including Senegal, Gambia, Liberia, Burkina Faso, Chad and São Tomé e Príncipe to cement ties with these nations.

24 — Jordan University confers an honorary doctorate upon Vice President Lien Chan. During his trip to Jordan, Lien also meets with top officials of the host nation to strengthen bilateral cooperative relations.

Mar.   4 — On his way back to Taiwan from a trip to Jordan, Bahrain and the United Arab Emirates, Vice President Lien Chan arrives in Kuala Lumpur for a four-day private visit. Lien is scheduled to meet with Malaysian Prime Minister Mahathir Mohamad and his deputy Anwar Ibrahim to discuss possible cooperative measures for tackling the current financial troubles in Asia.

Apr.   3 — The Ministry of Foreign Affairs announces that President Lee Teng-hui has been nominated for the 1998 Nobel Peace Prize. It is the second time in three years that President Lee has been nominated for the honor.

21 — Haitian President René Garcia Preval arrives in Taipei for a four-day state visit. He and President Lee will sign a communiqué to strengthen bilateral friendship and cooperation.

22 — A delegation sent by the Straits Exchange Foundation with its deputy secretary-general, Jan Jyh-horng, at the head arrives in Beijing. Jan is scheduled to meet with his ARATS counterpart and set agendas for the second round of Koo-Wang Talks

slated to be held in autumn. The visit marks the restoration of cross-strait consultation and negotiation, which were unilaterally broken off by Beijing since 1995 following ROC President Lee Teng-hui's journey to the US to visit his alma mater, Cornell University, in June of the same year.

24 — The ROC signs a memorandum of understanding on customs cooperation with the Slovak Republic.

— The ROC announces the severance of diplomatic ties with Guinea-Bissau of western Africa.

25 — Premier Vincent C. Siew starts his three-day visit to Kuala Lumpur to meet with high-ranking officials of the host nation. How to further bolster bilateral ties and deal with the Asian financial turmoil stand as the centerpiece of the meeting.

— The president of the Central Bank of China, Perng Fai-nan, leads a delegation to attend the 31st board director meeting of the Asian Development Bank in Geneva.

May 5 — Vice President Lien Chan, sent by President Lee as a special envoy, leaves for Costa Rica to attend the inauguration of President-elect Miguel Angel Rodríguez slated for May 8. Also included in his itinerary is a three-day visit to Grenada and meetings with heads of state of other Caribbean nations, which maintain diplomatic ties with the ROC.

11 — The ROC armed forces conduct their annual routine joint military exercise in the eastern Taiwan counties of Hualien and Taitung. The drill, code-named "Han Kuang No. 14" will serve as a review of the military's combat readiness and ability to ensure national security.

22 — ROC President Lee Teng-hui and Nauru President Kinza Clodumar sign a joint communiqué to reinforce bilateral cooperation. The head of the Republic of Nauru and his entourage pay a four-day visit to the ROC.

31 — Gyorgy Ujlaky, Hungary's newly appointed representative to the ROC, arrives in Taipei to set up a trade office in Taipei to promote bilateral exchanges. Following the Czech Republic and Poland, Hungary will become the third central European country to open a trade office in Taiwan.

June 1 — Premier Vincent C. Siew presides over the opening ceremony of the newly established Southern Taiwan Service Center in Kaohsiung City. The center aims to guarantee efficient service and decisive problem-solving for residents of the southern part of Taiwan.

15 — Democratic Republic of São Tomé e Príncipe President Miguel A.C.L. Trovoada and his wife arrive in Taipei for a five-day state visit.

July 2 — Premier Vincent Siew embarks on a nine-day Pacific trip to consolidate bilateral relation with ROC diplomatic partners in the region.

21 — The opening of the Taiwan International Mercantile Exchange is a milestone for Taiwan's financial sector.

Oct. 9 — The Legislative Yuan passes the statute to streamline the Taiwan Provincial Government, making the TPG a non-autonomous body under the central government.

13 — Daniel C. Tsui, member of the ROC's Academia Sinica, wins the 1997 Nobel Prize for physics.

14 — Straits Exchange Foundation Chairman Koo Chen-fu arrives in Shanghai to meet with his ARATS counterpart Wang Daohan. During his trip, Mr. Koo states that the conciliatory spirit of agreements signed between the two sides in Singapore five years ago will be restored.

Nov. 2 — The ROC severs diplomatic ties with Kingdom of Tonga.

3 — President Lee Teng-hui meets with former German Chancellor Helmut Schmidt to exchange views on world economic development.

9 — US Secretary of Energy Bill Richardson arrives in Taiwan to attend the 22nd annual USA-ROC Economic Council.

16 — Pin-kung Chiang, chairman of the Council for Economic Planning and Development, heads for Malaysia to attend the APEC annual conference on behalf of President Lee Teng-hui.

20 — The ROC and the Marshall Islands sign a joint communiqué to formalize diplomatic relations, as the Marshall islands becomes the ROC's 27th diplomatic ally.

Dec.　5 — Vice President Lien Chan leads a humanitarian delegation of government officials and representatives from charity and religious organizations on an 11-day visit to hurricane-stricken allies including Nicaragua, Honduras, El Salvador, and Guatemala.

— In the election for the Fourth Legislative Yuan, the ruling KMT secures 123 of the 225 seats and the DPP garners 70 seats while the rest goes to the NP and other minority parties. The KMT also triumphs in elections for Taipei mayor and councilmen of Taipei and Kaohsiung cities, but it loses the mayoral election in Kaohsiung City.

21 — Operations begin to streamline the provincial government, a vital part of the efficiency-oriented master plan to restructure the government in Taiwan.

1999

Jan.　9 — Premier Vincent C. Siew heads for the Dominican Republic, Haiti, and Belize to consolidate relations in the Caribbean.

12 — The Legislative Yuan unanimously abolishes the *Publication Law*.

26 — The ROC launches ROCSAT-1, its first wholly-owned and operated satellite, into orbit from Cape Canaveral, Florida, USA, marking the ROC's entry into the era of advanced space technology.

27 — The ROC and the Republic of Macedo-

nia sign a joint communiqué to establish formal relations. Macedonia thus becomes ROC's second diplomatic ally in Europe, after the Holy See.

Feb.　5 — President Imata Kabua of the Marshall Islands arrives in Taipei for a one-week visit.

Mar.　5 — Foreign Minister Jason C. Hu signs a memorandum with his Macedonian counterpart, Aleksandar Dimitrov, in Skopje to promote bilateral economic cooperation.

7 — The President of the Assembly of Macedonia, Savo Klimovski, arrives in Taipei for a six-day reciprocal visit.

17 — The Atomic Energy Council issues a permit for Taiwan Power Company to construct the ROC's fourth nuclear power plant.

22 — Costa Rican President Miguel Angel Rodriguez arrives in Taipei for a six-day visit.

29 — Former US President Jimmy Carter visits Taiwan at the invitation of a private think tank in Taipei.

Apr.　28 — The Embassy of the Republic of Macedonia commences operation with Verka Modanu as Macedonia's first resident envoy to the ROC.

30 — Foreign Minister Jason C. Hu arrives in the Marshall Islands for a three-day official visit to strengthen bilateral ties in such areas as tourism, fisheries, and investment.

May　27 — Premier Vincent C. Siew heads to the Central Caribbean to attend the inauguration of El Salvador President Francisco Flores. During his visit there, the premier meets with the Presidents of Nicaragua and Panama.

June　4 — The Legislative Yuan passes the third reading of the *Cigarette and Wine Management Law*, revoking the decades-old monopoly tax system.

6 — Macedonian President Ljubco Georgievski, head of a 59-member delegation, arrives Taipei for a six-day official visit. During his visit to the ROC, he

signs agreements on economic cooperation, investment guarantees, and prevention of the double taxation of investors to strengthen relations with the ROC government.

7 — In an international press conference, President Lee Teng-hui announces that the ROC will provide US$300 million Balkans aid package to ease the plight of Kosovo war refugees.

16 — The Legislature passes the third reading of the amendments to the *Public Lottery Act*, ensuring the right of lottery issuance by the central government.

23 — The ROC signs a press cooperation agreement with Panama.

24 — The *Domestic Violence Prevention Law* goes into effect.

July 9 — In an interview with the German Broadcasting company, Deutsche Welle, President Lee Teng-hui first announces the concept that Taiwan and the Chinese mainland have a "special state-to-state relationship."

— To enhance bilateral economic and trade ties, the ROC and Thailand sign pacts on aviation exchanges and avoidance of double taxation.

20 — President Lee Teng-hui further elaborates his recent remarks of the "special state-to-state relationship" between the two sides of the Taiwan Strait by saying that he did not put forth the statement to seek Taiwan independence but simply to reiterate the fact that both sides are separately governed.

Aug. 1 — Premier Vincent C. Siew, head of an 80-member delegation, departs for the Republic of Macedonia to enhance bilateral relations. During his visit to the ROC's new diplomatic ally in south Europe, the premier officiates at the groundbreaking ceremony for the Taiwan-funded export processing zone near Macedonia's capital city of Skopje.

30 — Premier Vincent C. Siew departs for Panama to attend the September 1 inauguration of Panamanian President-elect Mireya Moscoso.

Sept. 4 — The Third National Assembly passes a constitutional amendment which extends the current terms of the deputies from May 2000 to June 2002, and includes the appointment of all deputies on the basis of party proportional representation in the fourth Assembly.

7 — The second ROC-Central American summit is held in Taipei. During the summit, President Lee signs a joint communiqué with the leaders of seven Central American allies.

9 — Pin-kung Chiang, chairman of the Council for Economic Planning and Development, participates in the APEC leadership summit in Auckland, New Zealand as an envoy of President Lee Teng-hui.

20 — President Lee Teng-hui and Paraguayan President Luis Angel González Macchi sign a joint communiqué reaffirming the two countries' commitment to stronger cooperative relations. The 11th Economic Cooperation Conference between the ROC and Paraguay is also held in Taipei concurrent to González's state visit.

21 — Taiwan is hit by its deadliest earthquake in more than 60 years. The 7.3 magnitude quake claims more than 2,000 lives and injures over 8,000.

25 — President Lee issues an emergency decree to cut through red tape and expedite reconstruction work in the wake of Taiwan's devastating earthquake. The decree, which supersedes certain existing laws, is effective for six months.

Oct. 1 — The Civil Aeronautics Administration announces the indefinite suspension of direct flights between Taipei and Manila after a breakdown in negotiations on weekly passenger quotas.

20 — The ROC government extends its congratulations to Indonesia's President-elect Abdurrahman Wahid.

26 — The Taipei-based China External Trade Development Council opens a branch office in Bombay, India. The new office will play an extensive role in promoting the ROC's trade with India.

Nov. 6 — Independent candidate Chang Jung-wei wins the by-election for county magistrate in Yunlin County, beating rivals from the ruling Kuomintang and the main opposition Democratic Progressive Party.

7 — *Darkness and Light*, a film by Taiwan director Chang Tso-chi, is awarded the prize for best picture at the 12th Tokyo International Film Festival.

13 — Tokyo Governor Shintaro Ishihara arrives in Taiwan for a three-day visit at the invitation of President Lee Teng-hui. Ishihara has been the highest-profile Japanese official to visit Taiwan since the two countries cut diplomatic relations in 1972.

14 — Michael Campbell of New Zealand wins the 1999 Johnnie Walker Classic, held at the Ta Shee Golf and Country Club in northern Taiwan.

17 — The decision-making Central Standing Committee of the ruling Kuomintang approves a disciplinary committee proposal to oust independent presidential candidate James Soong from the KMT.

20 — President Lee greets visiting Nauru President Rene Harris and his wife in Taipei.

26 — Rene Liu of Taiwan wins the best actress award at the 1999 Asia-Pacific Film Festival, held in Bangkok, for her performance in *The Personals*.

Dec. 1 — President Lee presides over a welcoming ceremony for Malawi President Bakili Muluzi in Taipei.

— The ROC Ministry of Finance launches the National Welfare Lottery.

10 — Chen Shui-bian, presidential candidate of the main opposition Democratic Progressive Party, announces Taoyuan County Magistrate Lu Hsiu-lien as his running mate for the March 2000 election.

16 — The ROC is named a permanent observer of the Central American Parliament Speakers Forum at the ninth meeting of the CAPSF in Panama.

20 — ROC President Lee Teng-hui receives US Congresswoman Nancy Pelosi in Taipei.

28 — The ROC renames its representative office in Macau the Taipei Economic and Cultural Center.

30 — The ROC establishes formal diplomatic relations with Palau.

2000

Jan. 17 — President Lee Teng-hui receives a US congressional delegation headed by Representative Matt Salmon.

24 — Chen Wu-hsiung, vice chairman of the ROC Council of Agriculture, is elected vice chairman of the Asian-African Rural Reconstruction Organization. The AARRO is one of the few international organizations in which the ROC has participated in an official capacity.

Feb. 20 — A three-day joint conference of the Liberal International Congress and the Council of Asian Liberals and Democrats concludes in Taipei.

25 — President Lee Teng-hui and Liberian President Charles Ghankay Taylor sign a joint communiqué in Taipei to enhance bilateral cooperation.

29 — ROC Foreign Minister Chen Chien-jen and his Macedonian counterpart Aleksandar Dimitrov issue a joint statement in Taipei. The two sides have agreed to expedite the project to construct the Skopje Free Economic Zone in Macedonia and also to waive visa requirements for holders of diplomatic and official passports.

Mar. 7 — ROC Foreign Minister Chen Chien-jen and Palau Minister of State Sabino Anastacio sign a joint declaration in the South Pacific nation's capital, Koror, to strengthen bilateral cooperation.

9 — Lung Ying-tai, director of the Bureau of Cultural Affairs under the Taipei City

Government, delivers a speech in Sweden on Taiwan's future, the first public talk by an official from the ROC in the Scandinavian country.

18 — Democratic Progressive Party candidate Chen Shui-bian and his running mate Lu Hsiu-lien are elected president and vice president of the Republic of China, ending the KMT's more than 50-year hold on the presidency in Taiwan.

23 — US envoy Lee Hamilton meets with President-elect Chen Shui-bian to exchange views on future relations between Taiwan and the United States.

27 — Canadian Nobel laureate in economics Robert Mundell meets with ROC President Lee Teng-hui in Taipei.

31 — James Soong, the former Taiwan governor and Kuomintang maverick who lost his independent presidential bid, formally establishes the People First Party with himself as its chairman.

Apr. 5 — An international symposium on biodiversity is held in Taipei to discuss issues ranging from the latest developments in biodiversity research to key conservation efforts.

10 — President Lee Teng-hui confers the Order of Brilliant Star With Grand Cordon upon David Dean, former Taipei director of the American Institute in Taiwan, in recognition of the diplomat's contribution to US-ROC relations.

24 — The Third National Assembly approves a landmark amendment to drastically reduce its powers and functions. The Assembly will lose its status as a standing body and will convene only when proposals of impeachment, constitutional amendment and national boundary changes are initiated by the Legislature.

May 20 — Chen Shui-bian and Lu Hsiu-lien are sworn in as the ROC's tenth-term president and vice president, respectively, and Tang Fei takes office as the new premier.

21 — Taiwanese director Edward Yang wins a Golden Palm Award for best director at the Cannes Film Festival for *A One and A Two*.

June 9 — The 2000 Asia-Pacific Cultural Summit, sponsored by the Taipei City Government's Bureau of Cultural Affairs, begins a three-day conference in Taipei with the participation of mayors, officials, and delegates from 26 cities in the Asia-Pacific region.

11 — The 2000 World Congress of Information Technology, with more than 1,700 business leaders and executives from 82 countries participating, opens for a three-day run at the Taipei International Convention Center.

14 — US Secretary of Transportation Rodney Slater arrives in Taipei to attend the 24th joint conference of the ROC-US and US-ROC Business Councils.

23 — Taiwan democracy pioneers and former Democratic Progressive Party Chairmen Shih Ming-te and Hsu Hsin-liang leave for Warsaw to attend the World Democracy Forum.

25 — The Democratic Progressive Party elects Kaohsiung Mayor Frank Chang-ting Hsieh as its new chairman.

July 1 — Panamanian President Mireya Elisa Moscoso Rodríguez arrives in Taipei for a five-day state visit.

25 — Vice Premier Yu Shyi-kun resigns to take responsibility for failed rescue efforts that resulted in the deaths of four workers in a flash flood in Chiayi, southern Taiwan.

Aug. 1 — Chang Chun-hsiung of the Democratic Progressive Party succeeds Yu Shyi-kun as vice premier of the ROC.

13 — President Chen Shui-bian leaves for Los Angeles to conduct his first state visits to the ROC's diplomatic allies since assuming office on May 20. The 13-day journey takes Chen to the Caribbean nation of the Dominican Republic, and Nicaragua and Costa Rica in Central America,

as well as three African countries—the Gambia, Burkina Faso and Chad.

28 — Master Sheng Yen, the founder of Taiwan's Dharma Drum Mountain Buddhist Foundation, attends the Millennium World Peace Summit of Religious Leaders held in New York.

Sept. 1 — The ROC Ministry of Foreign Affairs announces that three representative offices in Congo, Angola and Madagascar are closed because they no longer serve their diplomatic function.

5 — The Fourth East Asian Women's Forum opens in Taipei with a focus on the "new era and modern women."

18 — ROC weightlifter Li Feng-ying wins the silver medal in the women's 53-kilogram category at the 2000 Olympic Games in Sydney, Australia.

22 — ROC Vice President Lu Hsiu-lien makes her first official foreign journey since taking office on May 20. Lu's four-state goodwill visit takes her to El Salvador, Honduras, Belize, and Guatemala.

23 — Singapore's Senior Minister Lee Kuan Yew arrives in Taipei for a four-day private visit.

Oct. 3 — Premier Tang Fei resigns and is succeeded by Vice Premier Chang Chun-hsiung.

15 — Former ROC President Lee Teng-hui attends the Forum 2000 conference in Prague.

27 — Premier Chang Chun-hsiung announces that the Executive Yuan is cancelling the partly built Fourth Nuclear Power Plant.

30 — Defense Minister Wu Shih-wen signs a memorandum on military cooperation with his Macedonian counterpart Ljuben Paunoski in Taipei.

Nov. 13 — The 11th Forum of Legislative Presidents of Central America takes place in Taipei.

15 — ROC Central Bank of China Governor Perng Fai-nan attends the APEC leaders summit in Brunei on behalf of President Chen Shui-bian.

17 — Lai Ying-li wins the gold medal in the

women's heavyweight category at the Third World Youth Tae Kwon Do Championship, held in Ireland.

23 — Kuomintang Vice Chairman Wu Poh-hsiung meets mainland Chinese Vice Premier Qian Qichen in Beijing.

28 — The 12th meeting of the East Asia Agricultural Organization Council is held in Taichung County, central Taiwan.

Dec. 9 — President Chen signs a joint communiqué in Taipei with his El Salvadorian counterpart, Francisco Guillermo Flores Pérez.

10 — Twenty-one prisoners, including 19 conscientious objectors, are released under an amnesty decree issued by President Chen Shui-bian.

10 — Taiwan director Chang Chih-yung wins the Best Director Award at the 2000 Asia Pacific Film Festival for his film *Lament of the Sand River*.

2001

Jan. 1 — The "Three Mini Links" (direct trade, postal, and transportation) between Taiwan's two frontline islands of Kinmen and Matsu and mainland China's Xiamen and Fuzhou harbors in Fujian Province are put into practice.

8 — President Yahya Jammeh of The Gambia arrives in Taipei for a six-day visit.

10 — President Chen meets with a US House of Representatives delegation headed by Eva Clayton and Danny Davis.

15 — The Council of Grand Justices rules that the Cabinet's controversial decision to halt work on the Fourth Nuclear Power Plant has "procedural errors," but refrains from declaring the action unconstitutional.

Feb. 6 — President Chen meets mainland Chinese-born Nobel literature laureate Gao Xingjian in Taipei.

11 — Taipei City Mayor Ma Ying-jeou arrives in Hong Kong for a four-day visit aimed at promoting city-to-city exchanges.

14 — Premier Chang Chun-hsiung makes an

official announcement to resume the construction of the Fourth Nuclear Power Plant.

18 — *Betelnut Beauty*, a film by Taiwan director Lin Cheng-sheng, wins a Silver Bear Award at the 51st Berlin Film Festival.

25 — *Crouching Tiger, Hidden Dragon*, directed by Taiwan-born director Ang Lee, wins four British Academy Awards. The martial arts film wins best director, best foreign-language picture, best soundtrack and best costume.

Mar. 15 — Burkina Faso President Blaise Compaore arrives in Taipei for a six-day visit.

24 — Dominican Republic President Hipólito Mejia arrives in Taipei for a five-day visit.

26 — The film *Crouching Tiger, Hidden Dragon* wins four Oscar awards at the 73rd Annual Academy Awards: best foreign-language film, best art direction, best cinematography, and best original score.

29 — Liberian President Charles Taylor arrives in Taipei for a weeklong visit.

30 — The Association of World Citizens, a non-governmental organization, holds its 11th World Citizen Congress in Taipei between March 30 and April 3.

31 — Tibetan spiritual leader Dalai Lama arrives in Taipei for a ten-day visit at the invitation of the Buddhist Association of the ROC.

Apr. 14 — President Chen Shui-bian receives a four-member US Senate delegation led by Senator Phil Gramm.

22 — Former President Lee Teng-hui arrives in Japan for medical treatment.

May 15 — ROC Council for Economic Planning and Development Chairman Chen Po-chih meets mainland Chinese President Jiang Zemin during a ministerial meeting on human resources at the APEC forum in Beijing.

16 — President Chen Shui-bian receives St. Vincent and the Grenadines Prime Minister Ralph Gonsalves.

21 — President Chen Shui-bian leaves for a 16-day, five-leg diplomatic journey to Latin America with transit stops in New York and Houston.

June 18 — The ROC severs diplomatic relations with Macedonia.

July 2 — President Chen Shui-bian decorates visiting Senegal President Abdoulaye Wade with the Order of Brilliant Jade in recognition of his efforts to strengthen relations between the two countries.

9 — Premier Vance W. Amory of St. Christopher and Nevis arrives in the Republic of China for a weeklong visit.

15 — Nicaraguan President Arnoldo Aleman arrives in Taipei for a four-day visit.

26 — President Chen receives former South Korean President Kim Young Sam in Taipei.

Aug. 14 — Five winners of the Nobel Peace Prize and representatives from several non-governmental organizations gather in Taipei for the 2001 Global Peace Assembly.

29 — President Chen receives US House Majority Whip Tom Delay in Taipei.

Sept. 1 — Premier Chang Chun-hsiung embarks on his first diplomatic trip to visit Taiwan's four diplomatic allies in the East Caribbean—St. Christopher and Nevis, the Commonwealth of Dominica, Saint Vincent and the Grenadines, and Grenada.

Nov. 6 — President Chen opens the 34th Baseball World Cup in Taipei, with 16 participating teams from around the world.

11 — The World Trade Organization approves Taiwan's entry at its fourth ministerial meeting in Doha, Qatar.

14 — First Lady Wu Shu-chen of the ROC receives the "2001 Prize for Freedom" in France bestowed on President Chen Shui-bian by the London-based Liberal International.

Dec. 1 — In the election for the Fifth Legislative Yuan, the DPP wins 87 seats of the 225 seats available, the KMT 68 seats, the PFP 46 seats, and the TSU 13 seats, while the rest go to minority parties and independents. In the election for county magistrates and city mayors, the DPP and the KMT each take nine seats out of the 23 seats available, the PFP wins two seats, the NP wins one seat, and the remaining two seats go to independents.

9 — Vice President Lu receives the World Peace Prize in Taipei for her work in promoting women's and human rights, democracy, and world peace.

10 — São Tomé e Príncipe President Fradique Banderira Melo de Menezes arrives in Taipei for a five-day visit.

19 — Vice President Lu departs for The Gambia to attend the inauguration of re-elected Gambian President Yahya Jammeh.

Appendix II

The History of the ROC Before 1949

Introduction

The Republic of China was established in 1912 after a revolution overthrew China's last dynasty, the Ching, and the last emperor abdicated. From its very beginning, the ROC faced enormous challenges that threatened its survival: division by warlords, political struggles, economic underdevelopment, and foreign colonialism and aggression. These weaknesses were taken advantage of when the Japanese invaded China in the 1930s and 40s, devastating the country and leaving millions dead. After the war, the Chinese communists also took advantage of a weakened ROC to wage civil war. In 1949, the ROC government was forced to relocate to Taiwan. While the ROC carried out agrarian reform, industrialization, and modernization on Taiwan, the communist People's Republic of China waged decades of political struggles on the mainland.

This chapter provides a brief summary of the history of the Republic of China prior to 1949.

Traditional China

Since the appearance of writing in China some 6,000 to 7,000 years ago, Chinese people have been recording the history of their families, clans, and dynasties. In time, many Chinese rulers and the large bureaucracies under them collated these various historical materials to write histories that highlighted the ruler's place in Chinese history. The resulting histories showed a "dynastic cycle" that began with the fall of a corrupt ruler and a weak dynasty followed by the rise of a new moral ruler and a strong dynasty. Many of these traditional histories are still extant and intelligible to readers of Chinese today. The Chinese people are thus the inheritors of the world's longest unbroken historical tradition.

The historical focus on political legitimacy and continuity was a powerfully conservative force in China. Traditional histories provided successive dynasties and governments with a set of precedents by which to rule. Thus, even though ruling power passed hands quite often in China, the way the country was ruled remained roughly the same. This lent a degree of stability to Chinese culture that was absent in the cultures bordering China.

One common explanation of the phenomenal endurance of Chinese civilization is that China was actually governed by an aristocracy of intelligentsia, which had been continuously revitalized by the introduction of new personnel. A civil service examination system, first implemented in the Sui dynasty over 1,400 years ago, allowed young men who were well schooled in China's historical and literary traditions to enter the government bureaucracy, regardless of their family's social, political, or economic status. Theoretically, even the son of commoners could become prime minister one day as long as he could pass a series of imperial examinations. When an emperor was deposed, it mattered little who would take his place, since the Chinese bureaucratic system continued to function.

Equally insulated from political infighting was the village economy, upon which China's agricultural civilization was based. Peasants seldom troubled themselves with national affairs unless war or imperial mismanagement threatened the livelihood of the village and its ability to raise grain, produce goods, and render the services of labor.

China's modern history began when the three pillars of Chinese stability—rule by historical precedent, bureaucratic conservatism, and village-based economics—were shaken by contact with the West. This chapter seeks to shed light on China's modern history and provide background information on the history of the Republic of China.

East Meets West

For thousands of years, China has maintained close relations with the nation states on its periphery. These periphery states often served as intermediaries between China and other major civilizations in India and the Middle East. As far back as the Han dynasty (206 B.C.–A.D. 221), China was exporting silk, porcelain, and other trade goods to the Roman Empire. During the Yuan dynasty (1279–1368), China's Mongolian rulers, especially Kublai Khan 忽必烈, brought a significant number of Persians, Turks, and

Chinese Dynastic Chronology

Dynasty	Divisions	Dates	Capital
Hsia 夏		2205–1766 B.C.	Anyi
Shang 商 (or **Yin** 殷)		1766–1122 B.C.	Anyang
Chou 周	Western Chou	1122–770 B.C.	Hao (Xian)
	Eastern Chou	770–221 B.C.	Loyi (Loyang)
	(Spring and Autumn Period)	770–476 B.C.	
	(Warring States Period)	475–221 B.C.	
Chin 秦		221–206 B.C.	Xienyang
Han 漢	Western Han	206 B.C.–A.D. 8	Changan (Xian)
	Hsin	8–25	Changan
	Eastern Han	25–220	Loyang
Three	Wei	220–265	Loyang
Kingdoms 三國	Shu	222–263	Chengdu
	Wu	222–280	Nanjing
Chin 晉	Western Chin	265–316	Loyang
	Eastern Chin	317–420	Nanjing
Southern	Sung	420–479	Nanjing
Dynasties 南朝	Chi	479–502	Nanjing
	Liang	502–557	Nanjing
	Chen	557–589	Nanjing
Northern	Northern Wei	386–534	Pincheng
Dynasties 北朝	Eastern Wei	534–550	Yeh (Honan)
	Western Wei	535–557	Changan
	Northern Chi	550–557	Yeh
	Northern Chou	557–581	Changan
Sui 隋		581–618	Changan
			Loyang
			Yangzhou
Tang 唐		618–907	Changan
			Loyang
Five	Later Liang	907–923	Kaifeng
Dynasties 五代	Later Tang	923–936	Loyang
	Later Chin	936–946	Kaifeng
	Later Han	947–950	Kaifeng
	Later Chou	951–959	Kaifeng
Sung 宋	Northern Sung	960–1127	Kaifeng
	Southern Sung	1127–1279	Hangzhou
Yuan 元		1279–1368	Beijing
Ming 明		1368–1644	Nanjing
			Beijing
Ching 清		1644–1911	Beijing

other peoples from Central Asia to work in the Mongolian administration. The great Italian traveler, Marco Polo, visited China during this time and is said to have worked for the Mongolians as a superintendent of trade in Lanzhou 蘭州.

Early in the 15th century, an ambitious Ming monarch, Cheng Tsu 成祖 (commonly referred to as the Yung Lo Emperor 永樂大帝), showed an intense interest in overseas exploration. He equipped scores of seafaring ships, manned by tens of thousands of sailors, and placed them under the command of one of his closest advisors, the eunuch Cheng Ho 鄭和. In the years between 1406 and 1433, Cheng Ho made seven voyages through the South China Sea, past the Malaysian Peninsula, into the Indian Ocean, and on to the east coast of Africa. His travels to more than 50 countries constituted the greatest overseas venture in Chinese history.

Two main sea routes linking the East and West were discovered during the Ming dynasty, and by the early 16th century, Portugal, Spain, Holland, and England were sending powerful fleets to Asian waters. The Portuguese were the first Europeans to reach China by sea. With the permission of Ming officials, the Portuguese set up an entrepôt at Macau in 1535. In the years that followed, many Christian missionaries came to China on Portuguese ships. In 1601, the Italian Jesuit Matteo Ricci was granted an imperial stipend to reside in Beijing 北京. Other missionaries soon followed in his footsteps. Julius Aleni, Johannes Terrens, Didacus de Pentoja, Johannes Adam Schall von Bell, and Ferdiandus Verbiest brought not only their religion, but also new concepts and ideas with respect to the arts, medical science, water conservancy, mathematics, geography, and astronomy, including the Gregorian calendar. As in the Yuan dynasty, some of these intrepid Christians even served as officials in the imperial bureaucracy.

China's Closed-door Policy

The Manchus established the Ching dynasty in 1644. During their rule over China, the Manchus subdued the remnants of Mongol resistance in the northwest, and conquered the Khalkhas, the Kalmuks, and the Turks. They also formally annexed Outer and Inner Mongolia, Xinjiang, Qinghai, and Tibet, thereby fixing the modern boundaries of China. In 1683, Ching forces took over Taiwan.

At the height of Ching power, the Manchus utilized the best minds and richest human resources of the country, regardless of race, to carry out many scholarly projects. However, Western missionaries—active in China since the end of the Ming—lost the trust of the Yung Cheng Emperor 雍正 because of their role in a power struggle for the throne. Christianity was thus banned in 1724, and the flow of Western technology into China soon slowed to a trickle. During the entire 18th century and the early 19th century, while Europe was being transformed and invigorated by the rise of rationalism, nationalism, colonialism, and the industrial revolution, the Ching court was adopting a virtual closed-door policy toward the Western world.

Breaking Down the Door

The Western powers, however, were not content to leave China isolated, as they coveted Chinese markets and resources. They were dissatisfied with perennial trade deficits with China; unhappy with being treated unequally by the royal court of China, which viewed trade as bestowing a favor; and chafed at being restricted to doing business in only a few small ports. High productivity in both light and heavy industries drove European countries (especially England) outward in search of new markets and resources. By the early 18th century, England dominated overseas trade, having gained dominance of the seas over Spain and Holland. During the next century, colonialism and resource exploitation backed by military force went hand in hand with the push by major European nations to develop overseas markets.

The seeds of the Opium War of 1839–42 were sown in a worsening trade relationship between Great Britain and the Ching court. The Ching government was gravely concerned about the loss of 1.8 million silver taels its populace was spending on 30,000 chests (each containing more than 100 catties) of opium each year. In January 1839, Ching Commissioner Lin Tse-hsu 林則徐 was made responsible for stamping out the opium trade. He closed down guilds in Canton 廣州 after foreign merchants, such as Lancelot Dent, refused to yield all the opium stored on Lingding Island 伶仃島. The foreign merchants finally gave in

515

and handed more than 20,000 chests of opium to Lin who, to the great dismay of the drug dealers, promptly burnt them all. In July 1840, British warships occupied Dinghai 定海 and in August attacked Dagu 大沽 near the northern port city of Tianjin 天津. A Ching official, Chi Shan 琦善, gave in to English demands for indemnity and ceded Hong Kong 香港 to England. However, the British government was not satisfied with the agreement and sent a new plenipotentiary, Henry Pottinger, who attacked Amoy 廈門 (Xiamen) in 1841, and Shanghai 上海 in 1842. The Treaty of Nanjing (Nanking) 南京條約 was consequently signed on August 29, 1842, and has proven to be one of the most influential treaties in China's modern history. Not only was it the first in a series of unequal treaties signed with Western powers, but it also marked the beginning of a long period of internal turmoil and external concessions for China over the next 150 years. The 13 articles in the treaty stipulated that five ports were to be opened for British trade and consulates; Hong Kong was to be ceded to England; and 21 million silver taels were to be paid in four installments. Supplementary clauses that were signed later further stipulated consulate jurisdiction over Englishmen residing in China.

After the Treaty of Nanjing, Belgium, Holland, Prussia, Spain, Portugal, the United States, and France also asked to establish consulates in China. In 1844, the Treaty of Wangxia 望廈條約 was concluded with the United States, which stated that the US would enjoy whatever privileges China granted to other nations. Later that year, a similar agreement, the Treaty of Whampoa 黃埔條約, was signed with France.

By signing the Treaty of Nanjing, China agreed to open five ports, including Canton, to foreign trade. However, the residents of Canton at first refused to allow Englishmen to enter the city and then attacked those already there. In early 1856, a French missionary was killed in Guangxi Province 廣西省. Later that year the Arrow Incident 亞羅號事件 occurred, in which the Arrow—a Hong Kong-registered ship under the protection of the English government—was searched in Canton by Ching soldiers and 12 of its sailors were arrested. These incidents eventually led to an Anglo-French expedition against Beijing in 1858 and the burning of the imperial summer palace by invading troops.

The Ching court was thus compelled to make further concessions in the 1860 Treaty of Beijing 北京條約.

The signing of these treaties led to a flood of Western merchants selling foreign goods: textiles, kerosene, lamps, cigarettes, and opium. Consequently, the old Chinese system collapsed, and the village economy that had served as the backbone of China's agricultural society and sustained Chinese civilization for several millennia was seriously disrupted.

The proud imperial bureaucracy and the mandarin elite were woefully ill-equipped to deal with this onslaught. They were ignorant of the new forces to which China was being subjected. Their training had been in the old Chinese classics, and their experience had not prepared them to meet these new challenges.

Reformers in the Ching court, however, were aware of the superiority of Western armaments. In 1861, Generals Tseng Kuo-fan 曾國藩, Li Hung-chang 李鴻章, and Tso Tsung-tang 左宗棠 were able to convince the Ching court to initiate a 30-year "self-strengthening" program. Under this new program, the Ching dynasty began to train translators, import Western military technology, and set up armories. The Tsungli Yamen 總理衙門 was established to manage foreign affairs.

The self-strengthening program, however, came too late. Further controversies with Russia in the northwest and with England and France in the southwest jeopardized the stability of the Ching dynasty. A war with France ended with the signing of the Treaty of Tianjin (Tientsin) 天津條約 in 1885. In the latter half of the 19th century, China lost its suzerain rights and sovereignty over the Indo-China Peninsula and large areas of the northwest.

During this period, Chinese and Japanese spheres of influence overlapped in Korea, and Japan was showing interest in taking over Taiwan. The Ching court sent Liu Yung-fu 劉永福 and his armies to safeguard the island. The military modernization undertaken during the self-strengthening program proved to be a complete failure when war between China and Japan finally broke out in 1894. Japan quickly breached the Chinese defenses and sank most of her northern navy. The Treaty of Shimonoseki 馬關條約 was signed the next year, compelling the Ching government to pay a huge indemnity, open its seaports, recognize the independence of Korea, and cede the Liaodong Peninsula 遼東半島, Taiwan, and the Pescadores to Japan.

The repeated defeats suffered by China at the hands of foreign powers, the weakness and incompetence of the Ching court, and the success of the Meiji Reformation in Japan prompted many Chinese to take action. Under the leadership of Kang Yu-wei 康有為 and Liang Chi-chao 梁啟超, a reform movement was initiated in 1898. The Kuang Hsu Emperor 光緒 sympathized with this movement, but met with strong opposition from his aunt, the Empress Dowager Tzu-hsi 慈禧太后, as well as from other conservative elements in the Ching court. The movement came to an inglorious end after only 100 days and was followed by a coup d'état in which the Kuang Hsu Emperor was imprisoned by the Empress Dowager and those who had played a leading part in the movement were executed or exiled.

Popular discontent with internal misgovernment and anti-foreign sentiment aroused by the unequal treaties combined to spark the Boxer Uprising 義和拳之亂 in 1900. The Boxers laid siege to the foreign legation in Beijing, where a combined force of Japanese, French, British, Russian, and American troops held out for over a month. The siege was broken when the forces of eight foreign powers marched from Tianjin and scaled the walls of Beijing. The foreign powers then took the opportunity to loot Beijing in one of the most disgraceful episodes of modern diplomatic history. In the signing of the Treaty of Beijing the following year, China was disarmed and forced to pay large indemnities. This treaty was regarded as the most humiliating of all the unequal treaties.

One of the foreign powers which sacked Beijing, Russia, also took this opportunity to occupy Manchuria. When the troops of the other foreign powers withdrew from Chinese territory, Russia refused to leave Manchuria, leading to conflicts with Japan and the outbreak of the Russo-Japanese War in 1904. Through the Treaty of Portsmouth signed in 1905, a victorious Japan obtained complete control over Korea and rights and interests in southern Manchuria, leaving the north to Russia. Thereafter, Manchuria and Mongolia became flash points of further conflict between Japan and Russia, with China the biggest loser of the three.

The Birth of the ROC

After decades of pain and frustration brought about largely by the weakness of the imperial government, many Chinese people were disillusioned with the Ching dynasty and began to take a keen interest in the revolutionary movement launched by Dr. Sun Yat-sen 孫中山 in the late 19th century. Dr. Sun set up a series of secret societies that operated in inland Chinese cities and overseas. In 1887, Dr. Sun even set up a secret society in Japanese-controlled Taiwan, from where he directed an uprising in Huizhou 惠州.

In 1905, Dr. Sun Yat-sen, who had been exiled from China for his involvement in the anti-Ching movement, organized the Revolutionary Alliance 同盟會 (Tung-meng Hui) in Tokyo. This organization sponsored a network of revolutionaries inside China. On October 10, 1911, Dr. Sun's supporters in Wuchang 武昌, fearing their cover was blown by the recent arrest of one of their agents, seized the initiative and raised the standard of revolt in Hubei Province. Drawing on a wellspring of popular support and the defection of numerous officers in the local garrison, the revolutionaries soon captured Wuhan 武漢. Two months later, revolutionaries fought and won a pitched battle in Nanjing 南京. On January 1, 1912, the Revolutionary Alliance, which by that time controlled 16 of the Ching dynasty's 22 provinces, established a provisional parliament in Nanjing and elected Dr. Sun Yat-sen to the provisional presidency of Asia's first democratic republic—the Republic of China.

Northern China, however, was effectively controlled by Yuan Shi-kai 袁世凱, who had served the Ching dynasty in a variety of high posts. To break the deadlock and unify China, a three-way settlement was reached between revolutionaries in the south and the military strongman Yuan in the north. On February 12, 1912, the last Ching ruler, Emperor Hsuan Tung 宣統, gave up his throne. The rule of the Manchus had lasted 268 years and spanned the rule of ten emperors. Dr. Sun Yat-sen agreed to relinquish the provisional presidency of the Republic of China to Yuan Shi-kai, and Yuan promised to establish a republican government.

Shaky Beginnings

The first half of the 20th century in China saw the gradual disintegration of the old imperial order.

Foreign political philosophies had halted the traditional dynastic cycle, and nationalism became the dominant force in China. Externally, China was still confronted by strong foreign powers and subject to the terms of unequal treaties. Domestically, the new republic was severely tested by its nominal leader Yuan Shi-kai.

As the former governor-general of Zhili 直隸, Yuan had trained the elite, Western-style Beiyang Army 北洋軍. He coerced the newly established parliament into formally electing him to the presidency, and was inaugurated on October 10, 1913. Upon his ascension to China's highest political office, Yuan Shi-kai sought to disband Dr. Sun Yat-sen's Revolutionary Alliance, which had been reorganized into the Kuomintang 國民黨. Yuan also dissolved the parliament and then assumed dictatorial powers. In an effort to appease China's rapacious neighbor in the northeast, Yuan Shi-kai agreed to Japanese demands, known as the Twenty-one Demands 二十一條款, for special rights and privileges in Shandong Province 山東省 in May 1915. As time passed, it became obvious that Yuan was planning to restore the imperial system with himself on the throne. Unmoved by the advice of foreign governments and opposition by the Kuomintang, Yuan Shi-kai declared himself emperor on December 12, 1915.

That same month, Chen Chi-mei 陳其美 led a revolt against the incipient restoration of monarchy in China. More significant was a military revolt in Yunnan Province 雲南省 led by Governor Tang Chi-yao 唐繼堯 and General Tsai O 蔡鍔. Joined by Lee Lieh-chun 李烈鈞 and other revolutionary generals, these men established the National Protection Army 護國軍 and demanded that Yuan cancel his plan to reestablish monarchal rule in China. During the spring and early summer of 1916, one after another, provinces and districts declared independence from the Yuan regime. As fate would have it, however, Yuan Shi-kai fell gravely ill and died on July 6, 1916. General Li Yuan-hung 黎元洪, vice president of the democracy that Yuan Shi-kai had sought to dismantle, succeeded to the presidency, and General Tuan Chi-jui 段祺瑞 retained his post as premier.

Highly ambitious and supported by many senior commanders from the old Beiyang Army clique, Tuan Chi-jui quickly began to strengthen his grip on power.

In February 1917 when the American government severed diplomatic relations with Germany and pressed China to do the same, President Li Yuan-hung strongly opposed the move, but Premier Tuan and his supporters were able to push through China's declaration of war on Germany on August 14, 1917. Despite sending over 100,000 men to France during World War I, China reaped little benefit from its entry into the war. It was assured a seat at the Versailles Peace Conference, but the Chinese delegation was stunned to discover that Germany's holdings in China would not be returned to the Chinese people. Rather, the Western powers had agreed to Japanese claims to the German concession in Shandong Province.

On May 4, 1919, students in Beijing protested the decision at the Versailles Peace Conference. A riot ensued and many students were arrested. Waves of protest spread throughout the major cities of China, merchants closed their shops, banks suspended business, and workers went on strike to pressure the government. Finally the government was forced to release arrested students and discharge some of the Chinese officials who had collaborated with Japan. Ultimately, the Chinese government refused to sign the Treaty of Versailles.

An intellectual revolution sparked by the events of May 4, 1919, referred to as the May Fourth Movement 五四運動, gained momentum during the first decade of the Republic of China. The movement was led by a new generation of intellectuals who scrutinized nearly all aspects of Chinese culture and traditional ethics. This new intelligentsia emerged in China after the traditional civil service examination system was suspended in 1905. New educational reforms enabled thousands of young people to study science, engineering, medicine, law, economics, education, and military science in Japan, Europe, and the United States. The "overseas students" returned to modernize China and, through their writings and lectures, exercised a powerful influence on the next generation of students. Guided by concepts of individual liberty and equality, a scientific spirit of inquiry, and a pragmatic approach to the nation's problems, the new intellectuals sought a more profound reform of China's institutions than what was accomplished by the self-strengthening movement of the late Ching dynasty or the republican revolution. Beijing University 北京大學, China's most prestigious institution of higher education, was transformed by its chancellor, Tsai Yuan-pei 蔡元培, who had spent many years in advanced study in Germany. Tsai made the university a center for scholarly research and inspired educators all over China. A proposal by Professor Hu Shih 胡適 that literature be written in the vernacular language rather than the classical style also won quick acceptance.

Important economic and social changes occurred during the first years of the Republic. With the outbreak of World War I, foreign economic competition against native industries abated, and state-run light industries experienced brisk development. By 1918, the industrial labor force numbered 1.8 million workers. A large portion of capital flowed from the agricultural sector to new industries in China's coastal provinces, and modern Chinese banks with growing capital resources were able to meet expanding financial needs.

In the 1920s the United States, Great Britain, and Japan seemed to be moving toward a new postwar relationship with China. At the Washington Conference (1921–22), the three major powers agreed to respect the sovereignty, independence, and territorial and administrative integrity of China; to give China the opportunity to develop a stable government; to maintain the principle of equal opportunity in China for the commerce and industry of all nations; and to refrain from taking advantage of conditions in China to seek exclusive privileges. The powers also agreed to take steps leading toward China's tariff autonomy and the abolition of extraterritoriality.

The Warlord Era

For a few years after the Washington Conference, foreign powers refrained from aiding particular Chinese factions in the recurrent power struggles. China was in turmoil; however, regional militarism was in full swell. During the first two decades of the Republic, China had been fractured by rival military regimes to the extent that no one authority was able to subordinate all rivals and create a unified and centralized political structure. The powerful Beiyang Army had split into two major factions: the Zhili faction led by Feng Kuo-chang 馮國璋 and the Anhui faction under Tuan Chi-jui. These two factions controlled provinces in the Yellow River and Yangtze River valleys,

and competed for control of Beijing. In Manchuria, Chang Tso-lin 張作霖 headed a separate army. Shaanxi Province 陝西省 was controlled by Yen Hsi-shan 閻錫山.

Having witnessed the collapse of the fledgling central government he had worked so hard to create, Dr. Sun Yat-sen turned south to his home province of Guangdong 廣東省, where he established a military government in August 1917. In 1919, Dr. Sun reorganized his party into the present-day Chinese Kuomintang (KMT, also known as the Nationalist Party), and in 1921, Dr. Sun Yat-sen assumed the presidency of the newly formed southern government in Guangdong. When war between the northern warlords erupted the following year, Dr. Sun issued a manifesto urging the reunification of China by peaceful means. A political idealist, Dr. Sun Yat-sen was to be disappointed by more years of sporadic fighting between warlords. Finally, in 1924, Dr. Sun Yat-sen and his southern government moved to set up a military academy that would train an officer corps loyal to the Kuomintang and dedicated to the unification of China. Dr. Sun appointed Chiang Kai-shek 蔣中正 as commandant of the Whampoa Military Academy 黃埔軍校.

On November 10, 1924, Dr. Sun Yat-sen called for the early convocation of a National People's Convention to bring each of China's regional leaders to the conference table. Two weeks later, Tuan Chi-jui became the provisional chief executive of the Beijing-based government and Dr. Sun Yat-sen, as head of the southern government, traveled north to hold talks with Tuan. While in Beijing, Dr. Sun succumbed to liver cancer and died on March 12, 1925, at the age of 59. His dream of a unified and democratic China freed of foreign constraint had yet to be realized.

Dr. Sun's untimely demise left the southern government in the hands of a steering committee. This 16-member committee established a national government in July 1925 and some 11 months later appointed Chiang Kai-shek commander-in-chief of the National Revolutionary Army 國民革命軍. In this capacity, Chiang Kai-shek launched a military expedition northward to eradicate various feuding warlords in central and northern China. This military campaign lasted three years and came to be known as the Northern Expedition 北伐. On March 22, 1927, the first troops of the National Revolutionary Army entered Shanghai and two days later, captured Nanjing. Despite a split between the right and left wings of the Kuomintang, Chiang Kai-shek was able to establish a new National Government in Nanjing on April 18, 1927, and the Northern Expedition continued without interruption.

The Japanese Invasion

By the spring of 1928, the National Revolutionary Army was approaching Jinan 濟南, the provincial capital of Shandong Province. Japan dispatched 3,000 soldiers to the city under the pretext of protecting Japanese residents. On May 3, two days after the National Revolutionary Army moved into Jinan, Japanese soldiers killed the Chinese negotiator Tsai Kung-shi 蔡公時. Thousands of Chinese soldiers and civilians were slaughtered by Japanese regulars in the ensuing massacre. Less than a month later, the Japanese followed this atrocity with the assassination of the Chinese warlord in northeast China, Marshal Chang Tso-lin, after he had expressed his intention to surrender Manchuria to the National Government. Manchuria was a huge and rich area of China in which Japan had extensive economic privileges. Japan dominated much of the southern Manchurian economy through a monopoly of the Southern Manchuria Railway 南滿鐵路. Manchuria's impending unification with the rest of China threatened Japan's economic privileges in central China and its domination in Manchuria.

The Chinese government realized the Jinan massacre and the assassination of Chang Tso-lin were premeditated actions designed by the Japanese militarists to provoke war while China was still divided. Chiang Kai-shek thus ordered the National Revolutionary Army to continue its northward march but to avoid Japanese-controlled areas in northern China. This strategy frustrated the Japanese schemes and effectively unified China under the National Government based in Nanjing.

Japanese militarists remained undaunted. Believing Manchuria to be strategically and economically vital to their plans for the conquest of all Asia, Japanese officers in Shenyang 瀋陽 (Mukden) sabotaged the Southern Manchuria Railroad on September 18, 1931, and ambushed the Northeastern Chinese Armies. On January 28, 1932, following a wave of murders

and arson by their agents in Shanghai, Japanese armies attacked that city. Chinese defenders resisted heroically, thereby drawing international attention. To deflect world opinion, which had condemned their actions, the Japanese installed a puppet regime known as Manchukuo 滿洲國 in 1932. The "land of the Manchu" proved to be no more than another stepping stone for the extension of Japanese aggression. In 1933, the humiliating Tanggu Truce 塘沽協議 was signed, which in effect yielded eastern Hebei Province 河北省 to the Japanese-controlled Manchukuo.

After long negotiations, Japan acquired the Soviet interests in the Chinese Eastern Railway 中東鐵路, the last legal trace of Russian influence in Manchuria. In 1935, Japanese armies attempted to detach Hebei and Jehol 熱河 provinces from Chinese control and threatened Shanxi, Suiyuan 綏遠, and Shandong provinces. The Japanese then set up the so-called East Hebei Anti-Communist and Self-Government Council 冀東反共自治會, another move after the Tanggu Truce to extend Japanese control over northern China.

The Rise of the Chinese Communists

The Japanese were not the only threat to the integrity of Chinese democracy. The Chinese communists, who had rebelled against the government of the Republic of China (ROC), established a provisional Soviet "government" in Jiangxi Province 江西省 on November 7, 1931, and created 15 rural bases in central China. The ROC launched five successive military campaigns to eradicate the communist threat to central authority. The communist armies were, in the end, forced to abandon their bases and retreat. Communist troops led by Mao Zedong 毛澤東, Zhu De 朱德, Zhou Enlai 周恩來, and Lin Biao 林彪 marched and fought their way across western China on the 6,000-mile Long March. By mid-1936, Nationalist forces had cornered the remnants of several communist armies in the impoverished area of Yenan 延安 in northern Shaanxi Province.

At this point, the Chinese communists opted for a new "united front" strategy against Japan. The ROC government, however, believed that the communists must capitulate to central authority before China could effectively repel Japanese encroachment. This policy, therefore, was one of "unity before resistance against foreign aggression." While further Japanese transgressions made this policy a costly one, Generalissimo Chiang Kai-shek was determined to carry on the anti-communist campaign. He ordered the Northeastern and Northwestern Armies to attack the communist forces in northern Shaanxi Province. When the Northeastern Army, commanded by Chang Hsueh-liang 張學良, disobeyed the order to pursue the war against the communists, Chiang Kai-shek flew to Xian 西安省 on December 12, 1936, to confront the general. Chang's army subordinates, however, shot Chiang Kai-shek's bodyguards and arrested the generalissimo. After a series of behind-the-scenes negotiations, Chang Hsueh-liang freed the generalissimo and escorted him back to Nanjing on December 25, 1936. The "Xian Incident" 西安事件 was a severe setback to Generalissimo Chiang's efforts to subjugate the communists.

The War Against Japan

On the eve of China's all-out war against Japan, the Japanese nation had a total of over 4.5 million soldiers. The total tonnage of its navy came to nearly two million, while its air force had 2,700 planes of various models. In comparison, the Chinese army had 1.7 million men, its navy had a total tonnage of 110,000, and its air force had 600 aircraft, only 305 of which were fighters.

On July 7, 1937, a minor clash between Japanese and Chinese troops near Beijing finally led China into war against Japan. (In Chinese, this conflict is called the Eight-year War of Resistance Against Japan 八年抗日戰爭.) From this point on, Chinese resentment of over half a century of Japanese aggression was expressed in the form of overt, concerted, and armed resistance. The war against Japan unfolded in three stages: a first stage of undeclared war beginning with the Marco Polo Bridge Incident 七七事變 (or 蘆溝橋事變) on July 7, 1937; an intermediate stage beginning in late 1938; and a third stage that began with China joining the Allied Forces after the Japanese bombing of Pearl Harbor. The war ended with Japan's surrender in 1945.

During the first stage of the war, Japan won successive victories. Tianjin was occupied in July 1937 and Beijing in August. After three months of fierce fighting, Shanghai was captured by the Japanese on November 11, 1937. The ROC capital, Nanjing, fell in December. The fall of the capital is now known as the "Rape of Nanjing" because Japanese forces occupying the city killed some 300,000 people (defenseless civilians and Chinese troops that had already laid down their arms) in seven weeks of unrelenting carnage. The loss of Nanjing forced the ROC government to move its capital up the Yangtze River to the city of Chongqing (Chungking) 重慶, which was shielded by mountains. By the end of this initial phase of the war, the ROC government had lost the best of its modern armies, its air force and arsenals, most of China's modern industries and railways, its major tax resources, and all the Chinese ports through which military equipment and civilian supplies might be imported. However, China had won a major battle at Taierzhuang 臺兒莊 on April 6, 1938.

In 1940, Japan set up a puppet government in Nanjing under Wang Ching-wei 汪精衛, but the Chinese people would not submit. Hundreds of thousands of patriotic Chinese continued to attempt the difficult trek to Chongqing. Students and faculties from most colleges in eastern China traveled by foot to makeshift quarters in distant inland towns. Factories and a skilled workforce were reestablished in the west.

The government rebuilt its scattered armies and tried to purchase supplies from abroad; however, the supply lines were long and precarious. When war broke out in Europe, shipments became even more scarce. After Germany's conquest of France in the spring of 1940, Britain bowed to Japanese demands and temporarily closed Rangoon, Burma, to military supplies for China. In September 1940, Japan seized control of northern Indo-China and closed the supply line to Kunming 昆明. While Japan had more than 1,000 planes, China had only 37 fighter planes and 31 old Russian bombers that were not equipped for night flying. The United States, however, had by then sold the Republic of China 100 fighter planes—the beginning of an American effort to provide air protection to the ROC.

By the summer of 1941, the United States knew that Japan hoped to end the undeclared war in China and was preparing for a southward advance toward British Malaya and the Dutch Indies, planning first to occupy southern Indo-China and Thailand, even at the risk of war with Britain and the United States. On July 23, 1941, US President Franklin D. Roosevelt approved a recommendation that the US send large quantities of arms and equipment to China, along with a military mission to advise on their use. The military mission arrived in October 1941. By December 1941, the United States had implicitly agreed to help create a modern Chinese air force, to maintain an efficient line of communication into China, and to arm 30 divisions of soldiers. The underlying goal was to revitalize China's war effort as a deterrent to Japanese military and naval operations in the south. The logistics line for all foreign aid depended on the 715-mile Burma Road, which extended from Chongqing to Lashio, the Burmese terminus of the railway and highway leading to Rangoon.

The third phase of the war against Japan began on December 7, 1941, when the Japanese bombed Pearl Harbor, and shortly afterwards the United States and Britain declared war on Japan. China, which also formally declared war against Japan after four years of staunch resistance, joined the Allies in waging the Pacific War. On January 2, 1942, Generalissimo Chiang assumed the office of Supreme Commander of the China Theater of War. This escalation of the Sino-Japanese conflict raised Chinese morale, but also damaged China's strategic position. With the Japanese conquest of Hong Kong on December 25, 1941, China lost its only air link to the outside world and one of its principal routes for shipping supplies. By the end of May 1942, the Japanese held most of Burma, and China was almost completely blockaded.

Following an initial grant of US$630 million in lend-lease supplies, the United States granted China a loan of US$500 million in February 1942, and Great Britain stated its willingness to lend £50 million. This helped to stabilize the Chinese currency and provided China with better terms of trade. A solution to the supply problem was found in an air route from Assam, India, to Kunming in southwest China—the dangerous "hump" route along the southern edge of the Himalayas. In March 1942, the China National Aviation Corporation 中國航空公司 (CNAC) began freight service over the hump, and the United States began a transport program the following month. It was not until December 1943 that cargo planes were able to equal the tonnage carried over the Burma Road by trucks two years before, but China's needs for gasoline, arms, munitions, and other military equipment were still not adequately met.

Both air force development and army modernization were pushed in early 1943. A training center was created near Kunming and a network of airfields was built in southern China. By the end of 1943, the China-based American Fifteenth Air Force had achieved tactical parity with the Japanese over central China, and began to bomb Yangtze River shipping. The Fifteenth Air Force even successfully raided Japanese airfields on Taiwan. China's determination was beginning to pay off. During November and December of 1943, the leaders of the Allied countries met in Cairo, Egypt. In the December 1st Cairo Declaration, the return of Manchuria, Taiwan, and the Pescadores was promised to China. The prewar system of extraterritoriality—whereby Chinese courts had no jurisdiction over any foreigner residing in China—was abolished. In addition, the Allies pledged themselves to "persevere in the prolonged operations necessary to procure the unconditional surrender of Japan."

On August 6, 1945, the United States dropped the first atomic bomb on Hiroshima, and three days later, a second was dropped on Nagasaki. The subsequent Japanese surrender was delivered to the Allies through Switzerland the next day, and on August 14, Japan announced its formal surrender in accordance with the terms of the Potsdam Declaration of July 1945 and declared that "the terms of the Cairo Declaration shall be carried out." The Japanese government accepted this in the instrument of surrender concluded on September 3, 1945, between Japan and the Allies. The Japanese armies on the Chinese mainland surrendered to the ROC government on September 9, 1945, in Nanjing.

Communist Rebellion

Even before Emperor Hirohito's announcement of Japan's surrender was known, the commander of the Chinese communist armies, Zhu De, ordered his troops to move into Japanese-held territory and seize Japanese arms. The American general, Douglas MacArthur, then ordered all Japanese forces in China to surrender their arms only to forces of the ROC government. Despite MacArthur's request, the Chinese communists sent tens of thousands of political cadres and soldiers into Manchuria. The Chinese communists took over most of the arms of the 600,000-strong Japanese army in Manchuria that had previously been confiscated by the Russians. The Soviet army dismantled most of the industrial machinery in Manchuria. The valuable equipment, so crucial to China's postwar revival, was shipped to the Soviet Union while immovable objects were mostly destroyed.

The government and the Chinese communists held peace talks that culminated in an agreement on October 10, 1945. The agreement called for the convening of a multiparty Political Consultative Council 政治協商會議 to plan for a liberalized postwar government and to draft a constitution for submission to a National Assembly 全國代表大會. When the Chinese communists continued to accept the surrender of Japanese garrisons, occupy cities, and confiscate property, Chiang Kai-shek ordered an offensive against them in November. Hostilities lasted throughout December and the early part of January 1946. Hoping to help end the fighting, US President Harry S. Truman dispatched George Marshall to China in December 1945. Marshall was able to negotiate several cease-fires during 1947, but a pattern of non-cooperation between the government and the communists soon escalated into open conflict.

While ROC troops were busily suppressing the incipient communist rebellion, many citizens were working to implement true democracy. On January 1, 1947, the *Constitution of the Republic of China* was promulgated. Within the year, members of the National Assembly, Legislative Yuan 立法院, and Control Yuan 監察院 had been elected, despite all sorts of difficulties and problems. In April 1948, the new National Assembly elected Chiang Kai-shek to the presidency of the Republic of China. These moves toward democratic government, however, were overshadowed by a communist offensive that cut Manchuria off from the rest of China.

The military setback in Manchuria was compounded by serious economic problems. Inflation continued unabated, caused principally by government financing of military and other operations, particularly for maintaining large garrison forces. Apart from the loss of millions of Chinese lives, the war against Japan had generated huge war debts, not to mention serious financial distress in the private sector. The government had run a budget deficit every year since 1928. Alarmingly, the money supply in China increased by 500 times between 1937 and 1945. Retail prices of daily necessities were so inflated that even middle-class families tottered on the brink of abject poverty. This unrestrained inflation triggered a national recession and alienated the public from its elected representatives.

By 1948, communist forces had cut lines of communication and destroyed vital outposts along the Longhai 隴海 and Pinghan 平漢 railways, isolating many cities. In December, the pivotal battle for Xuzhou 徐州 was lost. This defeat was followed by the fall of Tianjin and Beijing on January 19, 1949. Other cities in northeastern China were lost by March. In early 1949, Chiang Kai-shek began deploying a force of 300,000 troops in Taiwan backed by a few gunboats and some planes. After the Chinese communists had successfully crossed the Yangtze River, the government of the Republic of China began relocating its offices to Taiwan. As the mainland was falling to the communist forces, around one and half million people (mostly young and unmarried soldiers) accompanied the ROC government to the island of Taiwan.

(See Chapter 4 for information on the history of the ROC on Taiwan.)

Appendix III

The Constitution of the Republic of China and the Additional Articles

(Adopted by the National Assembly on December 25, 1946, promulgated by the national government on January 1, 1947, and effective from December 25, 1947)

The National Assembly of the Republic of China, by virtue of the mandate received from the whole body of citizens, in accordance with the teachings bequeathed by Dr. Sun Yat-sen in founding the Republic of China, and in order to consolidate the authority of the State, safeguard the rights of the people, ensure social tranquillity, and promote the welfare of the people, do hereby establish this Constitution, to be promulgated throughout the country for faithful and perpetual observance by all.

Chapter I. General Provisions

Article 1. The Republic of China, founded on the Three Principles of the People, shall be a democratic republic of the people, to be governed by the people and for the people.

Article 2. The sovereignty of the Republic of China shall reside in the whole body of citizens.

Article 3. Persons possessing the nationality of the Republic of China shall be citizens of the Republic of China.

Article 4. The territory of the Republic of China according to its existing national boundaries shall not be altered except by resolution of the National Assembly.

Article 5. There shall be equality among the various racial groups in the Republic of China.

Article 6. The national flag of the Republic of China shall be of red ground with a blue sky and a white sun in the upper left corner.

Chapter II. Rights and Duties of the People

Article 7. All citizens of the Republic of China, irrespective of sex, religion, race, class, or party affiliation, shall be equal before the law.

Article 8. Personal freedom shall be guaranteed to the people. Except in case of *flagrante delicto* as provided by law, no person shall be arrested or detained otherwise than by a judicial or a police organ in accordance with the procedure prescribed by law. No person shall be tried or punished otherwise than by a law court in accordance with the procedure prescribed by law. Any arrest, detention, trial, or punishment which is not in accordance with the procedure prescribed by law may be resisted.

When a person is arrested or detained on suspicion of having committed a crime, the organ making the arrest or detention shall in writing inform the said person, and his designated relative or friend, of the grounds for his arrest or detention, and shall, within 24 hours, turn him over to a competent court for trial. The said person, or any other person, may petition the competent court that a writ be served within 24 hours on the organ making the arrest for the surrender of the said person for trial.

The court shall not reject the petition mentioned in the preceding paragraph, nor shall it order the organ concerned to make an investigation and report first. The organ concerned shall not refuse to execute, or delay in executing, the writ of the court for the surrender of the said person for trial.

When a person is unlawfully arrested or detained by any organ, he or any other person may petition the court for an investigation. The court shall not reject such a petition, and shall, within 24 hours, investigate the action of the organ concerned and deal with the matter in accordance with law.

Article 9. Except those in active military service, no person shall be subject to trial by a military tribunal.

Article 10. The people shall have freedom of residence and of change of residence.

Article 11. The people shall have freedom of speech, teaching, writing and publication.

Article 12. The people shall have freedom of privacy of correspondence.

Article 13. The people shall have freedom of religious belief.

Article 14. The people shall have freedom of assembly and association.

Article 15. The right of existence, the right of work, and the right of property shall be guaranteed to the people.

Article 16. The people shall have the right of presenting petitions, lodging complaints, or instituting legal proceedings.

Article 17. The people shall have the right of election, recall, initiative and referendum.

Article 18. The people shall have the right of taking public examinations and of holding public offices.

Article 19. The people shall have the duty of paying taxes in accordance with law.

Article 20. The people shall have the duty of performing military service in accordance with law.

Article 21. The people shall have the right and the duty of receiving citizens' education.

Article 22. All other freedoms and rights of the people that are not detrimental to social order or public welfare shall be guaranteed under the Constitution.

Article 23. All the freedoms and rights enumerated in the preceding Article shall not be restricted by law except by such as may be necessary to prevent infringement upon the freedoms of other persons, to avert an imminent crisis, to maintain social order or to advance public welfare.

Article 24. Any public functionary who, in violation of law, infringes upon the freedom or right of any person shall, in addition to being subject to disciplinary measures in accordance with law, be held responsible under criminal and civil laws. The injured person may, in accordance with law, claim compensation from the State for damage sustained.

Chapter III. The National Assembly

Article 25. The National Assembly shall, in accordance with the provisions of this Constitution, exercise political powers on behalf of the whole body of citizens.

Article 26. The National Assembly shall be composed of the following delegates:

1. One delegate shall be elected from each hsien, municipality, or area of equivalent status. In case its population exceeds 500,000, one additional delegate shall be elected for each additional 500,000. Areas equivalent to hsien or municipalities shall be prescribed by law;

2. Delegates to represent Mongolia shall be elected on the basis of four for each league and one for each special banner;

3. The number of delegates to be elected from Tibet shall be prescribed by law;

4. The number of delegates to be elected by various racial groups in frontier regions shall be prescribed by law;

5. The number of delegates to be elected by Chinese citizens residing abroad shall be prescribed by law;

6. The number of delegates to be elected by occupational groups shall be prescribed by law; and

7. The number of delegates to be elected by women's organizations shall be prescribed by law.

Article 27. The function of the National Assembly shall be as follows:

1. To elect the President and the Vice President;

2. To recall the President and the Vice President;

3. To amend the Constitution; and

4. To vote on proposed Constitutional amendments submitted by the Legislative Yuan by way of referendum.

With respect to the rights of initiative and referendum, except as is provided in Items 3 and 4 of the preceding paragraph, the National Assembly shall make regulations pertaining thereto and put them into effect, after the above-mentioned two political rights shall have been exercised in one-half of the hsien and municipalities of the whole country.

Article 28. Delegates to the National Assembly shall be elected every six years.

The term of office of the delegates to each National Assembly shall terminate on the day on which the next National Assembly convenes.

No incumbent government official shall, in the electoral area where he holds office, be elected delegate to the National Assembly.

Article 29. The National Assembly shall be convoked by the President to meet 90 days prior to the date of expiration of each presidential term.

Article 30. An extraordinary session of the National Assembly shall be convoked in any of the following circumstances:

1. When, in accordance with the provisions of Article 49 of this Constitution, a new President and a new Vice President are to be elected;

2. When, by resolution of the Control Yuan, an impeachment of the President or the Vice President is instituted;

3. When, by resolution of the Legislative Yuan, an amendment to the Constitution is proposed; and

4. When a meeting is requested by not less than two-fifths of the delegates to the National Assembly.

When an extraordinary session is to be convoked in accordance with Item 1 or Item 2 of the preceding paragraph, the President of the Legislative Yuan shall issue the notice of convocation; when it is to be convoked in accordance with Item 3 or Item 4, it shall be convoked by the President of the Republic.

Article 31. The National Assembly shall meet at the seat of the Central Government.

Article 32. No delegate to the National Assembly shall be held responsible outside the Assembly for opinions expressed or votes cast at meetings of the Assembly.

Article 33. While the Assembly is in session, no delegate to the National Assembly shall, except in case of *flagrante delicto,* be arrested or detained without the permission of the National Assembly.

Article 34. The organization of the National Assembly, the election and recall of delegates to the National Assembly, and the procedure whereby the National Assembly is to carry out its functions, shall be prescribed by law.

Chapter IV. The President

Article 35. The President shall be the head of the State and shall represent the Republic of China in foreign relations.

Article 36. The President shall have supreme command of the land, sea and air forces of the whole country.

Article 37. The President shall, in accordance with law, promulgate laws and issue mandates with the counter-signature of the President of the Executive Yuan or with the counter-signatures of both the President of the Executive Yuan and the Ministers or Chairmen of Commissions concerned.

Article 38. The President shall, in accordance with the provisions of this Constitution, exercise the powers of concluding treaties, declaring war and making peace.

Article 39. The President may, in accordance with law, declare martial law with the approval of, or subject to confirmation by, the Legislative Yuan. When the Legislative Yuan deems it necessary, it may by resolution request the President to terminate martial law.

Article 40. The President shall, in accordance with law, exercise the power of granting amnesties, pardons, remission of sentences and restitution of civil rights.

Article 41. The President shall, in accordance with law, appoint and remove civil and military officials.

Article 42. The President may, in accordance with law, confer honors and decorations.

Article 43. In case of a natural calamity, an epidemic, or a national financial or economic crisis that calls for emergency measures, the President, during the recess of the Legislative Yuan, may, by resolution of the Executive Yuan Council, and in accordance with the *Law on Emergency Decrees,* issue emergency decrees, proclaiming such measures as may be necessary to cope with the situation. Such decrees shall, within one month after issuance, be presented to the Legislative Yuan for confirmation; in case the Legislative Yuan withholds confirmation, the said decrees shall forthwith cease to be valid.

Article 44. In case of disputes between two or more Yuan other than those concerning which there are relevant provisions in this Constitution, the President may call a meeting of the Presidents of the Yuan concerned for consultation with a view to reaching a solution.

Article 45. Any citizen of the Republic of China who has attained the age of 40 years may be elected President or Vice President.

Article 46. The election of the President and the Vice President shall be prescribed by law.

Article 47. The President and the Vice President shall serve a term of six years. They may be re-elected for a second term.

Article 48. The President shall, at the time of assuming office, take the following oath:

"I do solemnly and sincerely swear before the people of the whole country that I will observe the Constitution, faithfully perform my duties, promote the welfare of the people, safeguard the security of the State, and will in no way betray the people's trust. Should I break my oath, I shall be willing to submit myself to severe punishment by the State. This is my solemn oath."

Article 49. In case the office of the President should become vacant, the Vice President shall succeed until the expiration of the original presidential term. In case the office of both the President and the Vice President should become vacant, the President of the Executive Yuan shall act for the President; and, in accordance with the provisions of Article 30 of this Constitution, an extraordinary session of the National Assembly shall be convoked for the election of a new President and a new Vice President, who shall hold office until the completion of the term left unfinished by the preceding President. In case the President should be unable to attend to office due to any cause, the Vice President shall act for the President. In case both the President and Vice President should be unable to attend to office, the President of the Executive Yuan shall act for the President.

Article 50. The President shall be relieved of his functions on the day on which his term of office expires. If by that time the succeeding President has not yet been elected, or if the President-elect and the Vice-President-elect have not yet assumed office, the President of the Executive Yuan shall act for the President.

Article 51. The period during which the President of the Executive Yuan may act for the President shall not exceed three months.

Article 52. The President shall not, without having been recalled, or having been relieved of his functions, be liable to criminal prosecution unless he is charged with having committed an act of rebellion or treason.

Chapter V. Administration

Article 53. The Executive Yuan shall be the highest administrative organ of the State.

Article 54. The Executive Yuan shall have a President, a Vice President, a certain number of Ministers and Chairmen of Commissions, and a certain number of Ministers without Portfolio.

Article 55. The President of the Executive Yuan shall be nominated and, with the consent of the Legislative Yuan, appointed by the President of the Republic.

If, during the recess of the Legislative Yuan, the President of the Executive Yuan should resign or if his office should become vacant, his functions shall be exercised by the Vice President of the Yuan, acting on his behalf, but the President of the Republic shall, within 40 days, request a meeting of the Legislative Yuan to confirm his nominee for the vacancy. Pending such confirmation, the Vice President of the Executive Yuan shall temporarily exercise the functions of the President of the said Yuan.

Article 56. The Vice President of the Executive Yuan, Ministers and Chairmen of Commissions, and Ministers without Portfolio shall be appointed by the President of the Republic upon the recommendation of the President of the Executive Yuan.

Article 57. The Executive Yuan shall be responsible to the Legislative Yuan in accordance with the following provisions:

1. The Executive Yuan has the duty to present to the Legislative Yuan a statement of its administrative policies and a report on its administration. While the Legislative Yuan is in session, Members of the Legislative Yuan shall have the right to question the President and the Ministers and Chairmen of Commissions of the Executive Yuan.

2. If the Legislative Yuan does not concur in any important policy of the Executive Yuan, it may, by resolution, request the Executive Yuan to alter such a policy. With respect to such resolution, the Executive Yuan may, with the approval of the President of the Republic, request the Legislative Yuan for reconsideration. If, after reconsideration, two-thirds of the Members of the Legislative Yuan present at the meeting uphold the original resolution, the President of the Executive Yuan shall either abide by the same or resign from office.

3. If the Executive Yuan deems a resolution on a statutory, budgetary, or treaty bill passed by the Legislative Yuan difficult of execution, it may, with the approval of the President of the Republic and within ten days after its transmission to the Executive Yuan, request the Legislative Yuan to reconsider the said resolution. If after reconsideration, two-thirds of the Members of the Legislative Yuan present at the meeting uphold the original resolution, the President of the Executive Yuan shall either abide by the same or resign from office.

Article 58. The Executive Yuan shall have an Executive Yuan Council, to be composed of its President, Vice President, various Ministers and Chairmen of Commissions, and Ministers without Portfolio, with its President as Chairman.

Statutory or budgetary bills or bills concerning martial law, amnesty, declaration of war, conclusion of peace or treaties, and other important affairs, all of which are to be submitted to the Legislative Yuan, as well as matters that are of common concern to the various Ministries and Commissions, shall be presented by the President and various Ministers and Chairmen of Commissions of the Executive Yuan to the Executive Yuan Council for decision.

Article 59. The Executive Yuan shall, three months before the beginning of each fiscal year, present to the Legislative Yuan the budgetary bill for the following fiscal year.

Article 60. The Executive Yuan shall, within four months after the end of each fiscal year, present final accounts of revenues and expenditures to the Control Yuan.

Article 61. The organization of the Executive Yuan shall be prescribed by law.

Chapter VI. Legislation

Article 62. The Legislative Yuan shall be the highest legislative organ of the State, to be constituted of members elected by the people. It shall exercise legislative power on behalf of the people.

Article 63. The Legislative Yuan shall have the power to decide by resolution upon statutory or budgetary bills or bills concerning martial law, amnesty, declaration of war, conclusion of peace or treaties, and other important affairs of the State.

Article 64. Members of the Legislative Yuan shall be elected in accordance with the following provisions:

1. Those to be elected from the provinces and by the municipalities under the direct jurisdiction of the Executive Yuan shall be five for each province or municipality with a population of not more than 3,000,000, one additional member shall be elected for each additional 1,000,000 in a province or municipality whose population is over 3,000,000;

2. Those to be elected from Mongolian Leagues and Banners;

3. Those to be elected from Tibet;

4. Those to be elected by various racial groups in frontier regions;

5. Those to be elected by Chinese citizens residing abroad; and

6. Those to be elected by occupational groups.

The election of Members of the Legislative Yuan and the number of those to be elected in accordance with Items 2 to 6 of the preceding paragraph shall be prescribed by law. The number of women to be elected under the various items enumerated in the first paragraph shall be prescribed by law.

Article 65. Members of the Legislative Yuan shall serve a term of three years, and shall be re-eligible. The election of Members of the Legislative Yuan shall be completed within three months prior to the expiration of each term.

Article 66. The Legislative Yuan shall have a President and a Vice President, who shall be elected by and from among its Members.

Article 67. The Legislative Yuan may set up various committees.

Such committees may invite government officials and private persons concerned to be present at their meetings to answer questions.

Article 68. The Legislative Yuan shall hold two sessions each year, and shall convene of its own accord. The first session shall last from February to the end of May, and the second session from September to the end of December. Whenever necessary, a session may be prolonged.

Article 69. In any of the following circumstances, the Legislative Yuan may hold an extraordinary session:

1. At the request of the President of the Republic;

2. Upon the request of not less than one-fourth of its Members.

Article 70. The Legislative Yuan shall not make proposals for an increase in the expenditures in the budgetary bill presented by the Executive Yuan.

Article 71. At the meetings of the Legislative Yuan, the Presidents of the various Yuan concerned and the various Ministers and Chairmen of Commissions concerned may be present to give their views.

Article 72. Statutory bills passed by the Legislative Yuan shall be transmitted to the President of the Republic and to the Executive Yuan. The President shall, within ten days after receipt thereof, promulgate them; or he may deal with them in accordance with the provisions of Article 57 of this Constitution.

Article 73. No Member of the Legislative Yuan shall be held responsible outside the Yuan for opinions expressed or votes cast in the Yuan.

Article 74. No Member of the Legislative Yuan shall, except in case of *flagrante delicto,* be arrested or detained without the permission of the Legislative Yuan.

Article 75. No Member of the Legislative Yuan shall concurrently hold a government post.

Article 76. The organization of the Legislative Yuan shall be prescribed by law.

Chapter VII. Judiciary

Article 77. The Judicial Yuan shall be the highest judicial organ of the State and shall have charge of civil, criminal, and administrative cases, and over cases concerning disciplinary measures against public functionaries.

Article 78. The Judicial Yuan shall interpret the Constitution and shall have the power to unify the interpretation of laws and orders.

Article 79. The Judicial Yuan shall have a President and a Vice President, who shall be nominated and, with the consent of the Control Yuan, appointed by the President of the Republic.

The Judicial Yuan shall have a certain number of Grand Justices to take charge of matters specified in Article 78 of this Constitution, who shall be nominated and, with the consent of the Control Yuan, appointed by the President of the Republic.

Article 80. Judges shall be above partisanship and shall, in accordance with law, hold trials independently, free from any interference.

Article 81. Judges shall hold office for life. No judge shall be removed from office unless he has been found guilty of a criminal offense or subjected to disciplinary measure, or declared to be under interdiction. No judge shall, except in accordance with law, be suspended or transferred or have his salary reduced.

Article 82. The organization of the Judicial Yuan and of the law courts of various grades shall be prescribed by law.

Chapter VIII. Examination

Article 83. The Examination Yuan shall be the highest examination organ of the State and shall have charge of matters relating to examination, employment, registration, service rating, scale of salaries, promotion and transfer, security of tenure, commendation, pecuniary aid in case of death, retirement and old age pension.

Article 84. The Examination Yuan shall have a President and a Vice President and a certain number of Members, all of whom shall be nominated and, with the consent of the Control Yuan, appointed by the President of the Republic.

Article 85. In the selection of public functionaries, a system of open competitive examination shall be put into operation, and examinations shall be held in different areas, with prescribed numbers of persons to be selected according to various provinces and areas. No person shall be appointed to a public office unless he is qualified through examination.

Article 86. The following qualifications shall be determined and registered through examination by the Examination Yuan in accordance with law:

1. Qualification for appointment as public functionaries; and

2. Qualification for practice in specialized professions or as technicians.

Article 87. The Examination Yuan may, with respect to matters under its charge, present statutory bills to the Legislative Yuan.

Article 88. Members of the Examination Yuan shall be above partisanship and shall independently exercise their functions in accordance with law.

Article 89. The organization of the Examination Yuan shall be prescribed by law.

Chapter IX. Control

Article 90. The Control Yuan shall be the highest control organ of the State and shall exercise the powers of consent, impeachment, censure and auditing.

Article 91. The Control Yuan shall be composed of Members who shall be elected by Provincial and Municipal Councils, the local Councils of Mongolia and Tibet, and Chinese citizens residing abroad. Their numbers shall be determined in accordance with the following provisions:

1. Five Members from each province;

2. Two Members from each municipality under the direct jurisdiction of the Executive Yuan;

3. Eight Members from Mongolian Leagues and Banners;

4. Eight Members from Tibet; and

5. Eight Members from Chinese citizens residing abroad.

Article 92. The Control Yuan shall have a President and a Vice President, who shall be elected by and from among its Members.

Article 93. Members of the Control Yuan shall serve a term of six years and shall be re-eligible.

Article 94. When the Control Yuan exercises the power of consent in accordance with this Constitution, it shall do so by resolution of a majority of the Members present at the meeting.

Article 95. The Control Yuan may, in the exercise of its powers of control, request the Executive Yuan and its Ministries and Commissions to submit to it for perusal the original orders issued by them and all other relevant documents.

Article 96. The Control Yuan may, taking into account the work of the Executive Yuan and its various Ministries and Commissions, set up a certain number of committees to investigate their activities with a view to ascertaining whether or not they are guilty of violation of law or neglect of duty.

Article 97. The Control Yuan may, on the basis of the investigations and resolutions of its committees, propose corrective measures and forward them to the Executive Yuan and the Ministries and Commissions concerned, directing their attention to effecting improvements.

When the Control Yuan deems a public functionary in the Central Government or in a local government guilty of neglect of duty or violation of law, it may propose corrective measures or institute an impeachment. If it involves a criminal offense, the case shall be turned over to a law court.

Article 98. Impeachment by the Control Yuan of a public functionary in the Central Government or in a local government shall be instituted upon the proposal of one or more than one Member of the Control Yuan and the decision, after due consideration, by a committee composed of not less than nine Members.

Article 99. In case of impeachment by the Control Yuan of the personnel of the Judicial Yuan or of the Examination Yuan for neglect of duty or violation of law, the provisions of Articles 95, 97 and 98 of this Constitution shall be applicable.

Article 100. Impeachment by the Control Yuan of the President or the Vice President of the Republic shall be instituted upon the proposal of not less than one-fourth of the whole body of Members of the Control Yuan, and the resolution, after due consideration, by the majority of the whole body of Members of the Control Yuan, and the same shall be presented to the National Assembly.

Article 101. No Member of the Control Yuan shall be held responsible outside the Yuan for opinions expressed or votes cast in the Yuan.

Article 102. No Member of the Control Yuan shall, except in case of *flagrante delicto,* be arrested or detained without the permission of the Control Yuan.

Article 103. No Member of the Control Yuan shall concurrently hold a public office or engage in any profession.

Article 104. In the Control Yuan, there shall be an Auditor General who shall be nominated and, with the consent of the Legislative Yuan, appointed by the President of the Republic.

Article 105. The Auditor General shall, within three months after presentation by the Executive Yuan of the final accounts of revenues and expenditures, complete the auditing thereof in accordance with law, and submit an auditing report to the Legislative Yuan.

Article 106. The organization of the Control Yuan shall be prescribed by law.

Chapter X. Powers of the Central and Local Governments

Article 107. In the following matters, the Central Government shall have the power of legislation and administration:

1. Foreign affairs;
2. National defense and military affairs concerning national defense;
3. Nationality law and criminal, civil and commercial law;
4. Judicial system;
5. Aviation, national highways, state-owned railways, navigation, postal and telegraph service;
6. Central Government finance and national revenues;
7. Demarcation of national, provincial and hsien revenues;
8. State-operated economic enterprises;
9. Currency system and state banks;
10. Weights and measures;
11. Foreign trade policies;
12. Financial and economic matters affecting foreigners or foreign countries; and
13. Other matters relating to the Central Government as provided by this Constitution.

Article 108. In the following matters, the Central Government shall have the power of legislation and administration, but the Central Government may delegate the power of administration to the provincial and hsien governments:

1. General principles of provincial and hsien self-government;
2. Division of administrative areas;
3. Forestry, industry, mining and commerce;
4. Educational system;
5. Banking and exchange system;
6. Shipping and deep-sea fishery;
7. Public utilities;
8. Cooperative enterprises;
9. Water and land communication and transportation covering two or more provinces;
10. Water conservancy, waterways, agriculture and pastoral enterprises covering two or more provinces;
11. Registration, employment, supervision, and security of tenure of officials in Central and local governments;
12. Land legislation;
13. Labor legislation and other social legislation;
14. Eminent domain;
15. Census-taking and compilation of population statistics for the whole country;
16. Immigration and land reclamation;
17. Police system;
18. Public health;
19. Relief, pecuniary aid in case of death and aid in case of unemployment; and
20. Preservation of ancient books and articles and sites of cultural value.

With respect to the various items enumerated in the preceding paragraph, the provinces may enact separate rules and regulations, provided these are not in conflict with national laws.

Article 109. In the following matters, the provinces shall have the power of legislation and administration, but the provinces may delegate the power of administration to the hsien;

1. Provincial education, public health, industries and communications;

2. Management and disposal of provincial property;

3. Administration of municipalities under provincial jurisdiction;

4. Province-operated enterprises;

5. Provincial cooperative enterprises;

6. Provincial agriculture, forestry, water conservancy, fishery, animal husbandry and public works;

7. Provincial finance and revenues;

8. Provincial debts;

9. Provincial banks;

10. Provincial police administration;

11. Provincial charitable and public welfare works; and

12. Other matters delegated to the provinces in accordance with national laws.

Except as otherwise provided by law, any of the matters enumerated in the various items of the preceding paragraph, in so far as it covers two or more provinces, may be undertaken jointly by the provinces concerned.

When any province, in undertaking matters listed in any of the items of the first paragraph, finds its funds insufficient, it may, by resolution of the Legislative Yuan, obtain subsidies from the National Treasury.

Article 110. In the following matters, the hsien shall have the power of legislation and administration:

1. Hsien education, public health, industries and communications;

2. Management and disposal of hsien property;

3. Hsien-operated enterprises;

4. Hsien cooperative enterprises;

5. Hsien agriculture and forestry, water conservancy, fishery, animal husbandry and public works;

6. Hsien finance and revenues;

7. Hsien debts;

8. Hsien banks;

9. Administration of hsien police and defense;

10. Hsien charitable and public welfare works; and

11. Other matters delegated to the hsien in accordance with national laws and provincial Self-Government Regulations.

Except as otherwise provided by law, any of the matters enumerated in the various items of the preceding paragraph, in so far as it covers two or more hsien, may be undertaken jointly by the hsien concerned.

Article 111. Any matter not enumerated in Articles 107, 108, 109 and 110 shall fall within the jurisdiction of the Central Government, if it is national in nature; of the province, if it is provincial in nature; and of the hsien, if it concerns the hsien. In case of dispute, it shall be settled by the Legislative Yuan.

Chapter XI. System of Local Government
Section 1. The Province

Article 112. A province may convoke a provincial assembly to enact, in accordance with the General Principles of Provincial and Hsien Self-Government, regulations, provided the said regulations are not in conflict with the Constitution.

The organization of the provincial assembly and the election of the delegates shall be prescribed by law.

Article 113. The Provincial Self-Government Regulations shall include the following provisions:

1. In the province, there shall be a provincial council. Members of the provincial council shall be elected by the people of the province.

2. In the province, there shall be a provincial government with a provincial governor who shall be elected by the people of the province.

3. Relationship between the province and the hsien.

The legislative power of the province shall be exercised by the Provincial Council.

Article 114. The Provincial Self-Government Regulations shall, after enactment, be forthwith submitted to the Judicial Yuan. The Judicial Yuan, if it deems any part thereof unconstitutional, shall declare null and void the articles repugnant to the Constitution.

Article 115. If, during the enforcement of the Provincial Self-Government Regulations, there should arise any serious obstacle in the application of any of the articles contained therein, the Judicial Yuan shall first summon the various parties concerned to present their views; and thereupon the Presidents of the Executive Yuan, Legislative Yuan, Judicial Yuan, Examination Yuan and

Control Yuan shall form a Committee, with the President of the Judicial Yuan as Chairman, to propose a formula for solution.

Article 116. Provincial rules and regulations that are in conflict with national laws shall be null and void.

Article 117. When doubt arises as to whether or not there is a conflict between provincial rules or regulations and national laws, interpretation thereon shall be made by the Judicial Yuan.

Article 118. The self-government of municipalities under the direct jurisdiction of the Executive Yuan shall be prescribed by law.

Article 119. The local self-government system of the Mongolian Leagues and Banners shall be prescribed by law.

Article 120. The self-government system of Tibet shall be safeguarded.

Section 2. The Hsien

Article 121. The hsien shall enforce hsien self-government.

Article 122. A hsien may convoke a hsien assembly to enact, in accordance with the General Principles of Provincial and Hsien Self-Government, hsien self-government regulations, provided the said regulations are not in conflict with the Constitution or with provincial self-government regulations.

Article 123. The people of the hsien shall, in accordance with law, exercise the rights of initiative and referendum in matters within the sphere of hsien self-government, and shall, in accordance with law, exercise the rights of election and recall of the magistrate and other hsien self-government officials.

Article 124. In the hsien, there shall be a hsien council. Members of the hsien council shall be elected by the people of the hsien.

The legislative power of the hsien shall be exercised by the hsien council.

Article 125. Hsien rules and regulations that are in conflict with national laws, or with provincial rules and regulations, shall be null and void.

Article 126. In the hsien, there shall be a hsien government with a hsien magistrate who shall be elected by the people of the hsien.

Article 127. The hsien magistrate shall have charge of hsien self-government and shall administer matters delegated to the hsien by the central or provincial government.

Article 128. The provisions governing the hsien shall apply *mutatis mutandis* to the municipality.

Chapter XII. Election, Recall, Initiative and Referendum

Article 129. The various kinds of elections prescribed in this Constitution, except as otherwise provided by this Constitution, shall be by universal, equal, and direct suffrage and by secret ballot.

Article 130. Any citizen of the Republic of China who has attained the age of 20 years shall have the right of election in accordance with law. Except as otherwise provided by this Constitution or by law, any citizen who has attained the age of 23 years shall have the right of being elected in accordance with law.

Article 131. All candidates in the various kinds of elections prescribed in this Constitution shall openly campaign for their election.

Article 132. Intimidation or inducement shall be strictly forbidden in elections. Suits arising in connection with elections shall be tried by the courts.

Article 133. A person elected may, in accordance with law, be recalled by his constituency.

Article 134. In the various kinds of elections, the number of women to be elected shall be fixed, and measures pertaining thereto shall be prescribed by law.

Article 135. The number of delegates to the National Assembly and the manner of their election from people in interior areas, who have their own conditions of living and habits, shall be prescribed by law.

Article 136. The exercise of the rights of initiative and referendum shall be prescribed by law.

Chapter XIII. Fundamental National Policies
Section 1. National Defense

Article 137. The national defense of the Republic of China shall have as its objective the safeguarding of national security and the preservation of world peace.

The organization of national defense shall be prescribed by law.

Article 138. The land, sea and air forces of the whole country shall be above personal, regional, or party affiliations, shall be loyal to the state, and shall protect the people.

Article 139. No political party and no individual shall make use of armed forces as an instrument in a struggle for political powers.

Article 140. No military man in active service may concurrently hold a civil office.

Section 2. Foreign Policy

Article 141. The foreign policy of the Republic of China shall, in a spirit of independence and initiative and on the basis of the principles of equality and reciprocity, cultivate good-neighborliness with other nations, and respect treaties and the Charter of the United Nations, in order to protect the rights and interests of Chinese citizens residing abroad, promote international cooperation, advance international justice and ensure world peace.

Section 3. National Economy

Article 142. National economy shall be based on the Principle of the People's Livelihood and shall seek to effect equalization of land ownership and restriction of private capital in order to attain a well-balanced sufficiency in national wealth and people's livelihood.

Article 143. All land within the territory of the Republic of China shall belong to the whole body of citizens. Private ownership of land, acquired by the people in accordance with law, shall be protected and restricted by law. Privately-owned land shall be liable to taxation according to its value, and the Government may buy such land according to its value.

Mineral deposits which are embedded in the land, and natural power which may, for economic purposes, be utilized for the public benefit shall belong to the State, regardless of the fact that private individuals may have acquired ownership over such land.

If the value of a piece of land has increased, not through the exertion of labor or the employment of capital, the State shall levy thereon an increment tax, the proceeds of which shall be enjoyed by the people in common.

In the distribution and readjustment of land, the State shall in principle assist self-farming land-owners and persons who make use of the land by themselves, and shall also regulate their appropriate areas of operation.

Article 144. Public utilities and other enterprises of a monopolistic nature shall, in principle, be under public operation. In cases permitted by law, they may be operated by private citizens.

Article 145. With respect to private wealth and privately-operated enterprises, the State shall restrict them by law if they are deemed detrimental to a balanced development of national wealth and people's livelihood.

Cooperative enterprises shall receive encouragement and assistance from the State.

Private citizens' productive enterprises and foreign trade shall receive encouragement, guidance and protection from the State.

Article 146. The State shall, by the use of scientific techniques, develop water conservancy, increase the productivity of land, improve agricultural conditions, plan for the utilization of land, develop agricultural resources and hasten the industrialization of agriculture.

Article 147. The Central Government, in order to attain balanced economic development among the provinces, shall give appropriate aid to poor or unproductive provinces.

The provinces, in order to attain balanced economic development among the hsien, shall give appropriate aid to poor or unproductive hsien.

Article 148. Within the territory of the Republic of China, all goods shall be permitted to move freely from place to place.

Article 149. Financial institutions shall, in accordance with law, be subject to State control.

Article 150. The State shall extensively establish financial institutions for the common people, with a view to relieving unemployment.

Article 151. With respect to Chinese citizens residing abroad, the State shall foster and protect the development of their economic enterprises.

Section 4. Social Security

Article 152. The State shall provide suitable opportunity for work to people who are able to work.

Article 153. The State, in order to improve the livelihood of laborers and farmers and to improve their productive skill, shall enact laws and carry out policies for their protection.

Women and children engaged in labor shall, according to their age and physical condition, be accorded special protection.

Article 154. Capital and labor shall, in accordance with the principle of harmony and cooperation, promote productive enterprises. Conciliation and arbitration of disputes between capital and labor shall be prescribed by law.

Article 155. The State, in order to promote social welfare, shall establish a social insurance system. To the aged and the infirm who are unable to earn a living, and to victims of unusual calamities, the State shall give appropriate assistance and relief.

Article 156. The State, in order to consolidate the foundation of national existence and development, shall protect motherhood and carry out the policy of promoting the welfare of women and children.

Article 157. The State, in order to improve national health, shall establish extensive services for sanitation and health protection, and a system of public medical service.

Section 5. Education and Culture

Article 158. Education and culture shall aim at the development among the citizens of the national spirit, the spirit of self-government, national morality, good physique, scientific knowledge, and the ability to earn a living.

Article 159. All citizens shall have equal opportunity to receive an education.

Article 160. All children of school age from six to 12 years shall receive free primary education. Those from poor families shall be supplied with books by the Government.

All citizens above school age who have not received primary education shall receive supplementary education free of charge and shall also be supplied with books by the Government.

Article 161. The national, provincial, and local governments shall extensively establish scholarships to assist students of good scholastic standing and exemplary conduct who lack the means to continue their school education.

Article 162. All public and private educational and cultural institutions in the country shall, in accordance with law, be subject to State supervision.

Article 163. The State shall pay due attention to the balanced development of education in different regions, and shall promote social education in order to raise the cultural standard of the citizens in general. Grants from the National Treasury shall be made to frontier regions and economically poor areas to help them meet their educational and cultural expenses. The Central Government may either itself undertake the more important educational and cultural enterprises in such regions or give them financial assistance.

Article 164. Expenditures of educational programs, scientific studies and cultural services shall not be, in respect of the Central Government, less than 15 percent of the total national budget; in respect of each province, less than 25 percent of the total provincial budgets; and in respect of each municipality or hsien, less than 35 percent of the total municipal or hsien budget. Educational and cultural foundations established in accordance with law shall, together with their property, be protected.

Article 165. The State shall safeguard the livelihood of those who work in the fields of education, sciences and arts, and shall, in accordance with the development of national economy, increase their remuneration from time to time.

Article 166. The State shall encourage scientific discoveries and inventions, and shall protect ancient sites and articles of historical, cultural or artistic value.

Article 167. The State shall give encouragement or subsidies to the following enterprises or individuals:

1. Educational enterprises in the country which have been operated with good record by private individuals;

2. Educational enterprises which have been operated with good record by Chinese citizens residing abroad;

3. Persons who have made discoveries or inventions in the fields of learning and technology; and

4. Persons who have rendered long and meritorious services in the field of education.

Section 6. Frontier Regions

Article 168. The State shall accord to the various racial groups in the frontier regions legal protection of their status and shall give them special assistance in their local self-government undertakings.

Article 169. The State shall, in a positive manner, undertake and foster the development of education, culture, communications, water conservancy, public health, and other economic and social enterprises of the various racial groups in the frontier regions. With respect to the utilization of land, the State shall, after taking into account the climatic conditions, the nature of the soil and the life and habits of the people, adopt measures to protect the land and to assist in its development.

Chapter XIV. Enforcement and Amendment of the Constitution

Article 170. The term "law," as used in this Constitution, shall denote any legislative bill that shall have been passed by the Legislative Yuan and promulgated by the President of the Republic.

Article 171. Laws that are in conflict with the Constitution shall be null and void.

When doubt arises as to whether or not a law is in conflict with the Constitution, interpretation thereon shall be made by the Judicial Yuan.

Article 172. Ordinances that are in conflict with the Constitution or with laws shall be null and void.

Article 173. The Constitution shall be interpreted by the Judicial Yuan.

Article 174. Amendments to the Constitution shall be made in accordance with one of the following procedures:

1. Upon the proposal of one-fifth of the total number of the delegates to the National Assembly and by a resolution of three-fourths of the delegates present at a meeting having a quorum of two-thirds of the entire Assembly, the Constitution may be amended.

2. Upon the proposal of one-fourth of the Members of the Legislative Yuan and by a resolution of three-fourths of the Members present at a meeting having a quorum of three-fourths of the Members of the Yuan, an amendment may be drawn up and submitted to the National Assembly by way of referendum. Such a proposed amendment to the Constitution shall be publicly published half a year before the National Assembly convenes.

Article 175. Whenever necessary, enforcement procedures in regard to any matters prescribed in this Constitution shall be separately provided by law.

The preparatory procedures for the enforcement of this Constitution shall be decided upon by the same National Assembly which shall have adopted this Constitution.

The Additional Articles
of the Constitution
of the Republic of China

Adopted by the second extraordinary session of the First National Assembly on April 22, 1991, and promulgated by the president on May 1, 1991

Adopted by the extraordinary session of the Second National Assembly on May 27, 1992, and promulgated by the president on May 28, 1992

Adopted by the fourth extraordinary session of the Second National Assembly on July 28, 1994, and promulgated by the president on August 1, 1994

Adopted by the second session of the Third National Assembly on July 18, 1997, and promulgated by the president on July 21, 1997

Revised by the fourth session of the Third National Assembly on September 3, 1999, and promulgated by the president on September 15, 1999

The Council of Grand Justices, in its Constitutional Interpretation No. 499 on March 24, 2000, announced that the Additional Articles of the Constitution approved on September 15, 1999, were void, effective immediately. The revised Additional Articles promulgated on July 21, 1997 would remain in effect.

The revision of the Additional Articles of the Constitution of the Republic of China was approved by the fifth session of the Third National Assembly on April 24, 2000, and promulgated by the president on April 25, 2000.

To meet the requisites of the nation prior to national unification, the following articles of the ROC Constitution are added or amended to the ROC Constitution in accordance with Article 27, Paragraph 1, Item 3; and Article 174, Item 1:

Article 1. Three hundred delegates shall be elected by proportional representation to the National Assembly within three months of the expiration of a six-month period following the public announcement of a proposal by the Legislative Yuan to amend the Constitution or alter the national territory, or within three months of a petition initiated by the Legislative Yuan for the impeachment of the president or the vice president. The restrictions of Articles 26, 28, and 135 of the Constitution shall not apply. The election of the delegates by proportional representation shall be regulated by law.

The powers of the National Assembly shall be as follows, and the provisions of Article 4; Article 27, Paragraph 1, Item 1 through 3; Article 27, Paragraph 2; and Article 174, Item 1 shall not apply:

1. To vote, in accordance with Article 27, Paragraph 1, Item 4 and Article 174, Item 2 of the Constitution, on Legislative Yuan proposals to amend the Constitution;

2. To vote, in accordance with Article 4, Paragraph 5 of the Additional Articles, on Legislative Yuan proposals to alter the national territory; and

3. To deliberate, in accordance with Article 2, Paragraph 10 of the Additional Articles, a petition for the impeachment of the president or the vice president initiated by the Legislative Yuan.

Delegates to the National Assembly shall convene of their own accord within ten days after the election results have been confirmed and shall remain in session for no more than one month. The provisions of Articles 29 and 30 of the Constitution shall not apply.

The term of office of the delegates to the National Assembly shall terminate on the last day of the convention, and the provisions of Article 28 of the Constitution shall cease to apply. The term of office of the delegates to the Third National Assembly shall terminate on May 19, 2000. The Organic Law of the National Assembly shall be revised accordingly within two years of the adjustment of the powers and responsibilities of the National Assembly.

Article 2. The president and the vice president shall be directly elected by the entire populace of the free area of the Republic of China. This shall be effective from the election for the ninth-term president and vice president in 1996. The presidential and the vice presidential candidates shall register jointly and be listed as a pair on the ballot. The pair that receives the highest number of votes shall be elected. Citizens of the free area of the Republic of China residing abroad may return to the ROC to exercise their electoral rights and this shall be stipulated by law.

Presidential orders to appoint or remove from office the president of the Executive Yuan or personnel appointed with the confirmation of the Legislative Yuan in accordance with the Constitution, and to dissolve the Legislative Yuan, shall not require the countersignature of the president of the Executive Yuan. The provisions of Article 37 of the Constitution shall not apply.

The president may, by resolution of the Executive Yuan Council, issue emergency decrees and take all necessary measures to avert imminent danger affecting the security of the State or of the people or to cope with any serious financial or economic crisis, the restrictions in Article 43 of the Constitution notwithstanding. However, such decrees shall, within ten days of issuance, be presented to the Legislative Yuan for ratification. Should the Legislative Yuan withhold ratification, the said emergency decrees shall forthwith cease to be valid.

To determine major policies for national security, the president may establish a national security council and a subsidiary national security bureau. The organization of the said organs shall be stipulated by law.

The president may, within ten days following passage by the Legislative Yuan of a no-confidence vote against the president of the Executive Yuan, declare the dissolution of the Legislative Yuan after consulting with its president. However, the president shall not dissolve the Legislative Yuan while martial law or an emergency decree is in effect. Following the dissolution of the Legislative Yuan, an election for legislators shall be held within 60 days. The new Legislative Yuan shall convene of its own accord within ten days after the results of the said election have been confirmed, and the term of the said Legislative Yuan shall be reckoned from that date.

The terms of office for both the president and the vice president shall be four years. The president and the vice president may only be re-elected to serve one consecutive term; and the provisions of Article 47 of the Constitution shall not apply.

Should the office of the vice president become vacant, the president shall nominate a candidate(s) within three months, and the Legislative Yuan shall elect a new vice president, who shall serve the remainder of the original term until its expiration.

Should the offices of both the president and the vice president become vacant, the president of the Executive Yuan shall exercise the official powers of the president and the vice president. A new president and a new vice president shall be elected in accordance with Paragraph 1 of this article and shall serve out each respective original term until its expiration. The pertinent provisions of Article 49 of the Constitution shall not apply.

Recall of the president or the vice president shall be initiated upon the proposal of one-fourth of all members of the Legislative Yuan, and also passed by two-thirds of all the members. The final recall must be passed by more than one-half of the valid ballots in a vote in which more than one-half of the electorate in the free area of the Republic of China takes part.

Should a motion to impeach the president or the vice president initiated and submitted to the National Assembly by the Legislative Yuan be passed by a two-thirds majority of all delegates to the National Assembly, the party impeached shall forthwith be dismissed from office.

Article 3. The president of the Executive Yuan shall be appointed by the president. Should the president of the Executive Yuan resign or the office become vacant, the vice president of the Executive Yuan shall temporarily act as the president of the Executive Yuan pending a new appointment by the president. The provisions of Article 55 of the Constitution shall cease to apply.

The Executive Yuan shall be responsible to the Legislative Yuan in accordance with the following provisions; the provisions of Article 57 of the Constitution shall cease to apply:

1. The Executive Yuan has the duty to present to the Legislative Yuan a statement on its administrative policies and a report on its administration. While the Legislative Yuan is in session, its members shall have the right to interpellate the president of the Executive Yuan and the heads of ministries and other organizations under the Executive Yuan.

2. Should the Executive Yuan deem a statutory, budgetary, or treaty bill passed by the Legislative Yuan difficult to execute, the Executive Yuan may, with the approval of the president of the Republic and within ten days of the bill's submission to the Executive Yuan, request the Legislative Yuan to reconsider the bill. The Legislative Yuan shall reach a resolution on the returned bill within 15 days after it is received. Should the Legislative Yuan be in recess, it shall convene of its own accord within seven days and reach a resolution within 15 days after the session begins. Should the Legislative Yuan not reach a resolution within the said period of time, the original bill shall become invalid. Should more than one-half of the total number of Legislative Yuan members uphold the original bill, the president of the Executive Yuan shall immediately accept the said bill.

3. With the signatures of more than one-third of the total number of Legislative Yuan members, the Legislative Yuan may propose a no-confidence vote against the president of the Executive Yuan. Seventy-two hours after the no-confidence motion is made, an open-ballot vote shall be taken within 48 hours. Should more than one-half of the total number of Legislative Yuan members approve the motion, the president of the Executive Yuan shall tender his resignation within ten days, and at the same time may request that the president dissolve the Legislative Yuan. Should the no-confidence motion fail, the Legislative Yuan may not initiate another no-confidence motion against the same president of the Executive Yuan within one year.

The powers, procedures of establishment, and total number of personnel of national organizations shall be subject to standards set forth by law.

The structure, system, and number of personnel of each organization shall be determined according to the policies or operations of each organization and in accordance with the law as referred to in the preceding paragraph.

Article 4. Beginning with the Fourth Legislative Yuan, the Legislative Yuan shall have 225 members, who shall be elected in accordance with the following provisions, the restrictions in Article 64 of the Constitution notwithstanding:

1. One hundred and sixty-eight members shall be elected from the Special Municipalities, counties, and cities in the free area. At least one member shall be elected from each county and city.

2. Four members each shall be elected from among the lowland and highland aborigines in the free area.

3. Eight members shall be elected from among the Chinese citizens who reside abroad.

4. Forty-one members shall be elected from the nationwide constituency.

Members for the seats set forth in Item 3 and Item 4 of the preceding paragraph shall be elected according to a formula for proportional representation among political parties. Where the number of seats for each Special Municipality, county, and city as set forth in Item 1, and for each political party as set forth in Item 3 and Item 4, is not fewer than five and not more than ten, one seat shall be reserved for a female member. Where the number exceeds ten, one seat out of each additional ten shall be reserved for a female member.

When the Legislative Yuan convenes each year, it may hear a report on the state of the nation by the president.

Following the dissolution of the Legislative Yuan by the president and prior to the inauguration of its new members, the Legislative Yuan shall be regarded as in recess.

The territory of the Republic of China, defined by its existing national boundaries, shall not be altered unless initiated upon the proposal of one-fourth of all members of the Legislative Yuan, passed by three-fourths of the members of the Legislative Yuan present at a meeting requiring a quorum of three-fourths of all the members, and approved by three-fourths of the delegates to the National Assembly present at a meeting requiring a quorum of two-thirds of all the delegates.

Should the president issue an emergency decree after dissolving the Legislative Yuan, the Legislative Yuan shall convene of its own accord within three days to vote on the ratification of the decree within seven days after the session begins. However, should the emergency decree be issued after the election of new members of the Legislative Yuan, the new members shall vote on the ratification of the decree after their inauguration. Should the Legislative Yuan withhold ratification, the emergency decree shall forthwith be void.

Impeachment of the president or the vice president by the Legislative Yuan shall be initiated upon the proposal of more than one-half of all members of the Legislative Yuan and passed by more than two-thirds of all the members of the Legislative Yuan, whereupon it shall be submitted to the National Assembly. The provisions of Article 90 and Article 100 of the Constitution and Article 7, Paragraph 1 of the Additional Articles of the Constitution shall not apply.

No member of the Legislative Yuan may be arrested or detained without the permission of the Legislative Yuan, when that body is in session, except in case of flagrante delicto. The provisions of Article 74 of the Constitution shall cease to apply.

Article 5. The Judicial Yuan shall have 15 grand justices. The 15 grand justices, including a president and a vice president of the Judicial Yuan to be selected from amongst them, shall be nominated and, with the consent of the Legislative Yuan, appointed by the president of the Republic. This shall take effect from the year 2003, and the provisions of Article 79 of the Constitution shall not apply. The provisions of Article 81 of the Constitution and pertinent regulations on the lifetime holding of office and payment of salary do not apply to grand justices who did not transfer from the post of a judge.

Each grand justice of the Judicial Yuan shall serve a term of eight years, independent of the order of appointment to office, and shall not serve a consecutive term. The grand justices serving as president and vice president of the Judicial Yuan shall not enjoy the guarantee of an eight-year term.

Among the grand justices nominated by the president in the year 2003, eight members, including the president and the vice president of the Judicial Yuan, shall serve for four years. The remaining grand justices shall serve for eight years. The provisions of the preceding paragraph regarding term of office shall not apply.

The grand justices of the Judicial Yuan shall, in addition to discharging their duties in accordance with Article 78 of the Constitution, also form a Constitutional Court to adjudicate matters relating to the dissolution of unconstitutional political parties.

A political party shall be considered unconstitutional if its goals or activities endanger the existence of the Republic of China or the nation's free and democratic constitutional order.

The proposed budget submitted annually by the Judicial Yuan may not be eliminated or reduced by the Executive Yuan; however, the Executive Yuan may indicate its opinions on the budget and include it in the central government's proposed budgetary bill for submission to the Legislative Yuan for deliberation.

Article 6. The Examination Yuan shall be the highest examination body of the State, and shall be responsible for the following matters; and the provisions of Article 83 of the Constitution shall not apply:

1. Holding of examinations;

2. Matters relating to the qualification screening, security of tenure, pecuniary aid in case of death, and retirement of civil servants; and

3. Legal matters relating to the employment, discharge, performance evaluation, scale of salaries, promotion, transfer, commendation and award of civil servants.

The Examination Yuan shall have a president, a vice president, and several members, all of whom shall be nominated and, with the consent of the Legislative Yuan, appointed by the president of the Republic; and the provisions of Article 84 of the Constitution shall not apply.

The provisions of Article 85 of the Constitution concerning the holding of examinations in different areas, with prescribed numbers of persons to be selected according to various provinces and areas, shall cease to apply.

Article 7. The Control Yuan shall be the highest control body of the State and shall exercise the powers of impeachment, censure and audit; and the pertinent provisions of Article 90 and Article 94 of the Constitution concerning the exercise of the power of consent shall not apply.

The Control Yuan shall have 29 members, including a president and a vice president, all of whom shall serve a term of six years. All members shall be nominated and, with the consent of the Legislative Yuan, appointed by the president of the Republic. The provisions of Article 91 through Article 93 of the Constitution shall cease to apply.

Impeachment proceedings by the Control Yuan against a public functionary in the central government, or local governments, or against personnel of the Judicial Yuan or the Examination Yuan, shall be initiated by two or more members of the Control Yuan, and be investigated and voted upon by a committee of not less than nine of its members, the restrictions in Article 98 of the Constitution notwithstanding.

In the case of impeachment by the Control Yuan of Control Yuan personnel for dereliction of duty or violation of the law, the provisions of Article 95 and Article 97, Paragraph 2 of the Constitution, as well as the preceding paragraph, shall apply.

Members of the Control Yuan shall be beyond party affiliation and independently exercise their powers and discharge their responsibilities in accordance with the law.

The provisions of Article 101 and Article 102 of the Constitution shall cease to apply.

Article 8. The remuneration or pay of the members of the Legislative Yuan shall be regulated by law. Except for general annual adjustments, individual regulations on increase of remuneration or pay shall take effect starting with the subsequent Legislative Yuan. Expenses for the convention of the delegates to the National Assembly shall be regulated by law.

Article 9. The system of self-government in the provinces and counties shall include the following provisions, which shall be established by the enactment of appropriate laws, the restrictions in Article 108, Paragraph 1, Item 1; Article 109; Article 112 through Article 115; and Article 122 of the Constitution notwithstanding:

1. A province shall have a provincial government of nine members, one of whom shall be the provincial governor. All members shall be nominated by the president of the Executive Yuan and appointed by the president of the Republic.

2. A province shall have a provincial advisory council made up of a number of members, who shall be nominated by the president of the Executive Yuan and appointed by the president of the Republic.

3. A county shall have a county council, members of which shall be elected by the people of the said county.

4. The legislative powers vested in a county shall be exercised by the county council of the said county.

5. A county shall have a county government headed by a county magistrate who shall be elected by the people of the said county.

6. The relationship between the central government and the provincial and county governments.

7. A province shall execute the orders of the Executive Yuan and supervise matters governed by the counties.

The modifications of the functions, operations, and organization of the Taiwan Provincial Government may be specified by law.

Article 10. The State shall encourage the development of and investment in science and technology, facilitate industrial upgrading, promote modernization of agriculture and fishery, emphasize exploitation and utilization of water resources, and strengthen international economic cooperation.

Environmental and ecological protection shall be given equal consideration with economic and technological development.

The State shall assist and protect the survival and development of private small and medium-sized enterprises.

The State shall manage government-run financial organizations, in accordance with the principles of business administration. The management, personnel, proposed budgets, final budgets, and audits of the said organizations may be specified by law.

The State shall promote universal health insurance and promote the research and development of both modern and traditional medicines.

The State shall protect the dignity of women, safeguard their personal safety, eliminate sexual discrimination, and further substantive gender equality.

The State shall guarantee insurance, medical care, obstacle-free environments, education and training, vocational guidance, and support and assistance in everyday life for physically and mentally handicapped persons, and shall also assist them to attain independence and to develop.

The State shall emphasize social relief and assistance, welfare services, employment for citizens, social insurance, medical and health care, and other social welfare services. Priority shall be given to funding social relief and assistance, and employment for citizens.

The State shall respect military servicemen for their contributions to society, and guarantee studies, employment, medical care, and livelihood for retired servicemen.

Priority shall be given to funding education, science, and culture, and in particular funding for compulsory education, the restrictions in Article 164 of the Constitution notwithstanding.

The State affirms cultural pluralism and shall actively preserve and foster the development of aboriginal languages and cultures.

The State shall, in accordance with the will of the ethnic groups, safeguard the status and political participation of the aborigines. The State shall also guarantee and provide assistance and encouragement for aboriginal education, culture, transportation, water conservation, health and medical care, economic activity, land, and social welfare, measures for which shall be established by law. The same protection and assistance shall be given to the people of the Penghu, Kinmen, and Matsu areas.

The State shall accord to nationals of the Republic of China residing overseas protection of their rights of political participation.

Article 11. Rights and obligations between the people of the Chinese mainland area and those of the free area, and the disposition of other related affairs may be specified by law.

Appendix IV

ROC Government Directory

The most up-to-date information is always available on line at:
http://www.gio.gov.tw/info/chief

Office of the President 總統府

122 Chungking South Road, Section 1, Taipei
Phone: (02) 2311-3731
Fax: (02) 2331-1604
Website: http://www.president.gov.tw
E-mail: president@mail.oop.gov.tw
President: CHEN, Shui-bian 陳水扁
Vice President: LU, Hsiu-lien 呂秀蓮
Secretary-General: CHEN, Shih-meng 陳師孟

Academia Sinica 中央研究院
128 Yen Chiu Yuan Road, Section 2, Taipei
Phone: (02) 2782-2120
Fax: (02) 2785-3847
Website: http://www.sinica.edu.tw
E-mail: service@sinica.edu.tw
President: LEE, Yuan-tseh 李遠哲

Academia Historica 國史館
406 Pei Yi Road, Section 2, Hsintien
Taipei County
Phone: (02) 2217-5500
Fax: (02) 2217-0415
Website: http://www.drnh.gov.tw
E-mail: nha@academia.drnh.gov.tw
President: CHANG, Yen-hsien 張炎憲

National Security Council 國家安全會議
122 Chungking South Road, Section 1
Taipei
Phone: (02) 2371-8579
Fax: (02) 2371-8599
Chairman: CHEN, Shui-bian 陳水扁
Secretary-General: CHIOU, I-jen 邱義仁

National Unification Council 國家統一委員會
122 Chungking South Road, Section 1
Taipei
Phone: (02) 2311-5161
Fax: (02) 2314-1814

National Assembly 國民大會

53 Chung Hua Road, Section 1, Taipei
Phone: (02) 2331-1312
Fax: (02) 2314-2056
Website: http://www.nasm.gov.tw

Executive Yuan 行政院

1 Chung Hsiao East Road, Section 1, Taipei
Phone: (02) 3356-6500
Fax: (02)3356-6920
Website: http://www.ey.gov.tw
E-mail: eyemail@eyemail.gio.gov.tw
Premier: YU, Shyi-kun 游錫堃
Vice Premier: LIN, Hsin-i 林信義
Secretary-General: LEE, Ying-yuan 李應元

Ministers without Portfolio 政務委員
TSAY, Ching-yen 蔡清彥
HU, Sheng-cheng 胡勝正
CHEN, Chi-nan 陳其南
HUANG, Hwei-chen 黃輝珍
LIN, Sheng-feng 林盛豐
KUO, Yao-chi 郭瑤琪
YEH, Jiunn-rong 葉俊榮

Ministry of the Interior 內政部
5 Hsuchow Road, Taipei
Phone: (02) 2356-5000
Fax: (02) 2356-6201
Website: http://www.moi.gov.tw
E-mail: service@mail.moi.gov.tw
Minister: YU, Cheng-hsien 余政憲

Ministry of Foreign Affairs 外交部
2 Kaitagelan Boulevard, Taipei
Phone: (02) 2348-2999
Fax: (02) 2381-2703

Website: http://www.mofa.gov.tw
E-mail: eyes@mofa.gov.tw
Minister: CHIEN, Yu-hsin 簡又新

Ministry of National Defense 國防部
164 Po Ai Road, Taipei
Phone: (02) 2311-6117
Fax: (02) 2361-9368
Website: http://www.mnd.gov.tw
E-mail: mnd@mnd.gov.tw
Minister: TANG, Yiau-min 湯曜明
Chief of the General Staff: LEE, Jye 李傑

Ministry of Finance
2 Ai Kuo West Road, Taipei
Phone: (02) 2322-8000
Fax: (02) 2396-5829
Website: http://www.mof.gov.tw
E-mail: mof@mail.mof.gov.tw
Minister: LEE, Yung-san 李庸三

Ministry of Education 教育部
5 Chung Shan South Road, Taipei
Phone: (02) 2356-6051
Fax: (02) 2397-6949
Website: http://www.moe.gov.tw
E-mail: mail@mail.moe.gov.tw
Minister: HUANG, Jong-tsun 黃榮村

Ministry of Justice 法務部
130 Chungking South Road, Section 1, Taipei
Phone: (02) 2314-6871
Fax: (02) 2389-2164
Website: http://www.moj.gov.tw
E-mail: hotline@mail.moj.gov.tw
Minister: CHEN, Ding-nan 陳定南

Ministry of Economic Affairs 經濟部
15 Foochow Street, Taipei
Phone: (02) 2321-2200
Fax: (02) 2396-9098
Website: http://www.moea.gov.tw
E-mail: service@moea.gov.tw
Minister: LIN, Yi-fu 林義夫

Ministry of Transportation and Communications
交通部
2 Changsha Street, Section 1, Taipei
Phone: (02) 2349-2900
Fax: (02) 2389-6009
Website: http://www.motc.gov.tw
E-mail: motceyes@motc.gov.tw
Minister: LIN, Ling-san 林陵三

Mongolian & Tibetan Affairs Commission
蒙藏委員會
4th Floor, 5 Hsuchow Road, Taipei
Phone: (02) 2356-6467
Fax: (02) 2341-6837
Website: http://www.mtac.gov.tw
E-mail: mtacserv@mtac.gov.tw
Chairman: HSU, Chih-hsiung 許志雄

Overseas Chinese Affairs Commission
僑務委員會
16th Floor, 5 Hsuchow Road, Taipei
Phone: (02) 3343-2600
Fax: (02) 2356-6354
Website: http://www.ocac.gov.tw
E-mail: ocacinfo@mail.ocac.gov.tw
Minister: CHANG, Fu-mei 張富美

The Central Bank of China 中央銀行
2 Roosevelt Road, Section 1, Taipei
Phone: (02) 2393-6161
Fax: (02) 2357-1974
Website: http://www.cbc.gov.tw
E-mail: adminrol@mail.cbc.gov.tw
Governor: PERNG, Fai-nan 彭淮南

Directorate General of Budget, Accounting and Statistics, Executive Yuan
行政院主計處
1 Chung Hsiao East Road, Section 1, Taipei
Phone: (02) 2381-4910
Fax: (02) 2397-0196
Website: http://www.dgbasey.gov.tw
E-mail: dgbas@dgbas.gov.tw
Director-General: LIN, Chuan 林全

Government Information Office, Executive Yuan
行政院新聞局
2 Tientsin Street, Taipei
Phone: (02) 3356-8888
Fax: (02) 2356-8733
Website: http://www.gio.gov.tw
E-mail: service@mail.gio.gov.tw
Director-General: Arthur IAP 葉國興

Central Personnel Administration
Executive Yuan 行政院人事行政局
10th Floor, 2-2 Chi Nan Road, Section 1, Taipei
Phone: (02) 2397-9298
Fax: (02) 2397-5565
Website: http://www.cpa.gov.tw
E-mail: chief@cpa.gov.tw
Director-General: LEE, Yi-yang 李逸洋

Department of Health, Executive Yuan
行政院衛生署
100 Ai Kuo East Road, Taipei
Phone: (02) 2321-0151
Fax: (02) 2395-2907
Website: http://www.doh.gov.tw
E-mail: secgn@doh.gov.tw
Director-General: LEE, Ming-liang 李明亮

Environmental Protection Administration
Executive Yuan 行政院環境保護署
41 Chung Hua Road, Section 1, Taipei
Phone: (02) 2311-7722
Fax: (02) 2383-0455
Website: http://www.epa.gov.tw
E-mail: www@sun.epa.gov.tw
Administrator: HAU, Lung-bin 郝龍斌

Council for Economic Planning and Development
Executive Yuan 行政院經濟建設委員會
3 Pao Ching Road, Taipei
Phone: (02) 2316-5300
Fax: (02) 2370-0415
Website: http://www.cepd.gov.tw
E-mail: web@sun.cepd.gov.tw
Chairman: LIN, Hsin-i 林信義

Veterans Affairs Commission, Executive Yuan
行政院國軍退除役官兵輔導委員會
222 Chung Hsiao East Road, Section 5, Taipei
Phone: (02) 2725-5700
Fax: (02) 2723-0170
Website: http://www.vac.gov.tw
E-mail: eyes@mail.vac.gov.tw
Chairman: YANG, Te-chih 楊德智

National Youth Commission, Executive Yuan
行政院青年輔導委員會
14th Floor, 5 Hsuchow Road, Taipei
Phone: (02) 2356-6232
Fax: (02) 2356-6307
Website: http://www.nyc.gov.tw
E-mail: nyc@nyc.gov.tw
Chairperson: LIN, Fang-mei 林芳玫

National Palace Museum 國立故宮博物院
221 Chih Shan Road, Section 2, Wai-shuang-hsi
Shihlin, Taipei
Phone: (02) 2881-2021
Fax: (02) 2882-1440
Website: http://www.npm.gov.tw
E-mail: tu@npm.gov.tw
Director: TU, Cheng-sheng 杜正勝

Atomic Energy Council, Executive Yuan
行政院原子能委員會
67 Lane 144, Keelung Road, Section 4, Taipei
Phone: (02) 2363-4180
Fax: (02) 2368-3591
Website: http://www.aec.gov.tw
E-mail: public@aec.gov.tw
Chairman: OU YANG, Min-shen 歐陽敏盛

National Science Council, Executive Yuan
行政院國家科學委員會
106 Ho Ping East Road, Section 2, Taipei
Phone: (02) 2737-7992
Fax: (02) 2737-7566
Website: http://www.nsc.gov.tw
E-mail: nsc@nsc.gov.tw
Chairman: WEI, Che-ho 魏哲和

**Research, Development and Evaluation
Commission, Executive Yuan**
行政院研究發展考核委員會
6th-8th Floor, 2-2 Chi Nan Road, Section 2
Taipei
Phone: (02) 2341-9066
Fax: (02) 2396-9380
Website: http://www.rdec.gov.tw
E-mail: rdec@rdec.gov.tw
Chairman: LIN, Chia-cheng 林嘉誠

Council of Agriculture, Executive Yuan
行政院農業委員會
37 Nan Hai Road, Taipei
Phone: (02) 2381-2991
Fax: (02) 2331-0341
Website: http://www.coa.gov.tw
E-mail: coa@mail.coa.gov.tw
Chairman: FAN, Chen-tzung 范振宗

Council for Cultural Affairs, Executive Yuan
行政院文化建設委員會
30-1 Pei Ping East Road, Taipei
Phone: (02) 2343-4000
Fax: (02)2321-6478
Website: http://www.cca.gov.tw
E-mail: wwwadm@www.cca.gov.tw
Chairperson: TCHEN, Yu-chiou 陳郁秀

Council of Labor Affairs, Executive Yuan
行政院勞工委員會
6th Floor, 132 Min Sheng East Road, Section 3
Taipei
Phone: (02) 8770-1866
Fax: (02) 2514-9240
Website: http://cla.gov.tw
E-mail: cla@mail.cla.gov.tw
Chairperson: CHEN, Chu 陳菊

Mainland Affairs Council, Executive Yuan
行政院大陸委員會
15th Floor, 2-2 Chi Nan Road, Section 1
Taipei
Phone: (02) 2397-5589
Fax: (02) 2397-5300
Website: http://www.mac.gov.tw

E-mail: macst@mac.gov.tw
Chairperson: TSAI, Ing-wen 蔡英文

Fair Trade Commission, Executive Yuan
行政院公平交易委員會
12th-14th Floor, 2-2 Chi Nan Road, Section 1
Taipei
Phone: (02) 2351-7588
Fax: (02) 2397-4997
Website: http://www.ftc.gov.tw
E-mail: ftcpub@ftc.gov.tw
Chairperson: HWANG, Tzong-leh 黃宗樂

Council of Indigenous Peoples
Executive Yuan 行政院原住民族委員會
7th Floor, 3 Sung Jen Road, Taipei
Phone: (02) 8789-1800
Fax: (02) 2345-4323
Website:http://www.apc.gov.tw
Chairman: CHEN, Chien-nien 陳建年

Public Construction Commission
Executive Yuan 行政院公共工程委員會
9th Floor, 4 Chung Hsiao West Road, Section 1
Taipei
Phone: (02) 2361-8661
Fax: (02) 2331-5808
Website: http://www.pcc.gov.tw
E-mail: pccbox@mail.pcc.gov.tw
Chairman: KUO,Yao-chi 郭瑤琪

Consumers Protection Commission
Executive Yuan 行政院消費者保護委員會
1 Chung Hsiao East Road, Section 1, Taipei
Phone: (02) 2321-4700
Fax: (02) 2321-4538
Website: http://www.cpc.gov.tw
E-mail: tcpc@ms1.hinet.net
Chairman: LIN, Hsin-i 林信義

Central Election Commission
中央選舉委員會
10th Floor 5 Hsuchow Road, Taipei
Phone: (02) 2356-5484
Fax: (02) 2397-6900
Website: http://www.cec.gov.tw

E-mail: post@cec.gov.tw
Chairman: HUANG, Shih-cheng 黃石城

National Council on Physical Fitness and Sports
Executive Yuan 行政院體育委員會
20 Chu Lun Street, Taipei
Phone: (02)8771-1800
Fax: (02) 2552-3600
Website: http://www.ncpfs.gov.tw
E-mail: public@ncpfs.gov.tw
Chairman: LIN, Te-fu 林德福

Council for Hakka Affairs
Executive Yuan 行政院客家委員會
8th Floor, 3 Sung Jen Road, Taipei
Phone: (02) 8789-4567
Fax: (02) 8788-4568
Chairperson: YEH, Chu-lan 葉菊蘭

Coast Guard Administration
Executive Yuan 行政院海岸巡防署
296 Hsing Lung Road, Section 3, Taipei
Phone: (02) 2239-9201
Fax: (02) 2239-9258
Director General: WANG, Chun 王郡

Legislative Yuan 立法院

1 Chung Shan South Road, Taipei
Phone: (02) 2358-5858
Fax: (02) 2358-5255
Website: http://www.ly.gov.tw
President: WANG, Chin-ping 王金平
Vice President: CHIANG, Pin-kung 江丙坤
Secretary-General: LIN, Hsi-shan 林錫山

Judicial Yuan 司法院

124 Chungking South Road, Section 1, Taipei
Phone: (02) 2361-8577
Fax: (02) 2361-3295
Website: http://www.judicial.gov.tw
E-mail: judicial@judicial.gov.tw
President: WENG, Yueh-sheng 翁岳生

Vice President: CHENG, Chung-mo 城仲模
Secretary-General: YANG, Jen-shou 楊仁壽

Supreme Court 最高法院
6 Changsha Street, Section 1, Taipei
Phone: (02) 2314-1160
Fax: (02) 2375-1788
President: WU, Chii-pin 吳啟賓

Supreme Administrative Court 最高行政法院
1 Lane 126, Chungking South Road
Section 1, Taipei
Phone: (02) 2311-3691
Fax: (02) 2311-1791
President: JONG, Yaw-tarng 鍾曜唐

Commission on the Disciplinary Sanctions of
Public Functionaries 公務員懲戒委員會
3rd Floor, 124 Chungking South Road
Section 1, Taipei
Phone: (02) 2311-1639
Fax: (02) 2331-7908
Chief Commissioner: LIN, Kuo-hsien 林國賢

Examination Yuan 考試院

1 Shih Yuan Road, Taipei
Phone: (02) 8236-6000
Fax: (02) 8236-6100
Website: http://www.exam.gov.tw
E-mail: exam@exam.gov.tw
President: HSU, Shui-teh 許水德
Secretary-General: HSU, Ching-fu 許慶復

Ministry of Examination 考選部
1 Shih Yuan Road, Taipei
Phone: (02) 2236-9188
Fax: (02) 2236-2529
Website: http://www.moex.gov.tw
E-mail: boss@mis.moex.gov.tw
Minister: LIU, Chu-chi 劉初枝

Ministry of Civil Service 銓敘部
1 Shih Yuan Road, Taipei
Phone: (02) 8236-6666
Fax: (02) 8236-6448

Website: http://www.mocs.gov.tw
E-mail: mop@mocs.gov.tw
Minister: WU, Rong-ming 吳容明

Civil Service Protection and Training Commission
公務人員保障暨培訓委員會
1 Shih Yuan Road, Taipei
Phone: (02) 8236-7000
Fax: (02) 8236-6919
Website: http://www.csptc.gov.tw
Chairman: CHOU, Hung-hsien 周弘憲

Supervisory Board of the Civil Servants Pension Fund 公務人員退休撫卹基金監理委員會
1 Shih Yuan Road, Taipei
Phone: (02) 8236-7200
Fax: (02) 8236-7268
Website: http://www.fund.gov.tw

Control Yuan 監察院

2 Chung Hsiao East Road, Section 1, Taipei
Phone: (02) 2341-3183
Fax: (02) 2341-0324
Website: http://www.cy.gov.tw
E-mail: cymail@ms.cy.gov.tw
President: Fredrick F. CHIEN 錢復
Vice President: CHEN, Meng-ling 陳孟鈴
Secretary-General: TU, Shan-liang 杜善良

National Audit Office 審計部
1 Hangchow North Road, Taipei
Phone: (02) 2397-1366
Fax: (02) 2397-7889
Website: http://www.audit.gov.tw
Auditor-General: SU, Chen-ping 蘇振平

Taipei City Government 臺北市政府

1 Shih Fu Road, Taipei
Phone: (02) 2720-8889
Fax: (02) 2725-8677
Website: http://www.taipei.gov.tw
E-mail: mayor@mail.tcg.gov.tw
Mayor: MA, Ying-jeou 馬英九

Secretariat 秘書處
1 Shih Fu Road, Taipei
Phone: (02) 2725-6081
Fax: (02) 2725-6080

Bureau of Civil Affairs 民政局
1 Shih Fu Road, Taipei
Phone: (02) 2720-8889
Fax: (02) 2759-8799

Bureau of Finance 財政局
1 Shih Fu Road, Taipei
Phone: (02) 2720-8889
Fax: (02) 2759-5659

Bureau of Education 教育局
1 Shih Fu Road, Taipei
Phone: (02) 2720-8889
Fax: (02) 2759-3384

Bureau of Reconstruction 建設局
1 Shih Fu Road, Taipei
Phone: (02) 2720-8889
Fax: (02) 2759-6608

Bureau of Public Works 工務局
1 Shih Fu Road, Taipei
Phone: (02) 2720-8889
Fax: (02) 2725-6801

Bureau of Transportation 交通局
1 Shih Fu Road, Taipei
Phone: (02) 2720-8889
Fax: (02) 2729-1814

Bureau of Social Affairs 社會局
1 Shih Fu Road, Taipei
Phone: (02) 2720-8889
Fax: (02) 2720-6552

Bureau of Labor Affairs 勞工局
1 Shih Fu Road, Taipei
Phone: (02) 2720-8889
Fax: (02) 2720-6656

Taipei City Police Headquarters 警察局
96 Yen Ping South Road, Taipei

Phone: (02) 2331-3561
Fax: (02) 2331-8898

Bureau of Health 衛生局
1 Shih Fu Road, Taipei
Phone: (02) 2720-8889
Fax: (02) 2722-2427

Bureau of Environmental Protection 環境保護局
1 Shih Fu Road, Taipei
Phone: (02) 2720-8889
Fax: (02) 2759-7986

Bureau of Urban Development 都市發展局
1 Shih Fu Road, Taipei
Phone: (02) 2720-8889
Fax: (02) 2759-3321

Taipei Fire Department 消防局
1 Sung Jen Road, Taipei
Phone: (02) 2729-7668
Fax: (02) 2758-7865

Cultural Affairs Bureau 文化局
1 Shih Fu Road, Taipei
Phone: (02) 2345-1556
Fax: (02) 2725-3496

Department of Land Administration 地政處
1 Shih Fu Road, Taipei
Phone: (02) 2720-8889
Fax: (02) 2759-5123

Department of Public Housing 國民住宅處
9th Floor, 8 Roosevelt Road, Section 1, Taipei
Phone: (02) 2321-1828
Fax: (02) 2357-2864

Department of Information 新聞處
1 Shih Fu Road, Taipei
Phone: (02) 2720-8889
Fax: (02) 2345-4568

Department of Military Service 兵役處
9th Floor, 92 Roosevelt Road, Section 4
Taipei

Phone: (02) 2365-4361
Fax: (02) 2367-3072

Department of Budget, Accounting and Statistics
主計處
1 Shih Fu Road, Taipei
Phone: (02) 2720-8889
Fax: (02) 2720-3187

Department of Personnel 人事處
1 Shih Fu Road, Taipei
Phone: (02) 2720-8889
Fax: (02) 2720-9111

Government Ethics Department 政風處
1 Shih Fu Road, Taipei
Phone: (02) 2720-8889
Fax: (02) 2759-5690

Research, Development and Evaluation Commission 研究發展考核委員會
1 Shih Fu Road, Taipei
Phone: (02) 2720-8889
Fax: (02) 2759-3593

Commission of Administrative Appeals
訴願審議委員會
1 Shih Fu Road, Taipei
Phone: (02) 8780-1252
Fax: (02) 2759-3266

Rules and Regulations Commission
法規委員會
1 Shih Fu Road, Taipei
Phone: (02) 2720-8889
Fax: (02) 2759-6695

Council of Aboriginal Affairs
原住民事務委員會
1 Shih Fu Road, Taipei
Phone: (02) 2720-6001
Fax: (02) 2720-5996

Urban Planning Commission 都市計畫委員會
1 Shih Fu Road, Taipei
Phone: (02) 2720-8889
Fax: (02) 2759-3013

Department of Rapid Transit Systems 捷運工程局
7 Lane 48, Chung Shan North Road, Section 2
Taipei
Phone: (02) 2521-5550
Fax: (02) 2521-7639

Taipei Feitsui Reservoir Administration
台北翡翠水庫管理局
43 Hsin Wu Road, Section 3, Hsintien, Taipei County
Phone: (02) 2666-7811
Fax: (02) 2666-7264

Taipei Water Department 臺北自來水事業處
131 Chang Hsing Street, Taipei
Phone: (02) 8733-5678
Fax: (02) 8733-5824

Taipei Bank 台北銀行
50 Chung Shan North Road, Section 2, Taipei
Phone: (02) 2542-5656
Fax: (02) 2542-4396

Civic Worker Training Center
公務人員訓練中心
20 Lane 21, Wan Mei Street, Section 2, Taipei
Phone: (02) 2932-0212
Fax: (02) 2932-3588

Taipei Rapid Transit Corporation
臺北大眾捷運股份有限公司
7 Lane 48, Chung Shan North Road, Section 2, Taipei
Phone: (02) 2536-3001
Fax: (02) 2511-5003

Kaohsiung City Government

高雄市政府

2 Ssu Wei Third Road, Kaohsiung
Phone: (07) 336-8333
Fax: (07) 333-7633
Website: http://www.kcg.gov.tw
E-mail: mayor@mail.kcg.gov.tw
Mayor: Frank HSIEH 謝長廷

Secretariat 秘書處
2 Ssu Wei Third Road, Kaohsiung
Phone: (07) 332-3377
Fax: (07) 335-3132

Bureau of Civil Affairs 民政局
2 Ssu Wei Third Road, Kaohsiung
Phone: (07) 335-6111
Fax: (07) 331-5944

Bureau of Finance 財政局
2 Ssu Wei Third Road, Kaohsiung
Phone: (07) 334-7866
Fax: (07) 331-8859

Bureau of Education 教育局
2 Ssu Wei Third Road, Kaohsiung
Phone: (07) 334-0022
Fax: (07) 331-5736

Bureau of Reconstruction 建設局
2 Ssu Wei Third Road, Kaohsiung
Phone: (07) 336-6252
Fax: (07)331-6425

Bureau of Public Works 工務局
2 Ssu Wei Third Road, Kaohsiung
Phone: (07) 333-5386
Fax: (07) 331-5426

Bureau of Social Affairs 社會局
2 Ssu Wei Third Road, Kaohsiung
Phone: (07) 337-3365
Fax: (07) 331-5940

Bureau of Labor Affairs 勞工局
6 Chen Chung Road, Kaohsiung
Phone: (07) 812-4613
Fax: (07) 812-4783

Police Headquarters 警察局
260 Chung Cheng Fourth Road, Kaohsiung
Phone: (07) 261-3000
Fax: (07) 251-8241

Fire Department 消防局
3 Chung Cheng Third Road, Kaohsiung
Phone: (07) 227-1055
Fax: (07) 227-1058

Health Department 衛生局
261 Chung Cheng Fourth Road, Kaohsiung
Phone: (07) 251-4171
Fax: (07) 215-1752

Department of Environmental Protection
環境保護局
2 Ssu Wei Third Road, Kaohsiung
Phone: (07) 336-8333
Fax: (07) 331-6164

Department of Mass Rapid Transit 捷運工程局
2 Ssu Wei Third Road, Kaohsiung
Phone: (07) 337-3000
Fax: (07) 331-4366

Department of Land Administration 地政處
2 Ssu Wei Third Road, Kaohsiung
Phone: (07) 337-3445
Fax: (07) 331-4017

Department of Public Housing 國民住宅處
2 Ssu Wei Third Road, Kaohsiung
Phone: (07) 337-3517
Fax: (07) 331-5058

Department of Information 新聞處
2 Ssu Wei Third Road, Kaohsiung
Phone: (07) 333-3269
Fax: (07) 331-5017

Department of Conscription 兵役處
2 Ssu Wei Third Road, Kaohsiung
Phone: (07) 331-6502
Fax: (07) 331-6506

Department of Budget, Accounting and Statistics
主計處
2 Ssu Wei Third Road, Kaohsiung
Phone: (07) 334-1766
Fax: (07) 331-4803

Department of Personnel 人事處
2 Ssu Wei Third Road, Kaohsiung
Phone: (07) 337-3640
Fax: (07) 331-5652

Department of Government Ethics 政風處
2 Ssu Wei Third Road, Kaohsiung
Phone: (07) 330-6816
Fax: (07) 331-3655

Human Resource Development Institute
公務人力資源發展中心
801 Chung Te Road, Kaohsiung
Phone: (07) 342-2101
Fax: (07) 342-2124

**Research, Development and Evaluation
Commission** 研究發展考核委員會
2 Ssu Wei Third Road, Kaohsiung
Phone: (07) 330-3012
Fax: (07) 331-3975

Rules and Regulations Commission
法規委員會
2 Ssu Wei Third Road, Kaohsiung
Phone: (07) 335-6766
Fax: (07) 333-8191

**Commission for Examining Petitions
and Appeals** 訴願審議委員會
2 Ssu Wei Third Road, Kaohsiung
Phone: (07) 337-3690
Fax: (07) 330-8971

Commission of Indigenous Affairs
原住民事務委員會
2 Ssu Wei Third Road, Kaohsiung
Phone: (07) 337-3205
Fax: (07) 334-0804

Urban Planning Committee 都市計畫委員會
2 Ssu Wei Third Road, Kaohsiung
Phone: (07) 335-5766
Fax: (07) 336-3937

Directory of ROC Representatives Abroad

All information presented was accurate at press time; however, minor changes might have
occurred since then. The most up-to-date information is always available on-line at:
http://www.mofa.gov.tw

ROC Embassies and Consulates

Asia

Embassy of the Republic of China
Majuro, Republic of the Marshall Islands
P.O. Box 1229, Majuro
Marshall Islands, MH 96960
Phone: (+692) 625-4051
Fax: (+692) 625-4056
E-mail: eoroc@ntamar.com

Embassy of the Republic of China
Yaren, Republic of Nauru
P.O. Box 294
Republic of Nauru, Central Pacific
Phone: (+674) 555-4399
Fax: (+674) 444-3846
E-mail: rocnauru@cenpac.net.nr

Embassy of the Republic of China
Koror, the Republic of Palau
P.O. Box 9087
Koror, Republic of Palau
Phone: (+680) 488-8150
Fax: (+680) 488-8151

Embassy of the Republic of China
Honiara, Solomon Islands
1st Floor, East Wing
Panatina Plaza
Solomon Islands
Mailing Address:
P.O. Box 586, Honiara
Solomon Islands, South Pacific
Phone: (+677) 38-050
Fax: (+677) 38-060
E-mail: embroc@welkam.solomon.com.sb

Emabssy of the Republic of China
Funafuti, Tuvalu
P.O. Box 130, Funafuti, Tuvalu
Phone: (+688) 20-278

Fax: (+688) 20-277
E-mail: rocembassy@tuvalu.tv

Africa

Ambassade de la République de Chine
Ouagadougou, Burkina Faso
01 B.P. 5563, Ouagadougou 01
Burkina Faso
Phone: (+226) 316-195
Fax: (+226) 316-197
E-mail: ambachine@fasonet.bf

Embassy of the Republic of China
N'Djamena, Republic of Chad
Mailing Address:
B.P. 1150, N'Djamena, Chad
Phone: (+235) 524-405
Fax: (+235) 524-402
E-mail: ambchine@intnet.td

Embassy of the Republic of China
Banjul, Republic of The Gambia
26 Radio Gambia Road
South Kanifing, Banjul
Mailing Address:
P.O. Box 916, Banjul, The Gambia, West Africa
Phone: (+220) 374-046
Fax: (+220) 374-055
E-mail: rocemb@qanet.gm

Embassy of the Republic of China
Monrovia, Republic of Liberia
Tubman Blvd. Congo Town Monrovia, Liberia
Mailing Address:
P.O. Box 5970, Monrovia, Liberia (West Africa)
Phone: (+231) 228-024
Fax: (+231) 226-740
E-mail: chineseemb.monrovia@libnet.net

Embassy of the Republic of China
Lilongwe, Republic of Malawi
Area 40, Plot No. 9

Capital City, Lilongwe, Malawi
Mailing Address:
P.O. Box 30221
Capital City, Lilongwe 3, Malawi
Phone: (+265) 773-611
Fax: (+265) 774-812
E-mail: rocemml@malawi.net

**Embaixada da República da China
na República Democrática de
São Tomé e Príncipe**
Avenida 12 de Julho, Sao Tome
República Democrática de São Tomé e Príncipe
Mailing Address:
Caixa Postal 839
República Democrática de São Tomé e Príncipe
Phone: (+239-12) 23-529
Fax: (+239-12) 21-376
E-mail: rocstp@sol.stome.telepac.net

**Ambassade de la République de Chine Dakar
République du Senegal**
30, Avenue Nelson Mandela
Dakar, Senegal
Mailing Address:
B.P. 4164, Dakar
République du Senegal
Phone: (+221) 8219-819
Fax: (+221) 8219-821
E-mail: embchine@sonatel.senet.net

**Embassy of the Republic of China
Mbabane, Kingdom of Swaziland**
Warner Street, Mbabane
Kingdom of Swaziland
Mailing Address:
P.O. Box 56, Mbabane
Kingdom of Swaziland
Phone: (+268) 404-4740
Fax: (+268) 404-6688
E-mail: chineseembassy@iafrica.sz

Europe

**Embassy of the Republic of China
Vatican City, Holy See**
Ambasciata Delle Republica di Cina

Presso la Santa Sede
Piazza delle Muse, 7
00197 Roma, Italia
Phone: (+39) 06808-3166
Fax: (+39) 06808-5679
E-mail: ambacina@tuttomi.it

Central and South America

**Embassy of the Republic of China
Belize City, Belize**
3rd Floor, James Blade Building
Corner Huston/Eyre Street
Belize City, Belize
P.O. Box 1020, Belize City
Belize, C.A.
Phone: (+501) 278-744
Fax: (+501) 233-082
E-mail: embroc@btl.net

**Embassy of the Republic of China
San José, Republic of Costa Rica**
300 mts. al norte y 150 al este de la Iglesia
Santa Teresita, Barrio Escalante
San José, Costa Rica, C.A.
Mailing Address:
Apartado 676-2010 Zapote, Costa Rica
Phone: (+506) 224-8180
Fax: (+506) 253-8333
E-mail: oficon88@sol.racsa.co.cr

**Embassy of the Republic of China
Roseau, Commonwealth of Dominica**
Check Hall/Massacre
Commonwealth of Dominica
Mailing Address:
P.O. Box 56, Roseau
Commonwealth of Dominica
West Indies
Phone: (+1-767) 449-1385
Fax: (+1-767) 449-2085
E-mail: rocemb@cwdom.dm

**Embassy of the Republic of China
Santo Domingo, Dominican Republic**
Edificio Palic-Primer Piso
No. 952 Ave. Abraham Lincoln, Santo Domingo

República Dominicana
Mailing Address:
Apartado Postal 4797, Santo Domingo
República Dominicana
Phone: (+1-809) 562-5555
Fax: (+1-809) 563-4139
E-mail: e.china@codetel.net.do

Embassy of the Republic of China
San Salvador, Republic of El Salvador
Embajada de Republica de China
Avenida la Capilla No. 716
Col. San Benito, San Salvador
El Salvador, C.A.
Phone:(+503) 263-1330
Fax: (+503) 263-1329
E-mail: sinoemb@es.com.sv

Embassy of the Republic of China
St. George's, Grenada
Archibald Avenue, St. George's
Grenada, West Indies
Mailing Address:
P.O. Box 36, St. George's
Grenada, West Indies
Phone: (+1-473) 440-3054
Fax: (+1-473) 440-4177
E-mail: rocemgnd@caribsurf.com

Embassy of the Republic of China
Guatemala City, Republic of Guatemala
4a. Avenida, Zona 9
Guatemala City, Guatemala, C.A.
Mailing Address:
Apartado Postal 1646, Guatemala City
Guatemala, C.A.
Phone: (+502) 339-0711
Fax: (+502) 332-2668
E-mail: echina@intelnet.net.gt

Embassy of the Republic of China
Port-au-Prince, Republic of Haiti
16 Rue Leon Nau, Petion-Ville
Port-au-Prince, Haiti
Mailing Address:
P.O. Box 655, Port-au-Prince, Haiti

Phone: (+509) 257-2899
Fax: (+509) 256-8067
E-mail: ambrdc@acn2.net

Embassy of the Republic of China
Tegucigalpa, Republic of Honduras
Colonia Lomas del Guijarro
Calle Eucaliptos No. 3750
Tegucigalpa, M.D.C., Honduras, C. A.
Mailing Address:
Apartado Postal 3433
Tegucigalpa, M.D.C., Honduras, C.A.
Phone: (+504) 231-1484
Fax: (+504) 232-7645
E-mail: embchina@david.intertel.hn

Consulate General of the Republic of China
San Pedro Sula, Republic of Honduras
12 Ave. B, 11 y 12 Calle B
Col. Trejo, San Pedro Sula
Honduras
Mailing Address:
Apartado Postal 4298, San Pedro Sula
Republic of Honduras, C.A.
Phone: (+504) 556-8490
Fax: (+504) 556-5802
E-mail: consulchina@globalnet.hn

Embajada de la República de China
Managua, República de Nicaragua
Planes de Altamira, Lotes #19 y 20
Frente a la Cancha de Tenis, Managua 5
Nicaragua
Mailing Address:
Apartado Postal 4653, Managua 5
Nicaragua
Phone: (+505) 270-6054
Fax: (+505) 267-4025
E-mail: embchina@ibw.com.ni

Embassy of the Republic of China
Panama City, Republic of Panama
Edificio Torre Hong Bank
10 Piso, Ave. Samuel Lewis, Panama
Republic of Panama
Mailing Address:

Apartado 4285, Panama 5
Republic of Panama
Phone: (+507) 223-3424
Fax: (+507) 263-5534
E-mail: embchina@pan.gbm.net

Consulate-General of the Republic of China
Colon, Republic of Panama
Calle 8, Ave. Roosevelt, Casa #10-084
Colón, Republic of Panama
Mailing Address:
Apartado No. 540, Colón
Republic of Panama
Phone: (+507) 441-3403
Fax: (+507) 441-3784
E-mail: congencn@sinfo.net

Embassy of the Republic of China
Asunción, Republic of Paraguay
Avenida Mcal. López 1133, Asunción, Paraguay
Mailing Address:
Casilla de Correos 503, Asunción, Paraguay
Phone: (+595-21) 213-362
Fax: (+595-21) 212-373
E-mail: emroc@highway.com.py

Consulate-General of the Republic of China
Eastern City, Republic of Paraguay
No. 1349 Avda. Mcal. Estigarribia
(Ave. Lago de la Republica), Ciudad del Este
Paraguay
Mailing Address:
Casilla Postal No. 131
Ciudad del Este, Paraguay
Phone: (+595-61) 500-329
Fax: (+595-61) 510-931
E-mail: cogechcde@fnn.net

Embassy of the Republic of China
Basseterre, Saint Christopher and Nevis
Taylor's Range, Basseterre
Saint Kitts, West Indies
Mailing Address:
P.O. Box 119, Basseterre
Saint Kitts, West Indies
Phone: (+1-869) 465-2421

Fax: (+1-869) 465-7921
E-mail: rocemb@caribsurf.com

Embassy of the Republic of China
Kingstown, Saint Vincent and the Grenadines
Murray's Road
Saint Vincent and the Grenadines
Mailing Address:
P.O. Box 878
Saint Vincent and the Grenadines, West Indies
Phone: (+1-784) 456-2431
Fax: (+1-784) 456-2913
E-mail: rocemsvg@caribsurf.com

ROC Representative Offices

Asia

Taipei Economic and Cultural Office
in Brunei Darussalam
No. 5, Simpang 1006
Jalan Tutong, B.S. Begawan
Brunei Darussalam
Mailing Address:
P.O. Box 2172, B.S. Begawan, BS8674
Brunei Darussalam
Phone: (+673-2) 652-113
Fax: (+673-2) 651-245
E-mail: twnrocbr@pso.brunet.bn

Chung Hwa Travel Service
Hong Kong
40th Floor, Tower One, Lippo Centre
89 Queensway, Hong Kong
Mailing Address:
G.P.O. Box 13485, Hong Kong
Phone: (+852) 2525-8315
Fax: (+852) 2810-0591
E-mail: rochkg@netvigator.com

Taipei Economic and Cultural Center
in New Delhi
3A Palam Marg, Vasant Vihar, New Delhi
110057, India
Phone: (+91-11) 614-6881
Fax: (+91-11) 614-6880
E-mail: tecc@giasdl01.vsnl.net.in

**Taipei Economic and Trade Office
Jakarta, Indonesia**
Mailing Address:
P.O. Box 2922, Jakarta Pusat
Indonesia
Phone: (+62-21) 515-3939
Fax: (+62-21) 515-4626
E-mail: teto@uninet.net.id

**Taipei Economic and Cultural Representative
Office in Japan**
20-2 Shirokanedai 5-chome
Minato-Ku, Tokyo 108-0071
Japan
Phone: (+81-3) 3280-7811
Fax: (+81-3) 3280-7934
E-mail: teco-tky@www.roc-taiwan.or.jp

**Taipei Economic and Cultural Representative
Office in Japan, Yokohama Branch**
2nd Floor, Asahiseimei Yokohama Building
No. 60, Nihonohdori, Nakaku, Yokohama
Japan
Phone: (+81-45) 641-7736
Fax: (+81-45) 641-6870
E-mail: teco-ykh@ma.kcom.ne.jp

**Taipei Economic and Cultural Office
in Osaka**
4th Floor, 4-8 Nichiei Building
Tosabori, 1-chome, Nishi-Ku, Osaka
Japan
Phone: (+81-6) 6443-8481
Fax: (+81-6) 6443-8577
E-mail: teco-osa@ma.kcom.ne.jp

**Taipei Economic and Cultural Office in Osaka,
Fukuoka Branch**
12-42 Sakurazaka, 3-chome, Chuo-Ku
Fukuoka, Japan
Phone: (+81-92) 734-2810
Fax: (+81-92) 734-2819
E-mail: teco-fkk@ma.kcom.ne.jp

Taipei Mission in Korea
6th Floor, Kwang Hwa Moon Building
211 Sejong-Ro, Chongro-Ku

Seoul, Korea 110-050
Phone: (+82-2) 399-2767
Fax: (+82-2) 730-1296
E-mail: tmik@taeback.kornet.nm.kr

Taipei Economic and Cultural Center, Macau
Al. Dr. Carlos d'Assumpaco, N. 411-417
Edif. Dynasty Plaza, 6 Andar F-K
Macau
Mailing Address:
P.O. Box 3072, Macau
Phone: (+853) 306-282
Fax: (+853) 306-153
E-mail: tpe@macau.ctm.net

**Taipei Economic and Cultural Office
in Malaysia**
9.01 Level 9, Amoda Building
22 Jalan Imbi, 55100 Kuala Lumpur
Malaysia
Phone: (+60-3) 2142-5549
Fax: (+60-3) 2142-3906
E-mail: teco@po.jaring.my

**Taipei Economic and Cultural Office
in the Philippines**
28th Floor, Pacific Star Building
Sen. Gil J. Puyat Avenue
Corner Makati Avenue
Makati, Metro Manila
Philippines
Mailing Address:
P.O. Box 1097
Makati Central Post Office
1250 Makati, Metro Manila
Philippines
Phone: (+63-2) 892-1381
Fax: (+63-2) 811-5165
E-mail: tecoph@usinc.net

**Taipei Representative Office
in Singapore**
460 Alexandra Road
#23-00, PSA Building
Singapore 119963
Mailing Address:

PSA Building Post Office, P.O. Box 381
Singapore
Phone: (+65) 278-6511
Fax: (+65) 271-9107
E-mail: tperep@pacific.net.sg

**Taipei Economic and Cultural Office
in Thailand**
20th Floor, Empise Tower 195
South Satsorn Road, Yannawa
Bangkok 10120, Thailand
Phone: (+66-2) 670-0200
Fax: (+66-2) 670-0220
E-mail: teto@infonews.co.th

**Taipei Economic and Cultural Office
Hanoi, Vietnam**
5th Floor, HITC Building, Km 8, Highway 32
Caugiay, Hanoi, Vietnam
Mailing Address:
GPO Box 104, Hanoi, Vietnam
Phone: (+844) 833-5501
Fax: (+884) 833-5508
E-mail: tecohn@netnam.org.vn

**Taipei Economic and Cultural Office
Ho Chi Minh City, Vietnam**
336 Nguyen Tri Phuong
P.4Q.10 Tp. Ho Chi Minh
Vietnam
Phone: (+848) 834-6264
Fax: (+848) 834-6260
E-mail: tecotoh@tecohcm.org.vn

Oceania

Taipei Economic and Cultural Office, Australia
Unit 8, Tourism House, 40 Blackall Street
Barton, Canberra, ACT 2600, Australia
Phone: (+61-2) 6273-3344
Fax: (+61-2) 6273-3228
E-mail: oftpecbr@dynamite.com.au

**Taipei Economic and Cultural Office
Melbourne, Australia**
Level 46, 80 Collins Street

Melbourne, VIC 3000, Australia
Phone: (+61-3) 9650-8611
Fax: (+61-3) 9650-8711
E-mail: tecom@sprint.com.au

**Taipei Economic and Cultural Office
Sydney, Australia**
Suite 1902, Level 19, M.L.C. Center, King Street
Sydney, N.S.W. 2000, Australia
Phone: (+61-2) 9223-3233
Fax: (+61-2) 9223-0086
E-mail: syteco@magna.com.au

**Trade Mission of the Republic of China
Suva, Republic of Fiji**
6th Floor, Pacific House, Butt Street, Suva
Republic of Fiji
Mailing Address:
G.P.O. Box 53, Suva
Republic of Fiji
Phone: (+679) 315-922
Fax: (+679) 301-890
E-mail: tmroc@is.com.fj

**Taipei Economic and Cultural Office
New Zealand**
21st Floor, 105 The Terrace, Wellington
New Zealand
Mailing Address:
P.O. Box 10250, The Terrace, Wellington
New Zealand
Phone: (+64-4) 473-6474
Fax: (+64-4) 499-1458
E-mail: tecowlg@actrix.gen.nz

**Taipei Economic and Cultural Office
Auckland, New Zealand**
11th Floor, Norwich Union Building
Cnr. Queen and Durham Streets
Auckland, New Zealand
Mailing Address:
C.P.O. Box 4018, Auckland
New Zealand
Phone: (+649) 303-3903
Fax: (+649) 302-3399
E-mail: tecoakl@taiwan-roc.org.nz

Trade Mission of the Republic of China (on Taiwan)
Port Moresby, Papua New Guinea
6th Floor, Defense Haus, Hunter Street
Port Moresby, Papua New Guinea
Mailing Address:
P.O. Box 334
Port Moresby, Papua New Guinea
Phone: (+675) 321-2922
Fax: (+675) 321-3510
E-mail: taiwantramis@datec.com.pg

West Asia

Trade Mission of the Republic of China
Manama, State of Bahrain
Flat 1, Abulfatih Building, No. 172
Block 319, Road 1906
Al Hoora Area, Manama
State of Bahrain
Mailing Address:
P.O. Box 5806, Manama
State of Bahrain
Phone: (+973) 292-578
Fax: (+973) 293-852
E-mail: tmorocb1@batelco.com.bh

Taipei Economic and Cultural Office in
Tel-Aviv, Israel
Azrieli Center 1, Round Build, 21st Floor
132 Petach-Tikva Rd.
Tel-Aviv 67027, Israel
Mailing Address:
P.O. Box 6115, Tel-Aviv 61060, Israel
Phone: (+972-3) 607-4788
Fax: (+972-3) 695-4742
E-mail: mofa@teco.org.il

Commercial Office of the Republic of China
(Taiwan), Jordan
9 Jagboub Street, Amman
Mailing Address:
P.O. Box 2023, Amman 11181, Jordan
Phone: (+962-6) 593-1530
Fax: (+962-6) 593-2607
E-mail: kanda186@go.com.jo

Taipei Commercial Representative Office
in the State of Kuwait
House No. 18, Street No. 111, Block 6
Al-Jabriah, State of Kuwait
Mailing Address:
P.O. Box 732, 32008 Hawalli
Kuwait
Phone: (+965) 533-9988
Fax: (+965) 533-3497
E-mail: tseng@qualitynet.net

Taipei Economic and Cultural Office
Muscat, Oman
Mailing Address:
P.O. Box 1536, Ruwi
Postal Code 112, Muscat
The Sultanate of Oman
Phone: (+968) 605-695
Fax: (+968) 605-402
E-mail: taipei@omantel.net.om

Taipei Economic and Cultural Representative
Office in the Kingdom of Saudi Arabia
Diplomatic Quarter, Riyadh, Saudi Arabia
Mailing Address:
P.O. Box 94393, Riyadh 11693, Saudi Arabia
Phone: (+966-1) 488-1900
Fax: (+966-1) 488-1716
E-mail: tecroksa@shabakah.net.sa

Taipei Economic and Cultural Representative
Office in the Kingdom of Saudi Arabia,
Jeddah Office
Mailing Address:
P.O. Box 1114, Jeddah 21431, Saudi Arabia
Phone: (+966-2) 660-2264
Fax: (+966-2) 667-5843
E-mail: tecro@naseej.com.sa

Taipei Economic and Cultural Mission
in Ankara, Turkey
Resit Galip Cad. No. 97
Gaziosmanpasa, Ankara, Turkey
Phone: (+90-312) 436-7255
Fax: (+90-312) 437-6013
E-mail: chnkeng@domi.net.tr

Commercial Office of the Republic of China to Dubai, United Arab Emirates
Mailing Address:
P.O. Box 3059, Dubai, U.A.E.
Phone: (+971-4) 3977-888
Fax: (+971-4) 3977-644
E-mail: corocdxb@emirates.net.ae

Africa

Trade Mission of the Republic of China Port Louis, Mauritius
706 St. James Court, St. Denis Street
Port Louis, Mauritius
Mailing Address:
P.O. Box 695, Bell Village, Port Louis
Mauritius
Phone: (+230) 212-8534
Fax: (+230) 212-4587
E-mail: tmroc@bow.intnet.mu

The Trade Mission of the ROC (TAIWAN) Lagos, Federal Republic of Nigeria
292E Ajose Adeogun Street
Victoria Island Annex, Lagos, Nigeria
Mailing Address:
P.O. Box 80035, Victoria Island, Lagos
Nigeria
Phone: (+234-1) 261-6350
Fax: (+234-1) 288-1123
E-mail: roctm@alpha.linkserve.com

Taipei Liaison Office in the Republic of South Africa
1147 Schoeman Street, Haifield, Pretoria 0083
Republic of South Africa
Mailing Address:
P.O. Box 649, Pretoria 0001
Republic of South Africa
Phone: (+27-12) 430-6071
Fax: (+27-12) 430-5816
E-mail: embroc@icon.co.za

Taipei Liaison Office in Cape Town
10th Floor, 1004 Main Tower
Standard Bank Center, Foreshore, Cape Town
Republic of South Africa

Mailing Address:
P.O. Box 1122, Cape Town 8000
Republic of South Africa
Phone: (+27-21) 418-1188
Fax: (+27-21) 425-3022
E-mail: taiwan@iafrica.com

Taipei Liaison Office in Johannesburg
10th Floor, Rennies House, 19 Ameshoff Street
Braamfontein, Johannesburg 2001
Republic of South Africa
Mailing Address:
P.O. Box 32458 Braamfontein
Johannesburg 2017
Republic of South Africa
Phone: (+27-11) 403-3281
Fax: (+27-11) 403-1679
E-mail: roccon@icon.co.za

Europe

Taipei Economic and Cultural Office Institute of Chinese Culture Vienna, Austria
Wagramerstr. Strasse 19, 11OG., 1220
Vienna, Austria
Phone: (+43-1) 212-4720
Fax: (+43-1) 212-4703
E-mail: tecovie@atnet.at

Taipei Economic and Trade Mission in Minsk, Belarus
Mailing Address:
P.O. Box 149
220030 Minsk
Republic of Belarus
Phone: (+375-17) 223-9289
Fax: (+375-17) 210-5676
E-mail: pix6573@yahoo.com

Taipei Representative Office in Belgium
Avenue des Arts 41, 1040 Bruxelles
Belgium
Phone: (+32-2) 511-0687
Fax: (+32-2) 511-1789
E-mail: roc.bxl@pophost.eunet.be

Taipei Economic and Cultural Office
Prague, Czech Republic
Evropska 2590/33c
16000 PRAHA 6
Czech Republic
Phone: (+420-2) 3332-0606
Fax: (+420-2) 3332-6906
E-mail: tecoprag@mbox.vol.cz

Taipei Representative Office
in Denmark
Amaliegade 3, 2nd Floor
1256 Copenhagen K
Denmark
Phone: (+45) 3393-5152
Fax: (+45) 3393-2235
E-mail: trodnk@teliamail.dk

Taipei Economic and Cultural Office
Helsinki, Finland
Aleksanterinkatu 17, 4th Floor
00100, Helsinki, Finland
Phone: (+358-9) 6969-2420
Fax: (+358-9) 6969-2421
E-mail: taipei.economic@wtc.fi

Bureau de Représentation de Taipei
en France
78 rue de l'Université, 75007 Paris
France
Phone: (+33-1) 4439-8830
Fax: (+33-1) 4439-8871
E-mail: taipiao.brtf@magic.fr

Taipeh Vertretung in der Bundesrepublik
Deutschland, Büro Berlin
Markgrafen Strasse 35, 10117 Berlin
Germany
Phone: (+49-30) 2036-1160
Fax: (+49-30) 2036-1101
E-mail: taipeiwk@t-online.de

Taipeh Vertretung in der Bundesrepublik
Deutschland, Büro Hamburg
Mittelweg 144, 20148 Hamburg
Federal Republic of Germany
Phone: (+49-40) 447-788

Fax: (+49-40) 447-187
E-mail: 106266.1666@compuserve.com

Taipeh Vertretung in der Bundesrepublik
Deutschland, Büro München
Sonnenstr. 25
80331 München
Germany
Phone: (+49-89) 5126-790
Fax: (+49-89) 5126-7979
E-mail: 106224.1257@compuserve.com

Taipei Economic and Cultural Office
Athens, Greece
57 Marathonodromon Avenue
154 52 Psychico, Athens
Greece
Phone: (+30-1) 677-6750
Fax: (+30-1) 677-6708
E-mail: 777teco@otenet.gr

Taipei Representative Office
Budapest, Hungary
Rakóczi út 1-3/III em., 1088 Budapest
Hungary
Phone: (+36-1) 266-2884
Fax: (+36-1) 266-4003
E-mail: taipeiro@mail.elender.hu

Taipei Representative Office
in Ireland
8 Lower Hatch Street
Dublin 2, Ireland
Phone: (+353-1) 678-5413
Fax: (+353-1) 676-1686
E-mail: tpeire@indigo.ie

Ufficio Di Rappresentanza di Taipei
in Italia
Via Panama 22 PI, Int. 3
00198 Roma, Italia
Phone: (+39-06) 884-1362
Fax: (+39-06) 884-5772
E-mail: c.hsieh@flashnet.it

Taipei Mission in the Republic of Latvia
Room 602, World Trade Center

2a Elizabets Street, LV-1340, Riga
Latvia
Phone: (+371) 732-1166
Fax: (+371) 783-0125
E-mail: tmil@tmil.lv

**Taipei Economic and Cultural Office
Luxembourg**
50, route d'Esch, Luxembourg-Ville,
L-1470 Grand-Duché de Luxembourg
Phone: (+352) 444-772
Fax: (+352) 250-485

**Taipei Representative Office
in the Netherlands**
Javastraat 46-48
2585 AR, The Hague
The Netherlands
Phone: (+31-70) 346-9438
Fax: (+31-70) 360-3836
E-mail: tperep@wxs.nl

**Taipei Economic and Cultural Office
Oslo, Norway**
P.O. Box 2643 Solli
Riddervolds gate 3, 0203 Oslo
Norway
Phone: (+47) 2411-4260
Fax: (+47) 2256-2531
E-mail: twteco@online.no

**Taipei Economic and Cultural Office in
Warsaw, Poland**
4th Floor, Koszykowa Street 54
00-675 Warszawa, Poland
Mailing Address:
P.O. Box 51, ul. Senatorska 40
Urzad Pocztowo-Telekomunikacyjny
Warszawa 84, Poland
Phone: (+48-22) 630-8438
Fax: (+48-22) 630-8431
E-mail: taiwan@polbox.pl

**Centro Economico e Cultural de Taipei
Lisbon, Portugal**
Rua Castilho N 14-6, 1250 Lisbon, Portugal
Phone: (+351-21) 315-1279

Fax: (+351-21) 315-1288
E-mail: tecc.lisboa@ip.pt

**Representative Office in Moscow for
the Taipei-Moscow Economic and Cultural
Coordination Commission**
3rd Floor, 24/2 Tverskaya Street, Korpus 1
Gate 4, Moscow 103050
Russian Federation
Phone: (+7-503) 956-3786
Fax: (+7-095) 956-3625
E-mail: anhwei@aha.ru

**Oficina Económica y Cultural de Taipei
Madrid, España**
C/Rosario Pino 14-16
Piso 18 Dcha., 28020 Madrid, Spain
Mailing Address:
Apartado 36016, 28080 Madrid, Spain
Phone: (+34) 91571-4729
Fax: (+34) 91570-9285
E-mail: ofitaipei@retemail.es

Taipei Mission in Sweden
Wenner-Gren Center, 18tr., Sveavägen 166
S-113 46 Stockholm, Sweden
Phone: (+46-8) 728-8513
Fax: (+46-8) 315-748
E-mail: taipei.mission@tmis.se

**Délégation Culturelle et Economique de
Taïpei, Berne, Suisse**
Monbijoustrasse 30, 3011 Berne, Suisse
Phone: (+41-31) 382-2927
Fax: (+41-31) 382-1523
E-mail: taipei.delegation@spectraweb.ch

**Délégation Culturelle et Economique de
Taïpei, Bureau de Geneve**
56 rue de Moillebeau
1209 Geneve, Suisse
Phone: (+41-22) 919-7070
Fax: (+41-22) 919-7077
E-mail: tpe-gva@iprolink.ch

Taipei Representative Office in the UK
50 Grosvenor Gardens, London SW1W OEB

United Kingdom
Phone: (+44-20) 7396-9152
Fax: (+44-20) 7396-9145
E-mail: tro@netcomuk.co.uk

**Taipei Representative Office in the UK
Edinburgh Office**
1 Melville Street
Edinburgh EH3 7PE
United Kingdom
Phone: (+44-131) 220-6886
Fax: (+44-131) 226-6884
E-mail: troed@dial.pipex.com

North America

Taipei Economic and Cultural Office, Canada
Suite 1960, World Exchange Plaza
45 O'Connor Street, Ottawa
Ontario K1P 1A4
Canada
Phone: (+1-613) 231-5080
Fax: (+1-613) 231-7112
E-mail: teco@magi.com

Taipei Economic and Cultural Office, Toronto
151 Yonge Street, Suite 1202, Toronto
Ontario M5C 2W7, Canada
Phone: (+1-416) 369-9030
Fax: (+1-416) 369-0548
E-mail: tecotron@axxent.ca

Taipei Economic and Cultural Office, Vancouver
2008, Cathedral Place, 925 West Georgia Street
Vancouver, B.C. V6C 3L2, Canada
Phone: (+1-604) 689-4111
Fax: (+1-604) 689-0101
E-mail: tecovan@telus.net

Taipei Economic and Cultural Representative Office in the United States
4201 Wisconsin Avenue, NW
Washington, DC 20016-2137, U.S.A.
Phone: (+1-202) 895-1800 (20 lines)
Fax: (+1-202) 363-0999
E-mail: tecrotcd@erols.com

Taipei Economic and Cultural Office in Atlanta
Suite 1290, Two Midtown Plaza
1349 West Peachtree Street, NE Atlanta
Georgia 30309, U.S.A.
Phone: (+1-404) 872-0123
Fax: (+1-404) 873-3474
E-mail: tecoatl@mindspring.com

Taipei Economic and Cultural Office in Boston
99 Summer Street, Suite 801
Boston, MA 02110, U.S.A.
Mailing Address:
P.O. Box 120009, Boston, MA 02112
U.S.A.
Phone: (+1-617) 737-2050
Fax: (+1-617) 737-1684
E-mail: teco@epartner.com

Taipei Economic and Cultural Office in Chicago
Two Prudential Plaza, 57th & 58th Floors
180 N. Stetson Avenue, Chicago, Illinois 60601
U.S.A.
Phone: (+1-312) 616-0100
Fax: (+1-312) 616-1490
E-mail: tecochg@allways.net

Taipei Economic and Cultural Office in Guam
Suite 505, Bank of Guam Building
111 Chanlan Santo Papa Road
Hagatna, Guam 96910, U.S.A.
Mailing Address:
P.O. Box 3416, Hagatna, Guam 96932
U.S.A.
Phone: (+671) 472-5865
Fax: (+671) 472-5869
E-mail: tecogm@ite.net

Taipei Economic and Cultural Office in Honolulu
2746 Pali Highway
Honolulu, Hawaii 96817, U.S.A.
Phone: (+1-808) 595-6347
Fax: (+1-808) 595-6542
E-mail: tecohnl@hawaii.rr.com

Taipei Economic and Cultural Office in Houston
11 Greenway Plaza, Suite 2006
Houston, Texas 77046, U.S.A.
Phone: (+1-713) 626-7445
Fax: (+1-713) 626-1202
E-mail: tecohou@sprynet.com

Taipei Economic and Cultural Office in Kansas City, Missouri
3100 Broadway, Suite 800
Kansas City, MO 64111, U.S.A.
Mailing Address:
P.O. Box 413617
Kansas City, MO 64141
U.S.A.
Phone: (+1-816) 531-1298
Fax: (+1-816) 531-3066
E-mail: kcteco@penn.com

Taipei Economic and Cultural Office in Los Angeles
3731 Wilshire Boulevard, Suite 700
Los Angeles, CA 90010, U.S.A.
Phone: (+1-213) 389-1215
Fax: (+1-213) 389-1676
E-mail: info@tecola.org

Taipei Economic and Cultural Office in Miami
2333 Ponce de Leon Boulevard, Suite 610
Coral Gables, Florida 33134, U.S.A.
Phone: (+1-305) 663-3247
Fax: (+1-305) 444-4796
E-mail: tecomia@icanect.net

Taipei Economic and Cultural Office in New York
885 Second Avenue, 47th Floor
New York, NY 10017, U.S.A.
Phone: (+1-212) 317-7300
Fax: (+1-212) 754-1549
E-mail: tecony@abest.com

Taipei Economic and Cultural Office in San Francisco
555 Montgomery Street, Suite 501
San Francisco, CA 94111, U.S.A.

Phone: (+1-415) 362-7680
Fax: (+1-415) 362-5382
E-mail: tecosf@amer.net

Taipei Economic and Cultural Office in Seattle
Westin Building, Suite 2410
2001 Sixth Avenue, Seattle, WA 98121, U.S.A.
Phone: (+1-206) 441-4586
Fax: (+1-206) 441-4320
E-mail: teco@aa.net

Central and South America

Oficina Comercial y Cultural de Taipei en la República Argentina
Av. de Mayo 654, piso 4, C1084AAO 1084
Capital Federal, Argentina
Mailing Address:
Casilla de Correos No.196
1401 Capital Federal, Argentina
Phone: (+54-11) 4334-0653
Fax: (+54-11) 4334-5581
E-mail: taipei@impsatl.ar

Oficina Comercial-Consular de la República de China, La Paz, Bolivia
Calacoto, Calle 12, No. 7978, La Paz
República de Bolivia
Mailing Address:
Casilla 13680, La Paz, Bolivia
Phone: (+591-2) 797-307
Fax: (+591-2) 797-303
E-mail: oconstwn@entelnet.bo

Escritório Econômico e Cultural de Taipei Brasil
SHIS QI 09, Conjunto 16, Casa 23-Lago Sul
71.625-160-Brasilia-Distrito Federal
Brasil
Phone: (+55-61) 364-0221
Fax: (+55-61) 364-0234
E-mail: eect@brnet.com.br

Escritório Econômico e Cultural de Taipei Rio de Janeiro, Brasil
Rua Voluntârios da pátria
45 Sala 405 CEP, 22270-000

Rio de Janeiro-RJ, Brasil
Phone: (+55-21) 2535-0768
Fax: (+55-21) 2537-1031
E-mail: taipeirj@prolink.com.br

**Escritório Econômico e Cultural de Taipei
São Paulo, Brasil**
Av. Paulista, 2073-Ed. Horsa II
Conj. 1203 e 1204-12 Andar
01311-940-São Paulo, SP, Brasil
Phone: (+55-11) 285-6194
Fax: (+55-11) 287-9057
E-mail: mofasp@intercall.com.br

**Oficina Económica y Cultural de Taipei
Santiago, República de Chile**
Burgos 345, Las Condes, Santiago, Chile
Mailing Address:
Casilla 175-Santiago 34, Santiago, Chile
Phone: (+56-2) 228-2919
Fax: (+56-2) 206-3635
E-mail: oftaipei@vtr.net

**Oficina Comercial de Taipei, Santafe de
Bogotá, D.C., República de Colombia**
Carrera 11, No. 93-53, Of. 501
Santafe de Bogotá D.C., Colombia, S.A.
Mailing Address:
Apartado Aéreo No. 51620 (Chapinero)
Santafe de Bogotá, D.C., Colombia, S.A.
Phone: (+57-1) 635-0958
Fax: (+57-1) 635-1216
E-mail: oftaipei@impsat.net.co

**Oficina Comercial de la República de China
Quito, Ecuador**
Mailing Address:
Casilla P.O. Box 7-17-1788, Quito
Ecuador
Phone: (+593-2) 501-315
Fax: (+593-2) 501-747
E-mail: keting@uio.satnet.net

**Oficina Económica y Cultural de Taipei en
México**
Paseo de la Reforma 1945
Col. Lomas de Chapultepec
CP 11000, México D.F.
México
Phone: (+525) 596-1412
Fax: (+525) 251-0960
E-mail: taipeimx@infosel.net.mx

**Oficina Económica y Cultural de Taipei
Lima, República del Perú**
Av. Benavides No. 1780
Miraflores, Lima 18
Perú
Mailing Address:
Casilla: 18-1052, Lima 18, Perú
Phone: (+51-1) 242-1817
Fax: (+51-1) 447-1764
E-mail: oftaipe@amauta.rcp.net.pe

**Oficina Económica de Taipei
República Oriental del Uruguay**
Echevarriarza 3478, Montevideo
Uruguay
Mailing Address:
Casilla de Correo No. 16042
Distrito 6 C.P. 11600, Montevideo, Uruguay
Phone: (+598-2) 622-0801
Fax: (+598-2) 628-0263
E-mail: oetroc@adinet.com.uy

**Oficina Económica y Cultural de Taipei
Caracas, República de Venezuela**
Avenida Francisco de Miranda
Torre Delta, Piso 4, Altamira, Caracas, Venezuela
Mailing Address:
Apartado 68717, Altamira, Caracas 1062-A
Venezuela
Phone: (+58-212) 265-2184
Fax: (+58-212) 264-1163
E-mail: oectop@cantv.net

Appendix VI

Directory of Foreign Embassies and Representatives in the ROC

All information presented was accurate at press time; however, minor changes might have occurred since then. The most up-to-date information is always available on line at:
http://www.mofa.gov.tw

Foreign Embassies in the ROC

Embassy of Beliez
11th Floor, 9 Lane 62, Tienmou West Road
Taipei 111
Phone: (+886-2) 2876-0894
Fax: (+886-2) 2876-0895

Embassy of Burkina Faso
6th Floor, 9-1 Lane 62, Tienmou West Road
Taipei 111
Phone: (+886-2) 2873-3096
Fax: (+886-2) 2873-3071

Embassy of the Republic of Chad
8th Floor, 9 Lane 62, Tienmou West Road
Taipie 111
Phone: (+886-2) 2874-2943
Fax: (+886-2) 2874-2971

Embassy of the Republic of Costa Rica
5th Floor, 9-1 Lane 62, Tienmou West Road
Taipei 111
Phone: (+886-2) 2875-2964
Fax: (+886-2) 2875-3151

Embassy of the Dominican Republic
6th Floor, 9 Lane 62, Tienmou West Road
Taipei 111
Phone: (+886-2) 2875-1357
Fax: (+886-2) 2875-2661

Embassy of the Republic of El Salvador
2nd Floor, 9 Lane 62, Tienmou West Road
Taipei 111
Phone: (+886-2) 2876-3509
Fax: (+886-2) 2876-3514

Embassy of the Republic of The Gambia
9th Floor, 9-1 Lane 62, Tienmou West Road
Taipei 111
Phone:(+886-2) 2875-3911
Fax:(+886-2) 2875-2775

Embassy of the Republic of Guatemala
3rd Floor, 9-1 Lane 62, Tienmou West Road
Taipei 111
Phone: (+886-2) 2875-6952
Fax: (+886-2) 2874-0699

Embassy of the Republic of Haiti
8th Floor, 9-1 Lane 62, Tienmou West Road
Taipei 111
Phone: (+886-2) 2876-6718
Fax: (+886-2) 2876-6719

Embassy of the Holy See (Apostolic Nunciature)
87 Ai Kuo East Road, Taipei 106
Phone: (+886-2) 2321-6847
Fax: (+886-2) 2391-1926

Embassy of the Republic of Honduras
9th Floor, 9 Lane 62, Tienmou West Road
Taipei 111
Phone: (+886-2) 2875-5507
Fax: (+886-2) 2875-5726

Embassy of the Republic of Liberia
11th Floor, 9-1 Lane 62, Tienmou West Road
Taipei 111
Phone: (+886-2) 2875-1212
Fax: (+886-2) 2875-1313

Embassy of the Republic of Malawi
2nd Floor, 9-1 Lane 62, Tienmou West Road
Taipei 111

Phone: (+886-2) 2876-2284
Fax: (+886-2) 2876-3545

Embassy of the Republic of Marshall Islands
4th Floor, 9-1 Lane 62, Tienmou West Road
Taipei 111
Phone: (+886-2) 2873-4884
Fax: (+886-2) 2873-4904

Embassy of the Republic of Nicaragua
3rd Floor, 9 Lane 62, Tienmou West Road
Taipei 111
Phone: (+886-2) 2874-9034
Fax: (+886-2) 2874-9080

Embassy of the Republic of Panama
6th Floor, 111 Sungkiang Road, Taipei 104
Phone: (+886-2) 2509-9189
Fax: (+886-2) 2509-9801

Embassy of the Republic of Paraguay
7th Floor, 9-1 Lane 62, Tienmou West Road
Taipei 111
Phone: (+886-2) 2873-6310
Fax: (+886-2) 2873-6312

Embassy of Democratic Republic of São Tomé and Príncipe
3rd Floor, 18 Chilin Road, Taipei 104
Phone: (+886-2) 2511-4111
Fax: (+886-2) 2511-6255

Embassy of the Republic of Senegal
10th Floor, 9-1 Lane 62, Tienmou West Road
Taipei 111
Phone: (+886-2) 2876-6519
Fax: (+886-2) 2873-4909

Embassy of Kingdom of Swaziland
10th Floor, 9 Lane 62, Tienmou West Road
Taipei 111
Phone: (+886-2) 2872-5934
Fax: (+886-2) 2872-6511

Embassy of Solomon Islands
7th Floor, 9-1 Lane 62, Tienmou West Road
Taipei 111

Phone: (+886-2) 2876-6431
Fax: (+886-2) 2876-6442

Foreign Representatives in the ROC

American Institute in Taiwan, Taipei Office
7 Lane 134, Hsin Yi Road, Section 3, Taipei 104
Phone: (+886-2) 2709-2000
Fax: (+886-2) 2702-7675

American Institute in Taiwan, Kaohsiung Office
3rd Floor, 2 Chung Cheng Third Road
Kaohsiung 800
Phone: (+886-7) 224-0154
Fax: (+886-7) 223-8237

Argentina Trade and Cultural Office
Room 1003, 333 Keelung Road, Section 1
Taipei 110
Phone: (+886-2) 2757-6556
Fax: (+886-2) 2757-6445

Australian Commerce and Industry Office
Room 2608, 333 Keelung Road, Section 1
Taipei 110
Phone: (+886-2) 8725-4100
Fax: (+886-2) 2757-6074

Austrian Trade Delegation
Room 608, 205 Tun Hua North Road
Taipei 105
Phone: (+886-2) 2715-5220
Fax: (+886-2) 2717-3242

Austrian Tourism Office
5th Floor, 164 Fu Hsing North Road, Taipei 104
Phone: (+886-2) 2712-8598
Fax: (+886-2) 2514-9980

Belgian Trade Association, Taipei
Room 901, 131 Min Sheng East Road, Section 3
Taipei 105
Phone: (+886-2) 2715-1215
Fax: (+886-2) 2712-6258

Bolivian Commercial and Financial Representation
Room 7E-13, 5 Hsin Yi Road, Section 5
Taipei 110
Phone: (+886-2) 2723-8721
Fax: (+886-2) 2723-8764

Brazil Business Center
5th Floor, 197 Chung Shan North Road
Section 6, Taipei 111
Phone: (+886-2) 2835-7388
Fax: (+886-2) 2835-7121

British Trade and Cultural Office
9th Floor, 99 Jen Ai Road, Section 2
Taipei 100
Phone: (+886-2) 2322-4242
Fax: (+886-2) 2393-1985

British Trade and Cultural Office in Kaohsiung
3rd Floor, 6 Ming Chun 2nd Road
Kaohsiung 806
Phone: (+886-7) 337-7350
Fax: (+886-7) 536-4144

Canadian Trade Office in Taipei
13th Floor, 365 Fu Hsing North Road
Taipei 105
Phone: (+886-2) 2547-9500
Fax: (+886-2) 2712-7244

Chilean Trade Office, Taipei
Room 7B-06, 5 Hsin Yi Road, Section 5
Taipei 110
Phone: (+886-2) 2723-0329
Fax: (+886-2) 2723-0318

Czech Economic and Cultural Office
6th Floor-1, 51 Keelung Road, Section 2
Taipei 110
Phone: (+886-2) 2738-9768
Fax: (+886-2) 2733-3944

Danish Trade Organizations, Taipei Office
Room 1207, 12th Floor, 205 Tun Hua North Road
Taipei 105

Phone: (+886-2) 2718-2101
Fax: (+886-2) 2718-2141

Fiji Trade and Tourism Representative Office in ROC
Room 3212, 333 Keelung Road, Section 1
Taipei 110
Phone: (+886-2) 2757-9596
Fax: (+886-2) 2757-9597

Finland Trade Center
Room 7E-04, 5 Hsin Yi Road, Section 5
Taipei 110
Phone: (+886-2) 2722-0764
Fax: (+886-2) 2725-1517

French Institute in Taipei
Room 1003, 10th Floor, 205 Tun Hua North Road
Taipei 105
Phone: (+886-2) 2545-6061
Fax: (+886-2) 2718-4571

German Cultural Centre
11th Floor, 24 Hsin Hai Road, Section 1
Taipei 100
Phone: (+886-2) 2365-7294
Fax: (+886-2) 2368-7542

Deutsches Institut Taipei
4th Floor, 2 Min Sheng East Road, Section 3
Taipei 104
Phone: (+886-2) 2501-6188
Fax: (+886-2) 2501-6139

German Trade Office, Taipei
4th Floor, 4 Min Sheng East Road, Section 3
Taipei 104
Phone: (+886-2) 2506-9028
Fax: (+886-2) 2506-8182

Hungarian Trade Office
2nd Floor, 3 Chung Cheng Road, Section 2
Taipei 111
Phone: (+886-2) 2834-3701
Fax: (+886-2) 2837-7151

India-Taipei Association
Room 2010, 333 Keelung Road, Section 1
Taipei 110
Phone: (+886-2) 2757-6112
Fax: (+886-2) 2757-6117

Indonesian Economic and Trade Office to Taipei
12th Floor, 337 Nanking East Road, Section 3
Taipei 104
Phone: (+886-2) 8712-4570
Fax: (+886-2) 8712-4575

The Institute for Trade and Investment of Ireland
Room 7B-09, 5 Hsin Yi Road, Section 5
Taipei 110
Phone: (+886-2) 2725-1691
Fax: (+886-2) 2725-1653

Israel Economic and Cultural Office
Room 2408, 333 Keelung Road, Section 1
Taipei 110
Phone: (+886-2) 2757-9692
Fax: (+886-2) 2757-7247

Italian Economic, Trade and Cultural Promotion Office
Room 1808, 333 Keelung Road, Section 1
Taipei 110
Phone: (+886-2) 2345-0320
Fax: (+886-2) 2757-6260

Interchange Association (Japan), Taipei Office
10th Floor, 245 Tun Hua South Road, Section 1
Taipei 106
Phone: (+886-2) 2741-2116
Fax: (+886-2) 2731-1757

Interchange Association (Japan) Kaohsiung Office
10th Floor, 87 Ho Ping First Road
Kaohsiung 802
Phone: (+886-7) 771-4008
Fax: (+886-7) 771-2734

The Jordanian Commercial Office
1st Floor, 110 Chung Cheng Road, Section 2

Taipei 111
Phone: (+886-2) 2871-7712
Fax: (+886-2) 2872-1176

Korean Mission in Taipei
Room 1506, 333 Keelung Road, Section 1
Taipei 110
Phone: (+886-2) 2758-8320
Fax: (+886-2) 2757-7006

Malaysian Friendship and Trade Centre Taipei
8th Floor, 102 Tun Hua North Road, Taipei 105
Phone: (+886-2) 2713-2626
Fax: (+886-2) 2514-9864

Manila Economic and Cultural Office
4th Floor, 107 Chung Hsiao East Road, Section 4
Taipei 106
Phone: (+886-2) 2778-6511
Fax: (+886-2) 2778-4969

Manila Economic and Cultural Office Extension Office in Kaohsiung
2nd Floor, 146 Szu Wei Second Road
Kaohsiung 802
Phone: (+886-7) 331-7752
Fax: (+886-7) 331-7806

Manila Economic and Cultural Office Extension Office in Taichung
2nd Floor, 476 Chung Cheng Road, Taichung 403
Phone: (+886-4) 205-1306
Fax: (+886-4) 205-1317

Mexican Trade Services
Room 2905, 333 Keelung Road, Section 1
Taipei 110
Phone: (+886-2) 2757-6526
Fax: (+886-2) 2757-6180

Moscow-Taipei Economic and Cultural Coordination Commission in Taipei
10th Floor, 2 Hsin Yi Road, Section 5
Taipei 110
Phone: (+886-2) 8780-3011
Fax: (+886-2) 8780-2511